WRITING WITHOUT FORMULAS

WILLIAM H. THELIN
UNIVERSITY OF AKRON

HOUGHTON MIFFLIN COMPANY
BOSTON NEW YORK

Publisher: Patricia Coryell
Editor in Chief: Carrie Brandon
Senior Sponsoring Editor: Lisa Kimball
Senior Marketing Manager: Tom Ziolkowski
Senior Development Editor: Meg Botteon
Senior Project Editor: Samantha Ross
Art and Design Manager: Jill Haber
Cover Design Director: Tony Saizon
Senior Photo Editor: Jennifer Meyer Dare
Senior Composition Buyer: Chuck Dutton
New Title Project Manager: Susan Brooks-Peltier
Editorial Assistant: Sarah Truax
Marketing Assistant: Bettina Chiu
Editorial Assistant, Editorial Production: Andrew Laskey

Cover image: © Kasia Siwecka

Photos, page 244: *(left)* © Mary Evan Picture Library/The Image Works; *(right)* Adbusters.org
Text credits begin on page 517, which constitutes an extension of the copyright page.

Printed in the U.S.A.

Library of Congress Control Number: 2006938431

Instructor's examination copy
ISBN-13: 978-0-618-73248-7

For orders, use student text ISBN
ISBN-13: 978-0-618-38218-7

1 2 3 4 5 6 7 8 9 – CRS – 11 10 09 08 07

· CONTENTS ·

Preface xii

Introduction 1

PART I: KEY CONCEPTS OF WRITING 3

CHAPTER 1: REASONS FOR WRITING 5

READING Malcolm X, "Learning to Read" 6
- Writing from Personal Inspiration 11
  - Observation 11
  - Complaints 12

READING "Letter to a Restaurant Manager" 12
  - Reflection 13
  - Gratitude and Good Cheer 13
- Writing as a Citizen 14
  - Letters to the Editor 14
  - Political Action 15

READING TrueMajority, "'Computer Ate My Vote' Scores Coast to Coast Wins" 15
  - Public Presentations 17
- Writing in College 18
  - The Five-Paragraph Theme 18
  - The Modes of Discourse 18
  - Emphasis on Grammar 19
  - Formal Thesis Statements 19
- Writing in the Workplace 20
  - Cautious, Not Skimpy 20

READING Bill Thelin, "Norming Groups" 20
  - Finding Importance 21
  - Avoiding Deception 21
- *Summary 22*

CHAPTER 2: CRITICAL ANALYSIS FOR WRITING 23

STUDENT WRITING Sam Robinson, "The Car Accident" (draft) 23

STUDENT WRITING Sam Robinson, "The Car Accident" 25
- Interrogating the Obvious 28
  - Twisting the Cliché 28
  - Focusing on Interrelatedness of Key Elements 29

READING Lynne Luciano, "Male Body Image in America" 29
Finding What's Not There 35
READING Noreena Hertz, *from* The Silent Takeover 35
Investigating Assumptions 39
Race, Class, and Gender 39
Unearthing Agendas 40
READING Michael Kinsley, "The False Controversy of Stem Cells" 41
Seeing Patterns 42
READING Alfred Lubrano, *from* Limbo 43
Facts and Events as Examples 46
Who Profits? 47
READING Richard Meyer, "Curriculum Is a Political Statement" 47
Avoiding Poor Reasoning 50
Attacks Against Others 50
Diversions 51
Overgeneralizing 52
Summary 53

CHAPTER 3: AWARENESS OF AUDIENCE 54

STUDENT WRITING Anna Banks, "Sexuality Orientation" 55
Targeting Potential Readers 58
Common Knowledge 58
Cultural Considerations 59
Vocabulary 60
READING Mariah Blake, "Voices: The Damage Done: Crack Babies Talk Back" 60
Anticipating Reader Needs 63
Value Systems 64
READING Anna Quindlen, "Death Penalty's False Promise" 65
Life Experiences 67
READING Barbara Mellix, "From Outside, In" 67
Allusions 75
Responding to Possible Objections 76
Self-Reflection 77
Tone 78
STUDENT WRITING "Curse of the Ouija Board" 78
Refuting or Conceding 81
Using Real Readers in Peer Groups 82
Peer Review Writer's Discussion Guide 83
Peer Review Reader's Discussion Guide 84
Revision 84
Make Decisions 85
Receive Peer Feedback More Than Once 85
Summary 86

CHAPTER 4: STRATEGIES FOR ORGANIZING YOUR IDEAS 87

STUDENT WRITING Steve Windhorst, "Humor in Society" 87

READING Peter Singer, "Tools for Research" 91

READING Peter Wise, "The Problem with Being a Thing" 95

- Introducing Your Subject 98
  - Introductions Come Last 98
  - Finding Common Ground 99
  - General to Specific 99
  - Pivotal Scene 100
- Transitioning from Ideas 101
  - Increasing Levels of Specificity 101

READING Anastasia Toufexis, "The Right Chemistry" 101

- Contrast, Addition, Summary, and Exemplification 105
- Repeating Keywords 106
- Time and Place 106
- Subheadings 107

Placing Your Thesis 108

- Putting a New Twist on an Old Idea 108
- Using the Oreo Cookie Method 108

READING Amy Wang, "The Same Difference" 109

- Building Toward Consensus 112

Finishing Your Thoughts 113

READING Shirley Jackson, "The Lottery" 113

- Tying Points Together 120
- Call to Action 120

READING Fred Kaplan, "The Worst-Laid Plans: Why Was Emergency Planning So Awful?" 121

- Last Moment of a Narrative 123
- Selecting a Powerful Image 123

READING Gloria Naylor, "Mommy, What Does 'Nigger' Mean?" 123

Summary 126

CHAPTER 5: LANGUAGE CHOICES IN WRITING 127

STUDENT WRITING Ding Guang, "Negative Cliques in Schools" 128

- Mediating Experiences 130
  - Consensus Building 130
  - Naming the World 132
  - Figurative Language 132

READING Martin Luther King, Jr., "I Have a Dream" 132

- Describing and Shaping 136
  - Vague Words 136
  - Connotations 137

READING Mike Rose, *from* The Mind at Work 138

- Charged Language 139

Slang and Obscenity 140

READING Rick Bass, *from* The Lost Grizzlies 141

Euphemisms 144

READING David Cay Johnston, *from* Perfectly Legal 144

Filler Words 146

Bureaucratese 147

Sanitizing 147

READING William Lutz, "Life Under the Chief Doublespeak Officer" 148

Finding Your Voice 150

Choosing Your Words 151

Types of Words 152

Active Sentence Constructions 152

Summary 153

PART II: CONFRONTING WRITING TASKS 155

CHAPTER 6: DISCOVERING YOUR WRITING PROCESS 157

Seeing Your Own Patterns 159

Track Your Steps 160

Note What You Do Not Do 160

Breaking Through Writer's Block 161

Discovering Why You Are Blocked 162

READING Charlie Lau, Jr., *from* Lau's Laws on Hitting 162

Focused Freewriting 163

Starting with the Critical Analysis 164

Drawing a Tree 164

Discovering Strategies for Drafting and Revision 165

READING Jane Tompkins, *from* "'Indians': Textualism, Morality, and the Problem of History" 166

Focus on Revision 169

Create Options 169

Write Out of Order 170

Editing and Proofreading 171

Weaving in Analysis 171

Word Choice and Sentence Variety 172

Proofreading 173

Using Spelling and Grammar Checkers 173

Summary 175

CHAPTER 7: USES OF COLLABORATION 176

READING Marcus Laffey, "Inside Dope" 178

Beyond the In-Class Response Group 184

Face-to-Face Groups 185

Online Groups 186

Assigning Tasks in Group Projects 187
Selecting a Secretary 187
Strengths and Weaknesses 187
Keep a Progress Log 188

STUDENT WRITING "Jim's Progress Log" 188
Instructor Intervention 190
Synthesizing Ideas 191
Critiquing Peers' Work 192
Weaving Sections Together 193

READING Terry McCarthy, "Nowhere to Roam" 194
Stabilizing the Voice 195

READING Richard Corliss and Michael D. Lemonick, "How to Live to Be 100" 195
Taking Responsibility 202
Individual Evaluations 202
Teamwork 203

Summary 203

CHAPTER 8: PURPOSES AND STRATEGIES FOR READING 205

READING Jack Rasmus, "Executive Pay in the U.S." 207
Knowledge, Safety, and Awareness as Consumers 212
Warning Labels 212
Instructions 212
Contracts 213
Social and Civic Engagement 214
Voting 214
Protesting 214

READING Fairness and Accuracy in Reporting, "Smearing Anti-War Activists?: *NY Times* Op-Ed Laments Anti-War Funeral Protests" 215
Public Interest 216

READING Ohio Department of Public Safety, "Where to Ride on the Road" 217
Information Retrieval 219
Competition 219
Hobbies 219
Social Discourse 220

READING Jan Harold Brunvand, *from* The Vanishing Hitchhiker 220
Academic Achievement 224
Academic Learning 224
Learning for Future Application 225
Developing Reading Strategies for College 225

STUDENT WRITING Mandy Badar, "An Analysis of the Dietary Habits of a Known Bookworm" 226
Short Spurts 228
The Right Spot 229
Reading Planner 229

Comprehension 231
Focused Freewriting 232
STUDENT WRITING "Molly Egan's Freewrite"
Highlighting 233
Check Marks in the Margins 233
Summary 236

CHAPTER 9: WRITING WITH EVIDENCE 237
STUDENT WRITING Julie Springfield, "Sex and Religion" 237
STUDENT WRITING Brad Turner, "Instincts vs. Rules" (draft) 240
STUDENT WRITING Brad Turner, "Instincts vs. Rules" 241
Examining Evidence 243
Facts 245
Statistics 245
Witnesses 245
Personal Experiences and Observations 246
READING P. J. O'Rourke, "To Hell with Lipitor" 247
Establishing Criteria for a Claim 249
Ensuring the Relationship to the Claim 250
Establishing Substantive Criteria 250
Avoiding the Bandwagon Mentality 250
Checking Information 251
Beliefs, Histories, and Definitions 252
The Straw Man Fallacy 253
Dictionaries, Encyclopedias, and Websites 253
Integrating Sources 254
Extricating the Information 254
READING Nancy Roberts, *from* Blackbeard and Other Pirates of the Atlantic Coast 254
STUDENT WRITING "Extract from Claudia's Essay" 256
Paraphrasing 257
READING Paul Shepard, *from* The Tender Carnivore 257
STUDENT WRITING "Extract from Sherry's Essay" 259
Tag Phrases 259
Summary 260

CHAPTER 10: WRITERS AND RESEARCH 261
Locating Critical Knowledge 263
Mainstream Sources 264
Field-Specific Journals 264
Books 265
Alternative Magazines 265
READING Peter Phillips, Trish Boreta, and Project Censored, "The Top Censored News Stories of 2005–2006" 266

Evaluating Online Sources 276
Author 276
Citation of Sources 277
Updates of Sites 277
Agenda 277

READING Green Party website, "2006 Green Party Candidate Spotlight" 278
Fanatical Approach 279
When Sources Collide 280

READING Rick Reilly, "Questioned Marks" 281
Which Follows the Pattern? 282
How Do They Deal with the Other Side? 283

READING Leonard Peltier, "Statement to Judge Paul Benson" 283
Account for All Evidence 287
Giving Credit Where It Is Due 287
Include an Acknowledgement Page 288
Author, Title, and Publication Information 289
In-Text Citations 289
Distinctions Between Cited Materials 290

Summary 291

PART III: TOPICS FOR WRITING 293

CHAPTER 11: HOLIDAYS AND CELEBRATIONS 295

Overview 295
Openings for Writers 297
Religion and culture • "Hallmark holidays" • Origins of symbols • Arbitrariness of celebrations
Language 298
Holiday • Celebration • Ritual

READING Gerina Dunwich, "The Symbols of Halloween" 298

READING Leslie Pratt Bannatyne, "The Reformation and Guy Fawkes Day" 303
Assignment Ideas 305
Group Work 306

READING Elizabeth Pleck, "Festivals, Rites, and Presents" 307

READING Ellen Goodman, "Thanksgiving" 314

READING Arden Ranger, "A History of Anglo-Saxon Wedding Customs" 315

READING Brian Tokar, "The Twentieth Anniversary of Earth Day" 323

CHAPTER 12: HOBBIES 327

Overview 327
Openings for Writers 329
Childlike hobbies • Marketing • Gender and hobbies • Boredom in the adult world

Language 329
Hobby • Habitual • Maturation • Routine

READING Paul Roberts, "Risk" 330

READING Susan Sheehan and Howard Means, "Leonard Lauder: The Beauty of Small Things" 337
Assignment Ideas 342
Group Work 343

READING Michael Bamberger, "Con Games" 343

READING Chris Ballard, "Fantasy World" 350

READING David Sedaris, "Giant Dreams, Midget Abilities" 358

READING Debbie L. Sklar, "Indiana's Potato Chip Lady: Myrtle Young of Seyfert Foods, Inc." 365

CHAPTER 13: THE SUPERNATURAL 367
Overview 367
Openings for Writers 370
Rational explanations • Hoaxes • Wanting to believe • Faith and the supernatural
Language 370
Imagination • Coincidence • Bigfoot • ESP and UFO • Miracle

READING Robert Ellis Cahill, "Whitman's Haunted Bed" 371

READING Susan McClelland and John Betts, "UFOs, Skepticism, and Belief" 373
Assignment Ideas 377
Group Work 379

READING Jeff Parker, "Four Stops on a Bigfoot Hunt" 379

READING Jeff Chu, Broward Liston, Maggie Sieger, and Daniel Williams, "Is God in Our Genes?" 385

READING Associated Press, "Courthouse Camera Captures a Ghost" 392

READING Associated Press, "Courthouse Ghost Identified as Insect" 393

READING Matt Nisbet, "Talking to Heaven Through Television: How the Mass Media Package and Sell Medium John Edward" 394

CHAPTER 14: HUMOR 405
Overview 405
Openings for Writers 408
Comedians • Puns • Teaching and humor • Humor and tragedy
Language 408
Ridicule • Crudeness • Satire • Stereotypes

READING Joyce Carol Oates, "Is Laughter Contagious?" 409

READING "The Darwin Awards" 417
Assignment Ideas 420
Group Work 421

READING David Sedaris, "Me Talk Pretty One Day" 422

READING Warren St. John, "Seriously, the Joke Is Dead" 425

READING Marshall Brain, "How Laughter Works" 428

READING Glenn Garvin, "All I Think Is That It's Stupid: Dave Barry on Laughing at Very Big Government" 436

CHAPTER 15: HONESTY AND DECEPTION 449

Overview 449
Openings for Writers 452
Privacy • Embezzlers and frauds • Prioritizing values • Tall tales
Language 453
Stretching the truth • Justice • Honesty

READING Stephen L. Carter, "The Insufficiency of Honesty" 453

READING Al Franken, "I'm a Bad Liar" 458
Assignment Ideas 468
Group Work 468

READING Roger Henn, "The Lightning Struck Lost Mine" 469

READING Jim Ladd, "The Big Lie" 472

READING Steven Rendell, Jim Naurechas, and Jeff Cohen, "Censor or Victim of Censorship?" 479

READING Eric Dezenhall, "We Like Our Bad Guys to Be Honest About It" 481

CHAPTER 16: PETS, PESTS, AND BEASTS 484

Overview 484
Openings for Writers 486
Relationships with pets • Animal rights • Human destiny • Dealing with pests
Language 487
Master and owner • Obedience and disobedience

READING David Quammen, "Face of a Spider" 487

READING Jane Ganahl, "Women Like Men Who Like Cats" 491
Assignment Ideas 493
Group Work 494

READING N. Scott Momaday, "The Indian Dog" 495

READING Edward Abbey, "The Snake" 495

READING Scott McMillion, "Treat It Right" 499

READING Thomas McNamee, "Drainage Ditch" 512

Credits 517
Index 519

· PREFACE ·

I have taught first-year college composition courses in five different schools for close to twenty years. In many ways, I have been composing *Writing Without Formulas* ever since I started teaching. In every class, my students taught me something about teaching and writing that I pondered. Keeping a teaching journal and saving successful class plans, I amassed quite a bit of material, and a pattern emerged about the effective teaching of composition. Students needed to learn conceptually to incorporate skills and knowledge into their writing processes. They needed to see a purpose behind the writing task, decide how best to explore the topic, and then figure out the best way to revise their drafts for their intended audience. Although many compelling new approaches to teaching composition are published every year, I could not find a textbook that complemented what I was discovering in my own teaching and learning; so I decided to write one. *Writing Without Formulas* represents the best ideas, exercises, and assignments that I sifted from my experiences with hundreds of students and colleagues.

The underlying ethos of *Writing Without Formulas* is that when accomplished writers first examine a topic, they pose problems and uncover the critical matters that make for intriguing essays. Eschewing assignments and exercises that put structure before content, *Writing Without Formulas* invites students to make decisions about writing within the context of audience awareness and critical analysis. In *Writing Without Formulas,* arranging or organizing a piece of writing comes after the student has generated important ideas about the subject and knows the needs and concerns of the targeted audience. Each chapter emphasizes that a writer learns about and modifies the initial thesis by thoroughly understanding the rhetorical situation of the writing task. While much of value resides in the pages of books that structure themselves around the modes of discourse or genres, I intentionally diverged from that model to encourage students to understand important rhetorical concepts and arrive at effective ways to approach and arrange their writing.

Part I focuses on five concepts that successful student writers need to know and practice: determining the reason or purpose for writing, critically analyzing a topic, responding to audience needs and concerns, organizing an essay, and using language effectively. Each chapter guides students through a new concept, stimulating their interest with examples from both student and professional writing, and gives students ample opportunity to practice their understanding of the concept within rhetorical situations. Students will have many opportunities to apply the five concepts effectively in their formal essays.

Part II continues to help students develop effective writing and reading processes and introduces them to rhetorical situations encountered in collaboration, writing with evidence, and research. Students will discover practical advice on honing the processes they have begun to develop and will find ways to work through the challenges of group assignments, essays focusing on argument, and tasks requiring the use of sources. Diverse readings and compelling examples clarify important points, helping students understand the necessity of developing processes, establishing a writer's voice while working with peers and professional texts, and handling particular rhetorical situations.

Part III encourages students to apply the knowledge learned in Parts I and II. Students need to see a problem in order to revise effectively. Many students are interested in subjects that surround them daily. When we give them choices, they often gravitate toward their own experiences with our culture's and subculture's values, habits, and idiosyncrasies. Students who write about what they know often produce competent prose, but their theses tend to lack originality. Students resist revising the content of their essays because the material feels too close and comfortable. The lessons they learn about audience awareness and language choices during revision are too limited because they cannot see problems with their drafts.

I developed topics that interest students from varying regions and backgrounds and chose readings to help them defamiliarize their ideas. Defamiliarization makes ordinary experiences, customs, and feelings seem extraordinary or strange, provoking curiosity and stimulating interest, and thus allows students to critically locate their views within a larger framework. The process of defamiliarization creates rhetorical problems that open up students to revision.

Writing Without Formulas anticipates students' interest with chapters revolving around humor, the supernatural, and honesty and deception, among other topics. Part III defamiliarizes these topics with challenging questions and approaches. The readings and apparatus do not let students settle on pat conclusions; instead, their creative capacities are stimulated. This is accomplished in part through prompts that intensely question the details and language use of what students otherwise might perceive as common sense. The readings themselves pose problems by giving little-known facts and introducing marginalized ideologies. Students are gently urged to new levels of awareness, which creates cognitive openings for new knowledge about writing to enter. Further, the apparatus in Part III reminds students to integrate the rhetorical knowledge from earlier in the book into their writing, thus tying previous lessons into their actual writing activities.

Through this focus on content-driven writing assignments, students learn on a deeper level than when we give them formulas or rules to follow. They see the purpose for adding detail, for example, and they draft and revise to respond to their audience's needs, or to incorporate an insight derived from a critical analysis, or to nurture an idea springing from a particular choice of words. *Writing Without Formulas* gives sound advice about rhetorical concepts that lets students know *why* they are doing what they do. In keeping with the aphorism that still rings true, *Writing Without Formulas* shows students how to write instead of telling them.

Features

Detailed Discussion of Rhetorical Concepts

The first part of *Writing Without Formulas* focuses students on purposes for writing, critical analysis, audience awareness, organization of ideas, and language usage. Each concept is introduced by an actual classroom situation that lends itself to key questions about the rhetorical concept. The text answers these questions in a thorough review of how writers understand, respond to, and use the concept and introduces students to the necessity of weaving these understandings into writing tasks. It also provides readings and classroom activities to illuminate the concepts.

Writing Without Formulas does not ignore the skills instructors expect students to learn and use. In Part II, students learn about brainstorming and other activities associated with the writing process, investigate the best strategies for effective reading, see practical approaches to collaboration, and develop strategies for finding and using outside resources. As in Part I, the concepts that writers need to know are explained in great detail and are supported by concrete examples.

Critical Approach to Topics

Throughout *Writing Without Formulas,* materials and readings stimulate student thinking. In Part III, thematic chapters help students question the assumptions and practices of our culture. Each chapter begins with an overview of the topic that raises questions about our values, our relationship to one another, and the effects of our actions. Students are encouraged to do brainstorming and freewriting about critical areas and key terminology before turning to professional readings on the topic. Suggested assignments lead students toward situating their experiences or observations within the problems and debates brought up by the readings. Each chapter contains one assignment explicitly designed for groups of students. Finally, any easily drawn conclusions are countered by supplemental readings that seek to broaden the boundaries of the original set of readings. The multiple layers aid in development of students' critical thinking skills.

Creative Classroom Activities

Under the headings "Discussion," "Writing," "Collaborating," "Openings for Writers," "Language," and "Assignment Ideas," instructors will find multiple classroom activities that help students learn and practice the important concepts in the first two parts of *Writing Without Formulas.* These activities encourage the conceptual learning important to this text's foundation. Students are not asked to locate the thesis sentence of a reading or to do any other exercise that caters to formulaic understandings of writing. Instead, the activities ignite students' imaginations, placing them in hypothetical rhetorical situations or calling on their knowledge of contemporary culture to draw parallels to concepts crucial to good writing and communication. Sometimes students are asked to follow up on ideas introduced in student or professional readings; other times, they analyze the slang expressions they use; and still other times, they introduce people in their peer groups the way contestants on *Jeopardy* are introduced. Each activity strengthens student understanding of a concept and leads to the integration of the concept into student processes.

Readings

Throughout *Writing Without Formulas,* readers will find diverse selections that examine many different aspects of our culture. My vision of a classroom is a place of democratic, progressive goals in which students may challenge the status quo and investigate alternative perspectives and sources of information. Many of the readings, while not specifically aligned with a political party's platform, explore social issues from a variety of critical, personal, and political perspectives. Mainstream voices are prominent, but readers will also find marginalized social critics such as animal activists, Marxists, and paranormal investigators. I also have included several student essays. Perhaps more important are the many vignettes throughout the book; my experiences with students are crucial to understanding how I arrived at my conclusions about writing. Students will enjoy seeing how an instructor learned from his students.

Sustained Focus on Collaboration

Writing Without Formulas contains an informative chapter on student collaboration, but the emphasis on collaboration does not stop there. Collaborative activities and assignments can be found throughout the book. "Collaborating" and "Discussion" activities in Parts I and II invite students to work together to come to consensual understandings. The use of peer groups for sharing student writing is similarly explored.

Each chapter in Part III has a separate assignment designed specifically for collaborative writing. Each of these assignments incorporates enough work to ensure that students will want to collaborate rather than work individually. Yet, the assignments do not overwhelm students or ask them to do more than they are capable of doing. Instead, students will surmise that some writing activities need to be done together in order to accomplish the desired goal.

Flexible Organization

Instructors can enter *Writing Without Formulas* at just about any point and succeed in teaching their students how to write. They do not need to feel bound to a particular order or approach. The book can be followed chronologically, but instructors might want to dive right into one of the topics in Part III and incorporate lessons from the first two parts of the book as they assess student need. Instructors may also move to the concepts of writing they find most important and skip chapters without losing coherence. Clear illustrations of rhetorical concepts in Parts I and II through references to the selections in Part III give instructors opportunities to link rhetorical lessons to Part III topics. In addition, instructors can teach a Part III topic and refer to particular points in Part I or II as necessary to facilitate student learning.

Additional Resources

Instructor's Resource Manual

The Instructor's Resource Manual contains in-depth explanations on incorporating *Writing Without Formulas* into the classroom. Along with suggesting ways to use the classroom activities and assignments, the manual discusses ways to respond to student work that will help maintain consistency with the text. Instructors need not worry about student responses that seem to have gone awry. The activities and assignments have been tested in actual classrooms, and the manual demonstrates how to deal with student misunderstandings of the text's ideas.

Website

The website accompanying this text includes links to appropriate online sources that can supplement the readings. It also contains additional classroom activities to reinforce the important rhetorical concepts in each chapter. Additionally, apparatus from Houghton Mifflin is available through links, including important support for students' syntactical and grammatical difficulties. Both students and instructors can benefit from this website.

Acknowledgements

Every book is a collaboration. Too often, behind-the-scenes people are not given enough credit for the encouragement they supplied, the sacrifices they made, and the insights they provided. Some of these people might be obvious to those who have read such acknowledgement pages before, as it takes many employees of a publisher to produce a book. *Writing Without Formulas* would not have been completed without Meg Botteon, my development editor, who made me wise to the world of textbooks and kept me on a steady enough of a path to finish this. Thanks for putting up with me, Meg. Suzanne Phelps Weir was also instrumental to this project. As editor in chief at the time, she believed in my different approach to teaching composition and never lost faith in my abilities, even when I did. After Suzanne left Houghton Mifflin, I had the pleasure of working with senior sponsoring editor Lisa Kimball, who has been equally encouraging. In the final stages of this project, Samantha Ross, the senior project editor, and Sarah Truax, the editorial associate, were extremely helpful and, like poor Meg, had to put up with my idiosyncrasies and complicated life. Let me also mention Mary Wilkinson, the sales representative when I started at the University of Akron, who first heard my ideas for a textbook and passed them along, and Heather McMaster, Joanne DeLapa, and Tom Ziolkowski, whose enthusiasm in talking about possible adoptions renewed my zeal for the project when my spirits had temporarily waned.

As much as I am in the debt of the above named people, it is those who contributed in other ways, sometimes directly, sometimes indirectly, who I would most like to acknowledge. Chief among these people are, of course, my past and present students, who enabled me to learn how to reach them and figure out what I was doing. I have forgotten many of the names and even some of the faces have faded over time, but I cannot thank them enough. I only wish I could acknowledge each of them personally. And where would I have been as a professor if enthusiastic professors had not piqued my interest as a student? There are far too many, but Dr. Arthur Lane's wit and wisdom sticks out in my memory, as does the initial mentoring of Dr. Thia Wolf, who led me into the field of composition studies. Dr. Cherryl Smith was the first of many who had to put up with me for a long project, as she directed my Master's thesis and was quite kind and brilliant in helping me toward completion. Dr. Michael Williamson survived the task of directing my doctoral dissertation, giving me much direction and focus. I thank you all, as I feel your work with me has found its way into these pages. Since becoming a professor, many colleagues have given me similar guidance. John Tassoni, who has co-authored the Instructor's Resource Manual, continues to amaze me with his insights, and his advocacy of what I do humbles me. Ira Shor has influenced me perhaps more than any other colleague and has been a patient, good friend over the years. My colleagues in Rhetoricians for Peace and Working-Class Culture and Pedagogy have similarly given me many ideas to ponder that have shaped my thoughts and theories. I owe you all.

Perhaps most important are those who support me on a daily basis. On the top of this list are my wife, Leann, and my daughter, Katrina. They had to do without me many evenings and weekends so I could meet deadlines or brainstorm ideas. My father and mother, Howard and Vivien Thelin, have offered much encouragement and have helped out my family in many ways. Dr. Diana Reep and Dr. Tom Dukes from the University of Akron have been supportive in good times as well as bad and picked up the slack on occasion to allow me to work on the book. My workout partner and friend Bacari Brown always pushed me in the gym, letting me release stress and stay sane. And I cannot overlook the staff at Max McQ's. Lora Long and Nick Pulos lead the list of a lot of servers who poured my scotch just right while listening with a compassionate ear during those moments when I was discouraged or feeling overwhelmed. To all, you have no idea how important you have been to the completion of this book.

Finally, I would like to thank the many reviewers who read either the proposal or a draft and gave suggestions toward making *Writing Without Formulas* a successful book: Jennifer Beech, University of Tennessee at Chattanooga; Mary Ann Bretzlauf, College of Lake County; Avon G. Crismore, Indiana–Purdue University, Fort Wayne; Debra Dew, University of Colorado, Colorado Springs; Christina Fisanick, Xavier University; Shu-Huei Henrickson, Rock Valley College; Julie C. Kearney, Penn State, Harrisburg; Sophia Kowalski, University of Central Florida; Robert Lamm, Arkansas State University; Robert Lamphear, Oakland University; Nicole Montoya, University of Texas at El Paso; Kathleen Snow White, Pima Community College; Wayne Stein, University of Central Oklahoma; Theresa Trela, West Texas A&M University; and Kelly Wonder, University of Wisconsin–Eau Claire.

·INTRODUCTION·

The title of this textbook might strike you as strange. *Writing Without Formulas?* What does that mean? You are used to formulas in chemistry classes, I imagine, but not in courses about English. Writing does not involve calculations or memorizing steps in a process. It is not objective the way many other disciplines are. Naturally, then, you will be writing without a formula. Why state the obvious?

If these sentiments resemble your feelings, we are in agreement. A textbook should not need to declare itself formula-free. But it is necessary to make this statement about the title of my textbook. It reveals concerns I have had as a professor of English about how students have been taught writing. Too many textbooks and too many classrooms rely on formulaic methods to teach writing. But writing does not boil down to formulas.

This textbook avoids some of the formulaic strategies used by textbook writers. It does not discuss types of papers, such as expository essays or descriptive narrations. To do so puts structure ahead of the topic and limits your creativity as a writer. While published and student essays are used to illuminate points and stimulate your thinking, I do not talk about modeling your essays on them. Instead of copying the styles of professional and student writers, you will develop a style and a voice of your own.

The book does not instruct you to follow a set process for writing. Each writer must discover his or her own best approach to a writing task or situation. This book does not dictate what an "essay" should look like or how to go about writing a "paper." Such instruction regresses into formulas. I prefer that you discover knowledge about writing on your own, and I hope that you generate completely unique ideas, structures, and processes.

Instead of showing you formulaic techniques for replicating stale, stagnant models of prose, this textbook introduces important concepts about writing—such as "twisting clichés" and creating reality through language—that will breathe life into your work. Each chapter discusses how these concepts influence the decisions you make as a writer. Making decisions and anticipating reader response are what writing is about. To develop into a better writer, you must take chances. Through trial and error, you will see how to integrate these key concepts into your writing. My hope is that you will learn how to develop and express your thoughts and experience the excitement in writing.

Writing Without Formulas has been organized in three parts. Part I discusses the key concepts behind writing. Once you understand the reasons for writing and know how to develop a critical analysis, what audience concerns to keep in mind, what options to consider in structuring an essay, and why paying attention to language is important, you can begin exploring the next two parts. Part II discusses approaching a writing task, group work, overcoming resistance to reading, writing with evidence, and research. Each chapter in Part II integrates the key concepts into a discussion of common concerns students have about aspects of writing. Part III presents diverse readings on topics not seen in many composition textbooks, such as the supernatural, humor, and honesty and deception. Each chapter in Part III introduces issues within the topic, presents readings from which you can extract information or simply ponder in relation to the topic, and offers possible assignments.

You can write papers based on the chapters in Part III while you are learning the key concepts in Part I or are studying the common elements of writing addressed in Part II. The text has been designed to allow you and your instructor to jump back and forth. The questions and issues raised by the topics in Part III reinforce the understandings you will gain from Parts I and II, but you will become equally adept at writing if you work on assignments in Part III and refer back to the first two parts when you reach stumbling blocks.

Few students look forward to reading a required textbook, but I do hope you will find this one enjoyable and stimulating. I love to write, but I understand that not everyone does. My goal in *Writing Without Formulas* is not to try to convert you into a lover of writing. Rather, I want you to build confidence so that you can use writing effectively in your college courses, your activities as a citizen, and your career—and even for those times when you record your experiences and insights for no one other than yourself.

· PART I ·

KEY CONCEPTS OF WRITING

Good writing transcends formulas. As you have experienced in your own reading, good writing pleases, stimulates, coaxes, and consoles. A thoughtful author understands key concepts of writing rather than following a preset structure or copying someone else's style. In eliminating the common formulas of writing instruction (some of which are discussed in Chapter 1), this book invites a legitimate question: "What will be taught in their place?" This first part of *Writing Without Formulas* should answer that question. You will learn about the purposes of writing, about performing a critical analysis, about understanding the relationship between your writing and the audience, about structuring your writing, and about scrutinizing language choices. These key concepts form the basis of Part I. If you grasp them and try to implement them in all your reading and writing tasks, you will be able to make informed decisions that produce good writing.

The first chapter reviews the reasons that we write. Often, students do not see the purpose of learning to write. Many students perceive their first-year writing course as a requirement, a hoop to jump through. Chapter 1 focuses on the diverse situations where knowing how to write enhances your personal life, your responsibilities as a citizen, your college experiences, and your chosen career.

The second chapter explores the role of critical analysis in developing a meaningful thesis. Many student writers can tell good stories or relay information, but their essays fall short because they do not integrate a thesis into their writing. Chapter 2 shows the many different ways that a writer can approach and interpret a situation, an event, or a fact to reach a fresh, insightful point.

The third chapter explains the critical role that audience plays in writing. Over the years, many students have been told to add detail to their paper, to look at a topic from another perspective, or to clarify the ideas. All this advice stems from concerns about audience. Chapter 3 discusses how to understand the needs of potential readers and respond to their questions or objections to convey your ideas as clearly as possible.

The fourth chapter shifts to the matter of an essay's arrangement. A writer must take the audience into consideration when putting a paper in order, especially when a thesis challenges tenets of the status quo, as discussed in Chapter 2. Yet, the specific ways to tie together the introduction, body, and conclusion of an essay have been the main area in which formulaic instruction has misled student writers. Chapter 4 covers the structuring of writing independently, showing how to make organizational decisions.

The fifth chapter focuses on the use of language. Its concern is not so much with correct usage and grammar as it is with helping you understand the complexities of language as both a writer and a reader. Chapter 5 scrutinizes the way we construct information in our writing and shows the power of language in framing reality.

These concepts appear throughout *Writing Without Formulas,* as they are the basis behind making strong rhetorical choices when you write and producing effective essays, reports, and researched papers. Activities in each chapter will help you understand and implement the concepts in Part I.

While writing is rarely easy, the goal of this book is to empower you to make thoughtful, informed decisions as you write. Understanding the purposes of writing and grasping the key concepts presented here will allow access to that power. Making informed decisions will start you on the path toward becoming an effective writer.

CHAPTER 1

REASONS FOR WRITING

Last semester, an eighteen-year-old student sat in my office, listlessly gazing at the floor. Maria had hoped to learn the formula for revision so she could earn an A on her paper about her relationship with her ex-boyfriend. Unfortunately, I had no formulas to diagram for her. I discussed essential concepts, such as awareness of her audience and producing a thesis from an analysis, but she seemed to resist applying them to her writing. Finally, she let out an exasperated sigh and looked at me. "I just want to know how to fix this essay. I don't want to know this other stuff. I'm going to be an accountant. Why do I need to know how to write?"

Students like Maria often have limited experience with the various uses of writing. In fact, they dread the thought of writing because they connect it with tasks assigned in school and perhaps with unpleasant evaluations and comments from teachers. I talked to Maria about how interesting writing a paper could be and linked writing to objectives of our university, such as cultural literacy, critical thinking, and effective communication. I also mentioned that while papers for her classes did compel her to write, they comprise only one of the many reasons a person takes pen in hand or composes on a keyboard. Writing is a combination of thinking, communicating, and reflecting, I told her. As such, it offers a unique form of learning and allows for active participation in the world by accountants and everyone else.

Maria rolled her eyes. As in accounting, she wanted a step-by-step procedure that would work not just for this assignment but also for others. Perhaps you had the same reaction as Maria did to my explanation about the uses of writing. You might have groaned or shaken your head, since you have

This icon will direct you to web links and additional resources on the website college.hmco.com/pic/thelin1e

either heard it all before or think it sounds corny. The very words *learning* and *participation* hearken back to the rituals of school, even though I was trying to show the real-world application of writing. Let's face it; few people enjoy school. But there are legitimate reasons to write in the college classroom and elsewhere, and I would like you to share this belief. To try to convince you, I start with this premise: School is a game; education is not.

As I talked with Maria, I started to see that the rules she had learned about writing had more to do with formulas for school than with anything else. Writing had become a game of figuring out how to please her teacher through neatness and presentation. She had been rewarded for having correct margins, skipping exactly three lines between her title and her first paragraph, having a thesis statement in the first paragraph, and spelling correctly. She was also a well-behaved student who attended all of her classes and did not miss deadlines, and she received points for these accomplishments in her high school English classes. With this as her view of writing, no wonder she did not see its relevance to the world outside the classroom! Like other students, she had confused the *processes* of school with the *substance* of education. She had learned how to play a game, not to write effectively. When she recognized this distinction, she was able to start developing skills and applying knowledge. Writing began to have a real purpose for her.

I would like to help you see the relevance of writing to your life. I want to get past the games of school. Of course, I'm taking an awkward first step: You're reading a textbook, a staple of the schooling process, and you're doing it for a class, another familiar part of the process. I also cannot deny that I designed the techniques and topics you will find in this book to be taught in a course on composition in an educational institution. Like you and your previous teachers, I seem to be firmly embedded in the schooling process.

However, the most confining situations still let you learn if you allow for it. Malcolm X, the famous civil rights activist of the 1950s and 1960s, honed his reading and writing skills in prison. If he was able to increase his level of literacy and improve his eloquence while behind bars, the rest of us can learn despite the rules and prescriptive formulas that might get in our way.

MALCOLM X

Learning to Read

In reading this excerpt from his autobiography, notice how Malcolm X motivated himself to learn and then became consumed by knowledge. Broadening his literacy shaped his identity.

It was because of my letters that I happened to stumble upon starting to acquire some kind of a homemade education.

I became increasingly frustrated at not being able to express what I wanted to convey in letters that I wrote, especially those to Mr. Elijah Muhammad. In the street, I had been the most articulate hustler out there—I had commanded attention when I said something. But now, trying to write simple English, I not only wasn't articulate, I wasn't even functional. How would I sound writing in slang, the way I would *say* it, something such as, "Look, daddy, let me pull your coat about a cat, Elijah Muhammad—"

Many who today hear me somewhere in person, or on television, or those who read something I've said, will think I went to school far beyond the eighth grade. This impression is due entirely to my prison studies.

It had really begun back in the Charlestown Prison, when Bimbi first made me feel envy of his stock of knowledge. Bimbi had always taken charge of any conversations he was in, and I had tried to emulate him. But every book I picked up had few sentences which didn't contain anywhere from one to nearly all of the words that might as well have been in Chinese. When I just skipped those words, of course, I really ended up with little idea of what the book said. So I had come to the Norfolk Prison Colony still going through only book-reading motions. Pretty soon, I would have quit even these motions, unless I had received the motivation that I did.

I saw that the best thing I could do was get hold of a dictionary—to study, 5
to learn some words. I was lucky enough to reason also that I should try to improve my penmanship. It was sad. I couldn't even write in a straight line. It was both ideas together that moved me to request a dictionary along with some tablets and pencils from the Norfolk Prison Colony school.

I spent two days just riffling uncertainly through the dictionary's pages. I'd never realized so many words existed! I didn't know *which* words I needed to learn. Finally, just to start some kind of action, I began copying.

In my slow, painstaking, ragged handwriting, I copied into my tablet everything printed on that first page, down to the punctuation marks.

I believe it took me a day. Then, aloud, I read back, to myself, everything I'd written on the tablet. Over and over, aloud, to myself, I read my own handwriting.

I woke up the next morning, thinking about those words—immensely proud to realize that not only had I written so much at one time, but I'd written words that I never knew were in the world. Moreover, with a little effort, I also could remember what many of these words meant. I reviewed the words whose meanings I didn't remember. Funny thing, from the dictionary's first page right now, that "aardvark" springs to my mind. The dictionary had a picture of it, a long-tailed, long-eared, burrowing African mammal, which lives off termites caught by sticking out its tongue as an anteater does for ants.

I was so fascinated that I went on—I copied the dictionary's next page. 10
And the same experience came when I studied that. With every succeeding page, I also learned of people and places and events from history. Actually the dictionary is like a miniature encyclopedia. Finally the dictionary's A section had filled a whole tablet—and I went on into the B's. That was the way I started copying what eventually became the entire dictionary. It went a lot faster after so much practice helped me to pick up handwriting speed. Between what I wrote in my tablet, and writing letters, during the rest of my time in prison I would guess I wrote a million words.

I suppose it was inevitable that as my word-base broadened, I could for the first time pick up a book and read and now begin to understand what the book was saying. Anyone who has read a great deal can imagine the new world that opened. Let me tell you something: from then until I left that prison, in every free moment I had, if I was not reading in the library, I was reading on my bunk. You couldn't have gotten me out of books with a wedge. Between Mr. Muhammad's teachings, my correspondence, my visitors, . . . and my reading of books, months passed without my even thinking about being imprisoned. In fact, up to then, I never had been so truly free in my life.

The Norfolk Prison Colony's library was in the school building. A variety of classes was taught there by instructors who came from such places as Harvard and Boston universities. The weekly debates between inmate teams were also held in the school building. You would be astonished to know how worked up convict debaters and audiences would get over subjects like "Should Babies Be Fed Milk?"

Available on the prison library's shelves were books on just about every general subject. Much of the big private collection that Parkhurst had willed to the prison was still in crates and boxes in the back of the library—thousands of old books. Some of them looked ancient: covers faded, old-time parchment-looking binding. Parkhurst . . . seemed to have been principally interested in history and religion. He had the money and the special interest to have a lot of books that you wouldn't have in a general circulation. Any college library would have been lucky to get that collection.

As you can imagine, especially in a prison where there was heavy emphasis on rehabilitation, an inmate was smiled upon if he demonstrated an unusually intense interest in books. There was a sizable number of well-read inmates, especially the popular debaters. Some were said by many to be practically walking encyclopedias. They were almost celebrities. No university would ask any student to devour literature as I did when this new world opened to me, of being able to read and *understand.*

15 I read more in my room than in the library itself. An inmate who was known to read a lot could check out more than the permitted maximum number of books. I preferred reading in the total isolation of my own room.

When I had progressed to really serious reading, every night at about ten P.M. I would be outraged with the "lights out." It always seemed to catch me right in the middle of something engrossing.

Fortunately, right outside my door was a corridor light that cast a glow into my room. The glow was enough to read by, once my eyes adjusted to it. So when "lights out" came, I would sit on the floor where I could continue reading in that glow.

At one-hour intervals at night guards paced past every room. Each time I heard the approaching footsteps, I jumped into bed and feigned sleep. And as soon as the guard passed, I got back out of bed onto the floor area of that light-glow, where I would read for another fifty-eight minutes until the guard approached again. That went on until three or four every morning. Three or four hours of sleep a night was enough for me. Often in the years in the streets I had slept less than that. [. . .]

I have often reflected upon the new vistas that reading opened to me. I knew right there in prison that reading had changed forever the course of my life. As I see it today, the ability to read awoke inside me some long dormant craving to be mentally alive. I certainly wasn't seeking any degree, the way a college confers a status symbol upon its students. My homemade education gave me, with every additional book that I read, a little bit more sensitivity to the deafness, dumbness, and blindness that was afflicting the black race in America. Not long ago, an English writer telephoned me from London, asking questions. One was, "What's your alma mater?" I told him. "Books." You will never catch me with a free fifteen minutes in which I'm not studying something I feel might be able to help the black man.

Yesterday I spoke in London, and both ways on the plane across the At- 20
lantic I was studying a document about how the United Nations proposes to insure the human rights of the oppressed minorities of the world. The American black man is the world's most shameful case of minority oppression. What makes the black man think of himself as only an internal United States issue is just a catch-phrase, two words, "civil rights." How is the black man going to get "civil rights" before first he wins his *human* rights? If the American black man will start thinking about his *human* rights, and then start thinking of himself as part of one of the world's great peoples, he will see he has a case for the United Nations.

I can't think of a better case! Four hundred years of black blood and sweat invested here in America, and the white man still has the black man begging for what every immigrant fresh off the ship can take for granted the minute he walks down the gangplank.

But I'm digressing. I told the Englishman that my alma mater was books, a good library. Everytime I catch a plane, I have with me a book that I want to read—and that's a lot of books these days. If I weren't out here every day battling the white man, I could spend the rest of my life reading, just satisfying my curiosity—because you can hardly mention anything I'm not curious about. I don't think anybody ever got more out of going to prison than I did. In fact, prison enabled me to study far more intensively than I would have if my life had gone differently and I had attended some college. I imagine that one of the biggest troubles with colleges is there are too many distractions, too much panty-raiding, fraternities, and boola-boola and all of that. Where else but in a prison could I have attacked my ignorance by being able to study intensely sometimes as much as fifteen hours a day?

You must extract the substance of your education from the process of going to school. Only then will you see the importance of writing outside the context of college in order to understand its importance inside. My take on formulas about writing you might have learned in school, such as the five-paragraph essay, emphasis on grammar, and other issues, appears later in this chapter. For now, the following example should clarify my point about extracting substance.

Just about every child draws, colors, and paints. At an early age, we gravitate to reproducing or creating our world through art. Most parents do not initially interfere with their children's creative impulses, even if the children hold crayons awkwardly or make messes with glue. As we get older, producing scribbling and rough images no longer satisfies our needs. We want to improve so that our art captures our intentions more precisely. To make this transformation, we need to follow some rules.

Some parents purchase art kits for their children to begin the integration of rules and processes into the children's art. Other parents interact directly with their children, explaining that color must stay within the lines of a coloring book or that using pencil to outline a picture before using crayons or paint will let them correct mistakes. Computer programs allow for experimentation with the blending of colors and the structure of a drawing.

Art teachers in elementary school build on these lessons and introduce more complicated lessons, such as perspective, shading, and three-dimensional crafts. Children must learn the proper order for tasks within an art project and adhere to conventions in size and shape as well as behaviors such as neatness. As students, children receive grades for their finished products and might even have to compete against other students in school fairs and other contests. Eventually, children learn many rules and processes that seem to confine their freedom of expression, and they may start resenting the loss of fun in artistic endeavors. Like my student Maria, these children might not see the relevance of following rules for art, since they do not plan on being artists in the future.

But art lessons provide much needed information if children can extract the substance from the process. It is not always necessary to follow a strict order of idea, pencil outline, inking, coloring, and lettering when you are drawing a comic strip, for example, but having an image in mind before you start and understanding viewers' needs for clarity are important. These concepts will help later in the presentation of business reports, in the design of banners for parties or community carnivals, and in the creation of posters for political activism, such as for a protest march. You will want to produce something inspiring or provocative. You still have the trappings of school processes. Someone is going to assign you a task, and you must meet a deadline. You must obtain approval from someone above you, even if you are not receiving a grade, and your project will have requirements. Viewers will judge your final project. The difference is that you see the *purpose* for making something pleasing and you have extracted the substance from the processes taught to you. You do not look at these art projects as just another game in school.

The strategies you developed for coping with rules that accompany otherwise enjoyable activities are not as far removed from school and writing as you may think. The only difference comes from your understanding of the

DISCUSSION

Think of some concepts and skills that you apply frequently in your life. They can be anything—cooking, rapping, carpentry, etiquette—as long as you feel that you use these concepts or skills effectively in life outside of school. Where did you learn them? Were there rules you had to follow? How did you get past the parts of the process you did not like? Talk with your classmates about the parts of the learning experience that benefited you and the strategies you learned for coping with rules or processes that bothered you.

immediate applicability of the skills or concepts you know. Similarly, you need to see the purpose behind your education and understand how the application of concepts can help you beyond college. The grade on your transcript for this class, your diploma in four years, or other rewards (or fear of punishment) should not substitute for the substance of education. These motivators constitute external pressure for doing well. Authentic, purposeful writing involves a genuine reason for doing the task and a sense of self-satisfaction—not mere relief—on completion. Within the conventions of the schooling process, you can find the type of purpose—and, therefore, motivation—that you discovered for other activities you enjoy.

The first concept revolves around the reasons for writing. If you do not see writing as more than a vehicle of schooling, you will be back within a meaningless process. There are four main reasons to engage in writing: personal inspiration, the responsibilities of citizenship, the requirements of college, and the demands of the workplace. Yes, one of these reasons involves your college courses, but you may be surprised by the flexibility and creativity encouraged in this book. Throughout, we discuss concepts, techniques, and strategies for you to experiment with and apply when you are compelled by one of these reasons to write.

Writing from Personal Inspiration

On occasion, we want to record what we have experienced. Other times, we want to communicate an idea to a friend. Still other times, we need to vent to release pent-up anger or frustration, maybe to better understand its source. In these moments, our desires do not differ greatly from those of professional writers. Something has inspired us. We are writing because we want to.

Observation Sensual stimulation can cause us to want to remember something or to share it with others. The very act of writing commits an observation to memory and allows us to recall it. On a hike, maybe we came across a doe and a fawn, and our observation inspires us to think about the gracefulness of their motions or the subtlety of the maternal protective instinct. Wanting to share this observation, we re-create the scene in an email to a friend, or we jot a few notes on a piece of paper so as not to forget to tell our coworkers about it the next day. A professional writer takes this type of inspiration one step farther. He or she forms a thesis, perhaps comparing the scene to previous observations, and structures an essay around the encounter. We might think that professional writers are more talented than we are or that they have centered their careers on writing, but the truth is that published writers spring from all walks of life, starting with nothing more than the need to capture an inspiring moment and say something about it to a group of interested people.

Complaints Inspiration also comes when we're angry about experiences we have had as consumers. We write letters of complaint to credit card companies, businesses, and consumer agencies. These experiences have taught us the importance of knowing how much detail to include, what part of an incident to highlight, and why asking for a refund or other forms of redress is correct. You might be surprised by the results a well-written letter can get. Anger serves as fuel for hard-hitting writing, as long as it does not get out of hand, and writing can prevent retailers or others from taking advantage of us. When we tactfully word our frustration so that we communicate without insulting or alienating the audience (we discuss the audience in Chapter 3), a letter of complaint accomplishes much. The following example is a different sort of complaint in which a customer acted on behalf of a server at a local restaurant.

Letter to a Restaurant Manager

Dear Manager of LaLond's:

While I rarely write letters of complaint, my experience at LaLond's this past Wednesday night became very unpleasant due to the actions of the assistant manager on duty. My friends and I felt that he berated a server for no reason, and we hope the server will not be punished for a situation that was not her fault.

The server in question is named Sherry, and she served us promptly and professionally throughout the evening. However, a table of men across from us continually demanded her attention when she was serving us and other customers in the area. While they appeared at first to have a legitimate complaint about the temperature of their food, they hounded Sherry throughout the evening. She tried to be courteous and to respond to their requests, but the men became belligerent and made many hurtful comments to her that had nothing to do with the service she provided or the quality of the food. Sherry called over the assistant manager. Without listening at all to Sherry, he apologized to the men, bought them a round of drinks, and scolded Sherry. After they left, we could see and hear the assistant manager yelling at her in front of all patrons, telling her that she had to shape up or find another job.

Sherry has been our server many times, and we find her quite pleasant and highly competent. The men in question subjected Sherry to personal abuse, and the assistant manager should have sought out the facts before humiliating her. My friends and I regularly dine together on Wednesdays and will spend up to a hundred dollars on food and refreshments. I cannot see us returning to LaLond's for one of these nights unless we can be assured that servers will receive the respect they deserve from management.

Thank you,

Donna Sheffield

Donna Sheffield

Reflection People are also inspired to keep journals or blogs. A journal or a blog, like a trusted friend, can help you solve relationship, work, and other problems by reflecting on the experience through writing. Writing involves discovery. The act of writing pushes us to more complex understandings of ourselves and our world. Writing down a series of events casts it in a new light. The very words we choose help shape the reality of the situation, as is discussed in Chapter 5. Trying to precisely describe our emotions and experiences lets us understand smaller, hidden feelings and observations that come to light only through vocabulary choices. Most of the time, such entries go no farther than our own eyes, and they do not need to. Other times, journal entries can be the source of writing to be shared, such as a blog that allows reader comments and feedback.

Gratitude and Good Cheer Making people feel better is another reason to write. We might feel warmth in our hearts that inspires the desire to communicate special feelings, such as with a lover or a cherished relative. Receiving a gift makes us want to show our gratitude to the sender. Sorrow also might need to be expressed when someone suffers a loss. We want to express our connection to a specific person at such a time, letting him or her know our sentiments and hoping that we can demonstrate our love, offer comfort, or raise spirits. A phone conversation might be awkward or intrusive, depending on the circumstance. A personal note, though, gives you a chance to think through your message and choose the very best words to express your gratitude, joy, or remorse. The person on the other end can read your note at his or her leisure.

While greeting cards can send holiday and birthday wishes, the verses and messages often seem contrived when you want to express your sincere thanks, your emotion at an accomplishment such as a birth or graduation, or your support at a time of need. E-cards allow you to personalize your message by writing your own words in the section devoted to personal notes. You can use nicknames in personalized notes, refer to special times that only you and the other person know about, and say exactly how you feel. Even people who are strangers can benefit from words of commendation that lift their spirits. Workers appreciate your sending letters or email to their supervisors or to the corporate office when they have done something well. We often want to recognize a clerk or a staff person who has taken care of a problem or has performed a favor. Writing a note or email makes others feel better and gives us a feeling of accomplishment for recognizing the worth in others.

What does personal inspiration have to do with you as a college student? Simply put, you are more than just a student. You are a person with feelings and ideas. You already write all the time. Why else do you check your email and return messages with updates on your life? Why do you leave notes for your parents or write birthday cards to your grandmothers? Why do you participate in websites like Facebook and MySpace? Writing beyond the rules for school assignments is not remote from your everyday life.

The opportunity for reflection and personal growth attracts many people to writing. Writing what you like—writing to suit your needs—lets you apply lessons from education in a meaningful way. What better way to start than to use words to create meaning from something that matters to you?

WRITING

Have you ever been inspired to write for any of the reasons discussed above? Did you ever wish you had written to somebody or about something? Write about one of those moments when you wish you had shared an observation or idea with another person, had taken the time to complain to a person or an organization about a problem you experienced, or had written to yourself to sort through your feelings.

Writing as a Citizen

The letters to the editor sections in daily newspapers and online news sites show how engaged citizens communicate through writing. In a democracy, responsible people make their voices heard. Otherwise, as the saying goes, we have no one to blame but ourselves for laws, ordinances, and rulings that we do not like. At its best, effective writing increases public awareness and brings about change. When the stakes are high, the ineffective communication of ideas can undermine a whole platform.

Letters to the Editor Daily newspapers and online news services offer citizens the chance to publish counterarguments to editorials or to reveal the slant of articles. Citizens correct facts, show the personal effect of governmental actions, and share anger or distress about public events. Because letters to the editor are short and meaty, many government officials peruse them daily to get a sense of the community's reaction to events. Letters that get to the point, engage in critical analysis, or use humor have a better chance of getting published than those that repeat clichés or meander endlessly. Published letters have a chance of being read by someone in power, and that person can start remedying the situation. Even letters that go unheeded still remind other citizens of alternative ways of thinking, which can indirectly affect registering and voting practices.

Political Action Citizens committed to change also can start or work for nonprofit or special interest groups to get their messages heard. These groups use persuasive pamphlets, letters, websites, and email to ask for financial support, to lobby elected officials, and to educate voters. Writing that merely lists facts without clearly connecting them persuades no one. Writing that documents ineffectively or does not distinguish between credible and unreliable sources strains the patience of readers. Writing that rants and has no control over voice delegitimizes the entire agenda, causing group members to be dismissed as fanatics. Public officials and voters cannot afford to waste their time on absurdities.

Further, your name and email address are likely to be available, particularly when you contribute to a public listserv. Although electronic ethics suggest that posts or synchronous messages not be forwarded to nonsubscribers without the permission of the author, too often they are forwarded anyway. If you write something that is reactionary and that is not well thought out, your words could be circulated to thousands of people who do not share the sentiments of those on the listserv, which could damage your reputation and the reputation of the group you represent. Ultimately, the presentation of written materials can make the difference between a community's future being enhanced or jeopardized, depending on the severity of the problem under consideration.

TRUEMAJORITY

"Computer Ate My Vote" Scores Coast to Coast Wins

Here's an example of political advocacy from the political action group TrueMajority. Notice the upbeat tone in which the facts are presented. As a citizen, would this information influence you in any way?

Friends:

We're making waves and the tide is turning. The last week has been a big one for the Computer Ate My Vote campaign, and I wanted to share with you some of the progress we've been making.

In California, 50 TrueMajority members filled a Sacramento sidewalk last week calling for accountability from paperless electronic voting terminals. It was a fun event—our "hungry computer" prowled around for votes to eat and TrueMajority balladeer Laramie Crocker sang his ode to paperless voting, "Little Black Box," while the crowd urged state officials to dump California's unverified voting machines. The very next day California's Voting Systems and Procedures Panel said that's exactly what should be done. The panel recommended to California Secretary of State Kevin Shelley that he revoke the certification of the model TSx paperless electronic voting machine, made by Diebold Election Systems.

This is big news. California is the biggest market for election equipment in America. A rejection of paperless electronic voting terminals there will have ripple effects throughout the country, and we expect California Secretary of State Kevin Shelley to issue that decertification any day. We continue to work in California to extend the decertification of the Diebold TSx machines to *all* paperless electronic voting machines.

> On the day of the California announcement, TrueMajority members in Canton, Ohio, gathered outside the annual shareholders' meeting of Diebold Corporation. Ironically, Ohio is considering buying the very same Diebold TSx machines recommended for decertification in California.

A banner reading "Diebold Devours Democracy" floated from three helium-filled weather balloons outside the auditorium where Diebold CEO Walden O'Dell addressed shareholders and media. Activists gathered around a smoking, flashing mock-up of a malfunctioning Diebold voting terminal as TrueMajority organizers detailed the long list of failures by Diebold's machines in states across the nation. The event made news not only in Ohio newspapers and on Ohio television and radio but also throughout the country due to coverage by the national wire services.

Our work continues in Ohio, where the legislature is still debating a bill to require a paper trail (a TrueMajority organizer testified in favor of it). The bill doesn't go as far as we'd like—some counties would still be able to purchase paperless machines this year, and retrofit them later—but it's still a turnaround for a state which had been on the verge of locking *every* county into paperless voting for the foreseeable future. Diebold, meanwhile, seems to be changing its tune. Instead of claiming that paper trails are difficult to produce, as they did at the beginning of our campaign, company spokespeople said last week they'd be happy to make paper-capable machines for states that want them.

We reported to you earlier that eight states have required paper trails for their electronic voting terminals. Here's more good news—Maine just joined the club April 22, when Governor Baldacci signed LD1759 into law. State Rep. Hannah Pingree, the chief sponsor of the Maine bill, tells us that your messages to the secretary of state there softened the ground and were important in getting the law passed.

We're not stopping there, though. In addition to pushing on in Ohio and California, we'll soon be taking on the new federal Election Assistance Commission. That's the new board tasked with writing the standards for electronic voting machines. We'll be asking them to write "voter verified paper trail" into the federal standards, so all those states who are waiting until next year to buy voting machines will buy the right ones. Look for an alert soon on that topic.

More and more news outlets are waking up to this nationwide movement, and elected officials are listening. I'm glad to be able to work with all of you to protect our democracy.

Ben

Ben Cohen

President, TrueMajority.org

PS: For more information about our campaign, check out www.truemajority.org/voting.cfm. For more information about computer voting systems, check out www.verifiedvoting.org or www.calvoter.org/votingtechnology.html#resources.

Public Presentations Citizens who are rebutting government proposals, making statements to the press, or presenting at town hall meetings also use writing. Many people read their speeches verbatim from cue cards or notes, partly because extemporaneous public speaking terrifies individuals, but also partly because writing helps people find the best word choices. Speakers who have not prepared presentations often stumble in their delivery, even when they think they know what they want to say, losing the opportunity to deliver hard-hitting blows for their positions. In other cases, the heat of the moment will cause individuals to forget the tightly constructed phrases they put together. Even the best orators write down what they want to say and go through several drafts before committing a speech to memory.

COLLABORATING

Make a list of issues that concern you, even if you do not know many of the details. Feel free to list community concerns, concerns about things you heard on the radio, or concerns about global situations. Share this list with a group of three or four classmates, and pinpoint similar sentiments. What forum would be best to express these sentiments? Work together to write a paragraph to voice your collective views to that forum.

Writing in College

You may have noticed that you write more fluently and for longer stretches when you write about what you know. But if you were to write only about subjects that already interest you or that you understand thoroughly, you would never extend yourself as a writer. You need to extend yourself to improve your writing and to learn new concepts and ideas. Until you confront a problem while writing, you will not be able to respond effectively to assignments in other college courses, not to mention to civic writing or business writing tasks.

Putting an end to the game of giving teachers what they want will let you see that college writing assignments are opportunities to communicate what you have understood, developed, implemented, and discovered. You cannot change your assignments, but you can look at writing in your courses through a new lens. Your professors are interested in reading your work. They no more want you to adhere to formulaic conventions that stifle your thoughts and voice than you do. Certainly, you have to follow formats for particular types of college writing, such as lab reports and research proposals, and some professors do ask you to follow conventions to aid in careful reading of your work. But if you did not enjoy writing your paper, your professor is unlikely to enjoy reading it.

Many myths and fallacies about professors' standards have circulated throughout college campuses. You may have heard some of these mistaken notions about academic writing in high school or college classrooms. Let's review and critique some of the myths and fallacies and explore the reasons you should not follow these conventions in the classroom or in other types of writing:

The Five-Paragraph Theme In the five-paragraph theme, all points are presented in the introduction; the conclusion repeats the introduction; paragraphs are limited to five sentences each; and exactly three points are used in support of a thesis. While some essays are five paragraphs long, professional writing rarely uses the formulas found in this structure. The repetition bores readers, and the tight structure limits the author's voice.

The Modes of Discourse Although you might not be familiar with this term, you are familiar with assignments based on the modes, such as comparison and contrast, definition, cause and effect, and argument. The problem is that the modes favor structure over content, forcing you to look for a topic that fits the mode instead of for a mode that fits the topic. Most college assignments give students a subject or a choice of subjects and rely on the students to find the best ways to explore and present the topic. Beyond page limits, special formats, or other parameters set by your professor, you do not have to fit your writing into a particular structure if you choose to compare, describe, define, or argue something.

Emphasis on Grammar Surface-level correctness ensures that your reader can understand you. Too many mistakes can distract a reader from your point. However, a grammatically correct paper is not necessarily an effective paper. Without strong content, which is drawn from critical analysis, awareness of audience, and language choices, an error-free paper will not engage a reader. You need to focus on more areas of the writing process than just surface-level correction.

Formal Thesis Statements Starting your prewriting or drafts with a thesis statement restricts opportunities for exploration of your topic. A thesis should emerge from an essay, not be imposed on it. Once developed, the thesis does not have to be stated explicitly in the introduction. Some of the sciences do not like surprises coming at the conclusion of a paper, but a thesis implied elsewhere in an essay can be just as effective as a thesis statement in the introduction. When formal thesis statements are used in professional writing, they can be found in various places in an essay. Look at "The Insufficiency of Honesty" by Stephen Carter on page 453, Chapter 15. Where is his thesis statement?

You might still wonder how to generate excitement about topics and assignment requirements selected for you in college writing. The real lesson, however, revolves around your understanding of audience needs, your awareness of language usage, your decisions about organization, and your ability to critically analyze. If you can grasp these concepts in the different contexts in which they are presented in future chapters, you will find real-world applications to college writing.

But college writing also has the real purpose of communicating to your professors what you have understood, developed, implemented, and discovered. This communication allows professors across the curriculum to assess your knowledge more accurately. Poor writing can lead to grades that do not reflect how much you actually learned about a subject. Professors give advice and make recommendations based on what they believe students know and can contribute. Their judgments of you, especially within your major, can influence their decisions to invite you to participate in research, to write letters of recommendation for you, and to help you make contacts in the field, all of which will affect your career options.

DISCUSSION

List some rules or guidelines you acquired through your previous experiences with writing. Given what has been said in this chapter, how many of those rules or guidelines might be myths or fallacies? Why? Can you extract important concepts from your lists—ideas that might have been lost in your haste to conform to the rules or guidelines?

Writing in the Workplace

You might already have experience in the workplace. If so, you have a good idea of how valued strong writing skills are. Through email, memos, manuals, and reports, workers at many levels develop ideas and communicate them to people above and below them on the corporate ladder. Lack of clarity in a memo can lead to confusion about responsibilities and delegation of duties. Consumers can injure themselves or misuse products when manuals convey inconsistent or vague instructions. Innovations can be ignored if reports do not grab the attention of an executive. Carelessly written email messages can be used against individuals and corporations in lawsuits.

Much business or technical writing might seem dry when compared with opportunities for expression found in personal, civic, and even academic writing. Some businesses train executives to keep memos short and to avoid revealing too much of the reasoning behind decisions to workers. Some projects involve monotonous or bland research, making written reports dull. When dealing with consumers, many businesses resort to jargon or slogans and do not directly answer questions. However, examples of poor business writing reinforce the need to learn important concepts.

Cautious, Not Skimpy Little in this world is dull by nature, and new employees in a business do not have to reproduce dry writing. No rule keeps memos short and to the point, other than the fear of writing something that might get you or your business in trouble. Careful writing, not sparse writing, is the answer. Memos that can build the esteem of the recipient while giving clear information and instructions will succeed best.

BILL THELIN

Norming Groups

In the following office memo, you will notice that necessary details are available to the recipients who are addressed directly and to those copied on the memo. To help employees who may have forgotten the purpose for the venture, paragraph 2 outlines why faculty members are to meet for the norming sessions.

TO: Composition Faculty

FROM: Bill Thelin
Director of Composition

DATE: April 6, 2004

SUBJECT: Norming Groups

I am very pleased with the progress we have made in implementing our new system of portfolio assessment. I appreciate the effort and skill you are bringing to this project. Please continue to give me your input as we approach the end of the semester.

It is time again to form norming groups for Week 15. As you know, to ensure consistency in the program, we have instructors share a designated number of portfolios and calibrate grades together, producing a norm that we all follow. I have posted a schedule of times when you can meet for a norming session. Sign your name for the date and time that is most convenient for you. All faculty members are required to attend one session and bring at least three portfolios with them to share with other participants.

As always, feel free to come to me with any problems. I will again make myself available during all times listed to answer questions that come up, review particularly troublesome portfolios, or help in any other way.

Please sign up for a date and time by **Friday, April 16.**

CC: Diana Reep, Chair, Department of English
Thomas Dukes, Assistant Chair, Department of English

Finding Importance Before starting job-related writing, first determine why the writing is important—what purpose it will serve—and then find a way to make reading it compelling to the higher-ups who are its intended audience. Job-related writing is not busy work. Something is riding on it. Your research could be the basis of a request or a grant for funding, or you might be asked to write a request or grant yourself. Without the resources you are requesting, a product line might not be established. Assessment reports about personnel could be the basis for giving an employee a bonus or for terminating the employee. A productivity report might lead to downsizing or upgrading. Under such circumstances, you would not want to submit an inaccurate analysis of your company.

While this type of writing might seem tedious, it matters. Searching for the crucial details through critical analysis will enliven your writing strategies (see Chapter 2). By looking for a particular angle or finding something that is not obvious, you can motivate yourself to write a report that is both accurate and engaging.

Avoiding Deception Different perspectives and agendas cause many consumer complaints. Explaining your company's position clearly while showing that you understand the consumer's difficulty not only creates goodwill but

WRITING

Pretend that you are a member of a student committee. Your job is to write a portion of a request for a grant for new and/or updated computer labs. Your portion is the rationale. Rationales must persuade decision makers to release funds. In this case, you should show that the equipment requested will significantly add to student learning.

To gain an understanding of the importance of updated technology, visit the campus computer labs to assess their strengths and weaknesses or consult an instructor or lab technician about technology she or he would like to have available in the labs. Remember to give enough information to make the need clear. Do not gloss over your reasoning. At the same time, avoid deception. Do not overstate or understate the condition of the current equipment or make false claims.

can also lead to solutions. Straight answers when your business has erred—even when the truth might cost the business money—produce repeat business. Who would you rather deal with: a business that responds to questions with gobbledygook or a business that takes care of the problem? Of course, if your manager encourages you to shade the truth, it is up to you to make an ethical decision. Is this the type of company you want to work for? It is hard to label deliberate dishonesty or obfuscation "good writing." Just as with personal, civic, and college writing, the best prose cannot overcome weak content.

Summary

Good writing involves much more than applying formats and prescriptions. Learning to write means understanding concepts that you call on when occasions to write occur. While the classroom might seem like an artificial setting in which to hone writing skills, much can be accomplished that will have direct relevance to your future. As a student, you must separate the process of schooling from the substance of learning effective writing strategies. These strategies will aid you when occasions arise to write, whether those occasions involve communicating about personal inspiration, acting as a citizen, demonstrating knowledge in a college classroom, or performing duties in a business.

CHAPTER 2

CRITICAL ANALYSIS FOR WRITING

Sam wrote a pretty interesting account of a car accident in which he had been involved and presented it to a peer group workshop. The group members asked him for details in certain spots and prodded him to admit what he eventually did—that he had been drinking before the accident. They discussed organization, focused on some word choices, and seemed to be satisfied that they had critiqued Sam's paper thoroughly. But one woman, Jerusha, finally asked this question: "What is the thesis?"

Sam looked to the others and said, "Car accidents, right?" Indeed, his paper was about a particular car accident. But a thesis involves asserting or questioning something about the subject. An essay needs to have a thesis or a main point. If it does not, the essay is simply a story or a set of observations. What did Sam want to say about car accidents?

SAM ROBINSON

The Car Accident (draft)

When I started driving, I promised myself I would be very careful. But as I got more used to getting behind the wheel, I guess I got too confident. I didn't watch out for myself and what I was doing. I figured I knew how to drive so what was to worry. I can handle sharp corners. I know how long it takes to brake.

I went to a party last summer and drove my folks' car. I was with my friend Jimmy. We had a great time dancing, drinking, and laughing,

This icon will direct you to web links and additional resources on the website college.hmco.com/pic/thelin1e

> but it got time to go. I'd never been to this house before, so the road started looking unfamiliar. Jimmy and me wondered which turn to take and how to get back to the main road.
>
> He would point one way and I would say another, so we would go far in one direction until nothing looked familiar and then head back the other way. We kept looking for signs, as Jimmy thought he remembered the name of a street, but we couldn't read the street signs when we saw them. We even drove back to Carol's house just to see if we started out fresh from the beginning, could we make it? I was tired and getting madder and madder, and I jackrabbited the car at every stop sign. When I bothered to stop at them.
>
> Well, after traveling down another road we didn't recognize, I told Jimmy I think I remember this side street name, as I got out of the car and looked at the sign. He said it sounds right, so we started hauling down that street. I was driving too fast, I know, but I swear there was no sign that said we were on an "S." I only saw it under sunlight when I went back next week. I started swerving to stay on the road, but as I went left, then right, I couldn't control the car. We hit the barrier and came to a stop with the front two tires off the road. There was only a cliff beneath it. We could have been killed!
>
> We were able to get out of the car. Jimmy had a tough time as his side didn't have any roadway under it, as we had skidded right before hitting, but he made it out with my help. We walked until we found a house with a light on it, and the people were nice enough to let us in. We called my folks, who were hopping mad, and they called a tow truck and drove out there themselves to pick us up.
>
> The car's front end was all messed up, and we decided to total it. We didn't have collision insurance, so we got nothing for the car. Accidents are really scary and I'm just glad I got out of this one alive!

Sam studied his essay. "I guess I could say that you shouldn't drive drunk," he murmured.

"But if you were drunk, why did you leave that out?" Jerusha asked. "If that's the thesis of the essay, you would have mentioned it right away."

Jerusha was claiming that Sam was copping out, turning to the easy and obvious cliché about drunk driving that he thought would fit. Details that pop up later can add to or alter a thesis, but in this case, Sam avoided mentioning the drinking intentionally. The group felt compelled to explore why Sam would cop out if the drinking was important for his thesis. Jerusha and the others speculated that his avoidance could be a reaction to public scorn for drunk drivers. Maybe Sam wanted to avoid that label or avoid the responsibility it involves.

"But I wasn't really drunk," Sam contended. "I had only three beers." He explained that he did not want readers to think that drunkenness was the cause of the accident, because it wasn't. He talked about the darkness of the road he had been on and the sharp curves. As he answered his peer group's questions, an initial thesis took form: Drivers are only as good as the roads on which they drive.

Should Sam have avoided the details of drinking before driving? No. But to have used his easy thesis of not driving drunk would have shut off other possible avenues of exploration. Developing his thesis involved accounting for the social perception revealed in his peer group. By studying the ideas and reactions of his fellow students carefully, he better understood why he initially rejected the dominant social perception. Still, Sam needed to include the details of how much he drank and why he thought it was acceptable to drive. Otherwise, he would have little to examine in trying to find a relevant thesis. He needed the details to engage in the most essential activity in writing: critical analysis. A critical analysis of this draft would expose his assumptions to scrutiny, would make him see where they came from, would test their validity, and would let him form a generalization from the conflict between common societal values and his experience.

Such a process prevents writers from succumbing to clichés in their theses. Sometimes when we use the term *cliché,* we are referring to language that is repeated often and seems trite or bland. The expression "It was raining cats and dogs" is a cliché for this reason. It does not communicate precise detail, and it fails to evoke emotion in the reader.

In this chapter, however, we are interested in clichéd thinking and how to avoid it. Clichéd thinking occurs when a person applies a common societal belief to a situation too quickly. You might be tempted to use clichés because they seem to speak truth. In many ways, they are safe. But clichés fail to account for the variables in any given situation. A cliché needs to be modified or extended to convey a logical, meaningful thesis.

In Sam's case, the popular slogan "Don't drink and drive" would have functioned like a cliché because it mirrored what he and his peers had probably heard in alcohol awareness campaigns and driver's education seminars instead of resulting from careful analytic thought. Choosing "Don't drink and drive" or "Friends don't let friends drive drunk" as a thesis would have conveyed a clichéd attitude about the subject and would have undermined a legitimate warning about driving while under the influence. Fortunately, Sam worked through ideas—the possibility that alcohol consumption deludes us into thinking we are more "okay" than we think, the contention that even slight impairment of judgment renders a person unable to drive a car—before arriving at a thesis about the many factors that must coincide for an accident to occur. He believed that the driver's ability, whether impeded by alcohol, a natural lack of coordination, anger, or fatigue, is part of a much larger equation and that the societal focus on a driver's sobriety blinds us to other dangers on the road that could be more easily fixed.

SAM ROBINSON

The Car Accident

When I started driving, I promised myself I would be very careful. But as I got more used to getting behind the wheel, I guess I got too confident. I didn't take matters into consideration like I should have, such as road conditions, darkness, and fatigue. I figured I knew how to drive so what was to worry. I can handle sharp corners. I know how long it takes to bring my car to a full stop.

I went to a party last summer and drove my folks' car. I was with my friend Jimmy, and the house was located in the mountains, up some windy roads. We had a great time dancing and joking around with our friends. Alcohol was served at the party, and I drank three beers during the three hours we were at the party. When it was time to go, I quickly checked myself to make sure I was not impaired, as I never want to drive drunk. A person my weight, according to my driver's ed class, can consume one drink every hour without losing coordination. So I was safe.

I'd never been to this house before, so the road started looking unfamiliar. Jimmy and I wondered which turn to take and how to get back to the main road. He would point one way and I would say another, so we would go far in one direction until nothing looked familiar and then head back the other way. We kept looking for signs, as Jimmy thought he remembered the name of a street, but we couldn't read the street signs when we saw them, as it was so dark. We found our way back to Carol's house, and although I was frustrated, I sensed that I could figure out the directions better if we came back to our starting place. We should have just gone inside and asked for directions, but we didn't want to look like dweebs. We started back down the hill. I was tired and getting madder and madder. I jackrabbited the car at every stop sign, when I even bothered to stop at them.

After traveling down another road we didn't recognize, I told Jimmy I thought I remembered the name of a side street we had passed, but the moonlight was not enough for me to be sure, so I got out of the car and looked at the sign. He said it sounded right when I told him the name, so we started hauling down that street. I was driving too fast, I know, but I swear there was no sign on that next block that said we were coming to an "S" road—one that winds sharply like a snake. I started swerving to stay on the road, but as I went left, then right, I couldn't control the car. We hit the barrier and came to a stop with the front two tires off the road. There was only a cliff beneath them. We could have been killed!

We were able to get out of the car. Jimmy had a tough time as his side didn't have any roadway under it, as we had skidded to the right before hitting, so the passenger's side was practically hanging over the side of the mountain. He made it out with my help, as I made sure I didn't unbalance the car by exiting before he did. We walked until we found a house with a light on it, and the people were nice enough to let us in. We called my folks, who were hopping mad. They called a tow truck and drove out there themselves to pick us up.

The car's front end was all messed up, and we decided to total it. We didn't have collision insurance, so we got nothing for the car. I

> argued with my parents, who figured they had gotten me off a drunk driving charge by waiting until the next day to inform the police about the damage to the barrier. I insisted that I was not drunk, and I got the mother of the girl whose house it was to call my mom and tell her that I had been sober. We drove out there the next week in my mom's car, and although we saw the warning sign about an "S" curve, they agreed it would be hard to see in the dark. It was old and did not reflect well when headlights were on it. There were no street lights anywhere on that block and the lanes were very narrow. I didn't feel it at the time, but there were several deep potholes we noticed right around the place where my car hit the barrier. My ability to handle the car could have been affected by one of those potholes if I hit one. Jimmy said he did remember us hitting one.
>
> A lot of factors go into a car accident occurring. Our society likes to blame the individual and tries to find reasons that place the fault squarely on him. A driver's ability only contributes so much to an accident. Everyone cannot be a safe driver all the time, as mistakes are human. We get into cars when we're tired, angry, and distracted, and all drivers get lost some time, which reduces our natural caution when we're trying to find our way. Local and state governments can help to protect individuals against these moments by ensuring that roadways are safe. Street signs should be able to be seen in the dark. Street lights need to be installed in places that have a hazard potential. Roads need to be fixed. I'm a good driver, but some drivers start with coordination that is less than perfect, and some drivers do get drunk. We can protect them and any pedestrian or other vehicle they might run into by having better road conditions. So much focus on preventing drunk driving, while definitely something to avoid, blinds us to easier solutions towards road safety.

Sam engaged in critical analysis to reach his conclusion. Perhaps we would be more comfortable as readers if he had admitted more responsibility, but the point of critical analysis is not to reach a thesis that everyone agrees with. Rather, it is to reach a thesis that challenges preconceptions and can lead us toward fruitful paths of action. As much as we do not want people to drive after drinking, Sam's thesis offers a new perspective that can help reduce automobile accidents.

DISCUSSION

Writing that does not stir passion, that remains safe in clichés, offers little to the reader. Sam takes a risk with his ideas. Do you think that Sam's thesis is a denial of his own responsibility in the accident? What other conclusions could he have reached to avoid clichés?

COLLABORATING

Each member of your group should write down the details of an incident that taught her or him a lesson. Make sure to state what that lesson was. Each member should share the details of his or her incident with the group, and discuss other possible lessons that could have been learned from the incidents. Based on the details, could one or more of the other possibilities be valid? Could one or more of them be more valid than the initial lesson you learned? Why? Examine how you phrase this lesson. Is any part of it a cliché? Explain.

You might be wondering how to engage in critical analysis. What is the process? How can you do it? While no exact formula exists, the following sections give you the basic concepts behind critical analysis and let you practice this method of thinking.

Interrogating the Obvious

One way to engage in critical analysis and develop a unique, provocative thesis relies on intensive questioning of surface explanations for incidents. In other words, do not settle on your first instinct when searching for a thesis. Your first instinct might be correct, of course, or might be as close to accurate as possible, but the time you spend interrogating the obvious will remove nagging doubts from your mind and your readers' minds about the conclusions you have drawn from your subject. At its best, interrogating the obvious helps you take the significant parts of an incident into account and allows you to focus on the most relevant aspects of information or data. It might reaffirm some key tenets of what you first thought while adding or subtracting new elements for you to ponder. Developing the habit of interrogating the obvious also will aid you beyond the classroom in understanding world events, personal relationships, and the mechanisms of corporations.

Twisting the Cliché If you start with the most apparent explanation in your process of thinking, you are probably echoing a societal cliché. Try turning the cliché on its head. For instance, if you are thinking about the value of honesty, you may come up with the cliché "Honesty is the best policy." What if you were to seriously consider its opposite, "Honesty is the worst policy" or "Dishonesty is the best policy"? Can somebody think this way? What would motivate them to do so? How do those motivations differ from those of someone who advocates honesty?

This type of questioning of a common belief will produce an array of options for you to consider—in this case, perhaps places in the middle of the extremes of best and worst. The reasons most people shy away from complete truth-telling might help you produce an insight about honesty and be able to apply it to your subject. Instead of using the pat conclusion about honesty being the best policy, you can put a twist on the cliché, perhaps suggesting limitations to the use of honesty. Chapter 15 includes a reading by Stephen Carter called "The Insufficiency of Honesty" in which the author has wrestled with this issue and has decided that integrity is a better policy than honesty. You do not need to subscribe to the exact opposite of a cliché to make this exercise valuable. The exact opposite is simply a starting point for further questioning.

WRITING

Look at the chapter topics for Part III in the table of contents. Choose one of the topics, and write a statement about it that you would consider to be the most obvious. More than likely, this statement will contain clichéd language or attitudes. Write about the statement, using the method of twisting the cliché to question its legitimacy or accuracy.

Focusing on Interrelatedness of Key Elements Many explanations, whether clichés or not, isolate the key element or the triggering device in a subject. Interrogating the obvious asks you to find many variables and see how they connect to produce the results. You might have heard a chef or a cook discuss the secret ingredient that makes the difference between a mediocre entrée and a superb one. Yet, most cooks will tell you that no one ingredient makes the difference. The combination of subtle variations in preparation, such as cooking temperatures and the amounts of ingredients, produces the difference.

Thus, you should look in your subject for the interrelatedness of key elements and see how they connect. You can ask yourself how many of them you could tweak to produce a difference. While at times you might find one element that seems to be crucial, searching for more than one element will often let you notice subtleties that went unnoticed the first time around, subtleties that are worth mentioning when you form your thesis.

LYNNE LUCIANO

Male Body Image in America

Examine how this article ties together several factors in American society that have led to an obsession with appearance. It does not isolate one variable only but shows the interconnectedness of elements.

American men spent $3 billion on grooming aids and fragrances in 1997. They also spent nearly $800 million on hair transplants and $400 million on hairpieces. Sales of exercise equipment and health-club memberships raked in $4 billion. An estimated eighty-five million Americans, mostly male, are doing some kind of weight training. Even serious bodybuilding, once a fringe activity largely relegated to the lower classes, has gained middle-class status as upwardly mobile men of all ages grunt and strain for the blood-vessel-constricting high known as the pump. For men who have more fat than muscle, a lucrative foundation-garment industry offers Butt-Busters and Man-Bands to flatten bulges. Men are dieting in unprecedented numbers, and an estimated one million of them suffer from eating disorders commonly thought to afflict only women.

Also surprising is men's pursuit of beauty through the scalpel: in 1996, the bill for male cosmetic surgery was $500 million. Just under $200 million was spent on the two most popular surgeries, liposuction and rhinoplasty (nose jobs), with the rest going for esoteric surgeries like pectoral implants and the creation of cleft chins, not to mention the ultimate male surgery, penis enlargement. We are clearly witnessing the evolution of an obsession with body image, especially among middle-class men, and a corresponding male appropriation of, in the words of the feminist Barbara Ehrenreich, "status-seeking activities . . . once seen as feminine."

What, then, does it mean to be a man at the dawn of the twenty-first century? The historian and philosopher Elisabeth Badinter has concluded that models of masculinity haven't changed much over the centuries. She points to four "imperatives" for today's men: first and foremost, men must be men—"no sissy stuff"; second, they must be competitive, constantly demonstrating their success and superiority; third, they must be "detached and impassive"; and, finally, they must be willing to take risks and confront danger, even to the point of violence. These four imperatives have two qualities in common: they are diametrically opposed to what is generally regarded as feminine behavior, and they say nothing about how a man is supposed to *look*.

Until World War II, it is true, male attractiveness was derived from activity; how a man behaved and what he achieved were the true measures of his worth. In the immediate aftermath of World War II, it seemed these ideals would continue along their accustomed track. The American male would provide for his family, succeed at his job, and be strong, rugged, and virile. While women labored at self-beautification, men devoted themselves to more important matters. Men were not exactly indifferent to their bodies, but any man who overly emphasized his physical appearance risked being accused of vanity. Men who wore toupees aroused amused derision at best. Although obesity among Americans had reached alarming proportions by mid-century, men shied away from dieting, despite warnings about heart disease. Exercise, which at least had the cachet of being "masculine" because it was associated with action, didn't get much more strenuous than golf and gardening. Workouts that raised serious sweat had few middle-class adherents, and cosmetic surgery was regarded as the exclusive preserve of women. As for the body's most intimate parts, a cloud of secrecy shrouded them, as well as their function (and dysfunction), from public debate and public view.

5 What has caused American men to fall into the beauty trap so long assumed to be the special burden of women? Does men's concern about their

bodies mean they've become feminized? Have they been so addled by the women's movement that they are responding by becoming more like women? There is no simple, single answer. Rather, a confluence of social, economic, and cultural changes has been instrumental in shaping the new cult of male body image in postwar America.

The changing status of women brought about by second-wave feminism has radically reshaped how women view the male body. As long as men controlled economic resources, their looks were of secondary importance. Though feminism would have many, often conflicting, objectives, the liberal feminism that emerged mainly among professional and upper-middle-class women focused on social and legal constraints that denied women equal access to the workplace. As the role of breadwinner became a shared one, men's economic power and sense of uniqueness would be undermined.

The impetus behind the rising number of college-educated wives entering the workplace came less from the need to contribute to the family income, however, than from the diminishing attractions of the home. Avid middle-class pursuit of higher education, especially at graduate and professional levels, deterred growing numbers of young men and women from early marriage. At the same time, greater latitude for sexual experimentation made it less likely that women would marry just to legitimize sexual relations. An emphasis on the importance of self-fulfillment also undermined marriage as a priority for many young Americans. It was during the 1960s that the term *lifestyle* was first used in reference to being single: its significance lay in its suggestion of choice. Marriage was no longer expected but a matter of personal taste, as were its alternatives, divorce and cohabitation, which became ever more common.

By the end of the decade, the average age at first marriage had risen, and the marriage rate had begun to drop, and continued to drop through the 1970s. A survey of college students at that time showed that 82 percent of the women rated a career as important to self-fulfillment, whereas only 67 percent believed this was true of marriage. The *Cosmopolitan* editor Helen Gurley Brown, who had spent most of the 1960s trying to create an image of the *Cosmo* girl as mirror image of the sexually uninhibited *Playboy* man, emphatically agreed: marriage, she told her legions of female readers, was nothing more than "insurance for the worst years of your life."

Try as she might to turn men into sex objects, Brown was ahead of her time in 1962. For most women, being single was still stigmatizing rather than stimulating. And as Brown herself was quick to point out, sexual liberation didn't work without economic liberation, and that hadn't arrived yet. But as the decade progressed, single life took on new legitimacy and had wide-ranging social and economic effects. One of the most significant was that in the dating marketplace, single women were as likely to be doing the choosing—and rejecting—as men, elevating the importance of male looks to a whole new level. Why, demands the woman who works out rigorously to keep her body lean and fit, should I put up with a man who spends his leisure time sitting on a couch watching television? Or, as the feminist Germaine Greer inquired with some acerbity in 1971, was it too much to ask that women be spared "the daily struggle for superhuman beauty in order to offer it to the caresses of a subhuman ugly mate"?

10 Economic change wasn't limited to women's more substantial paychecks. World War II catapulted America into unprecedented power and prosperity. Lavish government spending, corporate expansion, and the development of a vast complex of technological industries based on the postwar symbiosis of military, government, and science created thousands of secure, well-paying white-collar jobs. As union wages rose, stimulated by cost-of-living increases and buffered by national prosperity, millions of working-class Americans could afford middle-class lifestyles and the accoutrements that defined them.

For nearly a quarter century, expectations of continued affluence and material progress were undimmed. But in the 1970s, America's virtually unchallenged global economic preeminence, as well as its internal prosperity, would confront foreign competition, inflation, declining corporate profits, and unemployment. In the ensuing downsizing that persisted well into the 1990s, hardest hit would be those most accustomed to job success and security—white males. To maintain an edge, it became important not just to be qualified for a job but to look as if one were; and that meant looking dynamic, successful, and, above all, young.

These changes are related to a more complex and extremely significant alteration in American life since midcentury: the rise of a culture increasingly based on self-fulfillment and the cultivation of self-esteem. Though many factors brought about this sea change, one of the most compelling was the proliferation of consumerism and its emphasis on the importance of self-image.

America's transformation from a culture of production to one of consumption was well under way by the turn of the nineteenth century. At that time, the basic needs of most middle-class Americans were being met, and manufacturers therefore sought to create desire in place of necessity. They were aided by advertisers who set out to convince consumers that their very identities depended on owning the right products, that they could be whatever they wished, as long as they purchased enough goods.

Advertising agencies appeared on the American landscape as early as the 1850s but remained on a small scale until World War I, when technological and cultural factors converged to create the modern advertising industry. New technologies like arc and neon lighting allowed ads to be displayed in more interesting and enticing ways, while advanced printing methods like lithography made it possible to copy images less expensively and more attractively. During the war, advertising and public relations joined forces with the U.S. government to generate propaganda and unifying symbols as a means of mobilizing support for the war among a fragmented and diverse population—an effort devoted more to popularizing and legitimizing the war than to disseminating real information. Afterward, products poured off booming American assembly lines, and advertisers mobilized consumer enthusiasm in much the same way. Ad agencies created personalities for their products, which were sold not on the basis of what they could do but on the basis of the image they projected—as one advertising mogul put it, they sold the sizzle, not the steak.

15 Advertising was helped in its crusade by the emergent popularity of psychology. Terms like *ego* and *repression* were bandied about in everyday conversation, and by the 1920s, the idea of complexes had moved out of medical circles and into the lives of ordinary people. Americans, buffeted by changes brought about by industrialization and the new public life of cities, had fallen prey to feelings of anxiety and insecurity. Magazines and self-help books asked, "Do you have an inferiority complex?" and emphasized the importance of self-scrutiny. Advertisers seized on the connection between the psychological and the physical, urging consumers to buy their products to overcome deficiencies ranging from dandruff to bad breath.

Well into the twentieth century, women were advertisers' main targets. Consumption—that is, shopping—was defined as women's work. Single women were encouraged to compete for men by buying commodities to make themselves more beautiful, and married women were encouraged to demonstrate their husbands' success by their purchasing power. But as commodities became increasingly central to defining self-worth, men, too, would be pulled into the vortex of consumerism, warned by advertisers that the wrong "look" posed a threat to career, love life, and self-esteem.

In its early days, advertising had been simply a means of linking buyer and seller by presenting basic information about a product—how big it was, for example, or how much it cost. But in an urbanizing and modernizing culture, advertising evolved from selling mere products to selling their benefits. Advertising is about image, self-esteem, and display of the self. It is *not* about what the psychologist Erik Erikson calls, in his studies of human psychological development, "the mature person's developing sense of the importance of giving something back to community and society." In a consumer society, a sense of responsibility to the larger community doesn't develop. As the sociologist Diane Barthel points out, every advertiser knows that the critical attribute of any product is "What will it do for *me*?" The line between commodity and individual has become blurred, so that we *are* what we buy. Americans have been beguiled by marketing acumen, and the body has become the ultimate commodity.

The importance of self-presentation originated early in the century, though initially it was more subtle than it is today. As early as the second decade, social critics were noting that America was shifting from a culture of character to a culture of personality. Character implies self-discipline and a sense of inner direction, whereas personality revolves around the ability to please others—not necessarily through real accomplishment but by winning friends and influencing people. While character is its own reward, personality demands external validation and appreciation.

By midcentury, the ethos of personality had almost entirely displaced older notions of character. Image is described by the historian Daniel Boorstin as "a studiously crafted personality profile of an individual . . . a value caricature, shaped in three dimensions, of synthetic materials." Like the right personality, it relies on external indicators to proclaim our personal worth and determine how others see and evaluate us. The right clothes, the right car, and even the right body and face—all can be purchased rather than cultivated.

20 The 1960s brought not only social upheaval but an emphasis on sexuality, self-expression, and youth. Commercial packaging of youth actually began in the 1950s, when marketers recognized teenagers' "purchasing power," a term first used after World War II. By 1959, teenagers controlled ten billion dollars in discretionary income, more than the total sales of General Motors. Teen society was grounded in a sense of acute difference from adult society and was primarily defined in terms of consumer choices, especially in fashion and music. Yet in other respects, adolescents in the 1950s appeared to want the same things as their parents: a mate, a family, a home in the suburbs. They spent a great deal of time practicing for their future by playing courtship games like going steady and getting pinned. Most girls looked forward to taking on the responsibilities of motherhood, and boys wanted to become men. As for adults, though they wanted to look attractive and have that elusive quality known as "sex appeal," they generally didn't wish to look, or behave, like teenagers. The culture of youth was distinctive *because* it was reserved for the young.

The cultural importance of youth surged in the 1970s, as prosperity continued to allow teenagers to pursue their distinctive consumerism and because so many defining aspects of the 1960s—fashion, hair, music, radicalism—had centered on young people, especially those of college age. Even the soldiers who fought in the Vietnam War were younger than those of any previous American war: their average age was nineteen, compared with twenty-four for soldiers in World War II. Although the end of the 1960s was marked by disillusionment over the decade's social and political turmoil, the desirability of being (and looking) young remained undimmed. Growing numbers of Americans, confronting the prospect of turning thirty, became determined never to leave adolescence—at least, not physically. Youth was no longer a stage of life to be passed through but one to be clung to tenaciously.

In the 1970s, the obsession with youthfulness combined with the emphasis on self-expression and acquisitiveness to create an entirely new culture grounded in the importance of self-esteem. Narcissism, identified in the 1960s by Erikson as a modern form of neurosis, was recast by the historian and cultural theorist Christopher Lasch into a theory of modern social history. According to Lasch, the bewildering array of images to which the average American was subjected led to a preoccupation with projecting the "right" image of oneself in order to confirm one's very existence. If the 1950s had been defined by conformity, the 1970s were characterized by a sense of selfhood "hopelessly dependent on the consumption of images" and consequently on relentless self-scrutiny. The marketing of commodities, Lasch cautioned, created a world of insubstantial images difficult to distinguish from reality. Within this world, images were incorporated into Americans' visions of themselves, with important implications for body image for both genders. Advertising and mass marketing held out the promise of self-fulfillment and eternal youth through consumerism—for everyone. Finally, as the historian Margaret Morganroth Gullette has observed, "the system that sells products based on fears of aging . . . turned its giant voracious maw toward that next great big juicy market, men."

In the 1990s, that "big juicy market" was the largest it had ever been—the baby boomers were entering middle age. These thirty-one million people—12 percent of the population—were beginning to experience the trauma of midlife crisis. In 1993, the National Men's Resource Center declared that all men undergo a midlife crisis and that a major manifestation of this was growing concern about the loss of physical appeal.

It's tempting to surmise that men's interest in body image, and their relatively recent concerns about physical attractiveness, along with sexualization of the male body, means they are becoming feminized. This, however, is decidedly not the case. Looking good is part of a quintessential male strategy whose ultimate aim is to make men more successful, competitive, and powerful. The means of achieving this goal may be new, but the objective is not.

Millions of American men have been transformed into body-conscious consumers of revealing fashions, seductive perfumes, and the services of hairstylists, personal trainers, and plastic surgeons. Due credit for this transformation must be given to advertisers, marketers, and self-esteem gurus, who have sold men—and all of us—a message of self-transfiguration through self-commodification. The traditional image of women as sexual objects has simply been expanded: *everyone* has become an object to be seen.

Finding What's Not There Essential components of a subject often are initially missed by a writer, sometimes because they seem obvious or not particularly relevant. Yet, readers will wonder about these components, just as Jerusha and the other group members wondered about the issue of drinking in Sam's essay about the car accident. Interrogating the obvious means reexamining what we have written and looking for elements that are not there. Traditional questions we can ask involve who, what, where, when, why, and how. You might not need to incorporate the answers to these questions into the final version of your essay, but you might find that one or two of the details can shed some light on your thesis.

NOREENA HERTZ

from The Silent Takeover

In this excerpt from The Silent Takeover, *Noreena Hertz questions what the public is not hearing in the official version of the success of the free market. Notice that she asks why, how, and what, then reveals missing details that lead her to believe that corporate behemoths are engaging in a "silent takeover" of the world.*

Benetton provides an apt metaphor for politics today. Over the last eighteen years this Italian fashion company has run the most provocative advertising campaigns ever seen. Twenty-foot billboards with the picture of a starving black baby; the AIDS victim at his moment of death; the bloodied uniform of a dead Bosnian soldier; the "United Killers of Benetton" campaign, a ninety-six-page magazine insert with photograph after photograph of condemned prisoners languishing on America's death rows. Benetton shocked us to attention, but shock is all it provided. It didn't rally us into action. Nor did it try and address these issues itself. Their advertising provided no exploration of the morality of war, there was no attempt to relieve poverty or cure AIDS. The only goal was to increase sales, not to start a discussion of the issues behind capital punishment. And if it profited from others' misery, so what?

We are living in a Benetton bubble. We are presented with shocking images by politicians who try to win our favor by demonizing their opponents and highlighting the dangers of the "wrong" representation. They speak of making a difference and changing our lives. Mainstream parties offer us supposedly different solutions and choices: Democrats tout liberal virtues, Republicans tout conservatism, all in an attempt to secure our votes.

But the rhetoric is not matched by reality. The solutions our politicians offer are as bogus as those of Benetton: a Chinese girl standing next to an American boy, a black woman holding hands with a white woman. Models with unusual faces, strong faces, sometimes beautiful, sometimes not. Multicolored people in multicolored clothes.

Political answers have become as illusory as the rows and rows of homogenized clothes, standard T-shirts, and cardigans folded in your local Benetton store. Commercialized conservatism and conformity par excellence. Politicians offer only one solution: a system based on laissez-faire economics, the culture of consumerism, the power of finance and free trade. They try and sell it in varying shades of blue, red, or yellow, but it is still a system in which the corporation is king, the state its subject, its citizens consumers. A silent nullification of the social contract.

5 But, I will argue, the system is undeniably failing. Behind the ideological consensus and supposed triumph of capitalism, cracks are appearing. If everything is so wonderful, why . . . are people ignoring the ballot box and taking to the streets and shopping malls instead? How meaningful is democracy if only half the people turn out to vote, as in the Bush–Gore presidential election, even though everyone knew it was going to be a close race? What is the worth of representation if . . . our politicians now jump to the commands of corporations rather than those of their own citizens?

It took time for people to rise up in protest, to see that the weightless state was unlikely to deliver the clean, safe world that they wanted their children to grow up in. For a long time people didn't question the one-ideology, homogeneous world. Why should they? For many, life was good and getting better. For most of the past twenty years the stock market has risen and interest rates fallen. More people than ever before own their own homes. Two thirds of us, in the developed world, have television sets of our own. Most of us, in the West that is, have cars. Our children wear Nike and Baby Gap. The middle class has grown and grown.

We are drip-fed images that reinforce this capitalist dream. Studios and networks beatify the very essence of capitalism. Prevailing norms and mainstream thoughts are recorded, replayed, and reinforced in Technicolor, while any criticism of the orthodoxy is consciously quashed. . . .

Such is our legacy. A world in which consumerism is equated with economic policy, where corporate interests reign, where corporations spew their jargon on to the airwaves and stifle nations with their imperial rule. Corporations have become behemoths, huge global giants that wield immense political power.

Propelled by government policies of privatization, deregulation, and trade liberalization, and the technological developments of the past twenty years, a power shift has taken place. The hundred largest multinational corporations now control about 20 percent of global foreign assets, and fifty-one of the one hundred biggest economies in the world are now corporations. The sales of General Motors and Ford are greater than the GDP of the whole of sub-Saharan Africa; the assets of IBM, BP, and General Electric outstrip the economic capabilities of most small nations; and Wal-Mart, the supermarket retailer, has higher revenues than most Central and Eastern Europe states.

The size of corporations is increasing. In the first year of the new millen- 10
nium, Vodafone merged with Mannesmann (a purchase worth $183 billion), Chrysler with Daimler (the merged company now employs over 400,000 people), Smith Kline Beecham with Glaxo Wellcome (now reporting pretax profits of $7.6 billion as GlaxoSmithKline), and AOL with Time Warner in a merger worth $350 billion—five thousand mergers in total in 2000, and double the level of a decade earlier. These megamergers mock the M&A activity of the 1980s. Each new merger is bigger than the one before, and governments rarely stand in the way. Each new merger gives corporations even more power. All the goods we buy or use—our gasoline, the drugs our doctors prescribe, essentials like water, transport, health, and education, even the new school computers and the crops growing in the fields around our communities—are in the grip of corporations which may, at their whim, nurture, support, or strangle us.

This is the world of the Silent Takeover, the world at the dawn of the new millennium. Governments' hands appear tied and we are increasingly dependent on corporations. Business is in the driver's seat, corporations determine the rules of the game, and governments have become referees, enforcing rules laid down by others. Portable corporations are now movable feasts and governments go to great lengths to attract or retain them on their shores. Blind eyes are turned to tax loopholes. Business moguls use sophisticated tax dodges to keep their bounty offshore. Rupert Murdoch's News Corporation pays only 6 percent tax worldwide; and in the U.K., up to the end of 1998, it paid no net British corporation tax at all, despite having made £1.4 billion profit there since June 1987. This is a world in which, although we already see the signs of the eroding tax base in our crumbling public services and infrastructure, our elected representatives kowtow to business, afraid not to dance to the piper's tune.

Governments once battled for physical territory; today they fight in the main for market share. One of their primary jobs has become that of ensuring an environment in which business can prosper, and which is attractive to business. The role of nation states has become to a large extent simply that of providing the public goods and infrastructure that business needs at the lowest costs while protecting the world's free trade system. . . .

Never before in modern times has the gap between the haves and the have-nots been so wide, never have so many been excluded or so championless. Forty-five million Americans have no health insurance. In Manhattan, people fish empty drink cans and bottles from trash cans to claim their five cents' redemption value, while in London, car windshield washers armed with squeegees and pails of dirty water ambush drivers at traffic lights. Americans spend $8 billion a year on cosmetics while the world cannot find the $9 billion the UN reckons is needed to give all people access to clean drinking water and sanitation. The British Labour party has gone on record as saying that wealth creation is now more important than wealth redistribution.

In America, during the ten years after 1988, income for the poorest families rose less than 1 percent, while it jumped 15 percent for the richest fifth. In New York City the poorest 20 percent earn an annual average of $10,700 while the wealthiest 20 percent earn $152,350. Wages for those at the bottom are so low that, despite the country's low unemployment figures, millions of employed Americans and one in five American children are now living in poverty. Never since the 1920s has the gap between rich and poor been so great. Bill Gates's net worth alone at the end of the last century, for example, equaled the total net worth of the bottom 50 percent of American families.

15 Capitalism has triumphed, but its spoils are not shared by all. Its failings are ignored by governments which, thanks to the very policy measures they introduced, are increasingly unable to deal with the consequences of their system.

COLLABORATING

Read the following simple story and determine its thesis. Next, by using one of the methods of interrogating the obvious, see if you can arrive at alternative theses or at least at questions that might lead you to a different thesis.

> A large male lion lorded over his terrain in a remote savannah in Africa. However, a drought dried up the watering holes that supplied his pride, so all of the lions had to migrate to a new area. As he had done in the old territory, the male lion established one watering hole that belonged exclusively to him. The pride drank from a separate watering hole that at first seemed sufficient. However, the lionesses came to feel that the male lion was hiding something from them. They started complaining about the bizarre behavior of the male lion, saying that his decisions were crazy and his actions outrageous. The rumor spread

quickly that the male lion had gone insane. The pride would no longer hunt for him and wanted to know what had happened to its wise, beloved leader.

The male lion could not understand the problem. He felt that he was acting the same as he ever had and thought that the pride had turned lazy and slothful. As his hunger grew, he planned to flee and hunt for himself. On the way out of the new territory, he stopped at the lionesses' watering hole to quench his thirst. He thought the water tasted particularly refreshing and drank for a long time. He did not feel like leaving any more, and his hunger seemed to wane. He strolled over to some of the lionesses and roared how much he had missed them. He agreed with them that hunting was not necessary and started questioning some of the decisions he had made since moving to the new territory. The pride rejoiced. Its leader had regained his sanity.

Investigating Assumptions

You have assumptions about how the world operates. Many of these assumptions seem like common sense. For example, eggs, cereal, and pancakes are commonsense options when you decide on breakfast. On a larger scale, the merits of competition are so ingrained in us that not only does our economic system depend on it but many leisure activities—playing cards, participating in sports, engaging in trivia challenges—also rely on it. Common sense relates to a value system constructed on cultural preferences about harmless matters like breakfast and more complex issues like competition.

When we extend these preferences to assumptions about individuals or groups of people, we create stereotypes, or unfair representations. The use of stereotypes in a thesis can alienate readers. Unexamined adherence to cultural assumptions or personal ones can do even more harm; they interfere with our understanding of our own actions and of how others react to us. Therefore, we must strive to investigate the assumptions behind our subjects as well as behind our lives.

Race, Class, and Gender

Assumptions about race, class, and gender abound in society. People growing up in previous generations used to find a color in a typical box of crayons called "flesh tone." The color resembled Caucasian skin, not African American, Hispanic, or any other group's skin. Airlines unabashedly segment members of differing social classes in "first class," "business class," and "tourist" seating. Golf courses around the nation still use the term "women's tees" for the starting spot for players who do not hit for long distances. All these instances show institutions adhering to assumptions about what is normal viewed through a lens of racial superiority, class privilege, or sexism.

When looking for the assumptions within a subject, ask questions about race, class, and gender. A white person who is trying to find a thesis for an essay based in personal experience might ask herself how her narrative might have been different if she or any of the people involved had been Korean, Navajo, or Caribbean. When arguing a point, another person might wonder what conditions of upper-class, middle-class, or working-class life factor into his position on an issue. In finishing a research component of a paper, he might check whether the likes and dislikes expressed in the library materials reflect a gender preference. The differences uncovered might be minimal or insignificant. But a combination of factors might enable these students to work toward theses that critique the influence of one or more of the assumptions on the subject.

WRITING

Many people do not like to write about racial, gender, or class privilege; they believe that such discourse divides us rather than unites us. Some prominent critics of political correctness say that we are all just people and that complaints based on race, gender, and class serve as an excuse for people not to succeed. While social class is important, let's stick to race and gender for now. To investigate the assumption that race and gender don't matter, freewrite in response to the following prompt, adapted from bell hooks's *Teaching Community*: If you were to die and could choose to come back as a white male, a white female, a black female, or a black male, which identity would you choose? Explain your choice, and decide whether your explanation refutes or supports the contention that race and gender matter.

Unearthing Agendas We often wonder about another person's true agenda, the genuine reasons the person reacts or feels a certain way. In sorting through the logic and evidence of an argument (discussed in Chapter 9), we sense that something has been left out, perhaps even buried so we won't find it. You might agree with Noreena Hertz's arguments (pages 35–38) about the concentration of wealth and its effects on justice and equity, but you might not believe that the capitalist system is "undeniably failing," as Hertz contends, and wonder why she has expressed such passion. You might start digging to unearth and bring to light her agenda. You speculate on her past experiences, and an Internet search reveals that she worked for International Finance Corporation before becoming a prominent academic. Might this color her view of the system?

You need also to examine your own reaction and interpretation. Why do you want to defend the system? Is there a reason you want to question or ignore the startling statistics Hertz presents? It is more difficult to dig deeply to unearth our own agendas than it is to critique those of others. Sometimes we find that a certain perspective, such as Hertz's, threatens our beliefs or our dreams. But if we start our investigation of assumptions with ourselves, we can clearly convey to readers what our agendas are and why facts or claims have not convinced us.

By unearthing our agendas, we avoid the appearance of deception and also learn about the legitimacy of our assumptions. What if our support for an English-only movement stems from our own insecurity about not speaking a second language? What if our belief in stereotypes about gang members fuels our distaste for rap music? These discoveries beg for self-reflection and change, both of which can start when we write about our feelings and bring our assumptions to the surface.

MICHAEL KINSLEY

The False Controversy of Stem Cells

If you think it through, the case for embryonic research is an easy one

Michael Kinsley has dug into the controversy over stem-cell research and suggests agendas for both the advocates and opponents of the destruction of human embryos. In this way, his ideas function as an example of trying to unearth agendas.

Congratulations to Representative Dana Rohrabacher, 56, and his wife Rhonda, 34, who gave birth to triplets last month. As we tend to suspect when a couple has triplets, the new parents used the services of a fertility clinic. Modern in-vitro techniques generally involve creating multiple embryos in the laboratory, transferring two or three and hoping that at least one will make it through to birth. Often it doesn't work. Sometimes it works unexpectedly well. Successful or not, the process creates many more embryos than babies. There is a built-in presumption—really, an intention—that even most of the transferred embryos will die. As for embryos that aren't transferred, they get destroyed or frozen indefinitely—unless, that is, they are used for stem-cell research.

So it's interesting that Rohrabacher has changed his position on the medical use of embryonic stem cells. The California Republican was a supporter of President Bush's three-year-old policy severely restricting government-funded stem-cell research, But he signed a recent letter to Bush from 206 members of Congress urging the President to reconsider that policy. Bush says he won't reconsider.

"Embryonic stem-cell studies are controversial because they involve the destruction of human embryos," the *New York Times* explained in a May 6 article reporting on the shifting politics of stem-cell research. (For example, Nancy Reagan, whose husband has Alzheimer's, has gone public with her opposition to the Bush restrictions.) But that can't be right. Fertility clinics destroy far more human embryos than stem-cell research ever would, yet they are not controversial. Death or deep freeze is the fate of any embryo spared by the Bush policy from the indignity of contributing to medical progress.

Stamping some issue as controversial can be a substitute for thinking it through. In the case of embryonic-stem-cell research, thinking it through does not require further study or commissions of experts. This is one you can feel free to try at home. In fact, thinking it through is a moral obligation, especially if you are on the side of the argument that wants to stop or slow this research.

5 It's not complicated. An embryo used in stem-cell research (and fertility treatments) is three to five days past conception. It consists of a few dozen cells that together are too small to be seen without a microscope. It has no consciousness, no self-awareness, no ability to feel love or pain. The smallest insect is far more human in every respect except potential.

Is destroying that microscopic dot the exact moral equivalent of driving a knife through the heart of an innocent 6-year-old girl? Some stem-cell enthusiasts think that even antiabortion absolutists can support stem-cell research, since it uses surplus embryos that are doomed anyhow. But that logic would justify Nazi experiments on doomed Jews in the concentration camps. If the microscopic dot is a human being with full human rights, the answer is easy: no stem-cell research.

But you don't have to be an abortion-rights advocate to reach the opposite conclusion. In fact, for abortion opponents whose views fall anywhere short of fanatical absolutism, the answer ought to be easy as well: full speed ahead. To the nonabsolutist, it ought to matter a lot that restricting stem-cell research doesn't actually spare the lives of any embryos. That means the lives of real people desperately awaiting the fruits of stem-cell research are being weighed against a purely symbolic message.

It also ought to matter to the nonfanatic that embryos are needed only to start the research process. Most of the research and all the treatments that come out of it will use so-called lines developed out of a few initial stem cells in the laboratory. That makes the stem-cell issue different from—and easier than—the one about fetal tissues a few years ago. Fetal-tissue treatments use brain tissue from several aborted fetuses for each patient. An embryo used in stem-cell research has nothing resembling a brain.

A difficult issue is one in which you hold two or more conflicting values. Stem cells are not a difficult issue: either you think a microscopic embryo has the same human rights as you and I, or you don't. Do you believe that a woman who gets an abortion should be prosecuted for murder, just like a mother who hires a professional killer to off her teenage son? Are you picketing around fertility clinics, which kill hundreds of thousands of unborn children—if that's what you believe a 5-day-old embryo to be—just like abortion clinics do? If so, you are entitled to oppose stem-cell research. If not, please get out of the way.

Seeing Patterns

While we are all individuals existing in space separate from other people, our backgrounds, opportunities, belief systems, and actual experiences have more in common with other people's than we often believe. Frequently, we focus on the small matters that distinguish us from others rather than looking at commonalities. We want to be unique. And we are in many ways. You were born on a specific date and time, grew up in a certain locale, and participated

COLLABORATING

What fuels Kinsley's passion for wanting to disentangle stem-cell research from the controversy over abortion? Might he have an agenda he has not reflected on or at least has not revealed? Do an Internet search about Kinsley to find out more about him. As a group, discuss how information about Kinsley's life affects the way you interpret his position. Does the information you found strengthen your perception of Kinsley's argument? Or are certain facts making you wondering about Kinsley's reliability?

in particular games and activities. No one else has experienced life precisely the way you have. In writing, however, focusing on such differences does not always amount to much. By settling on the uniqueness of a situation as part of a thesis, we can shut off critical analysis altogether.

One way to engage in critical analysis is to spot patterns, similarities, and connections between persons, places, and events. In the following excerpt from *Limbo,* Alfred Lubrano demonstrates how showing commonalities with the lives of others reinforces the importance of a personal experience and leads to critical analysis.

ALFRED LUBRANO

from Limbo

Rather than portraying himself as a hothead, Lubrano teases out a dilemma—a person from a blue-collar background in a white-collar environment. Lubrano discusses an experience from his days as a journalist, framing it with the similarities he finds with other people in this situation.

When I told my folks how much my first paper in Ohio was paying me, my father helpfully suggested I get a part-time job to augment the income. "Maybe you could drive a cab." Soon afterward, the city editor chewed me out for something trivial, and I made the mistake of telling my father during a visit home. "They pay you nothing and they push you around in that business," he told me, the rage building. "Next time, you grab the guy by the throat, push him against the wall, and tell him he's a big jerk."

"Dad I can't talk to the boss like that. And I can't touch him."

"Do it! You get results that way. Never take any garbage."

A few years before, a guy hadn't liked the retaining wall my father and a partner had built. They tore it down and did it again, but still the guy complained. My father's partner then shoved the guy into the freshly laid bricks. "Pay me off," my father said, and he and his partner took the money and walked. Blue-collar guys have no patience for office politics and corporate bile-swallowing. Just pay me off and I'm gone. . . .

If you come from the working class, you haven't got a clue how to conduct yourself when you first land in an office. You're lost if you can't navigate the landscape—if you follow blue-collar mores and speak your mind, directly challenging authority. Without tact and subtlety, without the ability to practice politics amongst the cubicles, an executive with a blue-collar background will not rise. And it's a drag watching others get promoted over you. . . .

5 Here's the dilemma: You come from a culture in which the boss is the common enemy and you're expected to be loyal to your fellow workers. People are not trying to work their way up to own the plumbing supply outfit in which they sweat. It's noble enough to hang in there and knock out those rent payments. Meanwhile, you go to college, then find yourself embarking on a white-collar career, where you are required to pledge allegiance to firm, not to your coworkers. And success is measured not by the secure stasis and comfortable consistency your parents struggled for but by constant movement upward, spurred by a class-taught, sleep-robbing dissatisfaction with your current spot on the corporate organizational chart. Stop climbing and you die. Which reminds me, because middle-class life can include frequent relocation ("We need you in Omaha yesterday, Don"), that creates still more problems for workers from blue-collar backgrounds, who traditionally live closer to extended family and feel a cultural obligation to remain nearer the clan. Oh, and by the way, to facilitate this grand journey, you might well have to shmooze a boss and kiss a fanny or two, anathema to your working-class forebears.

Okay, now try resolving all that.

Not everyone can. Myself, I've gotten into trouble by opening my mouth when I shouldn't have and speaking out when silence was the smart, middle-class alternative. Especially in the early days of my career, there was no such thing as an unexpressed thought. I believed it was more honest that way, more manly. If the boss is wrong, you tell him. You think the assignment is stupid or the editing bizarre? Just say it. That's what my father would have done. Growing up, blue-collar types have no reason not to speak their minds; there's nothing to lose when you're on the bottom. We tell you what we feel rather than what you want to hear.

As Signe Kastberg [an] Ithaca counselor . . . says, blue-collar people value the direct and honest approach. "I am," she tells me, "unable to be tactful. I cannot waste time figuring out 95 ways to say something that can be expressed in three blunt words. And I know that in some environments, that's not appreciated."

The blue-collar-born are committing faux pas left and right in the middle-class workplace, a panoply of mortal and venial sins of comportment, notes Laurene Finley, the psychologist who makes a specialty of treating people with working-class backgrounds. Meantime, people born in middle-class homes, who attended middle-class colleges, are making the relatively easy transition into the middle-class workplace.

"But when you don't know the politics of a place you can get slam-dunked." Finley says. Rife with enough difficulties, the office can be that much harder for a person who finds him, or herself tripping over the language and the furniture. Many may actually be ashamed of their backgrounds and try to hide the facts. Frustrated, working-class types sometimes make the mistake of hurling four-letter epithets at colleagues or even getting physical, as they resort to survival tactics from the old neighborhood when they feel threatened. "I've treated people who got directly into colleagues' faces, challenging them. They didn't fit into the culture at all. But nobody ever helped them belong." Needless to say, such folk are soon branded irritant, problem employees, and it isn't too long before bosses are "keeping paper on them"—compiling documentation in support of dismissal. Lots of people get lost, and corporate structure is not accommodating to those who are different. "I know many folks with talent who'll never make it in those circumstances," Finley concludes. 10

A sad friend of mine used to point out all her bosses' mistakes and found it hard to smile and give them what they wanted. "It may sound like I was being true to myself, but really, it was very self-defeating," she concludes. White-collar colleagues, she says, understand that the key to success is getting along with people. But she was raised on stories of the rotten foreman whom her father stood up to and threatened. She says her dad was a hero to his guys because he didn't take bull. But in the world she lives in now, you have to learn to get around the bull somehow. You can't keep calling the boss a jerk.

Over the years I've tried to improve my own manner, with marginal success. Now I say things like, "With all due respect . . . ." before I tell a boss I think he's wrong. I try not to be hostile. But I've got a glass head and I can't always hide my feelings, which stage three-act plays for everyone to see. I once told an editor, "With all due respect, I think that's a really bad idea." The man glared and was barely civil to me until he left the paper a year later. Not long after, my blue-collar persona shoved my white-collar self into a corner in a meeting with a top editor. I had challenged the guy, risking months of my work being thrown out and the real possibility of a permanent blackballing. Before doing the story, an examination of bad medical practices, I had elicited a promise from the editor that my wife's name would go on the bottom as a contributor. I wasn't trying to blow kisses to my honey. It's standard practice to include the name of a reporter who's helped substantively, and no financial compensation is involved. Linda, a freelance medical writer for MSNBC .com, Reuters.com, and the *New York Times,* didn't work for the newspaper but had given me numerous sources, in some cases calming skittish doctors who would never have talked to me if she hadn't intervened. Her involvement cut 30 days off the reporting process. Months before the meeting, before any reporting had been done on the story, I explained all this to the boss, a white-collar son of a white-collar dad, and asked his permission. He'd said it would be okay to publish Linda's name in the small print at the end of the story, giving her proper credit.

Suddenly, on the eve of publication, he was reneging. No explanation, really. He was just The Man and that was that. The five other editors in the room stayed mum and studied carpet patterns. But I had to show loyalty to my wife and coworker, in true working-class fashion, didn't I? Most white-collar guys in this situation would have finessed it, maybe met the editor afterward for a private chat. They certainly would not have challenged the big cheese in front of his own cabinet. "We had a deal," I told him candidly. "It was a promise you made. I wouldn't have done the story if you hadn't agreed to her tag line." As I spoke, I could feel my non–poker face register intensifying phases of red: fire truck, white guy yelling at a cop, lobster boiling. There was a loud noise in my head drowning out his equivocations, his smoothings. Brooklyn rose hot in my belly and I felt a righteous blue-collar fury erupting. Just then, my father's suggestion about grabbing my old boss seemed appropriate, almost justified. I didn't move, though. And the white-collar guy inside suddenly lunged for the controls, struggling to keep me employed and manfully preventing personal attacks and curses. "I guess we're at an impasse," I said. I'd decided I would remove my name from the story—a bald challenge to the boss, and tantamount to killing the work. No paper would print such a sensitive story without a byline, and the entire project would have been denigrated as a waste of time and money. As the room began to freeze over with tension, another editor piped up that maybe it wouldn't be so bad to have my wife's name at the bottom of the story. The big man saw a face-saving way out and relented. He also didn't talk to me for a long time. Needless to say, I never got any merit raises from the guy.

Let loose in shirt-and-tie America, the white-collar offspring of blue-collar parents report lots of self-inflicted career wounds. Maybe they try hard to fit in, maybe they don't try at all. Regardless, often enough, their true natures burble forth, and the authenticity isn't always appreciated.

While not ignoring the differences among the experiences we are comparing, we have to question how unique our personal experiences really are. People worry that a lack of uniqueness brings about conformity, a dull cooperation with popular trends, so they often want to stress features that set them apart from the crowd. For the purpose of critical analysis and building toward a theme, think of this type of uniqueness as a variable within similarity, something crucial to our sense of identity, perhaps, but not essential in generating an understanding of a person, place, or event. Following are ways to work toward finding patterns.

Facts and Events as Examples As a writer, look at any set of facts or description of events as an example of a larger trend in society. The September 11, 2001, attacks on New York City and Washington D.C., for instance, stand out as unique in the minds of many Americans; they appear to have no precursor. But when we probe the details, we find valid comparisons to previous events that did not immediately come to mind.

For instance, the pilots of the hijacked planes committed suicide for their political cause. Twentieth-century history provides many examples of suicide for political purposes, such as Japan's kamikaze pilots in World War II and the Buddhist monks who set themselves on fire to protest the policies of the Ngo Dinh Diem regime in South Vietnam. From here, a writer can look for other connections. Another detail of the September 11 attacks concerns the reaction of our government, such as the creation of the USA Patriot Act. At other times, have Americans curtailed civil rights in favor of national security? Examples abound. Woodrow Wilson and Abraham Lincoln, for example, both placed restrictions on citizens in ways similar to the Patriot Act. Once we see these similarities, others might surface.

The purpose of seeing seemingly unique occurrences as examples is that placing an event or set of facts into a context allows us to better understand it. We can think more clearly about what to do when we know that others have been in similar situations, and we can propose solutions that worked previously or raise objections to those that failed. When we spot a trend, we can evaluate it to see whether it affects our society positively or negatively. For example, knowing that our freedoms have been limited in the past could be either disturbing or comforting. We might notice a pattern of restrictions on individual pursuits of liberty that have gradually eroded our rights. On the other side, we might see a pattern of restoration of rights after temporary restrictions or increased safety as a result of permanent restrictions. Such critiques require first studying patterns by looking at the event as an example of something larger than just the unique occurrence it initially appears to be.

Who Profits? Sometimes the most penetrating critical analysis begins with the question, "Who stands to benefit the most if a situation remains the same?" Depending on the topic, we may be able to pinpoint specific individuals. But even profiles of the type of person who might profit can yield important insights, as long as we do not succumb to stereotyping or innuendo. Keep in mind that people profit in many different ways besides monetarily, such as by gaining power, earning acclaim, and maintaining their sense of respect or dignity. At times, you might shrug your shoulders over what you uncover using this analytic method; no one seems to be harmed when one person or a group profits. But when you see profiting disguised as taste, preference, or culture, you have to question why a person or group avoids being forthcoming about the profit element. Too often, many or the majority of people suffer when a small number profit.

RICHARD MEYER

Curriculum Is a Political Statement

Like many scholars who have researched how children learn to read, Richard Meyer believes that the widely taught phonics approach has tremendous flaws. In this passage, Meyer talks about decisions made regarding curriculum for reading classrooms. He has conducted research in a classroom taught by a woman named Karen, who was mandated to use a phonics curriculum. Notice that Meyer discusses both who wins and who loses when phonics are taught in the classroom.

As a scholar in education, Meyer uses the widely accepted American Psychological Association (APA) documentation style. You're probably already familiar with internal citations within a text. When an author quotes or paraphrases someone else's words, the author gives the specific page number on which those words first appeared. In academic writing, scholars such as Meyer also often refer to the works of other scholars to grant credence to their own ideas. Text is followed by the last name of another scholar plus the year of publication of the work that contains the idea in parentheses. So in the following excerpt, "(Wilson, 2000)" means that Meyer is building his ideas from previous scholarship, thus placing his ideas within an acceptable context in the field. If readers look at the reference list of the article (not reprinted here), they will find the article or book in question and can consult it if they so choose.

Curriculum is more than a set of materials. Curriculum, in Karen's case, signifies many decisions that were made. Karen was not included in those decisions, but she and her students must live with them—a view made clear to her by her administrators in the school and district.

Curriculum is political because it comes from some *place* and that place is a place (position) of influence and power. The claims that children can't read, aren't learning to read, schools must be bigger (read: more economical), and that all children must experience the same curricular materials (Wilson, 2000) are all serving someone. They are serving curriculum manufacturers, politicians who are serving individuals who want to do away with public schools (Ohanian, 2000), religious groups (Spring, 1997), and legislators who answer to industry (which supports their election). This is what Wilson (2000) called the "Emperor's new education" (p. 334). However, "unlike the small child who exposed the Emperor's nudity, in a related folk tale, no one has succeeded in exposing the Emperor's new education" (p. 334).

But I'm trying to expose it—its undemocratic views, its deprofessionalizing stances toward teachers, and its inhumane treatment of children. Paul (2000) reminded teachers to think about books like *The Giver* (Lowry, 1993), in which culture, differences, and even color are bleached away. Paul explained that "These are worlds uninhabitable to real people *who retain cultural memory* and who *recognize social conflict and complexity*" (p. 340; italics added). The phonics curriculum that Karen is using is creating uninhabitable literacy worlds for children. Any time we influence the worlds of children, we are making a political statement and engaging in political activity. The curriculum that is enacted is a political document because it touches children's and teachers' worlds. Karen "retain(s) cultural memory" and "recognizes social conflict and complexity" and this causes her pain—pain that I refer to as *curricular heartache.* It is a heartache born of the consciousness of a teacher knowing she can do better than the curriculum that is binding and limiting her and her students.

When a curriculum is enacted, it answers this question: What is a curriculum supposed to do? Perrone (1998) reminded us that "the content of schools seldom relates to what people in a particular community are worried about or care deeply about" (p. 61). He explained that much of what happens in schools is disconnected from the community and that the "disconnectedness trivializes much of what students are asked to learn" (p. 61). In previous school years, Karen saw her children become increasingly phonemically aware with the use of language activities that were relevant to the children. Now she and her students live with imposed irrelevance that ignores bodies of reading research.

5 When an approach to teaching reading discounts or dismisses huge bodies of research, such as the research on miscue analysis (Brown, Marek, & Goodman, 1996), *that* is a political act. Texas and California, two high-population states, influence the rest of the country when decisions are made in those states about the teaching of reading. They influence the rest of the country because publishers cater to high-population states, adjusting what is available for sale to meet the desire of those states' curriculum decision makers. The more publishers match the demands of the high-population states, the more money they make. Texas and California are known for statewide adoptions, meaning millions of dollars are at stake. When those two states became interested in more phonics instruction, publishers were quick to present programs to them (see Taylor, 1998). Those states made adoptions. Their adoptions were analyzed by Dressman (1999), who found that they "disregard or avoid . . . any research findings of the intervening 30 years that refute or adjust traditional beliefs about the efficacy of traditional practices" (p. 279). Dressman went on to say that:

> . . . these programs pay little if any attention to the communicative function of language, to the complex interrelations of the subcomponents of literacy, or to the agency of children as learners or adults as teachers. Instead, they prescribe programs of explicit, systematic instruction in the traditional subcomponents of reading and writing plus prerequisite screening and intervention via phonemic/phonological awareness activities . . . . They tacitly maintain that literacy is a cognitive issue that demands an almost exclusively cognitive approach to its instruction. (p. 279)

Dressman went on to describe the tediousness of these programs, referring to "reading a story aloud occasionally to break the monotonous labor of learning to read as an *unnatural* act" (p. 280; italics added).

Who gains when learning to read is a monotonous unnatural act? The children who rarely experience reading in other contexts aside from school lose; those that hear excited family members read to them outside of school also lose, just not as severely. When a curriculum teaches that reading is unnatural, it is making a political statement because those who have little power, who send their children to school with dreams of accessing power in the form of a better quality of life, are forced to stay marginalized. Their children are being edged out, pushed out, turned off, and disenfranchised from reading. They learn that reading is dull, unnatural, irrelevant, and dismissive of their lives outside of school. This is political work. It is political work that sounds like it would take place in a part of the world in which human rights are ignored, violated, or abused. It is happening here.

DISCUSSION

Can you think of ways that our culture demonstrates the value of individuality or uniqueness? Under what circumstances does our culture value conformity? Think of a time you witnessed or experienced a situation in which one person asserted the uniqueness of a person, place, or event while another person tried to show that the person, place, or event was not unique. What was at stake? Did anyone stand to lose or gain by the outcome? Compare your example with the examples of other students in class. Is there a discernible pattern to your experiences?

Avoiding Poor Reasoning

Critical analysis leads us toward challenging dominant thought in society. Often, we can fulfill a rebellious need through these types of critiques and build much enthusiasm when writing. However, we have to be careful to avoid confusing critical analysis and poor reasoning. Even intelligent people sometimes mistake the two.

Reasonable or rational thinking requires us to adhere to conventions of logic as well as ethics. Poor reasoning seeps into our ideas or arguments when we worry about persuading or convincing an audience or reader that we are correct. We reach for tactics that undermine our thinking and play on the emotions of others. In Part II, we examine the appropriate ways to work with evidence and to avoid lapses in logic, such as those that occur when writers succumb to the bandwagon mentality or straw-person arguments.

For now, we should monitor ourselves for any of the logical fallacies that often occur when a writer is trying to construct a powerful thesis. If you find that you are using any of the strategies discussed below to persuade an audience—whether that audience consists of other students, instructors, or a general readership—rethink your approach and revise accordingly.

Attacks Against Others

We are frequently tempted to discredit an idea or belief on the basis of who introduces it to us. We ignore logic and evidence in favor of the popularity of the person presenting an idea or belief to us. Generally, we attack a person's intellect by making such remarks as "Well, what does he know?" or by bringing up unfavorable characteristics, such as "She's a nerd, so of course she thinks that."

When we find ourselves using such devices, which are called ad hominem attacks, we are really making excuses to avoid pondering a position that threatens some aspect of ourselves. Aside from involving a lack of reflection, the ad hominem attack derives its strength from our hope that nobody we admire adheres to the belief under attack. What would happen if the nerd we degraded believes the same thing as our favorite musician or an admired intellectual or moral figure, such as Albert Einstein or Mahatma Gandhi? That would take us back to where we started, which is with the evidence and logic behind the idea.

Reasonable thinking demands not taking such detours. Questioning the credibility of a source is fine. For example, if a student in your class diagnoses your flulike symptoms as pneumonia, you would be reasonable in doubting her assertion because she is not a doctor. It would be unwise, in fact, to act as if you had pneumonia without getting a second opinion from somebody with a medical degree. Your classmate could be missing something essential in her diagnosis because of her lack of expertise and experience. You seek verification under such circumstances.

When wondering about the validity of facts that someone supplies, it is also perfectly acceptable to ask for verification. People have been known to misread books or to frame the results of a study to favor their own position. When examining eyewitness testimony or the truth behind a story someone tells you, consider the person's background, beliefs, and agenda before deciding about the person's reliability.

But when we dismiss an idea simply because of who says it, we are no longer being reasonable. In writing, it might appear easier to construct a thesis on the basis of an attack on an unpopular person or even to associate opposing viewpoints with unpopular terms you have heard. Radio commentator Rush Limbaugh frequently avoids critical analysis by labeling opponents "liberals" or "feminazis" and excoriating people who agitate for change on the basis of liberal or feminist ideology. The ideas of these opponents persist, though, precisely because they have not been defeated through a reasonable approach. Attacking others does not work because the substance of an idea is separate from the person who holds the idea.

Diversions While critical analysis calls for making connections that might not be apparent at first, writers have to be careful not to confuse an issue. Some professional writers, whether intentionally or unintentionally, divert an audience from the issue at hand to talk about another situation. This logical fallacy is called a "red herring."

A person, for instance, might want to argue that opening up federal land for oil exploration is necessary because of upcoming shortages. He might say, "If we do not get more oil, we will face higher prices and gasoline rationing, just as happened during the energy crisis of the 1970s. We all remember how bad that was." If the person continues to discuss the hardships brought on by the energy crisis thirty years ago without making direct comparisons to the current situation, he will be diverting the audience in unethical ways, trying to garner support by evoking deprivation. In so doing, he is not explaining anything about the current situation, why he thinks there will be shortages, or how opening up federal lands to exploration will prevent shortages.

A comparison might yield a pattern, as discussed in the previous section, but the focus should be on the pattern, not on the situation thirty years ago. In avoiding the facts of the current situation, the person is not critically analyzing the situation; he is avoiding analysis of the crucial facts and not supporting his position. Alert readers uncover such tactics quickly, which undermines the credibility of the writer's position and brings the writer's integrity into question.

Overgeneralizing

Writers forming generalizations from analyses need to adhere to certain constraints so that they do not apply their conclusions too broadly. Critical analysis uncovers insights and generates theories. However, the insights and theories are not proof. Rather, they suggest possible applications to other situations or point in directions where some ideas can be applied. When we claim that a conclusion applies to all situations, we are overgeneralizing.

For instance, you might write an essay about holidays and reach the conclusion that people have changed the purpose of holiday celebrations from commemoration to simply having fun. This thesis, though perhaps tied to a great deal of evidence about our culture's habits of celebration, cannot account for the somber commemorations on national holidays such as Memorial Day, when many people grieve for the dead at cemeteries. A more accurate thesis might be that many people have distorted the purpose of holidays to having fun. The qualification "many," instead of the implied "all" in the original statement, makes the difference.

Mistakes can also be made when we take one or two incidents, ignore important specifics from those situations, and reach a general conclusion. In the essay about holidays, you might decide that, based on the past two Fourth of July parties you attended, people no longer enjoy fireworks on Independence Day. Two parties supply very little evidence for such a sweeping statement. You might have overlooked the specifics of the situations, such as the age group of the partygoers, the region of the country, or the type of peo-

WRITING

Go to the website of your local newspaper, and read several days' worth of op-ed columns, which you will find on the editorial or opinion pages. How do the columnists support their ideas? Do the columnists appear to be reasonable? Did you notice any attacks on others, diversions, or overgeneralizations?

Choose one editorial that you agree with and another that you do not agree with. Write a one-paragraph summary of each editorial, then look again at the editorials to determine how the columnists dealt with people in opposition to them, comparisons to other situations, and generalizing from the evidence they presented. Write down your evaluation of the columnists' ideas, noting places where they might have succumbed to poor reasoning.

ple. A more accurate thesis would limit this conclusion, saying perhaps that you have noticed a decline in the popularity of Independence Day fireworks among people of your age group. The key word *might,* combined with the detail about your age group, keeps you clear of overgeneralizations.

Summary

All essays must have a thesis that logically derives from their content. The best way to avoid clichés in a thesis and to assert ideas that strike you as true is to engage in critical analysis. Critical analysis digs deep, looking at the content from several different perspectives and uncovering insights that lead to a strong thesis.

Critical analysis takes many forms: interrogating the obvious, questioning assumptions, and reconceiving uniqueness. When you employ any of these methods, you may discover ideas that you had not considered before. In conveying these ideas, however, you have to be careful to avoid poor reasoning; you can be perceived as illogical and unethical if you attack others, use diversions, or overgeneralize.

CHAPTER 3

AWARENESS OF AUDIENCE

Good writers use critical analysis to reach bold ideas. In expressing these ideas, writers have to be aware of their readers. These actual and imagined readers comprise what we will term the audience. The audience affects what a writer does in everything from how much detail to supply to where to place opposing points of view. An audience also determines the success of any piece of writing.

An audience judges writing on what writers compose. If the audience does not know the writer, either personally or through reputation, all judgments will come from the words the writer uses to establish his or her ethos on the subject. *Ethos* can be loosely defined as the ethical credibility of the writer. Writers demonstrate ethos through words. Authorial intention, or what a writer means to say through writing, does not control the reaction of an audience and cannot be relied on to clarify ambiguity or defend a point of view. A writer must be aware that she or he is constructing a writerly self or a persona that an audience will respond to either positively or negatively.

Anna, who took a course in English composition from me several years ago, wrote a paper about the social issues surrounding gays and lesbians on campus. She focused on the method of tolerance for alternative sexual lifestyles apparently advocated during a freshmen orientation seminar. She was having difficulty living up to this method's expectations, saying that being around people of the same gender who acted in ways indicative of same-sex relationships made her uncomfortable. In the draft of her paper that Anna presented in a whole-class workshop, she concluded that no one should force anyone else to be tolerant.

This icon will direct you to web links and additional resources on the website college.hmco.com/pic/thelin1e

ANNA BANKS

Sexuality Orientation

I do not like when other people's views are forced onto me. I think that the Freshman Orientation here at ___________ does not orient people to being able to live on campus. It brainwashes them into wanting to accept ideas that make them sick.

I try to keep an open mind about everything. The Freshman Orientation started out okay in this respect. I was told there might be some people born elsewhere who could be staying in my dorms, and I said to myself that I would tolerate their ways. I listened to advice on how to communicate when their English was not that good and thought I could offer help if needed.

After the Orientation people reviewed things on campus like speakers and activities, I thought I had heard all I wanted to. I really wanted to know how to find classes and to make sure I didn't get raped by some inbred wandering around. But I found out that the theme for the Orientation was diversity and tolerance. All of a sudden, they bring to the stage some gay and lesbian people.

The guy started by saying that about 10% of the population on the campus is gay and that some sort of research said that as many as 30% of the population could have hidden feelings like that. He then said that if you had ever noticed how well dressed a person of the same sex was or noticed the good figure on a girl or for guys, their muscles, you were displaying normal tendencies that involve homosexual feelings. Fortunately, he didn't say that made us lesbians, because I've noticed when friends are pretty and I know I don't go for chicks! But I felt pretty insulted anyway, as he wanted us to be like them.

A dyke took the stage and I thought she would have a really deep voice and act like a man, but she seemed pretty nice. She didn't try to tell us we were all lesbians, but instead talked about ways to respect gays and lesbians. She said that you shouldn't be uncomfortable around gay couples because they did not pose any threat to you. She said that most gay people did not get passionate in front of heteros, I didn't like how she termed all us that, and that the most you would probably notice would be hand holding or putting arms around each other. The same rules apply, as a "hetero" couple makes people uncomfortable with "public displays of affection" too.

The final guy talked about stereotypes of gays and claimed that some of them were very athletic and manly while lesbians could be feminine and have traditional values. He gave examples of friends of his who did mountain climbing and worked as an ambulance driver. He finished by saying we shouldn't assume we couldn't be friends with gays just because we weren't gays. He said we could still share interests and form friendships.

> I came back home and was thoroughly disgusted. I couldn't believe that people wanted me to tolerate gays and lesbians. When I think of them kissing and stuff like that, it makes me want to throw up. I don't feel right when I am around someone who acts gay or lesbian and don't want someone to force me to pretend to be comfortable. I don't think school should expect me to accept people I don't like. I definitely don't want to be friends with them because then people will think I'm a lesbo. I guess people can do what they like when they're alone, but they cannot expect normal people to agree with it and want to be around it. That's asking too much.

In the workshop, many of Anna's peers could not get past the thesis and what they considered to be her hostility toward gays and lesbians. While some members of the class agreed with her to an extent, the dominant sentiment seemed to be that gays and lesbians should be left alone, that as long as their lifestyle did not affect anyone else, other members of the campus should be tolerant. The students kept asking Anna to investigate her assumptions and unearth her agenda. It seemed that the students saw potential in her paper for self-reflection that would allow her to establish a stronger ethos for her audience. Several asked Anna if she had heard antigay sentiments in her household or among her peers. Anna became frustrated.

"I want to make this paper better," she said. "Give me some ideas I can use."

The students were momentarily stunned. A class leader named Jim broke the silence. "But that's what we're doing," he said. "You haven't given any reasons for not wanting to be around gays and lesbians. You described the seminar but that's about it."

A student named Sandra chipped in. "Yeah, you talk about all the good things said in orientation but not about why they didn't affect you."

"But this is my paper," Anna said. "I don't want it to explain everything."

"But if you want your readers to understand you," I said, "you have to give them your reasons."

"Right now," Jim said, "it sounds like you hate gays and lesbians and just want us to accept that."

Indeed, Anna's paper was expressing a strong opinion that lacked the forms of critical analysis discussed in Chapter 2. The only person who could read it and take her views seriously would be someone who shared Anna's feelings or experiences. Anna had failed to communicate the logical reasoning or personal convictions that would allow readers to receive her paper more sympathetically.

Anna kept her head down through most of this conversation, but she looked at me after Jim spoke. "So I have to change what I say to make this a good paper?" she asked.

In unison everyone said that wasn't the point. "People do not have to agree with me for me to listen to them," Jim said. "But they have to understand where I'm coming from if I'm going to listen."

"I can't take your ideas seriously," Sandra said, "because you haven't taken my ideas seriously." Sandra was referring to the persona Anna had created. While her fellow students knew a little about Anna through classroom activities, she could not rely on that information to establish ethos with them as readers.

Ultimately, Anna had failed to take the possible reactions of her audience into consideration when she had written this draft. The process of drafting acts as a time of discovery, as is discussed later in Chapter 6, and does not necessarily need to accomplish more than express thoughts and attempt to support them. In revising, however, writers need to consider who will be reading their words, what those readers already know and do not know, what they might believe, and where they might object to a position or statement. Writers also need to look within themselves and reflect on their ideas to build and maintain an ethos that will secure an audience's willingness to listen. Anna did not seem to feel that her audience mattered. Yet, words have no effect if they are not heard. In dismissing the importance of audience, Anna dismissed the communicative function of writing. She felt that her ideas and reasoning should be apparent, and she rejected notions that the experiences she described were a result of her prejudice.

Unfortunately, Anna never submitted a revision of that paper. Had she continued to revise, she may have decided to reflect and examine the prejudice in her thinking. She might have considered religious or moral views that made her oppose gay and lesbian lifestyles and attempted to explain those beliefs more clearly for an audience that she knew did not share these views. She could have revised her paper to critique the orientation seminar through logical means and possibly have found holes in its assumptions, reinforcing

DISCUSSION

What do you immediately see when you look at this drawing? Did other students see the same thing immediately? If not, why? Can you perceive the picture differently on a second look? Think about how valuable the audience (in this case, viewers rather than readers) is in interpretation. Does this picture have a definite, precise interpretation not constructed by the audience?

Old Woman . . . or Young Girl?

Hint: The old woman's nose is the young girl's chin.

beliefs she had learned while growing up. A successful revision could have considered the views of an opponent of her beliefs, someone who found that the freshmen orientation gave him or her a refreshing perspective on gays and lesbians. In her first draft, Anna might have intended to sound sympathetic to gays and lesbians and might have meant to say only that the lifestyle was not for her. In the end, we cannot know her intentions. Until she could establish her own ethos by explaining the assumptions on which her arguments rested, she could not hope to accommodate or understand her audience.

An audience constructs meaning from a piece of writing. The best opportunity for feedback between writers and potential readers is during a draft workshop or something like it. Once a piece of writing is published, submitted to a instructor for a grade, given to an executive board to act on, or sent over the Internet to readers, the writer has little control over interpretation. An audience will be puzzled, angered, dismayed, or unaffected if the writer did not anticipate the differing needs, backgrounds, and opinions of its members. Two people can look at the same object and see differing images.

Understanding the audience does not mean altering your intended meaning or disguising your intentions. If you establish a strong or consistent ethos, your audience will be more likely to listen, even if its members do not agree. You do not need to pander to readers in order to communicate. Yet, you do have to understand the diverse views of society and prepare for them. You also need to realize that what is perfectly clear to you might not be clear to someone else; a member of an audience probably has not experienced life the way you have, especially when it comes to specific experiences or other factors that have influenced your beliefs. The guidelines that follow should help you take the audience into account when you write.

Targeting Potential Readers

Not every possible reader warrants consideration when you write. If you were to write about the virtues of Ty Cobb as the greatest baseball player ever, for instance, you would have already targeted people who care about baseball. Someone who has no interest in the game will read no farther, so you do not have to worry about that person as a potential reader. Since baseball is not an obscure sport, you could assume that most potential readers do not need an overview of how the game is played (unlike an extreme sport such as wakeboarding), but you do face a decision about readers' knowledge of baseball history and the finer points of the game. For most writing, you need to factor in common knowledge, cultural considerations, and vocabulary to make decisions about how much information to provide. The following guidelines also determine the amount of research and evidence you need for academic writing.

Common Knowledge If you learned something in high school or before, you can consider that information to be common knowledge—that is, generally acknowledged to be true. For example, the capitals of states, the dates of major historical events, and the basic components of a cell are all common knowledge. In academic writing, you would not need to cite sources for these facts.

You also do not need to recount common knowledge in setting up your essay. If you provide too much remedial information, you risk insulting or boring your readers. Of course, people's experiences in high school differ, so what counts as common knowledge varies.

If you are worried that an audience will not recollect information important for the acceptance of your thesis, preface your overview with a brief summary of the key points, making it clear that you are supplying a review for the sake of convenience. Avoid condescending remarks or statements indicating that the information is obvious. Sometimes it is frustrating to include information that is second nature to you. You may wish that the audience can be counted on to know more so you can get right to the point. Keep in mind, though, that a condescending tone does not win friends. You probably develop a negative impression when someone implies that you are stupid because you do not already know something. Writing works the same way. If you do not strike a balance regarding common and specialized knowledge, you can lose your audience.

Cultural Considerations Writers have to understand that the culture in which they live might be unfamiliar to a larger audience. In fact, an audience might hold stereotypical beliefs about particular subcultures. Thus, what is second nature to us might confuse readers or be misunderstood. Consider the following passage from "Bloody Footprints" by Roxanne A. Dunbar.

> The poor whites (white trash) I come from, Okies and their descendents, were those who formed the popular base for the post–World War II rise of the hard right in Orange County, California. Richard Nixon the anti-Communist was their man. They were the "little people" and "silent majority" addressed by Richard Nixon as President, then by Ronald Reagan. They were among the bigots, including my father, who supported George Wallace. During the 1980s, they helped swell the ranks of the Christian Coalition, promoting anti-abortion and anti-gay initiatives.

Dunbar adds much detail to describe "poor whites" or "Okies" because she has anticipated that these terms might evoke another image for her

WRITING

In her effort to define the term *poor whites* for her audience, Roxanne Dunbar uses terms like *silent majority* and makes references to American historical figures like George Wallace. What cultural knowledge is needed to make sense of her description? Did you have trouble understanding her point about her family's background? Write an explanation of both the common knowledge and the cultural considerations needed to comprehend this passage fully.

audience. Writers need to examine their topics when revising and ponder whether examples, references, or points rely on specialized cultural or ethnic knowledge that needs further explanation. Weaving in short explanations keeps the audience within the targeted readership and might even pique interest in your particular culture, thus helping to deflate stereotypes.

Vocabulary Practically nothing alienates a reader more than the use of words and phrases that he or she does not understand. Writers need to use plain, clear English to communicate their ideas. A writer's sophistication, though, can evaporate if he or she tries to "dumb down" his or her vocabulary, and the writer might be perceived as condescending.

To reach your audience effectively, avoid jargon and imply the meaning of uncommon vocabulary words in the context of the sentence. Jargon consists of words and phrases that have developed in a workplace or culture to substitute for longer explanations of events, theories, or procedures. Sometimes jargon users invent words that are not in the dictionary. Other times, jargon is comprised of words already in general usage to mean something slightly or altogether different from the dictionary definitions.

Writers should also avoid unnatural, elevated vocabulary, which occurs when writers try to find too obscure of a synonym to express an ordinary word. To avoid repetition, inexperienced writers sometimes fall prey to using a thesaurus and end up writing sentences with words that they do not ordinarily use and that readers do not know (more on thesaurus usage in Chapter 5). Other times, writers with advanced knowledge or expertise unintentionally use words familiar to people like them but unfamiliar to a general audience. To target readers beyond the small circles where jargon and elevated vocabulary are appropriate, you must take steps to be inclusive. Small efforts to reach a targeted audience will keep its members reading and comprehending.

MARIAH BLAKE

Voices: The Damage Done

Crack babies talk back

Analyze how well this author targeted potential readers. Has she given enough background information, too much, or too little? What do you need to know about the media hype surrounding crack babies to understand the thesis? Is the vocabulary too elevated or full of jargon? Decide who the intended audience was.

Antwaun Garcia was a shy boy whose tattered clothes reeked of cat piss. Everyone knew his father peddled drugs and his mother smoked rock, so they called him a "crack baby."

It started in fourth grade when his teacher asked him to read aloud. Antwaun stammered, then went silent. "He can't read because he's a crack baby," jeered a classmate. In the cafeteria that day no one would sit near him. The kids pointed and chanted, "crack baby, crack baby." Antwaun sat sipping his milk and staring down at his tray. After that, the taunting never stopped. Unable to take it, Antawun quit school and started hanging out at a local drug dealer's apartment, where at age nine he learned to cut cocaine and scoop it into little glass vials. *"Crack baby,"* he says. "Those two words almost cost me my education."

Antwaun finally returned to school and began learning to read a year later, after he was plucked from his parent's home and placed in foster care. Now twenty, he's studying journalism at LaGuardia Community College in New York City and writing for *Represent,* a magazine for and by foster children. In a recent special issue he and other young writers, many of them born to crack addicts, took aim at a media myth built on wobbly, outdated science: crack babies. Their words are helping expose the myth and the damage it has done.

Crack hit the streets in 1984, and by 1987 the press had run more than 1,000 stories about it, many focusing on the plight of so-called crack babies. The handwringing over these children started in September 1985, when the media got hold of Dr. Ira Chasnoff's *New England Journal of Medicine* article suggesting that prenatal cocaine exposure could have a devastating effect on infants. Only twenty-three cocaine-using women participated in the study, and Chasnoff warned in the report that more research was needed. But the media paid no heed. Within days of the first story, CBS News found a social worker who claimed that an eighteen-month-old crack-exposed baby she was treating would grow up to have "an IQ of perhaps fifty" and be "barely able to dress herself."

5 Soon, images of the crack epidemic's "tiniest victims"—scrawny, trembling infants—were flooding television screens. Stories about their bleak future abounded. One psychologist told the *New York Times* that crack was "interfering with the central core of what it is to be human." Charles Krauthammer, a columnist for the the *Washington Post,* wrote that crack babies were doomed to "a life of certain suffering, of probable deviance, of permanent inferiority." The public braced for the day when this "biological underclass" would cripple our schools, fill our jails, and drain our social programs.

But the day never came. Crack babies, it turns out, were a media myth, not a medical reality. This is not to say that crack is harmless. Infants exposed to cocaine in the womb, including the crystallized version known as crack, weigh an average of 200 grams below normal at birth, according to a massive, ongoing National Institutes of Health study. "For a healthy, ten-pound Gerber baby this is no big deal," explains Barry Lester, the principal investigator. But it can make things worse for small, sickly infants.

Lester has also found that the IQs of cocaine-exposed seven-year-olds are four and a half points lower on average, and some researchers have documented other subtle problems. Perhaps more damaging than being exposed to cocaine itself is growing up with addicts, who are often incapable of providing a stable, nurturing home. But so-called crack babies are by no means ruined. Most fare far better, in fact, than children whose mothers drink heavily while pregnant.

Nevertheless, in the midst of the drug-war hysteria, crack babies became an emblem of the havoc drugs wreak and a pretext for draconian drug laws. Hospitals began secretly testing pregnant women for cocaine, and jailing them or taking their children. Tens of thousands of kids were swept into foster care, where many languish to this day.

Represent magazine was founded at the height of the crack epidemic to give voice to the swelling ranks of children trapped in the foster-care system. Its editors knew that many of their writers were born to addicts. But it wasn't until late last year, when a handful expressed interest in writing about how crack ravaged their families, that the picture snapped into focus. "I remember hearing about crack babies and how they were doomed,'" says editor Kendra Hurley. "I suddenly realized these were those kids."

10 Hurley and her co-editor, Nora McCarthy, had worked with many of the writers for years, and had nudged and coddled most through the process of writing about agonizing personal experiences. But nothing compared to the shame their young scribes expressed when discussing their mothers' crack use. Even the most talented believed it had left them "slow," "retarded," or "damaged." The editors decided to publish a special crack issue to help break the stigma and asked the writers to appear on the cover, under the headline "'Crack Babies'—All Grown Up." Initially, only Antwaun agreed. He eventually convinced three others to join him. "I said, 'Why shouldn't we stand up and show our faces?'" he recalls. "We rose above the labels. I wanted to reach other kids who had been labeled and let them know it doesn't mean you can't succeed."

As it happens, when the crack issue went to press, a group of doctors and scientists was already lobbying the *New York Times* to drop terms like "crack baby" from its pages. The group included the majority of American researchers investigating the effects of prenatal cocaine exposure or drug addiction. They were spurred to action by the paper's coverage of a New Jersey couple found to be starving their four foster children in late 2003. For years the couple had explained the children's stunted growth to neighbors and friends by saying, among other things, that they were "crack babies." The *Times* not only failed to inform readers that crack babies don't exist, but reinforced the myth by reporting, without attribution, that "the youngest [of the children] was born a crack baby."

Assistant Managing Editor Allan Siegal refused to meet with the researchers, saying via email that the paper simply couldn't open a dialogue with all the "advocacy groups who wish to influence terminology." After some haggling, he did agree to publish a short letter to the editor from the researchers. While the paper hasn't used "crack baby" in the last several months, it has referred to babies being "addicted" to crack, which, as the researchers told the editors, is scientifically inaccurate, since babies cannot be born addicted to cocaine.

The researchers later circulated a more general letter urging all media to drop the term "crack baby." But the phrase continues to turn up. Of the more than 100 news stories that have used it in the last year, some thirty were published after the letter was distributed in late February.

Represent's writers made a more resounding splash. National Public Radio and AP both featured them in stories on crack's legacy. Inspired by their words, the columnist E. R. Shipp called on New York *Daily News* readers to consider the damage the crack-baby myth has done. A July *Newsday* op-ed made a similar plea, and also urged readers to avoid rushing to judgment on the growing number of babies being born to mothers who use methamphetamines.

Still, a number of recent "meth baby" stories echo the early crack-baby 15
coverage. A July AP article cautioned, for instance, that an "epidemic" of meth-exposed children in Iowa is stunting infants' growth, damaging their brains, and leaving them predisposed to delinquency. In May, one Fox News station warned that meth babies "could make the crack baby look like a walk in the nursery." Research is stacking up against such claims. But, then, scientific evidence isn't always enough to kill a good story.

COLLABORATING

Spend time writing a three- or four-paragraph description of an activity you enjoy doing with your family or with a group of close friends. Assume you are writing for a general audience. Discuss what you do and why you like it.

Share your descriptions with your group. Look closely at each description to see where common knowledge has been considered, where cultural assumptions have been explained, and where jargon and elevated language have been avoided. Are there places where too much or too little background information is given? Has the writer failed to communicate something essential about his or her culture? Do any vocabulary choices confuse or alienate you? As a group, form a consensus about the type of reader who would understand and enjoy each paper, and discuss changes that could increase the number of readers.

Anticipating Reader Needs

Once we know our audience, we want to establish our ethos so that readers can relate to us and value our perspective as worthy of consideration. Writing is generally a matter of persuasion. We want readers to believe that the way we communicate a story is the way events actually transpired. We want readers to see our position on an important issue as the most correct and logical position. We want readers to feel so strongly about our thesis that they will respond to a call for action. Anna's draft from earlier in the chapter failed to target her audience, and her problems continued with not anticipating her readers' needs. She wanted to have her perspective valued and understood, but she did not seem to be concerned enough about her readers' needs to try to persuade them.

Persuasion begins with understanding that readers may have different values and experiences than you do. Allowing them to relate to you involves showing them the commonalities between your and their experiences or perspectives. The relationship you want to establish in every piece of writing will be determined by your purpose. Some forms of persuasion are almost invisible and might not be an overt part of your intentions. If you always keep possible differences between you and your audience in mind, you will be able to incorporate responses to your readers' needs in subtle ways.

Value Systems All of us believe in certain principles. If we feel that a particular set of ideas is beyond question, we have reached a conviction. Most readers have convictions that lead them to develop a system of values that guide their decisions in life. While we cannot possibly anticipate every reader's system, we can and should be aware of the dominant value systems of our community and society. Some of these systems conflict, as we see in the efforts at persuasion by members of opposing value systems in debates over social issues, such as abortion and capital punishment, and in elections, where representatives with differing value systems apply their convictions to foreign and domestic issues. If we are to do serious critical analysis, as advocated in the previous chapter, we need to persuade our audience to consider possibilities beyond its value system. To do this, we have to make a list of where our ideas might conflict with dominant systems and grasp common values that might bring the audience closer to our side.

For example, if you believe that children should take dancing lessons to develop grace and the ability to express themselves, you should anticipate that these ideas will conflict with some value systems. Listing the reasons that people might disagree with you is a good starting point toward finding common values. One such value might involve masculinity. Some fathers would shudder at sending their boys to dance lessons, thinking that such lessons might jeopardize the boys' development into masculine men. If you dismiss such sentiments as a knee-jerk reaction and ignore the need to relate to them in your writing, you will be appealing only to those who are predisposed to agree with you, which might be a very narrow readership. To relate to and even persuade an audience of concerned fathers who value masculinity, you would have to think about how dancing could help a young boy develop a sense of masculinity. Thus, you might talk about the physical strength needed by male ballet dancers. You might mention that Arnold Schwarzenegger, winner of multiple body-building competitions, took dance instruction. Finally, you might observe that good dancing skills in young men lead to attention from young women, which would be in keeping with a value of masculinity.

Knowing in advance what an audience will think and showing the similarities between your goals and theirs will help readers consider your point of view more thoroughly. You will also learn from comparing your ideas to dominant value systems and can either strengthen your position or understand its weaknesses, which perhaps might lead you to tailor what could be construed as an extreme position.

WRITING

Make a list of your values, and focus on one that you believe most conflicts with a dominant value in society. Narrate a specific experience or observation in which your value influenced the way you interpreted or described an event. Write down the ways you might be able to find common ground with people who did or might have disagreed with your interpretation of the incident.

ANNA QUINDLEN

Death Penalty's False Promise

Note where the author, Anna Quindlen, relates to the values of her anticipated audience.

Ted Bundy and I go back a long way, to a time when there was a series of unsolved murders in Washington State known only as the Ted murders. Like a lot of reporters, I'm something of a crime buff. But the Washington Ted murders—and the ones that followed in Utah, Colorado and finally in Florida, where Ted Bundy was convicted and sentenced to die—fascinated me because I could see myself as one of the victims. I looked at the studio photographs of young women with long hair, pierced ears, easy smiles, and I read the descriptions: polite, friendly, quick to help, eager to please. I thought about being approached by a handsome young man asking for help, and I knew if I had been in the wrong place at the wrong time I would have been a goner.

By the time Ted finished up in Florida, law enforcement authorities suspected he had murdered dozens of young women. He and the death penalty seemed made for each other.

The death penalty and I, on the other hand, seem to have nothing in common. But Ted Bundy has made me think about it all over again, now that the outlines of my 60s liberalism have been filled in with a decade as a reporter covering some of the worst back alleys in New York City and three years as a mother who, like most, would lay down her life for her kids.

Simply put, I am opposed to the death penalty. I would tell that to any judge or lawyer undertaking the voir dire of jury candidates in a state in which the death penalty can be imposed. That is why I would be excused from such a jury. In a rational, completely cerebral way, I think the killing of one human being as punishment for the killing of another makes no sense and is inherently immoral.

But whenever my response to an important subject is rational and com- 5
pletely cerebral, I know there is something wrong with it—and so it is here. I have always been governed by my gut, and my gut says I am hypocritical about the death penalty. That is, I do not in theory think that Ted Bundy, or others like him, should be put to death. But if my daughter had been the one

clubbed to death as she slept in a Tallahassee sorority house, and if the bite mark left in her buttocks had been one of the prime pieces of evidence against the young man charged with her murder, I would with the greatest pleasure kill him myself.

The State of Florida will not permit the parents of Bundy's victims to do that, and, in a way, that is the problem with an emotional response to capital punishment. The only reason for a death penalty is to exact retribution. Is there anyone who really thinks that it is a deterrent, that there are considerable numbers of criminals out there who think twice about committing crimes because of the sentence involved? The ones I have met in the course of my professional duties have either sneered at the justice system, where they can exchange one charge for another with more ease than they could return a shirt to a clothing store, or they have simply believed that it is the other guy who will get caught, get convicted, get the stiffest sentence. Of course, the death penalty would act as a deterrent by eliminating recidivism, but then so would life without parole, albeit at greater taxpayer expense.

I don't believe deterrence is what most proponents seek from the death penalty anyhow. Our most profound emotional response is to want criminals to suffer as their victims did. When a man is accused of throwing a child from a high-rise terrace, my emotional—some might say hysterical—response is that he should be given an opportunity to see how endless the seconds are from the 31st story to the ground. In a civilized society that will never happen. And so what many people want from the death penalty, they will never get.

Death is death, you may say, and you would be right. But anyone who has seen someone die suddenly of a heart attack and someone else slip slowly into the clutches of cancer knows that there are gradations of dying.

I watched a television re-enactment one night of an execution by lethal injection. It was well done; it was horrible. The methodical approach, people standing around the gurney waiting, made it more awful. One moment there was a man in a prone position; the next moment that man was gone. On another night I watched a television movie about a little boy named Adam Walsh, who disappeared from a shopping center in Florida. There was a re-enactment of Adam's parents coming to New York, where they appeared on morning talk shows begging for their son's return, and in their hotel room, where they received a call from the police saying that Adam had been found: not all of Adam, actually, just his severed head, discovered in the waters of a Florida canal. There is nothing anyone could do that is bad enough for an adult who took a 6-year-old boy away from his parents, perhaps tortured, then murdered, him and cut off his head. Nothing at all. Lethal injection? The electric chair? Bah.

10 And so I come back to the position that the death penalty is wrong, not only because it consists of stooping to the level of the killers, but also because it is not what it seems. Just before Ted Bundy's most recent execution date was postponed, pending further appeals, the father of his last known victim, a 12-year-old girl, said what almost every father in his situation must feel. "I wish they'd bring him back to Lake City," said Tom Leach of the town where Kimberly Leach lived and died, "and let us all have at him." But the death

penalty does not let us all have at him in the way Mr. Leach seems to mean. What he wants is for something as horrifying as what happened to his child to happen to Ted Bundy. And that is impossible.

Life Experiences Experience is a great teacher for most of us, and we often wonder about the experiences of others. Nothing piques a reader's interest more than hearing about the writer's experience with a topic. When writing, though, we have to remember that readers have not lived our lives and do not have access to our minds.

Details about life experiences help readers conjure up a sense of who you are and how much they can relate to you. As a writer, do not shy away from explaining the situations that led you to believe a certain way or find the importance in a certain subject. Use specific and concrete words so that your audience can envision a description of a personal experience as clearly as possible. Your words should evoke sight, sound, smell, touch, and taste in ways that are precise and vivid. It is one thing to be told that a forest is beautiful and full of life. It is another to experience a writer describing the rich and various shades of green as she treks through a damp, secluded section of Yosemite National Park, glimpsing deer bounding through a meadow and shuddering at the howl of coyotes at night. Readers will stay with you, even if they sense they disagree with your overall point, simply because they are interested in what happened to you.

Readers need to be invested in your writing and perhaps see their own life experiences reflected in it. Thus, life experiences can be used as a brief introduction to a topic, as examples to support a position, or as the basis from which to generalize. Remember again the example of Anna at the beginning of the chapter. The students in her class wanted to know more about her to understand her position on gays and lesbians. She could have included details from her upbringing or her young adult experiences to help her audience understand the development of her beliefs. In so doing, she might also have come to understand her ideas much better, which would have allowed her to establish her ethos much better. Anticipating the needs of an audience helps you develop as a writer.

BARBARA MELLIX

From Outside, In

Barbara Mellix uses her life as an example from which to generalize about African American language usage. While some readers might not share her values, the personal experiences she discusses compel readers to continue reading. While Chapter 5 will discuss the power of words in more detail, look at this selection to see how the author's language choices help the audience better understand her situation and thesis.

Two years ago, when I started writing this paper, trying to bring order out of chaos, my ten-year-old daughter was suffering from an acute attack of boredom. She drifted in and out of the room complaining that she had nothing to do, no one to "be with" because none of her friends were at home. Patiently I explained that I was working on something special and needed peace and quiet, and I suggested that she paint, read, or work with her computer. None of these interested her. Finally, she pulled up a chair to my desk and watched me, now and then heaving long, loud sighs. After two or three minutes (nine or ten sighs), I lost my patience. "Looka here, Allie," I said, "you too old for this kinda carryin' on. I done told you this is important. You wronger than dirt to be in here haggin' me like this and you know it. Now git on outta here and leave me off before I put my foot all the way down."

I was at home, alone with my family, and my daughter understood that this way of speaking was appropriate in that context. She knew, as a matter of fact, that it was almost inevitable; when I get angry at home, I speak some of my finest, most cherished black English. Had I been speaking to my daughter in this manner in certain other environments, she would have been shocked and probably worried that I had taken leave of my sense of propriety.

Like my children, I grew up speaking what I considered two distinctly different languages—black English and standard English (or as I thought of them then, the ordinary everyday speech of "country" coloreds and "proper" English)—and in the process of acquiring these languages, I developed an understanding of when, where, and how to use them. But unlike my children, I grew up in a world that was primarily black. My friends, neighbors, minister, teachers—almost everybody I associated with every day—were black. And we spoke to one another in our own special languages: *That sho is a pretty dress you got on. If she don' soon leave me off I'm gon tell her head a mess. I was so mad I could' a pissed a blue nail. He all the time trying to low-rate somebody. Ain't that just about the nastiest thing you ever set ears on?*

Then there were the "others," the "proper" blacks, transplanted relatives and one-time friends who came home from the city for weddings, funerals, and vacations. And the whites. To these we spoke standard English. "Ain't?" my mother would yell at me when I used the term in the presence of "others." "You *know* better than that." And I would hang my head in shame and say the "proper" word.

5 I remember one summer sitting in my grandmother's house in Greeleyville, South Carolina, when it was full of the chatter of city relatives who were home on vacation. My parents sat quietly, only now and then volunteering a comment or answering a question. My mother's face took on a strained expression when she spoke. I could see that she was being careful to say just the right words in just the right way. Her voice sounded thick, muffled. And when she finished speaking, she would lapse into silence, her proper smile on her face. My father was more articulate, more aggressive. He spoke quickly, his words sharp and clear. But he held his proud head higher, a signal that he, too, was uncomfortable. My sisters and brothers and I stared at our aunts, uncles, and cousins, speaking only when prompted. Even then, we hesitated, formed our sentences in our minds, then spoke softly, shyly.

My parents looked small and anxious during those occasions, and I waited impatiently for our leave-taking when we would mock our relatives the moment we were out of their hearing. "Reeely," we would say to one another, flexing our wrists and rolling our eyes, "how dooo you stan' this heat? Chile, it just tooo hy*ooo*-mid for words." Our relatives had made us feel "country," and this was our way of regaining pride in ourselves while getting a little revenge in the bargain. The words bubbled in our throats and rolled across our tongues, a balming.

As a child I felt this same doubleness in uptown Greeleyville where the whites lived. "Ain't that a pretty dress you're wearing!" Toby, the town policeman, said to me one day when I was fifteen. "Thank you very much," I replied, my voice barely audible in my own ears. The words felt wrong in my mouth, rigid, foreign. It was not that I had never spoken that phrase before—it was common in black English, too—but I was extremely conscious that this was an occasion for proper English. I had taken out my English and put it on as I did my church clothes, and I felt as if I were wearing my Sunday best in the middle of the week. It did not matter that Toby had not spoken grammatically correct English. He was white and could speak as he wished. I had something to prove. Toby did not.

Speaking standard English to whites was our way of demonstrating that we knew their language and could use it. Speaking it to standard-English-speaking blacks was our way of showing them that we, as well as they, could "put on airs." But when we spoke standard English, we acknowledged (to ourselves and to others—but primarily to ourselves) that our customary way of speaking was inferior. We felt foolish, embarrassed, somehow diminished because we were ashamed to be our real selves. We were reserved, shy in the presence of those who owned and/or spoke *the* language.

My parents never set aside time to drill us in standard English. Their forms of instruction were less formal. When my father was feeling particularly expansive, he would regale us with tales of his exploits in the outside world. In almost flawless English, complete with dialogue and flavored with gestures and embellishment, he told us about his attempt to get a haircut at a white barbershop; his refusal to acknowledge one of the town merchants until the man addressed him a "Mister"; the time he refused to step off the sidewalk uptown to let some whites pass; his airplane trip to New York City (to visit a sick relative) during which the stewardesses and porters—recognizing that he was a "gentleman"—addressed him as "Sir." I did not realize then—nor, I think, did my father—that he was teaching us, among other things, standard English and the relationship between language and power. 10

My mother's approach was different. Often, when one of us said, "I'm gon wash off my feet," she would say, "And what will you walk on if you wash them off!" Everyone would laugh at the victim of my mother's "proper" mood. But it was different when one of us children was in a proper mood. "You think you are so superior," I said to my oldest sister one day when we were arguing and she was winning. "Superior!" my sister mocked. "You mean I am acting 'biggidy'?" My sisters and brothers sniggered, then joined in teasing me. Finally, my mother said, "Leave your sister alone. There's nothing wrong with using proper English." There was a half-smile on her face. I had gotten "uppity," had "put on airs" for no good reason. I was at home, alone with the family, and I hadn't been prompted by one of my mother's proper moods. But there was also a proud light in my mother's eyes; her children were learning English very well.

Not until years later, as a college student, did I begin to understand our ambivalence toward English, our scorn of it, our need to master it, to own and be owned by it—ambivalence that extended to the public-school classroom. In our school, where there were no whites, my teachers taught standard English but used black English to do it. When my grammar-school teachers wanted us to write, for example, they usually said something like, "I want y'all to write five sentences that make a statement. Anybody git done before the rest can color." It was probably almost those exact words that led me to write these sentences in 1953 when I was in the second grade:

> The white clouds are pretty.
> There are only 15 people in our room.
> We will go to gym.
> We have a new poster.
> We may go out doors.

Second grade came after "Little First" and "Big First," so by then I knew the implied rules that accompanied all writing assignments. Writing was an occasion for proper English. I was not to write in the way we spoke to one another: The white clouds pretty; There ain't but 15 people in our room; We going to gym; We got a new poster; We can go out in the yard. Rather I was to use the language of "other": clouds *are,* there *are,* we *will,* we *have,* we *may.*

My sentences were short, rigid, perfunctory, like the letters my mother wrote to relatives:

> Dear Papa,
> How are you? How is Mattie? Fine I hope. We are fine. We will come to see you Sunday. Cousin Ned will give us a ride.
> Love,
> Daughter

The language was not ours. It was something from outside us, something we used for special occasions.

But my coloring on the other side of that second-grade paper is different. I drew three hearts and a sun. The sun has a smiling face that radiates and envelops everything it touches. And although the sun and its world are enclosed in a circle, the colors I used—red, blue, green, purple, orange, yellow, black—indicate that I was less restricted with drawing and coloring than I was with writing standard English. My valentines were not just red. My sun was not just a yellow ball in the sky.

By the time I reached the twelfth grade, speaking and writing standard English had taken on new importance. Each year, about half of the newly graduated seniors of our school moved to large cities—particularly in the North—to live with relatives and find work. Our English teacher constantly corrected our grammar: "Not 'ain't,' but 'isn't.'" We seldom wrote papers, and even those few were usually plot summaries of short stories. When our teacher returned the papers, she usually lectured on the importance of using standard English: "I *am;* you *are;* he, she, or it *is,*" she would say, writing on the chalkboard as she spoke. "How you gon git a job talking about 'I is,' or 'I isn't' or 'I ain't'?"

15 In Pittsburgh, where I moved after graduation, I watched my aunt and uncle—who had always spoken standard English when in Greeleyville—switch from black English to standard English to a mixture of the two, according to where they were or who they were with. At home and with certain close relatives, friends, and neighbors, they spoke black English. With those less close, they spoke a mixture. In public and with strangers, they generally spoke standard English.

In time, I learned to speak standard English with ease and to switch smoothly from black to standard or a mixture, and back again. But no matter where I was, no matter what the situation or occasion, I continued to write as I had in school:

> Dear Mommie,
> How are you? How is everybody else? Fine I hope. I am fine. So are Aunt and Uncle. Tell everyone I said hello. I will write again soon.
> Love,
> Barbara

At work, at a health insurance company, I learned to write letters to customers. I studied form letters and letters written by co-workers, memorizing the phrases and the ways in which they were used. I dictated:

> Thank you for your letter of January 5. We have made the changes in your coverage you requested. Your new premium will be $150 every three months. We are pleased to have been of service to you.

In a sense, I was proud of the letters I wrote for the company: they were proof of my ability to survive in the city, the outside world—an indication of my growing mastery of English. But they also indicate that writing was still mechanical for me, something that didn't require much thought.

Reading also became a more significant part of my life during those early years in Pittsburgh. I had always liked reading, but now I devoted more and more of my spare time to it. I read romances, popular novels. Looking back, I realize that the books I liked best were simple, unambiguous: good versus bad and right versus wrong with right rewarded and wrong punished, mysteries unraveled and all set right in the end. It was how I remembered life in Greeleyville.

Of course I was romanticizing. Life in Greeleyville had not been so very uncomplicated. Back there I had been—first as a child, then as a young woman with limited experience in the outside world—living in a relatively closed-in society. But there were implicit and explicit principles that guided our way of life and shaped our relationships with one another and the people outside—principles that a newcomer would find elusive and baffling. In Pittsburgh, I had matured, become more experienced: I had worked at three different jobs, associated with a wider range of people, married, had children. This new environment with different prescripts for living required that I speak standard English much of the time, and slowly, imperceptibly, I had ceased seeing a sharp distinction between myself and "others." Reading romances and mysteries, characterized by dichotomy, was a way of shying away from change, from the person I was becoming.

But that other part of me—that part which took great pride in my ability to hold a job writing business letters—was increasingly drawn to the new developments in my life and the attending possibilities, opportunities for even greater change. If I could write letters for a nationally known business, could I not also do something better, more challenging, more important? Could I not, perhaps, go to college and become a school teacher? For years, afraid and a little embarrassed, I did no more than imagine this different me, this possible me. But sixteen years after coming north, when my younger daughter entered kindergarten, I found myself unable—or unwilling—to resist the lure of possibility. I enrolled in my first college course: Basic Writing, at the University of Pittsburgh.

20 For the first time in my life, I was required to write extensively about myself. Using the most formal English at my command, I wrote these sentences near the beginning of the term:

> One of my duties as a homemaker is simply picking up after others. A day seldom passes that I don't search for a mislaid toy, book, or gym shoe, etc. I change the Ty-D-Bol, fight "ring around the collar," and keep our laundry smelling "April fresh." Occasionally, I settle arguments between my children and suggest things to do when they're bored. Taking telephone messages for my oldest daughter is my newest (and sometimes most aggravating) chore. Hanging the toilet paper roll is my most insignificant.

My concern was to use "appropriate" language, to sound as if I belonged in a college classroom. But I felt separate from the language—as if it did not and could not belong to me. I couldn't think and feel genuinely in that language, couldn't make it express what I thought and felt about being a housewife. A part of me resented, among other things, being judged by such things as the appearance of my family's laundry and toilet bowl, but in that language I could only imagine and write about a conventional housewife.

For the most part, the remainder of the term was a period of adjustment, a time of trying to find my bearing as a student in college composition class, to learn to shut out my black English whenever I composed, and to prevent it from creeping into my formulations; a time for trying to grasp the language of the classroom and reproduce it in my prose; for trying to talk about myself in that language, reach others through it. Each experience of writing was like standing naked and revealing my imperfection, my "otherness." And each new assignment was another chance to make myself over in language, reshape myself, make myself "better" in my rapidly changing image of a student in a college composition class.

But writing became increasingly unmanageable as the term progressed, and by the end of the semester, my sentences sounded like this:

> My excitement was soon dampened, however, by what seemed like a small voice in the back of my head saying that I should be careful with my long awaited opportunity. I felt frustrated and this seemed to make it difficult to concentrate.

There is a poverty of language in these sentences. By this point, I knew that the clichéd language of my Housewife essay was unacceptable, and I generally recognized trite expressions. At the same time, I hadn't yet mastered the language of the classroom, hadn't yet come to see it as belonging to me. Most notable is the lifelessness of the prose, the apparent absence of a person behind the words. I wanted those sentences—and the rest of the essay—to convey the anguish of yearning to, at once, become something more and yet remain the same. I had the sensation of being split in two, part of me going into a future the other part didn't believe possible. As that person, the student writer at that moment, I was essentially mute. I could not—in the process of composing—use the language of the old me, yet I couldn't imagine myself in the language of "others."

I found this particularly discouraging because at midsemester I had been writing in a much different way. Note the language of this introduction to an essay I had written then, near the middle of the term:

> Pain is a constant companion to the people in "Footwork." Their jobs are physically damaging. Employers are insensitive to their feelings and in many cases add to their problems. The general public wounds them further by treating them with disgrace because of what they do for a living. Although the workers are as diverse as they are similar, there is a definite link between them. They suffer a great deal of abuse.

The voice here is stronger, more confident, appropriating terms like "physically damaging," "wounds them further," "insensitive," "diverse"—terms I couldn't have imagined using when writing about my own experience—and shaping them into sentences like "Although the workers are as diverse as they are similar, there is a definite link between them." And there is the sense of a personality behind the prose, someone who sympathizes with the workers. "The general public wounds them further by treating them with disgrace because of what they do for a living."

What caused these differences? I was, I believed, explaining other people's 25
thoughts and feelings, and I was free to move about in the language of "others" so long as I was speaking of others. I was unaware that I was transforming into my best classroom language my own thoughts and feelings about people whose experiences and ways of speaking were in many ways similar to mine.

The following year, unable to turn back or to let go of what had become something of an obsession with language (and hoping to catch and hold the sense of control that had eluded me in Basic Writing), I enrolled in a research writing course. I spent most of the term learning how to prepare for and write a research paper. I chose sex education as my subject and spent hours in libraries, searching for information, reading, taking notes. Then (not without messiness and often-demoralizing frustration) I organized my information into categories, wrote a thesis statement, and composed my paper—a series of paraphrases and quotations spaced between carefully constructed transitions. The process and results felt artificial, but as I would later come to realize I was passing through a necessary stage. My sentences sounded like this:

> This reserve becomes understandable with examination of who the abusers are. In an overwhelming number of cases, they are people the victims know and trust. Family members, relatives, neighbors and close family friends commit seventy-five percent of all reported sex crimes against children, and parents, parent substitutes and relatives are the offenders in thirty to eighty percent of all reported cases.[12] While assault by strangers does occur, it is less common, and is usually a single episode.[13] But abuse by family members, relatives and acquaintances may continue for an extended period of time. In cases of incest, for example, children are abused repeatedly for an average of eight years.[14] In such cases, "the use of physical force is rarely necessary because of the child's trusting, dependent relationship with the offender. The child's cooperation is often facilitated by the adult's position of dominance, an offer of material goods, a threat of physical violence, or a misrepresentation of moral standards."[15]

The completed paper gave me a sense of profound satisfaction, and I read it often after my professor returned it. I know now that what I was pleased with was the language I used and the professional voice it helped me maintain. "Use better words," my teacher had snapped at me one day after reading the notes I'd begun accumulating from my research, and slowly I began taking on the language of my sources. In my next set of notes, I used the word "vacillating"; my professor applauded. And by the time I composed the final draft, I felt at ease with terms like "overwhelming number of cases," "single episode," and "reserve," and I shaped them into sentences similar to those of my "expert" sources.

If I were writing the paper today, I would of course do some things differently. Rather than open with an anecdote—as my teacher suggested—I would begin simply with a quotation that caught my interest as I was researching my paper (and which I scribbled, without its source, in the margin of my notebook): "Truth does not do so much good in the world as the semblance of truth does evil." The quotation felt right because it captured what was for me the central idea of my paper—and expressed it in a way I would like to have said it. The anecdote, a hypothetical situation I invented to conform to the information in the paper, felt forced and insincere because it represented—to a great degree—my teacher's understanding of the essay, her idea of what in it was most significant. Improving upon my previous experiences with writing, I was beginning to think and feel in the language I used, to find my own voice in it, to sense that how one speaks influences how one means. But I was not yet secure enough, comfortable enough with the language to trust my intuition.

Now that I know that to seek knowledge, freedom, and autonomy means always to be in the concentrated process of becoming—always to be venturing into new territory, feeling one's way at first, then getting one's balance, negotiating, accommodating, discovering one's self in ways that previously defined "others"—I sometimes get tired. And I ask myself why I keep on participating in this highbrow form of violence, this slamming against perplexity. But there is no real futility in the question, no hint of that part the old me who stood outside standard English, hugging to herself a disabling mistrust of language she thought could not represent a person with her history and experience. Rather, the question represents a person who feels the consequence of her education, the weight of her possibilities as a teacher and writer and human being, a voice in society. And I would not change that person, would not give back the good burden that accompanies my growing expertise, my increasing power to shape myself in language and share that self with "others."

"To speak," says Frantz Fanon, "means to be in a position to use a certain syntax, to grasp the morphology of this or that language, but it means above all to assume a culture, to support the weight of a civilization." To write means to do the same, but in a more profound sense. However, Fanon also says that to achieve mastery means to "get" in a position of power, to "grasp," to "assume." This, I have learned both as a student and subsequently as a teacher, can involve tremendous emotional and psychological conflict for those attempting to master academic discourse. Although as a beginning student writer I had a fairly good grasp of ordinary spoken English and was proficient at what Labov calls "code-switching" (and what John Baugh in *Black Street Speech* terms "style shifting"), when I came face to face with the demands of academic writing, I grew increasingly self-conscious, constantly aware of my status as a black and a speaker of one of the many black English vernaculars—a traditional outsider. For the first time, I experienced my sense of doubleness as something menacing, a built-in enemy. Whenever I turned inward for salvation, the balm so available during my childhood, I found instead this new fragmentation which spoke to me in many voices. It was the voice of my desire to prosper, but at the same time it spoke of what I had relinquished and could not regain: a safe way of being, a state of powerlessness which exempted me from responsibility for who I was and might be. And it accused me of betrayal, of turning away from blackness. To recover balance, I had to take on the language of the academy, the language of "others." And to do that, I had to learn to imagine myself a part of the culture of that language, and therefore someone free to manage that language, to take liberties with it. Writing and rewriting, practicing, experimenting, I came to comprehend more fully the generative power of language. I discovered—with the help of some especially sensitive teachers—that through writing one can continually bring new selves into being, each with new responsibilities and difficulties, but also with new possibilities. Remarkable power, indeed. I write and continually give birth to myself.

Allusions Sometimes, college or workplace writing assignments discourage the use of personal life experiences. Your readers still want something to grasp onto, some way to relate to a situation, something that makes your topic and your perspective matter. When the writing situation calls for more detachment, you might consider using allusions to popular culture or well-known events to connect the topic to the reader. Many writers, for instance, use verses from poems or songs to spring into their topics. If the audience knows the song or poem, it responds with interest. The same holds true for allusions to television shows or movies and to human-interest cases, such as publicized jury trials, tragedies, acts of courage, and criminal activity.

While some allusions can be used as support for a position, their most important function is to meet audience needs. Eric Dezenhall makes use of allusion in his essay, "We Like Our Bad Guys to Be Honest About It," in Chapter 15 (page 481). He mentions *The Sopranos* television show, and the movies *Analyze This* and the cult classic *Animal House,* among other allusions. Authors do not have to state that an allusion is coming. Take this example from Dezenhall's piece: "It's no coincidence that Butch and Sundance are lionized just as Don Corleone's Godfather is—though all are violent criminals." The smooth integration into his essay of these allusions builds his ethos in the mind of the audience; readers see Dezenhall as someone just like them. The thesis has relevance to television shows and movies they and Dezenhall have seen, so they can envision his main point better. While some audience members might not be familiar with your allusions, summaries and specific details will work the same way specific, concrete descriptions work. The audience's needs to be shown rather than simply told will be met.

COLLABORATING

Choose a topic for your group from among the following: knitting, gaining the trust of parents, choosing a car to buy, or behaving in an obnoxious way at a party. After you have chosen a topic, list these three specific audiences: a group of department store salespeople, members of an environmentalist organization, and fifteen-year-old girls. Decide what you want to say about your topic, and anticipate the needs of each audience. How can you get each to relate to you? What differences among these audiences will you have to respond to? What techniques will you have to use to get your point across? Write two paragraphs to each group that demonstrate your ability to make the same point while relating to the audience and possibly persuading its members to accept your point of view.

Responding to Possible Objections

Considering possible objections to your point of view differs slightly, but significantly, from anticipating readers' needs. While allowing the audience to relate to you is the desired outcome of anticipating their needs, responding to their objections means formulating specific strategies. You need to acknowledge differences of opinion and counter the beliefs and evidence of a reader on the opposite side of the political or social spectrum.

When you engage in this type of writing, your purpose is generally argument. Argument engages readers' minds, hearts, and agendas in an attempt to persuade them to take action, adopt a viewpoint, or arrive at a negotiated solution. Chapter 2 examined the critical analysis that can lead to effective argument. Chapter 9 covers the strategies you need to support an argument. We now examine what to do when you take a position that has strong advocates from different perspectives. You cannot ignore audience concerns that stem from objections to your points.

Self-Reflection At the beginning of the chapter, Anna asked whether she needed to change her position on gays and lesbians to improve her paper. Many student writers have asked their instructors similar questions or have felt that it would be best to give the instructor what she or he wants by taking a different point of view. It cannot be emphasized enough that changing your position does not make a paper better. Insincerity impresses no one, and you might lose the ethos you were beginning to develop in your draft.

When your instructor challenges your positions, her or his goal in presenting opposite points of view might differ considerably from her or his political or social perspectives on the world. Yes, instructors hold strong positions on issues, and these positions are often well-formulated, making some instructors reluctant to accept the viewpoint of a student writer. But look at that position for just what it is—a well-formulated counterargument to what you believe. If you are not persuaded by the counterargument, you need to reflect on your own values to see what is at their root.

Often we find that our identity influences our positions more than we would like to believe. Other times, we have emotional responses about an issue due to a life event. Sincerely considering the opposite perspective and modifying our beliefs mean changing who we are and coming to new understandings of our experiences. Such changes are opportunities for growth. You cannot become educated without changing. But your instructor does not expect your opinions to do a complete flip. Just as politicians are criticized for waffling to attract the greatest number of votes, writers who lack the courage of their convictions are difficult to trust. Change should come gradually. You need to reflect in order to check what you think and to make sure that you have not gotten so caught up in trying to win an argument that you have ignored crucial pieces of evidence on your side or the other side.

WRITING

Write about a time when you were directly challenged in class or when you witnessed such a challenge. How did you feel? Did you eventually grow or change? What resistance did you feel? Also consider the effects on other students in the classroom. Did any of them grow as a result of the experience?

Tone The method in which we convey our position to potential readers goes a long way toward securing understanding. While we need to support our points, expressing uncertainty—the possibility that we could be wrong—often produces positive effects on an audience. A writer whose voice takes a conciliatory stance, offering to examine the evidence and revealing a slight amount of doubt, might at first appear to be foregoing power. However, audiences tend to tune out the know-it-all who is too firm in her or his position. The purpose of persuasion becomes too blatant, and people in general resist overbearing attempts at being persuaded.

Think of your response to telemarketers. They act as if they know all about your needs and that their products are without doubt the best solution. Like most consumers, you may start to feel pressured and become defensive when they attempt to persuade you to try their products. This defensiveness turns into annoyance, and you resent the intrusion. You do not buy what they are selling, and you hang up more quickly when the next telemarketer calls. The tone that conveys a sense that no other way of thinking can be right carries a similar obvious attempt at persuasion, and it will produce similar reactions in readers.

Therefore, writers need to find a reasonable tone. To do so, they acknowledge multiple perspectives about an issue and phrase each perspective in a way that its proponents will agree is accurate. Writers find many ways to appear agreeable. Humor can be effective, as can concern or anguish.

Try the approach of uncertainty. Not only will you avoid a combative, off-putting tone, but you will also keep your own mind open to possibilities, which can lead to the discovery of commonalities with your perceived opponents as well as fresh ideas on a subject.

Curse of the Ouija Board

"Curse of the Ouija Board" was written by a student who prefers to stay anonymous. While the story keeps most readers interested, pay attention to how the student weaves uncertainty into her analysis and conclusion. She does not force the reader to agree with her, and she admits to not really knowing whether her perspective is correct. Do you think this method is effective in helping an audience keep an open mind about what amounts to a pretty incredible story?

I never believed in anything being able to predict the future, but an event that happened when I was sixteen years old made me wonder. It all started when my friend Michelle brought out a Ouija board at her party. Only a few of us were left and some of the guys were pretty buzzed. This Ouija board was not the new kind that you can find in a store, but a really old, creepy one. It was bound in a velvet cloth, and Michelle had to dust it off to even reveal the contents.

"My grandmother forbidded me from ever going near this board," Michelle said. "She claimed it was not like an ordinary Ouija board, but was cursed to deliver bad news to the most vulnerable person who plays it."

Everyone starting snorting, telling her to get off it, but she persisted. "She claimed this board predicted her death." Michelle's grandmother had died three or four months before, so the room fell silent. "She knew she was going to die when she was 73 and knew it would be from respiratory disease." I didn't know how old Mrs. Houston was when she died, but I did know it was from emphysema. I felt a little chill go down my back.

"She was only sixteen when she played it the first time," Michelle continued. "The board was given to her by a group of gypsies passing through town. The fortune teller who gave it to her told her that the board was not to be taken lightly, that the spirit within it, named Nazuela, preyed on unwary souls who could not confront their own mortality. She said the spirit demanded a blood sacrifice for every time it was played and could manipulate the future to accommodate its demands. 'Play with care and wisdom,' the fortune teller warned her.

"My grandmother tried to speak to Nazuela while playing, telling the spirit to not bring harm to anyone else and only to speak about her fate. Nazuela apparently granted her wish, because he spelled out her name, the word 'breath,' and the year 1998. My grandmother automatically knew what it meant, but could not stop playing the game. She remembered the gypsy woman's warning about a blood sacrifice, so she pricked her finger with a safety pin and forced out several drops of blood on the board. She wrapped the board up in a velvet cloth and meant to destroy it the next day, but she had a dream that night that said not to destroy the board or risk losing her life prematurely. So she instead bound the board up and hid it in her closet.

"One time when I was eleven or twelve, I found the board and was about to open it. But my grandmother stopped me and told me the story. Even though I was afraid for grandma, I felt compelled to open it. Grandma muttered something about fate eventually winning over, but demanded I swear an oath never to use it until after she was dead. She felt she could protect me if she were on the other side."

No one was laughing at all as Michelle opened the board. It resisted a little bit, as the cloth clung to the board, but it eventually popped open, revealing some dried crusty spots that looked like blood. Some people were saying to stop it, that they knew Michelle was kidding, but she just said no one had to play who didn't want to. The guys were too in to being men to admit they were afraid, but some of my girlfriends crept away, saying it was the devil's work. I felt drawn to the board even though I was doubtful and sat down across from Michelle. We started moving across the board and I swear I could not control where my hands were going. We spelled a "T," then an "A," followed by an "M." My girlfriend Tami started screaming, as she wasn't playing and didn't want to be involved. Michelle and I were focused on each other, but my friends later told me that Tami was about to interrupt the game, when all of a sudden the electricity went out.

Everyone started screaming and I could feel the board still drawing Michelle and I back and forth. A guy had a lighter and Michelle's best friend, Jody, found a flashlight somewhere. My hands and Michelle's had stopped four times while the lights were out. We were finishing when the flashlight came on the board. The final letter was "D." Tami was sure her name had been spelled out and that it meant she was dead. I was shaken by the whole incident and got up from the board. Michelle looked pale and seemed like she was in a trance. One of the guys wrapped the velvet cloth back around the board. Tami was crying and left. None of us knew what to think.

The next morning, my boyfriend called. Tami's brakes had gone out and she had been hit by a truck. She was dead upon impact. I started crying and felt I was responsible. I wanted to go back to Michelle's house and destroy that board, but for some reason, I never even called her. In fact, I've never seen her since, even though she still lives in Anderson and hasn't moved.

I talked to my parents about it, and they said it was just coincidence, to forget about spirits and fortune tellers. They said there was no proof that the board even belonged to Michelle's grandmother and that Michelle probably made up the story about the gypsies and the bad luck following the board. But what about the drops of blood on the board? Maybe they weren't really blood at all, and Michelle had just put some paint in there to fool us. But the dust on the velvet had accumulated over years, so Michelle couldn't have been playing a prank. She would have really had to have been telling a whopper to come up with the name of the spirit, Nazuela, and not mispronounce it at least once. The big thing, though, is that I felt the pull of the Ouija board. Maybe Michelle was really guiding our hands and the power of suggestion overtook me, but I could swear I even heard whispers in my ear, faint but definitely there, spelling out "Tami" and "Dead." Nonetheless, my parents kept insisting, even forcing me to believe, that Tami's car accident was just an unfortunate coincidence and nothing more.

I met the priest at Tami's funeral, but was afraid to ask him about Ouija boards at the time. But later in the week, I went to his parish residence and talked to him, crying about how I thought I was responsible. I thought he would be comforting, but deep inside, I knew why I had to see him, so I wasn't surprised when he met me with a stare and a shake of his head. "There are some things not of this world," he said. "Scripture is full of demons and foul, evil beings." He didn't accuse me of doing anything, nor did he say I was responsible, but he felt a cleansing was necessary. He blessed me, pulled out some prayer book and chanted in Latin. Then he encouraged me to pray

> every night and to read the Bible. "And never," he said, "fool with the supernatural."
>
> Now I have accepted at this point that I am responsible, or partly at least, for Tami's death. Even if the story behind the Ouija board was not true, Tami thought it was and her hysteria made her unfit to drive. I heard later that she knew her brakes were bad, so it wasn't like a master cylinder went out all of a sudden. But she would have been driving slower and more carefully if her mind hadn't been clouded by stories of her own death. I'm not sure the priest performed a real ritual on me or if he was just helping me get over my grief, but I felt better (and I've never missed a Sunday mass since!). But everything coming together the way it did makes me believe that this story was not a string of coincidences. It seems to me more logical to believe in a spirit guiding fate than in a whimsical world where my friend could be killed just because she thought she was going to die. I'll never really know, but I've grown up a lot since then and feel that the world has some order. Rivers flow in one direction. The sun rises every morning. Trees take in carbon dioxide. Water gives off oxygen. Everything has a reason and a purpose. Writing off any tragedy to coincidence is a way of avoiding responsibility. And I won't live in a world where people can't admit their guilt and move on to make the world a better place.

Refuting or Conceding In keeping with our discussion on tone, we must constantly remind ourselves that readers whose opinions differ from our own have valid points and evidence to support their perspective. As a writer, you should not avoid discussing evidence that supports the opposition if you want to impress those readers with your points. You will seem uninformed or deceitful if you do not address facts or logical reasoning that points in the other direction. Therefore, you need to present that evidence and either refute it or concede its validity. Refuting means disproving an account of something. If you happen to know that recent scientific inquiries have disproved long-held facts, your task is easy. But evidence often is based on logic or lore. You have to show holes in thinking to get your point across.

In "Death Penalty's False Promise," for instance, Anna Quindlen asks whether anyone still believes that the death penalty acts as a deterrent to criminals. If you were to try to refute her position in an essay, you would have to ask what evidence she has that supports this statement. You could easily determine that no one can directly track such information. If a crime has not been committed—in other words, if a would-be murderer has been deterred from killing—how would a person know that deterrence occurred or find out why it occurred? Generally speaking, people do not confess in public to murderous desires they have seriously considered acting on. Researchers do not know where to find such people, nor are they able to isolate capital punishment as the reason a murder was not committed. In this case, neither Quindlen nor anyone opposed to her assertion could offer direct evidence that capital punishment does or does not act as a deterrent. Through logic, you can refute the implication in Quindlen's argument that the matter of deterrence in capital cases has been settled.

But you also need to consider conceding a point when a particular piece of evidence stands up to scrutiny. You strengthen your case by admitting that evidence on the other side has legitimacy. Readers do not necessarily like to be shown that everything they have relied on in deciding their thinking on an issue is wrong. Their egos can be damaged, and they will revert to the emotional pull of their original position. A writer can be much more effective in establishing ethos by conceding that elements of the opposing position warrant consideration, but that after careful deliberation, those elements do not match the evidence for the writer's position.

Your position might be 100 percent correct, but if your reader will not listen, being right doesn't really matter. Conceding something to the opposition bestows dignity on proponents of that side and makes them more willing to consider opposing positions, even to the point of changing their minds.

WRITING

Think of a dispute you have had with friends, parents, teachers, or others. Make a list of the reasons you believed you were right. Then list the reasons your opponents disagreed with you. You might have already attempted to repair these differences, but look at the dispute as still active and assume that you want to resolve it. Why do you feel that your reasons are stronger than those of your opponents? What do you not believe about their perspective? Determine what elements are at the crux of the matter (facts, reasoning, agendas, morals), and write to the opponent, using a reasonable tone to assert your position while responding to the objections you listed.

Using Real Readers in Peer Groups

While an audience can consist of a group of imagined readers, feedback from real readers lets you test your ideas on an actual audience. Chapter 7 discusses writing as collaboration—the joint authorship of a piece of writing. Most writers of reports and business documents collaborate with others involved in a project or decision and work to make the prose as fluid and clear as possible. For now, let's look at peer feedback or workshopping. Peer feedback consists of sharing writing with people equally invested in similar writing activities who provide ideas for revision and a sense of the potential of a piece of writing. Peer feedback is not evaluation; it does not involve saying, "This is good" or "I can't stand this." Nor is it sentence-level editing, wherein a reader merely corrects mistakes. Rather, peer feedback involves recognizing an audience and the way a piece of writing affects that audience.

Peer feedback should give a writer suggestions to consider not only to improve the paper through greater clarity and description, but also to anticipate reader needs and respond to their objections. Actual readers' reactions to your stance and approach can be used to modify tone, add necessary introductory material, replace jargon, and make many other revision choices. Peer feedback can also be used to ensure that critical analysis has taken place and that the requirements of an assignment have been met.

A draft, by its very nature, is a first attempt at a writing task, and it needs further work to reach an acceptable level. Keep in mind that the main responsibility in securing strong feedback rests with the writer. The peer review writer's discussion guide should help you fulfill these responsibilities.

PEER REVIEW WRITER'S DISCUSSION GUIDE

- Prepare properly by first doing a self-evaluation of your own essay. Keep a blank piece of paper next to you, and read through the essay. For every concern you have, list the problem on the blank paper. If you're worried, for example, that your critical analysis does not make sense or is not leading to a strong thesis, make note of it. If you doubt that your introduction grabs your audience, write it down so that you do not forget. Whatever comes up when you're reading your own essay, write it down.
- Students often worry that they will hurt someone's feelings with negative comments, so invite your peers to discuss your writing seriously. Explain that you want genuine reactions that will help in revision. Show your seriousness by writing down what your peers say. If you're working online, make sure that you will have access to the dialogue for later use.
- Guide readers to the problem areas you isolated in your self-evaluation. If you do not know whether you have given too much or too little description, lead your readers toward this area. If you're worried that your thesis complicates an issue too much, talk about it with your peers. Do not let a peer group avoid or overlook issues.
- Read through the assignment sheet and have your peers show you the areas where you have fulfilled all of the listed criteria for the assignment.
- Review the instructions on critical analysis on pages 28–50 in Chapter 2, and allow your readers to engage in one or more types of analysis to see if the same conclusions are reached as in your thesis. When you show willingness to seek and take advice, your group members will respond.

As a reader in a peer group, you will learn a great deal by critiquing someone else's paper. If you recognize strengths and weaknesses in the writing of your peers, you gain confidence and start to bring that critical eye to your own writing. You should find this peer review reader's discussion guide helpful in committing yourself to being an effective reader in a peer group.

PEER REVIEW READER'S DISCUSSION GUIDE

- While you want to have a dialogue with the writer, write comments to him or her. If you are allowed to make notes in the margins of the writer's paper, do that. Otherwise, have a separate sheet of paper available to jot down your thoughts. Some online programs allow readers to write comments in a draft, so if you are working in an online environment, consider this option.
- Take your role seriously, and curb any instinct to say or write that a piece of writing is "great," "fine," or "nice." These evaluations do not help the writer, nor do they help you develop your critical skills.
- Write down the specific elements that, as a reader, keep your attention. This will let you see other elements that need refining or rethinking. If your initial impression is mostly favorable, find particular places that strike you as lively, amusing, or intriguing, and write what the author has done to produce this effect. Starting with compliments almost always allows more penetrating critiques to be considered constructively.
- Do not give insincere compliments, as they mislead a writer and damage your credibility. If your initial impression is unfavorable, look for the potential in the draft and start your commenting there. In the opening example in this chapter, the students in Anna's class attempted to find places in her writing that she could develop, trying to unearth the potential in a paper that offended many. You should try this method as well.
- Think about how the writer can get an audience to relate to his or her point, and write and/or talk about where you see attempts at targeting a particular readership.
- Write about the kernel of critical analysis that is trying to find its way out. From there, you can bring up your more negative reactions, such as confusion because of vague descriptions, a letdown due to clichés, or anger generated by a condescending tone. In all cases, be specific, and treat the writer as you would like to be treated.

Revision

After sharing your draft with a peer group, what do you do? Within just one peer group, you might receive differing reactions and conflicting advice. As a writer, you must understand that revision means more than "fixing" a paper. The insertion or deletion of a few details constitutes editing, not revision. Almost all drafts need revision—to be rethought, restructured, and rewritten. In using real readers, you have a chance to look at both global and local concerns in your draft before submitting the finished version for a grade.

Make Decisions Peer groups, your instructor, and the process of drafting will present you with options as a writer. You must decide what direction to pursue. The first step in making that decision comes during the peer review. At the end of the session, take out a separate piece of paper, think about the options you can see in your peers' comments, and summarize the major points made. Write fully your initial impressions of the dominant comments, especially those that contradict each other or otherwise send conflicting messages on how to revise. You might forget what was said if you do not record the conversation, and your initial reactions are important as well.

As the writer, you must make decisions about which, if any, of the choices to use in a revision. You do not need to bend to the will of the majority. Rather, listen to how your peers' reactions developed. Find patterns in their thoughts. If you guided your fellow students' responses as suggested above, your concerns or worries will be confirmed or alleviated, and you will have been alerted to other matters you had not thought of.

Look at the patterns to see what demands they are making on you as a writer. You can add detail or explanation, for instance, if readers have pointed out a need to do so, and that detail might open up possibilities regarding your thesis or main point. Perhaps your main point is really more complicated than you allowed for in your draft. If so, not only do you have to add details, but you also need to rethink your thesis. That might mean restructuring your introduction to prepare readers for a new thesis.

Peer feedback does not create a set of instructions for you to follow. Instead, it delivers options to explore. The writer must make the connection between the suggestions and the possible effect on the paper.

Receive Peer Feedback More Than Once You may disagree with the dominant sentiments springing from a session of peer feedback or feel uncomfortable about relying on them. You may understand the feedback but be uncertain about how well you can use it for revising. The solution is to have the peer group—or some members—read your revised draft. This has three benefits. First, you will see whether you understood the feedback. Second, you can test how readers react to your revision—whether you made the best decision based on the options in front of you. Third, you can look for signs of improvement and see if the direction of this revision is worth pursuing.

Discomfort or uncertainty can transform into excitement when you receive the approval of peers, and you will be able to start editing and polishing a paper with confidence. Nagging doubts can also be affirmed, which will send you in a more appropriate direction and help you avoid a bad grade. When you make changes to your paper that you disagree with, strange things can happen. Sometimes we disagree with the suggestions we most need to hear and act on. Every once in a while, it does not hurt to try an approach that we object to. In writing, acting on advice that we initially think is wrong can reap dividends.

COLLABORATING

Review the table of contents for Part III of this book, and select one topic that seems interesting. Freewrite on that topic for approximately twenty minutes, relating an experience or observation associated with it or a perspective you have. (Freewriting here means writing without stopping to check for correctness, clarity, or organization.)

In the time remaining in class, practice giving peer feedback on your freewrites to one another. While your in-class draft will not be as developed as most drafts you submit for peer feedback, it could lead to the eventual development of a paper for this course. Follow the instructions given for discussing writing in small groups, and be sure to take notes and write down summaries of your reactions to peer comments. Next, talk to each other about these reactions, concentrating on your sense of the advice you received. Be as honest as possible about how helpful your peers' comments could be when you revise this in-class draft. Make sure you explain to a writer if she or he misunderstood your comments, and find out if you have been too harsh, too nice, or not careful enough when responding to others' comments. You may be working with this group again, so work through the procedures, and find out what you need to do to improve the quality of your feedback.

Summary

Writing an essay, article, or report results in little if your audience does not understand you, cannot relate to you, or will not listen to you. As a writer, strive to keep both imagined and real readers in mind when constructing a draft and understand that establishing ethos or a credible writerly persona is crucial. You must recognize the type of person who is most likely to be interested in your subject and tailor the writing to fit that targeted reader. Your writing must also consider the audience's needs, especially the likely values and experiences of its members, and show commonalities that will allow readers to see differing perspectives. Establishing a coherent ethos gives you the authority to show those commonalities. If audience members might object to a point of view, the writer needs to respond to those objections and convey understanding and sympathy for opposing positions in order to avoid alienating the audience.

The best method to gauge possible audience reaction is to seek feedback from peers. While you need to listen to all suggestions and understand conflicting reactions, steering peer readers toward areas where you suspect problems or want more information or perspective will open up honest dialogue between writer and readers. You should expect to have difficulty in responding to some suggestions, but attempting revision in response to audience concerns often leads to deeper insights about your writing process, your topic, and yourself.

CHAPTER 4

STRATEGIES FOR ORGANIZING YOUR IDEAS

Every topic you consider as a subject for your paper presents a number of options for approaching it. Each approach leads to decisions about the arrangement of your paper, the organization or order in which you place sentences and paragraphs so that an audience can follow your train of thought. Many students have misconceptions about how to arrange writing and want to impose a preestablished structure onto their papers. This dilemma faced a student named Steve, who I was teaching in a writing class. While Steve put sentences together well, his essays lacked development, and each paragraph seemed like a separate idea, albeit on the same topic. I spoke with him about adding more detail to his first draft and exploring his thesis in greater depth. Steve's second draft contained incredibly long paragraphs where he had added details and ideas, and he expanded on his thesis statement in his introduction and conclusion. I still could not follow his train of thought.

I asked to see him after class, hoping to better understand his strategy for organization. Steve was an affable fellow and approached me with genuine willingness to learn. We sat at my desk and reviewed his introduction. Here's a copy of Steve's draft.

STEVE WINDHORST

Humor in Society

Humor is all around us in society. People like to laugh at other people, which is why comedians talk about well known politicians and actors. Slapstick humor is cruel, as it teases people for physical

This icon will direct you to web links and additional resources on the website college.hmco.com/pic/thelin1e

problems or for tragedies that occur. Jokes often are not funny when you are the one who is being targeted. People need humor to let off some steam, even if the jokes are mean-spirited, as they can avoid examining themselves for unpleasant characteristics they might have.

People like to laugh at other people, which is why comedians talk about well known politicians and actors. Every comedian I have seen talks about figures in society who everyone has heard of, like Michael Jackson or President Bush, and exaggerates their personalities. But comedians talk about all sorts of things other than politicians and actors. They also use stereotypes to talk about situations. There's a joke about the dumb blonde who is supposed to paint the porch for a guy. The guy is trying to rip her off, not telling her that the porch extends all the way around the house and having her do the job for a small amount of money. The blonde starts working and the guy goes back inside. After 10 minutes, she comes back inside and says she is finished. The guy knows she cannot have gotten the whole porch done. But before he says anything, she says, "I feel kinda guilty for just doing the Porsche. I have paint leftover. Do you want the SUV painted too?" We know nobody can be that stupid and the blonde is just a stereotype. It keeps us from worrying about really dumb things that people do. The same can be said about the redneck jokes that go around on the Internet or jokes about gays. Comedians want people to laugh, so they have to refer to something that everyone understands. Laughter is good for the soul. Everyone needs to laugh. Otherwise, we would always be feeling miserable and who wants a society of depressed people? I think comedians serve an important function in our society.

Slapstick humor is cruel, as it teases people for physical problems or for tragedies that occur. People laugh at other people all the time. If someone trips and falls, someone who sees it is bound to laugh. It's like with a food fight in the cafeteria. A lot of people think it is funny if they hit someone with a plate of spaghetti or throw a hard-boiled egg at someone. One time, this really heavy guy in our school named Kevin was minding his own business. He was walking with a tray of food. Some guy stuck out his foot and tripped him. Kevin fell face forward. The food ended up on the floor and Kevin's face and shirt were covered with it. People were laughing but that wasn't good enough. Some people from another table ran by and dumped milk and desserts on him. Everyone started throwing food at each other and laughing. No one knew that Kevin had hurt his knee. He twisted it or something and had to use crutches for about a week. Even then, people made fun of him for trying to get around on crutches. Here he was suffering, unable to walk well, and people were laughing at him! What really got me was all the fat jokes I heard. Some guy was saying that his knee couldn't support all of his lard and blamed him for the accident. I mean, this was cruel. There's all sorts of jokes and teasing you'll hear in high school about people. Then there was this one guy. I guess you would call him a midget, even though he wasn't that small. I guess he was about 5 feet tall in our senior year. He was an all right guy, but people found it so funny to constantly point out how short he was. One guy, who really wasn't all the much taller than him, used to put his elbow on the little guy's head and say, "A leaning post. Perfect height." They would scrunch down in their desks and wave their hand like they had an answer to a question, telling everyone they were like Watson, who was the little guy. We had some dances and most of the girls were taller than him. He still managed to get a few of them to dance with him, though, so the next Monday at school, guys were faking slow dances, commenting about where Watson's head would end up. I won't go into the details. People laughed. I think anything that mimics the physical problems of other people should not be used for jokes. Like some people don't have the normal speaking voices. Why do others think it is so funny to try to copy those voices? Is there a perfect way to sound? Then a lot of people will walk around, pretending to be walking like somebody else. I have seen people bust out laughing at people imitating swaggers, stiffness, and limps. This is just cruelty. More has to be done on high schools to prevent this type of slapstick humor. It's just not funny.

Jokes often are not funny when you are the one who is being targeted. Lots of jokes deal with people's race or gender or religion. For the most part, if you're the object of the joke, you're not going to laugh at it. Obviously, if something is making fun of your religion, you are going to get mad. Some jokes cannot be told in mixed company. But then there are people who make fun of themselves, talking about their religion or gender or even race! How can that be? I figured that these people make the jokes before somebody else can. That way, they are not the target. Or maybe they're really secure and don't have to worry about what people think. But it's weird how the same joke can be laughed at one time and won't be funny the next. I have heard a lot of girls make PMS jokes. They will laugh, sometimes too much. But if a guy repeats the joke elsewhere to a bunch of girls, he will be greeted with silence. It's like some jokes are permitted to be told by some people and others aren't. I guess you're not a target if you're making fun of yourself. My dad will always talk about his ugly ol' mug or his bald head. But I've noticed that if someone else makes a joke about his hairline, my dad doesn't share in the laugh. Maybe that's why we make jokes about others. If we feel we have been targeted one time, we have to make sure we're not the target the next time. I wish there was a better way. Laughing at real people doesn't help anyone.

Everyone likes to laugh, and it makes us feel better about ourselves. Comedians exaggerate things about well known people to take our minds off real problems. Slapstick humor makes people laugh at victims of pranks instead of with them and focuses on anything physical that seems odd. Some jokes can only be told by certain people for certain people or they won't be funny. Humor keeps people from examining themselves, which isn't bad, but we should try to avoid the mean-spiritedness that happens when we talk about people we know.

"You definitely have expanded on the thesis here," I said, pointing to the last sentence in his introduction. "But it doesn't seem to be woven into your essay very well. The body of your essay goes in so many directions."

"Yeah, I know," he said. "But each topic sentence comes from the introduction. Doesn't that make it okay?"

I reviewed the introduction and saw what he had done. He had taken a different phrase from his introduction to start each of the three body paragraphs he had used. I asked him why he had done this.

"That's what I was taught," he shrugged. "Isn't that right?"

"Well, look at your paragraphs," I said. "Don't you think you should break these down?"

"But I couldn't do that without breaking the structure," he countered.

"What structure?" I asked.

"You know," he said. "One paragraph of intro, three body paragraphs, and a conclusion."

I talked with Steve about some of the professional essays we had read during the semester and asked him if he could remember one that used that exact structure. He could not, so I wondered aloud why he was adhering to rules in his writing that professional writers did not follow.

"But what should I do, then?" Steve asked. "At least I know where to put everything when I follow this rule."

"The structure you are trying to follow takes away all of your natural tendencies to organize your ideas," I said. "You have things misplaced here and aren't considering the needs of your audience at all."

"What do you mean?" he asked.

"When you read," I responded. "What happens when you come to a paragraph that takes up a full page?"

Steve thought for a moment, trying to remember, I assumed, a book he had read with such paragraphs. He smiled. "I stop reading," he said. "I'm not getting a break so I tune out. Maybe I try it again later."

"And what happens when you have to go back to the introduction of an article to figure out why one paragraph follows the other?"

He didn't hesitate. "I stop reading."

"Then you can see why this structure might be alienating your audience," I said.

He nodded. Steve took his essay home to try to reorganize it. But like many students, he needed help in figuring out how to grab an audience with his introduction, how to make each paragraph flow into the next, and how to conclude without merely repeating what he had already said.

DISCUSSION

As a class, select one of the essays in Part III of this book. Have one student read the first paragraph aloud, then switch readers, and continue switching to new readers until you have read the whole article. What methods does the writer use to hold the essay together? How does each paragraph connect to the next? Where is the thesis statement in the text, or is it implied more than stated? What happens in the introduction? What happens in the conclusion? Discuss some of the strategies about arrangement that you can infer from this professional essay. What other options were there?

The above exercise should help you glean some basic ideas about the ways essays can look and be shaped. These discoveries must be placed within the understanding of an important concept: Content determines structure. Starting an essay with a structure limits your ability to develop your ideas and confuses your audience, just like Steve's essay did. The structure of a polished essay springs from a careful understanding of arrangement in relation to the content. But that structure applies to that essay and only that essay. Of course, you can repeat some of the strategies and concepts in different writing tasks, but you cannot reuse the same structure. Structure is not a pie tin that can be recycled for any number of pies. Rather, writing grows in different directions, and the writer must connect the ideas and shape them in some order to keep an audience interested and focused. Although there is no one formula for organizing essays, you can use some of the strategies discussed in this chapter to further your understanding of arranging and connecting different parts of an essay.

PETER SINGER

Tools for Research

The following two excerpts are written by activists for animal rights. Both Peter Singer and Peter Wise feel that animal experimentation is wrong. Even though their topics are similar, the two writers take considerably different paths to reach their points.

Anthony Hopkins of the Institute of Neurology, London, poisoned twelve adult and three infant baboons by injecting them with lead in varying doses for periods up to one year. Because earlier experiments on cats had shown that absorption of lead is more complete through the lungs, the doses were injected directly into the trachea, or windpipe, of each baboon, which was then held in an upright position so that the poison could "trickle" into its lungs. Before death occurred, loss of weight was "striking," five of the twelve adults losing

40 percent or more of their initial weight. Eight baboons had convulsive fits, thirty-four convulsive fits being observed, although "it is likely that others occurred when no observer was present."

In one baboon, seizures began with "twitching around the right eye, spreading to the rest of the right side of the face. During the next fifteen seconds the right arm became involved, and then seizures became generalized." Seizures were "occasionally preceded by a cry" and were sometimes "precipitated by a sudden movement of the animal as it tried to avoid transfer from one cage to another or whilst reaching up to take a banana." Other symptoms included bloody diarrhea, pneumonia, inflamed and bloody intestines, and liver degeneration. One baboon became so weak it could not stand up, and its left fingers could not grasp orange segments. For three weeks before it died this baboon was partially blind; it "groped for proffered fruit and on occasions appeared not to see it." Five of the baboons died in seizures; seven were found dead in their cages; the remaining three were "sacrificed."

When are experiments on animals justifiable? Upon learning of the nature of many contemporary experiments, many people react by saying that all experiments on animals should be prohibited immediately. But if we make our demands as absolute as this, the experimenters have a ready reply: Would we be prepared to let thousands of humans die if they could be saved by a single experiment on a single animal?

This question is, of course, purely hypothetical. There never has been and there never could be a single experiment that saves thousands of lives. The way to reply to this hypothetical question is to pose another: Would the experimenter be prepared to carry out his experiment on a human orphan under six months old if that were the only way to save thousands of lives?

5 If the experimenter would not be prepared to use a human infant then his readiness to use nonhuman animals reveals an unjustifiable form of discrimination on the basis of species, since adult apes, monkeys, dogs, cats, rats, and other mammals are more aware of what is happening to them, more self-directing, and, so far as we can tell, at least as sensitive to pain as a human infant. (I specified that the human infant be an orphan to avoid the complications of the feelings of parents, although in so doing I am being overfair to the experimenter, since the nonhuman animals used in experiments are not orphans and in many species the separation of mother and young clearly causes distress for both.)

There is no characteristic that human infants possess to a higher degree than adult nonhuman animals, unless we are to count the infant's potential as a characteristic that makes it wrong to experiment on him. Whether this characteristic should count is controversial—if we count it, we shall have to condemn abortion along with experiments on infants, since the potential of the infant and the fetus is the same. To avoid the complexities of this issue, however, we can alter our original question a little and assume that the infant is one with severe and irreversible brain damage that makes it impossible for him ever to develop beyond the level of a six-month-old infant. There are, unfortunately, many such human beings, locked away in special wards throughout the country, many of them long since abandoned by their parents. Despite their mental deficiencies, their anatomy and physiology is in nearly all respects identical with that of normal humans. If, therefore, we were to force-feed them with large quantities of floor polish, or drip concentrated solutions of cosmetics into their eyes, we would have a much more reliable indication of the safety of these products for other humans than we now get by attempting to extrapolate the results of tests on a variety of other species. The radiation experiments, the heatstroke experiments, and many other experiments described . . . could also have told us more about human reactions to the experimental situation if they had been carried out on retarded humans instead of dogs and rabbits.

So whenever an experimenter claims that his experiment is important enough to justify the use of an animal, we should ask him whether he would be prepared to use a retarded human at a similar mental level to the animal he is planning to use. If his reply is negative, we can assume that he is willing to use a nonhuman animal only because he gives less consideration to the interests of members of other species than he gives to members of his own—and this bias is no more defensible than racism or any other form of arbitrary discrimination.

Of course, no one would seriously propose carrying out the experiments described . . . on retarded humans. Occasionally it has become known that some medical experiments have been performed on humans without their consent, and sometimes on retarded humans; but the consequences of these experiments for the human subjects are almost always trivial by comparison with what is standard practice for nonhuman animals. Still, these experiments on humans usually lead to an outcry against the experimenters, and rightly so. They are, very often, a further example of the arrogance of the research worker who justifies everything on the grounds of increasing knowledge. If experimenting on retarded, orphaned humans would be wrong, why isn't experimenting on nonhuman animals wrong? What difference is there between the two, except for the mere fact that, biologically, one is a member of our species and the other is not? But *that*, surely, is not a morally relevant difference, any more than the fact that a being is not a member of our race is a morally relevant difference.

Actually the analogy between speciesism and racism applies in practice as well as in theory in the area of experimentation. Blatant speciesism leads to painful experiments on other species, defended on the grounds of its contribution to knowledge and possible usefulness for our species. Blatant racism has led to painful experiments on other races, defended on the grounds of its contribution to knowledge and possible usefulness for the experimenting race. Under the Nazi regime in Germany, nearly 200 doctors, some of them eminent in the world of medicine, took part in experiments on Jews and Russian and Polish prisoners. Thousands of other physicians knew of these experiments, some of which were the subject of lectures at medical academies.

Yet the records show that the doctors sat through medical reports of the infliction of horrible injuries on these "lesser races" and then proceeded to discuss the medical lessons to be learned from them without anyone making even a mild protest about the nature of the experiments. The parallels between this attitude and that of experimenters today toward animals are striking. Then, as now, the subjects were frozen, heated, and put in decompression chambers. Then, as now, these events were written up in a dispassionate scientific jargon. The following paragraph is taken from a report by a Nazi scientist of an experiment on a human being, placed in a decompression chamber; it could equally have been taken from accounts of recent experiments in this country on animals:

> After five minutes spasms appeared; between the sixth and tenth minute respiration increased in frequency, the TP [test person] losing consciousness. From the eleventh to the thirtieth minute respiration slowed down to three inhalations per minute, only to cease entirely at the end of that period . . . about half an hour after breathing had ceased, an autopsy was begun.

Then, as now, the ethic of pursuing knowledge was considered sufficient justification for inflicting agony on those who are placed beyond the limits of genuine moral concern. Our sphere of moral concern is far wider than that of the Nazis; but so long as there are sentient beings outside it, it is not wide enough.

10 To return to the question of when an experiment might be justifiable. It will not do to say: "Never!" In extreme circumstances, absolutist answers always break down. Torturing a human being is almost always wrong, but it is not absolutely wrong. If torture were the only way in which we could discover the location of a nuclear time bomb hidden in a New York City basement, then torture would be justifiable. Similarly, if a single experiment could cure a major disease, that experiment would be justifiable. But in actual life the benefits are always much, much more remote, and more often than not they are nonexistent. So how do we decide when an experiment is justifiable?

We have seen that the experimenter reveals a bias in favor of his own species whenever he carries out an experiment on a nonhuman for a purpose that he would not think justified him in using a human being, even a retarded human being. This principle gives us a guide toward an answer to our question. Since a speciesist bias, like a racist bias, is unjustifiable, an experiment cannot be justifiable unless the experiment is so important that the use of a retarded human being would also be justifiable.

This is not an absolutist principle. I do not believe that it could *never* be justifiable to experiment on a retarded human. If it really were possible to save many lives by an experiment that would take just one life, and there were *no other way* those lives could be saved, it might be right to do the experiment. But this would be an extremely rare case. Not one tenth of one percent of the experiments now being performed on animals would fall into this category.

PETER WISE

The Problem with Being a Thing

It is difficult, to handle simply as property, a creature possessing human passions and human feelings . . . while on the other hand, the absolute necessity of dealing with property as a thing, greatly embarrasses a man in any attempt to treat it as a person.

—Frederick Law Olmsted, traveling in the American South before the Civil War

Jerom's Story

Jerom died on February 13, 1996, ten days shy of his fourteenth birthday. The teenager was dull, bloated, depressed, sapped, anemic, and plagued by diarrhea. He had not played in fresh air for eleven years. As a thirty-month-old infant, he had been intentionally infected with HIV virus SF2. At the age of four, he had been infected with another HIV strain, LAV-1. A month short of five, he was infected with yet a third strain, NDK. Throughout the Iran-Contra hearings, almost to the brink of the Gulf War, he sat in the small, windowless, cinder-block Infectious Disease Building. Then he was moved a short distance to a large, windowless, gray concrete box, one of eleven bleak steel-and-concrete cells 9 feet by 11 feet by 8.5 feet. Throughout the war and into Bill Clinton's campaign for a second term as president, he languished in his cell. This was the Chimpanzee Infectious Disease Building. It stood in the Yerkes Regional Primate Research Center near grassy tree-lined Emory University, minutes from the bustle of downtown Atlanta, Georgia.

Entrance to the chimpanzee cell room was through a tiny, cramped, and dirty anteroom bursting with supplies from ceiling to floor. Inside, five cells lined the left wall of the cell room, six lined the right. The front and ceiling of each cell were a checkerboard of steel bars, criss-crossed in three-inch squares. The rear wall was the same gray concrete. A sliding door was set into the eight-inch-thick concrete side walls. Each door was punctured by a one-half-inch hole, through which a chimpanzee could catch glimpses of his neighbors. Each cell was flushed by a red rubber fire hose twice a day and was regularly scrubbed with deck brushes and disinfected with chemicals. Incandescent bulbs hanging from the dropped ceiling provided the only light. Sometimes the cold overstrained the box's inadequate heating units, and the temperature would sink below 50°F.

Although Jerom lived alone in his cell for the last four months of his life, others were nearby. Twelve other chimpanzees—Buster, Manuel, Arctica, Betsie, Joye, Sara, Nathan, Marc, Jonah, Roberta, Hallie, and Tika—filled the bleak cells, living in twos and threes, each with access to two of the cells. But none of them had any regular sense of changes in weather or the turn of the seasons. None of them knew whether it was day or night. Each slowly rotted in that humid and sunless gray concrete box. Nearly all had been intentionally infected with HIV. Just five months before Jerom died of AIDS born of an amalgam of two of the three HIV strains injected into his blood, Nathan was injected with 40 ml of Jerom's HIV-infested blood. Nathan's level of CD4 cells, the white blood cells that HIV destroys, has plummeted. He will probably sicken and die.

Sales Tax for Loulis

The biologist Vincent Sarich has pointed out that from the standpoint of immunology, humans and chimpanzees are as similar as "two subspecies of gophers living on opposite sides of the Colorado River." Rachel Weiss, a young Yerkes "care-tech" who watched Nathan being injected with Jerom's dirty blood and saw Jerom himself waste away and die, wrote about what she had seen. During the time she cared for the chimpanzees of the Yerkes Chimpanzee Infectious Disease Building, Rachel learned firsthand that chimpanzees possess "passions" and "feelings" that, if not human, are certainly humanlike. It made them no less "difficult to handle simply as property." She stopped thinking of them as "property" and resigned from Yerkes shortly after Jerom's death.

5 Seventeen years before Jerom's death, the primatologist Roger Fouts encountered Loulis staring at him through the bars of another Yerkes cage. Loulis's mother was huddled in a corner. Four metal bolts jutted from her head. Fouts doubted that the brain research she had endured allowed her even to know that Loulis was her son. He plucked up the ten-month-old, signed the necessary loan papers, then drove Loulis halfway across the United States to his adopted mother.

Washoe was a signing chimpanzee who lived on an island in a pond at the Institute for Primate Studies in Norman, Oklahoma. Loulis did not want to sleep in Washoe's arms that first night and curled up instead on a metal bench. At four o'clock in the morning, Washoe suddenly awakened and loudly signed *"Come, baby."* The sound jerked Loulis awake, and he jumped into Washoe's arms. Within eight days, he had learned his first sign. Eight weeks later, he was signing to humans and to the other chimpanzees in Washoe's family. In five months, Loulis, by now an accepted family member, was using combinations of signs. At the end of five years, he was regularly using fifty-one signs; he had initiated thousands of chimpanzee conversations and had participated in thousands more. He had learned everything he knew from the other chimpanzees, for no human ever signed to him.

As years passed, Fouts realized that Yerkes could call in its loan and put Loulis to the knife, as his mother had been. When Loulis was seventeen years old, Fouts sought to buy him outright. Yerkes agreed to sell for $10,000, which Fouts didn't have. After strenuous efforts, he raised that amount. But at the last second, a hitch developed. Ten thousand dollars was Loulis's purchase price. As if Yerkes were selling Fouts a desk or chair, Fouts was charged another 7.5 percent in Georgia sales tax.

The scientists who injected Jerom and Nathan kept the baker's dozen chimps imprisoned in a dungeon and invaded the brain of Loulis's mother, and the administrators who collected sales tax for Loulis believed that chimpanzees are things. But they didn't know why. Rachel Weiss and Roger Fouts show that we can come to believe—as they do—that chimpanzees are persons and not just things.

Demolishing a Wall

For four thousand years, a thick and impenetrable legal wall has separated all human from all nonhuman animals. On one side, even the most trivial interests of a single species—ours—are jealously guarded. We have assigned ourselves, alone among the million animal species, the status of "legal persons." On the other side of that wall lies the legal refuse of an entire kingdom, not just chimpanzees and bonobos but also gorillas, orangutans, and monkeys, dogs, elephants, and dolphins. They are "legal things." Their most basic and fundamental interests—their pains, their lives, their freedoms—are intentionally ignored, often maliciously trampled, and routinely abused. Ancient philosophers claimed that all nonhuman animals had been designed and placed on this earth just for human beings. Ancient jurists declared that law had been created just for human beings. Although philosophy and science have long since recanted, the law has not.

Legal personhood establishes one's legal right to be "recognized as a po- 10
tential bearer of legal rights." That is why the Universal Declaration of Human Rights, the International Covenant on Civil and Political Rights, and the American Convention on Human Rights nearly identically state that "[e]veryone has the right to recognition everywhere as a person before the law." Intended to prevent a recurrence of one of the worst excesses of Nazi law, this guarantee is "often deemed to be rather trivial and self-evident" because no state today denies legal personhood to human beings. But its importance cannot be overemphasized. Without legal personhood, one is invisible to civil law. One has no civil rights. One might as well be dead.

Throngs of Romans scoot past the gaping Coliseum every day without giving it a glance. Athenians rarely squint up at their Parthenon perched high on its Acropolis. In the same way, when we encounter this legal wall, it is so tall, its stones are so thick, and it has been standing for so long that we do not see it. Even after litigating for many years on behalf of nonhuman animals, I did not see it. I saved a handful from death or misery, but for most, there was nothing I could do. I was powerless to represent them directly. They were things, not persons, ignored by judges. But I was butting into something. Finally I saw that wall.

WRITING

Look at the different ways Peter Singer and Peter Wise structure their writing after similar beginnings, especially the way they weave in their support and the way they conclude their pieces. Write about the structural differences you see, such as the position of the thesis statements, the places you find evidence, and the flow from paragraph to paragraph. How do you think the content affected the authors' structural decisions? What do you believe was the effect of audience awareness (see Chapter 3) on how the authors organized the information?

Introducing Your Subject

The opening section of most pieces of writing is called an introduction. Its task is to capture readers' attention and orient them toward the subject. While some introductions contain thesis statements, these statements are not necessary components of introductions. Instead, introductions create interest by hinting at the thesis or suggesting the direction in which the essay might head. An introduction can be longer than one paragraph, especially if the author uses stark images or pivotal scenes to entice readers.

An introduction might be thought of as writing's version of a movie trailer. A good preview excites viewers and makes them want to see the whole movie. Audiences may know something about the plot, but if the preview gives away the surprise ending or explains everything that is going to happen, audience members will be less inclined to pay money to see the film when it is released. Previews, therefore, remain brief and hint at movies' highlights. While an introduction to a piece of writing cannot be as disjointed as a movie trailer or merely slap together snippets of scenes from the body, an introduction achieves a similar effect by creating the desire to read more.

Following are some suggestions to help you begin your essays. While many of them might be called "tricks of the trade," remember that the content of your essay should dictate what you do. Find the right type of introduction for your essay, keeping your audience's needs in mind.

Introductions Come Last Since a paper does not exist before you write it, you really do not know what you are introducing until you have established your paper's thesis. Many writers can put together a coherent introduction without first knowing what the content of the paper will be, but they run into trouble when the body of the paper leads in unanticipated directions. Equally troubling is a thesis that emerges from a critical analysis. The writer's discovery makes for a better paper for all the reasons discussed in Chapter 2, but the introduction might be preparing the audience for something much more pedestrian. In such cases, introductions have to be scrapped or at least reconceived. Therefore, writing the introduction last makes more sense than trying to write it first. You will know what your paper conveys and can think of the best ways to introduce it.

Finding Common Ground An introduction gives you an immediate opportunity to forge a relationship with your audience, in keeping with the discussion about ethos in Chapter 3. After developing the thesis, you can review your ideas and anticipate what your audience will need in order to understand your perspective and relate to you. You need to find common ground, in other words. You can display this common ground in your introduction with a quick reference to a popular icon of modern culture or a brief parallel to a famous occurrence that has relevance to your ideas. Sometimes you can spin a cliché to capture your audience's attention.

For Steve's topic of humor, for instance, we might come up with a variation of "Laugh with people, not at them." Steve's thesis concerned the uses of stereotypes in humor, concluding that people need to ridicule caricatures in order to distance themselves from annoying traits they themselves might embody. You can see that the first sentence of an introduction to this paper might use the cliché like this: "Many people believe that we need to laugh with people, not at them, since we reduce others to objects or stereotypes when we make them the butt of our jokes." The thesis could then be hinted at in the other sentences in the introduction; the introduction would move slowly away from the cliché to suggest something like "If we use caricatures instead of actual people as the butt of our jokes, we might reduce the harm of objectifying people while maintaining humor."

Another way to forge common ground is to ask the audience a question. When you ask a question, readers assume that you are addressing a person or a group of persons, which makes them see themselves as real entities whom you have considered when constructing your essay. Even if the question is rhetorical in nature and is answered by the writer, a good question has anticipated a genuine concern of an audience. Audience members feel that they have been addressed. Peter Singer makes use of this technique in "Tools for Research." While he grabs his audience's attention with the opening vignette of the poisoned baboons, the actual introduction starts with the question, "When are experiments on animals justifiable?"

General to Specific Starting with interesting information about the subject matter not only gives the audience clues about the topic, but could also be enough to hook audience members. This type of introduction begins with a general statement about the topic and gets more specific by adding facts or increasingly narrow ideas, usually culminating in something provocative. This type of introduction might reveal your thesis more than other types; in moving toward specifics, you draw closer to your actual points. Still, you do not want the information presented here to be repeated in the body of your essay. You are trying to attract readers with your introduction, not tell them the exact points you will make. Therefore, the information will create general interest. On page 123, Gloria Naylor uses this technique to introduce her essay. She starts with a description of the general subject of language, moves to the influence of language on reality, and narrows the topic toward one of her points—the power that societal consensus gives words. She orients readers without giving away too many details, and readers want to read more.

Pivotal Scene Many forms of writing include the narration of experience, whether the author's own or someone else's. Some pieces focus on a single event in the life of the writer or of a person he or she has interviewed; the story encompasses the body of the essay, with analysis woven throughout. There is nothing wrong with starting such a paper with an introduction that utilizes methods discussed above. However, consider Scott McMillion's essay, "Treat It Right," in Chapter 16 (page 499). McMillion starts with a pivotal scene from the story he tells about Buck Wilde, who comes on the remains of a mauled hiker. Instead of starting with Wilde's trip into the national park and telling everything he saw and heard before finding the injured man, McMillion puts the reader into Wilde's shoes, using a technique called the imperative voice to affect the reader as much as possible. McMillion continues with this pivotal scene, giving more and more details about what Wilde did to get help and protect other hikers, before going back to the beginning of the story in the first body paragraph, the one that starts "Wilde is an unusual man."

Narrative accounts like this allow a writer to grab the audience's attention by teasing the audience with a portion of the pivotal scene. The same technique can be used in recounting the details of a historical event or in relating case studies of actual human experience. Choosing an exciting part, one where an outcome hinges on the results, and giving the audience a taste of it will make people want to read more. Just make sure that you hint at the thesis or at least provide a clue that you will return to this key moment after recapping how you got there. Otherwise, you might confuse your audience instead of enticing it. Notice that McMillion asks a question early in his introduction: "Put yourself in Buck Wilde's shoes. What are you going to do?" This question hints about the point McMillion is driving toward.

COLLABORATING

Choose two people from your group and introduce them to the class by reading an introduction written collaboratively by the group. First find out some key details about each person. You will have a very boring introduction if you simply say, "This is Sandra, and she attends all the same classes I do." Conduct a brief interview if you are not familiar with the group members, or use the *Jeopardy* technique of having the people tell you a couple of unusual facts about themselves. With this information, use one of the strategies discussed above for introducing the first person and a different strategy for the second person. Each introduction should be no shorter than four sentences. When you present the introductions to the class, take note of what intrigues your peers and of what seems to create clarity for them. Do they want to hear more? Are they confused about anything? Get feedback and think of ways to rewrite the introductions to make them even stronger.

Transitioning from Ideas

The body of a piece of writing, whether a business report, a letter to a friend, or a project for college, constitutes its bulk. Unless the body consists mostly of a chronological retelling of a personal experience or observation, you will need to signal the relationship between each piece of information, especially from paragraph to paragraph. Such signals are called transitions, and they help the writer maintain order in a paper. They connect ideas and examples, allowing writers to construct a path that the audience can follow.

While writers sometimes use rhetorical devices as transitions, the best transitions come from logical sequencing. In other words, one idea naturally progresses into the next in response to audience needs. Again, writers do not conform to a preestablished structure to forge this relationship; instead, they try to arrange elements in their papers so that the audience can understand their train of thought.

No writer can predict what a finished essay will look like. The thesis will determine the audience's needs. Organization comes from coherence within thoughts and a sense of direction, meaning that every idea works toward a goal and each example illuminates those ideas. So when a writer speaks about the organization of an essay, he or she is really speaking of the way the text's ideas have been connected through transitions. The following methods of transition suggest ways to organize your writing.

Increasing Levels of Specificity Some writing tasks involve a high degree of explanation and support. When they do, you do not want to lose your audience's attention, so you can try the technique of slowly increasing the level of specificity to make sure your essay flows logically. The body of your essay can start with a general and familiar point and transition toward more specific explanations or forms of support.

ANASTASIA TOUFEXIS

The Right Chemistry

In "The Right Chemistry," Anastasia Toufexis critically analyzes traditional notions of romantic love, so she needs to explain herself clearly and offer much support for her ideas. She uses increasing levels of specificity as her organizational strategy.

> *Evolutionary roots, brain imprints, biological secretions. That's the story of love.*

O.K., let's cut out all this nonsense about romantic love. Let's bring some scientific precision to the party. Let's put love under a microscope.

When rigorous people with Ph.D.s after their names do that, what they see is not some silly, senseless thing. No, their probe reveals that love rests firmly on the foundations of evolution, biology and chemistry. What seems on the surface to be irrational, intoxicated behavior is in fact part of nature's master strategy—a vital force that has helped humans survive, thrive and multiply through thousands of years. Says Michael Mills, a psychology professor at Loyola Marymount University in Los Angeles: "Love is our ancestors whispering in our ears."

It was on the plains of Africa about 4 million years ago, in the early days of the human species, that the notion of romantic love probably first began to blossom—or at least that the first cascades of neurochemicals began flowing from the brain to the bloodstream to produce goofy grins and sweaty palms as men and women gazed deeply into each other's eyes. When mankind graduated from scuttling around on all fours to walking on two legs, this change made the whole person visible to fellow human beings for the first time. Sexual organs were in full display, as were other characteristics, from the color of eyes to the span of shoulders. As never before, each individual had a unique allure.

When the sparks flew, new ways of making love enabled sex to become a romantic encounter, not just a reproductive act. Although mounting mates from the rear was, and still is, the method favored among most animals, humans began to enjoy face-to-face couplings; both looks and personal attraction became a much greater part of the equation.

5 Romance served the evolutionary purpose of pulling males and females into long-term partnership, which was essential to child rearing. On open grasslands, one parent would have a hard—and dangerous—time handling a child while foraging for food. "If a woman was carrying the equivalent of a 20-lb. bowling ball in one arm and a pile of sticks in the other, it was ecologically critical to pair up with a mate to rear the young," explains anthropologist Helen Fisher, author of *Anatomy of Love.*

While Western culture holds fast to the idea that true love flames forever (the movie *Bram Stoker's Dracula* has the Count carrying the torch beyond the grave), nature apparently meant passions to sputter out in something like four years. Primitive pairs stayed together just "long enough to rear one child through infancy," says Fisher. Then each would find a new partner and start all over again.

What Fisher calls the "four-year itch" shows up unmistakably in today's divorce statistics. In most of the 62 cultures she has studied, divorce rates peak around the fourth year of marriage. Additional youngsters help keep pairs together longer. If, say, a couple have another child three years after the first, as often occurs, then their union can be expected to last about four more years. That makes them ripe for the more familiar phenomenon portrayed in the Marilyn Monroe classic *The Seven-Year Itch.*

If, in nature's design, romantic love is not eternal, neither is it exclusive. Less than 5% of mammals form rigorously faithful pairs. From the earliest days, contends Fisher, the human pattern has been "monogamy with clandestine adultery." Occasional flings upped the chances that new combinations of genes would be passed on to the next generation. Men who sought new partners had more children. Contrary to common assumptions, women were just as likely to stray. "As long as prehistoric females were secretive about their extramarital affairs," argues Fisher, "they could garner extra resources, life insurance, better genes and more varied DNA for their biological futures. Hence those who sneaked into the bushes with secret lovers lived on—unconsciously passing on through the centuries whatever it is in the female spirit that motivates modern women to philander."

> Love is a romantic designation for a most ordinary biological—or, shall we say, chemical?—process. A lot of nonsense is talked and written about it.
>
> —Greta Garbo to Melvyn Douglas in *Ninotchka*

Lovers often claim that they feel as if they are being swept away. They're not mistaken; they are literally flooded by chemicals, research suggests. A meeting of eyes, a touch of hands or a whiff of scent sets off a flood that starts in the brain and races along the nerves and through the blood. The results are familiar: flushed skin, sweaty palms, heavy breathing. If love looks suspiciously like stress, the reason is simple: the chemical pathways are identical.

Above all, there is the sheer euphoria of falling in love—a not-so surprising reaction, considering that many of the substances swamping the newly smitten are chemical cousins of amphetamines. They include dopamine, norepinephrine and especially phenylethylamine (PEA). Cole Porter knew what he was talking about when he wrote, "I get a kick out of you." "Love is a natural high," observes Anthony Walsh, author of *The Science of Love: Understanding Love and Its Effects on Mind and Body.* "PEA gives you that silly smile that you flash at strangers. When we meet someone who is attractive to us, the whistle blows at the PEA factory."

But phenylethylamine highs don't last forever, a fact that lends support 10
to arguments that passionate romantic love is short-lived. As with any amphetamine, the body builds up a tolerance to PEA; thus it takes more and more of the substance to produce love's special kick. After two to three years, the body simply can't crank up the needed amount of PEA. And chewing on chocolate doesn't help, despite popular belief. The candy is high in PEA, but it fails to boost the body's supply.

Fizzling chemicals spell the end of delirious passion; for many people that marks the end of the liaison as well. It is particularly true for those whom Dr. Michael Liebowitz of the New York State Psychiatric Institute terms "attraction junkies." They crave the intoxication of falling in love so much that they move frantically from affair to affair just as soon as the first rush of infatuation fades.

Still, many romances clearly endure beyond the first years. What accounts for that? Another set of chemicals, of course. The continued presence of a partner gradually steps up production in the brain of endorphins. Unlike the fizzy amphetamines, these are soothing substances. Natural pain-killers, they give lovers a sense of security, peace and calm. "That is one reason why it feels so horrible when we're abandoned or a lover dies," notes Fisher. "We don't have our daily hit of narcotics."

Researchers see a contrast between the heated infatuation induced by PEA, along with other amphetamine-like chemicals, and the more intimate attachment fostered and prolonged by endorphins. "Early love is when you love the way the other person makes you feel," explains psychiatrist Mark Goulston of the University of California, Los Angeles. "Mature love is when you love the person as he or she is." It is the difference between passionate and compassionate love, observes Walsh, a psychobiologist at Boise State University in Idaho. "It's Bon Jovi vs. Beethoven."

Oxytocin is another chemical that has recently been implicated in love. Produced by the brain, it sensitizes nerves and stimulates muscle contraction. In women it helps uterine contractions during childbirth as well as production of breast milk, and seems to inspire mothers to nuzzle their infants. Scientists speculate that oxytocin might encourage similar cuddling between adult women and men. The versatile chemical may also enhance orgasms. In one study of men, oxytocin increased to three to five times its normal level during climax, and it may soar even higher in women.

15 One mystery is the prevalence of homosexual love. Although it would seem to have no evolutionary purpose, since no children are produced, there is no denying that gays and lesbians can be as romantic as anyone else. Some researchers speculate that homosexuality results from a biochemical anomaly that occurs during fetal development. But that doesn't make romance among gays any less real. "That they direct this love toward their own sex," says Walsh, "does not diminish the value of that love one iota."

A certain smile, a certain face

— Johnny Mathis

Chemicals may help explain (at least to scientists) the feelings of passion and compassion, but why do people tend to fall in love with one partner rather than a myriad of others? Once again, it's partly a function of evolution and biology. "Men are looking for maximal fertility in a mate," says Loyola Marymount's Mills. "That is in large part why females in the prime childbearing ages of 17 to 28 are so desirable." Men can size up youth and vitality in a glance, and studies indeed show that men fall in love quite rapidly. Women tumble more slowly, to a large degree because their requirements are more complex; they need more time to check the guy out. "Age is not vital," notes Mills, "but the ability to provide security, father children, share resources and hold a high status in society are all key factors."

Still, that does not explain why the way Mary walks and laughs makes Bill dizzy with desire while Marcia's gait and giggle leave him cold. "Nature has wired us for one special person," suggests Walsh, romantically. He rejects the idea that a woman or a man can be in love with two people at the same time. Each person carries in his or her mind a unique subliminal guide to the ideal partner, a "love map," to borrow a term coined by sexologist John Money of Johns Hopkins University.

Drawn from the people and experiences of childhood, the map is a record of whatever we found enticing and exciting—or disturbing and disgusting. Small feet, curly hair. The way our mothers patted our head or how our fathers told a joke. A fireman's uniform, a doctor's stethoscope. All the information gathered while growing up is imprinted in the brain's circuitry by adolescence. Partners never meet each and every requirement, but a sufficient number of matches can light up the wires and signal, "It's love." Not every partner will be like the last one, since lovers may have different combinations of the characteristics favored by the map.

O.K., that's the scientific point of view. Satisfied? Probably not. To most people—with or without Ph.D.s—love will always be more than the sum of its natural parts. It's a commingling of body and soul, reality and imagination, poetry and phenylethylamine. In our deepest hearts, most of us harbor the hope that love will never fully yield up its secrets, that it will always elude our grasp.

With reporting by Hannah Bloch/New York and Sally B. Donnelly/
Los Angeles

Toufexis starts with a general explanation that love is "part of nature's master strategy" to aid in human survival. She follows with historical information, then transitions to analyzing specific patterns and emotions that people in love experience. In her tenth paragraph, she increases the level of specificity when she discusses the chemical substances that account for the "sheer euphoria of falling in love." She continues with these scientific explanations, each point responding to a specific, anticipated audience reaction, before transitioning toward her thesis. This structure ensures a logical flow and prevents her from confusing or alienating her audience.

Contrast, Addition, Summary, and Exemplification Rhetorical devices of transition help writers and readers locate the purpose of a piece of information quickly. While you do not want to overuse these devices, they can be helpful. The following table lists the most common rhetorical devices. A transition of contrast prepares the audience for a qualifier to a statement or for the presentation of the difference between one set of ideas and another. A transition of addition signals that you will make another point about the same subject. A transition of summary alerts the audience that you are concluding an idea or tying it together. A transition of exemplification lets you smoothly move into an example to support your idea.

Rhetorical devices can be placed at the beginning of a sentence or between the subject and predicate. They must occur early enough in the sentence for an audience to pick up on the relationship between the sentence and the next one or one paragraph and the next.

Contrast	Addition	Summary	Exemplification
However	And	Therefore	For example
But	Also	Then	For instance
Yet	Too	So	Specifically
Instead	Futhermore	Thus	In other words
Even though	In addition	Consequently	That is
On the other hand	Besides	As a result	Particularly
Nevertheless	Moreover	Accordingly	Namely
Although	Next	Hence	
Though	Finally		
Still	Similarly		
Despite	Likewise		
On the contrary			
In contrast			

Repeating Keywords You definitely want to avoid needless repetition in your paper. However, you can transition from one paragraph to the next by dropping a keyword from the previous paragraph into the first sentence of the next paragraph. You can repeat the word directly, use a different form of the word, substitute a synonym, or use a pronoun. Whatever shape it takes, this repetition provides a direct link from the previous paragraph to the next. So if the end of one paragraph reads, "The degree to which we react to fear limits our ability to confront our insecurities," the first sentence in the next paragraph could read, "Reactions vary in people." The same root word, *react*, appears in both sentences. The subtle shift from a verb to a noun helps prevent direct repetition, which allows for a better flow. Such links will keep your audience aboard, especially when material is complicated. You should use this technique sparingly, however, to avoid redundancy.

Time and Place Weaving in your critical analysis is crucial. In writing that uses elongated personal experiences within the body, however, the critical analysis can disrupt the chronological flow. You do not want your readers to be confused about where they left off, but a transition such as "As I was saying" is awkward and too talky; it seems like you have strayed from your point or are disorganized.

Instead, orient your audience to time or place in subtle ways. If a scene that has been interrupted takes place at night, show the continuation of the events with something like "Midnight drew near" or "My bedtime had passed three hours earlier." If a story involves a setting such as a barn, remind the audience where they are with a detail like "I noticed hay stuck in the cuff of my jeans."

Do not underestimate an audience's propensity to get lost. In "Me Talk Pretty One Day" (Chapter 14, page 422), David Sedaris disrupts his narrative of a French classroom to talk about his mother:

> I recalled my mother, flushed with wine, pounding the tabletop late one night, saying, "Love? I love a good steak cooked rare. I love my cat, and I love . . ." My sisters and I leaned forward, waiting to hear our names. "Tums," our mother said. "I love Tums."

Even though Sedaris's analysis and the vignette about his mother take only one paragraph, Sedaris makes sure the reader does not get lost by referring to the teacher and his own notepad in the opening sentence of the next paragraph, clearly placing the narrative in a classroom.

Remember that your readers did not experience the event you're writing about, so they do not know the sequence of events in advance. If your critical analysis is penetrating and you lingered on pertinent details appropriately or, like Sedaris, you included a relevant memory, your readers will be focused on those aspects and will need to have their memories jogged to get back into the narrative. Subtle hints can work wonders in ensuring that chronological organization does not get compromised.

Subheadings Reports often use subheadings as organizational tools. When a writer switches from one idea to the next, she or he inserts a heading, usually in a bold font, that prepares the reader for a shift in focus. This type of transition reduces the reliance on rhetorical devices of transition and on repetition of keywords. Subheadings also allow a reader to scan a document to locate desired information easily.

The subheading should summarize the focus of the next idea in a phrase or a single word. It should never be a full sentence. Look at Peter Wise's "The Problem with Being a Thing" on pages 95–97. Wise uses three subheadings: "Jerom's Story," "Sales Tax for Loulis," and "Demolishing a Wall." All three are phrases, not sentences.

WRITING

Use your current essay assignment to practice your use of transitions. Print your revision, and circle every rhetorical device of transition you have used in the body of the essay. Look at sentences or paragraphs where you have not used rhetorical devices. How are the sentences and paragraphs fitting together? Are ideas progressing from general to specific? Have you repeated keywords and phrases? If your piece is a narrative, have you stuck to chronological order? If you have disrupted that order, how have you transitioned back into the narrative? Did you try subheadings? Be able to identify how each sentence and paragraph connects to the next and how all parts of the body move toward the same goal. If sentences or paragraphs cannot be linked to what comes before and after, you will need to revise to find the proper place for them or make a decision about their worth for this paper.

Placing Your Thesis

Many myths revolve around the placement of the thesis in an essay. As Steve discovered, writers are not obligated to place a thesis statement in the introduction, much less as the last sentence in the introduction. A thesis also does not have to be directly repeated elsewhere in the essay once it is stated. In fact, a thesis does not really have to be stated, although an audience must come away from a piece of writing knowing what the point was.

A thesis is an idea that emerges from a critical analysis, as discussed in Chapter 2. The introduction should hint at it. The conclusion should build on it. Where should it go? You must consider the magnitude of your thesis and gauge possible reactions from your audience. Below are suggestions for determining the most effective placement.

Putting a New Twist on an Old Idea If your critical analysis has produced a variation of or wrinkle on a well-accepted idea, your strategy for placement will be different than if you are turning a societal norm upside down. You will not puzzle or alienate your audience by stating a new twist to an old idea immediately; in fact, you might intrigue readers, depending on how closely your thesis aligns to the norm. People tend to react well to the tweaking of things they are used to; their comfort level is unaffected, and the hope that your ideas might solve problems or contradictions in the old idea appeals to them. Thus, you can weave the thesis into the introduction or at least state it early in the paper without losing your readers.

Make sure you have assessed your audience correctly. While a group of retired people might welcome ideas to improve their health coverage, for instance, a group of upwardly mobile executives might see your slight changes to established procedures as an attempt at socialized medicine that would increase the tax burden and reduce treatment options. While you cannot always account for extreme reactions, you must guard against certain possibilities. That same group of executives might listen more attentively and be drawn into your argument if you do not reveal your thesis too quickly. You must judge any writing situation appropriately and evaluate the risks before deciding on the placement of the thesis.

> **WRITING**
>
> Look at Elizabeth Pleck's essay, "Festivals, Rites, and Presents," in Chapter 11. Pleck clearly is putting a new twist on old ideas through her look at sentimentality and postsentimentality. What audience has she targeted for this essay? How have her structural choices helped or hindered her in preparing the audience for her thesis?

Using the Oreo Cookie Method Some writers rely on shock value to keep audiences listening. In other words, audience members cannot believe what they are hearing, so they pay closer attention than they normally would.

Critical analysis can lead to harsh criticism of the status quo, producing a thesis that strongly challenges preconceived notions or shocks an audience. If your goal is to shake an audience out of its complacency, think about putting your thesis in the first sentence in the introduction.

Generally, readers will want to hear an explanation right away; if they do not, they may dismiss you. Therefore, the last sentence of the introduction does not work as well as the first sentence, since your audience will need assurance that your proposal has been thought through. Squeezing your thesis between some catchy opening ideas and an explanation or qualifier to ensure a sense of logic ensures that the audience absorbs the jolt but does not kill its interest. This placement is called the "Oreo cookie method," because it parallels the way an Oreo cookie surrounds the delicious cream with two otherwise bland chocolate cookies. It allows you to soften the blow without compromising what you have to say.

You have probably used a similar strategy in delicate social situations. You have news to deliver that you know your friend will not like, but you have to tell it anyway. You cannot wait to tell your friend until you are leaving; he or she needs time to get used to the news and might want you to spell out the positives as well as the negatives. Thus, you say, "I know how much you really like Ron, but he's not the guy you think he is. He just got arrested for dealing drugs. I know you find this hard to believe, but he has been living a double life for a long time." You then relate the details. The shocking statement is that Ron got arrested. The qualifier, "he's not the guy you think he is," prepares the friend for the news, and the statement about the double life leads to an explanation. Blurting out the news right away could cause panic and hysteria. Saving it until the end of the story would be cruel.

While a critical analysis cannot be accurately compared to bad news, a thesis springing from a critical analysis can have a similar effect on readers comfortable within the status quo. You must proceed cautiously when you have arrived at such a thesis.

AMY WANG

The Same Difference

Amy Wang grabs the attention of her audience early in this essay by recounting a childhood memory of racism. Her introduction hints at her thesis, but she builds sympathy with her audience before detailing her anger at white men and her thesis about the impossibility of white people understanding the worldview of people of color. She concludes with a conciliatory statement. Does the conclusion succeed in softening the blow without compromising Wang's position?

It was on my way home that the moment of truth swept by—again. There we were, a friend and I, heading north on the Pennsylvania Turnpike to central New York to visit my parents. Somehow our conversation had parted the curtains before my childhood memories, and before I knew it, I was telling him about an incident I have never quite forgotten.

As I spoke, it was almost as if my adult self were back in Pittsburgh, watching; strange how in my memory the sun is always glinting through a bright haze on that day. The trees are bare, or nearly so, with dark branches that reach out to splinter the sun's rays. I am walking alone, down a white concrete sidewalk littered with leaves, twigs, buckeyes. School is out for the day, and everyone is going home.

From behind come shouts, and I turn to see a group of children from school. A moment passes, and I realize they are shouting at me. I listen for several seconds before the words whip into clarity:

Chink! Hey, chink! Chinky chinky chink!

5 They are running. I am frozen, my heart the only part of me moving, and it is pounding. Then one of them stoops, picks up a twig and hurls it at me. It lands short, a foot away on the sidewalk. Then I turn, still blocks from home, and run. The twigs keep coming, clattering close behind as the others shout and follow. As I run, I think of the steep steps to the front door and despair.

But when I reach the steps and turn around, only silence follows. And when my mother answers the doorbell's ring, she sees only her daughter, cheeks a little flushed, waiting to be let in. Almost instinctively, I know I must not tell her. It would only hurt her, and there is nothing she can do. Besides, it is nothing I want to discuss.

"Wow," he said. "And you were in sixth grade when this happened?"

"Six," I said. "I was 6 when this happened. I was in first grade."

He was clearly appalled, his eyes in far focus as he tried to understand how such a thing could happen to a small child. I was concentrating on the road, but even a sidelong glance showed he did not, could not, quite understand. And it was then that I felt the familiar stab of disappointment: the realization that no matter how long we traveled together, we would always be on parallel roads, moving on either side of a great divide. I would never know his assurance as he made his way through a world where his skin color was an assumption, and he would never know my anxiety as I made my way through a world where my skin color was an anguish.

10 We were silent, and after a while he fell asleep. "Wake me up when we get to Allentown," he had said as he drifted off, and we both smiled, remembering a classmate who had once padded an expense account for profit by driving from New York to Allentown and back twice in two days.

The thought of the old mill town triggered memories of another old mill town, where I had gotten my first job out of college. It was at the local newspaper, working nights on the copy desk. Our shifts ended at 1 A.M., and I often drove home through deserted streets, the hush broken only by the whir of an occasional street-cleaning machine or the clanking of a distant garbage truck. The other drivers on the streets at that hour seemed just as weary, just as intent on getting to bed.

In such an atmosphere I often dream, and so to this day a shadowy, slowed-down quality suffuses the memory of turning my head and looking out the side window one night just in time to see an old red Dodge draw up in the next lane at a traffic light. Inside, four young white crewcut men dressed in denim and flannel strain toward me, their faces distorted with hate, their mouths twisted with invective. Our windows are closed, so I am spared their actual words, but their frenzied pantomime leaves little to be imagined.

When the light turns green I pull away hastily, but they cruise alongside for the next few blocks. By the time they tire of me and swing into a left turn, I am seething with fear and rage. I wait until they are committed to the turn, then raise my middle finger. One of them looks back for a final insult, sees my gesture, and gapes—but only for a moment. He turns, and I know he is screaming at the driver to turn back. I gun it.

They never come after me, and I make it home alive. Numb, I crawl into bed. It is only after I lie down that I realize how they might have hurt me, the four of them with their huge Dodge against my tiny Nissan, and I begin to shake. As my mind tumbles, the phone rings. For a moment I think it is them, and then logic returns. I answer, and it is my boyfriend, calling from Boston. I tell him what happened, melting into tears. He is sympathetic, but then he asks: "How do you know they weren't yelling at you because you were a woman?"

I don't, of course, but that is not the point. His whiteness rushes through 15
the line with the very question. "It doesn't matter," I tell him, and suddenly I can't stand to hear his voice. I tell him I don't want to discuss it anymore, and hang up.

Somewhere along Route 79 in New York he said, "This is beautiful." I smiled, remembering the years I spent in Finger Lakes country: middle school, high school, college. Here were trees I had climbed, hills I had sledded down, malls I knew by heart; here were roads that led to memories and people who knew my history.

And it was because I had to come back here that another He was able to betray me. It was during the first summer I spent away from home, working at a magazine in New York. Picture now a pavilion on the grounds of a quiet country club where the staff is enjoying the annual company picnic, and there I am by the jukebox, hovering over the glassed-in 45s as a light mist dampens the grass. As the Contours wail "Do You Love Me," I sway to the beat, attracting a stranger's eyes. In a moment he is introducing himself; in an hour he is sitting by me in the bus taking us back to the city; in a week he is asking me out to dinner.

I am no longer thinking clearly. On my last day at the magazine, he watches as I clean out my desk, then asks me, in a low but urgent tone, not to forget him. He tells me he wants my address, and a sudden foreboding chill nearly stuns me with its iciness, sending shivers through my hand as I write out the address and phone number. Then I ask for his address and phone number. I do not think to ask him not to forget me.

Weeks go by without a word, and then one night, I know. The chill comes back: For days I hate white men, all of them, they all bear the blame for his misdeed. But I have known too many good ones for my fury to last, and finally I am forced to admit that I have been a fool, and that this time, at least, it had nothing to do with race.

20 "It could have happened to anyone," a (white male) friend tells me. "It happens to everyone."

I am not immediately consoled. But time goes on, and finally, so do I.

By the time we pulled into my parents' driveway, it was nearly dinnertime. I sprang out, glad to stretch, and bounded into the house, but he was slow to follow, and I had discarded my shoulder bag and greeted everyone by the time he finally appeared in the doorway. I went to introduce him, wondering why he was hanging back. Then he raised his eyes to mine as he came up the stairs, and I realized he was nervous: He was in my world now, and he was finally getting an inkling of what I went through every day.

Payback time. At last.

Then my mother was there, smiling and shaking his hand, and my father was right behind her, also smiling.

25 "Welcome," he said.

For a moment, I could see the horizon, where parallel lines sometimes seem to meet.

Building Toward Consensus If your thesis does not necessarily shock anyone but still diverges from the societal norm, you might choose to place it toward the end of your essay. This way, you can take audience members along for the ride, giving them hints in the introduction and through the woven-in analysis, but not explicitly stating your thesis until you have completed your review of the salient points.

In a court of law, a judge uses this method to announce a decision on the admissibility of evidence, on a sentence, or on a verdict in small claims courts or nonjuried cases. If you have not seen an actual court case, you probably have seen dramas involving courtrooms or perhaps have watched *Judge Judy* and others on daytime television. A savvy listener will note where the judge lingers on evidence and will have a good notion of where he or she is headed, although that listener may not know exactly what the judgment will be. While you might disagree with the final judgment, you have listened the whole way. Sometimes your opinion and those of others might change, since the judge has built a consensus in the courtroom or in the homes of television viewers. More than likely, you will understand and respect the judgment.

An essay has to conclude, while the verdict in the courtroom is often the last or nearly the last thing said. But a thesis can work if placed toward the end and might grant more consideration from your audience than if you announced it immediately. Note the difference, though, between leading your audience toward a thesis you have developed through critical analysis and slapping a thesis onto the end of a paper to meet an assignment requirement. The former is based on audience awareness; the latter does not attempt the necessary critical analysis and the weaving of that analysis into the body. This distinction could not be more crucial.

COLLABORATING

Have each group member bring a news article from the local paper. Make sure it is a straightforward piece of reporting such as would be found on the front page, not an editorial or analysis. Because many readers only glance at headlines or read the first few paragraphs, news articles generally give the facts right away. As a group, decide what the thesis of each article is. Next, revise the articles, experimenting with different locations for the thesis. How does the content affect your choices in placing the thesis? What changes in arrangement are necessitated by different placement? Besides the ideas listed above, what strategies can you come up with in placing a thesis so that readers' expectations are fulfilled?

Finishing Your Thoughts

Writers may have more trouble with conclusions than with any other part of a paper. Some formulaic advice often given is to restate the thesis, rewrite the introduction, or end with a bang. The first two suggestions do not take into account how a paper progresses after the introduction and what strategies for arrangement are used. The last suggestion, though seemingly powerful, is vague. Introducing a surprise at the end of your paper might puzzle your audience. Even if you like the idea, how do you find a "bang"? How does it spring from an essay? The formulas do not help you figure out how to wrap up ideas, which is the purpose of the conclusion.

SHIRLEY JACKSON

The Lottery

This classic short story by Shirley Jackson does not reveal all the important details until the conclusion. Yet, the ending is plausible. When a reader reviews the story, he or she will see how Jackson makes the shock consistent with the body of the story. Jackson ends with a bang, but the details of the story support it.

The morning of June 27th was clear and sunny, with the fresh warmth of a full-summer day; the flowers were blossoming profusely and the grass was richly green. The people of the village began to gather in the square, between the post office and the bank, around ten o'clock; in some towns there were so many people that the lottery took two days and had to be started on June 26th, but in this village, where there were only about three hundred people, the whole lottery took less than two hours, so it could begin at ten o'clock in the morning and still be through in time to allow the villagers to get home for noon dinner.

The children assembled first, of course. School was recently over for the summer, and the feeling of liberty sat uneasily on most of them; they tended to gather together quietly for a while before they broke into boisterous play, and their talk was still of the classroom and the teacher, of books and reprimands. Bobby Martin had already stuffed his pockets full of stones, and the other boys soon followed his example, selecting the smoothest and roundest stones; Bobby and Harry Jones and Dickie Delacroix—the villagers pronounced this name "Delacroy"—eventually made a great pile of stones in one corner of the square and guarded it against the raids of the other boys. The girls stood aside, talking among themselves, looking over their shoulders at the boys, and the very small children rolled in the dust or clung to the hands of their older brothers or sisters.

Soon the men began to gather, surveying their own children, speaking of planting and rain, tractors and taxes. They stood together, away from the pile of stones in the corner, and their jokes were quiet and they smiled rather than laughed. The women, wearing faded house dresses and sweaters, came shortly after their men-folk. They greeted one another and exchanged bits of gossip as they went to join their husbands. Soon the women, standing by their husbands, began to call to their children, and the children came reluctantly, having to be called four or five times. Bobby Martin ducked under his mother's grasping hand and ran, laughing, back to the pile of stones. His father spoke up sharply, and Bobby came quickly and took his place between his father and his oldest brother.

The lottery was conducted—as were the square dances, the teen-age club, the Halloween program—by Mr. Summers, who had time and energy to devote to civic activities. He was a round-faced, jovial man and he ran the coal business, and people were sorry for him, because he had no children and his wife was a scold. When he arrived in the square, carrying the black wooden box, there was a murmur of conversation among the villagers, and he waved and called, "Little late today, folks." The postmaster, Mr. Graves, followed him, carrying a three-legged stool, and the stool was put in the center of the square and Mr. Summers set the black box down on it. The villagers kept their distance, leaving a space between themselves and the stool, and when Mr. Summers said, "Some of you fellows want to give me a hand?" there was a hesitation before two men, Mr. Martin and his oldest son, Baxter, came forward to hold the box steady on the stool while Mr. Summers stirred up the papers inside it.

5 The original paraphernalia for the lottery had been lost long ago, and the black box now resting on the stool had been put into use even before Old Man Warner, the oldest man in town, was born. Mr. Summers spoke frequently to the villagers about making a new box, but no one liked to upset even as much tradition as was represented by the black box. There was a story that the present box had been made with some pieces of the box that had preceded it, the one that had been constructed when the first people settled down to make a village here. Every year, after the lottery, Mr. Summers began talking again about a new box, but every year the subject was allowed to fade off without anything's being done. The black box grew shabbier each year; by now it was no longer completely black but splintered badly along one side to show the original wood color, and in some places faded or stained.

Mr. Martin and his oldest son, Baxter, held the black box securely on the stool until Mr. Summers had stirred the papers thoroughly with his hand. Because so much of the ritual had been forgotten or discarded, Mr. Summers had been successful in having slips of paper substituted for the chips of wood that had been used for generations. Chips of wood, Mr. Summers had argued, had been all very well when the village was tiny, but now that the population was more than three hundred and likely to keep on growing, it was necessary to use something that would fit more easily into the black box. The night before the lottery, Mr. Summers and Mr. Graves made up the slips of paper and put them in the box, and it was then taken to the safe of Mr. Summers' coal company and locked up until Mr. Summers was ready to take it to the square next morning. The rest of the year, the box was put away, sometimes one place, sometimes another; it had spent one year in Mr. Graves's barn and another year underfoot in the post office, and sometimes it was set on a shelf in the Martin grocery and left there.

There was a great deal of fussing to be done before Mr. Summers declared the lottery open. There were the lists to make up—of heads of families, heads of households in each family, members of each household in each family. There was the proper swearing-in of Mr. Summers by the postmaster, as the official of the lottery; at one time, some people remembered, there had been a recital of some sort, performed by the official of the lottery, a perfunctory, tuneless chant that had been rattled off duly each year; some people believed that the official of the lottery used to stand just so when he said or sang it, others believed that he was supposed to walk among the people, but years and years ago this part of the ritual had been allowed to lapse. There had been, also, a ritual salute, which the official of the lottery had had to use in addressing each person who came up to draw from the box, but this also had changed with time, until now it was felt necessary only for the official to speak to each person approaching. Mr. Summers was very good at all this; in his clean white shirt and blue jeans, with one hand resting carelessly on the black box, he seemed very proper and important as he talked interminably to Mr. Graves and the Martins.

Just as Mr. Summers finally left off talking and turned to the assembled villagers, Mrs. Hutchinson came hurriedly along the path to the square, her sweater thrown over her shoulders, and slid into place in the back of the crowd. "Clean forgot what day it was," she said to Mrs. Delacroix, who stood next to her, and they both laughed softly. "Thought my old man was out back stacking wood," Mrs. Hutchinson went on, "and then I looked out the window and the kids was gone, and then I remembered it was the twenty-seventh and came a-running." She dried her hands on her apron, and Mrs. Delacroix said, "You're in time, though. They're still talking away up there."

Mrs. Hutchinson craned her neck to see through the crowd and found her husband and children standing near the front. She tapped Mrs. Delacroix on the arm as a farewell and began to make her way through the crowd. The people separated good-humoredly to let her through; two or three people said, in voices just loud enough to be heard across the crowd, "Here comes your Missus, Hutchinson," and "Bill, she made it after all." Mrs. Hutchinson reached her husband, and Mr. Summers, who had been waiting, said cheerfully,

"Thought we were going to have to get on without you, Tessie." Mrs. Hutchinson said, grinning, "Wouldn't have me leave m'dishes in the sink, now, would you, Joe?" and soft laughter ran through the crowd as the people stirred back into position after Mrs. Hutchinson's arrival.

10 "Well, now," Mr. Summers said soberly, "guess we better get started, get this over with, so's we can go back to work. Anybody ain't here?"

"Dunbar," several people said. "Dunbar, Dunbar."

Mr. Summers consulted his list. "Clyde Dunbar," he said. "That's right. He's broke his leg, hasn't he? Who's drawing for him?"

"Me, I guess," a woman said, and Mr. Summers turned to look at her. "Wife draws for her husband," Mr. Summers said. "Don't you have a grown boy to do it for you, Janey?" Although Mr. Summers and everyone else in the village knew the answer perfectly well, it was the business of the official of the lottery to ask such questions formally. Mr. Summers waited with an expression of polite interest while Mrs. Dunbar answered.

"Horace's not but sixteen yet," Mrs. Dunbar said regretfully. "Guess I gotta fill in for the old man this year."

15 "Right," Mr. Summers said. He made a note on the list he was holding. Then he asked, "Watson boy drawing this year?"

A tall boy in the crowd raised his hand. "Here," he said. "I'm drawing for m'mother and me." He blinked his eyes nervously and ducked his head as several voices in the crowd said things like "Good fellow, Jack," and "Glad to see your mother's got a man to do it."

"Well," Mr. Summers said, "guess that's everyone. Old Man Warner make it?"

"Here," a voice said, and Mr. Summers nodded.

A sudden hush fell on the crowd as Mr. Summers cleared his throat and looked at the list. "All ready?" he called. "Now, I'll read the names—heads of families first—and the men come up and take a paper out of the box. Keep the paper folded in your hand without looking at it until everyone has had a turn. Everything clear?"

20 The people had done it so many times that they only half listened to the directions; most of them were quiet, wetting their lips, not looking around. Then Mr. Summers raised one hand high and said, "Adams." A man disengaged himself from the crowd and came forward. "Hi, Steve," Mr. Summers said, and Mr. Adams said, "Hi, Joe." They grinned at one another humorlessly and nervously. Then Mr. Adams reached into the black box and took out a folded paper. He held it firmly by one corner as he turned and went hastily back to his place in the crowd, where he stood a little apart from his family, not looking down at his hand.

"Allen," Mr. Summers said. "Anderson. . . . Bentham."

"Seems like there's no time at all between lotteries any more," Mrs. Delacroix said to Mrs. Graves in the back row. "Seems like we got through with the last one only last week."

"Time sure goes fast," Mrs. Graves said.

"Clark. . . . Delacroix."

"There goes my old man," Mrs. Delacroix said. She held her breath while her husband went forward. 25

"Dunbar," Mr. Summers said, and Mrs. Dunbar went steadily to the box while one of the women said, "Go on, Janey," and another said, "There she goes."

"We're next," Mrs. Graves said. She watched while Mr. Graves came around from the side of the box, greeted Mr. Summers gravely, and selected a slip of paper from the box. By now, all through the crowd there were men holding the small folded papers in their large hands, turning them over and over nervously. Mrs. Dunbar and her two sons stood together, Mrs. Dunbar holding the slip of paper.

"Harburt. . . . Hutchinson."

"Get up there, Bill," Mrs. Hutchinson said, and the people near her laughed.

"Jones." 30

"They do say," Mr. Adams said to Old Man Warner, who stood next to him, "that over in the north village they're talking of giving up the lottery."

Old Man Warner snorted. "Pack of crazy fools," he said. "Listening to the young folks, nothing's good enough for *them.* Next thing you know, they'll be wanting to go back to living in caves, nobody work any more, live *that* way for a while. Used to be a saying about 'Lottery in June, Corn be heavy soon.' First thing you know, we'd all be eating stewed chickweed and acorns. There's *always* been a lottery," he added petulantly. "Bad enough to see young Joe Summers up there joking with everybody."

"Some places have already quit lotteries," Mrs. Adams said.

"Nothing but trouble in *that,*" Old Man Warner said stoutly. "Pack of young fools."

"Martin." And Bobby Martin watched his father go forward. "Overdyke. . . . Percy." 35

"I wish they'd hurry," Mrs. Dunbar said to her older son. "I wish they'd hurry."

"They're almost through," her son said.

"You get ready to run tell Dad," Mrs. Dunbar said.

Mr. Summers called his own name and then stepped forward precisely and selected a slip from the box. Then he called, "Warner."

"Seventy-seventh year I been in the lottery," Old Man Warner said as he went through the crowd. "Seventy-seventh time." 40

"Watson." The tall boy came awkwardly through the crowd. Someone said, "Don't be nervous, Jack," and Mr. Summers said, "Take your time, son."

"Zanini."

After that, there was a long pause, a breathless pause, until Mr. Summers, holding his slip of paper in the air, said, "All right, fellows." For a minute, no one moved, and then all the slips of paper were opened. Suddenly, all the women began to speak at once, saying, "Who is it?" "Who's got it?" "Is it the Dunbars?" "Is it the Watsons?" Then the voices began to say, "It's Hutchinson. It's Bill," "Bill Hutchinson's got it."

"Go tell your father," Mrs. Dunbar said to her older son.

People began to look around to see the Hutchinsons. Bill Hutchinson was standing quiet, staring down at the paper in his hand. Suddenly, Tessie Hutchinson shouted to Mr. Summers, "You didn't give him time enough to take any paper he wanted. I saw you. It wasn't fair!"

"Be a good sport, Tessie," Mrs. Delacroix called, and Mrs. Graves said, "All of us took the same chance."

"Shut up, Tessie," Bill Hutchinson said.

"Well, everyone," Mr. Summers said, "that was done pretty fast, and now we've got to be hurrying a little more to get done in time." He consulted his next list. "Bill," he said, "you draw for the Hutchinson family. You got any other households in the Hutchinsons?"

"There's Don and Eva," Mrs. Hutchinson yelled. "Make *them* take their chance!"

"Daughters draw with their husbands' families, Tessie," Mr. Summers said gently. "You know that as well as anyone else."

"It wasn't *fair*," Tessie said.

"I guess not, Joe," Bill Hutchinson said regretfully. "My daughter draws with her husband's family, that's only fair. And I've got no other family except the kids."

"Then, as far as drawing for families is concerned, it's you," Mr. Summers said in explanation, "and as far as drawing for households is concerned, that's you, too. Right?"

"Right," Bill Hutchinson said.

"How many kids, Bill?" Mr. Summers asked formally.

"Three," Bill Hutchinson said. "There's Bill, Jr., and Nancy, and little Dave. And Tessie and me."

"All right, then," Mr. Summers said. "Harry, you got their tickets back?"

Mr. Graves nodded and held up the slips of paper. "Put them in the box, then," Mr. Summers directed. "Take Bill's and put it in."

"I think we ought to start over," Mrs. Hutchinson said, as quietly as she could. "I tell you it wasn't *fair*. You didn't give him time enough to choose. *Everybody* saw that."

Mr. Graves had selected the five slips and put them in the box, and he dropped all the papers but those onto the ground, where the breeze caught them and lifted them off.

"Listen, everybody," Mrs. Hutchinson was saying to the people around her.

"Ready, Bill?" Mr. Summers asked, and Bill Hutchinson, with one quick glance around at his wife and children, nodded.

"Remember," Mr. Summers said, "take the slips and keep them folded until each person has taken one. Harry, you help little Dave." Mr. Graves took the hand of the little boy, who came willingly with him up to the box. "Take a paper out of the box, Davy," Mr. Summers said. Davy put his hand into the box and laughed. "Take just *one* paper," Mr. Summers said. "Harry, you hold it for him." Mr. Graves took the child's hand and removed the folded paper from the tight fist and held it while little Dave stood next to him and looked up at him wonderingly.

"Nancy next," Mr. Summers said. Nancy was twelve, and her school friends breathed heavily as she went forward, switching her skirt, and took a slip daintily from the box. "Bill, Jr.," Mr. Summers said, and Billy, his face red and his feet over-large, nearly knocked the box over as he got a paper out. "Tessie," Mr. Summers said. She hesitated for a minute, looking around defiantly, and then set her lips and went up to the box. She snatched a paper out and held it behind her.

65 "Bill," Mr. Summers said, and Bill Hutchinson reached into the box and felt around, bringing his hand out at last with the slip of paper in it.

The crowd was quiet. A girl whispered, "I hope it's not Nancy," and the sound of the whisper reached the edges of the crowd.

"It's not the way it used to be," Old Man Warner said clearly. "People ain't the way they used to be."

"All right," Mr. Summers said. "Open the papers. Harry, you open little Dave's."

Mr. Graves opened the slip of paper and there was a general sigh through the crowd as he held it up and everyone could see that it was blank. Nancy and Bill, Jr., opened theirs at the same time, and both beamed and laughed, turning around to the crowd and holding their slips of paper above their heads.

70 "Tessie," Mr. Summers said. There was a pause, and then Mr. Summers looked at Bill Hutchinson, and Bill unfolded his paper and showed it. It was blank.

"It's Tessie," Mr. Summers said, and his voice was hushed. "Show us her paper, Bill."

Bill Hutchinson went over to his wife and forced the slip of paper out of her hand. It had a black spot on it, the black spot Mr. Summers had made the night before with the heavy pencil in the coal-company office. Bill Hutchinson held it up, and there was a stir in the crowd.

"All right, folks," Mr. Summers said. "Let's finish quickly."

Although the villagers had forgotten the ritual and lost the original black box, they still remembered to use stones. The pile of stones the boys had made earlier was ready; there were stones on the ground with the blowing scraps of paper that had come out of the box. Mrs. Delacroix selected a stone so large she had to pick it up with both hands and turned to Mrs. Dunbar. "Come on," she said. "Hurry up."

75 Mrs. Dunbar had small stones in both hands, and she said, gasping for breath, "I can't run at all. You'll have to go ahead and I'll catch up with you."

The children had stones already, and someone gave little Davy Hutchinson a few pebbles.

Tessie Hutchinson was in the center of a cleared space by now, and she held her hands out desperately as the villagers moved in on her. "It isn't fair," she said. A stone hit her on the side of the head.

Old Man Warner was saying, "Come on, come on, everyone." Steve Adams was in the front of the crowd of villagers, with Mrs. Graves beside him.

"It isn't fair, it isn't right," Mrs. Hutchinson screamed, and then they were upon her.

As with many aspects of writing, your thesis and the content will determine your approach to the conclusion. One size does not fit all. In wrapping up a paper, you must consider the emotional effect you have generated in readers so far and the feelings you want them to leave with. You have to ask questions such as these: Do I need to heighten the emotional pull? Do I need to bring them down from a fevered pitch? Do I want to direct them toward thinking or acting a certain way? Do I want to remind them of a particular point by leaving a certain image in their minds? Do I simply want to reinforce the points I made, or do I want to save my most powerful point to send a knockout punch in the conclusion?

In answering these questions, you might see whether any of the techniques below can aid you in developing the most effective conclusion.

Tying Points Together When a paper has been proceeding at a fairly even, pleasant pace, you do not want to change your tone dramatically to end with a bang. You need, instead, to make sure that your point is clear by reminding the audience of your goal and stating its implications. In tying points together, you might specifically state your thesis for the first time in your essay, following with its ramifications. With such a strategy, you would want to ease concerns about your point by reminding the audience of a lack of alternatives, given the evidence you have presented, and downplaying controversy.

Reread the last three paragraphs in Peter Singer's "Tools for Research" on page 94. His proposal to conduct no research on animals that we are unwilling to conduct on retarded humans might alarm some readers. However, he uses an even tone when he ties his points together, reminding his audience of the dangers of species bias but distancing himself from absolutist thinking.

Singer is advocating change, so he shows the logical progression toward his thesis before asserting it. Tying points together does not mean repeating points that you have already made verbatim. Repetition bogs down a conclusion, giving it a slow, plodding feeling. When you tie points together, you are creating something new from separate, perhaps disparate, parts. This new thing might reinforce old values; critical analysis does not necessarily guarantee fresh insights but rather lets you study the status quo closely. The conclusion that old values have merit brings together the points your analysis produced, so you can state that how intense study of the issue has brought you full circle to the original idea and then discuss what this discovery means to your readers.

Call to Action A strong critique of an existing situation often leads the writer to want to move his or her audience toward application of the ideas. Calls for action effectively conclude essays by giving audience members options to pursue. A call for action can be as obvious as explaining how to contact a U.S. senator to voice concerns about environmental policy or as subtle as suggesting that every person pick up one piece of trash a day to help in the battle against littering.

However, you cannot slap a call to action onto any essay. The body of your essay must build toward the need for action, and the thesis should closely align with the call. You also want to make sure that your call for action does not depart too radically from reasonable judgment. Demanding that citizens overthrow the government will leave your audience with questions about your credibility. Suggesting ways that voters can put more responsive candidates into office will be met with much less skepticism.

Most of all, a call for action must be sincere. If you do not want to lead the charge, you should not be advising others to do so, no matter how effective such an ending might be.

FRED KAPLAN

The Worst-Laid Plans

Why was emergency planning so awful?

Hurricane Katrina devastated New Orleans in 2005, and citizens across the country questioned the federal government's delays and confusion in bringing aid to victims. Fred Kaplan, writing three weeks after the hurricane, analyzes a manual that was supposed to guide the actions of the federal government in the event of fifteen types of disasters, including hurricanes. How does he build to a call for action?

When a new president of the United States takes office, one of his first tasks is to hear a briefing on the nuclear-war plan. Chances are nil that he'll ever have to carry out this plan. But if he did, his choice of action might be more fateful, and the consequences more catastrophic, than any event in human history. So, the briefing—or, as it's known, The Briefing—remains the first order of presidential business, the defining distinction of the job. A staff member on the National Security Council, if not the president himself, is routinely apprised of changes. The plan's logistical aspects are periodically rehearsed. A military officer carrying a briefcase that contains the nuclear-launch codes escorts the president constantly. The briefing, the officer, the plan, and the codes all remain the same, or gradually evolve, regardless of whether a Republican or Democrat has been elected. Nobody would think of appointing political hacks to run even the most trivial aspect of this well-oiled machine.

One lesson of Hurricane Katrina is that emergency-management planning ought to receive the same attention and professionalism as nuclear-war planning. Floods and hurricanes are less cataclysmic than nuclear war, but they're serious enough—and far more likely to happen.

This is a lesson for mayors and governors as well as presidents.

In 2000, Louisiana state officials produced a remarkably detailed "State Emergency Operations Plan," including an equally impressive "Southeast Louisiana Hurricane Evacuation and Sheltering Plan." If this plan had been followed, Katrina probably would have wrought far less havoc. But it seems to have been laid in a drawer and forgotten. An April 2005 update, issued by the state's office of homeland security and emergency preparedness, includes a page headlined "Record of Changes to Plan," with columns labeled "Change Number," "Date," "Part Affected," "Date Posted," and "Name of Poster." The page is blank; the plan had not been altered in the previous five years—a fairly sure sign that it hadn't been read, either.

5 On the federal level, it's not clear whether there *was* a plan worthy of the name. In July 2004, the Homeland Security Council—chaired by a White House adviser and consisting of 70 officials from 18 federal departments and agencies—published a manual titled *Planning Scenarios Created for Use in National, Federal, State, and Local Homeland Security Preparedness Activities.* The document laid out 15 scenarios for various types of disasters involving nuclear, biological, chemical, radiological, and cyber attacks, as well as major earthquakes and hurricanes. Each scenario outlined the likely damage and what steps should be taken in preparation, relief, and rescue.

What's striking about this document—the result of so much effort, devoted to such a high-profile issue of public policy, and designed to be distributed to emergency-management offices nationwide—is how useless it is. Take the chapter on major hurricanes. Its forecast of effects: "Casualties: 1,000 fatalities, 5,000 hospitalizations . . . Infrastructure Damage: Buildings destroyed, large debris . . . Economic impact: Millions of dollars . . . Recovery timeline: Months." One's first reaction, upon reading this: Any grade-school kid with an encyclopedia could have written it.

The list of recommended actions is no more reassuring. For instance: "Care must include medical assistance; shelter and temporary housing assistance; emergency food, water, and ice provision; and sanitary facility provision." Not only is this head-slappingly obvious, but when Katrina whirred its way up the coast, the officials in charge didn't follow even these elementary guidelines. Worse still, the chapters on planning scenarios for various terrorist attacks are no more informative or specific.

One could argue that these sorts of generalized guidelines are necessary first steps in the creation of an emergency-response strategy. But this document was published a year and a half after the Department of Homeland Security began operating. There's no good reason why it couldn't have appeared a *month* and a half after.

The DHS published an updated version of *Planning Scenarios* this past April. However, only officials with proper clearances can obtain or download a copy. Are all relevant federal, state, and local emergency-management officials cleared to read it? And is the second edition any better than the first? If an independent body gets around to investigating the terrible planning for Hurricane Katrina and the implications for future disasters, man-made or otherwise, these should be two of the questions.

Last Moment of a Narrative Papers that use extended narratives in the body can use the last part of the narrative as the conclusion. If you have woven critical analysis into the body and did not announce the thesis in the introduction, you can stop short of completing the story and instead discuss your thesis and end the paper by concluding the story.

For instance, if you had a story about the conflicting perceptions of the causes of an argument between you and your friend, you could narrate the events up to the final point of significance, then launch into your thesis. Your conclusion could pick up the story where you left off, or explain whether you ever came to terms with your friend, or describe what you do now when your perception differs from someone else's.

As long as you do not have more points of significance to analyze, you can wrap up the story with the narration, much like the final scene in a television drama. The climax has passed. Except for shows leaving viewers with a cliffhanger, the last few moments linger on one or two of the main characters, showing what they did or are doing after the fact. An essay with a narrative can end similarly.

Selecting a Powerful Image If you have used strong imagery in conveying a point, your conclusion can look again at a particularly strong image. Papers that describe the plight of the poor, for instance, may focus on a specific person, leaving an image for people to think about—a homeless person, perhaps, or a child going to bed hungry. If you have incorporated a case study in your paper, you can return to the case study in a manner similar to the strategy for the last moment of a narrative described above. What has happened to this person? Is his or her life continuing in the same way?

Lingering images can be effective when they leave the audience with something to ponder. Images personalize arguments, even if the images are of past events or inanimate objects, such as a mountain or a deserted street. Again, these images will not be effective if they have not been preceded by a discussion of your thesis so that your main point is clear to the audience.

GLORIA NAYLOR

"Mommy, What Does 'Nigger' Mean?"

Gloria Naylor analyzes the word nigger *in the following essay. She ends with an image that, while calm in tone, is emotionally disturbing to the reader.*

Language is the subject. It is the written form with which I've managed to keep the wolf away from the door and, in diaries, to keep my sanity. In spite of this, I consider the written word inferior to the spoken, and much of the frustration experienced by novelists is the awareness that whatever we manage to capture in even the most transcendent passages falls far short of the richness of life. Dialogue achieves its power in the dynamics of a fleeting moment of sight, sound, smell and touch.

I'm not going to enter the debate here about whether it is language that shapes reality or vice versa. That battle is doomed to be waged whenever we seek intermittent reprieve from the chicken and egg dispute. I will simply take the position that the spoken word, like the written word, amounts to a nonsensical arrangement of sounds or letters without a consensus that assigns "meaning." And building from the meanings of what we hear, we order reality. Words themselves are innocuous; it is the consensus that gives them true power.

I remember the first time I heard the word "nigger." In my third-grade class, our math tests were being passed down the rows, and as I handed the papers to a little boy in back of me, I remarked that once again he had received a much lower mark than I did. He snatched his test from me and spit out that word. Had he called me a nymphomaniac or a necrophiliac, I couldn't have been more puzzled. I didn't know what a nigger was, but I knew that whatever it meant, it was something he shouldn't have called me. This was verified when I raised my hand, and in a loud voice repeated what he had said and watched the teacher scold him for using a "bad" word. I was later to go home and ask the inevitable question that every black parent must face—"Mommy, what does 'nigger' mean?"

And what exactly did it mean? Thinking back, I realize that this could not have been the first time the word was used in my presence. I was part of a large extended family that had migrated from the rural South after World War II and formed a close-knit network that gravitated around my maternal grandparents. Their ground-floor apartment in one of the buildings they owned in Harlem was a weekend mecca for my immediate family, along with countless aunts, uncles and cousins who brought along assorted friends. It was a bustling and open house with assorted neighbors and tenants popping in and out to exchange bits of gossip, pick up an old quarrel or referee the ongoing checkers game in which my grandmother cheated shamelessly. They were all there to let down their hair and put up their feet after a week of labor in the factories, laundries and shipyards of New York.

5 Amid the clamor, which could reach deafening proportions—two or three conversations going on simultaneously, punctuated by the sound of a baby's crying somewhere in the back rooms or out on the street—there was still a rigid set of rules about what was said and how. Older children were sent out of the living room when it was time to get into the juicy details about "you-know-who" up on the third floor who had gone and gotten herself "p-r-e-g-n-a-n-t!" But my parents, knowing that I could spell well beyond my years, always demanded that I follow the others out to play. Beyond sexual misconduct and death, everything else was considered harmless for our young ears. And so among the anecdotes of the triumphs and disappointments in the various workings of their lives, the word "nigger" was used in my presence, but it was set within contexts and inflections that caused it to register in my mind as something else.

In the singular, the word was always applied to a man who had distinguished himself in some situation that brought their approval for his strength, intelligence or drive:

"Did Johnny really do that?"

"I'm telling you, that nigger pulled in $6,000 of overtime last year. Said he got enough for a down payment on a house."

When used with a possessive adjective by a woman—"my nigger"—it became a term of endearment for husband or boyfriend. But it could be more than just a term applied to a man. In their mouths it became the pure essence of manhood—a disembodied force that channeled their past history of struggle and present survival against the odds into a victorious statement of being: "Yeah, that old foreman found out quick enough—you don't mess with a nigger."

10 In the plural, it became a description of some group within the community that had overstepped the bounds of decency as my family defined it: Parents who neglected their children, a drunken couple who fought in public, people who simply refused to look for work, those with excessively dirty mouths or unkempt households were all "trifling niggers." This particular circle could forgive hard times, unemployment, the occasional bout of depression—they had gone through all of that themselves—but the unforgivable sin was lack of self-respect.

A woman could never be a "nigger" in the singular, with its connotation of confirming worth. The noun "girl" was its closest equivalent in that sense, but only when used in direct address and regardless of the gender doing the addressing. "Girl" was a token of respect for a woman. The one-syllable word was drawn out to sound like three in recognition of the extra ounce of wit, nerve or daring that the woman had shown in the situation under discussion.

"G-i-r-l, stop. You mean you said that to his face?"

But if the word was used in a third-person reference or shortened so that it almost snapped out of the mouth, it always involved some element of communal disapproval. And age became an important factor in these exchanges. It was only between individuals of the same generation, or from an older person to a younger (but never the other way around), that "girl" would be considered a compliment.

I don't agree with the argument that use of the word "nigger" at this social stratum of the black community was an internalization of racism. The dynamics were the exact opposite: the people in my grandmother's living room took a word that whites used to signify worthlessness or degradation and rendered it impotent. Gathering there together, they transformed "nigger" to signify the varied and complex human beings they knew themselves to be. If the word was to disappear totally from the mouths of even the most racist of white society, no one in that room was naïve enough to believe it would disappear from white minds. Meeting the word head-on, they proved it had absolutely nothing to do with the way they were determined to live their lives.

So there must have been dozens of times that the word "nigger" was spoken in front of me before I reached the third grade. But I didn't "hear" it until it was said by a small pair of lips that had already learned it could be a way to humiliate me. That was the word I went home and asked my mother about. And since she knew that I had to grow up in America, she took me in her lap and explained.

COLLABORATING

Pretend that each member of your group will be honored with an achievement award as a result of accomplishments in school, work, or life. Write three or four paragraphs about your own achievements, then pass that writing to the group member on your left. Each group member is responsible for crossing out all the personal pronouns in the writing they receive so that your writing is now in the third person. Next, group members should write conclusions for the papers in front of them, imagining that the papers will be read at an awards banquet. Group members should share their conclusions with the group and discuss their effectiveness. Which type of conclusion seemed to be the most appropriate? Why? Could more than one type of conclusion have been used? What revisions of the descriptions of accomplishments would have been necessary?

Summary

As a writer, know that your work need not conform to a predetermined structure. Instead, consider the purpose of the writing task, the needs you anticipate from your audience, and the effect of your thesis. The content dictates the strategies for arrangement of your ideas, although organization relies on an introduction, a body, and a conclusion.

The introduction should orient and entice the audience to read more. The body should contain the ideas, examples, and other types of support, including narratives, and the critical analysis should be woven through it. The conclusion wraps up the essay. The placement of the thesis is strategic and is not limited to just the introduction or conclusion.

CHAPTER 5

LANGUAGE CHOICES IN WRITING

Our language choices are crucial to our papers. While we use punctuation and other symbols for coherence, words constitute the bulk of our writing. Mark Twain once said that the difference between the right word and the nearly right word is the difference between lightning and a lightning bug. Language allows our audience to understand us or to miss—perhaps just slightly, but sometimes completely—what we mean.

Some students in a class I once taught suddenly made what I thought were peculiar language choices in their essays. One student, Marcus, seemed to have a large vocabulary but misused words frequently. For example, he used the word *talon* instead of *claw* in describing a cat's foot. His roommate, Craig, explained in one essay how he *arraigned* the guy down the hall of stealing from him; I thought *accused* fit the situation better. I was really thrown when yet a third student, Ding, described a goof-off in his high school as a *lotus-eater*. Since these three students usually sat together in class, I thought their strange language choices might be the product of their peer feedback to one another. So I sat with them during the next peer feedback session.

"When you guys look at each other's papers," I said, "pay close attention to the words you're choosing. It seems like you are trying to reach for larger words in your descriptions, and it confuses me when I am reading your papers."

"You mean you don't know the words?" Marcus smiled at me.

"It's not that," I said. "But I wonder if you are comfortable using these words. They don't sound like you."

"Well, we're writing," Craig said. "We're supposed to sound different."

This icon will direct you to web links and additional resources on the website college.hmco.com/pic/thelin1e

"We want to sound like we belong in college," Marcus chimed in.

"But what makes you think that these words make you sound smarter?" I asked. "I mean, come on, Ding. In your last paper you said a guy in your class was a lotus-eater. Have you ever heard anyone use that expression before?"

Ding shook his head. The only woman in the group, Melissa, was laughing. "I told them they shouldn't do it," she said.

"Do what?" I asked.

"They said we should use a thesaurus," Melissa announced. "But I told them it was a bad idea."

The men in the group looked sheepish. "It's not like we were cheating or anything," Marcus said.

Marcus, Craig, and Ding were not cheating, but they were depriving themselves of understanding the richness of language. They were also communicating poorly because they did not appreciate how language functions. While a term like *lotus-eater* might sound exotic, it carries a meaning that goes beyond the synonym Ding found in the thesaurus. A lotus-eater is someone who indulges in luxury, ignoring the concerns of day-to-day living. The term is archaic, referring to the people in Homer's *Odyssey* who ate fruit coming from a plant called a lotus that produced a dazed state. Did Ding mean to employ this term as a metaphor to implicate the class clown in drug use? Was he implying that the guy was a rich kid who had it made and didn't bother studying? Ding was not aware of the associations of the term, and using it in this context sounded strange. An audience could have easily misinterpreted him or could have read inaccurate implications into his story.

Here is the draft in which Ding used the term *lotus-eater*. Notice the other places where the vocabulary usage sounds strained.

DING GUANG

Negative Cliques in Schools

You can look at all different schools in America and they will have the same types of cliques. Students gain status by becoming associated with others on a social hierarchy. Often they will abandon their anomalous characteristics to match the habits and quirks of pupils more popular than themselves. This tendency allows for negative behavior to impinge upon the learning of others.

An observation conducted at a high school in the San Fernando Valley supports the contention that cliques will endanger both the person and the students surrounding them. Many negative cliques exist, but the ones that confine themselves to after school activities are relatively harmless. Skiers, jocks, and heavy metal enthusiasts will permit their ideologies to filter into the classroom and cafeteria, but their main actions engage elsewhere. They simply associate with others like them. The dangers, as documented here, come from the group who do not really have any activities except loquaciousness and tomfoolery.

Every class in this particular high school contained individuals who were too lazy to do their homework and constantly caused mischief. The main lotus-eater was a student named Kyle. He reclined in the back of his classes, his legs extended onto another desk, and refused to participate intelligently. He would remark on the answers given by other pupils, trying to take the attention off of them and onto himself. In so doing, he relegated their learning to an inauspicious endeavor and substituted his needs for the needs of others. Instructors tried to be patient, but they even would laugh and consort to banter with him.

For example, he had not studied for a certain quiz in history. The students only had 15 minutes to complete this quiz, but they had been given sufficient notice of it. While they struggled to recall answers to questions, Kyle would shout out ridiculous statements to the more studious pupils like, "Let me use your cheat sheet when you're through, Benson." The teacher issued a warning to Kyle, but since he was going to fail the quiz anyway, the warnings went unheeded. He fidgeted, tried to replicate from the student in front of him, and noisily ate a snack. Some pupils had difficulty concentrating and were unable to recall answers or did not finish.

Other students would mimic Kyle's persona and make jokes during crucial times in class. It appeared they had no incentive to perform adequately in school. Any class where the loafers attended ended up being disrupted through puerile behavior. The formation of this cabal resulted in reduced education for others. Therefore, cliques can give youths identity but they can be destructive if not properly monitored and curtailed.

DISCUSSION

Do you think Ding's vocabulary was influenced by the audience he perceived for this paper? Discuss Ding's intended audience and try to find more appropriate vocabulary to substitute for words or terms in the paper that sound awkward. What other types of audiences might a student target for a topic such as Ding's, and how would the audiences affect the word choices?

Vocabulary growth comes about gradually through experience, reading, and interacting in society. No one can develop a new, stronger vocabulary overnight, and finding synonyms in a thesaurus will not cover up other deficiencies in a paper. As a writer, you need to be aware of the strength of language and of how it operates, not just within a paper, but in society also.

We must search for precision in our language choices and also realize that we cannot completely control the effect words will have on people. Words can carry different meanings for different audiences, so again the influence of the reader is important as we prepare any piece of writing.

DISCUSSION

Think of the many terms, especially slang expressions, you may use or have heard in reference to the following items: home, boyfriend or girlfriend, police officers, free time, quality (when something is good or bad, whatever that thing might be). Have one class member write all of the terms you come up with on the board.

When you are finished, look at the lists, and discuss what you think might be the origins of some of the terms. What happens when you hear someone use these terms, especially the slang expressions, in contexts that do not reflect their origins? Do the terms lose their power? Do they take on new meanings? Do they adjust comfortably into new settings? Talk about why and how this process occurs.

Language can entrance readers, evoke pity, secure cultural bonding, produce outrage, and affect society in many other ways. As writers, we should understand the way language functions and the ways in which we manipulate it and it manipulates us.

Mediating Experiences

The world exists outside our perception of it. The only way we can understand it is through language. Without language, we cannot give meaning to the sensory impressions that barrage us. Furthermore, we need language to communicate with others—to share what we experience. Language mediates among the writer, the audience, sensory impression, and even nonsensory events in forming what we know as experience or reality. While language takes many forms, such as bodily gestures and signs, we'll concentrate on the written word.

If words mediate our experience, choosing the best words possible becomes vitally important. Every time we delete one word in favor of another, we subtly change the reality of a situation. We are helping create reality as we go. How do we know, then, what is appropriate and what is not in word choice? What is the difference between fabrication and the selection of words that enhance an experience? The following three tips help answer these questions.

Consensus Building When you experience an event, your memory records the details that you found most striking. You may miss other details. Our brains are so remarkable that they often store data that passed under our radar. Some activities, such as brainstorming and freewriting (see Chapter 6), can help us recall details we missed. However, sometimes we must rely on the recollections of others to construct the best understanding of what happened. Unless something happened to you alone, other people will have seen it. The news media and others often employ audiovisual equipment to record events of social or political importance.

You do not want to surrender your personal vision of an event, but when writing about it, you need to verify your impressions with others involved or check the records if the event was recorded or otherwise documented. By putting together several accounts, you can build a consensus, even if just a localized one, about the truth or reality of a situation. Once you establish the truth, you can choose words that accurately convey the consensus and, thus, avoid misleading your audience.

People's memories vary, and some recollections conflict in key ways. When this happens, you can account for differing perspectives by giving both versions and then expressing what you believe to be the case. For example, an American peace activist named Rachel Corrie visited the occupied territory of the Gaza Strip to investigate Israeli treatment of the Palestinians. On March 23, 2003, she engaged in a protest against the bulldozing of Palestinian homes in Rafah by Israelis. Very tragically, she was run over by a bulldozer and killed. This March 25, 2003, excerpt from CNN.com shows CNN accounting for two perspectives: that the bulldozer driver intentionally killed her, and that her death was accidental.

> "This morning, when she was killed, she was attempting to prevent the Israeli military from destroying Palestinian civilian homes," [Huwaida] Arraf [co-founder of the International Solidarity Group] said.
>
> "She was raising her hands and yelling at the bulldozer driver to stop," Arraf said. "The bulldozer driver paid no attention. . . . He buried Rachel with dirt, which ended up, obviously, knocking her down. Then he ran over her, and then reversed and ran over her again."
>
> Other witnesses, however, reported that Corrie had scaled a pile of dirt but then lost her footing and fell backward behind it, out of sight of the bulldozer operator. The bulldozer continued moving forward, covering Corrie with dirt and then crushing her.
>
> It was not clear whether the bulldozer operator could hear protesters' yells over the sound of the machine.
>
> A member of the solidarity group, who identified herself as Alice from London, said she and Corrie had sat for about three hours in front of houses belonging to their friends. The driver of the bulldozer must have seen them, she said, but drove over Corrie anyway.
>
> She emerged from under the bulldozer saying, "My back is broken, my back is broken," Alice told CNN.
>
> Tom Dale, who said he was about 10 yards from Corrie, said she was in plain view and was wearing an orange jacket. As the bulldozer lifted a pile of earth, it moved forward and caught Corrie under its blade, he said.

The repetition of the contention that the bulldozer driver acted either maliciously or carelessly clearly shows that the writer believes in the driver's culpability. Notice, however, that the writer includes the perspective of other witnesses. We talk about solo experience in the "Describing and Shaping" section later in this chapter.

Naming the World Use language that falls within the parameters of your vocabulary. A thesaurus may remind you of words you have forgotten, but you do not want to use the thesaurus the way Marcus, Craig, and Ding did in the opening example. You want to stretch your vocabulary by using appropriate words, and you want to acquire new words to build your vocabulary. However, always keep in mind the connection between reality and the language that mediates it.

Sometimes our minds search for a word to describe a situation, and we just do not feel right until we can remember what that word is. The reason for this feeling is the connection between language and experience. When we are not able to recall a particular word, we sense that we have not properly recaptured a moment or correctly expressed our feelings.

There are also times when we need new language in order to act, a process called "naming the world" by Brazilian educator Paulo Freire. In this process, individuals or groups empower themselves by utilizing terminology to cast a more appropriate light on a situation. At its best, naming the world allows for an understanding of forces that influence us in almost invisible ways. Feminists, for instance, use *patriarchy* to name the sense of oppression and dislocation women feel in a world dominated by men and male norms. Once a source of oppression can be named, action can be taken to correct the situation.

Figurative Language Writers name their worlds in many ways, such as by using metaphors and similes. These words allow for comparisons among events and feelings that are not literally similar. They attempt to convey an attitude or perspective by encouraging readers to transfer their feelings about one event to another. A writer might say, "With a gazelle-like burst, the runner sprinted to victory." A gazelle has four legs and many other features completely unlike human features. By using *gazelle-like,* the writer wants the audience to associate this particular sprint with the amazing speed of the animal, conjuring an image assumed to be familiar to all.

When you use the word *like* in a description, as in the above example, you have created a simile. In contrast, a metaphor implies rather than states a relationship with something literally dissimilar. Metaphors often appear in the form of a verb, as in the sentence "The news of his death crushed me." The news is not literally squashing the person, but the use of *crushed* conveys the pain the writer feels.

In the following reading, does the figurative language suggest more than a concrete description would?

MARTIN LUTHER KING, JR.

I Have a Dream

This famous speech by Martin Luther King, Jr., employs figurative language. Isolate and list the figurative language, and discuss its effect in this speech. King also makes use of allusions, which are references to famous works of art and literature, or, at times, historical events or persons. Do you think King's Biblical allusions function the same way his figurative language does?

Five score years ago, a great American, in whose symbolic shadow we stand, signed the Emancipation Proclamation. This momentous decree came as a great beacon light of hope to millions of Negro slaves who had been seared in the flames of withering injustice. It came as a joyous daybreak to end the long night of captivity. But one hundred years later, we must face the tragic fact that the Negro is still not free.

One hundred years later, the life of the Negro is still sadly crippled by the manacles of segregation and the chains of discrimination. One hundred years later, the Negro lives on a lonely island of poverty in the midst of a vast ocean of material prosperity. One hundred years later, the Negro is still languishing in the corners of American society and finds himself an exile in his own land.

So we have come here today to dramatize an appalling condition. In a sense we have come to our nation's capital to cash a check. When the architects of our republic wrote the magnificent words of the Constitution and the Declaration of Independence, they were signing a promissory note to which every American was to fall heir.

This note was a promise that all men would be guaranteed the inalienable rights of life, liberty, and the pursuit of happiness. It is obvious today that America has defaulted on this promissory note insofar as her citizens of color are concerned. Instead of honoring this sacred obligation, America has given the Negro people a bad check which has come back marked "insufficient funds." But we refuse to believe that the bank of justice is bankrupt. We refuse to believe that there are insufficient funds in the great vaults of opportunity of this nation.

So we have come to cash this check—a check that will give us upon de- 5
mand the riches of freedom and the security of justice. We have also come to this hallowed spot to remind America of the fierce urgency of now. This is no time to engage in the luxury of cooling off or to take the tranquilizing drug of gradualism. Now is the time to rise from the dark and desolate valley of segregation to the sunlit path of racial justice. Now is the time to open the doors of opportunity to all of God's children. Now is the time to lift our nation from the quicksands of racial injustice to the solid rock of brotherhood.

It would be fatal for the nation to overlook the urgency of the moment and to underestimate the determination of the Negro. This sweltering summer of the Negro's legitimate discontent will not pass until there is an invigorating autumn of freedom and equality. Nineteen sixty-three is not an end, but a beginning. Those who hope that the Negro needed to blow off steam and will now be content will have a rude awakening if the nation returns to business as usual. There will be neither rest nor tranquility in America until the Negro is granted his citizenship rights.

The whirlwinds of revolt will continue to shake the foundations of our nation until the bright day of justice emerges. But there is something that I must say to my people who stand on the warm threshold which leads into the palace of justice. In the process of gaining our rightful place we must not be guilty of wrongful deeds. Let us not seek to satisfy our thirst for freedom by drinking from the cup of bitterness and hatred.

We must forever conduct our struggle on the high plane of dignity and discipline. We must not allow our creative protest to degenerate into physical violence. Again and again we must rise to the majestic heights of meeting physical force with soul force.

The marvelous new militancy which has engulfed the Negro community must not lead us to distrust of all white people, for many of our white brothers, as evidenced by their presence here today, have come to realize that their destiny is tied up with our destiny and their freedom is inextricably bound to our freedom.

10 We cannot walk alone. And as we walk, we must make the pledge that we shall march ahead. We cannot turn back. There are those who are asking the devotees of civil rights, "When will you be satisfied?" We can never be satisfied as long as our bodies, heavy with the fatigue of travel, cannot gain lodging in the motels of the highways and the hotels of the cities. We cannot be satisfied as long as the Negro's basic mobility is from a smaller ghetto to a larger one. We can never be satisfied as long as a Negro in Mississippi cannot vote and a Negro in New York believes he has nothing for which to vote. No, no, we are not satisfied, and we will not be satisfied until justice rolls down like waters and righteousness like a mighty stream.

I am not unmindful that some of you have come here out of great trials and tribulations. Some of you have come fresh from narrow cells. Some of you have come from areas where your quest for freedom left you battered by the storms of persecution and staggered by the winds of police brutality. You have been the veterans of creative suffering. Continue to work with the faith that unearned suffering is redemptive.

Go back to Mississippi, go back to Alabama, go back to Georgia, go back to Louisiana, go back to the slums and ghettos of our northern cities, knowing that somehow this situation can and will be changed. Let us not wallow in the valley of despair. I say to you today, my friends, that in spite of the difficulties and frustrations of the moment, I still have a dream. It is a dream deeply rooted in the American dream.

I have a dream that one day this nation will rise up and live out the true meaning of its creed: "We hold these truths to be self-evident: that all men are created equal." I have a dream that one day on the red hills of Georgia the sons of former slaves and the sons of former slaveowners will be able to sit down together at a table of brotherhood. I have a dream that one day even the state of Mississippi, a desert state, sweltering with the heat of injustice and oppression, will be transformed into an oasis of freedom and justice. I have a dream that my four children will one day live in a nation where they will not be judged by the color of their skin but by the content of their character. I have a dream today.

I have a dream that one day the state of Alabama, whose governor's lips are presently dripping with the words of interposition and nullification, will be transformed into a situation where little black boys and black girls will be able to join hands with little white boys and white girls and walk together as sisters and brothers. I have a dream today. I have a dream that one day every valley shall be exalted, every hill and mountain shall be made low, the rough places will be made plain, and the crooked places will be made straight, and the glory of the Lord shall be revealed, and all flesh shall see it together. This is our hope. This is the faith with which I return to the South. With this faith we will be able to hew out of the mountain of despair a stone of hope. With this faith we will be able to transform the jangling discords of our nation into a beautiful symphony of brotherhood. With this faith we will be able to work together, to pray together, to struggle together, to go to jail together, to stand up for freedom together, knowing that we will be free one day.

This will be the day when all of God's children will be able to sing with a new meaning, "My country, 'tis of thee, sweet land of liberty, of thee I sing. Land where my fathers died, land of the pilgrim's pride, from every mountainside, let freedom ring." And if America is to be a great nation, this must become true. So let freedom ring from the prodigious hilltops of New Hampshire. Let freedom ring from the mighty mountains of New York. Let freedom ring from the heightening Alleghenies of Pennsylvania! Let freedom ring from the snowcapped Rockies of Colorado! Let freedom ring from the curvaceous peaks of California! But not only that; let freedom ring from Stone Mountain of Georgia! Let freedom ring from Lookout Mountain of Tennessee! Let freedom ring from every hill and every molehill of Mississippi. From every mountainside, let freedom ring.

When we let freedom ring, when we let it ring from every village and every hamlet, from every state and every city, we will be able to speed up that day when all of God's children, black men and white men, Jews and Gentiles, Protestants and Catholics, will be able to join hands and sing in the words of the old Negro spiritual, "Free at last, free at last; thank God Almighty, we are free at last!"

Building consensus and naming the world can serve many purposes. You can do it in numerous ways without having to use words that go beyond your vocabulary. Words you wield effectively can empower you. With that power, however, you have to be ethical. Figurative language can be misused, as we will see when we discuss euphemism and obfuscation later in this chapter. When you feel you have named the world accurately, you can feel confident that you have not fabricated and instead have enhanced your writing.

WRITING

Write a brief story about the very first memory you have. Describe the event or scene fully from your recollection, and try to find the right words to capture the sensation you remember. Do not settle for words that do not feel right. Feel free to use metaphors and similes.

When you are satisfied that you have recorded this event accurately, check with your parents or with other relatives who might have been there or might have seen what you remember. What can they add to your memory? Can you include their ideas to build a consensus that does not violate your sense of the event or scene?

When you discuss the stories in class, ask your fellow students if their memories take place before or after they were able to talk. With rare exceptions, you will find that first memories are of events or scenes from after they were able to use language. Otherwise, people struggle to remember what happened and have only vague impressions. They didn't have the language to interpret the events around them, so they cannot recollect those events now.

Describing and Shaping

Chapter 3 discussed the uses of specific and concrete words when writing about life experiences to appeal to the senses of readers. We mentioned that such words help readers relate to places and events that they have not experienced for themselves. When we describe situations, we are shaping the way readers will perceive these events.

When narrating a solo personal experience, you are your readers' only source about what transpired. The same is true when you summarize research from an obscure source or discuss world events not known to your audience, although ultimately this type of writing can be independently verified. While readers can judge the truthfulness of what you say through their sense of logic, probability, and common knowledge, they rely on you to give as accurate an account as possible and to keep them interested. The words you choose comprise their understanding of the event and re-create the person, place, or thing you describe. Be aware of the effects of your word choices.

Vague Words Perfectly good words in the English language do not always convey enough information to allow a reader to envision a situation. The verb *to see,* for instance, carries multiple meanings through its various usages and can elicit many different responses from a reader. The writer needs to narrow the meaning by choosing words that are more specific. A thesaurus can be handy at these times, if it is used properly. The synonyms found in a thesaurus cannot casually be inserted into a paper; substituting one word for another alters the reader's impression, even if only slightly. But the changes that a different word brings about might shape the reader's impression to a much more accurate representation of a situation.

Think of the different images called up by some of the synonyms of *to see* in the sense of looking: spot, stare, glance, spy, detect, notice, leer, gape, observe, peer, and ogle. Each of these synonyms evokes much more from a reader. Inserting one of them for *see* shifts the image conveyed to the reader. If the new image captures the situation accurately, the word should be used. If the word creates an impression that confuses the situation or incorrectly represents an element in it, the word should not be used.

WRITING

Look through your current writing assignment, and circle words that are vague—words that convey only a general impression of the subject or the action. Consult a thesaurus to find synonyms, and determine whether any of the choices better represent what you are describing. Do not simply substitute a synonym for the word you already have, especially if you have never heard the synonym before.

Connotations Words have common definitions that we call denotations. The denotations allow us to find synonyms for the words. But words that have essentially the same denotation hold further meanings that signal perspectives on a situation. These meanings, called connotations, are frequently subtle; they might be suggested by differing usages of the words in a subculture or in previous generations. Often, the dictionary alerts us to connotations through primary definitions or through secondary definitions.

For example, take two synonyms of *see—observe* and *spy*. Either word can be substituted in the sentence "I saw [observed/spied] a difference in her behavior." *Observe* implies close scrutiny; the person has studied and noticed a difference in behavior. Readers associate *spy* with a secretive type of seeing, as if the person were prying. The association comes from the noun form of the word *spy*, which conjures up images of espionage and secret agents. This association could cast a negative light on the person doing the seeing or make us wonder about the effect of the difference in behavior. The verb choice sets up an additional impression for the reader. The question is whether we want readers to have that impression.

We can convey much more with some words than with others. If our purpose involves displaying an attitude toward a certain act, understanding the connotations of words is important. Some connotations are fairly easy to apprehend, and the dictionary helps us. *Thin, slender,* and *skinny,* for instance, are synonyms, but the dictionary tells us that *skinny* means unappealingly thin, while *slender* implies attractively thin.

Sometimes we must rely on the audience's understanding of what a word connotes. For some audiences, the word *aggressive* connotes positive images. An aggressive ballplayer is someone we want playing on our team, and the term does not disturb most readers in this context. While we might want our doctor to exercise caution in diagnosing us, we also want him to seek a cure aggressively, and the description would give us confidence in the care we are receiving. But some audience members associate the term *aggressive* with violent, careless behavior, and they would react negatively to this description.

These readers might see the aggressive ballplayer as confrontational or perceive the aggressive pursuit of a cure as reckless behavior by the doctor.

Peer readers, as discussed in Chapter 3, can be of great value to writers in gauging how a larger audience might react. If we direct peer readers to look for language choices, they can tell us which words or phrases produced an association, whether that association was positive or negative, and whether it was within our goals or outside of them. Our sentences can be greatly strengthened through the proper understanding of the connotations of words, but they can also mislead readers and leave an impression outside our intention if we casually insert words that connote more than we realize.

MIKE ROSE

from The Mind at Work

In this brief excerpt from the introduction of The Mind at Work: Valuing the Intelligence of the American Worker, *Mike Rose analyzes the term* skill *in relation to intelligence by relating its connotations to readers. Does this analysis put Rose into a position to rename* skill, *as discussed in the subsection on naming the world?*

Within the West there are powerful research traditions that yield other conceptions of intelligence and other means to assess it. In various ways, these traditions posit, for example, that there are multiple components to intelligence, or even multiple intelligences; that intelligence is variable and dynamic; that social context is crucial to its emergence and display; that creativity, emotion, aesthetic response, and the use of the body—removed from traditional psychometric definitions and tests of intelligence—must be considered as aspects of intelligent behavior. And, finally, it is very important to note that any discussion of intelligence is culture-bound. Some aspects of what we consider intelligence might well overlap with definitions from other cultures, but many cultures posit a range of further or different attributes to intelligence, for example, the ability to live in harmony with others.

It is undisputed that formal education will affect one's score on an intelligence test, since the tests tend to be heavy on verbal and numerical items. The big challenge to test designers, then, is to create at least a few components that, in theory, will not be affected by schooling, for example, identifying the missing element in a visual pattern. Though the success of this endeavor is (yet another) contested issue, it seems pretty clear that it is difficult—some say impossible—to tease out the effects of education (including a familiarity with and investment in tests like these) from the effect of "pure" intelligence. Here's what concerns me. . . . If one does well on an intelligence test, that clearly indicates some kind of cognitive competence. But if one doesn't do well—and, historically, poor performers would include low-income, working people—then the meaning of the score is much less clear. So, we have a measure that works only at the upper end of the scale. To do well tells us something about intelligence—and, usually, schooling—but not to do well provides much less information about intellectual capacity . . . though that poor performance may speak volumes about educational opportunity. My worry is the ease with which poor performance gets interpreted as an accurate measure of intelligence, and the effect that interpretation has on the test-taker, both personally and societally.

This is not a call for a simplified egalitarianism. I am not denying the obvious fact that people come to any pursuit with different interests, talents, knacks for things, motivations, capabilities. Nor am I claiming that all bodies of knowledge and expressions of mind are of the same level of cognitive complexity and social importance. All the cultures I'm familiar with make judgments about competence in the domains that matter to them. (Though ours is more obsessed than any I know with developing measures of the mind and schemes to rank them.) No, the distressing thing is that both in our institutional systems and in our informal talk we tend to label entire categories of work and the people associated with them in ways that generalize, erase cognitive variability, and diminish whole traditions of human activity. Attributions of merit and worth flow throughout the process. We order, we rank, we place at steps upon a ladder rather than appreciating an abundant and varied cognitive terrain.

Skill. Let's begin with the *American Heritage Dictionary.* Skill is "proficiency, facility, or dexterity that is acquired or developed through training or experience." In traditional usage, this proficiency would be related to the use of body or hand, though more recently, the word *skill* has come to apply to a wide range of activities. We talk, for example, of communication skills or general problem-solving skills.

It is important to remember, however, that what gets defined as a skill 5
is historically and culturally determined, and this process is of special significance in labeling kinds of work. The politics and power plays by which particular interest groups get one kind of work categorized as "skilled" and another as "semiskilled" or "unskilled" have significant economic and social consequences. Another historical phenomenon to note here is the increasing role school has played over the past century in developing and certifying skills that, in previous eras, would have been developed within the job setting itself. The value that a skill has is also determined by time and place. In the rhetoric of the "new economy," for example, communication skills or general problem-solving skills or the ability to work in teams are privileged, while more specific mechanical skills—associated with conventional blue-collar work—tend to be perceived as less valuable. All of these processes of definition and the status they confer involve attributions of cognition and intelligence.

Charged Language Writers must strive to act ethically. A writer who resorts to name-calling, tries to establish guilt by association, or uses evocative language to arouse readers' fears and doubts has gone outside accepted ethics. Such tricks with words, called charged language, often damage the writer's credibility. Much like the person who spreads gossip, the writer might gain momentary popularity but soon establishes a reputation of untrustworthiness. More important, the writer polarizes audience members and undermines any attempt she or he has made to utilize critical analysis.

Name-calling tends to be blatant and is easy to avoid. If a writer has strong feelings about a person and considers that person to be an insensitive lout, terms that clearly express such sentiments can be weeded out in the revising process. The more subtle moments of charged language, though, can slip by. Sometimes, for example, writers defending one interpretation of the Second Amendment refer to gun control advocates as "anti-gun people" or contend that the first action of third-world dictators is to remove all weapons from the citizenry. The term *anti-gun* can conjure up negative images because *anti-* emphasizes oppositional behavior (advocacy groups usually emphasize what they favor: pro-life and pro-choice, for example). The reference to dictators associates gun control with tyranny. Not only does this language misrepresent the position of gun control advocates, but it also creates images that make engaging in critical analysis difficult. Danger lurks when a writer does not monitor her or his writing for such language choices. Readers might be angry if they feel a writer has tried to manipulate them, and they probably will not consider the writer's perspective further.

Slang and Obscenity Language serves many purposes. One of them is to unite groups. Another is to express the inexpressible. Slang and obscene words fulfill this purpose. Their place in writing, though, depends on a profound understanding of the context and audience. It can be argued that these words create a world of their own and, thus, shape reader perception better than more conventional word choices. A well-placed obscenity can perhaps make a description appear more real or down to earth. Similarly, slang shows membership in a group, conveying a sense of cool that might be compromised if replaced by other terminology.

Professional writers sometimes use slang and obscenity. You have probably read articles or web pages that use slang and obscenity extensively. However, the writers (and their editors) are aware of the possible consequences of such language choices. Much obscenity is linked to misogyny and racism. In other words, it degrades women and people of color. Slang tends to become out of date in popular culture and can be repetitious.

If you are quoting dialogue, it is fair and accurate to use the words that you heard. Narrative relies on a believable voice, something we discuss later in the chapter, and some writing situations call for the narrator to be trusted in the culture he or she describes. But the impression you convey matters. If your use of slang or obscenity deflects from your main point, you should edit it out.

Start by playing with the words that come to you immediately to see how they shape the reality you are creating for your reader, and test them on peer readers. Rather than reflexively self-editing language simply because some groups feel it is bad, think critically and carefully about your audience. If good reasons for change prevail—if, for example, you are not communicating effectively (some obscene words are used so frequently that they do not even work to intensify a situation) or if your audience feels insulted—revise accordingly.

RICK BASS

from The Lost Grizzlies

This excerpt comes from a firsthand account of searching for grizzly bears in the San Juan Mountains, where grizzlies are thought to be extinct. Rick Bass is describing the arrival of Doug Peacock to a preliminary meeting of an informal research group the two have organized. Decide how the use of obscenity shapes the reader's impression of Peacock in this passage, which is his first appearance in the book. Is something conveyed through the obscenity that could not have been conveyed through other words? How does it align with other characteristics revealed about Peacock shortly thereafter?

The next day, down in Colorado, when I reach Betty Feazel's ranch the aspens are as Doug had promised they'd be: in the full glory of autumn. I turn up the long gravel drive and see Peacock and Betty at the top. Peacock's walking around in shorts and hiking boots and a long flannel jacket. As usual, his wild thinning hair is askew. Dust still rises from the driveway; he's just arrived, too. He always reminds me of how good it feels to be alive. I get out of my truck and we shake hands, then hug.

"Wow," Peacock says, spreading his arms, "just look at this." Betty stands next to him, beaming, as if she'd planted these snow-crowned mountains herself. "Oh, shit," he says, and whirls around and stalks back to his Subaru. The tail end of the car nearly touches the ground under its load of bulging burlap sacks. "I forgot gifts. I was in Santa Fe last night. Jeez."

Empty beer cans, books on tape, canteens, and a pair of binoculars tumble out when he lifts the hatchback. He lunges, tries to catch each object as it falls.

"Aw, fuck it," he says, and crawls inside. The burlap sacks contain peppers, hundreds of big, red, spicy chili peppers. "Here," he says, wrestling one of the bags out. "To cook with. Where can I put this?"

Betty claps her hands, delighted. "In the basement," she says. 5

When I get within ten feet of Peacock's car, my eyes start to water and I sneeze.

"It was wonderful driving up here, breathing all that shit," he says, laboring beneath the bag. It looks like he's bought every pepper in Santa Fe. Just then Marty comes driving up in a dusty brown Volkswagen Rabbit. There is a big wolf-looking dog in the back seat of the car: his faithful, ancient Keetina.

We've come four thousand miles altogether, the three of us, and have arrived within ten minutes of one another. We go inside with Betty and Lucy and Bruce to reconnoiter—to look at photos and maps and listen to background information.

We'll only have a few days; I've got a grouse-hunting appointment with a friend back in Montana early the next week. This is mainly a trip to see and smell and feel the country, rather than to try to decide right away, yes or no, if there are any grizzlies left.

10 We sit like students at Betty's long dining room table. The farmhouse's windowpanes are wavy with age, bending the straw-colored sunlight that passes through them. Betty's energy is inspiring as she leans over the maps and points out areas where rumored sightings have occurred.

"Oh Jesus," Peacock says, looking at the topo maps. "Oh fuck, that's good country. Excuse me," he says to Betty, but she waves him off. "Oh fuck," he says again, "fuck yes."

The rumors are good. They're so similar to the rumors of the sixties and seventies that it seems certain a bear or bears are in there. A bear with a large hump was seen along Jo Jo Creek (most of the place names in the book have been changed to protect grizzly habitats). An outfitter saw what he believed were grizzly tracks—ten to twelve inches long, with big claws—along Blazo Creek in the summer of 1989. Sightings were reported along Wolf Creek Pass. The following year, Tony Povolitis, a senior scientist for the Humane Society, found a big track near Grizzly Creek and photographed it. We pass the photo around. It was taken in snow, and the track looks huge. We can tell where the claws landed. It's not conclusive, but it looks good.

Tom Beck is the biologist who headed the two-year Colorado Division of Wildlife study in the South San Juans in the wake of the Wiseman bear's "confirmation." Four trackers lived in tents from June to October, 1980 to 1982, and hunted for grizzly sign and set snares. Peacock bristles and huffs at this method; he's convinced that these bears won't be trapped and that all bears, especially grizzlies, know when they're being hunted.

Beck wrote, of that previous search, "Sometimes they'd trap a bear and really get excited because of its size, bleached tips on its brown fur, and the way it stood giving it a humped back, they'd swear they caught a grizzly." But all the trappers ever caught in their snares were black bears. Gary Gerhardt, a staff writer for the *Rocky Mountain News* who's been covering the rumors, wrote, "Beck said the division [of wildlife] assumes there aren't any grizzlies in Colorado, and it's going to take some strong documentation—such as a grizzly in a trap—for him to believe any are left in the San Juans."

15 One can imagine Peacock's terror at this philosophy. He's been trying to round up money to put a couple of fieldworkers in the San Juans, but he believes that they should engage in lower-impact methods to document grizzlies, such as photography or making casts of a track, but no trapping.

We could, of course, solve the problem quickly and simply. We could find grizzly sign or photograph a grizzly. I've got my camera. We could end all this political foolishness, all these abstractions. It might happen.

Now, in late September, the grizzlies are up high, getting ready to den. We aim to investigate the north-facing sides of the San Juans, and other places. We plan to do a lot of bushwhacking, crawling around in jungle and heavy windfall—which is not where bears typically hang out. But Peacock has a theory that any remaining San Juan grizzlies are atypical. They're smarter, and over the last forty years the mothers have raised their cubs to be solitary and to avoid humans. He's certain that these bears will by now be active primarily at night.

Before we begin to look for sign of them, we'll camp for two or three days at twelve thousand feet, so as to thin our blood and ready ourselves for the long hikes and heavy packs.

The next morning we say goodbye to Betty, Lucy, and Bruce and set off in two cars. We can feel their hopes riding with us like a net, a thing of a certain density, a specific weight. Of course the odds are long that in this brief trip we'll see a grizzly or find any sign of one, but there's always the chance. That empty place in our hearts.

20 He knows the habits of wild grizzlies better perhaps than anyone else in the country, and yet he abhors scientific meetings, academic conferences, and the like. He is an eloquent writer, and yet you absolutely cannot wring more than one or two sentences out of him concerning literature. He was a medic in Vietnam—a soldier, a warrior—and yet he dissolves into loving baby talk around children—around anyone under voting age.

For all of Peacock's complexity, however, he has basically two behavior patterns that I've observed. The first and most striking mode of behavior occurs when he's wired with an anxiety that leads to a mania reminiscent of the Bugs Bunny–Tasmanian Devil cartoons. When he's wound up that tight—twirling and blinking rapidly, owlishly, as if he can't believe how the world has turned against him—he'll invariably bolt, whether through a crowd of people or a heavy, tangled briar bush. Once spooked, he'll walk furiously away, his body seeking isobars of lower pressure—a calmer register of atmospheric conditions against his cells, is how I picture it. Peacock may be out of control, but it's nothing personal against the people who've spooked him. The second mode of behavior involves deep, unpretentious happiness, like the parody of a man in a beer commercial who takes a sip of fine brew, smacks his lips, and says "Ahhhhh!"

COLLABORATING

Your instructor will select two students who will go into the hall and then, one at a time, walk through the classroom door. As individuals, write down brief descriptions of what you saw. Compare notes with group members, looking at the words that you have used.

For each action verb in your description, such as *walk*, find three synonyms to describe the action. Do the same thing for each noun, then for any adjectives you used. Work with each other to avoid repetition. Does the description change through the use of the synonyms? Did the synonyms blur the situation or convey it more accurately? Discuss the effect of language on your descriptions, and decide what words best capture the situation.

Euphemisms

The previous section stresses the way language can shape a world for readers. While most writers want to be honest, some try to cover up the reality of a situation for their own purposes. As a reader, you want to be alert for euphemisms, expressions that make a painful or coarse situation seem less harsh. Euphemisms avoid bluntness. Instead of saying a woman is pregnant, some prefer to say she is "expecting" or use the archaic expression "in the family way."

Euphemisms present three problems. First, they can prevent clarity if the reader is not familiar with the expression that is substituted. Second, they can be used to mislead, as when a battlefield is called a "theater," thus equating killing with entertainment. And third, they tend to cover up natural experiences, thereby reinforcing ignorance and preserving a puritanical view, such as when "sins of the flesh" is substituted for direct reference to sexual acts.

Writers can drift toward these expressions if they grow overly concerned about audience reaction or want to sound more sophisticated or dignified. You do not want to sound prissy, though, and talk around your subject without ever naming it. Readers will think you are obfuscating your point, or trying to hide something. Furthermore, writing about the subject in direct terms will help in your critical analysis, as will studying the euphemisms society tries to substitute for concrete language.

DAVID CAY JOHNSTON

from Perfectly Legal

In this passage, David Cay Johnston shows how the manipulation of a term obfuscated an agenda and duped the public into supporting a tax break that benefited the extremely wealthy only.

Patricia Soldano owns Cymric Family Office Services in Costa Mesa, California, which takes the hassle out of everyday life for the rich extended families whose wealth it manages. Cymric creates budgets for family members, pays their personal bills, manages their investments, keeps track of all the paperwork and prepares their tax returns with a focus on paying as little as possible. The name Soldano gave her firm refers to an ancient breed of pussycat with a double coat of fur that requires special grooming.

A prim middle-aged MBA who maintains a laser focus on the problems and desires of her clients, Soldano decided one day in the early nineties that the best way to serve them better would be to get the estate tax repealed. When Soldano first raised the matter in her intensely private and wealthy circle in Orange County, she encountered doubt. "I was told it couldn't be done, that no one cared about the estate tax except the people paying it," Soldano said. It was at the time the conventional wisdom—no one cared about the estate tax except two groups. One was the very rich, or at least those among the very rich who hated it but figured they had no one with whom they could make common cause. The other group was wonks who believed it was critical to ensuring that America would be a meritocracy and not an aristocracy of inherited privilege and power. Soldano believed she could change that wisdom.

Soldano hired Patton Boggs, a Washington lobbying firm, and built alliances to wealthy families with privately held companies and a public history of hostility to taxes, notably the candy-making Mars and wine-making Gallo families. She founded the Center for the Study of Taxation. Despite its name there is nothing scholarly about the center. It publishes brochures opposing the estate tax, relying on anecdotes and witty quotes, not scholarship, to make its points. It is a pure marketing organization, no different from the big ad agencies except that it sells ideology instead of detergent.

She also hired Frank Luntz, the Republican pollster and idea man, to examine public attitudes toward the estate tax, along with pollster Peter Hart. Luntz believed that wording was crucial to shaping public opinion, that saying something the right way could sway voters and, if said the wrong way, could turn them off. That politicians did not seem to appreciate this and still got ahead fascinated him, as did the resistance of some of them to his ideas on the effective use of slogans.

5 "Classic example," Luntz said, "if you ask people, 'Would you be willing to pay more taxes to improve law enforcement?,' 51 percent of Americans would say yes. If you ask people, 'Would you be prepared to pay more taxes to halt the rising crime rates?,' 68 percent say yes. Same thing. Law enforcement is the process. Rising crime rate is the result. Half will pay more for process but two thirds will pay more for results. The key to this is how to wrap the language . . . the difference between a tax cut and tax relief. *Tax cut* is a political term that politicians offer in every election cycle. Tax relief is what the American taxpayer is actually looking for. They want a break. They don't want a political promise. They want their elected officials to give them a break."

Luntz didn't really want to do the Soldano project because he assumed, like her clients, that the estate tax was just a tax for the rich. There'd be no way to sell an effort to repeal it, he said, except to make it the caboose at the end of the tax cut train he was helping assemble in Washington.

But there was one little thing that intrigued Luntz, the phrase *death tax*. That phrase is usually attributed to James Martin, a conservative leader of older Americans. Luntz did not know or care where it came from, only how it played in focus groups and surveys. "I went out and looked at the difference between the estate tax, the inheritance tax and the death tax. And even back in '96, about half of Americans would support a repeal of the estate tax and 58 percent would support repeal of the inheritance tax and about 65 percent would support repeal of the death tax," he said.

After concluding that *death tax* was language he could change attitudes with, Luntz started selling. "I took it to every politician, every journalist, started using it in my own interviews, and right now, the only people who still call it the estate tax are lawyers. Now when you talk about repeal of the death tax, support is somewhere in the mid-70s, because the definition has changed. The same tax, roughly the same rates, but the definition of the tax, the focus of the tax, is no longer on millionaires, it's now on dying and death."

The term *death tax* is a superb example of marketing triumphing over reasoned debate. So thoroughly has the phrase been infused into Washington that many journalists, like White House correspondent David Gregory of the General Electric–owned NBC network, employ this term of advocacy instead of the neutral, and correct, term *estate tax,* without rebuke by their superiors. Even the usually scrupulously straight Dow Jones news wires used the phrase without qualification or explanation.

10 So had Luntz been advising the Democrats, what advice would he have given them to keep the tax?

"Honestly? They should raise the exemption from $1.5 million, raise it to $10 million, lower the top rate to 25 percent. If you cut the percentage to 25 percent, people think, Well hey, you still get to keep 75 percent. And you raise the exemption to $10 million, because Americans like round numbers."

And, he said, he would have taught the Democrats to always refer to "the billionaire's tax" because that was a fortune beyond the dreams of nearly all Americans. "We all want to be millionaires, but how many of us will actually ever be worth $10 million?"

You will find all sorts of assumptions embedded in language. In fact, euphemisms appear frequently in writing because writing often reproduces the language of society. Your goal should be clarity and critical insight, so you need to avoid the following types of euphemisms.

Filler Words Many writers have trouble breaking free of filler words. When we cannot figure out what to say, we will stall and claim that a dress is "nice," or that a book was "interesting," or that you consider a friend "special," or that the church service produced a "good" reaction from the parishioners. You might notice that these four words evaluate through summation; when used in writing, they fail to shape a situation or subject for a reader.

The harm of these filler words extends beyond evaluating for your audience. They are so vague and so overused that they have ceased to carry any meaning. In fact, we might mean something different from the dictionary definition of the words. Do we mean "pleasing" when we describe a blind date as "nice"? Does a counselor want "special" to be construed as "better than ordinary" when he or she talks about "a special case"? In both cases, the speakers are trying to avoid saying what they really mean. "Nice" might be a way of saying "not physically attractive but personable." "Special" might mean "troublesome." These types of euphemism, when written, produce a bland, blah feeling in readers, who sense that the writer is just filling up space. Filler words do not allow the writer to communicate sincere ideas and can mislead an audience.

Bureaucratese Writers often want the audience to believe they have more confidence and authority than they actually do. They will turn to a form of euphemism we call "bureaucratese"—the language of a bureaucrat. Bureaucratese, just like filler words, lulls the audience to sleep and does not help establish credibility. It evokes the blustery speeches of a mayor or the gibberish of a company spokesperson who wants to evade the central issue behind a legal probe.

Bureaucratese about a possible supernatural occurrence (a topic discussed in Chapter 13) might sound something like this: "While genuine concerns have been extended by esteemed members of the county board and good people of our city, the events in question are being investigated by top experts in our department to determine whether an apparition can be confirmed to reside on the top floor of city hall or anywhere else within this locale in which claims have been made to ensure the safety and well-being of our populace." In this stuffy, long-winded sentence, the writer (let's assume he is a man and has a position within a city government) is simply stating that he has assigned someone to look into reports of a ghost. The rest is gibberish and deception. Outside of largely discredited paranormal investigators, who are not usually on the payroll of a city, what government worker would be considered an expert on this? What qualifications would the person have? Would the government have so many of such people on board that two or more could be considered "top experts"? If this ghost were to be confirmed, what exactly would the writer do about it? How would he ensure the safety of the populace? Notice the language. The writer inflates it unnecessarily, referring to a ghost as an "apparition," for instance, and resorts to flattery early on to appease his audience. Despite the assurances to the audience, the writer uses no personal pronouns to assert his responsibility for the actions he has taken. This haughty persona, then, has no substance. More than likely, very little, if anything, is being done to investigate the reports of a ghost. The sentence uses a lot of words to send an empty message.

Since bureaucratese is deceptive and ineffective, you might be wondering how to establish confidence and authority when you write. The next section, on voice, helps in this area. Ultimately, you can establish confidence and authority only if you first have them. Do research and know your subject as well as you can. If you do not have confidence and authority, though, do not pretend that you do. Depending on the writing task, do your best to convey your ideas in your natural voice. Some writing tasks might demand establishing an ethos with which you're not entirely comfortable, but quite often audiences will not mind if you explore a topic with them. A questioning novice voice is always preferable to bureaucratese.

Sanitizing A dangerous type of euphemism occurs when writers sanitize events, policies, and positions for the audience. If an occasional euphemism displays a sense of delicacy in stressful situations—saying someone "passed away" rather than "died," for instance—sanitizing distorts to an unacceptable degree, trying to fool readers into believing that an event, a policy, or a position is not what it seems to be. The language used in sanitizing does not suggest a new perspective or a rosier way to view a situation. It constitutes a callous treatment of a subject and dodges responsibility. Calling a neutron bomb a "radiation enhancement device" does not change the destructive nature and devastating effects of the weapon. A temporary worker who has been told to "strengthen" her "relationship" with her employment agency will not feel better about being fired.

Writers use sanitizing to try to avoid a hostile audience reaction or to avert blame, figuring that readers are not intelligent enough to see through the obfuscation. Sanitizing often has the opposite effect, though. Instead of ameliorating a situation, it enrages people. Initial confusion evolves into anger. Citizens equate government euphemisms to lying and do not believe anything they hear. Former employees become upset by the deceptive way sanitizing hides a termination and accuse companies of unfair treatment, sometimes bringing lawsuits. As writers, we want to be careful to avoid confusing delicacy with duplicity. Some instances of sanitizing sound nice, and we might believe we are clever coming up with such colorful synonyms, but the effect will be reduced credibility.

WILLIAM LUTZ

Life Under the Chief Doublespeak Officer

William Lutz, a professor at Rutgers University, discusses sanitizing language that he calls "doublespeak" in this article. Some of his examples evoke the speech patterns of bureaucratese.

If there's one product American business can produce in large amounts, it's doublespeak. Doublespeak is language that only pretends to say something; it's language that hides, evades or misleads.

Doublespeak comes in many forms, from the popular buzzwords that everyone uses but no one really understands—"globalization," "competitive dynamics," "re-equitizing," and "empowerment"—to language that tries to hide meaning: "re-engineering," "synergy," "adjustment," "restructure," and "force management program."

With doublespeak, no truck driver is the worst driver, just the "least-best" driver, and bribes and kickbacks are called "rebates" or "fees for product testing." Even robbery can be magically transformed with doublespeak, as a bank in Texas did when it declared a robbery of an ATM to be an "unauthorized transaction." Willie Sutton would have loved to have heard that.

Automobile junkyards, junk and used car parts have become "auto dismantlers and recyclers" who sell "predismantled, previously owned parts." Don't want people to know you're in the business of disposing of radioactive and chemical wastes? Then call your company "U.S. Ecology Inc."

5 Wages may not be increasing, but the doublespeak of job titles sure has increased. These days, your job title has to have the word "chief" in it. How

many kinds of "chiefs" are there? Try these titles on for size: Chief Nuclear Officer, Chief Procurement Officer, Chief Information Officer, Chief Learning Officer, Chief Transformation Officer, Chief Cultural Officer, Chief People Officer, Chief Ethics Officer, Chief Turnaround Officer, Chief Technology Officer, and Chief Creative Officer. After all the "operations improvement" corporations have undergone, you have to wonder who all those "chiefs" are leading. Never before have so few been led by so many.

These days, a travel agent may be called a "travel counselor," "vacation specialist," "destination counselor," or "reservation specialist." As part of their merger, Chase Manhattan Bank and Chemical Bank decided that the position of "Relationship Manager" would be divided between executives of both banks. What is a "Relationship Manager"? Once upon a time this person was called a salesman. And if you're late in paying your bill after buying something from one of these "Relationship Managers," you'll be called by the "Persistency Specialist," or bill collector. If you're "downsized," the "Outplacement Consultant" or unemployment counselor will help you with "re-employment engineering," or how to find another job.

With doublespeak, banks don't have "bad loans" or "bad debts"; they have "nonperforming assets" or "nonperforming credits" which are "rolled over" or "rescheduled." Corporations never lose money; they just experience "negative cash flow," "deficit enhancement," "net profit revenue deficiencies," or "negative contributions to profits."

No one gets fired these days, and no one gets laid off. If you're high enough in the corporate pecking order, you "resign for personal reasons." (And then you're never unemployed; you're just in an "orderly transition between career changes.") But even those far below the lofty heights of corporate power are not fired or laid off. Firing workers is such big business in these days of "re-engineering," "restructuring," and "downsizing" that there are companies whose business is helping other companies fire their workers. (Think about that for a minute.) These companies provide "termination and outplacement consulting" for corporations involved in "reduction activities." In other words, they teach companies how to fire or lay off workers. During these days of "cost rationalization," companies fire or lay off workers many different ways. How do I fire thee? Let me count the ways.

Companies make "workforce adjustments," "headcount reductions," "census reductions," or institute a program of "negative employee retention." Corporations offer workers "vocational relocation," "career assignment and relocation," a "career change opportunity," or "voluntary termination." Workers are "dehired," "deselected," "selected out," "repositioned," "surplussed," "rightsized," "correct sized," "excessed," or "uninstalled." Some companies "initiate operations improvements," "assign candidates to a mobility pool," "implement a skills mix adjustment," or "eliminate redundancies in the human resources area."

One company denied it was laying off 500 people at its headquarters. 10
"We don't characterize it as a layoff," said the corporate doublespeaker (sometimes called a spin doctor). "We're managing our staff resources. Sometimes

you manage them up, and sometimes you manage them down." Congratulations. You've just been managed down, you staff resource you.

An automobile company announced the closing of an entire assembly plant and the elimination of over 8,000 jobs by announcing "a volume-related production schedule adjustment." Not to be outdone by its rival, another car company "initiated a career alternative enhancement program" that enhanced over 5,000 workers out of their jobs. By calling the permanent shutdown of a steel plant an "indefinite idling," a corporation thought that it wouldn't have to pay severance or pension benefits to the workers who were left without jobs.

Doublespeak can pay for the company, but usually not for the workers who lose their jobs.

As Pogo said, "We have met the enemy, and he is us." Or maybe Dilbert got it better: "Do we really get paid for writing this stuff?"

DISCUSSION

When have you found it appropriate to use euphemisms? For instance, can a euphemism for a job title enhance the dignity of the job? Some companies call their low-wage workers "partners." When I worked in a hospital years ago, I preferred the title of "courier" for my job of delivering and picking up medical charts instead of the usual name of "runner." Some trash collectors are referred to as "sanitation engineers." We also use euphemisms in personal relationships. In refusing a date or romantic overture, many people have said "we don't have chemistry" instead of "I find you unattractive" or other words of rejection. What is the effect? Do euphemisms soften the blow or create other problems?

Finding Your Voice

Words are essential for creating what is known as a narrative voice. This voice conveys the tone of the writing, such as humorous, conciliatory, ironic, or thoughtful, and conjures up an image of the writer for the audience. We want the narrative voice to be lively in our writing, not dry or dull, even when assignments call for a formal approach to a paper or project. We also want the voice to be genuine, portraying our sensitivities and passion.

Combined with the perspective that emerges from your critical analysis, the words you choose will shape an impression for the audience of your values, experiences, and attitude—the concept of ethos discussed in Chapter 3. Some audiences even form a physical description of the writer in their minds. The person they imagine you to be, whether pleasant or mean, influences how they receive your ideas. You can see, then, how important a narrative voice can be.

Constructing a voice that you deem to be genuine presents you with a challenge. Our voices change as we mature, discard old beliefs, embrace new ones, and stretch the boundaries of our identities. What happens if our personalities can be abrasive, especially when we talk about certain subjects? How can we be genuine, critically analytic, and audience-friendly all at the same time? Finding one consistent voice that is appropriate might seem impossible.

Identity, though, is not fixed. While weaknesses in our personalities will emerge during writing, just as they do in normal social interaction, we can control more than we might think. As during social interactions, we want to put our best face forward and make adjustments depending on the situation. We are not compromising our integrity or necessarily being insincere when we change our tone and vocabulary to accommodate those around us. If we want to impress a potential employer during a job interview, we monitor our use of slang and obscenity, extend courtesy, use appropriately intelligent language, and show enthusiasm. We could not do these things if they were not a part of us. Even if we fail to be polite more frequently than we like, prefer modest vocabulary when talking to our friends, and fend off bouts of depression instead of demonstrating exuberance, our identities are not limited to one set of traits. Our subtle alterations to adjust to shifting social environments are the type of changes to make when constructing the right voice in our writing.

Writing also allows you to test the limits of acceptability and, through revision, to find an appealing voice that is lively, critical, sensitive, credible, and still genuine. You will not have the advantage of using inflections in your voice, gestures, eye contact, and physical appearance, as you do when speaking, but you have the chance to do it over should you make mistakes in your word choices or in the arrangement of those words. Here are some ways to guide your decisions when it comes to finding voice.

Choosing Your Words

While voice is more than the catch phrases we see represented in some television sitcoms, people develop a set of terms or phrases that they feel comfortable using. When they are able to incorporate these words in their writing, part of them is down on the paper. I have a friend, for instance, who uses *copious* and *alarming* frequently in conversation. The words add a spark to his writing and convey a genuine narrative voice. Do you envision a certain type of person from these sentences? "After copious observation of the two neighbors at the party, I detected an unmistakable bond. It became alarmingly apparent to all as the evening progressed that the two were involved in an affair." The words fit naturally into the voice he has established, and an audience probably sees someone who is astute and maintains an air of decorum.

Of course, you want to avoid comfortable words that are too vague or clichéd, but sometimes a slang term or common saying can achieve voice. When a writer describes a character with the words, "He wasn't the sharpest knife in the drawer, if you know what I mean," I hear a voice, even though the metaphor is not original. The writer has adopted a colloquial, humorous voice. Filling an essay with such phrases would lessen their effect, but one well-placed expression that a writer is comfortable with can work toward constructing this voice.

Types of Words The words you select, especially the adjectives and verbs, help shape your voice. A writer who chooses a number of adjectives conveys an observant voice. A writer who understands distinctions, such as in color (the difference between mauve and purple, for instance) or in sound (a screech as compared to a scream), can construct a narrative voice that goes beyond being observant. The writer can display sensitivity and taste, for example, by describing details in the design of an old house that might escape the notice of a casual observer. A writer who uses action verbs throughout an essay and can distinguish between a car that is chugging down a street and a car that is creeping down a street constructs a voice that might be considered more pragmatic and subdued than the adjective-driven, observant voice but that is nonetheless dynamic and engaging. While no formulas exist for matching a voice to a subject or for creating a certain tone, attention to word types helps in a subtle way.

Active Sentence Constructions Arrangement of the words is the final piece to the puzzle of voice. Overuse of passive sentences creates a dry voice that might be appropriate for scientific reports, where the narrative voice does not concern the audience, but that takes life away from writing centered on civic concerns, social matters, and persuasion. A passive sentence construction uses compound verbs and moves or removes the actual subject of the sentence, known as the actor, to emphasize what should be the object. Typical examples of passive constructions are "The ball was hit by the boy" and "The ball was hit." The active sentence construction is "The boy hit the ball," where the actor, the boy, takes the prominent place in the sentence and acts on the object, the ball. Notice that the passive sentence construction forces the writer to use the *to be* verb, which, although essential in many places, is the weakest verb in the English language. The active sentence construction conveys movement, while the passive sentence construction emphasizes stasis. Thus, revising passive sentences into active sentences restores vigor to what might appear to be lifeless prose.

Writers should also look for expletive sentences, those that begin with variations of *there is* or *it is*. If *to be* is the weakest verb in our language, the pronouns *there* and *it* rank among the most boring subjects for a sentence. A sentence using the two in combination starts as poorly as possible. Consider this sentence: "There was a dog in our neighborhood that barked all the time." A simple revision changes it to "A dog in our neighborhood barked all the time." The sentence loses no meaning in the revision, and you can see how it rolls off your tongue better than the expletive beginning. Be aware of the arrangement of the words in your sentences; it can determine how much life your voice has.

COLLABORATING

Have everyone in your group bring an editorial from a local newspaper to class. Read through the editorials, and write a description of the voices you hear. How was each voice constructed? What made you think the narrator seemed dry, witty, intelligent, angry, pompous, or any other description you wrote? As a group, rewrite one of the editorials to create a different voice, whether better or worse than the one in the editorial, focusing on word choices and sentence arrangement. Be prepared to explain the effect you think you have achieved and how the voice differs from the original.

Summary

When all is said and done, writing comes down to words. Writers need to pay special attention to the choices they make and should not rely on gimmicks, such as a word search through a thesaurus, to build vocabulary. Words have the potential to create a world or a mindset for an audience; they mediate experience and shape events. While writers cannot control every association a reader might make with a particular word, they need to be aware of possible reader reactions and strive for precision.

Words can also mislead and deceive, as when writers employ euphemisms to avoid impoliteness or to cover up something unpleasant. Writers do not want to lose credibility by resorting to these tactics. Instead, writers can build credibility by using language to construct a genuine, vigorous narrative voice that is appropriate to the subject matter and audience.

· PART II ·

CONFRONTING WRITING TASKS

Now that you have increased your awareness of the key concepts behind writing, you can look at other issues that might confront you while producing an essay, researched writing, or a report. One or more of the key concepts—reasons for writing, critical analysis, audience, organization, and language usage—will factor into nearly all the other decisions you need to make when writing, but the areas discussed in the following chapters deserve special attention.

Chapter 6 discusses the writing process. The steps of the writing process vary with each writer and help divide the work into manageable tasks. However, some steps in an individual's writing process might actually hinder progress; other steps might better be done at a different stage of the process. Therefore, Chapter 6 reviews ways to get started on a project and to see it through to completion, all within the framework of the successful parts of the process you have already developed. While the reasons for writing will dictate much of what you do during your process, this issue needs to be discussed separately.

Some writing tasks will require you to work with others. Chapter 7 focuses on times when writers collaborate. Since most writing involves much work with other people, *Writing Without Formulas* treats collaboration separately from the major concepts. Many students enjoy the prospect of a group project but fear that one or two people will end up doing most of the work. In Chapter 7, you will find ways to effectively combine your strengths as a writer with those of your peers and make sure that everyone contributes equally.

Chapter 8 analyzes difficulties students typically encounter with college-level reading. Reading is a form of interpretation that does not differ all that much from other kinds of literacy we have developed. By drawing parallels to other forms of literacy, Chapter 8 seeks to help you develop an effective reading process that will work beyond your academic reading needs.

Chapter 9 looks at the specific issue of writing with evidence. While the chapter builds on the knowledge that can be found in the discussions about critical analysis, audience, organization, and language, it dives deeper to discuss problems that arise when writers use evidence. Chapter 9 contains information on what constitutes evidence, how to use it, when to use it, and why it can be integrated in some ways but not others.

Picking up on this information, Chapter 10 discusses the task of researching during a writing project. While the issues involved in research tie into the previous discussions on critical analysis and language, much remains to be discovered about the particulars of finding and evaluating sources. Chapter 10 reviews locating critical knowledge, evaluating your sources, untangling conflicting sources, and citing sources in a paper.

The information in Part II takes you directly into the realities of writing. You might not need to use every chapter for this class. For example, your course might not involve writing with research, or your instructor might not assign a group project. Still, the activities and advice will prove valuable in all sorts of future situations involving writing. You could be collaborating with co-workers during your first experience in a professional setting away from college. Knowing how to use evidence and do responsible research will matter in other courses as well as in civic activities. The suggestions in these chapters will add to your understanding of the key concepts and allow you to develop further as a writer.

CHAPTER 6

DISCOVERING YOUR WRITING PROCESS

During my early years as an instructor of writing, I told students to follow a writing process that had discernible stages. I broke down every assignment into prewriting, drafting, revising, more revising, and editing. I demanded that students turn in their work at every stage so I could check for improvement and make suggestions about critical analysis, audience considerations, and language. Some students turned in perfunctory prewriting or partially completed drafts, or they started editing during the revision stage, or their revisions looked no different than the previous versions. I deducted points and chastised students, trying to get them to conform to what I called the writing process. I must have been a holy terror.

It dawned on me how wrong I was to teach this way only after some students complained about my odd formula. They said that trying to conform to it made writing mechanical. It wasn't that they did not want to follow my assignments; they couldn't. My realization started with a conference I had with a competent writer named Akil. As we reviewed his revision, Akil grew more and more fidgety, asking if he could smoke and not seeming to agree with my comments that he had not revised sufficiently.

"I'll get to that," he told me about a lack of detail in his introduction. "I'm not ready right now."

"But you're not going to have time for proofreading and editing if you have to do all of these revisions in the next stage as well," I said.

"I do that as I go along," he said.

"But I told you guys to wait on that," I replied. "You're going to mess up

This icon will direct you to web links and additional resources on the website college.hmco.com/pic/thelin1e

the process and not get everything done." I shook my head and leaned back in my chair.

Akil leaned forward. "Look, I know what you're saying, but I don't write that way. This process is your process, not mine. I don't want you to get mad at me, but I don't do these things. Can't you help me work with *my* process?"

So that's what I did. I asked Akil to explain how he composed essays and tried to figure out a way to make his process work with the assignment. After he left, I thought about his resistance to the formula I had constructed. I wondered how many other students were having similar problems.

I started the next class session by talking about the approaches students took to writing assignments and wondering what students really do when they compose. I welcomed them to critique my formula, which they did, almost wildly, and I tried to group together ideas they used to get through an assignment. Each student wrote a list of his or her general writing steps, and we discussed the lists as a whole class. Ideas came flooding forward so quickly that I had trouble writing them on the board. When I had finished, I counted five patterns of composing. Although nearly every student had some variation and no two patterns were identical, they followed one of these five models, not the formula I had forced on them.

Of course, some of these models contained approaches to writing tasks that were not productive. Procrastination crept into many processes, forcing students to crank out drafts of papers the night before they were due. Other students did not know how to get through writing blocks and stared blankly at lined paper or computer screens. A couple of students became so caught up in proofreading that they were reluctant to revise beyond their first drafts, except for further proofreading. Some habits, then, needed to be changed, especially if the students found writing frustrating. The question was how to distinguish a strong writing process from a weak one. I needed to figure out how to tweak the individual processes so they could work better.

The five models I ascertained are as follows.

1. Write a partial draft, get feedback, complete it, and proofread.
2. Write a full draft in one session, edit while rereading, and submit it.
3. Jot down initial ideas, start the draft one day, revise and edit that part of it, finish the rest of it the next day, get feedback, add additional details, and proofread.
4. Think about what to write, do an outline, determine the thesis, do a rough draft (in one or more sessions), edit while you go, get some feedback, and do a final revision.
5. Wait until the last second to start the writing task, put something together, get feedback or directives, revise, get more feedback, revise again, and proofread.

Does one of these models look similar to what you do? I'm sure some approaches to writing are not represented fully, but you probably recognize the basic traits and the ordering of activities of your own writing. I believe we can find value in all of the models and find ways to make them productive. Four of the five, though, rely on being able to turn in drafts and receive feedback from peers or the instructor. In writing for civic purposes or personal expression, you may have to arrange for other forms of collaboration and feedback. We want to create models that can be used for writing activities beyond the classroom.

DISCUSSION

Talk about the approaches you take to activities other than writing. When you have household chores to do, do you make a plan? What if you are giving a party? What about crafts you might enjoy? Compare the ways you go about doing these and other activities. Which methods enable you to complete these tasks most efficiently? Which methods cause delays or problems?

This chapter should help you refine what you do when you have a writing task in front of you. You will understand what it means to prewrite, draft, revise, edit, and proofread. For many writers, these components or steps overlap; other writers separate them into discrete stages. Perhaps you do not need or want to incorporate certain components. Uncover what you do, and inject what you feel is missing, if anything, into your process. No one formula produces good writing.

Seeing Your Own Patterns

Do you take the same approach to differing writing tasks? Or does the purpose behind your writing dictate your process? For instance, if you are responding to a friend's email about your plans for the evening, you might pound out a quick answer without much planning. But if your friend wants to know whether you saw her boyfriend with another woman, you might not want to respond right away, especially if you witnessed her boyfriend stepping out on her. You have to consider whether you should mind your own business, how to break the news if you decide to tell her, how to avoid a gossipy tone and whether to use a sad, sincere one, and whether you should give advice. The two email messages demand differing approaches to what you write, so the processes have to be different.

Within all the disparate purposes, you should be able to discover patterns of how you approach a writing task. In other words, despite the differences the tasks call for, you will notice consistent tendencies. For example, I usually spend a short period thinking about any kind of writing I am doing, envisioning both the structure and the desired effect of the piece. I compose part of it, and then reread, inserting and deleting as appropriate to improve flow, correctness, and meaning. I then continue to write. Once I am finished, I reread at least twice to check for tone and for clarity and to do further proofreading. I always make sure that my audience has enough previous knowledge to understand the context of my communication, and I fill in details just to be on the safe side. I also am keenly aware of thoroughness. I do not want to leave anything out.

Before I deliver the writing to its intended audience, I think once more of the effect on that audience. Assuming that the purpose of writing is not to repeat something I have stated before (some email messages and memos do have the purpose of recapping prior exchanges), I want to make sure that I have added something to previous knowledge and that I have analyzed my ideas critically. If I see a problem, it might mean doing a global revision, the type of rewrite that leads to a change of perspective, structural alterations, or the revamping of a thesis. I might have to enlist somebody else to read the writing to check the need for local revision—the need for another example, the use of more concrete words, a snappier introduction, or other concerns that involve only insertion and deletion.

Finding such patterns in your approaches to writing is not that difficult. Try one of the following two methods to uncover them.

Track Your Steps The next few times you sit down to compose something, be aware of what you do when you write. Keep in mind your purposes and how they change your approach to writing. Look at your perception of quality. Do you tend to do your best writing in a journal you keep? How do you decide what and when to write in this journal? Perhaps you keep a blog. How do you go about conveying your ideas? Do you go back and edit, or do you edit while you are writing? Have you ever decided not to send something after having finished it? Why?

Don't forget classroom assignments. How do you prepare for an essay exam? How does that preparation differ from the way you prepare to write a longer paper? While it is not necessary to make a list of the persistent tendencies you note, you should get a sense of what components of your writing process keep reappearing and how the purpose changes what you do.

Note What You Do Not Do What you do not do in approaching a writing task can also reveal much. Perhaps you are at a loss for words to describe patterns within your process. You know that you do the writing involved, but beyond understanding your inspiration, or looking at the assignment, or reading the email you received, you cannot articulate anything other than that you put together a finished piece of writing.

Later this chapter discusses the differences between prewriting, drafting, revising, editing, and proofreading; for now, it is not necessary to use these terms. When my students discussed their practices and I drew up the list of the five models, we never used the term *prewriting,* for example, although two of the models describe activities that align with prewriting. If you describe what you do rather than trying to classify your activities into categories, you might find the patterns you are looking for.

Still, it might be easier for you to make a list of approaches you do not take in a given writing task. Anything that you do not write down or circle is likely to be part of your process. By understanding what you do not do, the process you use will become clearer, and you will give yourself ideas about where you need to tinker with it.

> **COLLABORATING**
>
> Look at the five models described by my students. Which of these models most closely aligns to your writing processes? Are there parts of each model or one model in particular that seems to be the opposite of what you do? Discuss the processes you use, compare them to the five models, and determine which components seem to be mentioned most often. What parts of the processes help produce successful writing? What parts interfere? Keep these in mind as you read through this chapter so as to determine which parts of your model need to be adjusted and which parts should be left alone.

Breaking Through Writer's Block

Many of my students have wondered how to get started writing. They experience what is known as a writer's block, the inability to respond to a writing task and put words on paper. Even professional writers confront a writing block at times. To some extent, every writing task initially produces a block. This is especially true of classroom assignments because, as students, you might not know what to write or even have much interest in the topic. You might also feel anxiety about being graded or evaluated.

Most writing teachers look to prewriting strategies to help students break through writing blocks and get started. When determining which strategy to use, the reason for the block has to be considered. For example, one type of block has to do with the inability to generate ideas. In such cases, group brainstorming is ideal; students, colleagues, or citizens can bounce ideas off each other and collectively help individuals who are stuck. Other times, writers might have so many ideas that they cannot focus on one good way to start. To clarify thinking and find relevant connections between possibly conflicting ideas, these writers can construct outlines to get started. But many other times, nothing more than just starting to write without stopping is needed.

Writers adapt this strategy, called freewriting, to break through writer's block. Freewriting involves continuously writing on the computer or on paper for five to seven minutes, even if only nonsense comes out. The act of nonstop writing enables the writer to get started. Start with what is on your mind: "I don't know what to write" or "I'm blocked." You can repeat that until another idea or phrase joins it. Often, freewriting serves a double purpose, both breaking the block and uncovering a thought or issue that might prove important for your paper. This strategy should help you get started on a writing task. Many writers will even use it in the middle of their drafting or revising to generate fresh ideas if a section or paragraph seems to have gone stale.

If you experience writer's block on a regular basis, consider incorporating prewriting into your process. Look at the following techniques to see if one or more respond to the reasons you get blocked.

Discovering Why You Are Blocked When a writing task confronts us, perhaps a paper for the classroom, perhaps a report for a business meeting, staring at the computer screen and hoping an idea will magically appear frustrates us and sometimes transforms a mild writing block into a severe one. Rather than trying ways to get started, many writers have success reflecting on the reasons for the block. In other words, they freewrite about the block, trying to figure out why they cannot find a way to begin. While this might sound like additional work that takes you away from the actual writing, it is not. You cannot write effectively until you understand why you're having problems. Trying to write without such understanding would be like running for office without knowing the identity and strategies of your opponent. Once you know the who and the what, you can respond.

Here is a checklist of questions designed to help you determine why you are blocked.

- Is the block caused by the particular task in front of you?
- What part of it can you single out as the primary problem?
- Are you worried that you do not have enough knowledge about the subject?
- Do you need more information on how to structure the writing?
- Do you have a clear idea of who your audience is?
- Are you worried about a negative evaluation from an instructor or manager?
- Do you feel that your writing does not express your thoughts well?
- Have you had trouble with sentence-level issues, and do you want to avoid making mistakes?

This list is not exhaustive, but the point is to ask yourself questions that will help you precisely nail down the issues you are facing. Once you can articulate the reason for your block, you will be one step closer to overcoming it. This reflection will allow you to figure out what you need to do next, whether it is to find out more information about the writing task, to do some reading to prepare you, to make time in your process for more editing and proofreading, or to use a specific prewriting strategy.

CHARLEY LAU, JR.

from *Lau's Laws on Hitting*

How is a writing block like other types of slumps? Read this excerpt about the hitting slumps of baseball players, and see if you can find similarities between the mental processes of hitting a baseball and of completing a writing assignment.

Ever notice when you get into a slump in any athletic endeavor the amount of people are eager to help you? Fall into a 1-for-25 slide in baseball and it seems everyone has a solution for you, from your teammates to your coach to your wife. Your head is pulling out. Your stance is all wrong. Your bat is too heavy. You name it: Everyone's identified the problem. The problem is, of course, that you can do more damage and prolong your slump by taking too much advice. Listening to everyone's suggestions often only clogs the mind. This is when the brain can get in the way of hitting. If the brain is trying to process too much information, the message it finally sends to the body is slowed. And hitting is all about timing and quick reactions. You want that message from the brain to the body to occur instantly. The point is this: When mired in a slump, be wary of taking in too much advice. Don't create an information overload.

Hey, the truth is, everyone goes into a slump. Everyone. Even the great hitters. In baseball, as with any other sport, you have to accept a certain degree of failure. As you've probably heard a million times, the best hitters in the game, the .300 hitters, fail seven out of 10 times. What keeps a great hitter great is his ability to fight through slumps. As I've pointed out before, there often is a mechanical reason for why a hitter isn't hitting well. Maybe he's not starting his swing soon enough. Maybe his top hand has become too dominant. But sometimes slumps occur simply because of your mental approach. You can't be successful at anything unless you first believe you can be successful. Yes, I believe in mind over matter. Your brain can do wonderful things if you let it and convince it to.

Focused Freewriting While much freewriting to generate ideas can be done on the spur of the moment, some of the most effective freewrites are focused around a central question, either a sticking point in a draft or a puzzling part of an assignment. A motivating question can arise from reflecting on why the writer has a block. If, for instance, you have narrowed down the problem to part of an assignment that asks for a summary of a difficult reading, a focused freewrite could start with the questions, "What do I understand about the reading? What don't I understand?" As with all freewrites, you must force words out of the keyboard or pen, even if just, "I don't know. I'm confused." You have the obligation to ask, "Why am I confused?" and to list specifics of what you already know and understand about a topic or assignment. Confronting the problem head-on is the start to breaking through the block.

A focused freewrite can also be beneficial in trying to understand what an audience needs in order to comprehend and consider your point of view. Freewriting in response to a simple question, such as "Who would disagree with my position?" will help you grasp and respond to the audience's perspectives as discussed in Chapter 3. Some blocks hit writers after they have received feedback from peers, teachers, or supervisors. Freewriting on a question such as "How can I restructure this paper to make it less confusing?" will generate possibilities for you to consider. Don't be afraid to do more than one focused freewrite, as many questions can be posed. A good freewrite will often generate questions that can be answered in another freewrite.

Starting with the Critical Analysis Writer's block can occur when you find it difficult to attach significance to the task at hand or perhaps even to your first draft. Your draft may sound clichéd, or a peer group may have told you that a stronger thesis is needed. Chapter 2 discusses critical analysis as a strategy for gaining insight and developing ideas. What better way to find significance and gain momentum in the writing process than to immediately get beyond clichés that can bog you down and make you think your writing is ordinary?

While some of the suggestions for critical analysis in Chapter 2 will work best after you have developed some content, the ideas in the section "Investigating Assumptions" on pages 39–50 can be used when you already have a topic. By critically analyzing the stereotypes that exist about a given topic, you can make a list of the ways race, class, and gender might influence first impressions. You can unearth agendas by freewriting about the reasons you and others feel a certain way about a subject. Critical analysis can give you a clear direction and shatter the writing block.

Drawing a Tree Visualizing your options in writing can help you to literally see the connections between seemingly disparate ideas. One visualizing strategy is to draw a tree about the broad topic of humor. The trunk represents the topic or assignment, and the branches represent major ideas. Each smaller branch can represent a new idea or connection. When you exhaust all ideas, go to another branch and begin to "grow" another idea. You can come back to any branch if necessary, but the idea is to see how all the branches grow from the same subject.

When you have drawn as many branches as possible, you might have a tree that looks something like the one on page 165. The main branch that is connected to the largest number of smaller branches probably has the most potential as a topic, but the connections can be clearly seen, too. For instance, one smaller branch is about the cruelty of humor. The even smaller branch that grows out of it, teasing an old softball mate, John, about his age, relates to the

DISCUSSION

What other ways do members of your class break through writing blocks? In the writing models listed earlier in this chapter, students mentioned jotting down notes and outlining. In this section, we discuss group brainstorming and freewriting, as well as drawing a tree and critical analysis. Are there others? Or has everyone used only the techniques mentioned in this chapter? Talk about the positive and negative results of any strategies for breaking through writing blocks that you can think of. How should these strategies blend into your individual writing process?

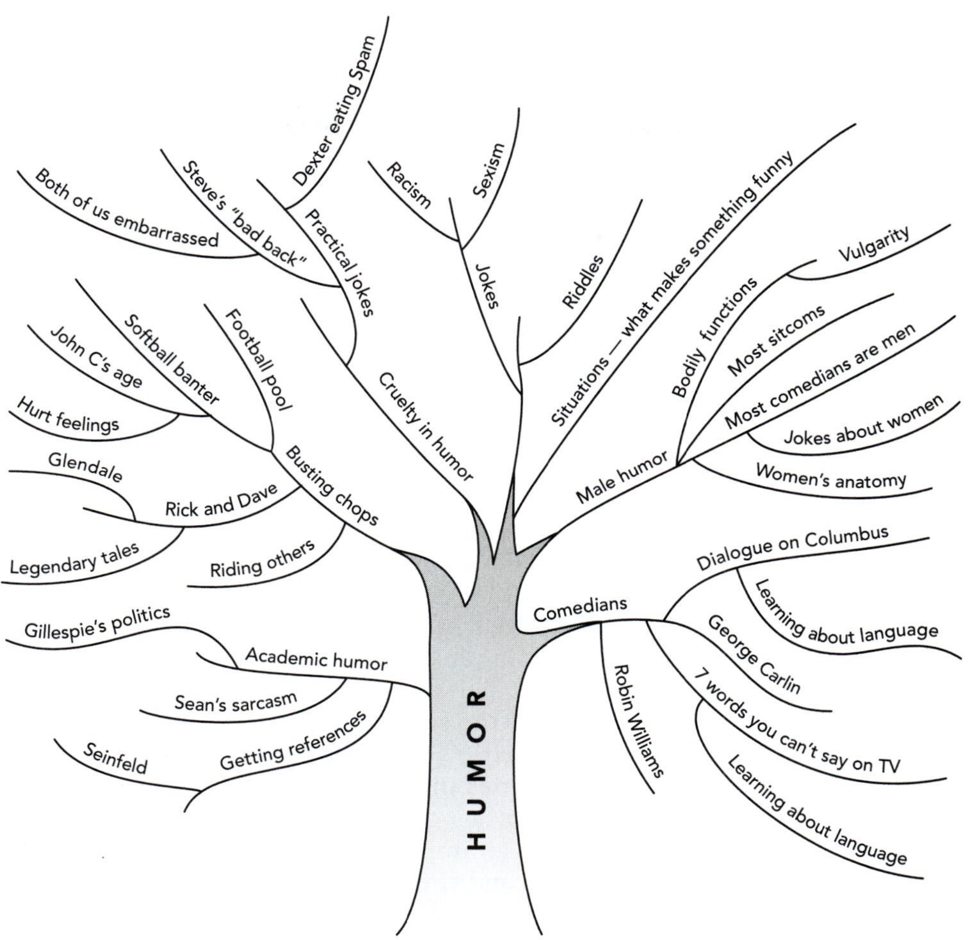

main idea. You can easily see that the theory represented in a main branch can be supported by the specifics laid out in a smaller branch. Such visual aids can make a writer move through a writing block toward a well-organized draft.

Discovering Strategies for Drafting and Revision

Have you ever been required to put together a rough draft for a deadline? If so, what did it mean to you? People know that drafting involves writing, but many are not sure what a draft of an essay or a research project is supposed to look like. A useful description springs from an understanding of the differences from similar activities, such as revising, editing, and proofreading. Drafting implies writing that is ongoing and is in a stage of construction beyond just notes, outlines, or ideas. When writing is being revised, a finished rough draft is being overhauled to make structural alterations, add or expand important elements, or change the focus. Inserting or deleting elements, rearranging the order, and refining an otherwise finished product constitute editing. Proofreading means giving a finished piece one final look to catch mistakes.

A rough draft looks like an attempt at completing a task. It might be strong in one area and weak in another. It might have sentence-level errors, such as verb tense problems or sentence fragments. Critical analysis might have been attempted, or audience expectations might have been taken into consideration. The writer has spent time thinking about the writing task, has shaped some paragraphs containing ideas that meet the crucial elements of the assignment, and knows that the piece needs further work.

Writers have differing ideas about how a rough draft should function. Some writers like to break drafting into several stages. To ensure that they are heading in the right direction, they might seek feedback on the first part of an essay before attempting to write more. They might like to review and edit one part of an essay before starting the next part. Sometimes what you should turn in when asked for a rough draft is not as clear as it should be. You need to ask your instructor about her or his expectations.

Being told to revise can be confusing as well. Often, if we have spent time on a rough draft—reviewing and editing on our own, for instance—we resist revision. We feel that we have done all the work for nothing, that our ideas and style have been harshly judged, or that we will make the essay worse by rethinking and restructuring major areas. Revision helps a piece of writing conform to its purpose, whether narrowing a focus for space requirements for an editorial for a newspaper, making sense of a personal experience in a journal, or simply meeting the instructor's expectations for an assignment in college. Most of the important activities involving critical analysis and audience awareness occur during revision.

Revision is an opportunity, not an impediment. It gives you a chance to look at the piece of writing for a second time, allowing for perspective, feedback, and new ideas to enhance what you started.

JANE TOMPKINS

from "Indians": Textualism, Morality, and the Problem of History

This excerpt from Jane Tompkins's essay concerns the multiple ways of trying to arrive at the truth behind an historical event. In her exploration of the American Indians' relationship with Puritan culture, she has to revise and continue to revise her initial views of Indians as she reads source materials. By looking critically at representations of Indians, she comes to understand the complications involved in making judgments about the European–Indian encounter while also knowing the moral imperative to do so. Her willingness to take a second look at her subject led to critical insights.

When I was growing up in New York City, my parents used to take me to an event in Inwood Park at which Indians—real American Indians dressed in feathers and blankets—could be seen and touched by children like me. This event was always a disappointment. It was more fun to imagine that you *were* an Indian in one of the caves in Inwood Park than to shake the hand of an old man in a headdress who was not overwhelmed at the opportunity of meeting you. After staring at the Indians for a while, we would take a walk in the woods where the caves were, and once I asked my mother if the remains of a fire I had seen in one of them might have been left by the original inhabitants. After that, wandering up some stone steps cut into the side of the hill, I imagined I was a princess in a rude castle. My Indians, like my princesses, were creatures totally of the imagination, and I did not care to have any real exemplars interfering with what I already knew.

I already knew about Indians from having read about them in school. Over and over we were told the story of how Peter Minuit had bought Manhattan Island from the Indians for twenty-four dollars' worth of glass beads. And it was a story we didn't mind hearing because it gave us the rare pleasure of having someone to feel superior to, since the poor Indians had not known (as we eight-year-olds did) how valuable a piece of property Manhattan Island would become. Generally, much was made of the Indian presence in Manhattan; a poem in one of our readers began: "Where we walk to school today/ Indian children used to play," and we were encouraged to write poetry on this topic ourselves. So I had a fairly rich relationship with Indians before I ever met the unprepossessing people in Inwood Park. I felt that I had a lot in common with them. They, too, liked animals (they were often named after animals); they, too, made mistakes—they liked the brightly colored trinkets of little value that the white men were always offering them; they were handsome, warlike, and brave and had led an exciting, romantic life in the forest long ago, a life such as I dreamed of leading myself. I felt lucky to be living in one of the places where they had definitely been. Never mind where they were or what they were doing now.

My story stands for the relationship most non-Indians have to the people who first populated this continent, a relationship characterized by narcissistic fantasies of freedom and adventure, of a life lived closer to nature and to spirit than the life we lead now. As Vine Deloria, Jr., has pointed out, the American Indian Movement in the early seventies couldn't get people to pay attention to what was happening to Indians who were alive in the present, so powerful was this country's infatuation with people who wore loincloths, lived in tepees, and roamed the plains and forests long ago. The present essay, like these fantasies, doesn't have much to do with actual Indians, though its subject matter is the histories of European–Indian relations in seventeenth-century New England. In a sense, my encounter with Indians as an adult doing "research" replicates the childhood one, for while I started out to learn about Indians, I ended up preoccupied with a problem of my own.

This essay enacts a particular instance of the challenge poststructuralism poses to the study of history. In simpler language, it concerns the difference that point of view makes when people are giving accounts of events, whether at first or second hand. The problem is that if all accounts of events are determined through and through by the observer's frame of reference, then one will never know, in any given case, what really happened.

5 I encountered this problem in concrete terms while preparing to teach a course in colonial American literature. I'd set out to learn what I could about the Puritans' relations with American Indians. All I wanted was a general idea of what had happened between the English settlers and the natives in seventeenth-century New England; poststructuralism and its dilemmas were the furthest thing from my mind. I began, more or less automatically, with Perry Miller, who hardly mentions the Indians at all, then proceeded to the work of historians who had dealt exclusively with the European–Indian encounter. At first, it was a question of deciding which of these authors to believe, for it quickly became apparent that there was no unanimity on the subject. As I read on, however, I discovered that the problem was more complicated than deciding whose version of events was correct. Some of the conflicting accounts were not simply contradictory, they were completely incommensurable, in that their assumptions about what counted as a valid approach to the subject, and what the subject itself was, diverged in fundamental ways. Faced with an array of mutually irreconcilable points of view, points of view which determined what was being discussed as well as the terms of the discussion, I decided to turn to primary sources for clarification, only to discover that the primary sources reproduced the problem all over again. I found myself, in other words, in an epistemological quandary, not only unable to decide among conflicting versions of events but also unable to believe that any such decision could, in principle, be made. It was a moral quandary as well. Knowledge of what really happened when the Europeans and the Indians first met seemed particularly important, since the result of that encounter was virtual genocide. This was the kind of past "mistake" which, presumably, we studied history in order to avoid repeating. If studying history couldn't put us in touch with actual events and their causes, then what was to prevent such atrocities from happening again?

For a while, I remained at this impasse. But through analyzing the process by which I had reached it, I eventually arrived at an understanding which seemed to offer a way out.

COLLABORATING

Jane Tompkins suggests that looking at the process that leads to a decision can help in finding solutions to a problem. We might have experienced this feeling of enlightenment when we retraced our steps in a mathematical problem. Can you think of any other situations where you analyzed the process and discovered a solution? Talk with your group about whether members have had similar experiences in which probing the process allowed them to see a situation better.

You need to incorporate revision into your writing process in such a way that it seems like a natural step toward adding depth to your paper. Revision should not worry or derail you. The suggestions that follow should help you discover a drafting and revising strategy that works for you.

Focus on Revision Some of the models discussed earlier broke the drafting of an essay into several parts. In other words, some writers don't crank out drafts in one sitting. If you work this way, you might think about utilizing the same process for revision. In fact, you should consider shifting the focus of your process to revision.

Revising a paper can seem daunting when you do it all at once. No wonder many students look at it as a chore. If the draft can become the preliminary step in which you test out ideas but do not worry about the shape of an essay, you can work through it much more quickly. The time you would normally put into drafting can be used for an extended revision period. You can do some of the revision on your own, and base some of it on feedback from others. Most important, you would not do the revising all in one sitting. You would be taking a crucial part of your own drafting process and applying it to your model of revision. By transferring your labor to the revision end of the process, you will be less likely to feel anxious about having to "redo" a paper. You will know in advance that you're going to make significant changes.

This method can accommodate the first-draft procrastinator as well. In many ways, there is nothing wrong with grinding out a draft at the last minute. Many of us work this way. We need to feel the pressure of an impending deadline to produce writing. The last-minute draft gets ideas on the paper in a presentable form. Unfortunately, if the writer also procrastinates on the revision process, the gains become losses. In other words, at some point revision must be thought out and suggestions implemented slowly. Time must also be budgeted for editing and proofreading.

Create Options Even when faced with a draft marked up with comments and corrections from an instructor, an editor, or a supervisor, a writer sometimes has difficulty envisioning anything other than the original writing. Feeling that a draft is set the way it is—that the structure cannot be changed by significant revisions of content—makes writers sensitive to judgment and resistant to audience needs.

If you have felt this way when a paper was returned for revision, you might try creating options for yourself before turning in the draft. For shorter writing tasks, a writer may create a draft, put it away, and then write another draft without referring to the first one. No one fully memorizes writing that quickly, so there will be differences between the two drafts, some more significant than others. Having two separate first drafts creates options that facilitate the revision process. Questions your instructor wrote in the margins, for example, might have already been answered in the alternative draft.

While you might not always want to rewrite a full draft, you might try this technique on an area in the first draft that is causing difficulty. You can try a different analysis, rewrite a poignant part of a narrative, or summarize support for your main point a second time. After receiving feedback, or maybe just on your own, you can compare the two versions to see which more closely addresses the needs of your audience. From bits and pieces of both drafts, you might be able to weave together a stronger critical analysis than you had in either. You might see openings that show how to restructure or develop your thesis.

You can also do this with revisions. If you do not know where to take your writing after submitting a draft, revise a section or even the whole paper one way, put the revision aside, and produce another revision. Whether you intend it to or not, the revisions will differ. You will be giving yourself choices. Again, you can compare the two revisions, combine them as you see fit, or look for further options. Try this if your revision process seems to be hampered by indecision or resistance to change. While the technique might sound like more work, producing two options on your own will make you feel more in control and more able to readily revise.

Write Out of Order During both drafting and revising, nothing compels you to proceed sequentially. As long as the version you show to others demonstrates order or structure, it does not matter how you arrived at it. Thus, you can break writing tasks into parts, starting with the easiest and moving gradually to the most difficult.

Many writers have difficulty writing introductions, for example. Writers often leave the introduction for last. They do not know what they want to introduce until the paper has a clear shape and purpose. If you have difficulty with introductions, try saving this part of your task until you have written other sections. Writers often leave the introduction for last, as discussed in Chapter 4.

As another example, some writers panic when confronted with too many revision suggestions. Perhaps a suggestion to add detail to an event you observed racks your brain; you cannot remember much more than what you have already recorded. Why not start with the revision of the critical analysis, even though it is interspersed throughout your paper? As long as you leave enough time to add to your description before the due date, the delay in addressing issues will not harm you.

Incorporating such techniques into your writing process allows for natural breaks in drafting and revising. The parts you finish first might give you hints about tackling the more difficult areas of the paper. Introductions do not magically appear, but a clear idea of your topic and thesis will make writing one less stressful. If you find that a critical analysis focuses on gender issues, it could lead you to remember details concerning male–female differences in an event you witnessed, for example. While your finished product should be organized coherently, your process needs to be logical only to you.

COLLABORATING

You might find this activity especially helpful if you are currently working on a draft. Make a list of what you do when you draft and revise. Share your list with your group. Refer to your draft to point out specific examples of techniques that seem to work, as well as those that cause procrastination, incomplete drafts, or poor revisions. Could any of the techniques in this section be integrated into your process? What modifications would you have to make? What obstacles would hinder you from making changes to the model you now use? Make sure each group member receives feedback and contributes ideas.

Editing and Proofreading

There is no right time to start editing and proofreading. Some of the students in my class incorporated editing early, but proofreading—when treated as a separate part of the process—always seems to be the last step a writer takes. As noted earlier in this chapter, revision is a chore when a writer has spent too much time proofreading a draft. No one wants to redo a paper that appears superficially polished and correct. The writer risks making more mistakes, and proofreading must be repeated.

Editing involves similar risks. A writer might have to delete a particularly clever phrase he or she spent time conceiving. Shuffling the order of ideas often means creating a new introduction. Choosing different words to avoid repetition, as Chapter 5 suggests, can create a perspective that you must take into consideration. The significant changes brought on by editing indicate why many writers do not wait for the end to engage in it. Editing can produce as much resistance as proofreading, so writers incorporate editing at different times in their processes to avoid the anguish of last-minute overhauls.

Although editing and proofreading differ from drafting and revising, making them completely separate stages is unnatural. We don't want editing and proofreading to interfere with the construction of a piece of writing. Getting sentences correct and paragraphs in the form you want takes time and can shut down creative and critical impulses of writers who focus on "making it right" early in the process. However, gradual editing and proofreading can help you avoid the anxieties associated with a full edit and full proofread of a writing assignment. The resistance at having to redo a seemingly finished draft or revision will be lessened because you will be used to inserting, deleting, or changing words, reordering, checking spelling, and looking for mistakes.

The following are suggestions on incorporating an ongoing process of editing and revision.

Weaving in Analysis Except for scientific reports, essays generally are not divided into discrete sections. (See Chapter 4 for information on structuring an essay.) While we can usually identify the introduction, body, and conclusion of an essay, writers weave analysis and detail throughout the body instead of moving sequentially from thesis to content to analysis. "Four Stops on a Bigfoot Hunt" in Chapter 13 serves as one example of analysis woven into the body of an essay.

Allow time in your editing to integrate the critical analysis throughout the body. In reviewing the body of your essay, find the points of significance on which your critical analysis rests, and linger on them to let the audience know their importance to your thesis. For an essay that uses narration in the body, lingering means disrupting the story to alert the audience to key elements. If you are using facts and research in your body, lingering means tying these elements together, showing how one builds on another. Jeff Parker slows his narration of the Bigfoot hunt, for example, by talking about the disagreements among Bigfoot researchers on matters as mundane as whether the plural of *Bigfoot* is *Bigfeet* and on more important matters about theories of what Bigfoot eats. All this speculation feeds into his ambivalent feelings about the purpose of Bigfoot research.

If you are describing a scene or relating an observation, lingering means slowing down your description to start explaining why you have emphasized a particular detail. This type of editing can take place at almost any point in your process. Some writers prefer to construct separate sections during drafting. They then cut and paste the critical analysis material, inserting relevant parts into significant text within the body. There should be obvious correspondence.

Other writers like this phase of editing to occur while they draft, making the review discussed above unnecessary. Based on freewriting that starts with the critical analysis (as discussed in the section on breaking through writing blocks), editing is incorporated when the writer sees a point of significance occurring, such as a detail about race or gender. Such writers rarely write separate analysis sections (except for the ideas generated through the freewrite); analysis is woven into their process, so the body leads directly to a conclusion.

Writers can mix these two editing strategies together as well, inserting a little analysis but also writing a critical analysis and reviewing the body during the revision process to see where more analysis can be woven in. The important point is that leaving this type of weaving until the end of your process will not allow enough time to consider structural changes that might be needed as a result.

Word Choice and Sentence Variety Editing and proofreading sometimes overlap in this part of the process. Most writers find it difficult, for instance, to check that they have not used filler words and then to return to the same sentence later to make sure words respond grammatically to the structure of the sentence. Generally, writers subconsciously do the editing (word selection) and the proofreading (checking for correctness) at the same time. Yet, catching mistakes differs from experimenting with words and rewriting sentences. Your process needs to reflect this distinction.

Although you can and should edit and proofread throughout your writing process, a final edit for word choice and sentence variety will not add an undue burden. Simply read your essay aloud from beginning to end, stopping when you notice too many short sentences in a row or too many long ones. You can combine some sentences with common connector words, such as *and* or *but,* and break up longer ones by deleting the same type of words and starting new sentences. While doing this final read, look for repetition of words and areas where your voice could come through more clearly. You probably used this strategy while you drafted and revised, but one final read will let you see the essay as a whole and fine-tune problem areas. When you insert a different word or revise a sentence, restart your oral reading at the beginning of the paragraph in which the change occurred. You want to make sure your rewrite fits into the flow of the paragraph.

Proofreading Writers stumble in proofreading because they do not know the rules. However, confusion caused by a lack of recognition of mistakes should not deter you from proofreading. The more you write, the more you will recognize what most writing teachers call patterns of error. Recognizing errors is the first step toward correcting them. For instance, if you know you have difficulty with comma placement, you will have spotted one such pattern. If you realize that the problems occur when you construct longer sentences, you will have a further understanding of the pattern. The more you narrow the pattern down, the closer you will be to finding the exact set of rules you need to understand and implement better.

Consult your teacher or see a writing center tutor to start working on the recognition of your errors. On your own, you can locate mistakes that you do recognize as well as other lapses, such as leaving out a word, by doing one more silent reading of your essay after your oral read for editing. For this final read, take each sentence out of context so that your mind does not play tricks on you. Because you as the writer know what you mean to say, you might subconsciously insert or delete words to match your prediction of what should be there.

We can often see the errors in other people's writing better than we can in our own because we do not know what to expect when we read their words, and we are aware of everything. Mistakes do not pass us by. To turn off the natural filter in your mind, you must stop reading for meaning. In the final read, look at the very last sentence in your paper. If it looks correct, go to the second-to-last sentence. If that seems all right, go to the third-to-last sentence. Follow this process until you have read your whole essay backwards, sentence by sentence. Make corrections when you see them, but do not read two sentences in a row or try to edit. By following this practice, you will slow down your reading and find mistakes that you previously failed to notice.

Using Spelling and Grammar Checkers Using a computer gives you an advantage in finding certain types of mistakes, since every word-processing program comes with a spelling and grammar checker. The checker highlights words that it cannot locate in its dictionary and sentences that do not seem to conform to the standard rules of grammar.

While these checkers come in handy, you need to understand their limitations. First, the spelling checker does not know what word you meant to spell. It will make suggestions from a list of words that look something like the word you spelled. You should not just click Change or Change All to fix a mistake. So what should you do when you do not know how to spell the word? Your program probably also includes a thesaurus. Run the suggested spelling through the thesaurus. If the synonyms listed match the meaning you want, then the word given by the spelling checker is correct. If not, seek alternate spellings.

Spelling and grammar checkers do not recognize most mistakes made that involve homophones (words with different meanings and spelling that sound alike, such as *there* and *their*). Study your own patterns of error concerning homophones, and pay special attention to them when you are doing your final proofread.

While grammar checkers are wonderful in locating sentence fragments or subject-verb agreement problems, the technology is far from perfect. Sometimes, a grammar checker will flag a sentence that does not need correction because it is unable to understand how a sentence functions in context. Other times, it confuses stylistic choices with mistakes. Consider the points the grammar checker makes, but do not click Change every time it flags a problem. Click the appropriate icon to get an explanation of the problem. If the explanation does not make sense in relation to your sentence, do not change it.

Also ask your teacher or a tutor for further guidance. There might be a pattern of error that you need help to recognize. In this case, talking with someone best helps you learn. Do not rely on spelling and grammar checkers to do your thinking. Learn to use these programs as aids, not as substitutes for skill development.

COLLABORATING

Practice the editing and proofreading techniques on a current writing assignment. Choose the group member who is farthest along in the process, and have him or her bring in enough copies of his or her paper for every member of the group. Use the techniques for weaving critical analysis into the body of the text, then do editing for word choice and sentence variety—having the writer read the paper aloud—and finish with a proofreading session in which the group reads the essay sentence by sentence in reverse order. Make changes that you can all agree on, and place check marks next to the lines that you wonder about. Consult with your instructor about the marked items. When you are finished, discuss the effectiveness of this strategy and its applicability to your individual processes. Can you think of ways to modify or otherwise tweak these suggestions so they work for you?

Summary

Writing processes are highly individualized. As you write more, you will develop a process that keeps the strong elements of the model you now use while allowing for changes that will improve the finished product. Some practices will help you accomplish this task. Understanding your current model and isolating problem areas in it are important. You must learn to recognize what causes writer's block and find methods to break it to ensure that it does not derail your ability to complete a task. Differentiating between drafting and revision, giving yourself options, and reorganizing your time to focus more on revision will help conquer your resistance to the process. Finally, weave editing and proofreading into your process so that they do not hinder the important areas of content development and analysis, but also do not leave everything to the very end. Final readings of an essay using various strategies will help you find the right words, ensure sentence variety, and catch mistakes.

CHAPTER 7

USES OF COLLABORATION

"Can't we get in groups to talk about this?"

I have heard this refrain from students many times. Students genuinely like working together. They can talk more freely among themselves than they can in larger groups. There is less fear of saying the wrong thing, appearing uninformed, or even sounding too smart. As a student, you probably enjoy active tasks more than lectures, so groups keep you attentive and allow you to learn more. And, yes, I know: When no teacher is hovering over you, you are freer to laugh and to get off task without reprimand. Groups can be fun, and they allow you to get to know the other students.

Based on requests and students' generally positive attitude toward group work, I decided years ago to extend in-class group work to out-of-class group work. My research told me that students were already consulting each other about editing, assignments, and other matters. I figured that a group project would give students a chance to continue enjoying the process of collaboration. Boy, was I wrong!

"One person always gets stuck doing all the work," my student Natalie complained when I introduced the final writing project of the year, a collaborative venture in which students would research the origins of their favorite holiday and compare purposes and intent with modern-day celebrations.

"Do we all get the same grade?" Nguyen chipped in. "That's not fair if my part of the project is good but the overall paper is bad."

"We should be able to select our own partners," Mildred said.

"Can I just do it on my own?" Kassim asked.

Online Study Center

This icon will direct you to web links and additional resources on the website college.hmco.com/pic/thelin1e

It seemed that the thought of sharing responsibility for a grade, especially with students who might drag them down, frightened my students. They could not imagine producing a stronger final piece through collaboration. I wondered why and asked. The students' past experiences had apparently been mixed.

Natalie had been grouped with slackers but would have felt like a snitch explaining to the instructor that the others had not contributed. "I wanted to help them, but they did not want to help me," she said.

Mildred felt she had been punished for her group's lack of caution in an experiment she reproduced as part of an oral group presentation in a chemistry class. "I did everything like I was supposed to, but the experiment did not reproduce like it was supposed to," she told everyone.

"I just could not work with these guys," Nguyen said, recalling a research report he had done on abortion. "They would not consider any argument about women having the rights to their own body."

Kassim was short and to the point. "I get everything done quicker if I do it alone."

Each of them had a valid point; yet, I knew that groups compose most professional and government documents. Few individuals produce a piece of writing to which no one else adds or on which no one else comments at some point in the process. Shouldn't we be teaching students how to collaborate?

Then it dawned on me: Teaching students how to collaborate is what I needed to do in class. While outcomes like the one Mildred described might still occur, experiences like Natalie's and Nguyen's could turn out better with guidance. If students like Kassim could see an advantage to working with others, the time involved might seem less important. I decided then and there that, rather than imposing collaboration on students, I would show them the benefits of working together and make them want to collaborate.

DISCUSSION

What have you experienced when working with groups outside of school projects? Make a list of the attitudes, actions, and discussions that helped the group function well. Make a similar list of behaviors that hindered the group. Discuss the attributes of functional and dysfunctional groups, and figure out how to avoid dysfunction. Can these ideas work in an academic project as well? What can each individual do to prevent dysfunction?

This chapter will help you learn to work together in an effective group. While these ideas can transfer to other disciplines, writing relies on collaboration more than does any other subject. Groups allow your strengths as a writer to shine through. A group will make use of these strengths, and areas in which you are perhaps weaker will be assigned to somebody else. Your weaknesses are probably somebody else's strengths. Working together, you can produce a much better finished product and enhance your skills as a writer.

MARCUS LAFFEY

Inside Dope

Many occupations use collaborative techniques to ensure that a job is done properly. In the following essay, a New York City police officer writes about his experiences arresting dope users. Pay attention to the necessity of collaboration. One person acting alone could not accomplish the goal.

If there were ever a Super Bowl matchup of junkies versus crackheads, it would be hard to figure which team the odds would favor. Both sides would most likely disappear during halftime. The crackheads would believe that they had won, and the junkies wouldn't care. If they did manage to finish the game, the smartest money would invest in a pawnshop next to the stadium, and within hours the investors would own every Super Bowl ring, for pennies on the dollar. Winners and losers would again be indistinguishable.

The war on drugs is a game for me, no matter how urgent it is for poor neighborhoods or how grave the risks are for cops. We call dealers "players," and there are rules as in chess, percentages as in poker, and moves as in schoolyard ball. When I went from being a beat cop to working in narcotics, the change was refreshing. For one thing, you deal only with criminals. No more domestic disputes, barricaded schizophrenics, or D.O.A.s, the morass of negotiable and nonnegotiable difficulties people have with their neighbors or boyfriends or stepchildren. Patrol cops deal with the fluid whole of people's lives, but usually when the tide's going out: people who have the cops called on them aren't happy to see you; people who call the cops aren't calling when they're having a good time. Now all I do is catch sellers of crack and heroin, and catch their customers to show that they sold it. The parts of their lives unaffected by coca- or opium-based products are none of my business. Patrol is politics, but narcotics is pure technique.

My unit, which consists of half a dozen cops and a sergeant, makes arrests for "observation sales." One or two of us go to an observation post ("the OP," and if you're in it you're "doing OPs") on a rooftop or in a vacant apartment to watch a "set," or drug operation, and transmit information to the "catch car," the unmarked van used to pick up the perps. The set might be a lone teenager standing on a corner with one pocket full of crack and another full of cash. Or it might be an organization of such intricate subterfuge—with lookouts, managers, moneymen, steerers (to guide customers), and pitchers (for the hand-to-hand transactions)—that you'd think its purpose was to deliver Soviet microfilm to covert operatives instead of a ten-dollar bag of junk to a junkie. But we watch, and give descriptions of buyers for the catch team to pick up, a few blocks away. Sometimes the dealers send out phantom or dummy buyers—people who appear to have bought narcotics but haven't—to see if they're stopped; we wait until we have a handful of buyers, then move in on the set. Most of the spots that we hit are well established, visited by both customers and cops on a regular basis; others pop up and disappear. You might drive around to see who's out—the faces at the places, the traffic pattern of steady customers and usual suspects. Sometimes you feel like the man on the catwalks over the casino floor, scanning the tables for the sharps and card counters, looking out for luck that's too good to be true. Other times, you feel as if you were watching a nature program, some *National Geographic* special on the felony ecology of the streets.

You read the block, seeing who moves and who stands still, their reactions and relations to one another; you sift the players from the idlers, the buyers from the passersby. Most people occupy their environment blithely, with only a slack and occasional awareness of their surroundings. A store window or a noisy garbage truck might distract them in passing, and they might look around before crossing the street, but the ordinary pedestrian is a poster child for daydreams and tunnel vision. Not so in the narcotics trade, where the body language of buyer and seller alike signals a taut awareness of opportunity and threat. There are distinctive addict walks, such as that of the prowler, who might be new to the spot, or sussing out an operation that has shifted to a more favorable corner. He hovers, alert for the deal, floating like a flake of ash above a fire. The addict on a "mission walk" moves with double-quick footsteps, leaning forward, as if against a strong wind, so as not to waste an extra second of his already wasted life. A player, on the other hand, has a self-contained watchfulness, a false repose, like a cat sunning itself on a windowsill, eyes half-closed but ready to pounce.

Every street set operates through an odd combination of aggressive mar- 5
keting and strategic defense, needing simultaneously to broadcast and to deny its function. The young man on the park bench should look like a high-school senior from thirty yards away but has to show he's a merchant at three yards, and he has to have the drugs near enough for convenience but far enough away to be out of his "custody and control" should he be stopped. If he's holding the drugs, he has to have an escape route—through a hole in a fence, say, or into an alley, or into the building where his grandmother lives. The man on the bench is just a man on a bench, after all, until his context proves him otherwise. But, as you watch, figures emerge from the flow of street life like coördinates on a grid, like pins on a drug map.

Say you're doing OPs from a rooftop, looking down on a street that has three young guys on the corner by the bodega, a couple with a baby in a carriage by the stoop, and a group of old men with brown-bagged brandy bottles by the vacant lot. A man on a bicycle moves in a slow, lazy slalom, up and down the street. The corner boys are the obvious pick, but I have to wait. When a buyer comes, he is easier to recognize, and his arrival on the set sends a signal, a vibration, like a fly landing in the web. The buyer is the bellwether and the bait: he draws the players out and makes them work, prompts them into visible display.

The buyer walks past the old men at the lot, the family on the stoop, to the corner boys, as expected. One corner boy takes the buyer aside and palms his cash, the second stands still, watching up and down the block, and the third goes to the family on the stoop and has a word with the woman with the baby. The woman steps inside the lobby for a few seconds—Thank God, I think, it's not in the carriage—and when she returns she hands something to the third boy, who meets up with the first corner boy and the buyer and hands off the product. The buyer walks away, retracing his route. The man on the bicycle follows him slowly.

I put the buyer over the air: "Hispanic male; red cap; Tommy Hilfiger jacket, blue; bluejeans. South on Third. Be advised, you got a lookout on a bike—white T-shirt, bluejeans, black bike—tailing him to see if he gets picked up. Let him run a couple of blocks, if you can."

Now I have a three-player set, with Mama and corner boys Nos. 1 and 3 down cold. The buyer should be taken, and No. 2 only observed for now. Mama's short time in the building tells me that the stash is not in an apartment but either on her person or right in the lobby, in an unlocked mailbox or a crack in the wall. Corner boy No. 2 is the one to watch, to see if he's the manager or a lookout, up a rank from the others or down. His position will become clear as I watch the group dynamic of the trio—the choreography of who stands where, who talks and who listens, who tells the jokes and who laughs, who's the one that runs to the bodega for the chips and soda. Until he participates in the exchanges, taking money or product, he's legally safe from arrest for an observation sale. If he's a manager, he's the one we want; if he's a smart manager, touching neither cash nor stash, he's the one we're least likely to get. In a sense, everybody wants the spot to get busy: the players grow careless as they get greedy, bringing out more product, paying more heed to the customer and less to us. The manager might have to step in and lend an incriminating hand. When the spot is slow, both groups—the cops and the players—have to be patient.

10 Even when nothing happens, there is much to interpret. Are they out of product, and will they re-up within ten minutes or an hour? Are they "raised"—afraid we're around—and, if so, is it because they saw our van (unmarked but patently obvious) or saw one of us peering over the roofline, or is it because a patrol car raced by, to a robbery three blocks away? Did they turn away another customer because he wanted credit, or because they thought he was an undercover cop, and were they right? Is the next deal worth the wait?

The wait can be the most trying part of the operation. I've spent hours on tar rooftops, crouched down till my legs cramped, sweating, shivering, wiping the rain from my binoculars every ten seconds. There have been times when I've forgotten to look down before I knelt by the ledge, and settled in beside piles of shit, broken glass, or syringes. On one rooftop, there was an ornate Victorian birdcage, five feet tall, bell-shaped and made of brass, and chained to it, still on a rotten leather leash, was the skeleton of a pit bull. You walk up dirty stairs to a dirty roof to watch a dirty street. At night, even the light is dirty, the sodium-vapor street lights giving off a muddy yellow haze. But sometimes, when something finally does happen, you realize that your concentration is perfect: you feel the cool, neutral thrill of being completely submerged in your task. The objects of surveillance inhabit a living landscape, and you can be struck by the small, random graces of the scene even as you transmit a streak of facts over the radio: "Gray livery cab, buyer in back seat, passenger side, possible white with white sleeves, U-turning now to the left. . . ."

A soap bubble, then two, then dozens rise up in front of me, iridescent, shimmering in their uncertainty. There is a child two floors below me, as rapt with the view above as I am with the view below.

"Arright, we got one, he's beelining to the player, they just popped into the lobby. . . . Now he's out—that's fast, he must have the stash on him. Arright, buyer's walking off now—Hold on, he's just kind of idling across the street. It's not an I-got-my-rock walk. I don't think he got done. Stand by. . . ."

A man standing on another tenement roof whirls an orange flag, and makes it snap like a towel. His flock of pigeons takes flight from the coop with a whoosh like a gust of wind, spiralling out in broadening arcs—showing the smoky gray of their backs as they bank out, the silver-white of their bellies as they circle in—rising up all the while.

"Player's walking off, he sent the last two away, he's out, he's raised, I don't know, but—Go! Go! Go! Hit the set!"

An incinerator chimney shoots out a lash of black smoke, which loops into a lariat before dissolving into the grimy sky.

At the other end of the OP is the catch car. You want a buyer's description, or "scrip," to have something distinctive about it—something beyond the "white T-shirt, bluejeans" of warm weather, "black jacket, bluejeans" of cold. You don't want "Male, walking three pit bulls." You're glad to hear about hot pink and lime green, or T-shirts with legible writing on them, or, even better, "Female in purple-and-yellow tracksuit, with a Cat-in-the-Hat hat, riding a tiny bicycle." For crackheads, as much as for any other species, protective coloration can be a successful evolutionary strategy.

Once you get the scrip and the buyer's direction of flight, you move in, allowing yourself some distance from the set, but not too much, or else the buyer will be home; in neighborhoods like this, people don't have to go far for hard drugs. Sometimes buyers run, and sometimes they fight, and sometimes they toss the drugs (though sometimes you can find those drugs later), and sometimes they eat them when they see you coming. There have been buyers who at the sight of me have reacted with a loss of bowel control, and control of the belly and the bladder as well. The truth is, I am the least of their problems: a night on a cell bench, with prison bologna sandwiches to eat, ranks fairly low amid the hazards of being at the bottom of the criminal food chain.

For crackheads, in particular, a stint as a model prisoner might be a career peak. While the street dealers at dope spots are often junkies themselves, crackheads can't be trusted with the stash—they can't even hold a job whose main requirements are to stand still and watch. The majority of them are figures from a famine: bone-thin and filthy. Months of that life take years from their lives, and thirty-year-olds can pass for fifty, burned out almost literally, with a red-hot core of desperation beneath a dead, charred surface. Junkies generally have a longer ride to the bottom, as the habit gradually slides from being a part of their lives to becoming the point of them. Heroin is purer now than it was in the past, and fewer than half the addicts I arrest have needles on them. They snort it instead of shooting it, which decreases the risk of disease and also seems to slow the forward momentum of addiction. But to me the terminal junkies are especially awful, because they have none of the trapped-rat frenzy of the crackhead; instead, they possess a fatal calm, as if they were keeping their eyes open while drowning. When you collar them, they can have a look of confirmed and somewhat contented self-hatred, as if the world were doing to them what they expect and deserve.

20 Addicts deserve pity, always, though often they inspire contempt. We collared one crackhead, bumping into him by accident as he stood in a project lobby counting out a handful of vials. He was a street peddler who sold clothing, and had about eighty dollars in his pocket. He had the shrink-wrapped look that crackheads get, as if his skin were two sizes too small. He moaned and wept for his infant child, who would starve, he said, without his support. Yes, he acknowledged, the baby lived with its mother, but he was the provider. The mother and child were only about ten blocks away, at a playground, so we drove to meet them. The mother was a pretty, well-dressed woman, though her soccer-mom wholesomeness may have been artificially heightened by the presence of her handcuffed mate. We called her over, and her look of mild confusion became one of mild dismay as she saw our back-seat passenger. She didn't look surprised, and didn't ask questions. He took out his wad of cash, peeled off four dollars, and handed it to me to give to her. "You gotta be kidding me," I said. "You give me all this father-of-the-year shit, just to throw her four bucks?"

"C'mon," he said. "When you get out of Central Booking, you're hungry, you want some real McDonald's or something."

I gave him back the four dollars and took the wad for the mother. "The Number Two Special, two cheeseburgers and fries, is three-twenty-nine," I told him. "It's what I get, and it's all you can afford." For an addict, the priorities are never unclear.

After you've collared the buyers, it's time to move in on the dealers. When you hit a set, there is always a charge of adrenaline, arising from the jungle-war vagaries of opponent and terrain. There are elusive adversaries, explosive ones, and lots of sitting ducks. Some dealers opt for a businesslike capitulation, aware that it's the way to go through the process with the least fuss. Others, especially lobby dealers with access to an apartment upstairs, tend to make a mad dash for freedom. The bust could be a surrender as slow and dignified as Lee's at Appomattox or it could be bedlam—roiling bodies and airborne stash. When you can't count the evidence at the scene, you have to at least control it—the hundreds of dollars in small bills, the fistfuls of crack slabs, the loose decks, the bundles of dope—so you jam it in your pockets like a handful of ball bearings, and all the while there may be a crowd screaming, or perps for whom the fight-or-flight reflex is not a simple either-or proposition.

The smarter dealers carry nothing on them, but you await information from the OP, sometimes with a distaste that verges on dread:

25 "It's in his sock."

"It's in the cast on his right hand—"

"It's in his cheek—sorry, guy, the other cheek. I mean, check between 'em, you copy?"

Stash can be hidden under a bottle cap or in a potato-chip bag, or strewn among heaps of noncriminal trash; it can be wedged in a light fixture in a hall or tucked inside the bumper of a car; it can be in a magnetic key case stuck to the iron bolt beneath a park bench; or it can be on a string taped to the wall and dangling down the garbage-disposal chute. A thorough search can lead to unexpected threats and rewards. Once, when I was rooting through a janitor's closet in a housing project after hitting a heroin set, I found a machine gun in the bottom of a bag of clothes. We continued to search the building and found more than a thousand dollars' worth of heroin, two more guns—a 9-mm. handgun and a .45 revolver—and also ammunition for another machine gun, an AK-47: copper-jacketed bullets more than two inches long, coming to a sharp, conical point like a dunce cap. An AK-47 can discharge bullets at a speed of more than two thousand feet per second, which would allow them to pass through my vest with barely a pause.

In the movies, there are a lot of drug-dealer villains, but those characters usually have to slap their girlfriends or kill a lot of cops to heighten the dramatic point of their bad-guyness. Because the victims of drug sales line up and pay, so to speak, for the privilege, the perpetrators don't have the forthright menace of violent felons. But most of the players I collar have a rap sheet that shows a more diversified criminal career—of earlier forays into robbery or theft—before they settled on the more lucrative and "less illegal" world of drug sales. And although some drug spots operate in a fairly quiet, orderly manner, as if a man were selling newspapers on the street, or a couple were running a catalogue business out of their apartment, most are established and maintained by means of assault, murder, and many subtler thefts of human dignity.

In New York, heroin dealers stamp brand names on the little wax-paper 30
envelopes in which the drug is packaged. This practice gives a glimpse not only of a corporate structure, when the same brands appear in different sites, but also of a corporate imagination, showing what they believe their product should mean to their customers. Some convey the blandly generic aspiration of quality—"First Class," "President," "Original"—that you might find on brands of cornflakes or of detergent in some discount supermarket. Others go for a racier allure, but the gimmick is so hackneyed in conventional advertising that the genuinely illicit thrill of "Knockout" or "No Limit" suggests the mock-illicit thrill of ads for perfume or fat-free ice cream. Topical references are common, from the flat-out copyright infringement of "DKNY" or "Ford" to the movie tagline "Show Me the Money." But the best brand names are the literal ones, which announce without apology the bad things to come: "911," "25 to Life," "Undertaker," "Fuck You." There is a suicidal candor to "Lethal Injection" and "Virus," a forthright finality to "O.D."—a truth in advertising here that few products can match.

Recently, I had a talk with one of my informants, a junkie with AIDS who sleeps in an alley. A few days before, I'd obtained a search warrant for a spot he visits several times a day, and he fervently wished me luck with the warrant's execution. That my success would cause him inconvenience in supplying his own habit was a mild irony that did not trouble him. He said, "I know you're a cop and I'm—" and there was a sliver of space before his next word, enough for me to wonder what term he might use for a shorthand self-portrait. And, knowing that there would be a measure of harsh truth in it, I was still surprised, and even felt sorry for him, when he said, "And I'm a fucking scumbag." But he was equally firm in his opinion of those who had benefitted from his self-destruction: "I done time, I'm no hero, but these people are blood-suckers. Them and rapists are as bad as people get. Those people are worse than rapists. Those dealers will suck you dry. I hope you get every last one of them."

Every day, we go out and hunt people. When we do well—picking off the customers with dispatch, swooping in on the dealers, taking trophies of their product and profit—we feel skilled and lucky at once, at the top of our game. We have shut down spots, reduced robberies and shootings, made whole blocks cleaner, safer, saner places. But other spots withstand daily assaults from us with negligible losses, and I've driven home after a twenty-hour day only to recognize, with the hallucinatory clarity of the sleep-deprived, the same man, on the same mission walk, that I'd collared the night before. Typically, buyers spend a night in jail and are sentenced to a few days of community service. Players might get less, odd as that may seem, if there weren't enough transactions in open view, or if no stash was recovered. We'll all meet again, soon enough. There are breaks and interruptions, retirements and replacements, but, no matter how often the whistle blows, the game is never over.

Beyond the In-Class Response Group

The most frequently used in-class collaborative task is a version of a peer response group. As discussed in Chapter 3, receiving feedback from readers allows a writer to ponder suggestions generated from actual responses and to use them in making decisions about revising. Outside of class, writers consult with people around them to get feedback. A writer contemplating the proper words in a note intended for a bereaved friend might share a version with someone who knows the person to make sure the note sounds sensitive without being sappy. A writer constructing a flyer to encourage people to come to a peace rally probably will let other organizers evaluate the strength of the appeal before printing several hundred copies. Peer response accompanies most writing endeavors.

Sometimes students shy away from organizing peer response groups outside of the classroom. You might feel comfortable having a family member or a roommate read an assignment you intend to submit to your instructor, but you do not look for advice from fellow students unless you have the opportunity during class time. You shut out the people who have the most knowledge about class lessons, teacher expectations, and assignment requirements. While the feedback you receive from others can be valuable, responses from your peers could be the difference between an A and a C on a final project.

You may have never considered forming peer response groups outside of class time, but you do not want to ignore this opportunity for important insights. Out-of-class response groups relieve some of the pressure of classroom tasks. They give you practice in the collaborating that will be fundamental in your professional and civic endeavors.

Response groups can meet at a time convenient for everyone. They can be done in conjunction with a potluck dinner or can take place during the first hour or so of a social outing. You can get together face-to-face or online. You can enjoy the time together as long as you attend to the writing part.

Face-to-Face Groups Weekend nights carry expectations that might undermine a serious effort at an out-of-class peer response group. Some students work at weekend jobs or return home for family visits. Thus, face-to-face groups should try to meet during the week. Ideally, the meeting should occur after everyone has attended his or her last class for the day. You can meet at a coffee shop, a dorm room, or anywhere that will be quiet enough for you to read and talk. Try to avoid more formal settings, such as a library or a vacant classroom, where the aura of schooling and the expectation of silence will be present.

Limit the number of people in a group, keeping it below five. More will make the session last too long and could shortchange writers whose work is considered toward the end of the session, when respondents are tired. Choose students with whom you can communicate. Sometimes the most popular or attractive person does not make the best group member. Rather, focus on students who participate effectively during class, usually come prepared, and show interest in improving as writers.

Skill level should not factor in as much as you might think. If you stack your group with the best writers in the class, you must be prepared to give as well as take, since they will have no incentive to help you if you do not offer substantial feedback. As long as a student has a desire to learn, he or she can contribute effectively to a group, despite skills that might be weaker. Everyone has the innate ability to judge, at some level, how well a writer has communicated to a reader. Everybody can give feedback on the important concepts of critical analysis, audience considerations, organization, and language.

If a piece of writing confuses a reader, no matter how good or bad a writer that person might be, his or her reaction can be probed for its usefulness in revision. Sometimes weak writers understand certain issues of critical analysis, audience, organization, and language better than strong writers. In matters related to proofreading, however, consult a handbook to verify the accuracy of feedback; when in doubt, consult your instructor.

To differentiate the out-of-class response group from the dominant mode of education—correction of error—the group should concentrate on matters of content. Members should bring copies of their essays for the other members to read (even if the group decides to read the essays aloud). Talk about ideas; keep the assignment handy to make sure requirements have been met; and make genuine suggestions about how to make the essay more insightful and stimulating.

Whether you are working on a draft, trying to start a revision, or testing a revision to see how an audience reacts to your attempts at improvement, out-of-class response groups can help. You can meet as often as you like, but scheduling meetings at a regular time every other week or so can make those meetings part of your routine that you arrange the rest of your life around instead of an obligation added to a hectic day. Remember to make it fun. Laugh, plan to see a movie afterwards, eat while reading, and get to know your peers. Learning involves discipline, but within the confines of responsibility and proper preparation, there is plenty of time for enjoyment.

Online Groups Online variations of out-of-class response groups include chat rooms and bulletin boards, such as those used in course management systems like Blackboard. Essays are posted so that peers in the group can review them. Responses can be sent as email messages or email attachments. Synchronous discussion of essays allows for dialogue and is therefore preferable to asynchronous postings.

Chat rooms can be established between pairs of students or the whole group, depending on members' preferences. Sometimes having too many respondents in a chat room makes following a strand of conversation difficult. One way to alleviate this problem is to establish rules. For instance, the writer could discuss the first peer reviewer's critique with that person only, while others listen. The other peers can voice agreement or disagreement with the first set of comments when it is their turn to critique.

Simple technology enables online discussions. For a course that uses Blackboard or another course management system, the instructor can allow the chat room capabilities to be used by the online group. Anyone who uses instant messaging can carry on a synchronous discussion. Arranging the online group is easier, too, by inviting classmates to join—perhaps by sending online invitations so as to weed out the technologically challenged—without having to find a place to meet or organizing transportation.

While the online option does not permit the socializing that face-to-face groups enjoy, contributors can instead establish different identities or play with text while engaging in the discussion. As is the case with the face-to-face groups, the group needs to focus on the important concepts of writing while resisting the temptation to proofread.

DISCUSSION

Talk about the strengths and the weaknesses of your first experience with in-class peer groups in this or other courses. What benefited you? What do you wish could have happened? Imagine that the peer group discussion had taken place in a location other than a classroom. What might have been different? How do the constraints or structure of the classroom hinder or help you in the task of responding to student writing? Discuss the structure that would make an out-of-class group utilize the strength of in-class groups while avoiding the problems that occur.

Assigning Tasks in Group Projects

Ideally, the group project assigned to you will have so many layers and require so much time that everyone will see the advantage of working with peers. But if the assignment is open-ended, the group must create tasks that will produce a final product above and beyond individual capabilities. Otherwise, you or another student might be tempted to take over the project should a problem emerge. If other members, particularly any who are inclined to be lazy, sense that one group member will pick up the slack, they may not work as hard. Furthermore, the instructor will expect more from a group of four or five students than from a single person. Match the teacher's expectations with a plan that will exceed what you could produce individually.

Assigning tasks to each member of the group is essential to the success of a group project. Collaboration starts with individual effort. As a member of a group, you must follow through on a specific part of the project that will link with the work turned in by the other students.

Selecting a Secretary Instead of electing a leader, have one person function as the secretary. The secretary should be responsible for taking notes at group meetings, organizing the deadlines for each phase of the process, and distributing the schedule and a list of everyone's tasks. The group should agree on the details of the schedule and the allotment of tasks; the secretary merely arranges and records the decisions.

The importance of having a secretary rests in writing down the agreements and making the list available, perhaps through email or on a temporary website such as one offered by FreeWebs or another online provider. If there are disputes about what tasks were assigned and when, the secretary can refer to an official record. If technology is not available, the secretary can record the important information on paper and give copies to all members to prevent legitimate mistakes and strengthen each person's sense of responsibility. The secretary's work puts the agreements reached in words and acts as a contract of sorts for the group.

Strengths and Weaknesses Tasks should utilize the best attributes of each member. If a project involves both library research and data gathering (Chapter 10 explains these elements of writing), the group members who best know the library databases should probably be assigned to this aspect. Members who are outgoing and who are comfortable approaching people might conduct interviews or collect questionnaires. Perhaps one member analyzes evidence well, so his or her task is to figure out the meaning of the results gathered in the data collection.

Tasks depend largely on the assignment. While writing should be done by everyone in the group, it may be easiest to have one person put together the whole first draft, to have two or three others work on the revision, and to have yet another do the final proofreading. In groups of four and five, you can also consider pairing a person strong in one area with a person who is weak in that area. The stronger person can teach the weaker person how to do something, and the weaker person can take the lead at some point. This type of task assignment helps everyone learn while completing the project. The strong person must not overstep boundaries so as not to compromise the learning and allow others to avoid doing any work.

Keep a Progress Log Too often, groups meet to discuss progress but do not have written material to show each other. This allows members to hide poorly done work or even to fabricate their efforts. The group then dives into writing the report or paper without any text to start from.

Groups should require each member to keep a progress log. The log should include specifics about what the member did—and where, how, and when he or she did it—and summarize important information. It will provide a chronological narrative of the task and will be especially useful in evaluating the work. Posting the progress logs online will give other group members access. Members can review and comment on one another's logs before group meetings.

A group cannot allow a member to summarize too broadly or to give details of some work and skim over the rest by saying, "There's much more, so we're okay." This line is frequently used by someone who has done the work at the last minute. Online intervention can urge the member to explain exactly what he or she did and prevent a member from covering up lax work. If an individual's task was to conduct a poll, the progress log should explain what was on the poll, where he or she approached people to get information, how people were selected to be polled, and when the polling took place. If the task was an online search for recent information on a topic, the log should explain what search engines and websites were used, with what key words, and when the search was completed.

It is also a good idea to include how many hours each member put into his or her part of the task. Although members might fudge a bit, this information will give an indication of everyone's involvement outside of the classroom. If a person claims to have worked ten hours but has a skimpy progress log, other members can ask how the time was spent and suggest better ways to get the work done.

Following is an example of a week's progress log that a student typed up and distributed to his group during the exploratory parts of a large research project.

Jim's Progress Log

The assignment was to research a historical mystery, uncover the political and social agendas that surrounded the mystery, and come to a conclusion about the influence of those agendas in preventing the mystery from being solved. While Jim seems frustrated with his research at times and wants to concentrate on specific information that he finds, he is recording relevant observations about the political battles surrounding his group's topic, the Dead Sea Scrolls, that may find their way into a final paper. It might have been best for Jim to give more detail about the articles he did not understand, but in at least mentioning them, he is showing a pattern in the published information that his group might be able to use as they synthesize the materials.

October 7: I spent 2 hours in the library trying to find articles about the Dead Sea Scrolls. I used Ohio Link and tried to find printable articles. There are several articles on the subject, most of them coming from a journal, Biblical Archaeology Review. I couldn't understand the points these articles were making. They were a bit over my head, so I stopped reading after a while. In 1982, an article called "Essene Origins—Palestine or Babylonia" talked about the Dead Sea Scrolls, but it was referring to terms and people that did not seem to concern our project. I don't know who the Essenes are or why the Hellenization of Judaism matters. I think this article was meant for a different type of audience. We might be able to make use of "Is the Vatican Suppressing the Dead Sea Scrolls?" I read more of it and printed it out. It's confusing, but I think it is talking about people's fears that the Dead Sea Scrolls would undermine Christianity and Judaism. It says there were no Jews on the editing team until after about 40 years and that the Vatican limited accessibility to the scrolls to only a few people. The author, Hershel Shanks, says that the scrolls do not challenge anyone's faith and that the Vatican was not trying to cover up anything about its content. It's from 1991.

October 9: I found another journal called Bible Review in our libraries' collection that had article on the Dead Sea Scrolls by James C. Vanderkam. It was from the issue in December 1991/February 1992 and was titled "The Dead Sea Scrolls and Christianity." It mentioned stuff that I could understand, like John the Baptist. I didn't read all the way through it, but it shows what the Dead Sea Scrolls could mean and how some people have misinterpreted them. For example, some people have claimed that Paul and even Jesus were meant when the scrolls referred to a "wicked priest." I think it is saying that the scrolls show us about the culture of early Christianity, but even though I tried, I couldn't finish it. I spent over an hour reading this article, so I didn't look for any more in this journal.

October 11: There was a book in our library called Who Wrote the Dead Sea Scrolls? by Norman Golb. I think it will help us because it gives a lot of background. The book is long, so I only skimmed it. One chapter talked about the same stuff as the article I found from Bible Review. There's a big struggle over who has the right to translate, edit, and interpret the scrolls. There's also a chapter about their discovery, which might help us, but it looks like the author is more interested in ownership of the scrolls, I guess. The more I look into this, the more it seems like historians want to argue over who said what and why their interpretation is better than others. This book has chapters like "The Deepening Scrolls Controversy" and "The New York Conference and Some

Academic Intrigues." I do not think it is really answering its question about the author or how the scrolls fit into Judaic and Christian beliefs. But the good thing is that the book has a glossary of all the important terms. It will make the chapters easier to understand. I just don't think we can read all of the book by our deadline. Maybe we can divide up chapters or something.

October 13: I visited the exhibit in our museum on the scrolls. I should have done this first! It actually had some of the scrolls on display! They had note cards which were written in pretty plain English that explained what the scrolls were supposed to mean and why they are important. I didn't bring a notebook with me, but I think we should go back together. I know I will understand the articles better if we take notes from the display. I think we can see what the real controversy is. One display said that a reference to a dying Messiah in the scrolls would be the first time a pre-Christian text mentions Jesus as Messiah. This is the type of stuff we're looking for. It's really pretty exciting, but I just can't remember everything. We need to go to the display.

Instructor Intervention What are your options if a group member is not contributing? You have three choices: Let that member's irresponsibility drag down the quality of the finished work; do the work and let the person receive credit for doing little or nothing; or arrange for intervention.

In the professional workplace, your employer is not going to accept excuses; a team member who does not carry his or her share has to be dealt with, not ignored. If a faulty product may be distributed to the public, you have to make someone aware. Ultimately, you will have to tell your employer that your group needs a replacement for the person. When raises and promotions are on the line, you want to get due credit. If you have been covering up for somebody, that person will reap the same rewards as you, perhaps even greater ones. Covering up enables the person to continue his or her unproductive ways. Since you have shown the ability to produce a good product while working with the person, you are bound to wind up on that team again, producing an ongoing cycle of unfair workloads. Clearly, you need to go to your manager and explain the unequal labor put into a task. Are these instances of ratting somebody out? Or are they responsible interventions?

The question is when to intervene when a classmate does not perform as required. The longer you wait, the worse the situation will become. To avert more negative consequences, speak to your instructor on the first missed due date or the second instance of sloppy work. Be sure to provide the group secretary's notes, materials from the group website, and relevant progress logs. The intervention should be done during conference time with the instructor in the presence of the less-productive team member, if possible. This allows the instructor to make recommendations to the student or the group, perhaps requiring the student to catch up quickly and turn in the work at the next class period. The instructor might replace the student with another student. Whatever the instructor's decision, group functioning probably will improve.

Asking the instructor to intervene also shows that you have been doing your part of the project. The instructor will likely continue to keep an eye on the group. Most important, intervention sends a message to the irresponsible student that you will not do his or her work and you will not put up with poor production.

While there could be initial social awkwardness if you travel in the same circles as the person, college functions differently from high school. Most college students understand the importance of doing good work and will not chastise a student doing a group project for making sure that everyone shares equally in the task.

COLLABORATING

Each group should select a topic from one of the Group Work sections in Chapters 11 through 16. Construct a plan for completing the project, including due dates and task assignments. Make sure your expectations are realistic and each member's task is clear. Assign a secretary to keep track of the group's meetings. When you have completed your assigned tasks, meet as a group, read each other's work, and discuss what else is needed. If you feel that each member has done his or her duty, follow the suggestions in the following section on synthesizing.

Synthesizing Ideas

Group projects usually involve tasks outside the classroom, such as observations, library research, experiments, data gathering, and analysis. If each member completes his or her task correctly, the group advances to the next step—synthesizing this information. Synthesizing means combining materials and drawing conclusions from the varying ideas presented in the group. For most projects, synthesis involves a written essay. If everyone has maintained a project log, you can start with the research summaries in putting together the first draft.

Some group members think they can just link the various contributions together to create a functional finished piece. This notion is mistaken. Every section must connect to the previous one, providing a smooth flow throughout the report. Group members must work together to ensure that the analysis is critical enough to produce an intriguing thesis, that the audience's needs are understood, that the best possible words have been chosen, and that the organizational strategy works well for the content. A final essay has to go beyond patching together pieces from sections.

However, the first draft should probably start with a rough connection of ideas. The member who has been assigned the task of assembling the first draft (it should be just one person to avoid too much confusion at this early stage) should put the sections together and propose a thesis statement, an introduction, and a conclusion. The initial draft should not go too far beyond this. The group member should email the draft to other members as an attachment or should post it to a website, so that the other group members may read and think about it.

Either electronically or face-to-face, group members must talk to one another, share critiques, and assess how the pieces fit together. Sometimes, even if each member was diligent in his or her research task, you might need more information. Some data and research raise questions that call for more data gathering and research. In the earlier example, Jim realized that the group had to do more than he initially accomplished alone. While we might fault Jim for not recording his visit to the museum appropriately, he intuitively realized that his group would profit by visiting the exhibit together. There's no shame in realizing that you need more information to produce coherence. Other times, you might have to rethink the thesis that the draft writer has produced.

Once you have the draft and one person's attempt at connecting together the sections, you are ready to proceed with real group synthesis. Following are some tips for synthesizing.

Critiquing Peers' Work Nothing is more important at this stage in a group project than being able to talk honestly and openly with one another. If you want a high-quality finished product, you must be willing to criticize group members' work constructively as well as receive criticism about your own contributions.

When you are assembling the parts of a project to give an essay its initial shape, you will see sections that are stronger than others, missing links between sections, and inconsistencies in tone. Often, some sections need more attention than others, which can frustrate the group and hurt the feelings of the individual whose section has been targeted. Cutting examples or sentences can also bruise a writer's ego, especially if these parts are done well but just do not fit the overall theme. Critiquing properly requires showing sensitivity toward others.

Many cooperative strategies will allow you to communicate. Here is one technique. First have everyone critique his or her own section, pointing out at least one strength and one weakness. Then, have each member critique every section in the report or paper, listing at least one strength but focusing on the weak areas and the possibilities for revision. Revision might include reorganizing, analyzing in more depth, adding more information, deleting parts, finding a more logical thesis, or rewriting for stronger language, audience awareness, or correctness. The revisions might extend from individual contributions all the way to the choices the draft writer made in putting the sections together.

This method will let you see the agreements among the group as well as each person's reasoning, and it will let the group reach consensus through the majority's opinions. Some individuals might spot unrealized potential or problem areas that did not occur to other members, but the group can voice its approval or disapproval even if individuals had not thought of these ideas originally.

Revision or editing suggestions do not need to be initially presented by a majority in order for them to be understood and agreed on by the majority when the group reaches consensus. Vote on each suggestion to ensure the participation of all group members. The secretary must keep especially good notes at this time, since two or three group members will implement the actual changes based on the agreements that have been reached.

With this technique or similar cooperative strategies, everyone will have an equal chance to give his or her opinion, and everyone's section will be discussed. Group decisions still might strike some members as adversarial, but this method softens seemingly harsh blows and yields a productive outcome.

Weaving Sections Together The two or three individuals who take responsibility for the revision of the essay should follow the guidelines set by the group. Yet, the group should not assume that they are robots who must merely follow instructions. Although specific suggestions will be made during the group critiques, transitioning from section to section involves initiative on the part of the writers. The analysis must be woven into the text. Each section must show awareness of the previous section, which calls for overlaps among sections as well as the use of transitions. The thesis must be introduced in a strategic area of the text. The only way to make such decisions is to try different approaches and see how they work. While you can implement many of the strategies suggested in previous chapters to make the strongest revision possible, transitioning from sections within a group project might involve some sticky issues. Frequently, the shift from one writer's research to the next disrupts the flow because of repetition or contradictions.

For example, if the topic is endangered species, the group might divide the tasks by having one member find information about specific species in danger of extinction, another find the history of laws designed to protect endangered species, and another look for conflicts between the economy and the survival of species. The first writer will probably uncover information about the grizzly bear and ranchers' complaints that not being allowed to shoot grizzlies who feed on livestock will run them out of business. In dutifully reporting this, the first writer has strayed into the territory of the other two, since the laws protecting grizzlies are the source of the ranchers' concerns about economic survival. Thus, the best of transitions will not link the two parts. Instead, the information has to be organized. You might choose to report on one animal at a time, including the information about laws and economics as they apply directly to that animal, or to separate the information into sections of general information (statistics about species size, descriptions, history), the laws (including specifics related to each animal), and the various economic effects. You will need to dissect information, placing some parts of a contributor's information here, other parts there.

When pieces of research contradict one another, you must account for these differences as well. Conflicts often emerge when one group member does library research and another does web-based research. In such cases, the revision writers must make decisions about the most reliable sources while still mentioning the other sources. For example, a revision about conflicting reports of bear attacks on cattle might read, "While online websites by ranchers paint a dire picture of their future cohabitating with grizzlies, current research by naturalists indicates that the financial losses caused by marauding bears are exaggerated." You would also have to document the sources.

Thus, weaving sections together involves much more than carrying out the instructions of the group. The revision writers play a key role in the success of the final paper or report.

TERRY MCCARTHY

Nowhere to Roam

In the following excerpt from "Nowhere to Roam," Terry McCarthy uses information from at least three different sources. Notice how he reports differences of opinion on the crucial issue of trophy hunting.

A Role for Trophy Hunting?

The Selous Game Reserve in Southeast Tanzania is the largest in Africa. Established in 1905 and stretching over 21,000 sq. mi., it is bigger than Switzerland and chock-full of wildlife: 4,000 lions, 110,000 buffalo, 50,000 elephants. But because it is hard to access, covered with dense scrub and lacking in the spectacular vistas found in the Serengeti to the north, it draws fewer than 5,000 visitors annually—less than 1% of tourists who visit Tanzania. To pay for the upkeep of the Selous and for antipoaching patrols over its vast area, the reserve's managers rely on another source of funding: big-game hunters. In Tanzania, hunters will pay up to $80,000 to shoot a lion. In 2002, 226 trophy lions were shot in Tanzania, many in the Selous reserve.

Conservationists used to choke on the topic of hunting, but increasingly they are prepared to accept some limited and tightly controlled hunts when they generate revenue for locals who might otherwise kill off the predators. "It seems counterintuitive that killing animals can be good for conservation," says Frank. "But trophy hunting is extremely lucrative, and in order to produce a few trophy males, it is a necessity to preserve vast ecosystems."

Lion hunting also provides revenue in Zambia, Zimbabwe and South Africa, though Kenya banned the practice in 1975. Most countries operate on a quota system. They estimate the lion population and set a sustainable quota for hunting. A study published this year by wildlife experts at the University of Minnesota has raised new interest in trophy hunting. Based on 40 years of data from northern Tanzania, the study showed that if hunters confined themselves to shooting male lions at least 5 years old, after they have bred and their cubs have matured, there's no noticeable long-term effect on the overall population. Researchers attribute this to the fact that male lions, while necessary for reproduction, do little to help raise their cubs. (Indeed, males typically kill the youngest cubs when they take over a pride.) Mature males also happen to be what trophy hunters prize, since a male's mane reaches its full glory after age 4. Lions 5 years or older can be identified by their noses, which are at least 50% black. Already the Tanzanian Wildlife Division and some professional hunters are advising clients to take aim at the older lions.

Still, many conservationists remain wary of trophy hunting in any shape or form. It works only with strict enforcement, says ecologist Craig Packer, who led the Minnesota study. "The temptation is to raise quotas to unsustainable levels because of the profit motive."

Stabilizing the Voice With so many different writers of project sections, prose styles and tones throughout your report or paper might conflict. Therefore, when the two or three revision writers present the revision to the larger group, one of your main functions will be to stabilize the voice in the paper.

Some areas are obvious. The group should not be referring to *I* or *me* in the paper. Sometimes, the use of *we* is inappropriate, such as in a personal experience used as an introduction or as an example. In cases like this, you should refer to the writer in the third person or introduce the experience with a phrase similar to this one: "One of our group members, Alan, reports on a personal encounter with an animal from an endangered species that adds support to our thesis. In Alan's words: . . ." You would then shift to a different font or block off the section to insert Alan's narrative. You could also continue with third-person reporting if it does not harm the flow of the narrative.

Some areas are not as obvious. All of us use expressions that are particular to ourselves. As discussed in Chapter 5, these expressions help establish our narrative voice. In a group project, however, the different voices might collide. Individuality must be assimilated into a group voice. Thus, the person responsible for the final proofreading and editing should eliminate places where such expressions give the impression that two different writers are speaking. The person should also make sure the diction is consistent throughout the essay. He or she will want to "revise upward" so that all sections match the best section in terms of vocabulary. As always, the person should make sure to avoid misusing words. Finally, combinations of sentences can reveal distinct styles and might give the sense of too many voices in a paper or report. Going through the sections to make sure all paragraphs use a variety of sentence lengths should solve such problems. Final editing and proofreading will not differ much from the editing and proofreading individuals do on a paper, but group work does demand stabilizing the voice.

RICHARD CORLISS AND MICHAEL D. LEMONICK

How to Live to Be 100

New research suggests that a long life is no accident. So what are the secrets of the world's centenarians?

Not only is this article cowritten, but it also had to smoothly incorporate information reported by seven contributors. How did authors Richard Corliss and Michael D. Lemonick achieve a stable voice?

Margaret Dell is 96, but you'd need to check the birth date on her driver's license to believe it. Sporting a baseball cap with a Harley-Davidson logo on it, she is the designated driver for her seventysomething friends who no longer feel comfortable behind the wheel. Last winter a snowfall threatened to keep her from her appointed automotive rounds. She took a shovel and cleared a path to her car. Driving keeps Dell young. That and knitting. She constantly knits. She makes baby booties and caps and blankets for friends and family whenever a baby arrives—the newborn getting an early blessing from the ageless. And every month, she donates several blankets to a charity for unwed mothers. Driving, knitting . . . and tennis. She plays two or three times a week. She has a much younger doubles partner who "covers the court. I'm a little afraid to run too much because of the circulation in my legs," she explains. When she was in her 80s, she played in a doubles tournament that required that the ages of both partners add up to at least 100. Her partner was in his early 20s; they won the tournament.

A lifetime nonsmoker and nondrinker, Dell lives alone in a two-story house in Bethesda, Md., her bedroom on the second floor. "I could stay on the first floor, but I try to make myself walk up those stairs and keep going that way." She buys her own groceries; don't even ask if you can shop for her. At home she likes a chicken or turkey sandwich for lunch. If she eats at the country club after tennis, she usually finishes only half and saves the rest for dinner. (The doggie bag is the senior citizen's medical-supply kit.)

Driving, tennis, knitting . . . and eating chocolates. She keeps them in a drawer by her easy chair. "I am very bad about those Hershey Kisses," she confesses. "And I love those little Dove ice cream things. I take one before I go to bed." That's the only medication Dell will take without a fight. She's no fan of doctors. Some years back, she took a fall, and her doctor prescribed an MRI. "I just refused to go," she says. "They were having a party. It was my 90th birthday." And the party girl left his office. Fortunately, nothing was broken. But Dell knew that.

More than what she knows, it's how she glows that impresses people. "She has a light in her eyes that is very alive, alert and interested," says Carole Dell. "It radiates over her whole face. Her face is kind of timeless. It's deeply lined, but she's actually beautiful." Spoken like a proud daughter-in-law with 96 reasons to be proud. Ninety-six and counting.

5 How does science explain someone like Margaret Dell? How can a woman closing in on the start of her second century be so robustly, almost defiantly, healthy, while men and women decades younger are languishing feebly in nursing homes, plagued with failing bodies and failing minds and wishing they hadn't been so unlucky as to live so long?

For most of human history, a long and healthy life has been shrugged off as a gift from the gods—or maybe the undeserved reward for a lifetime of plain cussedness. But to gerontologists, the vagaries of aging have become the focus of intense scientific research.

Scientists are as obsessed with the question of why the superold survive and thrive as Ponce de León was to find the Fountain of Youth. They want to understand why the Japanese islands of Okinawa are home to the world's largest population of centenarians, with almost 600 of its 1.3 million inhabitants living into their second century—many of them active and looking decades younger than their actual years. Like weekend visitors on the summer ferry to Martha's Vineyard, scientists and sociologists clog the boats to Sardinia and Nova Scotia, Canada, to see why those craggy locales harbor outsize clusters of the superold. (Gerontologists are not so beguiled by the Russian Caucasus, where exaggerated longevity claims sparked a series of Dannon yogurt commercials 30 years ago.)

As well as studying these populations intensively to unlock their secrets, scientists have also taken a hard look at the very old in the U.S., most notably in the New England Centenarian Study, led by Dr. Thomas Perls, a geriatrician at Boston University, and in a major study under way at the National Institute on Aging. While the very old are happy to offer homespun explanations for their longevity—"I never took a drink"; "I drank a shot of whiskey every day"—experts are trying to unravel and understand the biological factors that allow some people to reach 100 while others drop off in their 70s or 80s. Researchers are particularly interested in determining which factors allow up to 30% of those who reach 100 to do so in sufficient mental and physical health: a whopping 90% of centenarians, according to Perls, remain functionally independent up to age 92. "It's not 'the older you get, the sicker you get,' but 'the older you get, the healthier you've been,'" he says. "The advantage of living to 100 is not so much how you are at 100 but how you got there."

It's pretty obvious even to nonscientists that how you get there depends partly on the genes you are born with and partly on lifestyle—what and how much you eat, where you live and what types of stress and trauma you experience. How much depends on each factor, though, was unknown until Swedish scientists tackled the problem in 1998. They did it by looking at the only set of people who share genes but not lifestyle: identical twins who were separated at birth and reared apart. If genes were most important, you would expect the twins to die at about the same age. In fact, they don't, and the average difference convinced the scientists that only about 20% to 30% of how long we live is genetically determined. The dominant factor is lifestyle.

"You could have Mercedes-Benz genes," says Dr. Bradley Willcox, of the 10
Pacific Health Research Institute in Honolulu, "but if you never change the oil, you are not going to last as long as a Ford Escort that you take good care of. Those who have healthier genes and live healthier lives—those guys really survive for a long time."

Studies of Seventh-Day Adventists in Utah support this finding. Those unusually clean-living Americans are genetically diverse, but they avoid alcohol, caffeine and tobacco—and they tend to live an average of eight years longer than their countrymen. All of this is good news, with a Surgeon General's warning attached: you can't change your genes, but you can change what you eat and how much you exercise. "The lesson is pretty clear from my point of view in terms of what the average person should be doing," says Perls.

"I strongly believe that with some changes in health-related behavior, each of us can earn the right to have at least 25 years beyond the age of 60—years of healthy life at good function. The disappointing news is that it requires work and willpower."

At least that's true for many Americans, whose fat- and calorie-packed diets and largely exercise-free lives are a prescription for heart disease and plenty of other ills. For Okinawans, by contrast, the traditional way of life seems tailor-made for living forever—one day at a time.

Each day, Seiryu Toguchi, 103, of Motobu, Okinawa, wakes at 6 a.m., in the house in which he was born, and opens the shutters. "It's a sign to my neighbors," he says, "that I am still alive." He does stretching exercises along with a radio broadcast, then eats breakfast: whole-grain rice and miso soup with vegetables. He puts in two hours of picking weeds in his 1,000-sq.-ft. field, whose crops are goya—a variety of bitter gourd—a reddish-purple sweet potato called imo, and okra. A fellow has to make a living, so Toguchi buys rice and meat with the profits from his produce.

Since his wife Kame's death seven years ago, at 93, he has done all the housework himself. He rejected his children's suggestion to come live with them because, he explains, "I enjoy my freedom." Although his doctors insist Toguchi is in excellent health, the farmer takes no chances. "If he feels that something is wrong," says his daughter Sumiko Sakihara, 74, "even in the middle of the night, he calls a taxi and goes to the hospital." But he doesn't want the other villagers to worry, so, she says, "he writes a note explaining where he is and tapes it to the shutters."

15 At 12:30 Toguchi eats lunch: goya stir-fry with egg and tofu. He naps for an hour or so, then spends two more hours in his field. After dinner he plays traditional songs—a favorite is *Spring When I Was 19*—on the three-stringed *sanshin* and makes an entry in his diary, as he has every night for the past decade. "This way," he says, "I won't forget my Chinese characters. It's fun. It keeps my mind sharp." For a nightcap he may have a sip of the wine he makes from aloe, garlic and tumeric. And as he drifts off, he says, "my head is filled with all the things I want to do tomorrow."

Scientists working for the U.S. National Institutes of Health and Japan's Ministry of Health have been following oldsters like Toguchi since 1976 in the Okinawa Centenarian Study (OCS) and they've learned that he's typical. Elderly Okinawans tend to get plenty of physical and mental exercise. Their diets, moreover, are exemplary: low in fat and salt, and high in fruits and vegetables packed with fiber and antioxidant substances that protect against cancer, heart disease and stroke. They consume more soy than any other population on earth: 60–120 g a day, compared to 30–50 g for the average Japanese, 10 for Chinese and virtually 0 g for the average American. Soy is rich in flavonoids—antioxidants strongly linked to low rates of cancer. This may be one of many reasons why the annual death rate from cancer in Okinawa is far below the U.S. rate.

But it's not just what Okinawans eat; it's how much. They practice a dietary philosophy known as *hara hachi bu*—literally, eight parts out of 10 full.

Translation: they eat only to the point at which they are about 80% sated. That makes for a daily intake of no more than 1,800 calories, compared to the more than 2,500 that the average American man scarfs down. And as scientists have learned from lab animals, the simple act of calorie restriction can have significant effects on longevity.

Aging Okinawans also have a much lower incidence of dementia—Alzheimer's or other forms of senility—than their U.S. and European counterparts do. Part of that may also owe to diet; it's high in vitamin E, which seems to protect the brain. But perhaps just as important is a sense of belonging and purpose that provides a strong foundation for staying mentally alert well into old age. Okinawans maintain a sense of community, ensuring that every member, from youngest to oldest, is paid proper respect and feels equally valued. Elderly women, for example, are considered the sacred keepers of a family's bond with the ancestors, maintaining the family altars and responsible for organizing festivals to honor them. OCS data show that elderly Okinawans express a high level of satisfaction with life, something that is not as true in Western societies, where rates of suicide and depression are high among the elderly.

Need convincing evidence that our modern lifestyle can shorten lives? Look what happens when Okinawans move permanently off the island. They pick up the diet and cultural behaviors of their adopted country—and within a generation, their life-spans decrease and their rates of cancer and heart attack zoom. Even on the island, young males are following the seductive, virulent American style and renouncing imo for hamburgers. "Okinawan male life expectancy used to be No. 1 in Japan," says Dr. Makoto Suzuki, leader of the study of Okinawan elders. "It started to decline 10 years ago and hit 26th out of 47 prefectures in the 2000 census. I expect it to decline even further in the next census."

20 Oldsters in Sardinia, another wellspring of longevity, have many similarities to their Okinawan counterparts—except that the Sardinian ratio of centenarians is about equal for men and women (in most societies, 100-plus females outnumber males by 3 or 4 to 1). They maintain very active lives and powerful social networks; extended family and friends are available to share troubles and take some of the emotional burden out of life. Says researcher Gianni Pes, part of a team from Sardinia's University of Sassari, which is studying the group: "The 100-year-olds are less depressed than average 60-year-olds."

That makes perfect sense to Leonard Poon, director of the University of Georgia Gerontology Center. Since 1988 he has studied American centenarians—he calls them "expert survivors"—and compared them to people in their 80s ("master survivors") and to relative youngsters in their 60s. Poon found that out of 16 personality traits, the experts exhibited four coping mechanisms. First, he says, "centenarians are more dominant. They want to have their way," and they are not easily pushed around. Many are characterized by "suspiciousness. They do not take information on the superficial level" but will question an issue and think it through. They tend to be practical rather than idealistic. And in their approach to life, they are likely to be more relaxed. In other words, they are strong but not inflexible characters.

Poon also determined that people whose age reaches three figures tend to have a high level of cognition, demonstrating skill in everyday problem solving and learning. That's another reason exercise is important: to keep plenty of blood flowing to the brain as well as to stay in shape. Many of his subjects aren't rich; some of them have homes with mud floors. But they make good out of making do. "Many have their own gardens," he notes. "They can their own vegetables. They're living down to earth."

Like the Okinawans, Sardinians and Nova Scotians, the U.S. centenarians enjoy a strong social-support system. Few Americans live in a village anymore, but having outlived family and friends of the same age, the super-old find new helpers and confidants among people younger by a generation or more. It might be someone to help with groceries or car trips or simply a sympathetic voice on the other end of the line. Maintaining a connection with the world, with younger people, keeps their outlook youthful.

With so much evidence that lifestyle is the key to healthy aging, it might be tempting to ignore the role of genes altogether. That would be a mistake. Brothers of centenarians are 17 times as likely to live to 100 as are people without 100-year-olds in the family, while sisters of centenarians are 8.5 times as likely to live into their second century. Given statistics like that, says Winifred Rossi, director of the National Institute on Aging's study on exceptional survival, "we are interested in looking for some kind of genetic component to longevity." Her approach is to look at family members, especially the children, of centenarians. Says Perls, who does similar research: "Kids of centenarians who are in their 70s and early 80s are very much following in the footsteps of their parents, with a 60% reduced risk of heart disease, stroke and diabetes. They are the model for successful aging and a great group to study."

25 Indeed, despite what the Swedish and Adventist studies suggest, there's evidence that in some families, at least, genes exert pretty powerful effects on life-span. The centenarians registered in the New England Centenarian Study, for example, showed no consistent patterns in diet, exercise or healthy habits that could explain their extended years. About 20% had smoked at some point in their lives, and some had eating habits that should have made them obese or unhealthy but somehow did not. At least 10% to 15% had a history of heart disease, stroke or diabetes for more than 20 years. Something in that group's genes was protecting them from succumbing to diseases that had felled the average American decades earlier. "These people still get to 100," says Perls. "They seem to have a functional reserve or adaptive capacity that allows them to get disease but not necessarily suffer from it. The key seems to be resilience."

Some of that resilience may be linked to human leukocyte antigen (HLA) genes, a group clustered on chromosome 6 that affects vulnerability to such autoimmune diseases as lupus, rheumatoid arthritis and multiple sclerosis. Centenarians living in Okinawa, for example, have variants of HLA that tend to protect against those diseases. Perls has found a region on chromosome 4 that centenarians and their siblings and children in the U.S. seem to have in common and that sets them apart from shorter-lived individuals. The finding has not yet been replicated by other groups, but Perls expects to publish a paper in the next month detailing his results.

What exactly that stretch of DNA does remains to be discovered, but it may be a key not just to long life but also to the resilience found among U.S. centenarian-study participants, with their 20% smoking rate and imperfect eating habits. That group may be especially genetically blessed, and researchers are eager to tap its secrets.

We certainly need them. For as medical science adds years to our collective lives, we chip away at them by doing things—stewing at our desk jobs, eating fatty processed foods, blowing a gasket in a freeway traffic jam, exercising no more than our fingers at the computer—that centenarians can't imagine. Most of them were born into an America as remote from today's metaphorically as the craggy villages of Sardinia, Okinawa and Nova Scotia are geographically. In the early 1900s people walked miles to work not by choice but out of necessity; cars were still a luxury. People tilled the fields because their farmer parents needed cheap help. People ate what they grew because it was there. Most labor was manual then, and most nutrients were natural. Preserved food was what Aunt Maud sealed in a jar. Tobacco and alcohol were available, but most of today's centenarians didn't indulge to excess.

They trigger our awe and our nostalgia as representatives of a flinty, hardscrabble culture that hardly exists today. They lived out a parable of man at one with nature. They used their bodies as they were designed and programmed over the millennia: for walking, for working, for being fed from the earth's natural bounty. It makes one wonder whether the next generation of oldsters will last quite as long. They will need not just the luck of the genetic draw but also the strength to renounce the lure of fast-food days and couch-potato nights that add yards of butt lard and shorten life-spans by years.

Will Americans in the supersize age resolve to go medieval on their own 30
bodies? It would help, if they want to live to 100. As Poon says of his research pools, "I don't have any fat centenarians." And if research really does extend life by a vigorous couple of decades, the new millions of centenarians will need a support system that spreads beyond family and friends to include a hugely expensive Social Security and Medicare apparatus. The coming gerontocracy won't come cheap.

But that's for the future. Any child of today who hopes to live into the 22nd century without the aid of medical miracles should look to the past, and consider the lessons today's centenarians took from the 19th century. There's a poetry of common sense in their scheme for immortality. Eat sensibly. Keep walking. Keep knitting. If you can't keep friends, make new ones. Plan so much invigorating work that there's just no time to die. And no regret when you do. ***—Reported by Alice Park/New York; Melissa August/Washington; Anne Berryman/Athens, Georgia; Hanna Kite/Okinawa; Chris Lambie/Halifax; Jeff Israely/Sardinia; and Francis X. Rocca/Rome***

COLLABORATING

To practice this type of synthesis, group members should agree on an episode of a television series, a movie, a concert, or an event that they all saw and write about it. One person should write about the beginning; the middle can be divided up among two or three members; and one person can write what happened at the end. After finishing these pieces, the group's job is to put it together as a coherent piece of writing. Go through all the steps in "Synthesizing Ideas," but do the synthesizing, weaving, and checking for voice as a group. Make note of the parts of the process that cause difficulties for your group. Also observe which members seem to be best suited for the various tasks.

Taking Responsibility

Groups function most efficiently when every member takes individual responsibility for the project's success. This is easier said than done. As an individual, you can monitor yourself, but what about the others? Who ensures that they take the proper responsibility? As pointed out earlier in this chapter, groups must take action when a member does not fulfill his or her commitment to the group.

Sometimes a problem emerges gradually. A member's work deteriorates as the project goes on. Perhaps a person suffers an illness that sets him or her back a week. Maybe the member breaks up with a boyfriend or girlfriend, or homework for another course takes up more time than a person expected. Enthusiasm for a project can wane as well. The group cannot readily replace somebody late in the project, and it is possible that the final product will be affected.

If each person takes responsibility for failure to meet deadlines or to produce satisfactory work, others will find it easier to pitch in. Humans tend to dislike excuses. However, they respond to admissions of neglect and to the willingness to suffer consequences. There are two ways for a group to rescue itself when problems arise late in the project. Both hinge on individual group members acknowledging their failure to do their share of the work.

Individual Evaluations While you are functioning as a team, individual efforts must not be forgotten. When you submit your final paper or report, each group member should write to the instructor about his or her contribution to the project. Do not share the letters with other group members. If you have fulfilled your responsibility for all tasks assigned to you, you should be able to list them in specific terms and explain how well you did them. You should indicate which tasks you performed alone, which ones you did with one or two other group members, and which ones were a whole-group effort.

Take credit only for what you did. If two people take credit for the same task, or if one person fails to acknowledge a partner in a collaborative task, the contradictions will alert your instructor to problems. These letters should serve as a time for honesty and reflection.

Teamwork A group must make every effort to produce the best essay possible, even when one or two individuals fade at the end. Sometimes swapping duties will help. In a recent collaborative project, the lead writer of our group produced a functional first draft of an article with the help of one other co-writer. The lead writer wanted me to look at structure and tone, but I was too busy at the time. I asked another writer to step in and look at the structure and agreed to contribute more heavily during the revision and final polishing of the paper. She reviewed the structure, and I performed the majority of the duties later on. No one complained, since everyone did his or her share.

As long as people are capable of doing the task at hand, there is nothing wrong with veering from the plan and trading with somebody else. The key is to take responsibility and to tell the group what you haven't done or what you will not be able to do. If you delay in alerting the group, the essay will be affected. If you miss a meeting or give feeble excuses for failing to turn in materials, your group is likely to be disgusted. But people pitch in when they realize that one person cannot carry his or her load, as long as the person concedes the point and accepts the consequences.

Being a team member is much like being an understudy in a play. The understudy is responsible for taking the lead role in some performances (matinees, for instance) and for filling in when the lead actor is unable to act. The performance could be in jeopardy if the lead actor does not inform anyone in advance and just fails to show up or shows up with a litany of excuses about why he or she cannot go on that night. Disaster would also ensue if the understudy had not learned the lines. Strong teamwork does not necessarily demand equal production or the same quality from each person, but it does rely on individual responsibility.

DISCUSSION

Should the evaluations discussed in this section involve a critique of other group members' contributions? To what extent? Can you talk about what you did or did not do without comparing it or placing it in the context of the work done around you? Discuss ways you can write about the collaborative process without blaming group members for not fulfilling their responsibilities.

Summary

Most writing projects for business or community action involve the contributions of others. Therefore, writers need to practice collaborating with groups in the classroom. However, many students have had negative experiences in groups, with one member doing all the work or with the contribution of one member diminishing the overall quality of the project.

To avoid conflict and develop collaborative skills, students must understand behaviors that help and hinder effective group work. Taking classroom activities, such as peer response groups, outside of the classroom is one way to practice collaboration.

When an instructor assigns groups to collaborate on a writing project, group members must establish deadlines for each stage of the project, keep records, and hand out tasks according to ability. At each stage, group members must provide a complete written record of their individual work. Keeping a progress log ensures consistent recording of each member's work. If a member does not meet early deadlines, the group must ask for instructor intervention so that the member's lack of work does not snowball into an incomplete or poor final essay.

Even when individuals have done good jobs on their individual tasks, the group must make sure that the final essay is more than just strung-together individual sections. Drafting, revising, and editing must all be attended to by group members working separately and together. Individuals must be held accountable for their inability to fulfill their responsibilities as well as being given credit for success.

CHAPTER 8

PURPOSES AND STRATEGIES FOR READING

To develop a process and collaborate effectively, writers must move outside their immediate experience and learn about the world around them. While direct observation yields many insights, reading the ideas of others, especially ideas supported by research and facts, can stimulate you when you hit a writing block and can ensure the credibility of a group project. Yet, some students are reluctant to read materials that appear at first to be daunting.

Recently, a student named Ben complained to me about an assigned reading, "Executive Pay in the U.S." by Jack Rasmus. The assignment, one the students had helped me create, involved investigating the careers they hoped to enter upon graduation. I found the article to be extremely relevant; the statistics cited in it would have bearing on the students' futures. Ben could not make sense of the article, saying that he did not understand the references to the Enron scandal, earned income, and SERPS. He also felt overwhelmed by the sheer number of statistics given.

I recited the tired lines used by many professors: "When you have trouble understanding a passage, you should make a note in the margin and come to class prepared to ask questions about it. You can't just give up on the reading."

"But who wants to read this stuff anyway?" Ben asked.

Writing instructors often fail to realize that everyone does not enjoy reading as much as they do. Instructors see reading as a vital step in obtaining knowledge and heightening critical thinking skills as well as a source of entertainment and pleasure. They believe that people miss out on a lot of life

This icon will direct you to web links and additional resources on the website college.hmco.com/pic/thelin1e

if they do not exercise their reading skills. They can become defensive, too, and say things they perhaps shouldn't, as I did.

"What's the difference between a person who can't read and a person who doesn't read?" I asked.

Ben took up my challenge. "Newspapers are written so that a seventh grader can understand them," he observed. "Why do we have to do more than that for this class?"

"Because we're several years removed from seventh grade, aren't we?" I responded. "Do you want to remain at a seventh grade educational level for the rest of your life?" Most professors would probably respond to Ben the way I did, and even students would have to admit, albeit grudgingly, that I had a point. But as they were to teach me that day, Ben's question resounded with validity. Couldn't complex ideas be captured in plain language?

Moira was the next student to speak up. "Just because I don't like to read books doesn't mean I don't read," she said. "I read instant messages, signs, advertisements, gaming instructions, and all sorts of labels every day."

"Okay," I granted. "But don't you think more exposure to reading will make you better able to understand subtle parts of advertisements? Some instructions for gaming are complicated. Practice in reading difficult material beyond the seventh grade level will help you understand, right?"

Ben had given up on me, collapsing into his seat with a sigh of frustration. This was Moira's battle now. "Instructions usually come with diagrams. I can always ask someone if I don't understand some washing instruction on a label. And I can see through ads. I know they try to manipulate us. There's always something visual that goes with reading that helps me understand. That's how I comprehend all sorts of complicated stuff."

Moira was making sense, so I had to think for a second. "Aren't you doing a type of reading when you look at pictures and charts and everything? We talk about trying to read somebody, like in a poker game when you're trying to read somebody's face to see if they are bluffing."

"Yeah, I guess so," Moira said. "So reading is a way of interpreting and understanding something, right?"

I agreed.

"Then good writing should be easy to interpret and understand."

Some students clapped in approval. "Not necessarily," I said.

"Hold on a second," a student named Jasmine piped up. "There's different types of movies you like that require thinking. I wouldn't want every movie I see to be Disney or something like that. I want to be challenged sometimes. My feelings aren't simple. For a movie or a song or anything to get me to feel, it has to match my complexity. Same thing for writing, I suppose."

Jasmine's insight led the class to a rich discussion about the many kinds of reading we do. Students were able to see that more difficult reading might have a purpose—not as practice for the future, but as a way to evoke complicated feelings and ideas within us.

JACK RASMUS

Executive Pay in the U.S.

CEOs still take the money and run

Here is an excerpt from the article I assigned. Do you think the reading is too difficult? Does it appropriately match the complexity of the subject matter?

The most fundamental and singular result of corporate policies of the past 25 years has been a massive shift in relative income from the roughly 105 million workers to the wealthiest 10 percent of non-working class households in the U.S. This enormous income transfer grew in scope and magnitude annually throughout the 1980s and Reagan years, continued to expand steadily during the Clinton years, accelerated during the first term of George W. Bush, and now promises to exceed more than $1 trillion per year during the rest of Bush's second term.

Few groups within the ranks of the U.S. corporate elite have gained more from this historic income shift than the CEOs and senior managers of corporate America. In 1978, according to the *Wall Street Journal,* typical U.S. CEOs earned approximately 35 times the pay of the average paid worker in their company. In recent years CEO total compensation has risen to more than 500 times the average worker's pay, according to the conservative global business source, Reuters.

Defining Executive Pay

The typical worker in the U.S. receives about 90 percent of their earned income from their paycheck whether earned as an hourly wage or weekly salary. Not so for the typical CEO and senior manager. Historically only 7–10 percent of their income is earned from a salary as such. Focusing only on CEO salaries, therefore, totally misses the point and statistics quoting CEO salaries as the sole indication of executive pay levels should be especially suspect. At times the term "direct compensation" is used as an alternative measurement of executive pay. But that too underestimates such pay, as it excludes hidden indirect forms of compensation.

A slightly better term is "total compensation." It includes direct and indirect forms of executive pay. CEO total compensation may include salaries, bonuses (cash or other forms), stock options, stock grants and awards, long term incentive pay, deferred pay of various kinds, regular and supplemental management pensions, below market rate mortgage loans to managers by the company, write offs of personal loans by corporate boards, innumerable forms of perks with direct dollar value, prepaid charitable donations, lifetime use of corporate jets, company payment of CEO tax obligations (called "gross up" compensation), and so on in a long list of forms of creative and hidden pay. These and other non-salary forms of executive pay account for 90 percent or more of CEO and senior managers' total compensation.

5 But even "total compensation" is an inadequate indicator of executive pay. With hearings on executive pay by the U.S. Securities and Exchange Commission (SEC) to begin this spring, it is clear that many other forms of executive compensation remain hidden by opaque corporate accounting and reporting practices, are not counted as part of "total compensation," and are never communicated to the IRS.

During the Reagan years average CEO pay rose from just over $1 million a year to roughly $2.5 million by 1989. By 1992, at the close of the George Bush senior administration, it nearly doubled again to $4.5 million—despite the recession of 1990–91 and falling corporate profit performance. It more than doubled again under Clinton to $11.1 million by 2000, for a 342 percent gain over two decades. Some estimates placed the pay of the average U.S. CEO as high as $14.4 million by 2001.

According to a just released study by professors Lucian Bebchuk of Harvard Law School and Yaniv Grinstein of Cornell University, based on interviews of CEOs and top managers at the 1,500 largest publicly traded corporations in the U.S., the group of 5 top managers at the corporations received collectively $122 billion in compensation between 1999–2003 compared to $68 billion for the same group during 1993–1997. On top of these 1999–2003 gains, the Harvard–Cornell study estimates another 39 percent increase in average executive compensation in 2004 for the surveyed group of the largest corporations.

But even the Harvard–Cornell figures are underestimations as they exclude the lucrative and fast-growing supplemental pensions for executives, called Supplemental Executive Retirement Plans (SERPS). Some sources estimate SERPs constitute as much as an additional one-third of total executive compensation. Were SERPS and other supplemental retirement plans included in the Harvard–Cornell study estimates, the nearly doubling of executive pay that was estimated between 1999–2003 would have been even higher.

As corporations over the past decade have been busy reducing pension benefits for workers, under-funding and even abandoning their pension plans for workers, SERPs were being added across the board by corporations in the U.S. Changes in the tax laws in 1994 provided a strong incentive for creating SERPs for senior executives as a way to shelter more of their total compensation from taxation. Less than half of senior executives had supplemental pension plans prior to 1995; today more than 90 percent have such plans. Thus billions more have been squirreled away for CEOs and senior managers of the largest public companies over the past decade.

10 For CEOs of the largest corporations that means at least another $60 billion in addition to the $122 billion of the Harvard–Cornell study. But that additional $60 billion still does not include the rest of the 90 percent of corporations—apart from the 1,522 surveyed by Harvard–Cornell—that have also established SERPs today for CEOs and senior managers.

One of the great scandals at Enron when it went bankrupt was that Enron executives froze workers' pensions and did not allow them to take their money out as the company began to default, while those same executives were cashing out their pensions in a separate, supplemental management pension plan.

Other measures of growth in executive compensation corroborate the above trends and figures for executive pay. The non-partisan research group the Corporate Library recently surveyed "median" as opposed to average CEO pay. It estimated that median CEO compensation for 2003 rose 15 percent in 2003, followed by another increase in median executive compensation of 30 percent in 2004. No doubt results for 2005 will show a continuing accelerating trend.

Trading Jobs for Executive Pay

CEOs who have been doing especially well under George W. Bush are those companies that have been involved in aggressive offshoring of jobs. Approximately eight million quality, high paying jobs have been lost due to "free" trade policies and offshoring since the 1980s and the number continues to rise rapidly. Free trade policies and offshoring reflect the radical restructuring of trade relations and foreign direct investment strategies implemented by corporate America since Ronald Reagan. More than a million jobs have been lost due to NAFTA in the last decade alone and another 2.5 million have resulted from the granting of special terms of trade with China in 2000.

For dismantling of a good part of the U.S. manufacturing base, CEOs and senior managers of U.S. corporations involved in offshoring of jobs have been generously compensated compared to their already well-paid corporate peers. For example, a *Business Week* survey in 2003 of CEOs at the 50 largest U.S. companies that outsource the most showed that their CEOs enjoyed an average increase in compensation of 46 percent between 2001–03, earning as a group a reported $2.2 billion while sending an estimated 200,000 jobs offshore.

CEOs and managers are now compensated at record levels, not for their 15
contribution to the corporate bottom line anymore, but for selling off the company, for leaving quietly, or for gross performance failure. Thus Carly Fiorina, ex-CEO of Hewlett-Packard, departed last year with a package of more than $40 million. David Pottruck of Schwab left with around $50 million, and Craig Conway of Peoplesoft exited with a total package of more than $60 million. Among the biggest winners of CEO departees, however, were Phillip Purcell of the investment bank, Morgan Stanley, who left with a reported $113 million, and James Kilts of Gillette who walked out the corporate door with $165 million. Even more amazing was Steven Crawford, recent co-president of Morgan Stanley, who left after only three months of employment with $32 million—or a rate of pay of more than $10 million a month. Crawford's gain was more than matched in terms of the bizarre, though, by Daniel Carp, still CEO of Blockbuster Video Corp., who in 2004 received more than $50 million in compensation even though the company recorded a loss of $1.25 billion that year.

Comparing Pay

As previously noted, executive pay between 1980 and 2000 climbed an astounding 342 percent, outpacing the rate of inflation over the period by at least 4 to 1. In contrast, the average hourly wage for more than 100 million workers, when measured in 2003 dollars, rose from $14.86 at the start of 1980 to only $14.95 at the end of 2000. That's a 9 cents an hour gain after 20 years.

Furthermore, the average hourly wage today for 105 million workers after adjustment for inflation is exactly the same at year end 2005 as it was in 2001, according to the U.S. Department of Labor's statistics. In 2004–2005 it has fallen steadily as inflation has begun to accelerate. For the 60 million at the medium wage level or below, inflation the past two years has been rising at twice the rate of their hourly wage.

To compensate for stagnant and declining real hourly wages and earnings, U.S. workers have had to resort to alternative means to try to maintain income levels and spending. These alternatives to wage gains fall into three categories.

First, more U.S. families have been having other family members enter the workforce to supplement family incomes and/or have had to take on second part time jobs in addition to their normal job. U.S. families have increased the number of hours worked by more than 500 a year since 1980. Americans now work by far the greatest number of hours per year than workers in any of the other industrialized countries—approximately 1,970 hours each per year out of 2,040, based on a normal 40 hour work week. The next closest is Canada where workers average about 1,800 hours. Workers in industrialized economies of Europe average fewer hours worked, 1,600–1,800 hours per year.

Second, they have had to take on record levels of consumer and installment debt, levels that have doubled from $4 trillion to more than $9 trillion since Bush II took office.

Third, workers fortunate enough to own their homes have been refinancing those homes and using the proceeds as discretionary income to pay for major purchases such as medical expenses, education, and large ticket items—in effect living off their assets.

All three solutions to the stagnation and decline of real wages over the past quarter century, however, have their finite limits and cannot continue long term as safety valve alternatives to declining real wages, earnings, and incomes for the 105 million.

Ben, Moira, and Jasmine argued that reading is the understanding of a complex system of signs and that literacy is our determination of a person's ability to decode that system of signs. But reading and literacy encompass many complementary and competing elements.

Trailblazers, longhunters, and scouts in the eighteenth and nineteenth centuries had to "read" such signs as paw prints and footprints in the sand, broken twigs, and scat to determine the path of a herd, the whereabouts of outlaws, or the proximity of war parties. Many of these adventurers were illiterate in the sense of being able to decipher meaning from sentences written in our alphabet. Yet, they possessed a complicated and effective literacy in their understanding of the nuances of the land and of movements on it. In our century, an effective starting quarterback in the NFL must be able to "read" a defense as he approaches the line of scrimmage and to audible if the play he initially called does not align well against what he sees. The opposing team disguises its defense, so the quarterback has to pick out subtleties in order to predict the best play. Quarterbacks must be extremely literate to read these signs correctly.

The key element in reading is prediction. When game was plentiful, a longhunter such as Daniel Boone or Davy Crockett had no difficulty finding deer or elk. It was easy to predict where to go. But when game was scarce, initial predictions would prove unreliable, so Boone and Crockett had to look for deeper, less obvious signs to determine the location of a pack of animals. The ability to succeed in youth, high school, and even college football rests on being able to interpret obvious defensive formations. But when a quarterback is drafted into the NFL, he has less time to react to the game's fast pace and the defense's clever strategies. He has to predict what the defense will do based on previous knowledge of the team's habits and anything he can read from the alignment he sees.

This type of reading can lead to the creation of informed texts for others to follow. The focus of this book is on writing, but do not overlook oral text construction. Daniel Boone told other settlers about the areas he explored. When those settlers saw the places themselves, Boone's oral description provided a context through which they interpreted their observations. A map is a written form of such a description. In the twenty-first century, good readers of situations around them inform others through many text-bound activities, such as blogs, collaborative websites called wikis, and editorials. Critically reading not just their own experiences but also the writing of others allows them to create purposeful critical writing.

In reading written texts that others have created, we also use prediction. The more familiar we are with a genre or subject, the easier it is to read. When we know how stories or articles generally will unfold, we can read stories and articles quickly. If we uncover something we were not able to predict—the identity of a murderer in a mystery or information about how a cosmetic might react on our skin in a pamphlet—we become genuinely intrigued, so our reading is still not disrupted. Understanding one unfamiliar element is not difficult in the context of what we already know.

When our first set of predictions fails to unravel a text, our reading slows down. This is the point at which reading becomes difficult. Every paragraph seems to contain something we cannot predict. How can we penetrate this seeming barrier?

DISCUSSION

Think about the different types of literacy you possess beyond the ability to read books and articles. What skills—from car mechanics to fashion sense—do you possess? Do you need to read situations that involve those skills? List the characteristics of your types of literacy, and then talk about them with the group. Are you able to predict certain situations? What do you do when you cannot predict a situation, when a snag or a problem occurs?

This chapter considers the many purposes for reading and then explores strategies for reading effectively. Reading (in the broad sense) is essential to the type of critical analysis needed for effective writing. The four main reasons to read are for knowledge, safety, and awareness as consumers; for social and civic engagement; for information retrieval; and for academic achievement.

When you cannot easily predict a text or are not interested in a subject, you must develop strategies to break through reading blocks and to motivate yourself. Understanding the strategies you use in other types of reading will help. While individuals get pleasure and entertainment from personal reading, the social purposes for text reading supply the necessary motivation for required reading.

Knowledge, Safety, and Awareness as Consumers

It might sound strange that a process associated with mental activity can protect us. The concept of safety makes more sense in relation to the many ways we use reading as consumers. Purchasing even small items compels us to read. Sometimes we need to consult a resource, such as *Consumer Reports*, before we shop to know which products will serve our needs best. For dieting purposes, we read the ingredients on food labels, checking on calories, carbohydrates, or protein. To repair household items, we read instruction manuals, or we read the small print etched on equipment to make sure to buy the proper replacement parts. Reading in this sense is as an active component of empowerment.

Warning Labels Practically every product on the market comes with some sort of writing on its packaging that cautions consumers about proper and improper use. While we only scan this information if we have previously used the product or similar products, we look at the label closely if we are using it for the first time, especially if we perceive a possibility of danger. We have to be aware, for example, of the side effects of a medicine, and we have to avoid mixing it with other medication that might cause an adverse reaction.

Other types of warning labels protect us from improper usage of items we have purchased. We want to be able to wear clothes more than once, for instance, so we look at washing, drying, and ironing labels. Such labels rarely use full sentences, so a reader has to decipher the message. We usually do not give up when trying to understand warnings about line drying and using a cool iron. When we have invested money in a piece of clothing, we generally put in extra effort to achieve full comprehension.

Instructions Product instructions can be the most frustrating types of text. Many consumer items require assembly at home, and we need to protect ourselves from numerous hazards. Poor construction can be dangerous—improper wiring can cause fires; faulty assembly of a weight-bearing product can cause it to collapse. Damaging a part when attempting to put it where it doesn't belong can void a warranty.

Some people who are good with their hands might be able to put a bicycle together or assemble an entertainment center after quickly reviewing the instructions. Others may be guided by the drawings in the manuals. The rest of us must read the text, step by step, to construct something that resembles the picture on the packaging. We can distinguish instructions that are clear and detailed from those that are vague and skimpy.

Recipes are also instructions. While some cooks learn by watching others and relying on instincts thereafter, most of us have to follow the processes outlined in cookbooks. Otherwise, our meals can taste bland, overly spicy, dry, undercooked, or otherwise unsavory.

To install programs on computers, we also have to follow instructions. The directions that pop up on the computer monitor tell us what to do and when to do it. Few of us can override these instructions to install software on our own. If we want to use the program, we have to read the instructions.

Most instructions for consumer purchases demand full comprehension, so we have to scrutinize ambiguous passages. Consumers spend a lot of time making sure to do the right thing. Misreading could render the investment of money and time worthless.

Contracts Often, when we purchase items or make business agreements, we enter into contracts. While contracts usually concern payment plans, they also spell out our rights and responsibilities. Many include warranties or guarantees of which we need to be aware. Contracts with auto mechanics, carpenters, and repair people spell out the precise work they will do and our recourse if we are not satisfied.

Because of the importance of contracts, wise consumers read them, even when the contracts appear to be generic. While most businesses maintain honest standards, the old saying "let the buyer beware" applies. For example, many college students sign credit card deals with an average percentage rate (APR) of interest at 5.9 or 6.9 percent, only to find that the APR increases to 18.9 percent after a few months. While the advertisement says "fixed introductory rate," the rate is fixed, which means remains the same, only through the period the company deems to be "introductory." Everything purchased under that introductory agreement will be subject to the higher interest rate if it is not paid off completely before the introductory period ends. While such advertisements, though deceptive in this way, are legal, the contract must indicate the particulars of the agreement with the company. You might be willing to enter into the agreement if you need financing to buy some items, but the knowledge that comes with reading the contract will make you fully aware of the terms so that you can account for the payments in your budget.

Many students also enter into contracts for financial aid packages (student loans). Reading the contract makes you aware, for example, that you will never be able to default on the loan, even if you declare bankruptcy. You will also know the stipulations about the number of credit hours you must carry, about withdrawing from classes, and about extended illnesses or other emergencies that interfere with attending class. Awareness of the information in the contract can save you from serious financial problems later.

COLLABORATING

As a group, collect a warning label, a set of instructions, and a contract. Look at the language in each and determine its effectiveness. Does it appear to be consumer friendly? Opaque? Condescending? Unnecessary? Discuss the reasons for the language choices made by the writers of the label, instructions, and contract.

Social and Civic Engagement

Our responsibility as citizens is to ensure that our government responds to the needs of the people. We also have to do our part by engaging in socially responsible activities. To ensure that our local community and the nation prosper and offer all citizens freedom and opportunities for happiness, we need to do certain kinds of text reading. Not only must we be able to read documents that involve a higher level of prediction, but we must also examine them critically to uncover any manipulation of language. Chapter 5 discussed common misuses of language; this chapter focuses on the purposes for reading.

Voting We often are encouraged to "get out and vote." But a vote cast in ignorance of the candidates and the issues does not help the cause of democracy. Voting responsibly demands reading with a critical eye.

While television news programs, talk radio, and even advertisements offer information, the brevity of the information and the agendas behind it prevent citizens from making informed decisions. Citizens develop critical awareness in their reading and listening by arming themselves with information from a variety of sources and testing out its validity. (Chapter 10 discusses how to test the credibility of online sources.) They can then determine what propositions or platforms best benefit them, their community, and society as a whole.

Casting uninformed votes has consequences. Voting choices can mean the difference between job creation and job loss, clean water and polluted water, the right to free speech and the suppression of speech, and even hope for a better future and limited future prospects. Knowing the facts can help you make the best choices possible on your ballot and can influence the people you talk to into doing the same.

Protesting Protest can take a number of forms, including putting together petitions, forming advocacy groups, writing to government officials, and marching in the streets. Without doing the necessary reading, you are taking a chance when you raise your voice in protest. There are negative consequences to getting behind a cause and complaining, only to find out that you lacked accurate information.

For example, the American public supported the invasion of Iraq in 2003 under the impression that Iraq had weapons of mass destruction. Advocacy groups rallied in favor of the war to counter peace demonstrations that also took place across the nation. The public has since learned that the documents suggesting that Iraq had obtained uranium were falsified and that we were misled as to Iraq's capabilities of using weapons of mass destruction. That information had been available on the Internet and in alternative magazines before the invasion.

Critical awareness increases our chances of being aware that information is misleading or false. Basing our convictions on the most reliable information allows us to protest with knowledge and certainty.

FAIRNESS AND ACCURACY IN REPORTING

Smearing Anti-War Activists?: NY Times *Op-Ed Laments Anti-War Funeral Protests*

The watchdog group Fairness and Accuracy in Reporting (FAIR) advocates for ethical, informed news coverage. The following is an example of one of the Action Alerts in which the group documents distortions in major media outlets and demands better editorial oversight. Notice how a person who was not critically aware and who did not investigate could react inappropriately to the initial claim in the New York Times *article.*

A June 12 op-ed in the *New York Times* made a bold accusation: anti-war activists have targeted funerals of Iraq War soldiers with noisy protests. But evidence to back up that charge is nonexistent.

The author of the piece, writer Karen Spears Zacharias, recounted an interview with a war widow who said that "antiwar protesters . . . lined the streets across from the service . . . carried signs and . . . shouted as her husband's flag-draped coffin was carried past." Zacharias expanded on this claim when she wrote of the "hundreds of anti-war protestors who appear at military hospitals and funerals."

Following the op-ed's publication, several readers posted questions on Zacharias' website, asking if she could substantiate either the specific incident she had reported, or the broad claim that "hundreds" of anti-war activists have protested at multiple sites. The author responded by posting a link to a story on a conservative website about small vigils that were held at Walter Reed military hospital.

Many of the posts on Zacharias' website suggested that the funeral protests she was describing were more likely those organized by Fred Phelps' Westboro Baptist Church, a virulently homophobic group that celebrates U.S. military deaths as punishment for the military's "don't ask, don't tell" policy towards homosexuals. The Phelps group is by no reasonable definition anti-war.

5 In a response to one reader, Zacharias acknowledged that further research revealed that the widows she spoke with were all referring to Phelps' group.

Though the piece appeared on the *Times'* op-ed page, the paper has a responsibility to verify such claims—particularly when, as in this case, they serve as the premise of a column. Moreover, such anecdotes have the potential to smear an entire political movement, and live on long after they are published. Accounts of Vietnam vets being spit upon by anti-war protesters, for example, persist to this day (*Newsweek*, 6/12/06)—despite the fact that it is difficult to corroborate any of those alleged incidents (see *The Spitting Image: Myth, Memory, and the Legacy of Vietnam*, by Jerry Lembcke).

Action:

Contact the *New York Times* op-ed page and ask them to verify the claim that "hundreds of anti-war protestors" have demonstrated "at military hospitals and funerals." If they cannot, ask them to correct the record.

Public Interest True social engagement must start with one's own family. Problems that begin in the home often spill into society. Manuals produced by government health agencies and reliable advocacy groups offer accurate information on common social problems. For example, pamphlets on AIDS and other sexually transmitted diseases distinguish fact from fiction and give advice on preventing infection. Drug and alcohol awareness groups produce literature on the effects of addiction and options for treatment. In both cases, nipping a problem in the bud can prevent harmful social consequences, such as spreading a disease or driving while intoxicated.

Sometimes we want to trust our instincts rather than read information, only to find out later that we have done the wrong thing. For example, people who live near mountains or woods may encounter young, seemingly abandoned animals and may want to care for them. However, public service bulletins explain that such animals are probably only temporarily separated from their mothers. Their best chance for survival is for people to keep their distance; the scent of a human will keep such an animal's mother from retrieving it. A young animal taken to a person's home likely will die. To maintain a thriving, diverse ecosystem, humans often must forego their maternal or paternal instincts. Interference can lead to wilderness destruction and species endangerment in small and large ways.

Of course, bringing up our own children is tremendously important for society. Children who are not raised well may commit crimes, destroy property, and cost taxpayers money. Child-care pamphlets and books not only help parents ensure their children's health, but also give advice based on research to guide parents toward enacting proper discipline, creating acceptable boundaries, and establishing nurturing environments. Reading to ensure responsible personal behavior affects society positively.

OHIO DEPARTMENT OF PUBLIC SAFETY

Where to Ride on the Road

The following advice on bicycling comes from a manual produced by the Ohio Department of Public Safety. Read the instructions and determine whether the guidelines offer information about bicycling that you did not know. What are the social costs of bicyclists' not following such guidelines?

We've all seen bicyclists who wander from left side to right, who go from the sidewalk to the street and who weave in and out between parked cars. From moment to moment, nobody can tell what these bicyclists are about to do. Pedestrians jump back, and car brakes squeal as such bicyclists approach.

On the other hand, we've seen bicyclists who seem to blend into the traffic flow smoothly and effortlessly. You always know where they are headed and what to do around them, whether you're on a bicycle, in a car or on foot. They make bicycling look easy—but aren't they taking a risk? Isn't it safer to avoid the traffic as much as possible?

Part of the Traffic Pattern

With very few exceptions, *the safest way to ride is as part of the traffic,* going with the flow of the normal traffic pattern. Bicyclists who ride this way get where they're going faster and, according to scientific crash studies, have about five times fewer crashes than bicyclists who make up their own rules (J. Forester, *Effective Cycling.* Cambridge, MA: MIT Press, 1993).

Generally, the more you follow the normal traffic pattern, the safer and more predictable you become: The rules of the road set up a pattern for every situation, telling which driver has the right of way. Sometimes you have to wait for other drivers—for example, at a stop sign—but sometimes they have to wait for you. Bicyclists have the same rights—and responsibilities—as motorists.

In this way, the rules of the road protect you by making it clear what 5
you're going to do next.

If you ride in violation of the traffic laws, you greatly increase your risk of a crash. You also may give up all of your rights. If you get into a crash, the courts will almost always find that it was your fault!

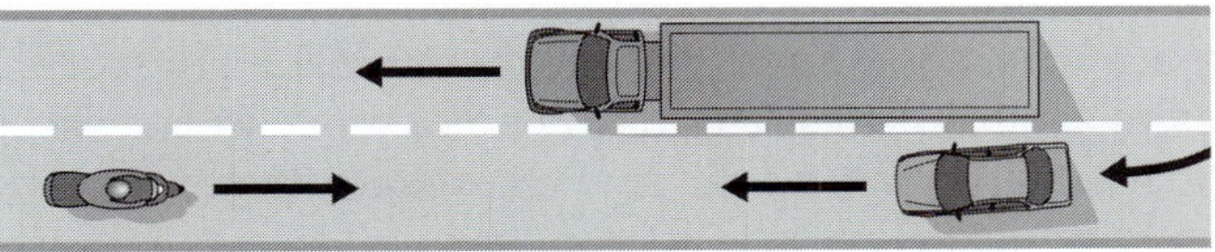

On a two-lane highway, be alert to drivers ahead of you pulling out to pass, especially if the lanes are narrow.

Understand that the law is on your side. The law gives you the right to use the road, the same as a motorist, and to make other traffic slow down for you sometimes. The driver approaching from the rear is always required to slow and follow if it's not possible to pass safely.

It may seem dangerous to make a motorist slow for you, but it's not. The usual reason that bicyclists feel unsafe on narrow roads is that they do not take control of the situation. Remember, the drivers behind you don't have room to pass you safely anyway. If you ride all the way over at the right, you're inviting them to pass you where the road is too narrow and, too often, you will get squeezed off the road. If you show clearly that it's not safe for drivers to pass you, they're unlikely to try.

Right

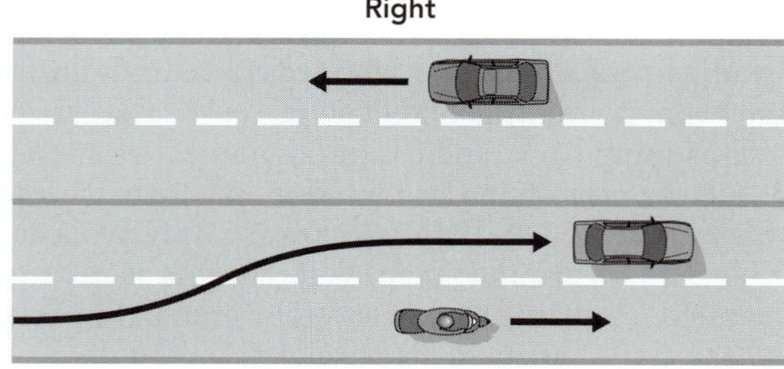

On a multilane road with a narrow right lane, ride in the middle of the right lane.

Wrong

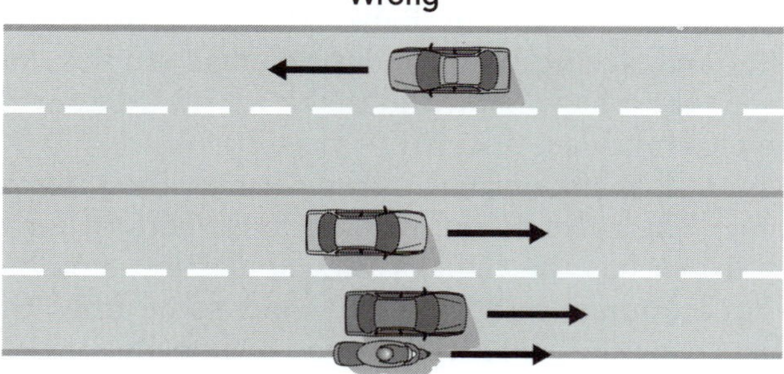

If you hug the edge, you are likely to get squeezed out.

But be courteous. When it becomes safe for the car behind you to pass you, give the driver a wave-by signal. If you block traffic for more than a short time, common courtesy suggests, and the law normally requires, that you pull to the side and let the traffic by when you can safely do so.

10 On a road with two or more narrow lanes in your direction—like many city streets—you should ride in the middle of the right lane at all times. You need to send the message to drivers to move to the passing lane to pass you. If you ride all the way to the right, two cars may pass you at the same time, side by side, and squeeze you off the road.

WRITING

Look on the Internet or in local newspapers to find stories on tragedies or waste that involved behavior inconsistent with authoritative information that the people involved could have learned by reading. What type of knowledge guided the people involved? Were they acting on instinct or responding to false information? Could prior reading have altered their actions? Make sure to verify your knowledge on the subject before making assertions about what the people should have done.

Information Retrieval

Much reading involves information retrieval. A person, place, or event intrigues us, and we want to know more. Workplace responsibilities sometimes require us to use information retrieval skills, whether in a library or on the Internet. If you look at the way you find information for personal purposes, you will be better able to carry out these other responsibilities.

Competition People compete in many ways. In American lore families often try to "keep up with the Joneses," meaning that when a family makes home improvements, their neighbors feel compelled to do something to their houses so as not to lag behind. Searching through magazines for ideas, finding regional trends on the Internet, and getting information on potential contractors from the Better Business Bureau will help them avoid costly mistakes.

As another example, many people play fantasy sports. Successful fantasy players read newspapers and surf the Internet for current information on athletes and teams. Reading about a coach's or manager's tendencies gives the fantasy player an advantage when deciding when to reserve or trade a player. Reading is the difference between winning and losing.

Still other people get hooked on trivia games. Perhaps they watch *Jeopardy* every night, play Trivial Pursuit with friends, or engage in electronically connected national rounds of Buzztime trivia in local taverns. Clearly, those who read and digest bits of information compete better than those who do not.

While competition sometimes serves negative purposes, it can also be fun. Reading can contribute to your enjoyment of the competition.

Hobbies Keeping up with trends in your hobby means reading. Sometimes you need to know what's new, such as about current stamps produced by the U.S. Postal Service, and have to scan popular websites or magazines to find the information. You discover the potential value of a set and decide whether to purchase it.

Other times, you might be trying to solve a problem. For example, perhaps, like many backpackers, you tend to get blisters. A technological innovation in hiking boots might make your next expedition more pleasurable. You doubt the salesperson's rating of boots because he is trying to earn a commission from your purchase. You need a source that evaluates new equipment, such as *Backpacker* magazine, for an unbiased assessment of new boots.

There is also the joy of experiencing a gathering of people with similar interests. Sometimes hobby conventions advertise on television and radio, but Star Trek conventions, for instance, do not necessarily receive that type of publicity. The only way to know that such an event is coming to your area is to stay current with fanzines and websites that have information about conventions.

In these and many other cases, reading helps you attend to your hobbies. Chapter 12 further discusses the intricacies of hobbies and their effect on our culture.

Social Discourse It's no fun to attend a social function and not be able to participate in the conversations. Whether your friends discuss celebrity gossip, music, current events, academics, or local happenings, you need to know something about contemporary culture to take part in the conversation. Reading serves this purpose better than any other medium. Not only does it keep you up to date on important local and national topics, but it can also give you information that is more precise and thorough than the sound bites others might have heard.

As mentioned earlier, we cannot completely trust the accuracy of television and radio sources. Respectable papers, magazines, and websites can keep us from succumbing to rumors and hate mongering. Sometimes, urban legends are spread at social functions because people do not have the proper information at their disposal. They enter into lively discourse without the context.

A student of mine once turned in an assignment detailing a "personal experience" of picking up a hitchhiker who later disappeared. According to his paper, an accident had occurred at the curve in the road where she vanished from his car. The student did not know that the legend of the vanishing hitchhiker is infamously just a myth. When confronted, the student claimed that the experience was not really his but a story he had overheard at a party that the storyteller claimed was true.

While we cannot be responsible for knowing about every subject, we can be held accountable for reading up on a subject before spreading a rumor. And, of course, no one should ever claim that an experience is his or hers just because it sounds like a good story! In any case, information gained through reading can prevent embarrassing social situations and can stop rumors from being circulated.

JAN HAROLD BRUNVAND

from The Vanishing Hitchhiker

In the following excerpt from The Vanishing Hitchhiker: American Urban Legends and Their Meanings, *Jan Harold Brunvand reviews variations of the same story, showing how features of the tale remain constant even when the details change. Think how stimulating it might be at a party to discuss the actual history and purpose of an urban legend rather than perpetuating the myth as a "true experience."*

Urban legends belong to the subclass of folk narratives, legends, that—unlike fairy tales—are believed, or at least believable, and that—unlike myths—are set in the recent past and involve normal human beings rather than ancient gods or demigods. Legends are folk history, or rather quasi-history. As with any folk legends, urban legends gain credibility from specific details of time and place or from references to source authorities. For instance, a popular western pioneer legend often begins something like, "My great-grandmother had this strange experience when she was a young girl on a wagon train going through Wyoming when an Indian chief wanted to adopt her . . ." Even though hundreds of different great-grandmothers are supposed to have had the same doubtful experience (being desired by the chief because of her beautiful long blond hair), the fact seldom reaches legend-tellers; if it does, they assume that the family lore has indeed spread far and wide. This particular popular tradition, known as "Goldilocks on the Oregon Trail," interests folklorists because of the racist implications of a dark Indian savage coveting a fair young civilized woman—this legend is familiar in the *white* folklore only—and it is of little concern that the story seems to be entirely apocryphal.

In the world of modern urban legends there is usually no geographical or generational gap between teller and event. The story is *true;* it really occurred, and recently, and always to someone else who is quite close to the narrator, or at least "a friend of a friend." Urban legends are told both in the course of casual conversations and in such special situations as campfires, slumber parties, and college dormitory bull sessions. The legends' physical settings are often close by, real, and sometimes even locally renowned for other such happenings. Though the characters in the stories are usually nameless, they are true-to-life examples of the kind of people the narrators and their audience know firsthand.

One of the great mysteries of folklore research is where oral traditions originate and who invents them. One might expect that at least in modern folklore we could come up with answers to such questions, but this is seldom, if ever, the case. . . . [M]ost leads pointing to possible authors or original events lying behind urban legends have simply evaporated. . . .

A prime example of the adaptability of older legends is "The Vanishing Hitchhiker"—*the* classic automobile legend. This returning-ghost tale was known by the turn of the century both in the United States and abroad. It acquired the newer automobile motif by the period of the Great Depression, and thereafter spawned a number of subtypes with greatly varied and oddly interlocking details, some of which themselves stemmed from earlier folk legends. Merely sampling some of the many "Vanishing Hitchhiker" variants that have been collected over a period of some forty years can help us trace the legend's incredible development. Surely most readers already know a local "true" account (or maybe two or three) similar to Example A, as told by a teenager in Toronto, Canada, in 1973:

A

Well, this happened to one of my girlfriend's best friends and her father. They were driving along a country road on their way home from the cottage when they saw a young girl hitchhiking. They stopped and picked her up and she got in the back seat. She told the girl and her father that she just lived in the house about five miles up the road. She didn't say anything after that but just turned to watch out the window. When the father saw the house, he drove up to it and turned around to tell the girl they had arrived—but she wasn't there! Both he and his daughter were really mystified and decided to knock on the door and tell the people what had happened. They told them that they had once had a daughter who answered the description of the girl they supposedly had picked up, but she had disappeared some years ago and had last been seen hitchhiking on this very road. Today would have been her birthday.

This version has the basic elements—not necessarily "original" ones—well known in oral tradition and occasionally reported in newspapers since the early 1930s. The stable story units have been labeled in brackets in the following text from South Carolina collected by workers of the South Carolina Writers' Project (Work Projects Administration) sometime between 1935 and 1941:

B

A traveling man [driver] who lived in Spartanburg [authentication] was on his way home one night [setting] when he saw a woman walking along the side of the road [hitchhiker]. He stopped his car and asked the woman if he could take her where she was going. She stated that she was on her way to visit her brother who lived about three miles further on the same road [her address]. He asked her to get in the car and sit by him, but she said she would sit in the back of the car [her choice of seat]. Conversation took place for a while as they rode along, but soon the woman grew quiet. The man drove on until he reached the home of the woman's brother, whom he knew [more authentication]; then stopped his car to let the woman alight. When he looked behind him, there was no one in the car [disappearance]. He thought that rather strange [curiosity or concern], so went into the house and informed the brother that a lady had gotten into his car to ride to see him, but when he arrived at the house the lady had disappeared. The brother was not alarmed at all and stated that the lady was his sister who had died two years before [identification]. He said that this traveling man was the seventh to pick up his sister on the road to visit him, but that she had never reached his house yet.

Variations on the basic story are endless, and trying to sort them out into any kind of possible chronological development is hampered by the fact that the date when a version happened to be collected and published bears little relationship to its possible age in tradition, and by the principle that legends become highly localized and rationalized with many circumstantial details whenever they are adopted into a particular context. For instance, the plot has several different twists and turns in this 1935 version (paraphrased by the collector) from Berkeley, California:

C

> This story was heard in a Durant Avenue boarding house, told several times as a true story. It happened to a friend of the narrator. This friend was driving up Hearst Avenue one rainy night. As he came to North Gate (Hearst and Euclid avenues) he saw a girl, a student with books under her arm, waiting for the streetcar. Since these had stopped running, he offered her a ride. She lived up on Euclid. They drove out along Euclid quite a way with some conversation. As they were crossing an intersection, another car came down the steep hill and they would have crashed if the girl had not pulled on the emergency brake [a unique detail in the story]. The fellow was flabbergasted and sat looking at the other car, which pulled around him and went on. When he remembered his companion and looked over, she was gone. Since it was near her home, he assumed she had simply gotten out to walk the rest of the way; but she had left a book on the seat. The next day he went to return the book. He found her father, an English professor, at home. He said that the girl was his daughter, that she had been killed in an auto accident at the same corner one or two years ago that very day. But since the fellow had the book, the father took it into the library, to look on the shelves for it—he found the place where it should have been vacant.

10 A strictly urban setting for the story allows for more precise and thorough double-checking of factual details. In 1941 Rosalie Hankey of the University of California, who was gathering materials for a lengthy study of "The Vanishing Hitchhiker," tried to verify specific accident reports from Berkeley. In one version the automobile crash in which the girl was killed was supposed to have happened in 1935 or 1936 at the corner of College and Bancroft. But in checking the Berkeley city records from 1934 to 1937, Hankey found that only a single accident involving personal injury, non-fatal, had occurred at that corner during the five-year period.

The specific "proof" in the story of the hitchhiker's actual presence in the car and her status as the ghost of a particular individual is always a key motif. Besides the book she leaves behind in Example C, the object may be a purse, a suitcase, a blanket, a sweater, a scarf or some other item of clothing, or simply footprints or water spots in the car. The identification of her at the family's home may depend upon showing the object to her relatives, or upon the driver's description of her, the girl's name, or a photograph of her which is displayed on the piano or mantel and which often shows her wearing the same party dress in which her ghost appears. One group of variants which includes either the clothing (hers or something borrowed from the driver) or the portrait detail (sometimes both) moves the climax of the story to a cemetery.

DISCUSSION

List every type of reading you did yesterday or today in order to retrieve information. Think of everything from box scores in the morning paper to listings of movie times while deciding which to see at a theater. Include any nontext reading, such as road signs without words and anything else you had to interpret. Share your information, and compare the amount of time you spent reading to the time your classmates spent. Was it more than you thought? Did you consider it a burden? Discuss the different purposes served by your reading.

Academic Achievement

When you consider your investment of money and time, doing well in college courses is a legitimate goal. Reading assigned texts can be the difference between succeeding and failing in a class. In the example at the beginning of this chapter, Ben and some of the other students would have suffered had there been a quiz on the Rasmus article. The farther you go in your education, the more important it is to read materials and be able to apply them on a test or in a paper.

Academic Learning

Many students do acceptable work in colleges and universities by listening to lectures, viewing presentations, and preparing for quizzes and tests. Some distinguish themselves by learning more through in-depth reading. These students become critically aware of the context surrounding the subjects they study. They grasp the real-life application of theories and research sooner than other students. They spot connections among the courses they take and can readily and accurately use that knowledge. They turn the game of school into a learning experience.

Sometimes textbooks can be boring, but they give learners a background in the subject that a lecture or project can enhance. Students with awareness of the subject beforehand have a better sense of what is and is not relevant and can thus take more accurate notes. They can better predict the information that is coming, even if the professor is updating or augmenting facts and theories. Textbooks also let students check facts. If you're not sure that you recorded something correctly in your notes, you can look in your textbook to confirm the information. Textbook reading can often lead to interest in primary sources, which might give you information that will surprise your professor. It feels good to know something that the teacher doesn't know, right? Critical awareness earns you respect and prestige.

Learning for Future Application Information gained through text reading has real-life applications. The reading for courses in your major prepares you for your career. Naturally, you want to pay particular attention to assigned texts, and you probably will have sufficient motivation to get through them. But what about the other reading you must do? What application can it have to your life?

Instructors in general education and specialized courses often assign reading that has relevance to your civic and social responsibility. You do not have to be a psychology major to appreciate information you find in the pages of a psychology textbook. You might learn to reflect on your own behavior better and to understand and accept the peculiarities of other people. The novels, poems, and plays you read in literature classes will be useful throughout your life as shared cultural icons that add depth to conversations or provide clear examples of complicated subjects.

Knowledge gained from reading can create indelible memories. When my daughter Katrina was young, she and I looked at the stars in the night sky. She could identify the Milky Way and other constellations, and I talked about the myths surrounding their creation based on knowledge from courses about mythology and told her scientific facts about the Milky Way, checking my old astronomy textbook to be accurate. Katrina and I would then make up our own stories about constellations in the sky. Later, I bought her a telescope, and we spent many nights looking for planets and trying to identify what we saw. We couldn't have enjoyed ourselves more. The applications of academic reading can surprise you.

COLLABORATING

Jot down information from a high school or college course that you applied to a real-life situation. What you record does not have to be a completely successful application of the material or have produced positive results, but be specific about the situation and the information you knew. As a group, review these applications and ask whether information beyond what was in the textbook or assigned reading could have augmented what transpired. In retrospect, would it have been the worth the effort to have read more?

Developing Reading Strategies for College

You may not need further convincing about the empowering aspects of reading. Your question may now be how to navigate through all the reading in college. It may still seem daunting. If you recognize the purpose of reading, you have the first key toward developing a strategy, but what about the rest? How does a reader move from reading he or she sees as purposeful or enjoyable to reading that is difficult? Student Mandy Badar discusses her development as a reader in an essay tracing different stages of her growth.

MANDY BADAR

An Analysis of the Dietary Habits of a Known Bookworm

How do you produce a bookworm? By what means do you cultivate a creature that devours texts insatiably? How do you stoke its hunger without starving it? How much do you feed it without causing it to choke or gag? And, most importantly, how do you get it to acquire the taste for books in the first place?

The way to whet the appetite for books is the same method by which you develop any other appetite. By this I mean that eating is an inextricable element of everyone's world. To encourage someone to develop healthy eating habits you draw on natural propensities and create conducive circumstances. Eating is simply something one must do. It is a basic need around which we build social, family, and other structures. It is also something that can be shaped by the behavior of the people one is surrounded by. If a child grows up eating healthy foods or exotic dishes, the child will not think that eating healthy or exotic foods is remarkable. Similarly, it would never occur to anyone to force feed a child to stimulate her appetite. Furthermore, it would not make sense to surround a child with unappetizing, unpalatable, or even inedible foods. Instead, one would surround her with enticing dishes and let her exercise her own culinary discretion. Nurturing a natural inclination and satiating varying appetites when they arise will make a bon vivant of most people.

Of course, one will not die if one does not get a regular dose of literature, but reading is still a skill that promotes survival. It's something almost everyone has to do to some extent to survive in a nation like ours. Reading is also a basic thing around which a much greater structure is built; it can be part of family life, the basis of social gatherings and much more. Reading habits and affinities can be shaped and encouraged by those around us. For example, if the people we see every day make reading a part of their lives, we will take for granted that reading is part of life. It cannot be inculcated by force, just as a liking for brussel sprouts cannot be ingrained by a parent's will. If one is brought up in a world of literature, if it is part of the backdrop of one's existence, then it is simply a matter of culturing the palate, determining from the choices by which one is surrounded which dish is most amenable to the tongue.

This is how I was turned, very early in life, from a bouncing baby girl to a ravenous bookworm. I was surrounded by reading material and constantly exposed to other readers. I had only one of those plastic, inane baby books; the rest of my numerous books were actual storybooks. My playroom was dominated by a bookcase, the contents of which grew and changed as I matured. At a mere four years of age my mom took me to story hour at the local public library. During these trips I listened to stories, picked out books, and played with other kids. As I grew older I raided the bookshelves of various family members and picked up whatever books Mom left lying around. Books were part of the lives of everyone I grew up around, and I took it for granted that they would be part of my life too.

Even though reading was a commonplace activity for most of the adults in my life, no one ever forced me to interact with texts. All too often I hear that someone was turned off to reading because her parents or teachers became unrelenting taskmasters who force-fed her "appropriate" literature. As a small child I was given the option of reading with my mom, along with many other choices. I am told that I opted for coloring as often as reading. Later, when I was able to read in my own right, I chose to join summer reading programs and to read for enjoyment, but no one ever forced me to make reading a daily or regimented activity. This is largely because I come from a blue-collar family, the members of which are not overly concerned with formal education. I am first-generation college-educated. To my knowledge, no family member before me was an outstanding student, let alone valedictorian. My eagerness to learn was regarded as a pleasant surprise, not a mandatory attribute. Thus, no one ever made reading (or any other educational activity) unbearable by demanding that I meet certain quotas or choose materials of a certain caliber. There was never any pressure to read, to read well, to read certain things, or to share my reading with others.

I was motivated to learn to read anyway. Although no external pressure was applied, I ached for the day when the secret of reading would be revealed to me. For so long I had watched the adults in my life sample a buffet of delights of which I could not partake. I wanted to sit at the grownup table and gorge myself on the delights I knew were there. In first grade, after half a year of drilling with letter flashcards, I got my chance. We were presented with primary readers and left to puzzle them out for ourselves. I knew that sounding out one word at a time was not reading because when my mom read to me at home the sense was immediately evident, whereas, when I tried to read at school, I would have to figure out all the words, then go back and re-read the sentence to get the meaning. I distinctly remember the day when it all came together. In a rush of understanding, a moment of epiphany, the text I had been laboring over suddenly made sense. The key turned in the lock and I was reading. I was so excited I refused to come back to my desk for my snack break. It was just like learning to ride a bike and the knowledge was just as irreversible. After that day I can't remember a time when a book was beyond my grasp, at least not until I took up Shakespeare, Chaucer, and a minor in philosophy, respectively.

Certainly, as with eating, some texts or authors are acquired tastes. One does not usually become a connoisseur of coffee or wine after the first sip. Becoming acclimated to and appreciative of Shakespeare, Chaucer, and philosophical texts was, for me, a great deal like developing a taste for wine. At first wine is harsh to the senses. It is unfamiliar; it is not immediately pleasurable; it can leave you with a massive headache. Similarly, delving into Chaucer's Troilus and Criseyde or plumbing the depths of Alvin Plantinga's Does God Have a Nature? is not immediately pleasurable and can certainly leave one with a terrific headache. Frankly, as with wine consumption, such reading endeavors often start for elitist, status-based reasons. It is impressive to be able to confidently assess a restaurant's wine list, and it is awe-inspiring to be able to read, understand, and expound upon Shakespeare, Chaucer, or philosophy. As time goes on, as with wine, familiarity engenders a comfort level with and appreciation for the experience. The antiquated or intensely cerebral language becomes familiar and discernible enough that the content becomes the focal point. It is like reaching the point at which you can tell a sangiovese from a shiraz, you know what glass and temperature are appropriate for serving, and even a dry white won't make you grimace. This is something that one achieves with practice and patience, and not a little desire, but the payoff for having mastered the medium is well worth it, especially socially.

Mandy's wine metaphor is useful for understanding that students can acquire a taste for reading. Reading is not beyond your capabilities as a college student. But many students want practical tips. To begin to develop an effective reading strategy, start by recognizing your processes of reading and comprehension.

You might be familiar with the situation where your mind is elsewhere but your eyes are still going down the paragraph. You have been reading, but you do not remember what you read. Strangely, if you reread the paragraph, you will remember bits and pieces of it. This situation usually occurs because of distractions. In developing a reading strategy, you must first eliminate the physical and psychological barriers that keep you from your purpose. See what you do when you're engaged in nontext reading. Draw parallels so that you understand how the process of prediction is most readily enabled.

Short Spurts When I take novices on backpacking trips, some tire quickly. The increase in altitude, the weight of the pack, and the number of miles in front of us often combine to make them want to quit. To keep them going, I usually devise short-term goals. I will point to a tree and say, "Let's reach that. We'll rest there." When we arrive, everyone feels a sense of accomplishment. This makes my companions more willing to continue after resting. I repeat this process whenever spirits ebb and my companions think they cannot go on. By not conjuring images of all the land in front of us, I am able to get the group to keep pushing, and eventually we reach our destination.

A similar process works when you have required reading to do. Count the number of pages you have to read, and divide them into manageable units. For example, if you have to read fifty pages, break the assignment into five separate goals. If the class meets at the end of the week, read ten pages on Saturday, ten pages the next day, and so forth so that you are done by the day of the class. If on Monday you are assigned fifty pages to read by Wednesday, use the same system, but find two or three specific times during the day to squeeze in a reading of ten pages, such as before breakfast or during lunch. These chunks are manageable, and you can read more in a sitting if your interest increases.

The Right Spot Finding a quiet spot to read can be especially challenging when you juggle school, work, and family responsibilities. Often, physical comfort is not as important as solitude when it comes to focused reading. You have to eliminate the parts of your life that act as distractions when you are reading.

If you need familiar surroundings to be comfortable, your dorm room or bedroom at home might be the best place. This allows you to fix a snack or to prop up your feet when you read. Perhaps you need space and cannot read if you are surrounded by clutter. The backyard or a balcony might be the best spot. Or getting out of a wooden chair into something soft that you can sink into is what matters most. The point is to make yourself comfortable and avoid distractions.

Turn off your cell phone. If the crowd noise from the ballgame on television is going to cause you to look away from your reading, turn off the game and put some music on. Don't be afraid to ask your roommates or family members to respect your study time and space. You will be amazed by the increase in your level of comprehension and the speed at which you read when you are in the right environment.

READING PLANNER

Compile a list of the reading you have to do for your courses for this week or next week. Follow these directions and fill in the chart on the next page.

- In the first column, list the course by its number or abbreviated title.
- In the second column, give an abbreviated title for each book from which reading has been assigned. Also list the titles of handouts or other assigned reading materials.
- In the third column, list the total number of pages you must read, such as "50 pages."

READING PLANNER

Course	Book	No. of Pages	Sun.	Mon.	Tues.	Wed.	Thurs.	Fri.	Sat.

- In the fourth through tenth columns, write the page numbers you will read from the text under the days of the week you will read them—for example, "pages 20–29." Make sure you divide the total number of pages from each book into equal and manageable units. Put a simple abbreviation next to the page numbers to indicate where you will do the reading (H for home, CS for coffee shop, L for library, and so on).
- On a given day, you might read from more than one book. Just make sure that the total number of pages does not exceed what you can realistically do, so as not to defeat the purpose of filling out the chart. Also make sure that you do not schedule the reading of two different books at the same time.
- Remember deadlines. If you have a quiz on reading materials on Wednesday, do not schedule reading from that book for Thursday or Friday. Prioritize your reading on the basis of the due dates your instructor gives you.
- Make sure to take into consideration the time you will be attending class, deadlines for reading, obligations to friends and family, work schedules, and other constraints, such as exercise routines and church services. Do not overlap reading with other commitments that will make adherence to the reading chart impossible.
- Do not designate a place for reading that your schedule will not allow. If you're going to try to read ten pages between classes, you will need to find a spot on campus that suits your needs, since you will not have time to get home to that favorite couch or chair.

Once you compile this chart, give it a trial run. If it helps you achieve your reading goals, constructing a chart every week will help you meet deadlines. If it does not seem to work, tweak it. Figure out what got in the way of following the schedule, and account for that in a new schedule. Unexpected occurrences may still get in the way, but the point is to use short spurts to accomplish your reading. A chart will aid you in avoiding destructive habits, such as procrastination. Work with it so that it becomes an effective tool for reading.

Comprehension

After you have eliminated the barriers to reading, you must make sure that you comprehend the material in front of you. You have to be able to understand what you read in order to apply it. In college, one of the purposes of reading is writing.

Textbooks generally help you in the process of comprehending for writing purposes by putting key terms in boldface or italic type. Textbooks usually are also broken into easily digestible sections in which the main point is stated in the first paragraph and summarized at the end. However, you might read primary sources in some courses, which are structured differently than textbooks.

Primary Sources	Secondary Sources
Material appeared in this form originally	Material reproduced in this form
Author conducted research and suggested a theory	Author summarizes research and repeats theories
Intended audience is made up of people knowledgeable about and/or interested in the topic	Intended audience is students or those who prefer more general information

For academic proficiency as well as for some civic responsibilities, you have to reach the same level of comprehension of primary sources as you do of textbooks. Here are some useful strategies.

Focused Freewriting After you finish one of your short spurts—or perhaps after going through the whole reading task in front of you—write down what you think you have learned through the reading. At this point, your writing does not have to accurately summarize the reading you have done, but you should make an honest attempt at conveying what you learned. Such focused freewriting, discussed in Chapter 6, should help improve your comprehension.

Think of this step as part of your reading process. Budget it into the time you spend on reading. What ideas can you articulate without going back to the text and copying it? What were the main points? What happened? You will discover that you understood more than you realized at first. Remember the phenomenon of not recalling what you just read until you reread it? Your brain is functioning in ways that you might not understand. It can predict and fill in blanks even when you might not consciously realize that it is doing so. By writing, you are activating the same processes used in rereading.

When you do a focused freewrite, do not be afraid to take educated guesses—to predict, in other words—about what your mind tells you must have been a part of your reading. You can go back and check what you wrote to see if it captures the spirit of the text. You can cross out and insert paraphrases as necessary. This activity will enable you to start putting ideas in your own words so that you can later use them in a paper.

Molly Egan's Freewrite

Here is a student example of a focused freewrite based on the excerpt from The Vanishing Hitchhiker.

It seems like urban legends always happen to other people. I wonder if there are any first hand accounts of this story. What's weird about it is that they persist even when people come out and say that they are fake. The one person did research and proved that the accident could not have taken place as the story said. Just the fact that versions of the story have occurred at all these different times and places should clue

> people in. But I guess the point that Brunvand is getting at is that people keep telling the stories because it fulfills a need in our culture. I'm just not sure I understand what that need is. Perhaps we have to maintain a belief in the fantastic or the nearly unbelievable. I think he said that we prefer to tell stories of escaped lunatics, which could happen, rather than of aliens or monsters, which couldn't. But I don't know what the moral of the Vanishing Hitchhiker is. Maybe this legend confirms for people that there is an afterlife. I'm not sure what Brunvand thinks it does.

This student takes educated guesses when she does not exactly understand Brunvand's ideas. In so doing, she takes the opportunity to extend Brunvand's ideas for a possible writing assignment on the topic. This focused freewrite will also guide her rereading and highlighting when she looks for places where she does not exactly understand the author's point.

Highlighting Underlining or highlighting text helps us concentrate on important or difficult sections and facilitates reviewing them. Be careful about highlighting or underlining too much; highlighting half the book defeats the purpose of the process and also slows down your reading.

Try highlighting after you have gone through one of your short spurts. Ten pages or so will be fresh in your memory, so you can easily go back and highlight important information. This makes referencing the text later that much easier. Highlight only key facts and theories. Often, examples are not as important as the main point, but sometimes it is difficult to tell an example from a fact or theory. Remember that an example is a specific instance of a larger point. Highlighting the key facts and theories will separate the important information that you can use later as evidence, as discussed in Chapter 9.

Check Marks in the Margins Do not get bogged down by strange allusions or vocabulary. If a text uses an allusion or a word that you do not understand, place a check mark in the margin and move on (use pencil if you have borrowed the book from the library or a friend). Even if the word or reference seems essential for full comprehension, you do not need to stop reading to go to a dictionary or an encyclopedia. Doing so will frustrate you and distract you from your reading task. Much comprehension can be gained from understanding the context around the word or reference. If you are reading the text for a class, you can assemble a set of questions for the instructor or listen for the answers during the lecture. The good thing about this process is that it tends to stick with you. You increase your vocabulary and recognize allusions the next time around.

> *This passage from* The Vanishing Hitchhiker *is an example of how to highlight important points and use check marks to identify strange words and references.*

Urban legends belong to the subclass of folk narratives, legends, that—unlike fairy tales—are believed, or at least believable, and that—unlike myths—are set in the recent past and involve normal human beings rather than ancient gods or demigods. Legends are folk history, or rather quasi-history. As with any folk legends, urban legends gain credibility from specific details of time and place or from references to source authorities. For instance, a popular western pioneer legend often begins something like, "My great-grandmother had this strange experience when she was a young girl on a wagon train going through Wyoming when an Indian chief wanted to adopt her. . . " Even though hundreds of different great-grandmothers are supposed to have had the same doubtful experience (being desired by the chief because of her beautiful long blond hair), the fact seldom reaches legend-tellers; if it does, they assume that the family lore has indeed spread far and wide. This particular popular tradition, known as "Goldilocks on the Oregon Trail," interests folklorists because of the racist implications of a dark Indian savage coveting a fair young civilized woman—this legend is familiar in the *white* folklore only—and it is of little concern that the story seems to be entirely apocryphal.

In the world of modern urban legends there is usually no geographical or generational gap between teller and event. The story is *true*; it really occurred, and recently, and always to someone else who is quite close to the narrator, or at least "a friend of a friend." Urban legends are told both in the course of casual conversations and in such special situations as camp-fires, slumber parties, and college dormitory bull sessions. The legends' physical settings are often close by, real, and sometimes even locally renowned for other such happenings. Though the characters in the stories are usually nameless, they are true-to-life examples of the kind of people the narrators and their audience know firsthand.

One of the great mysteries of folklore research is where oral traditions originate and who invents them. One might expect that at least in modern folklore we could come up with answers to such questions, but this is seldom, if ever, the case. . . . [M]ost leads pointing to possible authors or original events lying behind urban legends have simply evaporated. . . .

A prime example of the adaptability of older legends is "The Vanishing Hitchhiker"—*the* classic automobile legend. This returning-ghost tale was known by the turn of the century both in the United States and abroad. It acquired the newer automobile motif by the period of the Great Depression, and thereafter spawned a number of subtypes with greatly varied and oddly interlocking details, some of which themselves stemmed from earlier folk legends. Merely sampling some of the many "Vanishing Hitchhiker" variants that have been collected over a period of some forty years can help us trace the legend's incredible development. Surely most readers already know a local "true" account (or maybe two or three) similar to Example A, as told by a teenager in Toronto, Canada, in 1973:

A

> Well, this happened to one of my girlfriend's best friends and her father. They were driving along a country road on their way home from the cottage when they saw a young girl hitchhiking. They stopped and picked her up and she got in the back seat. She told the girl and her father that she just lived in the house about five miles up the road. She didn't say anything after that but just turned to watch out the window. When the father saw the house, he drove up to it and turned around to tell the girl they had arrived—but she wasn't there! Both he and his daughter were really mystified and decided to knock on the door and tell the people what had happened. They told them that they had once had a daughter who answered the description of the girl they supposedly had picked up, but she had disappeared some years ago and had last been seen hitch-hiking on this very road. Today would have been her birthday.

This version has the basic elements—not necessarily "original" ones—well known in oral tradition and occasionally reported in newspapers since the early 1930s. The stable story units have been labeled in brackets in the following text from South Carolina collected by workers of the South Carolina Writers' Project (Work Projects Administration) sometime between 1935 and 1941: 

B

> A traveling man [driver] who lived in Spartanburg [authentication] was on his way home one night [setting] when he saw a woman walking along the side of the road [hitchhiker]. He stopped his car and asked the woman if he could take her where she was going. She stated that she was on her way to visit her brother who lived about three miles further on the same road [her address]. He asked her to get in the car and sit by him, but she said she would sit in the back of the car [her choice of seat]. Conversation took place for a while as they rode along, but soon the woman grew quiet. The man drove on until he reached the home of the woman's brother, whom he knew [more authentication]; then stopped his car to let the woman alight. When he looked behind him, there was no one in the car [disappearance]. He thought that rather strange [curiosity or concern], so went into the house and informed the brother that a lady had gotten into his car to ride to see him, but when he arrived at the house the lady had disappeared. The brother was not alarmed at all and stated that the lady was his sister who had died two years before [identification]. He said that this traveling man was the seventh to pick up his sister on the road to visit him, but that she had never reached his house yet.

Variations on the basic story are endless, and trying to sort them out into any kind of possible chronological development is hampered by the fact that the date when a version happened to be collected and published bears little relationship to its possible age in tradition, and by the principle that legends become highly localized and rationalized with many circumstantial details whenever they are adopted into a particular context.

> **COLLABORATING**
>
> Select one of the readings from Part III of this book to read as a group. On your own, read the selection and do a freewrite. As a group, compare freewrites and see which aspects of the essay appear in all of the freewrites. Use your findings as the basis of highlighting and check marking the text. Make sure to differentiate between facts and examples in highlighting, and do not highlight more of the text than is necessary.

As with all the strategies suggested in this book, find what works for you. Analyze what you do to make accurate predictions about nontext reading, and apply that to text reading. Reading can be bearable and even fun if you develop strategies that make you a critical reader and support you as a writer.

Summary

Even people who do not read many books or magazine articles engage in acts of interpretation that can form the basis of a strong reading process. As a reader, you unconsciously try to predict texts. Difficulty in reading arises when texts are not easily predictable, and you may give up on your reading at this juncture. You need to see the purpose for reading to get through such blocks. With motivation established, you can develop a reading strategy that will get you through the actual reading and enhance your comprehension. You must attempt different processes to find out what works best for you.

CHAPTER 9

WRITING WITH EVIDENCE

Recently, students in my class selected the sensitive subject of religion as an essay topic. I expected some awkward moments during our whole class workshops, where we would critique student work and make suggestions for improvement. Since religion is, by its very nature, a matter of faith, not of fact, many students wrote drafts that lacked evidence to support their contentions. I was not asking students to prove that God exists or to defend their personal faith. Rather, I was asking them to explain the beliefs in their religions, describe the religion's appeal for them (or, if students had turned away from their religions, they could explain that choice), and generalize through examples to arrive at a thesis. One discussion from the workshop has relevance to this chapter.

Julie volunteered to be in the first group of students whose drafts were critiqued. The other students and I read her essay and came to class prepared to comment. Julie had been raised a Baptist and liked her religion very much, but she did not like its prohibitions against premarital sex. She argued logically for her position. Her peers, however, spotted a problem with her reasoning.

JULIE SPRINGFIELD

Sex and Religion

I love my church and would never think of changing religions. Ever since I can remember, I was a Baptist and went to the Antioch Baptist Church. I liked the feeling of praying together and being

Online Study Center

This icon will direct you to web links and additional resources on the website college.hmco.com/pic/thelin1e

reminded to live a good life. We believe that Jesus is our savior and that he died for our sins. We believe in the truth of the Bible. We believe that the Ten Commandments are God's laws for us. We reject the devil and all he stands for. We believe everyone should try to be a good Christian and not to sin.

Despite this, I do not understand why premarital sex is wrong. I have heard people condemn it and talk about the deterioration of morals and values because couples will not wait until they get married to have sex. Some people in my church have formed coalitions against television shows which allude to sexual situations or where men's and women's bodies are not concealed by heavy layers of clothing. They also don't believe in giving out birth control because they think it encourages sex.

I respect that they want to follow God's law, but I do not see the sense in it. Sex is very natural. While one of its purposes is for reproduction, just like the church people say, I do not think God would have created urges in all of us if that was all it was for. People will say that if you wait until you find the right person and get married, you will experience sex in a better way than if you have multiple partners. But how would they know? If you only experience sex with one person, you cannot tell if there is anything better or worse.

I do not believe people should be sleeping around casually with each other. But I think if you're in a relationship and you are in love, you shouldn't have to get married to have sex. You want to be closer to your boyfriend, but you cannot really know how mature or caring he is if you keep him at a distance. If you marry him and then discover that he has trouble with intimacy or needs freaky things to make him satisfied, you are stuck in a marriage. It is better that you know as much as you can about a guy before marriage. If you find out that he is not the guy you want to marry, you can go your separate ways without having to go through a divorce or anything.

I do not understand who anyone is hurting by having premarital sex. As long as you are careful with your birth control and stick to one guy at a time, you are not going to get pregnant or catch a disease. It's really no one else's business. You are not breaking any laws or causing anyone else harm. You are just making a decision about a relationship that influences you and nobody else.

When I turned sixteen, I did not go to church as often as I used to. It seemed the sermons did not talk as much about what Jesus wanted from us as much as what he did not want. I wanted to do good things to keep my walk with Jesus strong, but I had to let people know how I felt about sex. Especially in Youth Group, where they kept telling us not to succumb to temptation, I had to make my feelings known. All of a sudden, Mrs. Jorgenson, who led the group, automatically thought that I was having sex, which I wasn't. She went from being a kindly second mother to me to being a cold, intolerant old lady. She would scoff at me, make comments about my activities, and say that Jesus did not care for

> my activities. I stopped going to Youth Group and only showed up for Sundays once in a while.
>
> I missed going so last year, I talked to Mrs. Jorgenson and I practically apologized for thinking like I did. I told them I realized I was wrong and that I had drifted away from my walk. I started going back to church and tried not to think about this conflict. I feel good about my church and I want to be a good Christian. I believe what the Baptist religion tells me on most things. But I think its stance on premarital sex is wrong.

"Are you questioning what the Bible says?" Lester asked Julie.

"I don't think so," she said.

"Well, what does the Bible say about sex?" Lester continued.

"I guess it says it's bad," Julie replied with a shrug.

"How do you know that?" I asked.

"Well, people tell me that," she answered.

A student who was familiar with the Bible suggested that Christ's advice to the prostitute he saved from death to "sin no more" clearly indicated that sex was a sin. Julie said she would look for other places to support this point.

"That's not what I meant," Lester said. "If you're a Baptist, you should be taking the Bible literally, right?" Julie didn't know what he meant. "You can't pick and choose," he emphasized. "The Bible is the authority on these matters."

"I'm just saying that I don't see the logic behind not having premarital sex," Julie said. "I don't think it should be a sin."

"But that's not being a Baptist," Lester said. "If you choose to have premarital sex, you are choosing to defy God, right? Because it is in the Bible, and the Bible is God's word."

"Well, maybe not," Julie said, looking confused.

"That's my point," Lester said triumphantly. "By questioning this one rule, you are contradicting yourself. A Baptist believes that the Bible is God's word. Aren't I right, Dr. Thelin?"

"Did you look into the basis of your religion?" I suggested to Julie. "Do you know why John Smyth started the denomination? Do you know about the principles of your faith?"

"I don't," she said. "I was just stating what I believed in."

The mistake Julie made was to think that she could assert something without producing evidence. In this case, she needed to check her knowledge about her religion before asserting its beliefs. For that part of the assignment, she had listed information she thought she understood without verifying it. She simply repeated basic fundamentals of many Christian denominations without talking about the specifics of her denomination. Thus, she did not take the opportunity to critically explore her religion in a way that could have helped her better understand and convey the dilemma between her reasoning and the Bible.

Even though the subject of religion might touch on personal areas that some students find uncomfortable, in another section of the same course students wanted to invent a philosophy of life that would make the world a better place. We decided that critiquing the values they personally adhered to could make for interesting essays and discussions. The students were supposed to explore the principles that they felt their lives stood for and critically assess whether the world would be better or worse if everyone followed these principles. Brad, a student in this class, submitted a very short draft to the whole class workshop in which he asserted that people should not worry about rules and should follow their instincts instead.

BRAD TURNER

Instincts vs. Rules (draft)

I have worked ever since I turned sixteen years old. Not a summer went by that I didn't have to earn my keep, and even during school, I had chores to do before class and a job picking up scrap at construction sites after school ended. I work forty hours a week now and then make some spare cash working on folks' cars on weekends. I haven't had much time to worry about my principles or philosophies, as I think you just have to live.

People talk about rules you have to follow, but I won't have any of that. You should do your job, take care of yourself, and just follow your instincts about right and wrong. I don't need anyone telling me that I can't do this or I can't do that. There are things that aren't healthy for you, but you have to decide that. What people tell you is not always the truth, either. Some people mind your business better than they mind their own. You got to decide what you want to do, then do it.

So people have to just do what comes natural. I'm a good person by anyone's definition. Instincts can guide you toward right and wrong. You don't need to list principles or say that you're following some guidelines to end up in the right place. If people just stuck to this, the world would be a better place.

The class had all sorts of questions. "How can you call yourself a good person and talk about right and wrong if you don't have any values?" Roger asked Brad. Brad shrugged his shoulders and looked at me.

"Does Roger mean that right and wrong have to relate to some sort of code?" I asked the class. "Do good and bad have any meaning otherwise?"

"They can have different meanings," Patricia said.

"But it's got to come back to something," Desmond stated. He turned to Brad. "It's like you just want us to accept that you know right and wrong without telling us what they are."

"I'm just saying that it's inside all of us what's right and what's wrong," Brad answered. "You don't have to get all fancy about it."

"To make that claim," I said, "you must show how you know what most people believe about right and wrong. You would have to give examples to support your belief in instinct."

"But all I'm trying to say is that my life works for me," he responded.

"No," I replied. "You're suggesting through this paper that people in general—not just you—could live better if they did not burden themselves with rules. Am I right?"

"Yeah," Brad said. "What's wrong with that?"

"How do you know others could live better if you don't know how they're living?" Patricia asked.

"Right," Desmond said. "You're just dissing the values of others because you can't hang with them."

"And what evidence do you have that you're living better than you would?" Roger followed.

"But it's my opinion," Brad stated adamantly.

Like Julie, Brad had assumed that he did not need to support what he said because the assignment included a personal component. But even when writing tasks seem to call for your opinion, you must supply evidence. In academic papers and in most forms of public writing, you are making a claim, which can be defined as a position you hold or that you believe has validity for others. A mere opinion has little meaning for a reader if it is not supported by evidence.

You also cannot divorce your experiences from the larger context of the rest of the world. You have a perfect right to hold an opinion in your personal life that is not supported by evidence or to follow ideas that are inconsistent with the public beliefs with which you identify them. But in academic and professional writing, your ideas must be supported so that they make sense to an audience. You must transform these beliefs into claims for them to be worthy fodder for an essay and to keep your readers' interest. Just as if a narrative contained a feat that defied the known natural laws of this world, readers will scoff at explanations or opinions that show no understanding of the context in which crucial components of the argument take place.

Brad's initial resistance softened, and he produced a revision that supplied evidence for his claims.

BRAD TURNER

Instincts vs. Rules

I have worked ever since I turned sixteen years old. Not a summer went by that I didn't have to earn my keep, and even during school, I had chores to do before class and a job picking up scrap at construction sites after school ended. I work forty hours a week now and then make some spare cash working on folks' cars on weekends. I haven't had much time to worry about my principles or philosophies, as I think you just have to live. But my experiences working gave me a code that helped shape my instincts about right and wrong.

People talk about rules you have to follow, but I won't have any of that. The only rules a person should follow are the responsibilities that are laid out to them. Life is like a job. You hire on to do what is needed and you know what you're going to get for it. You know what you're supposed to do. You do it without whining. You get paid at the end. Beyond that, I don't need anyone telling me that I can't do this or I can't do that. For example, with my girl, I knew what it meant to commit. The codes behind getting into a relationship are no different than signing up for a job. I'm supposed to take her out and treat her good. I'm not supposed to mess with other girls. I'm supposed to help her out when she needs it. I'm not supposed to be rude or disrespectful. It doesn't take a philosophy in life to figure these things out.

In the same way, there are things that aren't healthy for you, and you have to decide what risks you want to take. If you want to party it up, that's okay, but you got to take responsibility for what you say and do. You can't make excuses the next day that you didn't know what you were saying or you didn't mean to start that brawl or whatever. If you're sick or your liver gives out or you get addicted to drugs and have to go to rehab, well, you knew what could happen when you started partying. No one's broken any promises. You got high, which is what you wanted, but you knew there was a limit and you got what you knew you would get when you went past it.

What people tell you is not always the truth, either. You have to be wise and let your instincts guide you. You know that if someone is offering something that seems too good to be true, it probably is. You don't need laws to protect you when your common sense will do just as well. Also, some people mind your business better than they mind their own. You got to decide what you want to do, then do it. Just like at the job, pay attention to what you're doing and make sure it's done right. Don't worry about what they're saying or doing.

People have to just do what comes natural. I'm a good person by most people's definition, and I think if people listened to me, they would live a better life. If people didn't try to get more than they deserve and made sure they deserve what they got, we would have a better world. This instinct can guide you toward right and wrong. You don't need to list principles or be reminded of rules or say that you're following some guidelines to end up in the right place. The world is a job. If you get it done right in the first place and don't try to cut corners, you don't have to go back and do it a second time.

COLLABORATING

Brad improved his essay by adding evidence to support his claim. What do you think of his point? As a group, decide if you agree with Brad's point, and write down evidence from your experiences or observations that could either support or refute his ideas.

WRITING

Think of a person who you think is the best at doing a particular activity. Write a short essay in which you state your opinion on this matter. You can write about a football player, a singer, a corporate leader, or anyone else. How do you support your contention that this person is the best? In other words, how is he or she better than the other persons in that category? Be specific, and make sure to give several different reasons for your opinion. Once you are done, ask yourself how much of what you claimed is supported by clear evidence. What other information would you have to obtain to support your point if all your claims aren't supported by clear evidence?

This chapter discusses the ways writers use different forms of evidence. Chapter 10 goes into more detail about the research process; this chapter covers what is necessary to transform an opinion, which is an unsubstantiated claim, into a supported position. It also examines the necessity of verifying your understandings of the world. Keep in mind that supporting a claim requires evidence. The most insightful critical analysis will fall flat if the body of your argument does not support it with evidence.

Examining Evidence

We must distinguish evidence from proof. Evidence consists of verifiable details that have relevance to a claim a writer makes. It suggests that a particular thesis, argument, or line of reasoning is valid. Proof, on the other hand, is undeniable evidence in support of the claim. When you have proof, you have established validity to the extent that the proof can be applied to your claim. In casual conversation, people use these terms interchangeably, but when you write—and when you evaluate claims made by other writers—you must be keenly aware of the distinction.

Our writing frequently deals with issues that contain much uncertainty. An audience would have little interest in reading about a position that has no reasonable counterargument. For instance, we have proof that Richard Ramirez, the infamous "Night Stalker," committed a string of serial killings in Los Angeles during the 1980s. He never seriously denied his guilt and has been convicted. Writing a paper to assert his guilt would be a ridiculous endeavor, since no reasonable person would disagree with it. Writers deal with subjects about which they feel passionate and about which reasonable counterclaims can be made.

Sometimes a topic has to be explored deeply to find an issue. For example, many students in my classes have written about smoking. The thesis that results from their research is that smoking is bad. Is there any reasonable counterargument to this? Medically speaking, there is not. Smoking seriously harms people, affecting their lungs and hearts and putting them at risk for cancer. An essay's thesis that claims that people should not smoke because of the medical evidence has merely stated the obvious. Scientific research has proven the point beyond any reasonable doubt. Yet, people still smoke. Thus, the claim could consider the reasons people smoke even though they have full knowledge of the dire consequences. Perhaps smoking can be seen as good psychologically, as it eases tension in a unique way. Maybe the rewards outweigh the risks for smokers. More compellingly, though, a writer could argue that advertising aimed at teenagers, who generally do not have as clear a sense of their mortality as adults, piques their spirit of rebellion. People will debate this point. It has not been proven. Thus, a writer can explore it and can supply evidence to support or refute the claim.

COLLABORATING

What sensibilities about smoking are represented in this vintage ad for Camel cigarettes and in the recent antismoking ad with Joe Chemo? Could looking into advertisements make an investigation into smoking worthwhile? As a group, reach a consensus on the type of evidence you would need to make a claim about the influence of cigarette and antismoking advertisements.

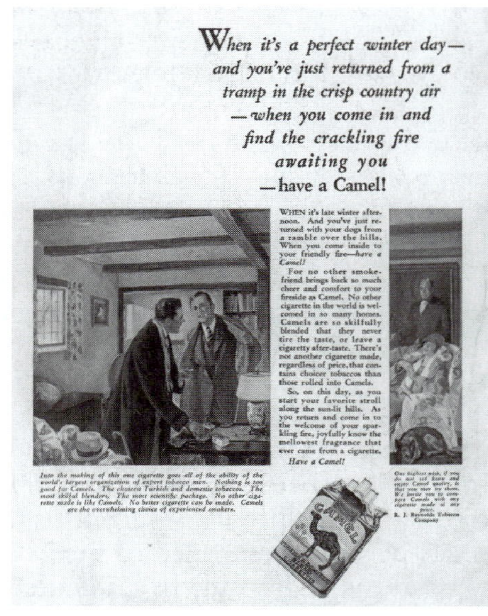

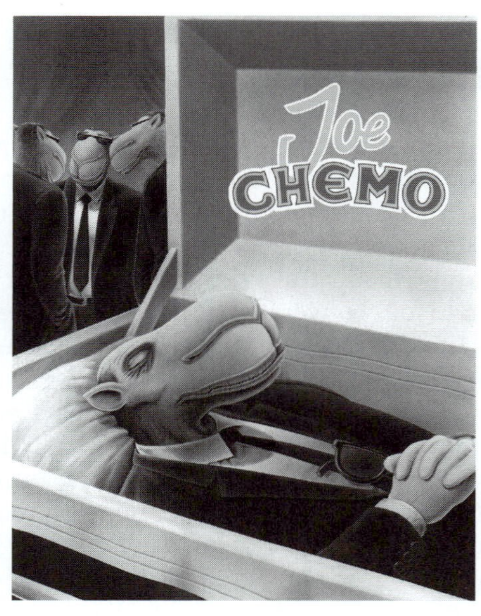

Some forms of evidence carry more weight than others. The more a writer relies on weaker forms of evidence, the more his or her claim has to suggest a conclusion rather than asserting it. Personal experiences, for instance, can help an audience relate to a claim, but they are the weakest type of evidence. When compiling evidence, you must examine each piece and understand what type of evidence you need to support your thesis.

Facts The strongest type of evidence is a fact. Facts cannot be disputed. They span a range of disciplines. In history, for example, we cannot dispute that Abraham Lincoln was the president of the United States during the Civil War. Many scientific discoveries and theorems, such as the laws of gravity, can be considered facts, although new discoveries will displace some of them as scientists progress in understanding the natural world.

Facts are neutral. For example, the short article "Courthouse Camera Captures a Ghost" in Chapter 13 discusses a peculiar light that appeared in a Maryland courthouse. The most important fact was a surveillance tape that showed a light with no apparent source moving on a stairwell. No one could dispute that something was showing up on the tape. Some people tried to interpret the fact as evidence of a ghost, while others felt it was evidence of a malfunctioning camera. (You can read the follow-up article on page 393 to learn what the mysterious light actually was.) The point here is that it is important to understand the difference between facts and the way people try to interpret them. Facts have no bias and usually are the strongest type of evidence for a claim. The claim can be disproved, but the facts cannot.

Statistics Statistics are the result of a formal study—an experiment, a survey, a protracted qualitative research project, a questionnaire, or a review of data. They strongly support claims when used. But the facts in statistics are limited by when the statistics were compiled, what sampling size was used, and other matters about how the researchers conducted the study.

The numbers produced from research come from interpretation of the information in the study. Interpretations can be and often are challenged, leading to follow-up studies that produce statistics that counter the previous study. The agenda of a research team, especially of its sponsor or financier, can call into question not just the interpretation of the results, but also the validity of the study itself. People can manipulate statistics to hide obvious points while highlighting less sustainable ones. The source of statistics, then, must be considered when using the statistics. Furthermore, statistics springing from surveys and questionnaires can be understood only in the historical moment. As evidence, they are limited to sentiment on a particular date and time and thus can support a claim only marginally.

Writers also need to avoid inadvertently implying the use of statistics. Even statements that start with "the majority feels" or "most people think" indicate statistical numbers, since both phrases are understood in relation to the marker of 50 percent. Writers must be careful about making such statements without support of a formal study. Qualifiers, such as "from my observation" or "I imagine" can be used when no statistical evidence is available, as can vague statements like "quite a few" or "many." Such phrases do not count as statistical evidence.

Witnesses Writers use firsthand accounts as evidence. Although witness statements rely on subjective observation, making them a weaker type of evidence than facts or statistics, firsthand accounts can verify the initial observation of an event and lend it credibility. Readers tend to be suspicious of a single account of an episode. When several witnesses recount essentially the same event, readers believe that the episode unfolded the way the initial person claimed it did. In an essay, being able to cite more than one person who perceived the same thing aids in the acceptance of your thesis.

Even a witness who saw something similar helps verify a previous account. For example, I grew up near a mountainside in northern Glendale, just outside Los Angeles. Coyotes, deer, and rattlesnakes visited our neighborhood every year. One neighbor claimed to have seen a mountain lion, a very rare animal in that part of California. Nobody believed him, even after his dog was killed by a large animal that came down from the hills. Less than a year later, another neighbor spotted what he described as a bobcat. With two claims, the other neighbors started believing that some large feline was roaming around, even though they were not certain of the species. Both neighbors could have been mistaken about what they saw, so their witness statements are a far cry from facts, but they do support a basic claim that some sort of wildcat was prowling in the neighborhood. A letter to the newspaper editor or a flier circulated in the neighborhood could have used this evidence effectively in warning parents to be watchful when their children played in the area.

Personal Experiences and Observations Our personal experiences and observations have a lot to do with shaping our view of the world. Yet, the narratives or examples we form from these experiences and observations are the least reliable type of evidence a writer can use. This statement puzzles many students, as some of our greatest lessons have come from learning from mistakes, growing through a tragic event, or succeeding when a challenge was put before us. The problem resides in the inability of an audience to verify the writer's personal experiences. Readers cannot simply believe everything a writer tells them. Many writers exaggerate experiences. Others remember details incorrectly. Still others leave out parts of a story that might complicate the point. Hard as it might be to believe, some writers simply lie about what happened or what they observed. For example, James Frey wrote a memoir in 2003 called *A Million Little Pieces* that he claimed was a completely true portrayal of his alcohol and drug addiction along with his criminal exploits. The book was selected for Oprah Winfrey's book club, and Frey became famous from his appearance on her television show. He even wrote a follow-up book, *My Friend Leonard.* In January 2006 The Smoking Gun, an investigative website, revealed that little in Frey's memoir actually happened.

Narratives or personal examples also tend to serve the interests of the person telling them. Their subjective nature leaves them vulnerable to opposing narratives. You might recount an experience about the hazards of bicycling at dusk, for instance. A reader might dismiss your account simply because he or she has ridden at dusk without incident on many occasions. One narrative cannot disprove the other, so you are left at a standstill.

Yet, narratives and personal examples can be used as evidence. Sometimes the body of a paper will be an extended personal example. You just have to temper your thesis statement, understanding that your personal examples can allow you to build a theory and share insights with an audience, but that your ideas need to be supported by more than just your experiences to gain validity. In "Face of the Spider" (Chapter 16), David Quammen narrates a story about his encounter with black widow spiders in his house. Rather than using the story as the sole piece of evidence for his theorizing, Quammen places his dilemma about whether to kill the spiders in the context of what other people think and feel about killing other forms of life, thereby giving his ultimate decision much more impact.

P. J. O'ROURKE

To Hell with Lipitor

P.J. O'Rourke supports his claim about Medicare with facts and projections about the national budget. Notice how he inserts his personal observations about senior citizens without relying on them as the sole means of evidence.

The Medicare Prescription Drug, Improvement, and Modernization Act of 2003 will—let's say—improve and modernize Medicare, mostly by giving old people money for drugs, at an expenditure of whatever, to be funded somehow. In his State of the Union address the President said the ten-year cost would be $400 billion. Medicare's chief actuary, Richard Foster, had informed the Administration that the cost would be more than $500 billion. He was told he'd lose his job if he let Congress know. Senator Trent Lott now estimates "closer to $600 or $800 billion." Good health is priceless. So are old people's votes.

Three quarters of seniors already had some prescription-drug coverage that cost Medicare nothing. The act "improves and modernizes" this, giving subsidies of $70 billion to employers and retirement plans that provide drug benefits.

Starting in 2006, Medicare recipients can enroll in government-approved private prescription-insurance plans (also subsidized) for about $35 a month. After a $250 deductible, 75 percent of drug costs will be covered up to $2,250; then no costs will be covered up to $5,100; then all costs will be covered except for five percent that won't be. Until 2006 government-approved private prescription-discount cards will furnish 15 to 25 percent savings (just in time, with wholesale prices for brand-name prescription drugs having risen 27.6 percent since 1999). Low-income beneficiaries will get $600 a year credited to these cards, which are free unless they use them. (There's a co-pay of five to 10 percent.)

Insert the phrases "a bewildering array of" and "until costs skyrocket" into each of the preceding sentences for a better understanding of new Medicare drug benefits.

5 These benefits were exhaustively explained in May, at a senior center in Nashua, New Hampshire, by Congressman Charles Bass, by an AARP representative, by the House Energy and Commerce Committee's chief health

counsel, and by the New England regional director of the Department of Health and Human Services. The audience's questions were acute: Preferred-drug lists and plan formularies? Benefit carry-overs? Calculation of income for assistance threshold? Multiple entitlement eligibilities?

Anyone who has experienced a Greatest Generation soliloquy on macaroni coupon rebates knows that this age cohort can shop. The HHS regional director, Brian Cresta, gave the audience his phone number: "Call me personally if you still don't understand the discount cards."

"I've given my number in dozens of meetings," Cresta said later. "I haven't gotten a call yet."

The old people weren't confused. And they weren't grateful. Tell kids they deserve a treat. Then give them 15 percent of a Snickers, or a little more if it's some generic candy bar. Tell them how, in two years, they can have candy free—if they pay for part of it and a bite has been taken out of the middle.

There must be a better way to give old people money for drugs—such as giving old people money for drugs. For Medicare recipients, average out-of-pocket spending on prescriptions in 2003 was $999. Pay them each $600 a year and the Prescription Drug Act's cost is slashed to $242.2 billion.

10 "How come," a man in the Nashua audience asked, "Canada can have the same drugs and pay less? [*applause*] Why don't they get some brain power down in Washington and lobby these drug companies down in price? [*applause*]"

The act in fact bans reimportation from Canada—devil take NAFTA principles—and forbids Medicare to bargain with pharmaceutical companies, although the Department of Veterans Affairs successfully does so.

But we might not want to cut drug prices too much. America is the last important free market for pharmaceuticals. Perhaps coincidentally, America produces two thirds of all "innovative drugs." Twenty years ago a more laissez-faire Europe produced two thirds of all innovative drugs, perhaps coincidentally. Anyway, drugs account for only 10.5 percent of health-care costs.

Which still leaves us wondering where to get that $242.2 billion or $400 or $500 or $600 or $800 billion, not to mention the $27.7 trillion in unfunded liability that Medicare's trustees say Medicare faces over the next seventy-five years. (Picture nonagenarian ravers demanding coverage for Ecstasy prescriptions.) Americans are now spending $1.55 trillion a year on health care. There's no way to cut these costs, because there's no way Dad's going to Dr. Bob's Cut-Rate Osteopath Shop.

We could raise taxes. (A lot. Medicare will consume half of all federal income-tax revenue by 2039 if current trends continue.) We could means-test fairly—by including the incomes of the people who owe everything to Medicare recipients: their kids. (That's me. Scratch that.) Or we could privatize Medicare. U.S. median household income is around $40,000. The federal Medicare tax is 2.9 percent. Invest that $1,160 a year, from age twenty-five to age sixty-five, at a six percent return, and you'd have $215,589. But that's in forty years.

15 Until then we have a choice: a realism about what Medicare can do, or a reality in which it can't do much. Perhaps the latter option isn't unthinkable.

At the Nashua senior center a Mr. Kim, who looked well into his seventies, addressed the audience. After apologizing for his English, he said, "To hell with Lipitor, a hundred and fifty dollars a month! I decided to hell with it. If I die, I die. I exercised. I lowered cholesterol level. Ran half marathon!"

DISCUSSION

Explore the following claim: "Corporal punishment serves to reinforce the use of violence as a solution to problems. Might becomes right, producing a child with limited self-discipline and a tendency to comply with authority out of fear." After mulling over this statement, explore its implications. If it was supported by facts, statistics, and witness statements, how would we negotiate our own experiences of discipline into the evidence, especially if the evidence conflicted with our experiences? Do we defend what we experienced no matter what the evidence? Do we deny our experiences in deference to the evidence? Find a strategy for dealing with such situations, and relate the strategy to writing tasks you have had.

Establishing Criteria for a Claim

Evidence for a claim makes sense only if it is compared or applied to an agreed-on standard by which it can be evaluated. The agreed-on standards by which we base claims are called criteria. Think of criteria as categories. Each category is an area needed in order to make a decision or form a thesis. The category headings are the criteria you have established. You will measure your evidence by how well it aligns with the categories.

In a writing activity earlier in this chapter (page 243), you were asked to make a claim about someone who is the best at doing an activity. In writing this essay, did you arrange evidence in categories so as to make comparisons to other people who do the same activity? If so, you established criteria by which to rank these people. When you determined criteria, you gave yourself a way to make clear decisions and to make your evidence better understood by your audience.

While a comparison uses criteria in an obvious way, an essay like Brad's also needs criteria. Brad's thesis was that people could live better lives if they followed their instincts instead of society's rules. Look back on your group writing about the evidence in Brad's claim on page 241. Did his evidence fit people's assumptions about a "better life"? In other words, did Brad anticipate audience needs and construct criteria about a better life? Were categories such as "personal responsibility" and "self-discipline" obvious, even if not stated explicitly in his text? For an essay to be effective, the writer's implied criteria should organize the essay and be clear to the audience.

Without the structure of criteria, your argument might haphazardly include information without showing its relevance. If you have anticipated audience needs well enough, your evidence should support your claims, even if audience members disagree with some of the criteria you used. When determining the criteria—something to think about early in your writing process—you should keep certain matters in mind.

Ensuring the Relationship to the Claim Writers should fill the bodies of their papers with evidence that is relevant to the claims. Thus, the criteria they establish should directly bear on the claims. Writers can become distracted when they know a great deal about a subject. If research has been done, they sometimes desire to show what they know and forget that some of the information is irrelevant to supporting a suitable thesis.

For example, if you were assigned to show why a historical figure should be considered heroic and decided that Mother Jones, the famous labor agitator, would be a good subject, you might become captivated by her biography. Mother Jones traveled from Europe to Canada to the United States, personally heard Lincoln speak, and experienced the advent of the industrial age firsthand. These facts might not work toward a thesis about heroism. Mother Jones suffered personal tragedy during the Chicago fire of 1871 and in one week lost her husband and all four of her children to an outbreak of yellow fever. This information, though interesting, still might not be relevant to your paper; overcoming personal crisis does not necessarily make for heroism. More relevant information includes her sacrifices for coal miners, her advocacy of oppressed Mexican revolutionaries in the Southwest, and her work in founding unions and political parties for working people. In other words, these accomplishments comprise the most worthy set of criteria because they have more to do with standard definitions of heroism. While background information might set the stage for your evidence, establishing criteria to make that information sound like evidence would dilute your thesis.

Establishing Substantive Criteria Criteria not only have to be relevant; they have to be substantive. Establishing superficial criteria does little except make the writer seem to be avoiding the real issues. Writers tend to succumb to superficiality when they worry about the validity of their theses. If establishing a criterion might jeopardize a point, some writers disregard that criterion and slip in something less deep.

Instead of establishing superficial criteria, try one of these two options. First, as was mentioned in earlier chapters, acknowledge the validity of opposing points of view. Explain that your point might seem weaker when viewed through this set of criteria, but establish why the criteria you chose more appropriately assess the situation. Second, rethink your thesis. If your point falls apart when serious criteria are applied, it probably has less value than you initially thought.

Look again at your writing about the person who is best at an activity to see whether other criteria might have been more appropriate for your claim.

Avoiding the Bandwagon Mentality Some criteria seem valid but actually do little to supply evidence for a point. One common mistake writers make is to use popularity as evidence. On the surface, popularity appears to be a good method of persuading an audience. If one of your criteria is that many people should agree with a point of view for it to be worthy, supplying evidence that people do, indeed, support your point seems helpful in securing the acceptance of your claim by readers. But this criterion is flawed. As we all know, the majority can be wrong. Further, a genuine critical analysis does not kowtow to the status quo. Critical analysis seems fresh and astute for the very reason that it does not produce the most popular or obvious points of view. Therefore, stating that your claim is correct because it is popular constitutes a logical fallacy that undermines your credibility.

Do not jump on the bandwagon when you are considering evidence. The bandwagon mentality appeals to prejudicial ideological assumptions. While few writers intentionally establish a criterion that relies on racism or sexism, this type of appeal does slip in. If a person were writing a paper about John Stockton, who holds the NBA record for assists, and established a criterion that Stockton was one of the few white stars in basketball when he played, the argument could be interpreted as racist, even though the writer did not say anything negative about other races. When writers establish categories that connote civic pride, patriotism, manhood, or other ideological constructions, they are committing the logical fallacy of the bandwagon argument. If your claim is so weak that you need bandwagon criteria to categorize your evidence, you need to reexamine the claim.

COLLABORATING

As a group, collect several different reviews of the same recent movie. Determine the implicit criteria the critics used in evaluating the movie. A critic rarely states such criteria explicitly. For example, a review will not state that a good movie must contain convincing performances. However, if the critic mentions flawed acting during the review and has an overall unfavorable opinion of the movie, you can ascertain that one criterion is the acting ability of the cast. Note how the criteria are woven into the reviews, and decide how valid they are to the critic's final judgment.

Checking Information

Whether your writing task involves asserting a claim, suggesting a possibility, or weaving in another type of thesis, you need to critically examine the information you use to support your reasoning. Novice writers frequently consider themselves to be experts and do not bother to verify their facts. Other times, knowledge that has been passed down, perhaps by their families, proves to be incorrect or less broad in application than they anticipated.

In the draft presented at the beginning of this chapter, Julie assumed quite a bit about her religion and its relationship to the Bible. Julie's claim about premarital sex needed to be understood in the context of Baptist beliefs on the primacy of the Bible. During the process of revision, Julie researched Baptist doctrine. She never knew, apparently, about key tenets of the denomination, and she came to understand that she would have to equate her logic to the word of God in order to validate her argument for a Baptist audience. Julie had never thought of this. She and her friends had talked about the issue, and relying on logic had worked in other academic arguments she made. She assumed that her opinion always mattered because "that's the way it was." She further assumed that she completely understood the position of her faith on the issue, but she really knew a simplified version. This led her to make a claim that did not accurately convey the complexity of Baptist beliefs.

Julie was willing to check her information when confronted with the possibility that she was wrong. But when armed with the facts, she found that she did not have a claim to make. For some reason, however, she did not want to reconceive her paper, so she turned in a revised piece that still had the glaring inconsistency. If she had checked her information first, she could have detected the problem much sooner and have taken the paper in a different direction. Following are guidelines about what information to check, how much information to check, and where to check the information.

Beliefs, Histories, and Definitions Writers should verify information about the beliefs of an institution or person, the history of a person, place, or institution, and the definition of key terms. Beliefs can be slippery, so you want to represent what somebody else feels in words that the person would see as accurate. As a citizen, for example, you might believe that your governor lacks commitment to cleaning up the environment. However, you would need to find a statement by your governor that supports your view, since you could be misinterpreting his or her actions. The governor might, in fact, believe wholeheartedly in cleaning up the environment but has not prioritized it. A more accurate statement would be that cleaning up the environment is not among his or her top priorities.

History is usually a matter of facts or of well-supported theories, although the perspectives and biases of those who narrate and interpret historical events have been questioned. For example, a student wrote in an essay that eight thousand people were killed in the September 11, 2001, attack on the World Trade Center. That figure was an estimate made at the time of the attack; the number was changed in subsequent days until the government arrived at the much lower tally of just over three thousand people. With some fact-checking, this student could have provided more accurate information. Any reference to past events, even recent ones, should be verified.

Confirming the definition of a key term can prevent embarrassing moments. Keep the advice about language in Chapter 5 in mind. An additional tip is to look up concepts that an instructor introduces in class. For example, the word *feminism* evokes many reactions. If you use the term, make sure you understand its meaning and the specific context in which it is used so as to not misuse it. In a recent class, a student essay talked about "feminism" when the student clearly meant "sexism." The two terms are not synonymous but are instead in opposition to each other.

The Straw Man Fallacy The straw man fallacy is an argument that does not represent the opposing side in a substantial, truthful way. Sometimes writers who are passionate about a claim see the opposition as unreasonable, perhaps even ignorant and immoral. In writing about opposing arguments, they create a caricature of the actual evidence and claims. If you have written a very negative description of counterarguments to your claim or of the people making a counterargument, check your information carefully. Research the purpose of the opposition and the ways the opponents construct their arguments. Consider the logic behind their goals and the strong points in their claims. To do otherwise is to succumb to the straw man fallacy, which many audiences consider unethical.

Dictionaries, Encyclopedias, and Websites Verify your information in reliable reference sources, both print and online, that provide concise and accurate information. In college-level writing, do not use a dictionary or an encyclopedia as a primary source of a paper that requires research. However, you can use such reference materials to check accuracy and to give you a starting point for more detailed research.

Dictionaries should be consulted for basic definitions. However, some concepts are better explained in extended form. For example, a philosophical movement, such as stoicism, existentialism, or postmodernism, needs more than a thumbnail sketch to be accurately represented. An encyclopedia or a website would supply more thorough information about these belief systems. The reference librarian at your campus library can direct you to the best sources for specific subjects.

For historical facts, encyclopedias or websites will give enough information to verify most information you might use. When using websites, confirm that they are legitimate. Keep the perspective of the person or organization running the website in mind. A pro-Palestinian website, for instance, will discuss the history of the West Bank much differently than a pro-Israeli website. Confirm controversial or sensitive information through several websites just to make sure. We discuss this issue more thoroughly in Chapter 10.

COLLABORATING

In your peer response group, share drafts of your current essays. Underline or highlight every sentence that states what a person or institution believes; that refers to the history of a person, place, or institution; and that uses a key concept. Figure out what the writer needs in order to verify this information. If you are working online, look together for reliable resources. If you come across a source that contradicts a claim in one of the drafts, how might the new information affect the essay's argument? Should the writer consider altering the claim?

Integrating Sources

You need to integrate evidence from sources into your essay as smoothly as possible. Plopping a quotation into the middle of an essay does not help the audience understand its context or relevance. You must take responsibility for clearly signaling that you understand the material and that you have a purpose for presenting it in the essay.

The key issue in integrating sources is for you to retain your own voice. An essay should not be an amalgamation of different sources but rather the coherent argument of a writer who uses different sources to support a claim. While using full quotations can be appropriate at times, this section suggests ways to locate key words within a quotation and to paraphrase so the voices in sources supplement rather than supplant your voice. Effective paraphrases extract evidence from source materials. Whether you are using ideas, facts, witness statements, or statistics, you need the information, not the words in which it is embedded.

The next chapter discusses how to use citation systems. The following ideas explain how to integrate evidence from sources into your writing.

Extricating the Information Often, writers simply need information from a source. In such cases, it makes no sense to retain the original words or sentence structures. Instead, you need to extricate the information. Claudia, a student in my class, discovered the story of Anne Bonny, an eighteenth-century pirate, while researching an essay about female outlaws. Claudia claimed that female criminals can be as brutal as male criminals, and Bonny's story supplied evidence. Consider this excerpt from Nancy Roberts's *Blackbeard and Other Pirates of the Atlantic Coast.*

NANCY ROBERTS

from *Blackbeard and Other Pirates of the Atlantic Coast*

Captain Rackham is the notorious pirate, "Calico" Jack Rackham. Bonny became attracted to him shortly after she married James Bonny, whom she grew to despise because he betrayed former mates for reward money. Rackham was hanged in November 1720, but not until Anne Bonny condemned him as a coward for not fighting hard enough in his last battle.

According to the law of the day the punishment for a woman who left her husband for another man was a public flogging. Though this punishment was seldom carried out, the governor threatened Anne with this treatment if she didn't return immediately to James Bonny. By this time Rackham was already plotting with Anne to steal a sloop and put to sea. When the governor's threat reached the pair, they accelerated their plans, and by dawn the next morning Rackham was sailing his new, ill-gotten ship with a new crew member on board—a woman.

Anne was faithful to her pirate captain. Writer Daniel Defoe says that a young crewman once made advances to Anne, and she beat him so badly that no one else tried to seduce her again. But she did give Rackham some jealous moments. After a time she became fast friends with a new pirate who had joined the crew, and the pair were constantly seen together, sometimes walking the deck arm-in-arm. This infuriated Captain Rackham.

"If I see you with that little fop again, I'll slit his throat!" he roared. In order to calm his rage, Anne asked that they have a private meeting with the new pirate in Rackham's cabin. He consented reluctantly, fingering the handle of his dagger and muttering, "I would rather solve the problem my way."

When the three were alone, Anne's pirate friend said in a soft voice, "I'm no threat to you, Captain Rackham." To Rackham's astonishment the pirate opened "his" shirt to partially reveal the breasts of a woman! The new crew member was a young widow named Mary Read, and she was the only woman friend Anne had ever known. Later Mary married one of the crewmen, and she and Anne remained close friends.

Then Anne began to have a much more serious problem. To her distress, 5
she noticed her agility lessening, her footing becoming unsteady, and her dagger thrusts finding their mark less often as she fought the crews of the vessels Rackham plundered. Sometimes, to her humiliation, her blows missed altogether. She was pregnant.

When Anne told Rackham, he suggested that they put aside piracy briefly and seek a more peaceful environment. They sailed for Cuba—a haven for pirate families, where husbands returned periodically for whatever semblance of home life pirates could have. Some women stayed there the year around, but not Anne, for she loved the sea. Scarcely risen from her childbed, she gave the baby up to another family in the pirate colony and was soon back on board ship, fighting at Rackham's side, capturing and plundering one ship after another.

During October of 1720, Rackham's ship *Curlew* attracted the interest of the governor of Jamaica. He had given the Brethren of the Sea offers of pardon if they would surrender, and many had done so. But some of the more stubborn had lacked gratitude for this generous treatment, and Rackham was one of them. This angered the governor, who sent an armed British sloop to attack the pirate captain's vessel.

The sloop took the *Curlew* by surprise. Soldiers and marines clambered over the side with swords drawn and revolvers firing. After running two Britishers through with her sword, Anne Bonny turned just in time to catch sight of most of her fellow pirates scrambling down the ladder to take refuge below deck. Captain Rackham, too, disappeared, and she and Mary Read, with the help of one man, found themselves holding off the attackers.

"Come up and fight, you sea scum!" Anne called out. Mary angrily fired her pistols into the hold to shame—perhaps rally—the crew, killing one pirate and wounding several others. "Fight, you cowards, or you'll hang!" Anne raged at them from the top of the ladder, but neither Rackham nor any of his crew emerged from the hold to defend themselves.

"Surrender! We don't want to kill women," a British marine shouted to Anne and Mary.

10 Then one of the soldiers closed in and began tearing at the beautiful red-haired pirate's clothing. Whirling, Anne jabbed him in the groin with a blow of her knee. "Get back! I'll die before you bloody scoundrels touch me."

"Let her alone!" shouted an officer, and he grasped her with a vise-like grip. "You wildcat!" he said with some respect as she continued to fight him. "Be still, and I'll make sure that you're not molested."

At the same time Anne glanced up to see the ominous black pirate flag of the *Curlew* lowered and the British Union Jack being raised in its stead. She ceased struggling. Everyone aboard was taken prisoner, and the two women, so that they would not be subjected to crude remarks, were led to the captain's cabin.

When the pirates were tried in Jamaica, spectators jammed the courtroom of St. Jago de la Vega. Crewmen who were able to prove they had been forced into piracy were soon acquitted, and Mary Read's husband was one of them. But there could be no plea of "being forced" for Anne Bonny and Mary Read. Both were still defiant, and the testimony of the crew members of the *Curlew* did not help them.

"No one was more ready to attack a ship and fight in hand-to-hand combat than these two women," the men testified. Their accounts of the women's ferocity horrified spectators and jury alike.

15 Anne Bonny, pregnant for the second time, entered the courtroom, striking even in tattered men's clothing.

"Look at that red-haired monster," women murmured as she passed. "To think she's going to be a mother!" The male spectators and even officers of the court regarded her warily, as if she were a tigress who might leap at them. But many found it impossible not to admire the proud way she held herself, staring straight before her, head high, oblivious to insulting remarks. There was a hush as she passed through the crowd, for she drew their attention like a magnet.

Claudia did not need to quote large extracts from Roberts's account of Bonny. Instead, she jotted down the facts in her own words: "Bonny beat with her fists any crewman who tried to seduce her; she plundered ships while pregnant; she shot and killed fellow pirates who would not fight when her ship was boarded." Claudia realized that she had to document where this information came from, but she knew that the facts could be effectively and accurately paraphrased. Roberts's purpose was to tell stories about different pirates. Claudia's purpose was to find women outlaws who were brutal. She wove the evidence from Roberts's biography into her own sentences, relying on her criteria for brutality as the frame for the information. Consider the following paragraph from Claudia's essay.

Extract from Claudia's Essay

Throughout history, women have performed acts as horrendous as men when put into unfortunate circumstances. For instance, Anne Bonny, an 18th century pirate, fought with her fists against men,

> plundered many ships, even when pregnant, and was not averse to killing her fellow crewman when they did not do as she demanded. Bonny seemed to excel at criminal acts at times when her crewmates were less inclined toward violence (Roberts 109–11). It is the greatest irony that she was released from her sentence of hanging because she was pregnant.

The voice in this excerpt is not the voice of Roberts, but of Claudia, using the facts for her purpose.

Paraphrasing Effective paraphrasing extracts ideas and information from a source. Paraphrasing is not changing a word or two in a sentence and calling it your own. That kind of carelessness is plagiarism. Rather, paraphrasing involves summarizing the ideas of a source while still retaining the flavor by using key words or phrases. In college writing, many instructors prefer students to paraphrase rather than to quote, as paraphrasing shows that the students understand the source material.

In most cases, paraphrasing provides greater clarity and consistency of tone than does simple quotation. To paraphrase properly, you need to read the source carefully. You should not be rooting through it, looking for a good quotation, but instead you should be trying to comprehend the overall point. Once you have finished your reading, write down in your own words what you believe to be key pieces of information or the main points of the arguments. Next, look for words or phrases in the selection that might give your paraphrase more precision.

For example, the first chapter of Paul Shepard's book *The Tender Carnivore* explains his theory that the advent of agriculture brought crisis, not progress, to Earth.

PAUL SHEPARD

from The Tender Carnivore

Often considered to be the father of ecopsychology, Paul Shepard linked contemporary environmental problems to humanity's desire to separate itself from its natural habitat.

The destructive combination of hydraulic agriculture and theocratic state has been the major force in the creation of our over-dense society and apocalyptic culture. Outside the great valleys other combinations have been chewing at the earth's skin just as effectively though less dramatically. In Morocco, pastoral nomadism and other grazing, charcoal-making, wood-burning, and land-clearing by fire have combined to deforest a once verdant and shady country. It is difficult to overestimate the extent of the damage by that arch destroyer, the goat.

Historians have blamed the Moroccan demise on Arab nomads who hated trees, just as the Mongols were blamed for the collapse of the

Mesopotamian irrigation systems. Ideology has been used to explain ecological situations. It is as though there were some cultural block against recognizing the fatal mishandling of the natural environment by the agricultural society and its urban overlords.

In China men struggled to control the Yellow River for four thousand years, while at the same time other men ravaged the upper watershed, creating gullies 600 feet deep. The mud that came down settled in the river bed, gradually lifting it high above the surrounding flood plain, and the river was contained entirely by manmade dikes. Flooding runoff from the denuded slopes occasionally overtopped the dikes. The great flood of 1852 shifted the mouth of the river 400 miles and drowned hundreds of thousands of people. The Biblical Flood of the Old Testament, about fifty-five hundred years ago, which was probably the Tigris River, had the same basic cause. There is evidence that the early Sumerian civilizations did not know floods of the Tigris, and that flooding began with upper-watershed destruction. The soils that fathered the first domestic plants and animals were ripped off the earth by hooves and teeth and sent down the Tigris and Euphrates, forming a delta that advanced 180 miles into the Persian Gulf, as though the skin had been peeled from the whole land and heaped into the sea, making 35,000 square miles of salt marsh from the topsoil.

The destruction was not necessarily the result of poor agricultural practices. It was rather the nature of husbandry itself. The record of agriculture everywhere on the planet is that of a blind force extending sand dunes and other wind damage by excavation and burial, lowering water-tables, increasing flooding, altering the composition of plant and animal communities, and diminishing the nutritive quality and stability of ecosystems. The loss of certain substances from the soil reservoir—especially phosphates, nitrates, and calcium—decreases crop food value. Change in floral composition affects a complex, stable species by replacing it with a simpler, shifting association. A forest may remain a forest, or grassland remain grassland, yet be drastically altered in richness, productivity, resistance, and soil-building ability. Changes in composition are brought about directly by overgrazing and indirectly by the cultivation of surrounding lands; they are invisible to most people, even cattlemen and other pastoralists.

5 No other organisms are more intricately associated with civilization than the cereals—wheat, barley, rye, corn, rice: modified annual grasses on whom the masses of mankind depend. Ecologically, the cereals are takers, not makers of soil. By contrast, perennial wild grasses work as pumps; their deep roots bring fresh nutrient minerals to the surface and structure the soil. They live in conjunction with a wide variety of flowering legumes and composites, two groups of plants essential for good soil formation, which are dependent on insect pollinators for their continued existence and in turn support a rich animal life.

As men undertook the cultivation of vast fields of cereals, they turned away from an ancient relationship with the wild nectar- and pollen-seeking bees, flies, butterflies, and beetles. Such insects had made possible the arboreal life of early primates in flowering and fruit-making tropical forests.

Then they were instrumental in the evolution of prairies and savannas, which supported the first pre-human ground apes. Finally, pollinating insects supervised the evolution of the steppe and tundra flora, where the great herds of Pleistocene mammals fostered the final hunting phases of mankind.

The earliest subsistence agriculture did not abandon its dependence on flowering plants and their pollinators, but when men moved into the great river valleys and planted vast fields of grain they in part repudiated ancient connections with a host of tiny animals who compose the richest and most diverse fauna on our planet. The cereals are wind-pollinated annuals, shallow-rooted, ephemeral, without soil-forming virtues, and their association with flowering forms or pollinator insects is minimal. By supporting large, minimally nourished human populations and by their destructive effects in the environment when grown in cultivated uniformity, the cereals are truly the symbol and agent of agriculture's war against the planet.

A student named Sherry was developing a claim that explored the negative aspects of farming. She paraphrased Shepard's key ideas accurately, integrating his insights with her own voice.

Extract from Sherry's Essay

Paul Shepard, a professor of human ecology and an environmental activist, believes much of our current environmental crisis can be traced back to the advent of agriculture. He accuses aspects of nomadic life, such as the domestication of animals and the clearing of land, as "chewing at the earth's skin," and he gives examples of agricultural practices that alter ecosystems (23–24). He feels that the harvesting of grains, in particular, symbolizes farming's "war against the planet" because it disconnects humans from natural fauna (25).

Sherry used Shepard's exact words twice in this paragraph, but she did not merely rewrite his sentences. Instead, she integrated them through paraphrasing, being careful to use quotation marks to distinguish between Shepard's words and her own. She chose these words because they demonstrate Shepard's passion and give the reader a context in which to place his ideas. She documented the page number from which she took those precise words, and she succeeded in writing an accurate paraphrase of Shepard's ideas.

Tag Phrases When you use a quotation or a paraphrase, you must introduce the source and briefly establish the author's credibility. Employ tag phrases to attribute the quotations to their source. While tag phrases such as "he said," "she asked," "we replied," and so forth are common in narratives with dialogue, different tag phrases are used with evidence. They introduce the author you are citing and indicate why the source is important.

When writing about music, for example, you might state that music allows listeners to relax. In introducing your support, you would write, "According to Alan Wells, who conducted research into the relationship between moods and music," and work in the relevant statistics from Wells's piece. "According to" is a standard tag phrase, and the following clause gives the audience a sense of why you are referring to this author. Another tag phrase is "Alan Wells, a qualitative researcher, finds that music . . . ." Depending on the evidence you have extracted, you can use the terms *claims, asserts, suggests, questions, states, believes,* or *cites.* The relationship to the paper makes the tag phrase different than the tag phrases used in dialogue. Once you have introduced the author, however, you do not have to continue to explain who he or she is in subsequent paragraphs. You can simply write, "On this point, Wells asserts, . . . " and paraphrase or quote his ideas.

COLLABORATING

Read a magazine article on a topic of your choice, and write a one-paragraph paraphrase that includes a direct quotation from the author, as in Sherry's paraphrase. Under your paragraph, list facts you found in the article. In your group, exchange your paragraph with another person. Read that person's paragraph as well as the listed facts, and write your own paragraph based on what is in front of you. Feel free to incorporate one or two items from the list of facts if they seem appropriate. You can use the direct quotation as is, shorten it, or leave it out. Have each group member read the original paragraph and the second one. How do the second paragraphs compare with the originals? Did not having the article to work from harm your ability to paraphrase?

Summary

Writers need evidence to support their claims. Personal experience alone is not sufficient to support academic essays and arguments. When making a claim, be aware of the relative worth of certain types of evidence. Facts carry the most weight, followed by statistics, witnesses, and experiences. To be understood by an audience, evidence needs to be selected according to appropriate criteria. These criteria must relate to your claim, must have the necessary depth, and must not commit the bandwagon fallacy. When writing about subjects you know well, confirm the information, especially when discussing beliefs and historical facts or relying on the definition of a key concept. In all forms of writing, be aware of how to integrate evidence into an essay, argument, or other genre of academic, professional, or civic writing. Quotations are not always necessary; you often need the evidence from a source, not the exact words. When you do want to retain the flavor of a source, you can paraphrase, but you must still correctly cite and credit the original source.

CHAPTER 10

WRITERS AND RESEARCH

Students often become overwhelmed by the information now available at libraries. The many computers, audiovisual materials, journals, magazines, newspapers, and microfilm machines, as well as the stacks and stacks of books, can make a library intimidating. Although search engines and the Internet are said to have made research easier than it was in the past, more than ever students need to participate in library orientation, make use of the services of reference librarians, and ask questions of their instructors.

I once took a class to the library to conduct research on political parties. Virtually all the students knew something about Republicans and Democrats, but they did not know the origins of either party or much detail about party platforms. Some students also wondered about alternative parties, such as the Libertarians, the Green Party, and the Labor Party. They worked in groups to see what they could find, and I circulated among them, fielding questions. The students gravitated to sites about the alternative parties. Their questions about the process of investigation and the quality of information could apply to any topic.

"Where do we go from here?" Kevin asked. His group had found a website that listed political parties, www.Politics1.com. This website gave thumbnail sketches of all known American political parties.

"How do we find out more about this group?" Patty asked. Her group had stumbled across the Pansexual Peace Party, a Wicca-based group that desired to free Americans from sexual repression.

This icon will direct you to web links and additional resources on the website college.hmco.com/pic/thelin1e

"Are these guys serious?" Pablo asked. He and Kevin were looking at the Constitutional Action Party, whose platform included banning abortion and doing away with the federal income tax.

Hilary's group felt that the Natural Law Party was on to something with its members' belief in transcendental meditation and yoga. Josh was amazed that the Nazis and the Ku Klux Klan had formal platforms. The many communist and socialist websites fascinated more than one group. Everyone wanted to know what to do with this information. How could they find out more? How could they be sure that they weren't being pulled into an elaborate joke? What type of people started and/or joined alternative parties?

All the groups logged into the first website Kevin's group had found, www.Politics1.com. It provided links to parties' web pages and to major figures, so students could see how party members viewed themselves and wanted others to perceive them. Students spent time reviewing platforms and statements of principles. Their explorations made some students curious to learn more about political parties that seemed to reflect their ideals.

"Why don't you send an email to the address provided?" I asked Hilary.

She stared at the screen. "Do you think it would be a good idea?" she asked. "I mean, couldn't I be hooking up with some crazies?"

"Yeah," Kevin joined in from a nearby terminal. "If these groups are so great, how come I never heard of them before?"

"People would be scared of this group," Patty said, fascinated by the platform of the Pansexual Peace Party. "People would be afraid that everyone would join. Students would join if these guys put more out there."

"So what is it you want to know?" I asked, as students in adjacent terminals looked at the sites others had found.

"Well," said Kevin, "how do we trust them? How can we tell if they're legit? Is it worth our time?"

"And what happens if we contact them directly, then get caught in something?" Pablo asked. "If we signed up, then they end up being traitors or something, we're like branded for life."

"So you guys don't trust what you're reading?" I asked.

"I don't believe nothing I read," Kevin responded. "I got to hear it from someone reliable."

"For a paper, the info's good, I guess," Patty mumbled.

"But for your life, it isn't?" I asked.

All of them stopped talking, some smiling awkwardly, others looking away. "I guess maybe if we don't trust it for life, we shouldn't trust it for school either," Pablo said slowly. "But what do we do? How do we find out?"

My students had identified a crucial problem of researching online. Like many people, students often too readily accept what they read on the Web. As long as the information seems pertinent to an assignment topic, they print it out or save it and use it indiscriminately. But for important decisions that may have a direct effect on their personal lives, they need more convincing. The verification they insist on before registering for a political party, paying membership dues to a club, moving to a new apartment, making sure a tattoo artist knows what he or she is doing, and other things does not carry over into their schoolwork.

Recognizing this inconsistent behavior is one thing. Changing it is another. As discussed in Chapter 1, students sometimes mistake the process of education for its substance, so they deem finding any source that seems to meet assignment requirements a success. Other students simply do not know where to go or what to do in working with sources for college assignments. They think they have to be let in on some secret or a magical formula for distinguishing legitimate from phony sources. As with so much in writing, though, the strategies students use in real life can be translated into academic researching methods.

DISCUSSION

What does a person have to do for you to trust him or her? When do you become skeptical of information a trustworthy friend gives you? Why does knowing the truth matter more in some types of situations? Make a list of the characteristics of a trustworthy person and another list of the type of situations that would make you doubt the information provided by a trustworthy friend. What characteristics or situations could you apply to your research for a paper? When does trusting the source matter?

While this chapter discusses specific research methods, you will find that most of the information parallels the strategies you use to make sound decisions in your daily life. Writing with research can frighten students, but armed with information, your task is not as daunting as you think.

Locating Critical Knowledge

Most instructors expect students to draw from a range of sources. They want you to avoid relying on superficial listings of facts and opinions, which will lead you to an analysis and a thesis that just repeat the same old thing. Beyond consulting some journals with small print runs and, of course, books, you can do most of your research from a computer terminal. You will run into the same problem whether you use paper or online sources: Which sources constitute merely surface knowledge, and which will give you an angle that can lead to a critical analysis?

Generally speaking, college-level papers, business reports, and documents constructed for citizen action should not use popular entertainment magazines. While *People, Us,* and others might relieve boredom while you are standing in line at the supermarket or waiting at the doctor's office, they do not have the depth or focus needed for serious research. Similarly, corporate websites and personal web pages generally do superficial analyses of products and issues, depending on their agendas. Blogs and wikis sometimes do excellent jobs of critically analyzing and debating current events, but contributors are not necessarily experts on the subjects they write about. Newsletters and fanzines are dedicated to a certain readership and can gloss over important information. You should be wary, too, of magazines or websites that propound extreme political views; they may distort the truth, despite coming up with fresh twists on issues. Following is a review of some sources that will help you critically analyze your subject and construct a sound thesis:

Mainstream Sources Some instructors are critical of weekly news publications, such as *Time* and *Newsweek*, and online news sources, such as websites for CNN and Fox News. Their criticism stems from legitimate concerns about ideology and bias. Most mainstream sources do not question underlying assumptions about our culture, so they tend to operate under the auspices of patriotism and capitalism with lingering sentiments of sexism and racism. Since laws no longer prevent multiple ownership of media outlets, the same few people own most of the prominent American television and radio stations, newspapers, and magazines. Furthermore, pack journalism and embedded reporting, wherein reporters receive most of their information from government sources, seriously hamper investigative reporting for mainstream publications. So the same ideology is present in all mainstream sources.

This does not necessarily imply bias. People who rant and rave about the liberal slant of the news media, for instance, often simply are unhappy that mainstream sources show sensitivity to minority opinions, something the media must do to try to maintain objectivity. Mainstream sources are not and should not be conduits for either conservative or liberal platforms, although the lingering sentiments mentioned above are stronger or weaker depending on ownership of the media outlet. Once a reader gets beyond the legitimate concerns, he or she will see that these sources approach their subjects seriously, do the necessary background checks, and aggressively pursue stories within certain boundaries. The stories generally reflect important national and world concerns. The information found at these sources can serve as a start toward doing serious critical analysis.

Field-Specific Journals Much prominent knowledge is generated by research from intellectuals. Mainstream media sometimes report on their findings. A substantial archeological discovery, for example, will likely be summarized in a newspaper article. The summaries often come from field-specific journals, and they are generally written on the day the journal publishes the article or the next day.

A field-specific journal is a serial publication that focuses on a particular subject matter. *College Composition and Communication*, for example, is published six times a year and focuses on the theories and experiences of teachers of writing. For the most part, field-specific journals have more rigorous standards than do mainstream publications. Many are published by universities or research institutes. Their goal is to disseminate higher levels of information than that found in mainstream publications. Their authors assume basic subject knowledge on the part of the readership and may use technical language and rhetorical forms in making their points. Since professors and professional researchers publish in these journals, the information generally is high quality. With little or no monetary profit at stake, the facts and theories distance themselves more freely from the ideology of mainstream publications.

Much critical knowledge is never summarized in mainstream publications because it is not accessible to or of interest to most people. However, with careful reading, you can extract much from field-specific journals that can be of help in your own writing.

Books Knowledge found in nonfiction books is probably safe for use in your research with the exception, perhaps, of some trade nonfiction. While books may be beholden to the ideology of the publishing house, they are likely to provide more detailed, in-depth information simply because of the extended number of pages devoted to the subject. Libraries have vast collections, including books from academic and specialized publishers that might not be found in mall bookstores.

Books are reservoirs of cultural knowledge. Critical information compiled in books might have been common knowledge years ago, but now seems fresh and intriguing. When the background of a situation needs to be understood, a book may give the most detailed information.

Some books, called anthologies, bring together the ideas of many different authors, so that each chapter contains a separate point or worldview. Some students shy away from books because they don't have time to do that much reading. An anthology allows you to browse until you come on a chapter that reveals the information you need.

Not all books go through rigorous editing and fact-checking. Rush Limbaugh's *The Way Things Ought to Be,* for instance, contains glaring errors about history and scientific discovery. Though widely read, the book is not a legitimate source for a college-level paper. Academic presses publish the most credible books. In deciding what information to use, follow the same guidelines presented in the section on evaluating online sources later in this chapter.

Alternative Magazines Many voices from the margins of society find homes in the multitude of alternative magazines available in paper form and online. Some students automatically dismiss such sources because the information seems too far removed from the mainstream. However, alternative magazines are among the best sources for critical knowledge. Since they challenge the cultural assumptions on which our society rests, they give many facts and viewpoints that will allow students to construct striking critical analyses.

People debate the distinguishing characteristics of alternative magazines. *The National Review,* for example, is hardly a mainstream publication, but its writers do not challenge dominant ideology as much as they expand on it. The magazine aligns its views with factions of the Republican Party and does not offer a fresh perspective. Its heavy funding further eliminates it from consideration. It can be best thought of as political commentary by conservatives and, as such, certainly offers facts and statistics that students can make use of, but it is not an alternative magazine.

Alternative magazines can have a conservative viewpoint, but most contain articles that lean left. *Z Magazine, The Progressive, UTNE,* and *The Nation* are examples of publications that are not in any way influenced by the Democratic Party, but that favor politics from the left. These magazines collect viewpoints from independent reporters around the world. Advertising revenues are limited, and they rely on reader subscriptions to stay in existence. Professors and instructors tend to take information in these magazines seriously because the reporting is not tainted by large media companies. Some stories that alternative magazines publish have been suppressed or censored by mainstream magazines because of the sensitivity of advertisers or the challenge to dominant ideology. While innuendo and shaky testimonials do find their way into the pages of these publications, most facts can be confirmed by experts. Readers can disagree with an analysis but still find value in the critical knowledge contained in it.

PETER PHILLIPS, TRISH BORETA, AND PROJECT CENSORED

The Top Censored News Stories of 2005–2006

Here are examples of censored stories compiled by writers from Spinwatch.org.

For 30 years, Sonoma State University's Project Censored has released an annual list of the most important news stories not covered by the corporate media in the United States. Here again are the Top 10 news stories that didn't make much news.

1. Net Neutrality

Throughout 2005 and this year, a largely underground debate has raged regarding the future of the Internet. More recently referred to as net neutrality, the issue has become a tug of war with cable companies on the one hand and consumers and Internet service providers (ISPs) on the other. Yet despite important legislative proposals and Supreme Court decisions throughout 2005, the issue was almost completely ignored in the headlines until 2006. And except for occasional coverage on CNBC's *Kudlow & Kramer,* mainstream television remains hands-off to this day.

Most coverage of the issue framed it as an argument over regulation, but the term "regulation" in this case is somewhat misleading. Groups advocating for net neutrality are not promoting regulation of Internet content. What they want is a legal mandate forcing cable companies to allow ISPs free access to their cable lines (called a "common carriage" agreement). This was the model used for dial-up Internet, and it is the way content providers want to keep it. They also want to make sure that cable companies cannot screen or interrupt Internet content without a court order.

Those in favor of net neutrality say that lack of government regulation simply means that cable lines will be regulated by the cable companies themselves. Internet service providers will have to pay a hefty service fee for the right to use cable lines (making Internet services more expensive). Those who could pay more would get better access; those who could not pay would be left behind. Cable companies could also decide to filter Internet content at will.

Source: "Web of Deceit: How Internet Freedom Got the Federal Ax, and Why Corporate News Censored the Story," by Elliot D. Cohen. Buzzflash.com, July 18, 2005.

2. Halliburton and Iran

According to journalist Jason Leopold, sources at Dick Cheney's former com- 5
pany, Halliburton, allege that as recently as January 2005, Halliburton sold key components for a nuclear reactor to an Iranian oil development company. Leopold says his Halliburton sources have intimate knowledge of the business dealings of both Halliburton and Oriental Oil Kish, one of Iran's largest private oil companies.

Halliburton has a long history of doing business in Iran, starting as early as 1995, when Vice President Cheney was chief executive of the company. In an attempt to curtail Halliburton and other U.S. companies from engaging in business dealings with rogue nations such as Libya, Iran, and Syria, an amendment was approved in the Senate on July 26, 2005. The amendment, sponsored by Sen. Susan Collins, R-Maine, would penalize companies that continue to skirt U.S. law by setting up offshore subsidiaries as a way to legally conduct business and avoid U.S. sanctions under the International Emergency Economic Powers Act.

A letter, drafted by trade groups representing corporate executives, vehemently objected to the amendment, saying it would lead to further hatred and perhaps incite terrorist attacks on the United States and "greatly strain relations with the United States' primary trading partners." The letter warned that "foreign governments view U.S. efforts to dictate their foreign and commercial policy as violations of sovereignty often leading them to adopt retaliatory measures more at odds with U.S goals."

According to Leopold, during a trip to the Middle East in March 1996, Dick Cheney told a group of mostly U.S. businessmen that Congress should ease sanctions in Iran and Libya to foster better relationships, a statement that, in hindsight, is completely hypocritical considering the Bush administration's foreign policy.

"Let me make a generalized statement about a trend I see in the U.S. Congress that I find disturbing, that applies not only with respect to the Iranian situation but a number of others as well," Cheney said. "I think we Americans sometimes make mistakes. . . . There seems to be an assumption that somehow we know what's best for everybody else and that we are going to use our economic clout to get everybody else to live the way we would like."

Cheney was the chief executive of Halliburton Corporation at the time he uttered those words. It was Cheney who directed Halliburton toward aggressive business dealings with Iran—in violation of U.S. law—in the mid-1990s, which continued through 2005 and is the reason Iran has the capability to enrich weapons-grade uranium.

It was Halliburton's secret sale of centrifuges to Iran that helped get the uranium enrichment program off the ground, according to a three-year investigation that includes interviews conducted with more than a dozen current and former Halliburton employees.

If the United States ends up engaged in a war with Iran in the future, Cheney and Halliburton will bear the brunt of the blame.

Source: "Halliburton Secretly Doing Business with Key Member of Iran's Nuclear Team," by Jason Leopold. GlobalResearch.ca, Aug. 5, 2005.

3. World Oceans in Extreme Danger

Oceanic problems once found on a local scale are now pandemic. Data from oceanography, marine biology, meteorology, fishery science, and glaciology reveal that the seas are changing in ominous ways. A vortex of cause and effect wrought by global environmental dilemmas is changing the ocean from a watery horizon with assorted regional troubles to a global system in alarming distress.

The oceans are one, say oceanographers, with currents linking the seas and regulating climate. Sea temperature and chemistry changes, along with contamination and reckless fishing practices, intertwine to imperil the world's largest communal life source.

In 2005, researchers from the Scripps Institution of Oceanography and the Lawrence Livermore National Laboratory found clear evidence that the ocean is quickly warming. They discovered that the top half-mile of the ocean has warmed dramatically in the past 40 years as a result of human-induced greenhouse gases.

One manifestation of this warming is the melting of the Arctic. A shrinking ratio of ice to water has set off a feedback loop, accelerating the increase in water surfaces that promote further warming and melting. With polar waters growing fresher and tropical seas saltier, the cycle of evaporation and precipitation has quickened, further invigorating the greenhouse effect. The ocean's currents are reacting to this freshening, causing a critical conveyor that carries warm upper waters into Europe's northern latitudes to slow by one-third since 1957, bolstering fears of a shut down and cataclysmic climate change. This accelerating cycle of cause and effect will be difficult, if not impossible, to reverse.

Atmospheric litter is also altering sea chemistry, as thousands of toxic compounds poison marine creatures and devastate propagation. The ocean has absorbed 118 billion metric tons of carbon dioxide since the onset of the

Industrial Revolution, with 20 to 25 tons being added to the atmosphere daily. Increasing acidity from rising levels of CO_2 is changing the ocean's pH balance. Studies indicate that the shells and skeletons possessed by everything from reef-building corals to mollusks and plankton will begin to dissolve within 48 hours of exposure to the acidity expected in the ocean by 2050. Coral reefs will almost certainly disappear and, even more worrisome, so will plankton. Phytoplankton absorb greenhouse gases, manufacture oxygen, and are the primary producers of the marine food web.

Mercury pollution enters the food web via coal and chemical industry waste, oxidizes in the atmosphere, and settles to the sea bottom. There it is consumed, delivering mercury to each subsequent link in the food chain, until predators such as tuna or whales carry levels of mercury as much as 1 million times that of the waters around them. The Gulf of Mexico has the highest mercury levels ever recorded, with an average of 10 tons of mercury coming down the Mississippi River every year, and another ton added by offshore drilling.

Along with mercury, the Mississippi delivers nitrogen, often from fertilizers. Nitrogen stimulates plant and bacterial growth in the water that consumes oxygen, creating a condition known as hypoxia, or dead zones. Dead zones occur wherever oceanic oxygen is depleted below the level necessary to sustain marine life. A sizable portion of the Gulf of Mexico has become a dead zone—the largest such area in the United States and the second largest on the planet, measuring nearly 8,000 square miles in 2001.

20 It is no coincidence that almost all of the nearly 150 (and counting) dead zones on earth lie at the mouths of rivers. Nearly 50 fester off U.S. coasts. While most are caused by river-borne nitrogen, fossil-fuel-burning plants help create this condition, as does phosphorous from human sewage and nitrogen emissions from auto exhaust.

Meanwhile, since its peak in 2000, the global wild fish harvest has begun a sharp decline. Progress in seagoing technologies and intensified fishing have stimulated unprecedented decimation of sea life. Long-lining, in which a single boat sets line across 60 or more miles of ocean, each baited with up to 10,000 hooks, captures at least 25 percent unwanted catch. With an estimated 2 billion hooks set each year, as much as 88 billion pounds of life a year is thrown back to the ocean either dead or dying.

Additionally, trawlers drag nets across every square inch of the continental shelves every two years. Fishing the sea floor like a bulldozer, they level an area 150 times larger than all forest clear-cuts each year and destroy sea floor ecosystems.

Aquaculture is no better, since 3 pounds of wild fish are caught to feed every pound of farmed salmon. A 2003 study out of the University of Nova Scotia concluded, based on data dating from the 1950s, that in the wake of decades of such onslaught, only 10 percent of all large fish (tuna, swordfish) and ground fish (cod, hake, flounder) are left anywhere in the ocean.

Other sea nurseries are also threatened. Fifteen percent of sea grass beds have disappeared in the last 10 years, depriving juvenile fish, manatees, and sea turtles of critical habitats. Kelp beds are also dying at alarming rates. While at no other time in history has science taught more about how the earth's life-support systems work, the maelstrom of human assault on the seas still continues. If human failure in governance of the world's largest public domain is not reversed quickly, the ocean will soon and surely reach a point of no return.

Source: "The Fate of the Ocean," by Julia Whitty. Mother Jones, *March/April 2006.*

4. Poverty Increasing in the United States

25 The number of hungry and homeless people in U.S. cities continued to grow in 2005 despite claims of an improved economy. Increased demand for vital services rose as needs of the most destitute went unmet, according to the annual U.S. Conference of Mayors Report, which has documented increasing need since its 1982 inception.

The study measures instances of emergency food and housing assistance in 24 U.S. cities and utilizes supplemental information from the U.S. Census and Department of Labor. More than three-quarters of cities surveyed reported increases in demand for food and housing, especially among families. Food-aid requests expanded by 12 percent in 2005, while aid center and food bank resources grew by only 7 percent. Service providers estimated 18 percent of requests went untended. Housing followed a similar trend, as a majority of cities reported an increase in demand for emergency shelter, often going unmet due to lack of resources.

President Bush's proposed budget for fiscal 2007, which begins October 2006, includes a Commerce Department plan to eliminate the Census Bureau's Survey of Income and Program Participation. The proposal marks at least the third White House attempt in as many years to do away with federal data collection on politically prickly economic issues.

Founded in 1984, the Census Bureau survey follows American families for a number of years and monitors their use of Temporary Assistance for Needy Families, Social Security, Medicaid, unemployment insurance, child care, and other health, social-service, and education programs.

Some 415 economists and social scientists signed a letter and sent it to Congress shortly after the February release of Bush's federal budget proposal, urging that the survey be fully funded as it "is the only large-scale survey explicitly designed to analyze the impact of a wide variety of government programs on the well-being of American families."

30 Supporters of the survey elimination say the program costs too much at $40 million per year. They would kill it in September and eventually replace it with a scaled-down version that would run to $9.2 million in development costs during the coming fiscal year. Actual data collection would begin in 2009.

Sources: "New Report Shows Increase in Urban Hunger, Homelessness," by Brendan Coyne. TheNewStandard.com, December 2005. "U.S. Plan to Elimi-

nate Survey of Needy Families Draws Fire," by Abid Aslam. OneWorld.net, March 2006.

5. High-Tech Genocide in Congo

The world's most neglected emergency, according to Jan Egeland, the U.N. Emergency Relief Coordinator, is the ongoing tragedy in the Congo, where 6 million to 7 million have died since 1996 as a consequence of invasions and wars sponsored by Western powers trying to gain control of the region's mineral wealth. At stake is control of natural resources that are sought by U.S. corporations: diamonds; tin; copper; gold; cobalt, an element essential to nuclear, chemical, aerospace, and defense industries; and, more significantly, coltan and niobium, two minerals necessary for production of cell phones and other high-tech electronics. Eighty percent of the world's coltan reserves are found in the Democratic Republic of Congo (DRC). Niobium is another high-tech mineral with a similar story.

The high-tech boom of the 1990s caused the price of coltan to skyrocket to nearly $300 per pound. In 1996, U.S.–sponsored Rwandan and Ugandan forces entered eastern DRC. By 1998, they had seized control and moved into strategic mining areas. The Rwandan army was soon making $20 million or more a month from coltan mining. Though the price of coltan has since fallen, Rwanda maintains its monopoly on coltan and the coltan trade in DRC. Reports of rampant human-rights abuses pour out of this mining region.

Coltan makes its way out of the mines to trading posts where foreign traders buy the mineral and ship it abroad, mostly through Rwanda. Firms with the capability turn coltan into the coveted tantalum powder, and then sell the magic powder to Nokia, Motorola, Compaq, Sony, and other manufacturers for use in cell phones and other products.

Yet as mining in the Congo by Western companies proceeds at an unprecedented rate—some $6 million in raw cobalt alone exiting DRC daily—multinational mining companies rarely get mentioned in human-rights reports.

Sources: "The World's Most Neglected Emergency: Phil Taylor Talks to Keith Harmon Snow," The Taylor Report, *March 28, 2005. "High-Tech Genocide," by Sprocket.* Earth First! Journal, *August 2005. "Behind the Numbers: Untold Suffering in the Congo," by Keith Harmon Snow and David Barouski.* Z Magazine, *March 1, 2006.*

6. Whistleblower Protection in Jeopardy

Special Counsel Scott Bloch, appointed by President Bush in 2004, is overseeing the virtual elimination of federal whistleblower rights in the U.S. government.

The U.S. Office of Special Counsel (OSC), the agency that is supposed to protect federal employees who blow the whistle on waste, fraud, and abuse, is dismissing hundreds of cases while advancing almost none. According to the Annual Report for 2004 (which was not released until the end of first quarter of the 2006 fiscal year), less than 1.5 percent of whistleblower claims were referred for investigation while more than 1,000 reports were closed before they were even opened. Only eight claims were found to be substantiated, and one of those included the theft of a desk, while another included attendance violations. Favorable outcomes have declined 24 percent overall, and this is all in the first year that Bloch has been in office.

Bloch, who has received numerous complaints since he took office, defends his first 13 months in office by pointing to a decline in backlogged cases. Public Employees for Environmental Responsibility executive director Jeff Ruch says, "Backlogs and delays are bad, but they are not as bad as simply dumping the cases altogether." According to figures released by Bloch in February 2005, more than 470 claims of retaliation were dismissed, and not once had he affirmatively represented a whistleblower.

In fact, in order to speed dismissals, Bloch instituted a rule forbidding his staff to contact whistleblowers if their disclosure was deemed incomplete or ambiguous. Instead, the OSC would dismiss the matter. As a result, hundreds of whistleblowers never had a chance to justify their cases. Ruch notes that these numbers are limited to only the backlogged cases and do not include new ones.

On March 3, 2005, OSC staff members, joined by a coalition of whistleblower protection and civil rights organizations, filed a complaint against Bloch. The complaint specifies instances of illegal gag orders, cronyism, invidious discrimination, and retaliation by forcing the resignation of one-fifth of the OSC headquarters legal and investigative staff. The complaint was filed with the President's Council on Integrity and Efficiency, which took no action on the case for seven months.

This is the third probe into Bloch's operation in less than two years in office. The Government Accountability Office and a U.S. Senate subcommittee both have ongoing investigations into mass dismissals of whistleblower cases, crony hires, and Bloch's targeting of gay employees for removal while refusing to investigate cases involving discrimination on the basis of sexual orientation. The case has since been supplemented with allegations of Bloch supplying Congress with misleading information and misusing his office to support a person espousing creationist views even though his office had no jurisdiction to do so.

The Department of Labor has also gotten on board in a behind-the-scenes maneuver to cancel whistleblower protections. If it succeeds, the Labor Department will dismiss claims by federal workers who report violations under the Clean Air Act and the Safe Drinking Water Act. Government Accountability Project general counsel Joanne Royce sums up major concerns: "We do not want public servants wondering whether they will lose their jobs for acting against pollution violations of politically well-connected interests."

Source: All stories by Jeff Ruch, Public Employees for Environmental Responsibility website. "Whistleblowers Get Help from Bush Administration," Dec. 5, 2005; "Long-Delayed Investigation of Special Counsel Finally Begins," Oct. 18, 2005; "Back Door Rollback of Federal Whistleblower Protections," Sept. 22, 2005.

7. U.S. Operatives Do Torture

The American Civil Liberties Union released documents of 44 autopsies held in Afghanistan and Iraq on Oct. 25, 2005. Twenty-one of those deaths were listed as homicides. The documents show that detainees died during and after interrogations by the Navy Seals, military intelligence, and other government agencies.

"These documents present irrefutable evidence that U.S. operatives tortured detainees to death during interrogation," said Amrit Singh, an attorney with the ACLU. "The public has a right to know who authorized the use of torture techniques and why these deaths have been covered up."

The Department of Defense released the autopsy reports in response to a Freedom of Information Act request filed by the ACLU, the Center for Constitutional Rights, Physicians for Human Rights, Veterans for Common Sense, and Veterans for Peace.

One of 44 U.S. military autopsy reports reads as follows: "[A] 27-year- 45
old Iraqi male died while being interrogated by Navy Seals on April 5, 2004, in Mosul, Iraq. During his confinement, he was hooded, flex-cuffed, sleep-deprived, and subjected to hot and cold environmental conditions, including the use of cold water on his body and hood. The exact cause of death was 'undetermined,' although the autopsy stated that hypothermia may have contributed to his death."

An overwhelming majority of the so-called natural deaths covered in the autopsies were attributed to "arteriosclerotic cardiovascular disease" (heart attack).

The Associated Press carried the story of the ACLU charges on their wire service. However, a thorough check of LexisNexis and Proquest electronic data bases, using the keywords ACLU and autopsy, showed that at least 95 percent of the daily papers in the United States didn't pick up the story.

Sources: "U.S. Operatives Killed Detainees During Interrogations in Afghanistan and Iraq," American Civil Liberties Union website, Oct. 24, 2005. "Tracing the Trail of Torture: Embedding Torture as Policy from Guantánamo to Iraq," by Dahr Jamail. TomDispatch.com, March 5, 2006.

8. Pentagon Exempt from FOIA

The Department of Defense has been granted exemption from the Freedom of Information Act (FOIA). In December 2005, Congress passed the 2006 Defense Authorization Act, which renders Defense Intelligence Agency (DIA) "operational files" fully immune to FOIA requests, the main mechanism by which watchdog groups, journalists, and individuals can access federal documents. Of particular concern to critics of the Defense Authorization Act is the DIA's new right to thwart access to files that may reveal human-rights violations tied to ongoing "counterterrorism" efforts.

The rule could, for instance, frustrate the work of the ACLU and other organizations that have relied on FOIA to uncover more than 30,000 documents on the U.S. military's involvement in the torture and mistreatment of foreign detainees in Afghanistan, Guantánamo Bay, and Iraq—including the Abu Ghraib scandal.

50 Several key documents that have surfaced in the advocacy organization's expansive research originate from DIA files, including a 2004 memorandum containing evidence that U.S. military interrogators brutalized detainees in Baghdad, as well as a report describing the abuse of Iraqi detainees as violations of international human rights law.

According to Jameel Jaffer, an ACLU attorney involved in the ongoing torture investigations, "If the Defense Intelligence Agency can rely on exception or exemption from the FOIA, then documents such as those that we obtained this last time around will not become public at all." The end result of such an exemption, he told TheNewStandard.com, is that "abuse is much more likely to take place, because there's not public oversight of Defense Intelligence Agency activity."

Jaffer added that because the DIA conducts investigations relating to other national-security-related agencies, documents covered by the exemption could contain critical evidence of how other parts of the military operate as well.

The Newspaper Association of America informs that due to lobbying efforts of the Sunshine in Government Initiative and other open-government advocates, congressional negotiators imposed an unprecedented two-year "sunset" date on the Pentagon's FOIA exemption, ending December 2007.

Source: "Pentagon Seeks Greater Immunity from Freedom of Information," by Michelle Chen. TheNewStandard.com, May 6, 2005.

9. World Bank Funds Israel-Palestine Wall

Despite the 2004 International Court of Justice (ICJ) decision that called for tearing down the Wall and compensating affected communities, construction of the Wall has accelerated. The route of the barrier runs deep into Palestinian territory, aiding the annexation of Israeli settlements and the breaking of Palestinian territorial continuity. The World Bank's vision of "economic development," however, evades any discussion of the Wall's illegality.

55 The World Bank has meanwhile outlined the framework for a Palestinian Middle East Free Trade Area (MEFTA) policy in its most recent report on Palestine published in December 2004: "Stagnation or Revival: Israeli Disengagement and Palestinian Economic Prospects."

Central to World Bank proposals is the construction of massive industrial zones to be financed by the World Bank and other donors and controlled by the Israeli occupation. Built on Palestinian land around the Wall, these industrial zones are envisaged as forming the basis of export-orientated economic development. Palestinians imprisoned by the Wall and dispossessed of land can be put to work for low wages.

The post-Wall MEFTA vision includes complete control over Palestinian movement. The report proposes high-tech military gates and checkpoints along the Wall, through which Palestinians and exports can be conveniently transported and controlled. A supplemental "transfer system" of walled roads and tunnels will allow Palestinian workers to be funneled to their jobs, while being simultaneously denied access to their land. Sweatshops will be one of very few possibilities of earning a living for Palestinians confined to disparate ghettos throughout the West Bank.

In breach of the ICJ ruling, the United States has already contributed $50 million to construct gates along the Wall to "help serve the needs of Palestinians."

Sources: "Cementing Israeli Apartheid: The Role of World Bank," by Jamal Juma. Left Turn, *issue No. 18. 'U.S. Free Trade Agreements Split Arab Opinion,' by Linda Heard.* Al-Jazeera, *March 9, 2005.*

10. Expanded Air War in Iraq

There is widespread speculation that President Bush, confronted by diminishing approval ratings and dissent within his own party, as well as within the military itself, will begin pulling American troops out of Iraq this year. A key element of the drawdown plans not mentioned in the president's public statements, or in mainstream media for that matter, is that the departing American troops will be replaced by American air power.

Writing in *The New Yorker* magazine, Seymour Hersh quotes Patrick Clawson, the deputy director of the Washington Institute, whose views often mirror those of Dick Cheney and Donald Rumsfeld, as saying, "We're not planning to diminish the war. We just want to change the mix of the forces doing the fighting—Iraqi infantry with American support and greater use of air power."

While battle fatigue increases among U.S. troops, the prospect of using air power as a substitute for American troops on the ground has caused great unease within the military. Air Force commanders in particular have deep-seated objections to the possibility that Iraqis will eventually be responsible for target selection. Hersh quotes a senior military planner now on assignment in the Pentagon as saying, "Will the Iraqis call in air strikes in order to snuff rivals or other warlords, or to snuff members of their own sect and blame someone else? Will some Iraqis be targeting on behalf of al Qaida or the insurgency or the Iranians?"

Visions of a frightful future in Iraq should not overshadow the devastation already caused by present levels of American air power loosed, in particular, on heavily populated urban areas of that country. The tactic of using massively powerful 500- and 1,000-pound bombs in urban areas to target small pockets of resistance fighters has, in fact, long been employed in Iraq. No intensification of the air war is necessary to make it a commonplace.

Sources: "Up in the Air," by Seymour M. Hersh. The New Yorker, *Dec. 5, 2005. 'An Increasingly Aerial Occupation,' by Dahr Jamail. TomDispatch .com, December 2005.*

COLLABORATING

Agree on a topic, perhaps one from Part III of this book, and have each group member find a source that in some way connects with the topic. Make sure that each type of source discussed in this section is represented. Separately, each group member should make a list of the facts or perspectives contained in the source (the person doing a book should cover just one chapter). As a group, compare what you found. Is information repeated from one source to another? What stands out as common knowledge? What stands out as not so well known? Prepare a brief statement explaining which source could give you the best insights for constructing a critical analysis.

Evaluating Online Sources

While all sources need to be scrutinized, writing instructors are especially suspicious of information from the Internet. Thus, in writing for an academic assignment, pay extra attention to the information you collect from the Web. Anyone can publish on the Internet. Home pages, websites, blogs, and listservs do not answer to any editor. While people monitor contributions and uphold standards for some online publications, the checking and double-checking of facts that ensues during publication of a print journal or magazine does not occur for most Internet sources.

As mentioned, many print sources are uploaded to the Internet, and the same information you find in a magazine or journal can be found online. These sources of information do not necessarily need to be scrutinized any more than print sources. However, be aware that some publishers try to lure potential subscribers to the online services of print products by putting abridged material on a website. Some tease you with an opening line, an article title, or the first page or two. Others delay online publication so as not to compete with the print product or deny general access to the product to give their online subscribers, who have passwords and have paid money, the advantage in securing information. You will not be getting a complete article if you download or print a teaser, a preview, or an abstract.

To evaluate other online sources, look for the following.

Author If a website has an anonymous author or the writer uses a pseudonym, the source cannot generally be considered credible. But just because a person takes credit for a website does not instantly grant the site authority. You have to ask who the writer is. If the person claims expertise, you can check that claim in an online search of her or his name.

If the person has credentials—is an MD if the article concerns medicine, for instance—you can assume that the website has credibility up to a point. Sometimes people falsify credentials. You cannot be responsible for tracking down every possible case of fraud, though, so you have to grant credibility in such cases, unless you spot inconsistencies that make you suspicious or if the website fails to meet standards discussed below.

Citation of Sources When an Internet source presents information, whether a theory supported by evidence or facts about a subject, you can gauge its reliability by seeing whether the author has cited his or her sources. When a site conveys information, in other words, the author will explain how he or she has come to know and believe the facts and perspectives presented.

The most legitimate websites give enough information for you to find the original source (systems of citation are discussed in the last section of this chapter). The writer uses quotation marks when appropriate, announces clearly when material is paraphrased, and usually confirms the results of studies, statistical analyses, or other research by citing the places he or she found them. If words in a website appear in other places on the Web without attribution, someone has plagiarized. Be suspicious of information on a website if you discover that the writer has plagiarized any material. If no citations are given, question the credibility of the source.

Updates of Sites Most legitimate Internet sources are consistently updated and post the dates of the most recent updates. If your online source has not been updated for a long time or includes many broken links, you should wonder about the information you collect from it. There's a good chance that the person or organization behind it is not reliable and therefore not credible.

When my students conducted research on political parties, they had to search for dates to see how committed a group was. Josh discovered a political party that was compatible with his beliefs, but it seemed that the group's commitment did not extend beyond the last election, when it ran a candidate for a seat on a local council. All the information ended at the time of the election. The site did not even announce the results of the election. Thus, Josh had to wonder whether the site was a hoax or was run by people not committed to a party platform as much as they were interested in getting a particular person elected. The information about their beliefs and principles and the facts they presented in support of their platform had to be questioned.

If a website does not indicate how often it is updated, question how much you can rely on the information. Look for contact information—an email address or phone number. If you cannot find the information or if it is no longer valid, factor this into your evaluation of the source.

Agenda Is the website trying to sell you something? Has it been created to promote a product? If you answer "yes" to either question, be careful about the information you gather from the site. It is not always true that such websites cannot be trusted, but the agenda behind the persons or organization must be critically analyzed. The people in charge of the site want you to believe certain principles or facts so you will spend money on their product. When a website is blatant and leads you to a catalog and product descriptions, you know the agenda and can take it into consideration. If a site looks to be informational at first but then prompts you to buy a book or purchase a membership, you must question the credibility. The site is being run for profit and is not being upfront about it.

This does not automatically disqualify the site as a legitimate source of information. For instance, people get sports statistics from ESPN's website. The site is not a public service. Advertisers pay to promote their products there, and the site has links to let you purchase merchandise from ESPN. But the statistics can be trusted. It would be foolish to set the information aside in search of a nonprofit site. You do, however, have to be careful about ESPN's self-promotion; don't use ESPN's references to itself as the number-one sports network as evidence in a paper rating cable sports channels.

More subtle agendas also need to be unearthed. In the political websites my students found, the information had to be considered in its context. While the students could confidently state that the Green Party stood for environmental protection and could relate information about its platform without hesitation, they could not use the Green Party web page (or those of its local chapters) to confirm that its candidates did not compromise their principles, backed their words with actions, or had better qualifications than their opponents. The Green Party would have a strong incentive to state those things and would be disinclined to publish information that would undermine its candidates. This agenda would bring the information it publishes into question. This is not to cast aspersions on the Green Party, which is an admirable organization. Rather, it suggests that a smart reader looks for confirmation elsewhere for any information or perspectives gathered from a website that has an agenda. Consistent confirmation of information or perspectives first gathered from a site give the site credibility over time.

GREEN PARTY WEBSITE

2006 Green Party Candidate Spotlight

http://www.gp.org/

This screenshot from the Green Party's home page offers a critique of Howard Berman. Students wanting to use this information would need to confirm the assertions made here, as the Green Party has an agenda to paint Berman in an unfavorable light. Also, notice that the party is soliciting donations. While other links from this page give you more specific information about the election, all the information you could gather would come from a group with an agenda.

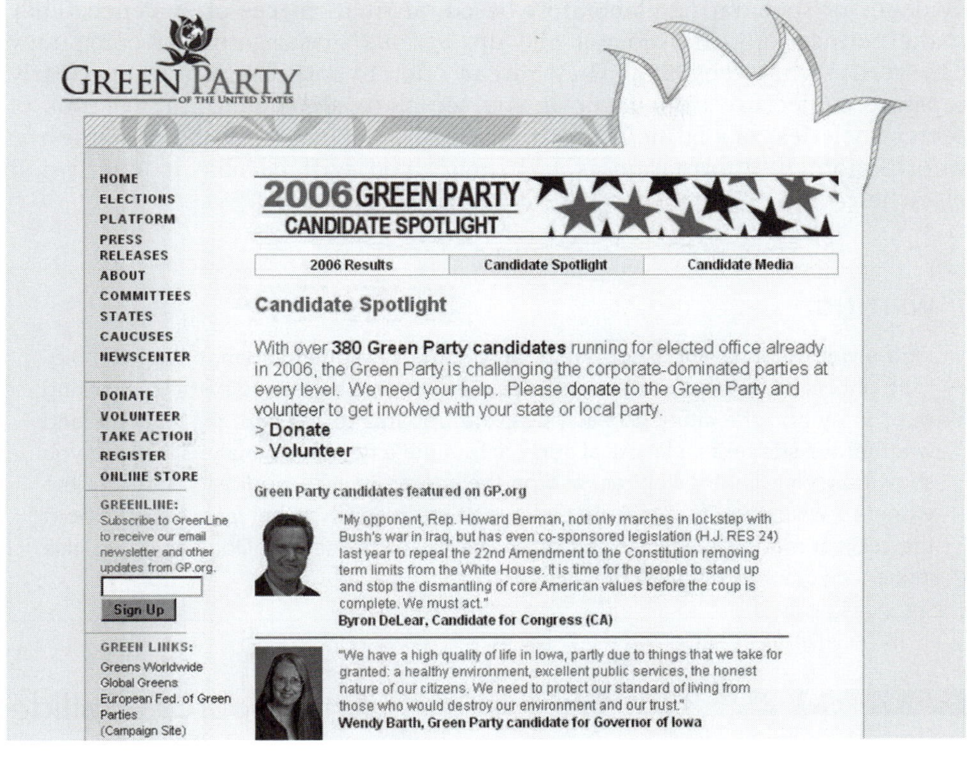

Fanatical Approach Some websites, frankly, are run by kooks. For example, look at the number of websites that discuss alien abductions. While you should never discount something simply because it defies common assumptions, the sheer lack of evidence that any human has encountered an alien should alert you to the possibility that a person claiming to have alien implants or to have been surgically probed on a spaceship suffers from a delusion or trauma.

More worrisome are extremist groups that base beliefs on racism, sexism, and jingoism. If you come across a website that uses charged language repeatedly, makes claims that appeal to prejudices, and misrepresents the ideas of opponents, you should dismiss the facts or perspectives you find there. Such sites take a fact or a legitimate perspective and twist it until it serves their cause. The sources consist of materials written by people who think just like they do.

Conspiracy theorists are another type of fanatical group. While legitimate sites discuss conspiracy theories about the assassinations of John and Robert Kennedy in the 1960s, the Iran-Contra scandal in the 1980s, and the 2000 presidential election, illegitimate conspiracy theorists make numerous claims that cannot be supported. They're missing key pieces of evidence or speculating elaborately based on small pieces of evidence. They make connections that do not add up. Serious investigators of conspiracy can verify what they say. They might offer hypotheses, but they clearly separate conjecture from facts. If you see charged language, allegations of secret societies, or claims of destruction of evidence, be wary of using the information. If information is legitimate, you will be able to confirm it elsewhere.

WRITING

Find a website involving a supernatural occurrence—guardian angels, UFOs, Bigfoot, ghosts, or another such occurrence. Evaluate the site's credibility by checking out the author, the citation of sources, the updates to the site, the agenda, and whether the site takes a fanatical approach. Write a two-page analysis in which you show how your findings either validate the site or limit its credibility. Indicate the extent to which you find the site to be legitimate and whether your beliefs about the subject matter have changed at all due to your checking. Does anything else influence your evaluation of the source?

When Sources Collide

When you separate the legitimate sources of information from the illegitimate, you still will run into conflicting evidence and perspectives. If your topic has depth and intrigue, experts will weigh in with differing positions. The "facts" you hear from one side might contradict the "facts" you hear from another. You probably will wonder why, since facts by their nature are beyond dispute. Facts do not change unless new discoveries upend long-established knowledge.

To determine what sources to use or follow in your analysis, consider how facts are interpreted, how much a writer emphasizes them, and how much facts that do not fit the agenda of the writer have been dismissed. You may find some instances in which facts support two or more different understandings of an issue or event.

Since you want your thesis to be as original as possible, you probably do not want to simply accept reputable sources that favor a majority opinion. In other words, if three sources agree on an interpretation of an event and one source offers an alternative, you should not necessarily believe the three sources at the expense of the one. In challenging the status quo, professional writers often depart from the mainstream. Since the ideas they have formulated do not work to the advantage of powerful forces, those ideas do not get published as often. Lack of publicity or popularity does not make an idea less valid, as discussed regarding the bandwagon fallacy in Chapter 9.

RICK REILLY

Questioned Marks

In this article from Sports Illustrated *written shortly before baseball's Ichiro Suzuki broke the single-season record for most base hits in a season, Rick Reilly shows how the media ignore important facts and statistical information to create a better story.*

Did you know that 49.2% of all statistics are misleading? It's true. Take, for instance, Seattle Mariners leadoff hitter Ichiro Suzuki and his quest to break the 84-year-old record of 257 hits in a season, set by George Sisler.

As Ichiro dramatically chases the hallowed mark with the games dwindling to a precious few, please join me in standing and saying, in unison, "What a load of Bushido!!!"

As of last Saturday the Mariners had played 154 games, the schedule Sisler had in 1920, and Ichiro was still seven hits short of breaking the record. End of story. Sorry. Enjoy the fishing season in Kobe. See you at spring training.

Al Simmons, Lefty O'Doul and Bill Terry came within a cross-eyed official scorer of Sisler's holy grail but ran out of games. So Ichiro gets eight free extra games? What's he, our millionth customer? Is he your kid sister and gets four strikes, too?

But do the TV stat boys tell you that? No. Do they mention that Ichiro 5
has collected more singles than a skycap (44 more than Sisler at week's end)? No, because these guys are not into style points. They are gigageeks, grown males who love stats. In other words, they have not had sex since Kirstie Alley was a size 6.

We need a new stat notation: SS (Stupid Stat). Whenever a player gets a record that is misleading, corrupt and/or downright immoral, we simply add an [SS] to it. For instance:

John Salley is the only player in NBA history to win world championship rings with three different teams—Detroit, Chicago, and L.A.[SS] Then, in four-point type, the footnote would read, SS—For the last two, Salley was on the floor less than the guy with the T-shirt bazooka.

Bernie Williams of the New York Yankees passed Mickey Mantle for alltime postseason home runs.[SS] (Please. In Mantle's day there was only one playoff round—the World Series. Williams has played 39 more postseason games than Mantle did. Get that stat outta here!)

Bruce Smith is the NFL's alltime sack leader.[SS] (No, Bruce Smith is the all-post-1982 sack leader, because that's the year the league started keeping track of the damn things. My favorite NFL player ever, Deacon Jones, used to get four or five sacks in a quarter—it's just that nobody was counting.)

The six biggest home run years in major league history have come in the 10
last six years.[SS] (The balls, players and stadiums are all juiced.)

All of us aren't born with Spackle for brains. Don't give us all-time PGA money leaders. (Jack Nicklaus is 102nd, just behind Tom Byrum.) Give us all-time PGA tournament wins. (Nicklaus is second, behind Sam Snead.) Don't give us 1,000-yard rushing seasons. (My God, Kevan Barlow of the San Francisco 49ers ran for 1,000 yards last year, and he needs two forms of I.D. in his own kitchen.) Give us 100-yard-game rushers. (Jamal Lewis of the Baltimore Ravens led the NFL in 2003, with 12.)

Just because it appears on the ticker across the bottom of the screen doesn't make a stat worth typing. *Only two teams held Michael Jordan to fewer than 25 points per game in his Chicago Bulls career: Toronto and Vancouver.* Held? No, Jordan sat down because his team was ahead by 220 points. *Lenny Wilkens is No. 1 among coaches in NBA wins.* Yeah, and he's No. 1 in losses, too.

That's another notation we need to start sticking in the record books—PU (Propped-Up stat). *Cal Ripken Jr. owns the major league record for consecutive games played.*[PU] (Yeah, but in 1990 he hit .250. You think maybe a little pine time might've helped him and the Baltimore Orioles?)

A.C. Green holds the Ripken record in the NBA.[PU] (Yeah, except after he caught an elbow in the mouth and lost two teeth, he twice propped it up by coming off the bench and standing on the floor for about 10 seconds and then sitting down again. What are we trying to prove—that he can climb out of a hospital bed?)

15 *Jerry Rice caught at least one pass in 274 straight games.*[PU] (Yeah, wonderful, epic player—except that for a couple of years the Oakland Raiders propped up that streak like the guy in *Weekend at Bernie's.* Early in every game it was slant to Rice, step-back toss to Rice, one-yard buttonhook to Rice. And when the streak ended recently, the usually elegant Rice threw down his helmet in disgust—in a Raiders *win.*)

Michael Adams held the NBA record for most consecutive games making a three-point shot.[PU] (Unfortunately, Adams got so desperate to keep the streak alive, he was jacking up threes one step off the bus. No wonder a lot of these streaks come with another streak at no charge—a losing streak.)

I mean, if we're going to keep track of pointless stuff like that, then let's keep consecutive games with a flop (Vlade Divac). Consecutive plate appearances in which batter readjusted his wristbands, helmet, pants and groin after *every* freaking pitch (Nomar Garciaparra). Lockouts nobody noticed until six weeks after the season was supposed to have started (NHL).

Anyway, sorry, I had to rant. I'll see you next week, as usual.[PU]

To develop a critical analysis, consider marginalized ideas. Instead of dismissing the minority opinion, look at the other possibilities for resolving the problem when legitimate sources collide.

Which Follows the Pattern? If a source too easily or obviously supports dominant ideology, consider the opposing alternative. The status quo operates on what looks to be common sense. As discussed about investigating assumptions in Chapter 2, society acknowledges some basic assumptions so readily that discussion rarely ensues about them. Other assumptions are repeatedly discussed.

For example, everyone has heard about the need for more personal responsibility. It appears to be obvious that we should take care of ourselves. Yet, politicians, the media, and corporations constantly repeat the need for citizens to take responsibility for their actions and indicate that people are slacking off or are blaming difficulties on others. When you read about lawsuits against corporations, it often seems like the complainant is trying to take advantage of the system by blaming a wealthy business or individual for something the complainant should have known not to do. The implication is that the complainant is refusing to take personal responsibility. If you use information about someone who sued because a cup of coffee was too hot or because he or she gained weight from eating too much fast food, your critique turns the issue into a matter of personal responsibility and aligns with the status quo.

An alternative look at lawsuits would show you that some corporations have been negligent in their treatment of workers, causing acute as well as chronic difficulties, and have not been willing to make things right unless faced with lawsuits. Your alternative look would show you the many times corporations have taken advantage of vulnerable populations—people who cannot afford lawyers—and have covered up their misdeeds with small hush payments. The majority opinion, then, cannot always be trusted, even though its position is supported by some facts. It might not serve your purposes to always believe the position or evidence you find most represented in sources.

How Do They Deal with the Other Side? You might not always want to disavow the status quo. A thorough critical analysis might take you back to dominant ideology. One strategy is to see how opposing sources deal with one another's positions. If a source appears fair and rational when discussing tenets of opponents, the source probably has little to conceal and has arrived at its conclusion intelligently. If the source sounds condescending toward the other side or represents opponents as buffoons or villains, it might have something to hide.

This being said, authors who feel slighted by the mainstream or who have suffered injustice might be harsh in writing about the other side. For example, the writings of Leonard Peltier, a member of the American Indian Movement, use charged language and bitter accusations about opposing perspectives.

LEONARD PELTIER

Statement to Judge Paul Benson

Leonard Peltier, a Chippewa, made the FBI's 10 Most Wanted Fugitive List in the mid-1970s following his alleged involvement in a shootout on the Pine Ridge Indian Reservation. Peltier was eventually apprehended in Canada, extradited, and convicted of two murders. He is serving life imprisonment in a U.S. penitentiary but has always maintained his innocence.

There is no doubt in my mind or my peoples' minds you are going to sentence me to two consecutive life terms. You are, and have always been prejudiced against me and any Native Americans who have stood before you. You have openly favored the government all through this trial, and you are happy to do whatever the FBI would want you to do in this case.

I did not always believe this to be so! When I first saw you in the courtroom in Sioux Falls, your dignified appearance misled me into thinking that you were a fair-minded person who knew something of the law and who would act in accordance with the law! Which meant that you would be impartial and not favor one side or the other in this lawsuit. That has not been the case and I now firmly believe that you will impose consecutive life terms solely because that's what you think will avoid the displeasures of the FBI. Neither my people nor myself know why you would be so concerned about an organization that has brought so much shame to the American people. But you are! Your conduct during this trial leaves no doubt that you will do the bidding of the FBI without any hesitation!

You are about to perform an act which will close one more chapter in the history of the failure of the United States courts and the failure of the people of the United States to do justice in the case of a Native American. After centuries of murder of millions of my brothers and sisters by white racist America, could I have been wise in thinking that you would break that tradition and commit an act of justice? Obviously not! Because I should have realized that what I detected was only a very thin layer of dignity and surely not of fine character. If you think my accusations have been harsh and unfounded, I will explain why I have reached these conclusions and why I think my criticism has not been harsh enough:

First, each time my defense team tried to expose FBI misconduct in their investigation of this lawsuit and tried to present evidence of this you claimed it was irrelevant to this trial. But the prosecution was allowed to present their case with evidence that was in no way relevant to this lawsuit—for example, an automobile blowing up on a freeway in Wichita, Kansas; an attempted murder in Milwaukee, Wisconsin, for which I have not been found innocent or guilty; or a van loaded with legally-purchased firearms, and a policeman who claims someone fired at him in Oregon State. The Supreme Court of the United States tried to prevent convictions of this sort by passing into law that only past convictions may be presented as evidence if it is not prejudicial to the lawsuit, and only evidence of said case may be used. This court knows very well I have no prior convictions, nor am I even charged with some of these alleged crimes; therefore, they cannot be used as evidence in order to receive a conviction in this farce called a trial. This is why I strongly believe you will impose two life terms, running consecutively, on me.

5 Second, you could not make a reasonable decision about my sentence because you suffer from at least one of three defects that prevent a rational conclusion: you plainly demonstrated this in your decision about the Jimmy Eagle and Myrtle Poor Bear aspects of this case. In Jimmy's case, for some unfounded reason that only a judge who consciously and openly ignores the law would call it irrelevant to my trial; in the mental torture of Myrtle Poor

Bear you said her testimony would shock the conscience of the American people, if believed! But you decided what was to be believed and what was not to be believed—not the jury! Your conduct shocks the conscience of what the American legal system stands for—the *search for the truth* by a jury of citizens. What was it that made you so afraid to let that testimony in? Your own guilt of being part of a corrupted pre-planned trial to get a conviction no matter how your reputation would be tarnished? For these reasons, I strongly believe you will do the bidding of the FBI and give me two consecutive life terms.

Third, in my opinion, anyone who failed to see the relationship between the undisputed facts of these events surrounding the investigation used by the FBI in their interrogation of the Navajo youths: Wilford Draper, who was tied to a chair for three hours and denied access to his attorney; the outright threats to Norman Brown's life; the bodily harm threatened to Mike Anderson; and finally, the murder of Anna Mae Aquash, must be blind, stupid, or without human feelings so there is no doubt and little chance that you have the ability to avoid doing today what the FBI wants you to do—which is to sentence me to two life terms running consecutively.

Fourth, you do not have the ability to see that the conviction of an AIM activist helps to cover up what the government's own evidence showed: that large numbers of Indian people engaged in that fire fight on June 26, 1976.

You do not have the ability to see that the government must suppress the fact that there is a growing anger amongst Indian people and that Native Americans will resist any further encroachments by the military forces of the capitalistic Americans, which is evidenced by the large number of Pine Ridge residents who took up arms on June 27, 1975, to defend themselves. Therefore, you do not have the ability to carry out your responsibility towards me in an impartial way and will run my two life terms consecutively.

Fifth, I stand before you as a proud man; I feel no guilt! I have done nothing to feel guilty about! I have no regrets of being a Native American activist—thousands of people in the United States, Canada, and around the world have and will continue to support me to expose the injustices which have occurred in this courtroom. I do feel pity for your people that they must live under such an ugly system. Under your system, you are taught greed, racism, and corruption—and most serious of all, the destruction of Mother Earth. Under the Native American system, we are taught all people are brothers and sisters, to share the wealth with the poor and needy. But the most important of all is to respect and preserve the Earth, who we consider to be our Mother. We feed from her breast; our Mother gives us life from birth and when it's time to leave this world, who again takes us back into her womb. But the main thing we are taught is to preserve her for our children and our grandchildren, because they are the next who will live upon her.

10 No, I'm not the guilty one here; I'm not the one who should be called a criminal—white racist America is the criminal for the destruction of our lands and my people; to hide your guilt from the decent human beings in America and around the world, you will sentence me to two consecutive life terms without any hesitation.

Sixth, there are less than 400 federal judges for a population of over 200 million Americans. Therefore, you have a very powerful and important responsibility which should be carried out impartially. But you have never been impartial where I was concerned. You have the responsibility of protecting the constitutional rights and laws, but where I was concerned, you neglected to even consider mine, or Native Americans', constitutional rights. But, the most important of all—you neglected our human rights.

If you were impartial, you would have had an open mind on all the factual disputes in this case. But, you were unwilling to allow even the slightest possibility that a law enforcement officer would lie on the stand. Then, how could you possibly be impartial enough to let my lawyers prove how important it is to the FBI to convict a Native American activist in this case? You do not have the ability to see that such a conviction is an important part of the efforts to discredit those who are trying to alert their brothers and sisters to the new threat from the white man, and the attempt to destroy what little Indian land remains in the process of extracting our uranium, oil, and other minerals. Again, to cover up your part in this, you will call me a heartless, cold-blooded murderer who deserves two life sentences consecutively.

Seventh, I cannot expect a judge who has openly tolerated the conditions I have been jailed under to make an impartial decision on whether I should be sentenced to concurrent or consecutive life terms. You have been made aware of the following conditions which I had to endure at the Grand Forks County Jail, since the time of the verdict:

(1) I was denied access to a phone to call my attorneys concerning my appeal;

(2) I was locked in solitary confinement without shower facilities, soap, towels, sheets or pillow;

(3) the food was inedible, what little there was of it;

(4) my family—brothers, sisters, mother and father—who travelled long distances from the reservation, were denied visitation.

No human being should be subjected to such treatment; and while you parade around pretending to be decent, impartial, and law-abiding, you knowingly allowed your fascist chief deputy marshal to play stormtrooper. Again, the only conclusion that comes to mind is that you know and always knew that you would sentence me to two consecutive life terms.

Finally, I honestly believe that you made up your mind long ago that I was guilty and that you were going to sentence me to the maximum sentence permitted under the law. But this does not surprise me, because you are a high-ranking member of the white racist American establishment which has consistently said, "In God We Trust," while they went about the business of murdering my people and attempting to destroy our culture.

Should Peltier's ideas be dismissed because of his clear disregard for Judge Benson and the justice system? Hardly. Peltier believed his activism was the catalyst for prosecution, and the investigative process and trial did appear to be tainted by racism, obstruction of justice, and induced perjury. He is on Amnesty International's list of political prisoners. Another person admitted on *60 Minutes* that he, not Peltier, committed the murders. Yet, Peltier still remains in prison. It should surprise no one, then, that Peltier comes off as a bit testy when trying to defend himself.

A side that supports the status quo has fewer legitimate reasons for reactive rhetoric than do oppressed proponents of an opposing position. The perspective supporting the status quo prospers because of it. Thus, if you see name-calling, dismissive attitudes, or misrepresentations from a source aligned with the status quo, you should wonder about the perspective, even if the source has solid evidence to back the claims. While supporters of the status quo might feel threatened by alternative perspectives, they should be able to show why an opposing idea has less merit than their own, and they should deal with the other side fairly.

Account for All Evidence In understanding that sources should deal fairly with the other side, you should also see the necessity for a source to account for all evidence. A source that ignores pertinent evidence that you find in another source must be questioned.

A source that has nothing to hide will wrangle with counterevidence by refuting it, explaining how it might fit into a different interpretation, or acknowledging its validity while still maintaining that its side is correct. The evidence will not be misrepresented or dismissed. In shorter op-ed pieces where space is at a premium, writers might not discuss counter-information thoroughly, so they might generalize about opposing evidence instead of analyzing it. In such cases, use another source that does account for counterevidence to confirm the perspective. If all the sources you consult avoid serious discussion of opponents' evidence, you should probably ask why. The source that can best explore opposing perspectives often winds up being the best source.

WRITING

For your current research project, find two articles from legitimate sources that present opposing positions. Putting aside for the moment what you personally believe, analyze the two articles in the three ways listed above. Write one or two paragraphs about each article, making sure to cover their relationship to dominant patterns, their treatment of opposing positions, and their accounting for all evidence. Which source is most valid? Why?

Giving Credit Where It Is Due

A writer must indicate how and where sources were used in an essay or report. A responsible writer has to distinguish among quotations, paraphrases, references to statistics, facts not commonly known, and theories or ideas that she or he gained from research. All must be documented with enough information to make it possible for a reader to find the sources and locate the information.

Documentation systems have been designed to give academic writers—not just students—a common structure to use in citing sources. Unfortunately, this commonality has been complicated by the use of many different systems of documentation. At some time during your academic career, you will see or use such systems as MLA (Modern Language Association) style, APA (American Psychological Association) style, and one of the documentation styles from the *Chicago Manual of Style*. All are valid.

When writing with research, ask your instructor which system she or he prefers. In this section, you will not follow any particular system but instead learn about the basic information you need for any of these systems.

Some students complain about having to cite sources. They point out that newspapers and magazines do not have bibliographies or internal citation systems such as footnotes or parenthetical documentation. The difference is that professional publications have editors and fact-checkers who research and confirm facts. If reporters or publications falsify information, use sources inaccurately, or do not give credit for words or ideas garnered from others, they are subject to lawsuits and other sanctions. Consequences for these kinds of unethical behavior are severe as well as embarrassing.

Reporters often work with primary sources, so quotations come directly from people who are interviewed. When they work with facts and evidence, they refer to archival information, which has been researched and confirmed by others, or they explain who or where the information came from. Students, as well as researchers publishing in discipline-specific journals or books, use documentation systems to verify that their information is accurate, to place it in a context, to give credit to original sources, and to avoid accusations of plagiarism.

In the workplace, plagiarism or dishonest use of information can get a writer fired and an organization sued. Universities do not take issues of academic dishonesty lightly either. Every instructor hates to give a student an F on a paper or for an entire course because the student copied from sources without crediting the original author. A student who downloads a paper from an Internet source or cuts and pastes sections from several such papers intends to deceive and deserves punishment. What is unfortunate is when a student makes mistakes that can be misinterpreted as an attempt to cheat.

Your handbook or research guide has detailed information on citation styles. Here, based on my own students' concerns, are some additional strategies.

Include an Acknowledgement Page In my courses I ask students to submit an acknowledgement page at the ends of their papers. In books and discipline-specific journals, authors give credit to all the people who helped them put together their work—from research assistants to peer reviewers to typists to babysitters. Everyone who deserves credit receives it.

For the acknowledgement pages in my class, students list the members of their peer groups, roommates who helped them proofread, friends who found websites for them, and television shows that gave them ideas for topics, analyses, or theses. They also list the books, websites, journals, and magazines they consulted to get information. I ask them to be specific about what they found, where they found it, and where in their papers they used it. So if one book gave a student all the facts needed for the paper, the student mentions the book, the library where it was found, and the section in the paper where its information appears. The student may also name the research librarian who helped her find the book. Perhaps an article gave a very specific example that another student used, so he tells me the article's name, where he found the journal or magazine, and the point in the paper he used the example. Maybe a website provided a summary of an event that proved helpful, so another student explains that her friend surfed the Internet one night and located the site, tells about the location, and shows where she used the information. Before you turn in a paper, construct an acknowledgement page of your own, whether or not your instructor asks you to include one.

The acknowledgement page does not take the place of a formal Works Cited (MLA) or References (APA) list, but it alerts you to problems in your documentation. You might realize, for example, that you would have had no way of knowing about a case study you used unless you had read it in a book that was neither listed in your bibliography nor referred to in your paper. You understand that you cannot borrow the case study without acknowledging its source. You might discover that you cited only one of two sources concerning an opposing position.

It also feels good to give credit to a parent or a significant other who helped you reword a few sentences or figure out an organizational strategy. On top of that, you can look back at how much work you did and be proud. Much like a journal entry, an acknowledgement page can be cathartic.

Author, Title, and Publication Information For every college assignment that requires research, no matter what documentation system the instructor follows, you need the same information from your sources. You should note the name of the author, the title of the book or article, and the date of publication. With books, you also need to find the city of publication and the publisher's name. For journals, the city and publisher are not necessary, but you should include the name of the journal, the volume and issue numbers, and the page numbers on which the article appeared. Magazines are similar to journals in that you need to name the magazine title and note the page numbers, but you do not need the volume and issues numbers. For websites, locate the address, the title of the web page (if different from the article name), the date of publication, and the date you found the information. When you have this information, you will be able to construct a Works Cited or References page at the end of your essay and insert all necessary information in accordance with the documentation system you use.

In-Text Citations All documentation systems require in-text citations to go with the Works Cited or References page. In-text citations are used in conjunction with the bibliographical information. You need to note the exact pages on which you found information you are quoting, paraphrasing, or otherwise using.

Note that you must use in-text citations for more than just quotations. You must give an in-text citation everyplace you relied on a source for information, even if you completely reworded the exact phrases. Some documentation systems require footnotes that include the author's last name, the title, and the page number.

Most in-text citations use a type of parenthetical reference. After a quotation, paraphrase, set of statistics, facts not commonly known, or ideas, you put a parenthesis, write the last name of the author, write the page number on which the information can be found, close the parenthesis, and add the end punctuation, usually a period. Some systems suggest putting in the year of publication. If you used two articles or books by the same author, you need to distinguish between them by including the year of publication or an abbreviated title. Check the rules of the documentation system you are using to make sure.

Distinctions Between Cited Materials When using an exact quotation, put quotation marks around the entire quotation. As discussed in Chapter 9, quotations should be used sparingly. It is best to paraphrase or to weave facts into your sentences. Paraphrases sometimes rely on the use of a key word or two. You can put these in quotation marks, but place the parenthetical reference at the end of the sentence. Make sure you introduce the paraphrase with a tag phrase so that your instructor knows that you are giving credit to the source. For summaries that do not contain key words, you can put your parenthetical reference at the end of the paragraph.

Facts not commonly known and statistics indicate by their very nature that they were found through research. In other words, readers automatically know this type of information has come from a source. As long as you have not copied sentences or phrases exactly, you do not need quotation marks or tag phrases. Just make sure to put a parenthetical reference immediately after the information. It is often difficult to know when a fact constitutes common knowledge that does not need to be documented. A guideline to keep in mind is that if you learned the fact through your research, document it. You might find out later that the fact is a common one, but it is best to err on the side of caution when making these determinations.

COLLABORATING

As you move from class to class, you will be asked to use different documentation systems. To familiarize yourselves with the differences, take the one you are using for this class and one other that your teacher assigns to your group. The rules for using these systems can be found in your handbook or the documentation system's web pages. Your instructor might provide handouts. Using one group member as a secretary, record all the differences you find between the two systems. In what ways does the bibliography differ? What about the in-text citations? Discuss your findings with the class as a whole, and decide which system you like best and why.

Summary

Much library research is now done in front of a computer screen. With the increased ease of locating sources, however, it is more important than ever to learn how to critically evaluate potential sources. Many search indexes refer writers to research sources, such as discipline-specific journals, mainstream magazines, books, and alternative magazines. These sources can provide critical knowledge and usually do not have to be closely scrutinized to determine legitimacy.

Online sources can be just as valuable, but writers need to evaluate the credibility of the information, since websites and other online sources often do not benefit from checking and cross-checking of facts. Even when sources have been determined to be credible, they may contradict one another. You need to decide what perspectives to believe, keeping in mind that the most familiar or comfortable is not always the best when critically analyzing a subject.

Once you have determined which sources to use and how to work them into your paper, you must abide by the requirements of a documentation system for a bibliography and in-text citations. You must account for the places where quotes, paraphrases, statistics, facts not commonly known, and ideas have been used.

· PART III ·

TOPICS FOR WRITING

The following chapters will introduce you to a variety of topics that may be used for writing assignments. The topics spring from aspects of our culture, common emotions, and ideas and ideals often thought to be in conflict with one another. Each chapter pushes for understandings that critically analyze the familiar. In other words, the chapters encourage your pursuit of the type of critical analysis discussed in Chapter 2 by questioning societal assumptions, looking beyond obvious conclusions and interpretations, and perhaps making familiar topics a bit strange or unfamiliar.

Each chapter begins with an overview of the topic. The overviews discuss common beliefs and begin the process of critical analysis by raising questions about the topic. They give a perspective from which you, the writer, can start your analysis.

The overviews lead into sections called "Openings for Writers." They contain brainstorming and freewriting activities that will help you work through any writing blocks that might have developed. While your instructor—or perhaps your instructor and the class in tandem—may choose ideas from the overview or may construct writing assignments based on beliefs about holidays, honesty, animals, or the other topics, the "Openings for Writers" sections will point you to other possibilities.

The sections on language pick up on the issues discussed in Chapter 5. Instead of providing vocabulary quizzes or definitions, these sections ask you to scrutinize your understanding of keywords used in the overviews and to see how your examination extends or limits the ideas in the overview. This scrutiny can help you analyze the perspective offered in the overviews, extend into your understanding of the readings in each chapter, and give you practice in paying close attention to your own use of words.

The next part of each chapter consists of selected readings on the topic. Some of these readings present information that you can extract and use in your writing. Other times, they add to the process of critical analysis by pursuing issues brought up in the overviews or by offering a differing perspective. The readings are intended to make you pause and consider a particular angle on a subject, and they serve as the focus of some of the assignment options.

The "Assignment Ideas" that follow this first cluster of readings are not meant to limit your choices but rather to focus you on possibilities. The prompts remind you of the importance of audience considerations from Chapter 3 and ask you to utilize ideas you generated in your brainstorming or freewriting. The options consist of questions based on the readings, extensions of the overview, or ideas that spring from or draw parallels to key issues surrounding the topic.

"Group Work" ideas give your class the option to pursue a collaborative research project. The questions break down a pertinent issue drawn from the chapter and start the process of assigning tasks, as discussed in Chapter 7. The questions are not more complex than those under "Assignment Ideas," but they have been designed to be most easily completed in a group situation.

The final sections consist of additional readings that provide supplementary information and perspective on the topics. Some are personal experiences, while others offer facts to consider. They often narrow the broad topic heading, going from a general topic like the supernatural in Chapter 13 to specific looks at Bigfoot researchers and at psychic John Edward. All ground the issues presented in the overview and the first set of readings and give extra perspectives to ponder.

Do not be afraid to veer away from the perspectives offered in the overviews and readings. Critical analysis must come from you. It does not involve nodding your head in agreement with a perspective that seems to be challenging the status quo. These chapters are designed to help you reexperience the ordinary. In your writing, you can extend the ideas more or draw back to a place you find more reasonable. The point is to go through the process of critical analysis to develop your critical faculties.

Part III lets you implement the important concepts introduced in Part I while allowing you to experiment with your writing and reading processes, use of evidence and research, and collaboration as discussed in Part II. You will become a stronger writer and reader by thinking through your ideas in relation to the perspectives in the following chapters and by analyzing them to reach a thesis interesting to you and your audience.

CHAPTER 11

HOLIDAYS AND CELEBRATIONS

Overview

Every year, Americans veer from their normal schedules to celebrate uniquely American holidays, days of remembrance, the reenactment of famous events, religious festivals, ethnic rituals, and other assorted occasions honoring aspects of our culture. Other celebrations are personally festive, such as weddings, anniversaries, and birthdays. On any of these days, we tend to dress up and party, sometimes after a solemn rite, but often enough the day is just a beginning-to-end enactment of merriment, filled with high spirits, desserts, and presents. Holidays and celebrations share two characteristics—a celebration of some sort and a break from routine, often with a day off from work or the closing of government offices. Most people look forward to celebrations and holidays, and official commemorations and related activities remind us of the traditions associated with each of them.

As individuals and as a culture, we seem to enjoy some holidays more than others. A few holidays have become controversial. Others have faded or changed in significance over the years. Yet, nothing seems to cheer people up more than the prospect of a special day on the calendar. Children become especially excited by holidays, even minor ones, such as April Fools' Day. On occasion, the reasons for this excitement cause concern in some corners of America. One of the main criticisms often heard about holidays stems from their perceived loss of meaning, as a focus on festivities distracts from more solemn or spiritual traditions. More than one parent has bemoaned children's preoccupation with gifts on Christmas morning, which comes at the expense

This icon will direct you to web links and additional resources on the website college.hmco.com/pic/thelin1e

of religious reflection. Patriots seethe at the manner in which Memorial Day has become the unofficial inaugural weekend of summer rather than a solemn remembrance of those fallen in war. Traditionalists groan about the transformation of Thanksgiving from a reenactment of gratitude and praise to a marathon of shopping and football.

Even if some holidays have become disconnected from their origins, Americans cherish the traditions and uniqueness of holidays. Despite the many city-sponsored fireworks displays before, during, and after Independence Day, for example, Americans still light their own fireworks, often illegally and dangerously. Americans want to partake in celebrations rather than just watch them. Numerous attempts to curtail trick-or-treating and mischief on Halloween have also failed miserably. October 31 is not a day off for schools, businesses, or government offices, although some Catholic schools do close the next day in honor of All Saints' Day, but people still decorate their houses and give candy to children.

Personal celebrations demonstrate a similar pattern. Weddings involve meticulous planning for many months before the event and cost considerably more than most people would spend if partying were the only purpose. Yet, many brides and grooms refuse to cut corners, even if selecting just the right flowers or music or dresses takes hours of time. These rituals persist not because of the excuse to celebrate, but because the break from the routine and the ordinary has significance.

Advocates even fight to preserve holidays with fewer traditions and celebrations. Earth Day, not forty years old, has no deeply engrained traditions behind it, but attendance at Earth Day celebrations increases each year, as do the number of environmental protests that go with it. Opposition groups have launched campaigns to undermine Earth Day, claiming, among other things, that the get-togethers produce waste for landfills, but so far nothing has deterred Earth Day's continuance.

We now have evidence that Christopher Columbus was not the first European to "discover" the Americas and that he was not as honorable or as brave as people once thought. In fact, some people contend that his explorations were the start of genocide of the native peoples of the Western Hemisphere. Yet, attempts to remove Columbus Day from the calendar meet with political resistance and have largely failed, even though Columbus Day celebrations consist of little more than parades.

Greeting card companies have cashed in on holidays and celebrations. They have also been instrumental in promoting, if not inventing, other types of holidays, such as Grandparents Day, Sweetest Day, and Administrative Professionals Day. Recognition of Kwanzaa has increased in part due to the marketing of holiday cards. Cynics call such celebrations ploys based in profit. But to the grandparents, significant others, and office workers who receive gifts, visits, lunches, or simple cards, the days are something special. A broad range of cards is available for birthdays, including cards developed for "special" birthdays such as "Sweet Sixteen." These and other special events mark breaks in routine and times to celebrate, if only for small related or connected groups.

Some celebrations and holidays receive much more attention in particular regions of the country. For years Groundhog Day has been a special occasion for all-day partying in Punxsutawney, Pennsylvania, following the official ritual of the groundhog's emergence to determine how much longer winter would last. Mardi Gras belongs to New Orleans; its parades and concomitant debauchery are known across the country but never successfully mimicked. Cinco de Mayo enjoys great popularity in the Southwest and on the West Coast but causes barely a ripple in most other regions.

The most interesting aspect of celebrations and holidays revolves around the history of such ancient festivals as Christmas, Easter, and Halloween. Not many people question why they are decorating trees, coloring eggs, or wearing masks, respectively, and some might be surprised to find out that they are reenacting pagan rituals. When the Catholic Church was trying to convert pagans to Christianity, its leaders incorporated native cultures in order to bring the people to the faith. They placed Christian commemorations on the dates of important pagan festivals. Although Church followers suppressed pagan worship, their merging of holidays—such as spring equinox and Easter—brought on long-term, if uneasy, acceptance of Christian ways. Today, families and communities unite during holidays and celebrations, so we must wonder whether the ancient symbols or original purposes behind the holidays matter any longer. Can we disconnect from the past and just have fun?

Perhaps celebrations boil down to individual memories. We do not want to tarnish our innocent childhood recollections by interrogating what exactly it is we're doing as a culture. But how do Native Americans feel about Thanksgiving and Columbus Day? Why honor one individual just because that was the day he or she was born? Why hasn't the Hindu festival of Diwali been transformed into an American holiday, given that we have converted a celebration of another religion, Christianity, into the secular holiday Christmas? In our need to break from routine, we have left much unanswered.

Openings for Writers

1. **Religion and culture** How are religion and culture kept separate in American holiday celebrations? Where do they merge? Do patriotic holidays contain elements of religion? Do religious holidays contain elements of culture?
2. **"Hallmark holidays"** In your own words, how would you define "Hallmark holiday"? Do you recognize the legitimacy of such commemorations? Have you observed or otherwise celebrated any of them?
3. **Origins of symbols** Many people do not know the relevance of the symbols of their favorite celebrations or holidays. Think of some of your favorite symbols and their place in a particular festive custom. What do you think is the meaning behind them? How does the meaning relate to your understanding of what the celebration is commemorating?
4. **Arbitrariness of celebrations** Although the fashion in which cultures, religions, and events have earned a place in our holiday system might appear random, a close look at the symbols and rituals of holidays reveals

certain patterns of American celebration. What features or ideals are repeated? What is not present? How many patterns can you find?

Language

1. **Holiday** The overview gives characteristics of holidays. What definition is implied by these characteristics? How would an alteration of the definition change the theme or main points?
2. **Celebration** Discuss the differences between the term *celebration* and similar words such as *commemoration, honoring,* or *festivity.* What does each connote? Do the different connotations shed light on any aspect of the overview?
3. **Ritual** Does the word *ritual* alter your conception of an activity, such as a wedding or bar mitzvah? Does it imply rigor or seriousness? How does it differ from the word *custom*?

GERINA DUNWICH

The Symbols of Halloween

Halloween has its origins in the ancient Celtic festival of Samhain (pronounced So-wen). Celtic peoples traditionally believed that the barrier between the worlds of the living and the dead was at its weakest on this night, allowing contact to be made between the two worlds. Although information from departed loved ones was welcomed, unwanted spirits were also believed to be set free. To avoid being haunted by malicious ghouls, the Celts wore costumes to fool them. This is the origin of our current practice of dressing up on Halloween.

In this selection from The Pagan Book of Halloween, *Gerina Dunwich explores the origins of many other Halloween symbols. Dunwich is a Wiccan, a modern-day practitioner of witchcraft, who keeps pagan tradition alive. Wicca is a religion and, despite modern day confusion, does not have any connection to Satanism. Wiccans (or witches) worship their deities and practice their religions in ways as varied as the many denominations of Christianity. They are sensitive to their history of persecution, represented in Dunwich's reference to the "Burning Times," and to misrepresentations of their beliefs by the dominant culture.*

Halloween's sinister reputation may be attributed to its symbols, most of which are of a macabre nature. As Halloween approaches, images of ghosts, goblins, black widow spiders, hideous old hags wearing pointed black hats, and jack-o'-lanterns with gruesome-looking faces make their annual appearance, stirring up the subconscious fears of both death and the unknown that inherently dwell within the minds of most human beings.

However, the origin of these symbols, which today are used by advertisers to sell Halloween candy and costumes, date back to pre-Christian times and are connected in one way or another with the Old Religion and its Pagan faithful.

The symbols of Halloween and the history that lies behind each one are important to Witch and Cowan (non-Witch) alike. They not only guide us on our quest to discover the true meaning of Halloween, but, in many cases, they enable us to observe the complex realms of human nature and the mind of man when we see how these symbols and their meanings evolved.

On a magickal level, symbols have played an important role in the Craft since olden times. They continue to be used by Witches as amulets and talismans, and as magickal tools to increase spellcasting powers, protect against evil, conjure forth spirits and elementals, and represent Deity in all of Her/His many guises. Together, they hold important clues to the ancient history and true meaning of Halloween for Witches around the world.

The Bat

A popular Halloween symbol, the bat is connected with sorcery and death in 5
various cultures. Its long-time association with the darker side of folklore and superstition no doubt has much to do with its habits of nocturnal flight and roosting in places such as caves and old, ghostly ruins.

Bats were first linked with Witches (another popular Halloween symbol) in the Middle Ages when it was widely believed that all Witches and Warlocks were assisted by demons who assumed the forms of animals. One of the animal shapes commonly used by these demons (or "familiars," as they were often called) was the bat. Bats and their blood were also used in the casting of spells (especially those of black magick), the brewing of potions, and the preparation of flying ointments. When Witches became firmly ensconced within Halloween tradition, all things associated with the practice of the Old Religion, such as the cauldron, the broomstick, and the bat, became connected with Halloween as well.

Today, bats are feared in many parts of the world, and are believed by many to be creatures of evil. They are commonly used by practitioners of the Black Arts, and Voodoo. Hoodoos (men and women who practice a type of folk magick similar to Voodoo and popular in many rural communities of the southern United States) have also been known to employ bats in many of their love spells, healings, and curses.

The bat is featured in a number of superstitions, many of which are quite ominous. For instance, a bat that flies thrice around a house, crashes into a windowpane, or flies inside of a house is supposed to be an omen of death for one of the occupants. If a bat shows up inside a church during a wedding ceremony, it is an omen of doom for the impending marriage. The behavior of bats has also been used by diviners to forecast the weather, and in some cultures it was once believed that bats were actually Witches in disguise! If a bat was seen flying straight up into the sky and then dropping back to Earth, this was a sign that the witching hour had arrived.

Luckily for the bat, just as it has sinister associations in many parts of the world, there are other places that regard the bat as a good omen. In Poland and China, the bat symbolizes happiness and longevity, and they are greatly respected by the Australian aborigines, who dare not harm or kill a bat in the belief that doing so takes years off of a person's life. In some cultures, the bat is regarded as a bringer of good luck, and is referred to as a "soul-symbol" in Barbara G. Walker's *The Women's Encyclopedia of Myths and Secrets.*

To many modern Witches and Pagans, especially those who follow a shamanistic or Native American-influenced path of spirituality, the bat is a creature that represents protection, good fortune, and rebirth. It is said to be a guardian of the night and a guide to past lives.

To keep bad luck at bay, many practitioners of Hoodoo folk magick prescribe the wearing of a mojo bag containing a bat's bone as a lucky charm.

When painted or engraved upon a bloodstone or heliotrope, the symbol of a bat is said to add great power to a Witch's incantations, and endow all practitioners of the magickal arts with the power to conjure, control, and banish demons.

The Jack-O'-Lantern

To most folks, Halloween just wouldn't be the same without the delightfully eerie glow of jack-o'-lanterns, which are often placed on the front porch of a house or on a windowsill as a traditional Halloween decoration. The very sight of a pumpkin with a wicked "face" illuminated by a candle helps to put most of us in the Halloween mood and also serves to welcome the costumed children who go door to door trick or treating.

The carving of a pumpkin is a fun activity for everyone—young and old. However, this custom is far from being a modern one. In fact, it is a well over two thousand years old.

The origin of the jack-o'-lantern can be traced back to Ireland, where hollowed-out turnips, rather than pumpkins, were carved with simple faces and used as hand-held lanterns. They were used not only to help light the way for those traveling the dark roads on Halloween night, but to scare away evil earthbound ghosts—especially those who pursued the spirits of deceased loved ones and prevented them from finding their way to peace in the Land of the Dead.

In Scotland, jack-o'-lanterns were originally fashioned from the thick stem of a cabbage plant. They were called "kail-runt torches" and were used in the same way as their turnip counterparts were used in Ireland.

Their protective powers are reflected in the lines from a traditional Halloween song from Scotland:

> *Hallowe'en a nicht o' tine* (night of fire),
> *A can'le* (candle) *in a custock* (cabbage stem),
> *A howkit neep wi' glowerin' een* (A turnip lantern with glowing eyes),
> *To fleg baith* (scare both) *witch and warlock.*

Eventually the use of cabbage stems and turnips for lanterns grew unpopular, and the pumpkin became the vegetable of choice and undoubtedly the most prevalent symbol of Halloween for Witches and non-Witches alike.

It is believed that faces, rather than other images or symbols, were originally carved onto the pumpkin because they gave the jack-o'-lantern the look of a head. The Celts of ancient times believed that the head was the most sacred part of the human body, for it housed a person's immortal soul.

20 Each year on a night that is the Japanese equivalent of Halloween, a glowing paper lantern takes the place of a carved and candle-lit pumpkin. Traditionally hung near garden gates, they welcome home the ancestral spirits and keep all evil-natured, light-fearing demons at bay.

The phrase "jack-o'-lantern" was at one time used as a name for the unexplained phosphorescent light that sometimes appears in swamps and marshlands after sunset. Also known as "will-o'-the-wisp" in the United States, "corpse light" in England, "fox fire" in Ireland, and "witch-fire" in Africa, this natural phenomenon understandably strikes fear in the hearts of many who encounter its eerie luminous glow.

According to European folk legend, the mysterious jack-o'-lantern light is a wandering soul that has been turned away by both Heaven and Hell, and is condemned to spend eternity earthbound and restless. It is dangerous to see one, some say, because they have often been known to beckon humans to follow them into the marshes where they ultimately drown or mysteriously disppear and are never heard from again.

The curious name of the jack-o'-lantern appears to reflect the Church's early efforts to link Halloween and its Pagan customs to Christianity's fearful Prince of Darkness, as Jack is another name for the Devil (especially in England). Yet an old folktale that hails from Ireland attributes the invention of the jack-o'-lantern to a man whose name was Jack.

Disliked by nearly everyone in his village, Jack was notorious for his drunkenness and mean disposition. He was drinking in the local pub when the time came for the Devil to claim his doomed soul. He talked the Devil into having one last drink with him before taking him to Hell, but after they finished their drinks, Jack informed the Devil that he did not have enough money on him to pay for the drinks. He cleverly convinced the Devil to change himself into a sixpence, and then change back to his true form after Jack "paid for the tot of grog." The Devil agreed to the plan. But as soon as he transformed himself into a shiny new sixpence, Jack snatched the coin from the tabletop and, without hesitation, deposited it in his coin purse, which had a silver catch in the shape of a cross. The Devil, rendered powerless by the cross, was trapped inside the coin purse and unable to escape.

25 Upon his death, Heaven would not permit Jack to enter the Pearly Gates because he was filled with too much greed. He was also denied entry into Hell because he had managed to trick the Devil, which understandably angered his Satanic Majesty to an extent that no mortal had ever angered him before. Jack was eating a turnip when the irate Devil threw him a lighted coal from the fiery pit of Hell. (How the Devil managed to escape from the coin purse and return to his infernal abode is not made clear.) Jack picked up the coal and placed it inside the turnip, creating a lantern which he used to illuminate his way as his restless spirit wandered the earth in search of a final resting place.

Modern Witches often use jack-o'-lanterns as Samhain altar decorations. One is placed at each cardinal point of the magick circle and lit at the start of a Samhain ritual to symbolize each of the four ancient elements: Air, Fire,

Water, and Earth. They also serve as a beacon of light to welcome the spirits of all deceased loved ones who return to the world of the living on this night.

Ghosts and Skeletons

Ghosts and skeletons are significant Halloween symbols as they communicate this holiday's ancient link to the cycle of death and rebirth.

Samhain, when spirits of the dead and other supernatural entities were believed to travel freely between their world and ours, was the Celtic feast of the dead, celebrated on November 1. All Souls' Day (November 2) is the Christianized version of Samhain. In many parts of the world, blessings for the dead are performed on Halloween and All Souls' Day. Death symbols are prominently displayed (particularly in Mexico) and are believed to impart good luck among the living who recite prayers and sing hymns for the souls of the deceased.

In the United States, ghosts and skeletons remain popular symbols of the Halloween season and can be found in abundance as costumes and party decorations. However, today the true meaning behind these symbols of death and the spirit world is largely misunderstood, and they are relegated to the same category as vampires, werewolves, and other supernatural creatures whose sole purposes at Halloween are for entertainment and macabre mood-setting.

Many modern Witches display images of ghosts and skeletons at Halloween not to instill fear, create morbidity, or raise the dead, but to celebrate the strong belief in reincarnation that nearly all traditions of Wicca and Neo-Paganism retain. In these religions, death is not regarded as a finality. It is believed to be merely a part of the perpetual cycle of birth, death, and rebirth, which is clearly evidenced in all aspects of nature. Therefore, Witches display these symbols of death to honor this sacred cycle as well as to honor the darker aspects of the Goddess and Horned God who reign supreme at the end of October.

It is customary for many modern Witches to adorn their Sabbat altars at Halloween with images of ghosts and skeletons, especially in the form of candles. When the shadows of this night grow long and dark and the restless spirits of the dead begin to take flight, these waxen representations of death are lit to signify the start of the Sabbat ritual, to welcome the returning spirits of deceased loved ones, and to keep malevolent supernaturals at bay.

The Black Cat

To many people around the globe, black cats are the ultimate representation of the mystery and sorcery that have played a major role in the celebration of Halloween practically since the Celtic order of Druids originated in Gaul (now France) circa the second century B.C.

Black cats are thought to be sinister creatures in the United States, as well as in several other countries, and chance encounters with them are considered to be extremely unlucky omens. The crossing of one's path by a black cat, especially on Halloween night, is an event that strikes terror in the hearts of a vast number of individuals who subscribe to superstitious thought. To counteract the bad luck believed to be brought on by the presence of a black cat, various magickal antidotes have been devised over the centuries. Some of these include spitting on the ground, turning oneself completely around three times, walking backward to retrace one's steps, recitation of special incantations, and, most drastically, the maiming or killing of the cat.

In ancient Egypt, the goddess Bastet (also known as Bast or Pasht) was worshiped in the form of a lean, short-haired black cat, and sometimes as a female human having the head of a cat. Her worship was widespread throughout Egypt and she was one of the most popular and beloved deities belonging to the mythos of that ancient culture. She was a benevolent goddess, and the domestic cat was the animal most sacred to her. So sacred, in fact, that at one time, the very harming of a cat in Egypt carried the price of execution. In mythology, Bastet was a deity who possessed nine incarnations, which may explain the concept of cats having nine lives.

The black cat is also associated with the Greek goddess Hecate (a de- 35
ity with a strong connection to the practice of Witchcraft) and to the Norse goddess Freya (who rode in a chariot drawn by cats, and was condemned as a sorceress of the black arts by the early Christians in their conquest of Paganism).

In the Middle Ages, the black cat became a symbol of the Devil and his disciples. Most Europeans at that time also believed the cat to be the animal form most assumed by the Witches' familiar (an imp, or demonic entity, dispatched by the Lord of Hell to serve a Witch as both a companion and an assistant in all of her magickal workings). Throughout the period of history known as the "Burning Times," an untold number of cats—especially black ones—were put to death alongside their Witch mistresses and Warlock masters in the name of God.

The cat has long held a reputation for being an animal possessing both psychic and magickal powers. With its unbreakable link to Witches, Pagan goddesses, divination, and all things of a magickal nature, it seems only logical that the black cat was destined, sooner or later, to become one of the prevalent symbols of the Witches' most favorite holiday.

LESLIE PRATT BANNATYNE

The Reformation and Guy Fawkes Day

This excerpt from Halloween: An American Holiday, an American History *reviews one of the many transformations of Halloween from its Celtic roots. Pope Gregory III of the mid-eighth century is credited with transferring All Saints' Day from May 13 to November 1, to coincide with Samhain celebrations in Europe. The eve of All Saints' Day became the "Hallowmas," and the church allowed the many rituals of Samhain to continue under this name. When Europeans started colonizing America, the Puritan settlers banned October 31 celebrations, believing them to be devil worship. The tradition of Halloween arrived in the United States largely through Irish immigration in the nineteenth century. However, as Leslie Bannatyne reminds us, Halloween was reincarnated in other ways, showing the persistence of holiday traditions.*

It was on Halloween—October 31, 1517—that Martin Luther initiated a religious reformation that was to put a halt to the observance of Halloween for many Europeans. Influential theologians, such as Luther in Germany and the Frenchman John Calvin in Geneva, convincingly put forth a new concept of man's relationship with God. They said man worshiped with faith and good deeds rather than through the "icons," or symbols, of the Catholic church. They rejected the authority of the pope and looked exclusively to the Bible for guidance.

The individual man-to-God relationship struck a chord with many, and new Protestant sects formed throughout western Europe. Lutherans and Calvinists were pitted against Catholics in over 200 years of bitter battles. The Reformation eventually established freedom of dissent, but the price was dearly paid with lives and political tyranny.

Among the practices of the Catholic church to be abandoned by Reformation Protestants was the observance of saints' days. And without All Hallows' Day on the Protestant church calendar, there was of course no All Hallows' Eve.

But again, tradition would die hard. Much as Celtic Samhain was wed with the Roman festival of Pomona and much as these pagan feasts merged with Catholic custom, the English Protestants preserved an annual autumn fete in their secular rites. It was known as Guy Fawkes Day.

> Please to remember the fifth of November
> Gunpowder, treason and plot
> I see no reason
> Why Gunpowder treason
> Should ever be forgot!
>
> —Guy Fawkes Day song lyrics, sung in the 17th and 18th centuries

5 The anniversary of the gunpowder plot, better known as Guy Fawkes Day, dates from the heyday of Protestant-Catholic enmity in England. Fanatical Catholic leaders Robert Catesby and Thomas Winter (with the help of fellow Catholic revolutionary Guy Fawkes) devised a plot to blow up the Protestant-sympathetic House of Lords when Parliament met on November 5, 1605. The plan was foiled at the last minute, and Fawkes was captured as he entered the building's cellar to set his storehouse of gunpowder on fire. Fawkes was immediately arrested and later executed; the other conspirators soon met similar fates. Parliament passed an act in January 1606 declaring November 5 a day of national thanksgiving—a celebration of the triumph of Protestants over Catholics. Although people in Scotland, Ireland, Wales and some parts of western and northern England continued to celebrate Halloween in the late autumn, many English men and women eschewed it for Guy Fawkes Day.

The proximity of the celebrations—Guy Fawkes Day followed All Hallows' Eve by only six days—allowed for a great borrowing of traditions. Guy Fawkes Day was marked with bonfires, and celebrants carried lanterns of hollowed-out turnips that had been fashioned into grotesque faces. The eve of Guy Fawkes Day became "mischief night" across most of northern England, an occasion for pranks and skylarking. Where once they had begged for "soul cakes" in commemoration of All Saints' Day, boys now dressed in costume and begged for lumps of coal to burn their effigies of Guy Fawkes. By the time King George III took the throne, just 15 years before the onset of the American Revolution, children had combined the Catholic soul-cake song with the Protestant coal-begging song:

Soul! Soul! for a lump of coal
A stick and a stake for King George's sake
Please to give a lump.

In the strongest Protestant regions of England, effigies of the pope were burned along with those of Guy Fawkes, and the holiday was known as Pope's Night. (Other luminaries enjoyed the same privilege over history: effigies of the Old Pretender, Napoleon, Cardinal Weisman, Nan Sahib, Kaiser Wilhelm II and Colonel Nasser were also burned in England.) In Lewes, where 17 Protestant martyrs were burned at the stake, children were more likely to sing

A rope, a rope, to hang the Pope
A piece of cheese to toast him,
A barrel of beer to drink his health,
And a right good fire to roast him.

Indeed, the fireworks, fires, masquerades, politics, pumpkins and pranks of Guy Fawkes Day were very much a part of the English fabric at the time of American colonization.

Assignment Ideas

In responding to one of these prompts for an essay, refer to your discussion of the words *holiday, celebration,* and *ritual,* as the connotations might influence how your audience will react to your thesis. Try to weave in definitions if possible, and be precise and consistent in your usage. Keep in mind, also, the possible beliefs and sensitivities of readers when you are forming your thesis. What would they object to, and how could you respond to their needs in your essay?

1. Dunwich investigates some common symbols of Halloween, and you might have guessed by now that symbols from other older holidays are steeped in pagan lore. Even celebrations like weddings have symbols tracing back to paganism (see "A History of Anglo-Saxon Wedding Customs" on page 315). Research the origins of two of the symbols from your brainstorming list. In an essay, discuss your participation in rituals involving those symbols, and explore any conflicts that emerge between the intended

meaning of the symbols and your use of them. Can you disconnect a symbol from its origins and still enjoy it? Or does what you have found out compromise your purpose for engaging in the ritual, the holiday, or the celebration associated with it?

2. England's Guy Fawkes Day shows the transformation of Halloween customs into a patriotic ritual. In the United States, Halloween has been transformed in a similar way, seemingly becoming a secular tradition. Keeping in mind your prewriting about religion and culture, write an essay discussing Halloween's function in today's society. Does it keep myth and superstition alive? Is it an approved societal release of darker emotions? Does it trivialize beliefs that run counter to the status quo? Does it celebrate a unique American character? Whatever you decide, evaluate that function and weave it into your thesis. Your brainstorming or freewriting on the arbitrariness of our holidays might be of help here also.
3. If you were to establish a special day of your own, what would it commemorate or ritualize? What customs would you establish, and why? Would you make it fun, solemn, or a mixture of both? You might want to consult the excerpt from Brian Tokar's "The Twentieth Anniversary of Earth Day" (page 323) to see how a fairly new holiday was conceived and enacted. Look also at your prewriting on the arbitrariness of holidays to see how your holiday would fit into the fabric of American traditions. Also compare it to your reaction to the "Hallmark holidays." Why should other people celebrate a holiday of your invention?
4. In an essay, discuss a celebration outside your religion or culture in which you do not participate. Do research to understand this celebration accurately. Discuss how and why aspects of the celebration, such as symbols and rituals, could be incorporated into the U.S. mainstream on a day set aside for the celebration. How would you feel if this or a similar day was forced on you as an American holiday? Remembering your freewriting about religion and culture, draw a parallel to other American citizens who might feel excluded by widely celebrated holidays that are in some way based on religious beliefs.

Group Work

Choose one holiday, and have each group member look into how it is currently celebrated in a country other than the United States. How do the celebrations reflect the culture from which they come? Has any essential meaning been lost in the translation from culture to culture? Can we reflect on what we do in light of these celebrations and critique our own culture?

Additional Readings

The following readings offer historical facts on celebrations as well as perspectives to consider. "Festivals, Rites and Presents" and "Thanksgiving" might allow insight into the first question under "Assignment Ideas," since both suggest that the purpose for celebrating is more a matter of family unity than of the history of holidays. The third reading provides facts about the rituals and symbols of weddings, and the fourth discusses the co-optation of Earth Day celebrations. As you read these four articles, think about the writers' purposes for presenting the holidays and celebrations the way they do. How do their agendas differ? What is accomplished by learning about these perspectives? Has any custom been ruined for you, or do you have a deeper appreciation of the rituals surrounding holidays and celebrations?

ELIZABETH PLECK

Festivals, Rites, and Presents

An easy way to understand the significance of American family rituals is to demonstrate their economic importance to the modern American economy. Every October the sale of Halloween supplies such as Ross Perot masks, Count Dracula fangs, and miniature peanut butter cups contributes $400 million to the gross domestic product. In 1996, weddings generated revenues of $31 billion a year; funerals brought in about $11 billion; and the greeting card industry earned $6.3 billion. Christmas, which I call a "family ritual" (or "domestic occasion") but is also considered a holiday, accounted for about $149 billion in gift and card purchases in November and December 1996.[1] Nearly one fourth of all yearly retail sales in the United States in 1992 came from Christmas purchases. That year even supermarkets generated 20 percent of their receipts and made 30 percent of their profits between Thanksgiving and New Year's.[2] If it is true, as Joyce Hall, the founder of Hallmark, claimed, that "sentiment sells," then even these partial sales figures suggest that sentiment, expressed in family rituals, adds up to almost $200 billion a year.

The commercialism of so many family rituals causes great unease. The din of the cash register during the Christmas season, the "jingle of gilded trinkets," it is said, drowns out the religious meaning of the holiday. Almost everyone complains that Christmas is too commercialized. The public castigates merchants, advertisers, manufacturers, and even guileless consumers taken in by Muzak and colored lights. Many cultural critics argue that consumer culture has not only cheapened the meaning of Christmas and other holidays but has created ersatz ones as well. Greeting card manufacturers, confectioners, and florists sugar-coated Mother's Day, transforming what had been a day to contemplate world peace into a holiday to send flowers to mother. Advertisers and neckwear manufacturers made Father's Day, a holiday that many men considered silly, into a fixture on the American calendar. Kodak and Hallmark, AT&T and Macy's, Coca-Cola and Montgomery Ward have shaped American celebrations, creating new representations of Santa, new folkloric figures (such as Rudolph the Red-Nosed Reindeer), new rituals (such as parades), and new visual images of ritual, all in the service of encouraging consumers to buy their products and services.

Such complaints are neither of recent origin nor unique to late-twentieth-century America. But celebrants often designed the postsentimental occasion as an active critique of the values of home, family, and woman's place honored in the sentimental occasion, in addition to complaining about excessive commercialism. Because the postsentimental approach depends on parody or critique of American sentimentality, it requires the continued existence of sentimentalism. In the postsentimental era of celebration, sentimentality has not disappeared, but instead has become a subject of debate.

Just as the sentimental occasion was the ideal form of festivity for the affectionate family, so too the postsentimental occasion fit the reality of postmodern family life.[3] According to anthropologist Judith Stacey, who coined the term "postmodern family," the American family since the 1970s has no longer had a single dominant form; there has been a great deal of public debate about what the family should be; and family life has become highly fluid and flexible. The male breadwinner–female homemaker family is no longer the universal standard for the family, nor is it even the most frequent household type. These changes were caused by a series of overlapping revolutions in attitudes toward sex, contraception, and abortion; intermarriage across religious, ethnic, and racial lines; women's roles; race; homosexuality; and divorce. Family residential arrangements changed. Many people, especially the elderly, lived in single-person households. Cohabitation became an alternative to marriage as well as a stage prior to it, and became more acceptable among the privileged classes, rather than a way of life found mainly among the poor. Such vast, sweeping changes led to acceptance of new styles of living as well as to backlash against the changes. A political and cultural shouting match began in the late 1970s, which invoked the much-disputed term "family values." One side advocated a single standard of family life and sexual morality; the other held that Americans had to accept cultural pluralism and diversity of sexual mores and family forms.

5 Of the wrenching changes that affected the American family between the 1960s and the 1980s the most important, from the point of view of family ritual, was the growth in married women's employment. From temporary work before marriage and after their children were of school age, women moved to a more or less permanent commitment to paid work. This single dramatic change reverberated in almost every facet of the marital relationship. Pursuing an education and having a job, in some cases a career, women were beginning to put their own happiness and independence first, and even postponed marrying.

As part of the postsentimental era, magazines and newspapers began to print articles on how to combat "holiday blues." Families began to use celebrations as a special time to assert a waning ethnic identity. Women put in less time organizing and preparing postsentimental occasions and as a result experienced less affirmation of their central role in the family. People brought new values to understanding such rituals: they saw them through the prism of their search for privacy, personal fulfillment, happiness, and individuality. Sociologist Robert Bellah nicely summarized the postsentimental desire for family privacy combined with the quest for self-realization. In the nineteenth century, he argued, writers often described the family as the refuge from individualism. In the last third of the twentieth century, he added, "individualism is in the family as well as outside it."[4]

Most students of U.S. history date the emergence of postsentimental values to the 1890s or even earlier, because so much of postsentimentalism partakes of consumerism and individualism, traces of which can be found in America as early as the eighteenth century.[5] One characteristic of individualism—noted even in the earliest novels—was the wish to marry for love. Another was the desire for personal fulfillment through marriage. The United States has always had the highest divorce rate in the industrialized world because more U.S. couples than elsewhere try to realize their expectations for personal happiness through marriage—and end up disappointed.

As for consumerism, the desire to seek personal fulfillment, and even identity, through purchases had for centuries been an element of celebrations among the elite. Mass production and mass consumption made luxury items available to the average American. In addition, as early as around 1900 American advertising and movies appealed to the emotions and reinforced values already present: that one should seek pleasure, gain satisfaction, realize one's fantasies, find the man or woman of one's dreams. Films, magazines, and advertisements conveyed the view that the American consumer—often seen as a woman—could take on a new, improved identity (as a fairy princess or queen for a day, for example). What changed was less the desire for personal satisfaction and happiness than the means available to the average person to realize that desire. Thus, the precise dating of the holiday consumer economy varies by holiday and commodity. Most Americans did not buy candy bars as an everyday treat until the 1920s; the average working-class family did not own a radio (to listen to a football game on Thanksgiving) until the 1930s. Overall, by the 1950s the white working class, and in the 1960s the emerging black middle class, began to live in an economy of abundance rather than scarcity. They may have wanted to buy and spend before that, but could not afford to, except for an occasional splurge.

This view of the decline of the carnivalesque and the rise of the sentimental and then the postsentimental is quite different from Caplow's* and from popular understanding. Most people believe the contemporary family is in a state of moral decline. To them the past is the place where virtue resides. The transformation of some rituals and the disappearance of others furnishes evidence of the demise of the family and its moral lapse. There are two forms of discourse about family decline, one for the American mainstream, and another for ethnic groups perceived as being outsiders to the mainstream.

Commentators on mainstream culture invariably bemoan one symptom 10
of family decline, the disappearance of the family meal. Families, they claim, lack any fixed time when they converse and eat a leisurely meal together. With the decline in a set meal time, critics argue, a sense of common family

---

* Theodore Caplow, an American sociologist, argues that the purpose of holidays is to celebrate an idealized version of the family.

purpose and a feeling of togetherness have been lost. When employed mothers are not blamed, the problem is said to arise from divorce, the decline in religious belief and practice, the effects of a narcissistic, individualistic culture, the overly scheduled life children lead, and the omnipresent television set.

In the ethnic discourse about family decline, the main target is not consumer culture, but the demise of a sense of kinship, family solidarity, and community within the ethnic group. Many "ethnic" films express this theme, among them Francis Ford Coppola's *The Godfather* (1970). The movie portrays a close-knit Sicilian-American family, presided over by a Mafia chieftain, who, although a criminal, is deeply committed to family solidarity and his own code of ethics. After the godfather dies, so does the sense of community and family solidarity he stands for. Many social critics, such as Stephen Steinberg, agree with Coppola's point of view. Steinberg argues that ethnicity in modern America consists "mainly of vestiges of decaying cultures that have been so tailored to middle-class patterns that they have all but lost their distinctive qualities."[6] Unlike in the mainstream jeremiad, in this one ritual persists, but has lost its authenticity with the decline in community.

Research has shown, however, that many so-called traditions practiced in America are little more than a century and a half old. Historians Eric Hobsbawm and Terence Ranger coined the term "invented tradition" to describe a ritual that implies continuity with the past, even though that continuity is largely fictitious.[7] Hobsbawm and Ranger traced the history of public, not private, rituals, especially in the late nineteenth century, although their concept is elastic enough to pertain to both. Invented traditions, they note, are a social construction, created by people in the present out of a need for a sense of connection with the past, and from a desire to stop the clock in order to keep at least one small part of life always the same.[8] In their view invented traditions are indications of change, not stability. Hobsbawm and Ranger noted that Bastille Day, kilt-wearing, the Olympics, and the pledge of allegiance are all "traditions" that originated since the eighteenth century, the last three being created in the late nineteenth century. These were entirely new ceremonies, they argued, intended to create the fiction of shared national identity and national unity during times when national unity appeared fragile.

Kwanzaa, devised by Ron (Maulana) Karenga in 1966, conforms most closely to Hobsbawm and Ranger's concept of an invented tradition. Kwanzaa was a nationalist—specifically, black nationalist—holiday and had a specific creator, who designed it as a celebration of the African harvest, with the intention that American blacks, in exile from their African homeland, would continue tradition and celebrate their African heritage. Fifty-eight years earlier Anna Jarvis had invented another American family ritual, Mother's Day. A church organist and Sunday school teacher, Jarvis, mourning the loss of her mother, helped organize Mother's Day services in her hometown of Grafton, Virginia, and in Philadelphia. A few years later Sonora Dodd of Arizona suggested a day for fathers to honor men like her own father, who raised her and her siblings after her mother's death. Kwanzaa, Mother's Day, and Father's Day, created by specific individuals for specific purposes, fall at one end of the scale. At the other are family rituals such as graduation parties, wedding anniversaries, and family reunions that have no explicit creator and no single date of origin.[9]

Four centuries ago the annual cycle of holidays and feasts was either simple and sparse or raucous and communal. As a result of the Reformation, many Protestants turned away from the pagan rituals of recognizing life and death at the winter solstice and celebrating the rebirth of spring to make the Sabbath their major weekly ritual, indeed their most important one. Among American Puritans, for example, family rituals were few and modest. They opposed celebrating Christmas and Easter, since they viewed these holidays as "papist," and observed only one occasion—the Sabbath—regularly. Even their funerals and weddings were relatively simple affairs, at which kin were not expected to gather. The Puritans are significant both for the nature of their ritual—its lack of seasonality and its simplicity—and for their attitude toward celebration. Religious leaders in the Protestant Reformation defined ritual as a legitimate subject of controversy. By singling out Catholic practices they did not approve of, Protestant reformers developed the idea of ritual as a distinct form of rote, often liturgical, action. From them we also derive some of our condemnation of false or hollow celebration as "mere" ritual.[10]

At the same time, holidays for the popular classes, at least for non- 15
Puritans, varied from today's in a quite different respect. These people celebrated some of their festivals as community events or as carnivals, times for begging and ritualized aggression, cross-dressing and masquerading, gluttony and sexual license. Wearing costumes and masks, revelers had a great deal of freedom to misbehave. The celebrants often inverted class or racial hierarchy and lampooned the ruling elite, violating rules governing ordinary behavior with seeming impunity.[11] In this way the elite, by permitting some social conflict to be expressed, defused it and rendered it harmless. The day after the carnival, the world returned to normal, unchanged. In both premodern Europe and America carnival was a time of disorder, but only in Europe did rowdies turn into rebels, causing riots and murders, resulting in celebrants occasionally being forbidden to wear masks.[12] American masking and mumming could be disorderly, but it was less political. Carnival processions and dances usually took place out-of-doors. Men pulled down their pants and joked; women watched and laughed. People also celebrated much more as communities rather than as nuclear families. Thus, for example, in many rural areas and especially among slaves and ex-slaves, corn shucking was a special time—an outdoor gathering that combined work, food, drinking, singing, and conviviality.[13]

Because the growing middle class saw carnivalesque celebrations as lawless and debauched, they tried and mainly succeeded in stamping them out. They regarded the carnival style as an improper way to celebrate Christmas, Thanksgiving, and many other holidays. As a result, a sentimental and commercial style of celebration, the form preferred by the more powerful and respectable bourgeoisie, became dominant, just as the urban middle class itself triumphed in short stories and sentimental novels. In the nineteenth century this stratum of society had the means to purchase both metal caskets for funerals and rocking horses as Christmas gifts. The Victorians (whose era

I roughly define as the decades from 1820 to 1890) virtually created the child-centered, sentimentalized occasion. Wealthy and middle-class Victorians wanted to make their family events displays of new standards of etiquette, respectability, beauty, and wealth.

They invented a long list of new holidays and made their rites of passage into beautiful pageants. During these seven decades Santa Claus and the Christmas tree entered the parlor. Family, friends, and sweethearts began to send lace paper greetings on St. Valentine's Day. The white wedding—a bride in white, a wedding cake in white—departed dramatically from the plain, informal services that had been the norm. Couples married for decades began to hold formal gatherings to commemorate the anniversary of the date of their wedding. Parents took note of the date of a child's birth by hosting a special party. After a death, the wake went on for several days; the funeral service took place in a church, and hundreds of men and women might walk or ride in carriages from there to the grave. In wearing mourning clothes grieving relatives were a living symbol of how death sundered family ties. As for happier occasions, middle-class families sought a pastoral setting away from the home for a family vacation. The Protestant Sabbath became child-oriented and mother-directed.

The Victorians dressed up some of the grandest rituals of the modern calendar—Thanksgiving, Christmas, and Easter—and added glamour to celebrations of the major transitions of life. It is at first easy to conclude, as Caplow did, that people in the contemporary United States are simply drawing on Victorian style, using little embellishments (such as "Jingle Bell Rock" or *The Grinch Who Stole Christmas* for that holiday, for example) as modern additions. Moreover, some of the key meanings of these festivals have also been passed down—Thanksgiving as a holiday of the family and of a nation blessed with liberty and bounty, Christmas and Easter as special times for children. By these standards, the twentieth century may appear to be culturally impoverished. However, some highly popular traditions were invented then, such as baby showers, Mother's Day, Father's Day, Kwanzaa, and Superbowl Sunday.

Though it is true that the time pressures of modern life have generally caused family rituals to be shortened and simplified, and many traditions to be cast aside entirely, at the same time, weddings have become more elaborate, expensive, and time consuming. By making the lavish wedding the grandest occasion of all, Americans, who define the wedding as the essence of family, are actually rejecting Victorian beliefs about the sentimental occasion. Part of the essence of sentimentalism was that the sad event was more significant than the happy one, and that families needed to gather for all the special times in the life cycle. Thus, Victorians gave about equal attention to christenings as to weddings, and made funerals the grandest occasion of all.

20 Postsentimentalism gives less attention to the sad occasion, in part because of the desire to deny death, in part because of an optimistic consumer and popular culture that defines spending as a means to achieve happiness. Family parties after christenings, first communions, and confirmations have become optional. But since the 1960s, the church wedding followed by a large reception has become very grand. Bar and bat mitzvahs and quinceañeras

(a girl's fifteenth birthday celebration among Hispanics) have also grown fancier, taking on all the trappings of a lavish wedding.

Notes

1. Leigh Eric Schmidt, *Consumer Rites: The Buying and Selling of American Holidays* (Princeton: Princeton University Press, 1995), pp. 16–17; *New York Times,* Oct. 28, 1997, p. C1; Shannon Durtch, "Greetings America," *American Demographics* 19 (February 1997): 4.
2. "Supermarkets Find Once-Joyful Holidays Are Now the Time to Give Away the Store," *Wall Street Journal,* Dec. 8, 1992, p. B1.
3. Judith Stacey, *Brave New Families: Stories of Domestic Upheaval in Late Twentieth Century America* (New York: Basic Books, 1990). For an argument that the central characteristic of postmodern ritual is a "fragmented" identity, see David Parkin, "Ritual as Spatial Direction and Bodily Division," in Daniel de Coppet, ed., *Understanding Rituals* (London: Routledge, 1992), pp. 11–25.
4. Robert N. Bellah, Richard Marsden, William M. Sullivan, Ann Swidler, and Steven M. Tipton, *Habits of the Heart: Individualism and Commitment in American Life* (New York: Harper and Row, 1985), p. 90. In this book I study the "discourse" of occasions, a term introduced by French historian and philosopher Michel Foucault. By discourse, Foucault meant not simply rhetoric or discussion but also social practice, cultural imagery, and the relationship between representations, discussions, and reality. As Foucault pointed out, ideas and practice are related, but may fit together poorly. Rituals may express contradictory views, or may contradict the ideas prevalent in magazines and newspapers. Michel Foucault, *The History of Sexuality,* vol. 1, trans. Robert Hurley (New York: Pantheon Books, 1978), pp. 100–102.
5. See Cary Carson, Ronald Hoffman, and Peter J. Albert, eds., *Of Consuming Interests: The Style of Life in the Eighteenth Century* (Charlottesville: University Press of Virginia and U.S. Capital Historical Society, 1994).
6. Stephen Steinberg, *The Ethnic Myth: Race, Ethnicity, and Class in America* (New York: Atheneum, 1981), p. 63.
7. Eric Hobsbawm, "Introduction: Inventing Traditions," in Eric Hobsbawm and Terence Ranger, eds., *The Invention of Tradition* (Cambridge: Cambridge University Press, 1983), pp. 1–14.
8. Ibid., p. 2.
9. For more about the development of Victorian rituals, see John R. Gillis, *A World of Their Own Making: Myth, Ritual, and the Quest for Family Values* (New York: Basic Books, 1996), pp. 61–132.
10. Peter Burke, "The Repudiation of Ritual in Early Modern Europe," in Peter Burke, ed., *The Historical Anthropology of Early Modern Italy: Essays on Perception and Communication* (Cambridge: Cambridge University Press, 1987), pp. 223–238; Edward Muir, *Ritual in Early Modern Europe* (Cambridge: Cambridge University Press, 1997), pp. 155–228.
11. Victor Turner studied ritual inversion in *The Ritual Process: Structure and Anti-Structure* (Chicago: Aldine, 1969).
12. Natalie Zemon Davis, *Society and Culture in Early Modern France* (Stanford: Stanford University Press, 1975), pp. 97–123.
13. Roger D. Abrahams, *Singing the Master: The Emergence of African American Culture in the Plantation South* (New York: Pantheon Books, 1992).

ELLEN GOODMAN

Thanksgiving

Soon they will be together again, all the people who travel between their own lives and each other's. The package tour of the season will lure them this week to the family table.

By Thursday, feast day, family day, Thanksgiving day, Americans who value individualism like no other people will collect around a million tables in a ritual of belonging.

They will assemble their families the way they assemble dinner: each one bearing a personality as different as cranberry sauce and pumpkin pie. For one dinner they will cook for each other, fuss for each other, feed each other and argue with each other.

They will nod at their common heritage, the craziness and caring of other generations. They will measure their common legacy . . . the children.

5 All these complex cells, these men and women, old and young, with different dreams and disappointments will give homage again to the group they are a part of and apart from: their family.

Families and individuals. The "we" and the "I." As good Americans we all travel between these two ideals.

We take value trips from the great American notion of individualism to the great American vision of family. We wear out our tires driving back and forth, using speed to shorten the distance between these two principles.

There has always been some pavement between a person and a family. From the first moment we recognize that we are separate we begin to wrestle with aloneness and togetherness.

Here and now these conflicts are especially acute. We are, after all, raised in families . . . to be individuals. This double message follows us through life.

We are taught about the freedom of the "I" and the safety of the "we." The loneliness of the "I" and the intrusiveness of the "we." The selfishness of the "I" and the burdens of the "we."

10 We are taught what André Malraux said: "Without a family, man, alone in the world, trembles with the cold."

And taught what he said another day: "The denial of the supreme importance of the mind's development accounts for many revolts against the family."

In theory, the world rewards "the supreme importance" of the individual, the ego. We think alone, inside our heads. We write music and literature with an enlarged sense of self. We are graded and paid, hired and fired, on our own merit.

The rank individualism is both exciting and cruel. Here is where the fittest survive.

15 The family, on the other hand, at its best, works very differently. We don't have to achieve to be accepted by our families. We just have to be. Our membership is not based on credentials but on birth.

As Malraux put it, "A friend loves you for your intelligence, a mistress for your charm, but your family's love is unreasoning: You were born into it and of its flesh and blood."

The family is formed not for the survival of the fittest but for the weakest. It is not an economic unit but an emotional one. This is not the place where people ruthlessly compete with each other but where they work for each other.

Its business is taking care, and when it works, it is not callous but kind.

There are fewer heroes, fewer stars in family life. While the world may glorify the self, the family asks us, at one time or another, to submerge it. While the world may abandon us, the family promises, at one time or another, to protect us.

So we commute daily, weekly, yearly between one world and another. 20
Between a life as a family member that can be nurturing or smothering. Between life as an individual that can free us or flatten us. We vacillate between two separate sets of demands and possibilities.

The people who will gather around this table Thursday live in both of these worlds, a part of and apart from each other. With any luck the territory they travel from one to another can be a fertile one, rich with care and space. It can be a place where the "I" and the "we" interact.

On this day at least, they will bring to each other something both special and something to be shared: these separate selves.

ARDEN RANGER

A History of Anglo-Saxon Wedding Customs

Something old,
Something new,
Something borrowed,
something blue
and a sixpence for her shoe.

After several weekends spent shopping for wedding dresses with my best friend's fiancée, we were both ready to throw in the towel and I was more than ready to help them elope. Sitting over a much-needed margarita, we discovered that we really had no idea where many of our wedding traditions came from. Since my S.O. and I are planning on flouting many of these traditions if we ever decide to get married, I thought it might be nice to know just exactly what the things we were throwing away meant. Thus began an unending journey into our ancient pasts. Between my S.O. and myself, we cover the heritages of Italy, Ireland, Scotland, England, and the American Indian. My friend and his fiancée added Germany, France, and Denmark into the mix. Since the scope of this is far too broad for a single paper or wedding, I will focus on the customs that have become part of today's traditional weddings.

Stag Parties

The Stag or Bachelor party had its beginnings with the ancient Spartans. Spartan soldiers would hold a great feast for their comrades who were about to be married the night before the wedding. There he would bid goodbye to his bachelorhood and swear unending allegiance to his comrades in arms. Knowing ancient history, I have to believe that these gatherings, like the ones that every modern bride fears, involved more than a little sex. For to the ancient Greeks, only a man could truly enjoy sex. Women were not capable of the higher emotions involved and were only for providing heirs.

Engagements

The modern engagement is rooted in the Medieval customs of publishing the banns and handfasting. The handfasting ceremony usually took place when the couple was very young, often many years before the actual wedding. It was this ceremony, not the wedding, that produced the exchange of vows which are now part of the Anglican wedding ceremony (where the couple vows to marry and be faithful). This was also time for bride price and dowry to be exchanged. The ceremony was sealed with a drink and a kiss. (Wet bargains were considered more binding than dry ones; if the kiss did not take place, and the parties later decided to back out, they both had to return any betrothal gifts. If the kiss did take place the man had to return all but the woman only half). This custom of keeping engagment gifts, specifically the ring, was recently shot down in the Kansas Supreme Court's decision in the case of *Parrish* v. *Heiman*. The judge declared that an engagement ring was a conditional gift, the condition being the wedding. Therefore, the woman had to return the ring even though it was the man who had broken off the engagement. In the 1300s the Archbishop of Canterbury decreed that all weddings should be preceded by the reading of the banns for three consecutive Lord's days (holidays). Banns are a public declaration of a couple's intent to wed, like today's engagement announcement that is published in the newspaper.

Weddings

The first marriages were by capture. The groom, with the help of his warrior friends (his best men), would steal into another tribe's camp and kidnap the woman of his choice. His friends covered his back and fought off any others with an interest in the woman. As the invading party fought off the other men, he would hold her with his left hand because his right hand was his sword hand. This is believed to be the root of the custom of the bride standing on the groom's left in the wedding ceremony. It was also the duty of his friends to hide the couple so her family couldn't find her. Because honey and the moon were tied to fertility, the couple drank only honey mead and remained in hiding for one full lunar cycle (twenty-eight days), a honey-moon. By the time they were found, the bride was already pregnant.

5 Marriage by purchase became the preferred practice, being less stressful for all involved. The word wedding is from the Anglo-Saxon word "wedd," meaning to wager or gamble. It referred to the vow the man gave to marry

another man's daughter or to the goods or bride price. Women were bought for breeding purposes by the grooms and sold for land, status, or political alliances and, occasionally, cash.

Arranged marriages also took place and neither the bride or groom had a say in it. Most of these deals took place at the birth of the girl for the same purposes as marriage by purchase. Some couples never saw each other until the groom lifted the bride's veil at which point, if either one didn't like what they saw, it was too late.

Church Weddings

Britain gradually converted to Christianity after Rome pulled out in 410 AD. One of the first things it took on was the wedding. While Roman upper classes had long been married by priests with nuptial sacrifices to the gods, the common people had not. With the involvement of the Church came marriage by purchase. The modern practices of the bride and groom exchanging wedding gifts and whose family pays for what are rooted in the ancient customs of bride price and dowry. After the families were agreed on the price, goods were exchanged at the handfasting, with the local priests among the witnesses. In the beginning, couples only went to the Church to have the union blessed. But the Church soon took over the whole operation. From witnesses, they moved to the blessing of the ring and the joining of hands; soon they turned a business arrangement into a full religious affair. The Archbishop of Canterbury ordered that all weddings be publicly announced for three Lord's days, and marriages should be celebrated in the church, with reverence, in daylight, in the face of the congregation. Priests were to use the threat of excommunication to prevent secret engagements and weddings. Any priests caught knowingly performing an illegal wedding would be punished. Originally, the ceremony itself was performed on the steps of the church, with everyone moving inside for Mass. Until the reign of Edward the VI, this was how it was done for everyone. Many reasons have been put forward for this, from the indecency of granting permission for a man and woman to sleep together inside the church, to the last-minute bargaining that went on just before the ceremony, to the more possible theory that it was a last-ditch effort to keep weddings out of the clutches of the clergy. It didn't work.

Giving the Bride Away

[This tradition] directly descended from marriage by purchase when the father handed his daughter over to her new master. In the Middle Ages, in the age of courtly love and the romantic ideal, it became "Coemptio," a letting go, a mock purchase. Today it is connected with the love between the father and his daughter. The father hands over the responsibility of caring for his daughter to the man she has chosen to marry.

The Bride Wore White. . . .

The white wedding that all mothers dream of from the day their daughters are born did not become popular until the Victorian Era. The brides of the ancient world did not associate white with brides or purity. For centuries after the Romans, there were no "wedding dresses"; a wealthy bride wore fancier versions of her everyday clothes; and the poor and middle classes wore their best dress, often fancied up with ribbon and garlands.

10 In Ancient Rome, the dress itself was less important than the accessories. As long as the dress was vertically woven and tied with a woollen girdle (belt), there was no special color called for.

The first mention of a white wedding dress in history is Anne of Brittany in 1499. There is not another mention of this occurrence until 1530, when the daughter of Henry VII, Margaret Tudor, married James IV of Scotland. Both bride and groom wore white damask edged and lined in crimson velvet. In 1558, Mary, Queen of Scots wore white when she married the Dauphin of France. She defied tradition by doing so; white was then the mourning color for French queens. The fact that these were described in such detail makes them remarkable. The practice was to have a few outfits and wear them until their state of wear was beneath your station, at which time they were cast-off. It was a mark of wealth and power to have clothing made for specific occasions in the Middle Ages and Renaissance.

The most popular colors for special occasion dresses (weddings, coronations, presentation to the Crown, etc. . . .) were purple, crimson, and royal blue. These rich jewel tones were difficult dyes to obtain and the colors themselves hard to mix; who could wear them was decreed by the rigid sumptuary laws of the day. During the reign of Elizabeth I, Royal Purple was decreed to be only worn by Her Majesty. It was also during this time that white became a symbol of pure, young maidenhood and an automatic choice for many brides, although still not thought of as the bridal color. It was the formidable Queen Victoria who started the white wedding dress custom that we know today.

Veils

The veil tradition of today is tied to the arranged marriage practices mentioned above and as a symbol of virginal humility. Yellow was the color of weddings, and the bride wore a yellow veil that covered her from head to toe. It covered her from the time she left her mother's house until her bridegroom unveiled her on the wedding night.

During the Dark Ages, blue veils became the symbol of purity for brides. The Virgin Mary is always portrayed as wearing blue, and that color became the mark of virginity. Some sources state that the belief in blue symbolizing purity originated in biblical times, when both bride and groom wore a band of blue around the hem of their garments. This belief would explain why Mary was always portrayed in that color.

Bridesmaids

15 The bride's maid is another tradition we owe to the Anglo-Saxons. Before Christianity, when Druids ruled Britain, it was believed that evil spirits, jealous of the happiness of the couple, would try to make mischief with them. To confuse the spirits, brides (the most common target) and their grooms surrounded themselves with close friends. All members of the "wedding party"

were dressed identically to the bride and groom to ensure that the jealous ones could not pick them out.

With Christianity, the belief in evil spirits faded, but the custom did not. Medieval brides surrounded themselves with unmarried friends, the senior one attending her for several days beforehand to help make the decorations for the wedding feast and the floral garlands with which the bride and groom would be crowned after the blessing in church.

Flowers

Since ancient times, every flower has had a magical significance, and different colors of a flower had an even more specific message. Carrying, wearing, giving, or receiving certain flowers conveyed deep meaning. The modern bridal bouquet has its origins in antiquity. In ancient Rome, Greece, and Egypt, brides carried sheaths of wheat, a strong fertility symbol. They also wore chaplets of flowers on their heads. Fertility symbols such as nuts and grains, as well as whatever local flora, would grant them happiness, fidelity, and wealth.

With This Ring . . .

In ancient times, a coin was broken by a young man and half given to his intended and half kept for himself. The broken coin represented his intent to return and "make what is broken whole." In the Middle Ages, coins were replaced with rings which continued to be broken for many years. The woman would wear her broken half on a ribbon around her neck to advertise the fact that she was betrothed. Eventually, the custom became two rings instead of a broken one: one for the engagement and another for the wedding. These rings were usually simple bands with romantic sayings engraved along the outside. A few of these phrases are: Till Death Divide (Nemo nisi Mors), In Good Faith (Tout pour bien Feyre), Love Conquers All (Amot vincit Om), May we Love Forever (Semper Amenus), You Have my Heart (Mon Coeur Avez), Two Bodies One Heart (Deux Corps une Coeur)

Italians were the first to associate the fiery brilliance of a diamond with the fires of love and have given diamonds as betrothal gifts for generations. It was believed for centuries that a diamond in an engagement ring would inevitably bring bad luck to the wearer and her husband, because the interruption of the perfect circle destroyed the eternal love that the unbroken circle symbolized. But the diamond engagement ring became fashionable in the 15th century when Mary of Burgundy received one from her fiancé, Archduke Maximilian of Austria.

The tradition of wearing the wedding ring on the third finger of the left 20
hand stems from the ancient Greek belief that a nerve ran directly from that finger to the heart, giving the groom the illusion that he had placed a ring around the bride's heart. Another explanation is that the ring is worn on the left hand to signify the subjugation of the bride to her husband. The right hand signifies power, independence, and authority. Another, more practical, belief is that the third finger can't be straightened unless the other fingers are extended, which makes the ring safer there. Also, since left-handed people

were considered sinister and of the devil, no one used that hand predominantly, so a ring there is safer than a ring on the right hand.

The Cake

There has always been a cake. The ancient Greeks, Romans, and Egyptians crumbled grain cakes over the head of the bride to symbolize her fertility. In the Middle Ages, it became popular to have the bride and groom try to kiss over a tower of smaller cakes. Success meant prosperity for the couple.

It is believed that a baker, on his way to a large wedding, was the first to frost a wedding cake. After several stops to restack the piles of individual wedding cakes on his carts, the exasperated man mixed a sticky paste from sugar and water, which he had his assistants pour between the layers and over the top of the piles. The baker then continued happily on his journey without interruption. Edible centerpieces known as sublities were popular in the Middle Ages and grew to extravagant heights in the Renaissance. It was during the reign of Charles II of England that the extravaganza we know today as the wedding cake became popular. It became customary at that time to build it as a palace, iced with white sugar, complete with figures of the new "Lord and Lady of the Manor," gardens, and horses.

In the 1700s it became the tradition to thread a small piece of the cake through the wedding ring a certain number of times (nine being the most magical number) and sleep with it beneath the pillow. Over time, it became the custom to box up small pieces of this cake for the maids and bachelors to take home. Before going to sleep a "prayer"* was said. Being as the civilized world was Christian, no one openly called it a spell, but it is a commonly held belief that it is just that, its origins lost in antiquity. The cake, with the aid of God, the saints, angels, or Venus, was said to grant the sleeping person dreams of their future marriage partner.

But madam, as a present take
This little paper of bride-cake;
Fast any Friday in the year,
When Venus mounts the starry sphere,
Thrust this at night in pillowbeer:
In morning slumber you will seem
T' enjoy your lover in a dream.

Tossing the Bouquet and Garter

Ancient traditions involving wedding "tokens" are many and varied. Anything associated with the bride was considered not only lucky, but magical as well. During the early Middle Ages, rare was the bride that made it to her new home with her garments intact. After the feast, the couple was carried by their friends and family to the nuptial chamber and taken inside by their

* (I defiantly recall hearing the spell. It was recited at a medieval style wedding of a friend several years ago; however, I am unable to find a copy of it now.)

closest companions. It should be noted that, by this time, everyone involved was roaring drunk. While the attendants undressed and prepared the couple, everyone else stood outside the closed door shouting encouragement and singing bawdy songs. When the couple was naked and laid out on their marriage bed, the attendants sat on the edge of the bed with their backs turned to the bride and groom and threw stockings over their shoulders. Whoever threw the stocking that hung on the bride or groom's nose would be the next to marry.

The wedding garter and the husband's removal of it represented the 25
bride's virginity and the symbolic relinquishing of that status. In the 14th century, brides had gotten tired of drunken male guests growing impatient and trying to remove it themselves. It was a lot less trouble just to throw the bouquet at them. It wasn't until late in the 19th century that the bouquet and garter toss became segregated affairs, and nowhere is the event as rowdy and injury-causing as in the United States.

Wedding Favors

During the Renaissance, taking a piece of the bride's wedding attire was lucky for the guests, disastrous for the bride. It was during this time that Italian brides began tacking flowers or bows to their gowns to give the guests something to take without leaving the bride in rags. This later evolved into the giving of wedding favors. For centuries, the brides of Italy have given little bags of confetti and candy-covered almonds to their guests, representing the bitter and the sweet of married life. Known today as Jordan almonds, they still grace many a reception table worldwide. Today's wedding favors are as diverse as the weddings, running the gambit between personalized chocolates and matchbooks to saplings and wildflower seeds.

Tying Shoes to Car Bumpers

This practice represents the powerful symbolism of shoes in antiquity. This seemingly innocent foot covering was the instrument with which the victor, putting his heel on the neck of a conquered enemy, would demonstrate the subjugation of the fallen foe. When the father of the bride in ancient Egypt gave his daughter to the groom, he also gave him her sandals to show whose property she was.

The Anglo-Saxon groom also received one of the bride's slippers from her father to show the transfer of authority. He then used the shoe to bop her on the head to show her who was the master in their relationship. It was then carried into the bridal chamber and placed over the husband's side of the bed. If the wife was later accused of having a temper, someone would invariably sneak into the room and transfer the shoe to the bride's side of the bed.

In Germany, the bride throwing her shoe was akin to tossing the bouquet. In time it became the custom in many places to throw shoes at the bridal couple; this continued through Victorian times. With the invention of the automobile, it became more practical for the guests to tie the shoes to the departing vehicle; in this way, the shoes still followed behind the couple.

Flower Girls and Throwing Rice

In ancient Greece, after the wedding feast, everyone walked with the bridal couple to their new home. Their path was littered with flower petals by the singing crowd to release the flower's magical fragrance into the air. Petals and grains were also thrown over the couple to ensure happiness and fertility.

The flower girl of today is performing a symbolic reflection of that age-old custom when she drops her petals down the aisle. Although today it is considered a way to get the younger member of the family involved in the ceremony, as well as a culmination of a lifetime of fairy tale princess walking down flower-strewn paths—a purely Victorian addition.

The ancient fertility custom of throwing grain at the departing couple never went away. When rice became cheaper than other grains, as well as its being white, it became the popular aerial weapon. When environmentalists made us aware of the danger rice posed to birds when they ate it, we moved to birdseed. However, this posed its own problems. Birds congregating at the doorway often left an unsightly mess in their wake, and brides began complaining of the difficulty of getting the seeds out of their hair. Today, the fertility meaning is lost, but the ritual goes on. Helium balloons enjoyed a brief popularity until the dangers to wildlife were pointed out. I attended a wedding several years ago of two magic enthusiasts where white doves were released. I have to say that it was a stunning effect from across the street where the video camera was, but it was a nightmare to be in the middle of it. Now, couples opt for bubbles, confetti, and the release of butterflies.

Something Old . . .

The well-known rhyme that opens this essay is often described as ancient, but various older texts from the 16th century-on do not bear this out. It appears to be yet another Victorian invention. While the superstitions themselves have their roots in antiquity, the rhyme does not. "Something old" refers to the belief in sympathetic magic—wearing great-grandmother's locket bestows your ancestor's blessings on your union. "Something new" calls up many things. It is bad luck to set up a new household with an old broom, wearing someone else's dress could give you their troubles, and the ring itself should be new to represent your new love. "Something borrowed" is based on the belief that to borrow something from a happily married woman will ensure your happiness. "Something blue" goes back to the ancient custom of wearing blue to symbolize the bride's purity, the purity of the Virgin Mary. The "silver sixpence for her shoe" is thought to come from the ancient Greek custom of the bride carrying three silver coins on her wedding day; one for her mother-in-law, one for the first person met on the road after the wedding, and one to carry to her new home to ensure prosperity.

Today's wedding heritage is rich and diverse, but many modern brides are turning their backs on many long-held traditions. Today's couple doesn't necessarily opt for the formal, white-church wedding. Many ceremonies are held in parks, gardens, hot-air balloons, skating rinks, shopping malls, stadiums, on motorcycles, in caverns, in Las Vegas one-hour wedding chapels complete with Elvis, and, in a little town in Tennessee, the feed store. Where once the theme was solemn, today's wedding themes include Western, Mardi Gras, Winter Wonderlands, Medieval, Italian Renaissance, Carnival, Holidays, Gothic Vampires, and even Circuses. In an age of easy divorce, second and third weddings are common. Returning brides wear white, feeling every woman deserves to get married in white, ivory, or pastels, if they're feeling traditional or whatever suits their fancy. Fairy-tale dresses or thigh-high cocktail dresses, suits and tuxedos—there are no rigid rules for the brides of today.

My friend and his fiancée had a traditional wedding, "for the parents." 35
However, their shared interest in vampires was reflected in the black invitations with embossed red rosebuds and silver ankh seals, the ankh-shaped tuxedo button covers and cake decorations, gothic organ music, the starkness of the all black and white wedding, and the formal pictures of the wedding party in custom-made fangs. The groom was Catholic, the bride divorced; by Church law, he is excommunicated, so there was no priest, befitting the joining of two vampiric ones.

Richard and I, if we do finally get married, know that our wedding will be a lot like our friends'. Maybe not the theme, although we do have that in common, but in the less-than-traditional aspect. There will be no bridesmaids—my best friends are all men—so they'll be my honor attendants, which seems only right since they are the ones who have defended my honor for the past few years. Richard's attendants will include his ex-wife (it's a long story), my daughter, and his token male friend who just happens to be gay. A practicing pagan will be singing "The Lord's Prayer," and my son will escort me down the aisle. For any number of reasons, not the least of which is that I look horrible in it, I will not be wearing white. We are planning on marrying at St. Andrew's Episcopal Church (I'm almost 40 years old and I still make concessions for Daddy: "If it doesn't happen in a church, it isn't a wedding."), but Mother Mary, not Father Bob, will conduct the ceremony. Not just any ceremony—the original ceremony from the 1662 Book of Common Prayer. We too, like many of our contemporaries, are defining ourselves and creating our own traditions.

BRIAN TOKAR

The Twentieth Anniversary of Earth Day

The year 1990 was an auspicious one for environmental activists in the United States. The twentieth anniversary of the original Earth Day was on the horizon, and it appeared as though everyone wanted to be an environmentalist. The widespread popularity of environmental concerns was reflected in the rapid growth of environmental organizations, the appearance of new publications, and some of the first glossy catalogs of environmental products. Expressions of concern for the environment adorned politicians' stump speeches, both in the United States and overseas. Environmental scientists and activists widely agreed that the 1990s would be a critical decade to stem the course of environmental degradation, and political and cultural trends offered many people a renewed hope that this was indeed possible.

A *New York Times*/CBS News poll announced that people firmly supported environmental protection, despite perceptions of a growing conflict between ecology and job growth. Seventy-one percent agreed that "we must protect the environment even if it means increased government spending and higher taxes." Fifty-six percent said they would opt for environmental protection even at the expense of local job losses.

Politicians of all stripes were quick to jump on board. President George Bush, a former Texas oil developer, declared himself "tough" on the environment, even though he had lobbied for oil drilling in the Arctic National Wildlife Refuge just weeks after the tragic 1989 Exxon Valdez oil spill marred some 900 square miles of Alaskan coastline. EPA chief William Reilly was credited with "greening the White House," even as he faced possible criminal charges in a case in which the EPA had pressured the state of North Carolina into hosting a commercial toxic waste dump. Senator Al Gore, the 1988 presidential campaign's leading Democratic hawk, began speaking out about global warming and other environmental threats. Internationally, Britain's "Iron Lady," Prime Minister Margaret Thatcher, called herself a "green," and even World Bank president Barber Conable managed to win praise from several environmental publications for voicing concerns about the Bank's role in environmental destruction.

The coming Earth Day celebrations aroused a mixture of hope and cynicism on the part of longtime activists. The hope lay in the vast numbers of people from all walks of life who were working to make Earth Day a celebration of their own communities' concerns for the fate of the earth. The cynicism was fueled by much of the literature emanating from the official Earth Day organizations that had been established throughout the country. They had apparently decided that Earth Day was going to be a politically safe event: symbolic tree plantings, "educating our leaders," "a galaxy of celebrities," and the like. Their pronouncements included almost nothing about the institutions or the economic system responsible for ecocide, nothing about confronting corporate polluters, nothing about changing the structures of society.

5 The overriding message was simply, "change your lifestyle": recycle, drive less, stop wasting energy, buy better appliances, etc. And while the 1990 national Earth Day organization turned down more than $4 million in corporate donations that did not meet their quite flexible criteria, celebrations in several major U.S. cities were supported by some of the country's most notorious polluters—companies like Monsanto, Peabody Coal, and Georgia Power, to name just a few. Everyone from the nuclear power industry to the Chemical Manufacturer's Association took out full-page advertisements in newspapers and magazines proclaiming that, for them, "every day is Earth Day." The now-familiar greenwashing of Earth Day had clearly begun.

This turn of events proved disconcerting to many activists. In much of the movement's lore, Earth Day had become a symbol of the emergence of environmentalism as a social movement in its own right. Countless popular organizations traced their origin, directly or indirectly, to that auspicious day in April of 1970 when some twenty million people participated in a diverse and colorful outpouring of public concern about the natural environment. Why had things changed so dramatically two decades later?

Activists began to probe the history of Earth Day, and their investigations revealed, to the surprise of many, that even the original Earth Day was largely a staged event. It was initiated by politicians like Senator Gaylord Nelson and supported, though not without controversy, by establishment institutions such as the Conservation Foundation, the corporate think tank founded in 1948 by Laurance Rockefeller. Following President Nixon's rather suspect New Year's proclamation that the 1970s would be the "Environmental Decade," most anti-Vietnam War activists had come to view Earth Day as a devious attempt to divert attention from the war and from the anti-war movement's planned Spring Offensive, as well as from the common underlying causes of war, poverty, and environmental destruction. An editorial in *Ramparts,* the leading activist journal of the period, described Earth Day as "the first step in a con game that will do little more than abuse the environment even further."

The Earth Day issue of *Ramparts* featured a story on "The Eco-Establishment," which focused on the corporate think tanks that were helping to shape the new environmental legislation. Following the descriptions of corporate reorganization and a "grosser national product," . . . the authors continued:

> The seeming contradictions are mind-boggling: industry is combating waste so it can afford to waste more; it is planning to produce more (smog-controlled) private autos to crowd more highways, which means even more advertising to create more "needs" to be met by planned obsolescence. Socially, the result is disastrous. Ecologically, it could be the end.

As journalist I. F. Stone wrote in his famous investigative weekly,

> Just as the Caesars once used bread and circuses so ours were at last learning to use rock-and-roll idealism and non-inflammatory social issues to turn the youth off from more urgent concerns which might really threaten the power structure.

Reviewing this history intensified many activists' feelings of betrayal, and many responded by organizing more politicized local Earth Day anniversaries of their own. These events focused on local environmental struggles, inner-city issues, the nature of corporate power, and other concerns that had been largely excluded from the official Earth Day. The most ambitious of these was a demonstration in New York City called by members of the Greens and Youth Greens from throughout the Northeast, with the aid of environmental justice activists, Earth First!ers, ecofeminists, urban squatters, and many others. Early Monday morning, April 23, the day after millions had participated in polite, feel-good Earth Day commemorations all across the country, several hundred

CHAPTER 12

HOBBIES

Overview

Barbie dolls, baseball cards, stamps, coins—hobbies often entail collecting items available in a limited supply. Hobbies can also be activities that people enjoy that do not involve their jobs or schooling. Although some people turn their hobbies into professional pursuits—fascination with dinosaurs can lead to a career in paleontology, for example, or a skateboarder might compete professionally—most people use their hobbies for relaxation. We humans need activities to help us unwind or to relieve monotony. Hobbies also often help us create private, fanciful identities for ourselves that make us part of communities of people with similar interests.

The important criterion for calling something a hobby is choice. Once an activity is imposed on us, it ceases to be a hobby. When I was a child, I filled many free hours playing baseball. Besides playing in Little League and other organized programs, I pored over baseball encyclopedias, listened to Dodgers' games, and read biographies of great players. I even enjoyed a game called dice baseball in which I played the commissioner and made up fantasy rosters for teams that competed by my rolling the dice for each player's "at-bat" and comparing the numbers on the dice with a chart I had devised. Baseball was my hobby, and I loved it. Yet, when my dad took my brothers and me to the batting cage to teach us the nuances of hitting, which should have been fun, I did not enjoy myself as much. Even though I wasn't bad at hitting, batting cage night was a chore, not an extension of my hobby, because I did not feel I could choose whether to participate.

This icon will direct you to web links and additional resources on the website college.hmco.com/pic/thelin1e

The hobbies we choose—and many of us have more than one—can tell us something about ourselves as well as about the culture in which we live. In gravitating toward an activity and gaining insights or skills, we reflect part of our inner selves. Some people fear embarrassment if they reveal too much of their inner selves, and they keep their hobbies private. For teenagers and young adults, especially, hiding a hobby can become as much of a preoccupation as the hobby itself, as the approval of one's peers makes many people want to appear to conform to standard tastes and interests. A young man might conceal his collection of toy soldiers when friends come over. A young woman might be reluctant to admit that she follows professional wrestling. Even a hobby as common and stimulating as reading can make a person feel like an outcast if his or her peers do not read—or do not read the same things. We do not want the private selves that enjoy gothic romances or science fiction to be scrutinized by others.

Thinking of reading as a hobby might confuse some people, as many readers do not consider relaxing with a book to be a hobby. But reading, just like music, dancing, carpentry, or cooking, is a hobby when we invest energy in becoming a member of a community of people who share our interests. This might seem to fly in the face of the need to protect our inner selves, but hobbyists do in fact want to share. The sharing comes with a mutual understanding that during the time two or more people are in the world they have created, all that matters is that world. So ballroom dancers who have made dancing into a hobby spend hours looking at or making costumes, attending socials, practicing, and imagining a world of grace and grandeur. A person can read sword-and-sorcery fiction without considering it a hobby, but a reader who seeks out sword-and-sorcery conventions, reads webzines, and participates on blogs is a hobbyist.

Knowing that an activity can be discussed only among certain individuals not only defines it as a hobby but also shows us something about our society. We often intuitively understand societal norms. Women know that they can safely discuss and openly participate in hobbies like cooking. Men recognize that backpacking can be brought up freely in conversation, even with people who do not enjoy it.

Not only gender but also expectations about maturation factor into the sense of acceptability of hobbies. For example, target shooting's masculine aura makes it an acceptable hobby for men, but the subset of cowboy shooting—in which participants dress up as gunslingers from the Old West and adopt stage names such as "Six-Gun Steve" and "Kenny the Kid"—may be considered childish, and participants might refrain from discussing it freely.

Our culture's perception of grown-up behavior could be what gives childlike hobbies such allure for many people. We have to grow up quickly in today's society, and perhaps we leave childhood behind sooner than we like. Childlike hobbies seem to allow us to retain some part of childhood. Are we trying to recapture the excitement and creativity we indulged in as children? If so, that indicates a lack of imagination in adulthood—an absence of mystery, adventure, intrigue, or even hope. This indictment of the routine nature of our adult lives might not be immediately evident, but a close study of hobbies suggests that they take us away from the world more than bring us into it, even when we desire peers' approval.

The hobby of rappelling takes enthusiasts into the mountains, away from buildings, traffic, advertisements, and people. The enthusiast might try to interest friends in the activity, but rappelling still takes people away from society and its norms. Collecting stamps means understanding a specific language to grade the condition of stamps, barter with other collectors, and recognize rarity. When dedicating time to this hobby, stamp collectors seal themselves away from others while studying their collections or unwinding with other collectors at a store or convention. Both physically and mentally, they are removed from the workings of the world.

At some level, the pursuit of just about any hobby can reveal a degree of displeasure with the culture in which we live. We create space for ourselves to ignore some of its tacit rules. And we also reveal the extent of our imagination in creating these spaces. For in gravitating toward certain hobbies and choosing the number of hours, days, or weeks to devote to them, we have indicated what we cherish, and we have found a way to secure it.

Openings for Writers

1. **Childlike hobbies** What attributes might cause people to designate a hobby as childlike? Do you know anyone who engages in hobbies that you consider childlike? How do you react to this person's enjoyment of his or her hobby? Think of the ways that our culture dictates which attributes you name and how you react to the person.
2. **Marketing** Some people claim that the private enjoyment of a hobby is co-opted when the hobby gains popularity and merchandise connected to it saturates the market. What part does marketing play in the enjoyment of hobbies? Explain your answer by describing specific examples.
3. **Gender and hobbies** In what ways are hobbies connected to gender? Some people argue that differences between males and females can be found even in hobbies that appeal to both genders, like music. Think of some hobbies, and determine the extent to which gender might be a factor.
4. **Boredom in the adult world** List ways other than hobbies that adults relax and enjoy themselves. If your list includes many items, try to explain the preponderance of hobbies. Why do we engage in hobbies when there are so many other things to do? Is it possible that hobbies keep us from enjoying aspects of our society?

Language

1. **Hobby** Research the etymology of *hobby.* Now that you know about its origins, how would you define the word's use in today's culture?
2. **Habitual** What makes an activity habitual? At what point does a habit become an addiction? Does a comparison of *habit* and *addiction* lead to any insights about hobbies?

3. **Maturation** People sense the boundaries of mature behavior better than they can articulate what maturation is. What characteristics do you associate with maturation? What do the words on the list you made connote?
4. **Routine** Does the word *routine* bring comfort and security to you, or does it conjure images of boredom? Can it do both at the same time? Find a connection between impressions of or reactions to *routine* and the differing needs of individuals for hobbies.

PAUL ROBERTS

Risk

Many hobbies involve an element of danger. In this article, Paul Roberts concentrates on the conflict between thrills and safety by focusing on the perilous hobby of mountain climbing. Roberts does not dismiss risk takers as foolhardy. Rather, he believes that risks connect us to progress and individuality. Many avenues for adventure have been curbed by our society's craving for protection. If we follow Roberts's logic, we can extend his argument about mountain climbing to include all hobbies.

In the land of seatbelts and safety helmets, the leisure pursuit of danger is a growth industry. Some experts say that courting uncertainty is the only way to protect the inner force America was founded on. Or to define the self.

Risky business has never been more popular. Mountain climbing is among America's fastest growing sports. Extreme skiing—in which skiers descend cliff-like runs by dropping from ledge to snow-covered ledge—is drawing wider interest. Sports like paragliding and cliff-parachuting are marching into the recreational mainstream while the adventure-travel business, which often mixes activities like climbing or river rafting with wildlife safaries, has grown into a multimillion-dollar industry. "Forget the beach," declared *Newsweek* last year. "We're hot for mountain biking, river running, climbing, and bungee jumping."

> Thirty-six year-old Derek Hersey knew a thing or two about life on the edge. Where most rock climbers used ropes and other safety gear, the wiry, wise-cracking Brit usually climbed "free solo"—alone, using nothing but climbing shoes, finger chalk, and his wits. As one climbing buddy put it, Hersey went "for the adrenaline and risk," and on May 28, 1993, he got a dose of both. High on the face of Yosemite's Sentinel Rock, Hersey met with rain and, apparently, slick rock. Friends who found the battered body reckon he fell several hundred feet. In the not-too-distant past, students of human behavior might have explained Hersey's fall as death-wish fulfillment. Under conventional personality theories, normal individuals do everything possible to avoid tension and risk.

In fact, as researchers are discovering, the psychology of risk involves far more than a simple "death wish." Studies now indicate that the inclination to take high risks may be hard-wired into the brain, intimately linked to arousal and pleasure mechanisms, and may offer such a thrill that it functions like an addiction. The tendency probably affects one in five people, mostly young males, and declines with age. It may ensure our survival, even spur our evolution as individuals and as a species. Risk taking probably bestowed a crucial evolutionary advantage, inciting the fighting and foraging of the hunter-gatherer.

In mapping out the mechanisms of risk, psychologists hope to do more 5
than explain why people climb mountains. Risk taking, which one researcher defines as "engaging in any activity with an uncertain outcome," arises in nearly all walks of life. Asking someone on a date, accepting a challenging work assignment, raising a sensitive issue with a spouse or a friend, confronting an abusive boss—all involve uncertain outcomes, and present some level of risk. Understanding the psychology of risk, understanding why some individuals will take chances and others won't, could have important consequences in everything from career counseling to programs for juvenile delinquents.

Researchers don't yet know precisely how a risk taking impulse arises from within or what role is played by environmental factors, from upbringing to the culture at large. And, while some level of risk taking is clearly necessary for survival (try crossing a busy street without it), scientists are divided as to whether, in a modern society, a "high-risk gene" is still advantageous. Some scientists, like Frank Farley, Ph.D., a University of Wisconsin psychologist and past president of the American Psychological Association, see a willingness to take big risks as essential for success. The same inner force that pushed Derek Hersey, Farley argues, may also explain why some dare to run for office, launch a corporate raid, or lead a civil-rights demonstration.

Yet research has also revealed the darker side of risk taking. High-risk takers are easily bored and may suffer low job satisfaction. Their craving for stimulation can make them more likely to abuse drugs, gamble, commit crimes, and be promiscuous. As psychologist Salvadore Maddi, Ph.D., of the University of California–Davis warns, "high-risk takers may have a hard time deriving meaning and purpose from everyday life."

Indeed, this peculiar form of dissatisfaction could help explain the explosion of high-risk sports in America and other post-industrial Western nations. In unstable cultures, such as those at war or suffering poverty, people rarely seek out additional thrills. But in a rich and safety-obsessed country like America, land of guardrails, seat belts, and personal-injury lawsuits, everyday life may have become too safe, predictable, and boring for those programmed for risk taking.

In an unsettling paradox, our culture's emphasis on security and certainty—two defining elements of a "civilized" society—may not only be fostering the current risk taking wave, but could spawn riskier activities in the future. "The safer we try to make life," cautions psychologist Michael Aptor, Ph.D, a visiting professor at Yale and author of *The Dangerous Edge: The Psychology of Excitement,* "the more people may take on risks."

Unique Wavelengths

10 In Icicle Canyon, a towering rocky corridor in the Cascade Mountains of Washington State, this strange interplay between safety and risk is a common sight. When weather permits, the canyon's formidable walls swarm with fit-looking men and women, using improbably small ledges and cracks to hoist themselves upward. For novices, risk can be kept to a minimum. Beginners' climbs are "top-roped" by a line running from the climber to a fixed cliff-top anchor and back down to a partner on the ground.

Even so, the novice can quickly experience a very realistic fear—what veterans call "getting gripped." Halfway up one short cliff, a first-timer in a tee shirt and shorts stabs out beneath a rock overhang. Unable to find a foothold, the climber peels off the cliff like wet wallpaper and dangles limply from the rope. His partner lowers him back to safety, where he stands white-faced, like someone emerging from an auto accident. Five minutes later, he is back on the cliff.

It's easy to see why high-risk sports receive so much academic attention. Climbers, for example, score higher on risk-preference tests than nearly all other groups. They show a strong need for intense stimulation and seek it in environments—sheer cliffs or frozen waterfalls—that most humans seem genetically programmed to avoid.

Climbers' own explanations for why they climb illustrate the difficulty of separating genetic, environmental, and cognitive components of this or any other behavioral trait. Many say they climb for decidedly conscious reasons: to test limits, to build or maintain self-esteem, to gain self-knowledge. Some regard it as a form of meditation. "Climbing demands absolute concentration," says Barbara, a lithe, 30-ish climber from Washington State. "It's the only time I ever feel in the moment."

Yet even the most contemplative climbers concede that their minds and bodies do operate on a unique wavelength. As Forrest Kennedy, a 32-year-old climber from Georgia, bluntly puts it, "What we do for kicks, most people wouldn't do if you held a gun to their heads."

15 Many climbers recognize that their commitment to the sport borders on addiction, one that persists after brushes with injury and death. Seattle attorney Jim Wickwire, for example, is probably best known for being on the first American team to summit Pakistan's 28,250-foot K-2, second highest peak in the world and arguably the most challenging. (The movie *K-2* was based on his story.) Yet this handsome, soft-spoken father of five is almost as well known for his obstinacy. On K-2, Wickwire lost several toes to frostbite and half a lung to altitude sickness. A year before, in 1977, he'd seen two climbing partners fall 4,000 feet. In 1981 on Alaska's Mount McKinley, he watched helplessly as another partner froze to death after becoming wedged in an ice crevasse.

Wickwire vowed then never to climb again. But in 1982, he attempted 29,028-foot Mount Everest, the world's tallest peak—and there saw yet another partner plunge 6,000 feet to her death. In 1993, as Wickwire, then 53, prepared for a second Everest attempt, he told a climbing magazine that he'd "stopped questioning why" he still climbed. Today, he seems just as uncertain.

"The people who engage in this," Wickwire says, "are probably driven to it in a psychological fashion that they may not even understand themselves."

Until recently, researchers were equally baffled. Psychoanalytic theory and learning theory relied heavily on the notion of stimulus reduction, which saw all human motivation geared toward eliminating tension. Behaviors that created tension, such as risk taking, were deemed dysfunctional, masking anxieties or feelings of inadequacy.

A Craving for Arousal

Yet as far back as the 1950s, research was hinting at alternative explanations. British psychologist Hans J. Eysenck developed a scale to measure the personality trait of extroversion, now one of the most consistent predictors of risk taking. Other studies revealed that, contrary to Freud, the brain not only craved arousal, but somehow regulated that arousal at an optimal level. Over the next three decades, researchers extended these early findings into a host of theories about risk taking.

Some scientists, like UC-Davis's Maddi and Wisconsin's Farley, concentrate on risk taking primarily as a cognitive or behavioral phenomenon. Maddi sees risk taking as an element of a larger personality dimension he calls "hardiness," which measures individuals' sense of control over their environment and their willingness to seek out challenges. Farley regards risk taking more as a whole personality type. Where other researchers speak of Types A and B personalities, Farley adds Type T, for thrill-seeking. He breaks Type-T behavior into four categories: T-mental and T-physical, to distinguish between intellectual and physical risk taking; and T-negative and T-positive, to distinguish between productive and destructive risk taking.

A second line of research focuses on risk's biological roots. A pioneer in 20
these studies is psychologist Marvin Zuckerman at the University of Delaware. He produced a detailed profile of the high-sensation seeking (HSS) personality. HSS individuals, or "highs," as Zuckerman calls them, are typically impulsive, uninhibited, social, intend toward liberal political views. They like high-stimulus activities, such as loud rock music or pornographic or horror movies, yet are rarely satisfied by vicarious thrills. Some level of actual risk—whether physical, social, or legal—seems necessary. Highs tend to be heavy bettors. They may try many kinds of drugs and favor sports like skiing or mountain climbing to running or gymnastics. Highs also show a clear aversion to low-sensation situations, otherwise known as boredom.

High-sensation seeking plays a huge role in relationships. Highs favor friends with interesting or offbeat life-styles, and avoid boring people. They're also far more sexually permissive, particularly in the number of sex partners, than lows. Highs favor mates with similar proclivities for stimulation, while lows generally pair off with other lows. And woe, apparently, to those who break this rule. "The combination of a high- and a low-sensation seeker," says Zuckerman, "seems to put the marriage relationship at risk."

Indeed, one benefit of such research is that it can be applied to many areas of everyday life. Those seeking mates, the University of Wisconsin's

Farley says, should focus on those who share their level of risk taking, particularly in terms of sexual habits. Likewise, thrill seekers should also look for the right level of on-the-job excitement. "If you're a Big T type working on a microchip assembly line, you're going to be miserable," Farley predicts. "But if you're Big T on a big daily newspaper or a police force, where you never know what you'll be doing next, you're probably going to thrive."

Many climbers fit the HSS profile. Many report difficulty keeping full-time jobs, either because the work bores them, or because it interferes with their climbing schedule. Long-term relationships can be problematic, especially where climbers marry nonclimbers, or where one partner begins losing interest in the sport. Nonclimbing partners often complain that their spouses spend too much time away from home, or refuse to commit to projects (children, for example) that might interfere with climbing. Relationships are also strained by the ever-present threat of injury or death. As one Midwestern climber puts it, "the possibility that I might miss dinner, forever, doesn't make things any smoother."

Further, while many climbers are models of clean living, the sport has its share of hard-partiers. Some even boast of making first ascents while high on marijuana or hallucinogens like LSD. Climbers say such drugs enhance or intensify the climbing experience. But studies suggest that the drugs may also mimic the process that pushes climbers in the first place.

Wired for Thrills

25 Researchers have long known of physiological differences between high- and low-sensation seekers. According to Zuckerman, the cortical system of a high can handle higher levels of stimulation without overloading and switching to the fight-or-flight response. Psychologist Randy Larsen, Ph.D., at the University of Michigan, has even shown that high-sensation seekers not only tolerate high stimulus but crave it as well.

Larsen calls high-sensation seekers "reducers": Their brains automatically dampen the level of incoming stimuli, leaving them with a kind of excitement deficit. (Low-sensation seekers, by contrast, tend to "augment" stimuli, and thus desire less excitement.) Why are some brains wired for excitement? Since 1974, researchers have known that the enzyme monoamine oxidase (MAO) plays a central role in regulating arousal, inhibition, and pleasure. They also found that low levels of MAO correlate with high levels of certain behaviors, including criminality, social activity, and drug abuse. When Zuckerman began testing HSS individuals, they, too, showed unusually low MAO levels.

The enzyme's precise role isn't clear. It regulates levels of at least three important neurotransmitters: norepinephrine, which arouses the brain in response to stimuli; dopamine, which is involved with the sensation of pleasure in response to arousal; and serotonin, which acts as a brake on norepinephrine and inhibits arousal. It's possible that high-sensation seekers have lower base levels of norepinephrine and thus, can tolerate more stimulation before triggering serotonin's dampening effect. High-sensation seekers may also have lower levels of dopamine and are thus in a chronic state of underarousal in the brain's pleasure centers.

Such individuals may turn to drugs, like cocaine, which mimic dopamine's pleasure reaction. But they may also use intense and novel stimulation, triggering norepinephrine's arousal reaction and getting rewarded by the dopamine pleasure reaction. "What you get is a combination of tremendous arousal with tremendous pleasure," Zuckerman speculates. "And the faster that arousal reaches its peak, the more intense your pleasure." Just as important, individuals may develop a tolerance for the pleasure reaction, and thus may need ever higher levels of stimulation—of risk—to achieve the same rush.

Today such an addictive dynamic may seem largely problematic. In prehistoric times it was very likely essential. Dopamine, for example, has known links to various "approach" behaviors: feeding, fighting, foraging, and exploration. Probably, the same mechanism that gave people like Derek Hersey a rush from climbing also rewarded their predecessors for the more necessary acts of survival.

Psychologist Aptor suggests that the willingness to take risks, even if 30
expressed by only certain individuals, would have produced benefits for an entire group. Upon entering a new territory, a tribe would quickly need to assess the environment's safety in terms of "which water holes are safe to drink from, which caves are empty of dangerous animals." Some risk takers would surely die. But, Aptor points out, "it's better for one person to eat a poisonous fruit than for everybody."

Climbers are understandably leery of such explanations. They admit that they may be more inclined to take risks than the average human. But that inclination's ultimate expression, they argue, is largely a matter of personal volition. "At some level, there is a reason, chemical, mechanical, or whatever, for why we climb. But doesn't that take the human element out of it, and make us all robots?" grouses Todd Wells, a 40-year-old climber from Chattanooga. "I climb so I don't feel like a robot, so I feel like I'm doing something that is motivated by the self."

Even physiologically oriented scientists like Zuckerman admit the dopamine reaction is only part of the risk taking picture. Upbringing, personal experience, socioeconomic status, and learning are also crucial in determining how that risk taking impulse is ultimately expressed.

Culture of Ascent

Although many climbers report a childhood preference for thrills, their interest in climbing was often shaped externally, either through contact with older climbers or by reading about great expeditions. Upon entering the sport, novices are often immersed in a tight-knit climbing subculture, with its own lingo, rules of conduct, and standards of excellence.

This learned aspect may be the most important element in the formation of the high-sensation-seeking personality. While risk taking may have arisen from neuro-chemicals and environmental influences, there is an intellectual or conscious side to it that is now not only distinct from them but is itself a powerful motivator. Working through a challenging climbing route, for example, generates a powerful sense of competence that can also provide climbers with a new-found confidence in their everyday life. "There is nothing more empowering than taking a risk and succeeding," says Farley.

35 No wonder scaling the face of a cliff is a potent act that can penetrate to the very essence of self and help reshape it. Many climbers report using that empowering dynamic to overcome some of their own inner obstacles. Among these, fear—of heights, of loss of control, of death—is the most commonly cited.

Richard Gottlieb, 42-year-old climber from New York, is known for climbing frozen waterfalls, one of the riskiest facets of the sport. But as a kid, he was too scared even to go to summer camp. "Yet there was something in me that wanted to get into some swashbuckling adventure," he says. Climbing satisfied that impulse while helping him overcome his fearful nature. Gottlieb believes climbing has helped him cope with his fear of death: "We open the door, see the Grim Reaper right there, but instead of just slamming the door, you push him back a few steps."

New Outlets

Traditional outlets for the risk taking impulse have been disappearing from everyday life. As civilization steadily minimized natural risks, Aptor says, and as cultures have sought to maintain their hard-won stability through repressive laws and stifling social mores, risk takers have been forced to devise new outlets. In the 20th century, that has brought about a rise in thrill sports. But Aptor believes the tension between civilization and risk taking dates back eons. Aptor wonders how much of the British Empire "was built up by people trying to escape the desperately conformist society of Victorian England."

When channeled into sports like climbing, where skill and training can minimize danger, or into starting a new business, risk taking may continue to be a healthy psychological outlet. It may provide a means to cope with boredom and modern anxieties, to bolster self-esteem. Risk taking may provide a crucial sense of control in a period where so much of what happens—from crime and auto accidents to environmental disasters and economic downturns—seems almost random.

Unfortunately, the risk taking impulse doesn't always find such healthy outlets. Many high-sensation seekers don't have the money or the role models for sky-diving or rock-climbing, Zuckerman notes. "In such groups, the main forms of sensation seeking include sex, drugs, heavy drinking, gambling, and reckless driving." Indeed, sensation seeking may emerge as a critical factor in crime. No surprise, then, that some researchers place the risk taking personality in the "abnormal" category and regard high-risk takers almost as an evolutionarily obsolete subspecies. Maddi suggests that well-adjusted people are "good at turning everyday experience into something interesting. My guess is that the safecracker or the mountain climber can't do that as well. They have to do something exciting to get a sense of vitality. It's the only way they have of getting away from the sense that life sucks." Larsen is even blunter: "I think risk takers are a little sociopathic."

Farley is more optimistic. Even civilized society, he says, holds ample opportunity for constructive risk taking: investing in a high-stakes business venture, running for political office, taking an unpopular social stand. Farley argues that history's most crucial events are shaped by Big T behavior and Big T individuals, from Boris Yeltsin to Martin Luther King, Jr. The act of emigration, he says, is an intrinsically risky endeavor that selects individuals who are high in sensation seeking. Consequently, countries built upon immigrant population—America, Canada, Australia—probably have an above-average level of risk takers. He warns that much of the current effort to minimize risk and risk taking itself runs the risk of eliminating "a large part of what made this country great in the first place."

For all the societal aspects of this peculiar trait, the ultimate benefits may continue to be purely personal. "There's a freshness to the [climbing] experience that clears away the weariness of routine and the complexity of social norms" says Seattle climber Bill Pilling. "Climbing brings you back to a primal place, where values are being created and transformed."

To push away from society's rides and protections, Farley suggests, is the only way to get a sense of where "society" ends and "you" begin. "Taking a risk, stepping away from the guardrails, from the rules and the status quo, that's when you get a sense of who you are," he says. "If you don't stretch, try to push past the frontiers, it's very difficult to know that."

SUSAN SHEEHAN AND HOWARD MEANS

Leonard Lauder

The beauty of small things

Some hobbies do not involve traditional pursuits and might strike us as strange. Authors Susan Sheehan and Howard Means profile some unusual leisure-time activities in their book, The Banana Sculptor, the Purple Lady, and the All-Night Swimmer: Hobbies, Collecting, and Other Passionate Pursuits. *As you read the following excerpt, think about the multiple purposes served by the hobby.*

Leonard Lauder, the CEO of Estée Lauder Companies, Inc., is in the library of his Fifth Avenue penthouse. On the library's walls are two paintings by Gustav Klimt that almost every museum in the world would be delighted to own. Tilted against a wall are a Picasso and a Braque that almost every museum in the world would be delighted to own—and would not place on a floor. Lauder and his wife, Evelyn, have one of the finest collections of Vienna Secessionist and Cubist art in the country.

There is a door in the library wall that doesn't look like a door. Lauder, a trim, courtly man with gray hair, opens this door and emerges from a small room hidden behind it, carrying several albums of picture postcards.

"Evelyn and I collect art and go hiking together," Lauder says. "Evelyn's personal interest is photography. Mine is postcards. I have the same affection for the postcards as for the Picassos." Lauder has the finest postcard collection in the country. He has about two hundred thousand cards.

By the time Lauder purchased his first Fernand Léger, he had already bought a great many postcards. He grew up in Manhattan and, as a child, often went out walking with his nanny. When he was five, he spent his weekly nickel allowance at Woolworth's, buying five postcards that cost a penny apiece, each showing the same picture of the Empire State Building. "They were so lovely I couldn't resist," he says.

During the late nineteen-thirties and early forties, Lauder went on vacation with his parents to Florida, and attended boarding school in Miami Beach. He opens a leatherette album with Mylar pages. Encased in the "archivally correct" Mylar are postcards showing art deco hotels in Miami Beach, arranged in alphabetical order. "I picked up all these cards as a kid, starting from the age of six," he says. "There's the Hotel Arlington. There's the Cadillac Hotel. On the card, it stands alone. There were buildings right next to it but they aren't shown. They were airbrushed out. We used to stay at the Charles Hotel."

5 He fast-forwards down the alphabet. "Here's the Roney Plaza," he says. "It used to be restricted. No Jews were permitted, so we didn't stay there. The Roney has been torn down, but most of these other hotels are still standing. The cards are linen-y. Linen went out in the late forties or early fifties and was replaced by chromes—photographic reproductions. These cards had no value until a few years ago, when the world rediscovered art deco and South Beach. To me, this is my childhood collection and I treasure it.

"When I was in high school I joined the oldest ongoing postcard club in America, the Metropolitan Postcard Club. I'm member number seventy-five. I'd swap cards with other collectors. Cards were worth between one cent and five cents. If we swapped, I might owe you ten cards or you might owe me twenty."

Lauder went off to college and to the navy, then came back to work for the cosmetics company his mother founded. He married and had two sons. "I was preoccupied," he says. "I didn't do much with postcards for fifteen years. Around 1965, I was building our company in England and I spent a lot of time in London. One weekend, I stumbled on some postcard dealers who had a stand on the Portobello Road. I became reinterested in postcards and started buying them. When I returned to the postcard scene in New York, the concept of exchanging was disappearing because the value of cards had gone up rapidly. You couldn't swap card for card. You'd wind up swapping value for value, which very quickly became buying and selling. The best way to collect was to go to postcard shows and make the rounds of the forty or fifty dealers who had tables at these bourses, and to buy the best of the best."

At these three-days shows, Lauder says, everyone was looking for something else. "A person would say to a dealer, 'Do you have any baseball stadiums?' Another would say, 'Do you have any dogs?' When I hear of people who collect postcards of cats or canaries, I'm not interested in them. That's never been the way I've collected cards. I collect cards that I think are beautiful—I'll get to that later—and cards I believe are of historical, sociological, or anthropological interest. I'm also interested in communication. The postcard has its place in the history of communication."

The telephone rings. Lauder answers it, looks at a calendar on his desk, and makes a tentative dinner date with a friend. After putting the receiver down and writing the date on a piece of paper, he says, "It's important to remember now that we're at the beginning of the twenty-first century that at the beginning of the twentieth century most people were unlikely to have telephones in their homes. Let's pretend the year is 1905 and I want to confirm a dinner date. I would probably do it by postcard.

"The first American government postal cards date back to 1873. Businesses bought these cards from the post office for a penny and had them printed with advertisements, greetings, or illustrations. In 1898, Congress put privately printed postcards, which had cost two cents [to send], on an equal footing with government-issued cards by cutting their price in half. It was the establishment of rural free delivery around the same time that made sending postcards a way of life.

"Free mail delivery in cities began in 1863, and home delivery was made to residents of towns with populations of at least ten thousand, but it was not until sometime between 1896, when RFD began, and 1906, when RFD was fairly well established, that farmers no longer had to travel considerable distances to the nearest post office to send or receive mail. Many had made this trip only once a week. Now the mail arrived every day, in cities sometimes two or three times a day, so people used the mail more often. You could send a card in the morning saying you expected someone for dinner at seven, certain in the knowledge that the dinner guest would receive the card well before seven o'clock. A penny postcard was a bargain. It was half the price of a letter and required less effort on the sender's part. The price of the penny postcard only went up to three cents in 1958."

Germany and Austria had started to produce beautiful postal cards in the eighteen-sixties, Lauder continues. Other countries soon followed, and a postcard-sending and postcard-collecting craze swept through a good part of Europe. "After 1898, the so-called golden age of postcards embraced America, and that age lasted for about twenty years," Lauder says. "I've read that in 1906 over a billion postcards were sent through the mail in Germany. By 1913, close to a billion postcards were mailed in the United States."

In that halcyon period between the Spanish-American War and the beginning of the First World War, people sent each other commercially produced postcards on birthdays and on holidays. Not just on Valentine's Day, Saint Patrick's Day, Easter, Thanksgiving, and Christmas, and other current greeting-card-industry holidays, but on Groundhog Day, Lincoln's Birthday, Washington's Birthday, Leap Year, April Fool's Day, Decoration Day, and Labor Day. They sent scenic views from their travels.

"Postcards also became a source of instant news," Lauder says. "If there was a fire in a small town, the local photographer took a picture of it, then went to a studio and produced fifty or a hundred photo postcards of the fire. That afternoon or the next day you could buy a postcard of the event and send it to your mother or your aunt who lived elsewhere and tell them, 'This is where we had the fire' or 'This is where we had the trolley car accident,' and your relatives could see what these disasters looked like. Small newspapers of that era did not reproduce photographs. Larger papers printed only photographs of important events and people, in a separate gravure section of the Sunday paper, so photographs of news events were generally made available by other means, primarily the photographic card."

In 1903, Eastman Kodak manufactured a camera that was designed to take postcard-size negatives. Adults had their own photographs taken and their children's photographs taken and printed on postcard-size stock and dispatched them for a penny. Many professional photographers found it lucrative to produce nothing but postcards.

"Some photographers went to the workplace and took photos of you and your mates," Lauder says. "Each of you would buy one to have. Except for my childhood collection of the hotels on Collins Avenue in Miami Beach, I don't collect touristic cards, although I'll send them from my travels if I spot some pretty ones. I don't collect postcards of movie stars either, but one of my granddaughters loves Shirley Temple and I was delighted to buy some Shirley Temple cards for her. The American photographic cards, known as 'real photographic cards,' to which I am partial, include views of people in the streets. I like scenes showing knife vendors and chestnut sellers. I'm fascinated by the small tradesmen of times gone by. I think the highest-quality American cards were produced by the Detroit Publishing Company.

"Detroit hired William Henry Jackson, one of the best-known photographers in America, as its manager and chief photographer. They got him a railroad car, which had in it a developing lab, and sent him around the country. From 1898 to 1914 he photographed America. Many other photographers worked for Detroit, which produced about sixteen thousand cards. They're numbered. I have most of them in my collection. I've already given away my Detroit duplicates to the New York Public Library.

"Most of the time I remember whether I've seen a card before, and whether I own it, but when you buy collections, as I do from time to time, you invariably acquire duplicates. You also get duplicates when you have a card and you have a chance to buy one in better condition and you upgrade. I have dealers looking for the missing Detroits on my behalf. Raphael Tuck's cards are also outstanding. Without postcards, we wouldn't have the incredible visual record of America that we do. And of a good part of the rest of the world, for that matter."

One of Lauder's favorite categories is transportation. He turns to a photographic card that shows the *Hindenburg,* the famous German airship, under construction. "That photo wasn't taken for a newspaper," he says. "It was taken for a postcard." He turns to a card showing the *Normandie,* a French luxury liner, while it was under construction. "That photo wasn't taken for a newspaper, it was taken for a postcard," he reiterates. He repeats these words as he goes through albums with cards showing more airships, or zeppelins, as they were called ("a moment in aviation history"); cards of the rue des Juifs in Toulon and a deserted street in a Moroccan ghetto; and streets in turn-of-the-twentieth-century Berlin and Moscow.

He holds up a postcard of Adolf Hitler, wearing white tie, in a box at the opera house in Dresden, taken between 1933 and 1939; people in the orchestra section below, wearing white tie, black tie, and business suits, are saluting him. Then Lauder proffers a postcard of the *Titanic* lifeboats, shot by a photographer aboard the *Carpathia.* "When that photographer boarded the *Carpathia,* he expected to take pictures of the Pierrot parties and other festivities on board," Lauder says. "When the *Carpathia* came to the rescue of the unsinkable ship's more fortunate passengers, he shot these historic photographs and turned them into postcards."

He studies another historic photograph-turned-postcard. "That picture was taken in Sarajevo on June 28, 1914, just moments after Gavrilo Princip, a Serbian high school student and nationalist, assassinated the Austrian Archduke Francis Ferdinand and his wife," he says. "You can see the Austrian automobiles and policemen chasing Princip. That assassination was an immediate cause of the First World War. I have postcards of the Russian revolution and of the German revolution right after World War One. It's extraordinary that such records of events and of revolutions exist."

Lauder speaks of another of his cards, which shows a ship that was part of the U.S. Navy's Great White Fleet approaching Japan. "I have a wonderful subcollection of about thirty thousand Japanese cards," he says. "I believe in collecting at great depth. Alone, a card often means little, but as part of a group it has meaning."

"The best of the best." Lauder repeats these words and glances at the Picasso and the Braque on the library floor. "Those two pictures were done at the same moment in time," he says. "The artists copied each other. Braque was the more creative of the two. Picasso was the better artist. These works of art speak to each other. If you put a Monet and a Lichtenstein next to each other, they would not have a dialogue. I think my best postcards are those done by expressionist artists like Oskar Kokoschka and Egon Schiele, and over forty other artists for the Wiener Werkstaette, and cards done by artists, among them Lyonel Feininger, for the Bauhaus.

"The Wiener Werkstaette, founded in Vienna in 1903, was an arts and crafts cooperative that created fine furniture, carpeting, wallpaper, silverware, and crystal for the home, fashionable clothes, and postcards. The postcards financially supported the other activities of the Viennese Workshop and advertised its other endeavors. These postcards are the top of the top because they are all original lithographs. Artists were commissioned to do these lithographs. They're the twentieth-century equivalent of a Rembrandt etching. They're a reproduction of nothing. The same is true of the Bauhaus cards. If a museum wanted to have a definitive collection of the works of Kokoschka, it would have to own the cards he did for the Wiener Werkstaette. I have collected early twentieth-century posters. A century ago people frequently collected posters and postcards. Posters very often appeared on postcards. Postcards did not become billboards."

Lauder says that he has most of the Wiener Werkstaette cards, but dealers are still searching on his behalf for the ones he is missing. He is ambivalent about completing this collection. "Until recently I was missing one of

Eugène Atget's eighty photographs showing tradesmen in Paris that were put out only on postcards," he says. "A while ago I met a dealer who knew of two men in France who had retired from working as flight attendants for Air France. They decided after their retirement to become postcard dealers. I sent them a list of cards I needed. To my astonishment, they had the Atget my collection lacked. I was momentarily pleased. And then I was disappointed. I had no more Atgets left to look for."

Almost as soon as Lauder completes a set of postcards, he starts looking for cards of a different variety. "I'm now collecting so-called rack cards," he says. "They're advertising cards, and of course in my line of work, advertisements are of the greatest importance." He pulls a few cards for Absolut vodka out of a Clinique bag he has brought home from his office. "I'm told that you can find these cards on racks in medium-priced restaurants between the men's and the ladies' rooms," he says. "I don't frequent such restaurants, so dealers buy them for me."

He also plans to collect postcards showing all the works of art displayed at the 1913 New York Armory Show, a pivotal point in the history of modern art. And he has started to collect photographic postcards from black Africa taken between 1895 and 1935.

"Missionaries were sent down there not only with crosses but with cameras," he says. "They captured a world that has disappeared. These cards are real anthropological statements and they give me a great deal of pleasure. As this is a new collection, I don't have to worry that I will complete it anytime soon. For me, the pleasure is in the chase, and for a while in the acquisition. Possession is far less exciting. I don't ever really want to have a complete collection. I prefer infinity to completion."

Assignment Ideas

Your ability to detail and describe hobbies, including their emotional allure, will enable a critical analysis of your topic. Pay attention to small details, as they may provide crucial hints to both yourself and your audience regarding the function of hobbies in today's culture. Try to make your descriptions as detailed as possible in the draft. You can edit out irrelevant material during your revision.

1. Compare and contrast the hobby in Roberts's essay or in the essay on Lauder to a specific hobby that you think functions in a similar way. Reflect on this function in light of your brainstorming or freewriting about boredom in the adult world. What conclusions can you reach about our culture? In what ways does this hobby reflect a dominant pattern in society? (Refer to Chapter 3 for strategies for critical analysis.) Feel free to incorporate insights from the additional readings.
2. Do you engage in a hobby that another person might find childlike? Discuss this hobby, and describe how you deal with the tension between the expectations of adulthood and the fulfillment you receive from your

hobby. Do you talk about your hobby freely? Do other people seem interested? Do you have to deal with teasing? Analyze the value of your hobby in the context of the conflict between childhood and adulthood.

3. What is the allure of collecting something? Many people think that a hobby like collecting stamps or baseball cards—which involves storing items more than displaying them—does little to relieve stress. Take a position on this issue, and give several examples of collecting something that demonstrates your point. The essay about Myrtle Young on page 365 can serve as an example of collecting something unusual.
4. Activities involving music—dancing, singing, collecting concert memorabilia, or just listening to CDs—have both private and public aspects and are related to peer approval. Talk about a hobby you have that involves music, such as karaoke or choreography, and discuss where and when this hobby remains private and where and when it becomes public. What, ultimately, is the importance of music to our culture? David Sedaris's "Giant Dreams, Midget Abilities" (page 358) might help by showing some of the different reasons people involve themselves in music.

Group Work

Interview several people about their favorite hobbies. Explore what your interview participants gain from the hobby, how they feel society perceives the activity, and how much of their time it occupies. Use this information to generate a thesis that responds to one or more of the theories presented in the overview or in Roberts's article. Does your group have a theory about the enjoyment of hobbies?

Additional Readings

The following four readings discuss hobbies ranging from chess to collecting potato chips. Hobbies often affect people other than the participants. As you read these selections, look for what might be called the "fallout" of these hobbies. Do the participants better themselves? Are other people affected by the time the participants spend with their hobby? Can you think of activities that might be as fulfilling as the ones described here but that better use the time?

MICHAEL BAMBERGER

Con Games

The passenger in my car, Samson Julius Benen, was the best chess player at Princeton. With his smart-kid cheekiness, he made you think of the actor Matthew Broderick as Ferris Bueller. But you couldn't blame him. He grew up affluent in New York City, the only child of devoted parents. As a schoolboy he was a chess prodigy, and now he was a freshman economics major at a university that had long trained the best and the brightest. When I asked him to name his favorite stock of the moment, he touted Sara Lee in such a knowing way that I almost turned over my 401(k) to him. His mother, he said, had already given him control of hers.

It was early on a cold, rainy weekday morning in April, and we were driving the 15 miles from the Princeton campus to Trenton State Prison, the only maximum-security correctional facility in New Jersey. Benen was going to referee the final matchup in the prison's chess tournament, then take on the winner.

"Nobody in there is going to beat me," Benen said, explaining that there were, at best, 200 players in the U.S. who were better than he was, and not one was doing time in a Jersey big house.

I handed him two pieces of paper, the closest thing there was to a tournament press packet. They were rap sheets for the finalists, Carl Gooding and Jay Rutherford. I had been making regular visits to the prison for six weeks. I knew that Rutherford had an easy smile and a relaxed manner and that Gooding did not.

5 Benen was 19 but looked as if he were preparing for his bar mitzvah. He considered the inmates' mug shots and vital statistics: birth dates, body measurements, aliases, criminal offenses, incarceration histories.

"Murder," Benen said. He turned the page. "And . . . murder. Wow."

One day late last year I read a story in my morning newspaper, *The Philadelphia Inquirer,* about four players from the Princeton chess club who had visited the New Jersey State Prison, as the Trenton penitentiary is officially known, to play 55 inmates. It wasn't serious chess. Each student played 13 or 14 prisoners at the same time. The score was Princeton 50, Trenton State 2, with three draws. I wondered how good the best player at Trenton State might be, and how his mind might work.

It was easy to identify the best player at Princeton. Sam Benen, class of '07 and one of the four students who played the inmates, was a chess master (the equivalent of a scratch golfer, and then some). His International Chess Federation rating was a flashy 2,320. (The highest-rated U.S. player, Alexander Onischuk, has a 2,652.) From the third through 12th grades at Hunter, an elite public school in Manhattan, he won seven national scholastic chess titles.

Identifying the best inmate chess player was another matter. Roy Hendricks, the Trenton State warden (administrator, technically), was immediately open to SI's idea of holding a prison chess tournament and then having the winner play the Princeton kid. Since the state of New Jersey had put the kibosh on prison boxing programs about a decade ago—fear of HIV transmission and taxpayers' objections to inmates' engaging in the violence of boxing—Hendricks, a large, bearded and pensive man who played tackle on his high school football team in Utica, N.Y., had been eager to find programs to enrich the lives of his 1,940 inmates, 85% of whom were on death row or had been sentenced to life without parole. He invited inmates to participate in the tournament, beginning with the first round in early March. Thirty-two signed up. March Madness came to Trenton State.

The hulking prison comprised connected buildings from different cen- 10
turies, the whole complex outlined by a 20-foot-high wall topped with razor ribbon. It is in downtown Trenton, in a poor, largely Hispanic neighborhood. Hendricks lives in a magnificent 1797 stone house attached to the prison. The inmates live in small, bare cells—one or two to a cell—in which they spend roughly 16 hours a day. "I get the worst of the worst," Hendricks said as we watched inmates play chess, a game that seems genteel but is rooted in war. The eyes of a guard nearby darted constantly, watching not the games but the players' hands. "You can never forget what they're in for and that they'd escape if they could."

Most of the inmates were in for murder. Some were famous, at least in New Jersey: The recent trials of two prisoners, one a contract killer for the mob and the other a rabbi who had his wife killed, got a lot of ink. Rubin (Hurricane) Carter, the former boxer and the subject of a Bob Dylan song, did time at Trenton State.

To enter the prison, you walk through a metal detector, get frisked and then head down a succession of windowless corridors and through a series of heavy metal doors with electronic locks, each closing loudly behind you before the next one opens. The journey in, particularly the first time, is unnerving, even with a visitor's badge on your lapel and a guard at your side.

The five rounds of the tournament were conducted over five weeks in a prison meeting room that looked like a high school cafeteria, except that the windows to the adjacent courtyard did not open and the doors were guarded and locked. Refreshments—juice and butter cookies—were served. Before the first round, two inmates set up 16 rubber chessboards and the corresponding 512 plastic chess pieces, looking like overworked busboys laying out silverware.

The 32 players had to remove their shoes and submit them for inspection. (During a recent religious service, one inmate had stabbed another with a metal shank he had hidden in his shoe.) The inmates all wore khaki pants, and most wore khaki shirts: they expressed their individualism through their hair and words. There were shaved heads and crewcuts and dreadlocks. One player, Phillip Dixon, had a Jimi Hendrix–style Afro and answered questions in long soliloquies. His chess game was deliberate. In one round he took nearly nine hours to play three games. When you're doing life, there's no real incentive to play fast.

One day Dixon gave me an envelope filled with his neatly typed poems, 15
mostly about the black experience in America. One stanza of a poem called *Nat Turner's Blade* was about hero worship:

> *YOUR CHILDREN SCREAM MY NAME—*
> *HOPING FOR A SCRIBBLED SIGNATURE*
> *ON A PIECE OF LAMINATED CARDBOARD.*

Between games Dixon and I talked about his experiences playing football and basketball while growing up in Camden, N.J., and about how Dajuan

Wagner, a 2001 graduate of Camden High, was making out in the NBA. When the field was down to Gooding and Rutherford, Dixon made his rooting interest clear. Rutherford was a Camden man, which gave Dixon reason enough to pull for him, and Gooding was from Philadelphia, which gave Dixon "all the more reason to hate him," he said. In an ill-considered attempt at defending Gooding's native city, I told Dixon that I lived in Philadelphia. "That don't change my opinion none," he said.

As the field was whittled over the next four weeks, the losing contestants became committed spectators, murmuring about moves they did not like. Don Mee, a veteran prison supervisor, said he had never witnessed a prison event, including religious services, in which the inmates had become so absorbed. A few of the players carried chess books that had been donated to the prison library by BeneCard, a New Jersey benefits company at which chess is part of the corporate culture the way golf is at other companies. There was more trash talk than at an ordinary chess tournament. A young player defeated a fellow inmate nearly twice his age and said, "Time for your nap, old man!" There were arguments, of course: You lifted your finger off the piece, dude! You own that move! On the other hand, you saw few of the facial tics and strange, repetitive body movements seen among players at a typical chess tournament. Mostly, you saw men in khaki shirts huddled over boards, lost in concentration. They were playing for keeps.

When he's not a resident of a suite in one of the Gothic dormitories at Princeton, Sam Benen lives with his parents in a two-bedroom apartment on lower Fifth Avenue in Manhattan. His mother, Jennifer Hershey, manages a consortium of five Broadway theaters, and his father, Neil, is a water-systems engineer who runs his own water-equipment distribution company. The family apartment is steps from Washington Square Park, the epicenter of chess hustling in Manhattan, and several blocks from the Marshall Chess Club, the old and famous sanctuary of elite chess players in the city. Those were the two main haunts of Josh Waitzkin—the child prodigy depicted in *Searching for Bobby Fischer*—and of Sam Benen too. When he was in sixth grade, Sam appeared on *The Late Show with David Letterman,* playing chess against the host.

20 Growing up, Sam was a Little League second baseman who played on asphalt diamonds, a child actor with bit parts in two films, a devoted fan of the New York Yankees, an elevator operator at the St. James Theatre (where he met the real Matthew Broderick), a straight-A student, and a TV and film fanatic. He was particularly fond of crime shows, *The Godfather* movies and *The Shawshank Redemption,* a film about a wrongly accused banker who uses a rock pick to chip through his cell wall to freedom. One of the most disappointing moments of Sam's young life came when he was rejected by Yale.

When he and I arrived at Trenton State, he carried an official chess time clock for the Gooding-Rutherford final and for his match against the winner. He handed over his dorm-room keys and his cellphone to a prison guard and made the depressing walk into the heart of the prison.

I had interviewed Gooding and Rutherford, separately and at length, several days before their tournament final. Rutherford, 30, started playing chess after he went to prison at 18. He was convicted of killing, by a gunshot to the head, the owner of a Camden grocery store during a 1992 robbery and is serving a life sentence. "I just wish I'd discovered chess when I was 10," he said. Winning the prison chess title would be his greatest accomplishment, he added, and would prove to his mother that "I'm doing something good with my life."

Gooding, who turns 40 in June, said he started playing as a boy in North Philadelphia. He even scored well enough on a test to get into Central, one of the city's elite public high schools, but was thrown out after his freshman year for poor attendance. He said he seldom played chess in prison because there wasn't enough competition for him. He was sentenced to life for fatally shooting a North Philadelphia man during a drug deal in 1987 and handed another life sentence for wounding two people in a shooting spree at a Camden apartment complex a day after the first incident. In '90, while serving time at Holmesburg Prison in Philadelphia, a decrepit 19th-century fortress of a penitentiary, Gooding and another inmate used small tools to chip through a two-foot-thick stone wall before being caught on the outer prison grounds.

I asked Gooding what he thought the Princeton campus was like. "I know exactly what it's like," he said.

"How's that?"

"I've been there. I had an uncle who went there, Frederick Gooding. My mother's brother. He went to Princeton, and then he went to medical school at Howard. Now he's a doctor. I visited him at Princeton when I was a little kid."

With inmates, you can never be sure. I called Princeton. Frederick Gooding was right there in the alumni records, class of '73, which means that Carl was nearly nine when his uncle graduated.

Don Mee introduced Sam Benen to the finalists and the 30 inmate spectators. Benen explained that no serious, competitive chess is played without a clock and said that each player would be given 30 minutes per game. He also said there would be a tiebreaker, with its own set of rules, if the players split the two scheduled games. There was some grumbling. Gooding hadn't played on a clock in 25 years, and Rutherford never had. They had played best of three, without a clock, throughout the tournament, with the third game played the same way as the first two.

Gooding drew white for the first game, meaning he would make the first move, which gave him a considerable advantage. He moved his pieces forcefully, landing them with a decisive thud, but his play was conservative. Rutherford was wearing on his right wrist a rubber band on which he had written the letters WFMM, for Win For My Mom. His play was aggressive—if there was a piece to capture, he'd capture it—but his manner was not. During the most tense moments of the match the only sound you could hear in the warm room was the whirring of giant fans. In a quiet voice Benen told me that the players' moves were "unorthodox, untrained, but not illogical."

For most of the first game Rutherford had a slight edge. On Move 24, however, he blundered, capturing a pawn but leaving his queen unprotected.

Two moves later Gooding cornered and checkmated him. The second game, in which Rutherford played white, was a reverse of Game 1 with Rutherford winning in 22 moves.

During the pause before the tiebreaker, Benen re-created from memory every move in both games and explained superior moves with which either player could have won. It was all black-did-this and white-did-that and black-should-have-done-this. The players and the spectators huddled around the board, awed by how quickly and precisely Benen worked. Minutes later, when he explained the International Chess Federation rules for a tiebreaker, nobody fussed at all.

Rutherford drew black, which gave him two handicaps: He would play second, and he would have only five minutes on his clock, while white would have six. But he had one major advantage: Under the tiebreaker rules, a draw for black would be considered a win.

From the first move, the room was tense. The tournament had taken on an outsized importance because there's little chance of being recognized for anything when serving a life sentence. Gooding went up a pawn early and won in 27 moves. He shook Rutherford's hand with a slap, high-fived his friends, poured himself a cup of coffee and prepared for Benen.

Gooding drew white for the first game against the Princeton kid. For much of the game he sat with his head in his hands, hunched over his pieces. Benen's eyes wandered all over the room. Hendricks thought it was an act, to give the impression that the match didn't require his full attention, but at a certain point it did. Benen kept waiting for Gooding to make a mistake, but Gooding made one sound move after another. The final two minutes of the game were played at a furious pace: Make a move, hit the clock; make a move, hit the clock. It was like the final seconds of a prizefight that's tied on points, when the boxers, sucking wind, get in a flurry of last-chance punches. It was a monster of a game. Benen won after his 56th move, when Gooding ran out of time. The inmate was spent. In the second game Benen played white and won easily.

When it was over, Benen told Gooding, "At Move 44 [of the first game] you could have had me." He quickly re-created their positions on the board. "Had you done this, this and this"—he went through a long series of moves and countermoves—"you could have drawn me."

I asked Roy Hendricks if he would consider allowing a rematch. "Yes," he said. "This was good."

"How about a home game for Sam?" I asked, meaning Gooding would go to Princeton, three decades after his uncle had left.

"No," the warden said slowly. "No. No. No. No way."

The inmates had surrounded Benen, looking to get his autograph. Phillip Dixon, the poet of "scribbled signatures," was among them.

Before Gooding went back to his cell, he said to me, "I played him better than you ever thought I could, didn't I." He wasn't asking a question. He doesn't do that much. He was stating a fact.

A couple of weeks later, back in Philadelphia, I looked up a man named Otis Burgess, who had taught Gooding chess in the late 1970s when Carl was in middle school. Burgess knew that Gooding was doing a long sentence but not much else. After not hearing from him for years, Burgess received a prison call from Gooding in the mid-'90s. "He kept saying, 'They're trying to execute me,'" Burgess told me.

Burgess had learned chess in the late 1960s, while serving 18 months in a Pennsylvania prison for a robbery conviction. Now he worked in a restaurant kitchen and played chess over the Internet, through the mail and, on certain Sunday evenings, at the McDonald's where we were meeting.

"I remember hearing about this little kid who would sit on his stoop with his chessboard and challenge grown-ups," Burgess said. "I put fliers up and down his block, looking for kids who wanted to play. He answered that. We'd go all over the city playing tournaments—at schools, at the Holiday Inn in Center City, sometimes over to Jersey. The whole experience of chess was a mindblower for him."

Burgess said he had met Carl's mother. "She had her hands full," he said. The boy did not have a father at home. Burgess knew that Carl needed a father figure but that he was not the one. He remembers Gooding getting thrown out of Central and getting into cocaine and street crime. They fell out of each other's lives. "He always had a temper," said Burgess, "but he never showed it on me."

I handed Burgess a recent mug shot of Gooding, the same one Benen had 45
seen. "You see, that's not the Carl I knew," Burgess said. "The Carl I knew was from a long time ago."

I visited Carl's mother, Carole, in her bright row house in West Philadelphia. She had Carl when she was 15. Carl's father, she said, was an 18-year-old, low-level mob street hustler in South Philadelphia. When Carl was born, Carole took him to his father's house. The father's mother answered the door. Carole says the lady looked at the infant and said, "Get that n—— baby off my step."

Carole eventually got a high school diploma, a college degree, a master's degree and then became a Philadelphia middle school teacher. She said she had applied for an assistant-principal position. She talked to Carl almost daily on the phone and visited him about once a month. "All he talks about now is chess, chess, chess," she said. "He wants chess books and magazines. He wants Mr. Burgess's address. He says he needs better competition."

Carl Gooding was high on cocaine when he shot the two people in the Camden apartment complex in 1987. One of the victims was left a paraplegic. There was an address for him in Philadelphia, in a subsidized apartment complex, but residents said he had never lived there. The other victim was Lloyd Wallace, a retired Philadelphia police officer who lived in an apartment in Atlantic City. Seventeen years ago Gooding broke in on him and shot him in the face—amazingly, the wound was superficial—and Wallace shot back at Gooding, grazing him. Wallace testified during Gooding's trial that he was sorry he hadn't killed Gooding, and Wallace told me that he did not regret his testimony. "He was trying to kill me," Wallace said.

Still, he was pleased to hear that Gooding had won the Trenton State Prison chess championship. "A man's got to do something with his life," Wallace said. "Otherwise, it's all just a waste."

CHRIS BALLARD

Fantasy World

It is 82° and sunny outside the Rio Hotel and Casino in Las Vegas, the type of brilliant March afternoon that feels like a misplaced slice of summer. Inside, however, it is 73°, and the night is, as always, just beginning. On the casino floor lights flash, slot machines emit their electronic gurgle and women in too-short skirts serve beers to men who beg for an ace or a face card, goddammit. Off to one side, a long hallway leads away to a maze of enormous, high-ceilinged conference rooms, all sparsely furnished, windowless and disorienting in their sameness. In one of these rooms, under a hazy fluorescent sun, 19 men sit at a U-shaped table and mull the value of New York Yankees first baseman Jason Giambi.

These men are not scouts, nor are they general managers or even, for that matter, Yankees fans. Rather, each has traveled to Vegas and paid $1,250 for the opportunity to draft a team in the National Fantasy Baseball Championship. As a result, they care deeply about Giambi—or at least the statistics he produces—because he could carry a fantasy team. He could also be an injury-riddled bust. So the men consult their laptops and frown deep frowns and grunt little grunts and generally look as if they all ate the same bad fish for lunch. So intense is their manner that one might mistake them for a secretive high-level government committee, if, that is, members of such a committee drank Bud Light and wore T-shirts that read MY KIDS THINK I'M AN ATM.

Some of the men arrived a few days early in order to attend the National Fantasy Trade Association's annual meeting, a two-day affair that featured everything from seminars on legal and technological issues to "expert" panels stocked with the Warren Buffetts of the business, men like Brandon (the Gamer) Funston of Yahoo and Eric Karabell of ESPN.com. Others came in expressly for the draft or the accompanying auction, among them the rock singer Meat Loaf, whose name is Michael Aday but who prefers to be called Meat (a moniker that is printed in red letters on the back of his baseball cap). So far, his National League–only team in the auction game, the Bats Out of Hell—named for his breakthrough 1977 album—includes Bobby Abreu, Luis Castillo and, much to Meat's later chagrin, Mets shortstop Jose Reyes, who will start the season on the disabled list.

Meat Loaf is a fantasy addict. He has been playing since the '80s and once participated in 56 football leagues in a single season. For this draft he drove in the night before from Los Angeles, not long after arriving on a plane from New Zealand, where he had been on tour. "I'm amazed I made it," he says during a break in the auction. "I'm pretty crispy right now. But I was determined not to miss this draft."

Meat Loaf is not alone in his devotion. In the ranks of the famous, team 5
owners also include star USA Softball pitcher Jennie Finch, Boston Red Sox pitcher Curt Schilling, former Miami Dolphins and current CBS analyst Dan Marino, R.E.M. bassist Mike Mills, and actors Vince Vaughn and Michael J. Fox. Once considered the province of Bill James–worshipping stat geeks, fantasy sports have become big, big business. More than 15 million people play, and fantasy has grown into a billion-dollar industry. Perhaps the only business more ready-made for the Internet is pornography. Though they all had their genesis in a game started by a group of New York literary types 25 years ago, fantasy sports have evolved—some might say metastasized—into a nationwide obsession. There is fantasy NASCAR and fantasy bass fishing, fantasy golf and fantasy cricket and even, absurdly, fantasy professional wrestling. Fantasy football, the most popular game, threatens to co-opt coverage of the NFL, as evidenced by the fact that there are now three times as many fantasy football preview magazines as actual football preview magazines.

As a result many fans now have a stronger allegiance to individual players than to teams, unless, of course, it is allegiance to their *fantasy* teams. For those teams they will spend hours checking box scores and scanning the waiver wire, not to mention ignoring less-pressing concerns such as, say, their jobs. For those who don't play but have to endure the obsessive yammering of those who do—the Rotisserie widows and friends who have no vested interest in who starts at tight end for the Colts—it can seem like the tech boom of the late '90s all over again, when nothing was quite as boring as hearing about someone else's portfolio.

Eventually, though, the tech boom went away; fantasy sports, like video games, are here to stay.

To understand the phenomenon of fantasy sports, one must first understand their origin, and for that one must talk to Dan Okrent, the founding father of Rotisserie baseball. Okrent is built like a catcher, short-legged and low to the ground. He has thick gray hair, a thatch of which is constantly on the verge of falling into his eyes, and a habit of sitting cross-legged as he talks. He is 56 years old and exceedingly accomplished in his field, having written for and edited at several of the world's most prominent magazines (including SI) and written four books. In his apartment on the Upper West Side of Manhattan there is a framed drawing of him and his wife by cartoonist Jules Feiffer titled "Dance to Okrents." He is currently the first public editor of *The New York Times.*

Despite his résumé Okrent is still known to many as the Guy Who Invented Rotisserie Baseball. He estimates that he has been interviewed on the subject more than 200 times in the past 25 years and in 2000 was one of the first two inductees (along with fellow Rotisserie pioneer Glenn Waggoner) into the Fantasy Sports Hall of Fame. Though Okrent holds out hope that his new job at the *Times* may alter his legacy—"Some people say that's why I took this job, so it would change my epitaph," he says, only half joking—he is of two minds about his creation. "I feel the way J. Robert Oppenheimer felt after having invented the atomic bomb: If I'd only known this plague that I've visited upon the world . . . ," he says with a laugh. "Though on one level I'm proud, certainly, to have created something that millions of people want to do. It's a contribution of sorts."

It was while flying from Hartford to Austin in the fall of 1979 that Okrent first came up with the idea. At the time he was working as a consultant for *Texas Monthly* magazine, a job for which he commuted every four weeks from his home in Worthington, Mass. His passion, however, was baseball. Before saber-metrics, Theo Epstein and the box-score orgy that is the *USA Today* sports section, Okrent was crunching numbers, editing a tome called the *Ultimate Baseball Book* and espousing the merits of an obscure Kansas writer named Bill James (who at the time self-published a mimeographed pamphlet on baseball tendencies). Since taking a class at Michigan a decade earlier with a professor named Bob Sklar—who had played a crude prototype of Rotisserie ball—Okrent had also been puzzling over how to create a game that realistically mimicked a baseball season.

Thousands of feet up he had a moment of inspiration and, as he now jokes, "carved the rules into the stone tablets." After some tweaking, they were (and still are) as follows. Teams each receive a budget of $260 to draft 23 players from either the American or National League, filling slots by position: nine pitchers, five outfielders, one shortstop, etc. Players are auctioned off to the highest bidder (a nod to the then fledgling age of free agency), and each team's performance is based on the cumulative stats of its players in eight categories: batting average, home runs, RBIs, stolen bases, wins, ERA, saves and WHIP, the ratio of walks and hits to innings pitched (then a virtually unheard-of statistic that now, thanks to Rotisserie, has wide currency).

Eager to test his creation, Okrent introduced it to his compatriots in the Phillies Appreciation Society, an informal crew who met monthly at New York City's La Rotisserie Française, a long-since-shuttered East Side restaurant (and the genesis of the game's tag). Okrent picked up a few converts and recruited the rest from among his extended circle of friends. On the first Sunday after Opening Day of the '80 season, the 11 owners of the 10 teams gathered at the home of Corlies Smith for the first Rotisserie draft (which included players from only the National League). Besides Okrent (owner of the Okrent Fenokees), the assemblage included a veritable Who's Who of the publishing world: Smith (owner of the Smith Coronas), a book editor for Viking Press; Bruce McCall, a writer-illustrator and contributor to *The New Yorker* (his McCall Collects lasted but one season); Sklar (owner of the Sklar Gazers), now a professor of cinema studies at NYU; screenwriter, novelist and editor Peter Gethers and co-owner Waggoner, a Columbia administrator who, thanks to his Rotisserie involvement, went on to become an editor at *ESPN the Magazine* (together, they formed the Getherswag Goners); Valerie Salembier (of the Flambés), now publisher of *Harper's Bazaar*; Michael Pollet (G.M. of the Pollet Burros), a lawyer who has argued before the Supreme Court; author and then *Esquire* editor Lee Eisenberg (owner of the Eisenberg Furriers); Tom Guinzburg (owner of the Guinzburg Burghers), then president of Viking Press; and Rob Fleder (mastermind behind the Fleder Mice), now an executive editor at SI. By all accounts it was a heady time. "When I first saw the rules, it was like seeing the Rosetta stone translated for the first time," says Waggoner. "It was"—he pauses—"the perfect game."

To be sure, the original owners (joined the next year by then SI baseball writer Steve Wulf, owner of the Wulfgang) took the game very seriously—they went on field trips to spring training every March to scout players, and Okrent estimates he burned up more than $1,000 a year on phone, travel and other Rotisserie expenses—but they also approached the whole thing with what Waggoner calls "a sense of whimsy." At the end of the season the winner got a ceremonial Yoo-Hoo shower (said to be good for the hair), and the 11 annual editions of *Rotisserie League Baseball Book,* written by committee, were as funny as they were informative. As Wulf wrote of those early days in a 1984 piece in SI, "The Rotisserie League is silly, and we know that. We also know that it has caused great changes in the lives of each and every one of us, mostly for the better. We play for money, of course, but we also play for friendship, competition, life, liberty and the pursuit of happiness."

Because of the group's media connections, Rotisserie spread at the speed of newsprint. In 1980 Fred Ferretti of *The New York Times* wrote about the league, which in turn spurred innumerable beat writers to start their own leagues, each of which inevitably inspired a column during the dog days of August. By '83 even major leaguers were aware of the fantasy game. "I remember I was behind the batting cage at Shea Stadium, and this shadow came over me," says Wulf, now an executive editor of *ESPN the Magazine.* "It was Dale Murphy, and he said, 'How's your Rotisserie team doing?' He told me he'd read the book, and he really liked the concept. That's when I knew this thing was really getting big."

15 By the late 1980s the game had surpassed its cult status. In '89 *The Sporting News* estimated that nearly 500,000 people played. Mario Cuomo was in a league, Bryant Gumbel played, the Philadelphia Phillies front office took the game nearly as seriously as their actual jobs, and Red Sox outfielder Dwight Evans became a fantasy player and reportedly traded himself for pitching help late in the season. So many Roto freaks were calling teams to get injury reports that they were overwhelming p.r. staffs. In an attempt to realize some profits from their creation, Okrent and the other founders trademarked the name Rotisserie and made halfhearted efforts at running a stats service. None of it came to much. "The brilliant thing about the game is that the rules are so simple that all you need are the rules," says Okrent. "That's also why we never figured out a way to make money off the thing."

Others eventually would. By the early '90s Rotisserie baseball led to Rotisserie football and basketball, which spawned a multitude of other fantasy sports. But the number of leagues and players was limited by the man-hours required; stats had to be calculated by hand or laboriously entered into Excel spreadsheets. The late '90s Internet boom changed the game: Now all a player had to do was wake up and check his team's stats online, after which he could shoot off a couple of ludicrous trade proposals by email. "It used to be thought of as [something for] just geeks and hard-core fans," says Greg Ambrosius, the president of the Fantasy Sports Trade Association (FSTA). "But this isn't a small closet hobby anymore. This sumbitch is a big, big industry, and it's all due to the Internet."

Were it not for the explosion of fantasy on the Web, a guy like Clark Olson would not be asked his opinion regarding Alfonso Soriano's tendency to swing at bad pitches. And he certainly wouldn't have been in Vegas in March wearing a matching hat and T-shirt embossed with 2003 ESPN FANTASY BASEBALL LEAGUE CHAMPION and toting a Fujitsu Stylistic ST5000D tablet PC while inspiring fear and reverence, expressed in whispered tones. No, Olson would be renowned primarily—and rightly—for his work on the Mars Rover. First at the Jet Propulsion Laboratory in Pasadena, Calif., and now as an assistant professor of computer and software systems at the University of Washington's Bothell campus, Olson has worked with computer vision, mobile robot navigation and terrain mapping techniques to make the Rover more effective. But no one cared about that in Vegas.

Olson is part of the new generation of fantasy player. Thirty-five years old, he looks a bit like Leonardo DiCaprio, were DiCaprio to play the role of a bookish rocket scientist. Olson began playing fantasy sports 18 years ago as a student at the University of Washington and, after some early success, started competing in the ESPN.com Über, a sort of fantasy pentathlon in which players accumulate points based on multiple entries from 33 games offered. The prizes include an expenses-paid trip to the ESPY Awards. Out of hundreds of thousands of players, Olson finished third in 2002 and was second last year. To do so, he says, he competed in 12 baseball leagues, one hockey league, six basketball leagues and about 10 football leagues, at a cost (reduced by discounts and packages) of $400.

Do the math, and it's easy to understand why so many companies are suddenly so smitten with all those fantasy geeks. Players like Olson and Meat Loaf—himself a top-200-ranked Überplayer on ESPN.com—spend hours each week scrutinizing websites to track their multiple teams and, not so incidentally, have plenty of disposable income.

20 The new fantasy economy was on full display at the trade association conference. Given the reputation of Roto players, one expected a brown-bag-lunch crowd—a bunch of friendly (if nerdy) guys who, had they been toting comics rather than pre-season fantasy guides, could have been mistaken for the X-Men Appreciation Society. But while there was a whiff of dorkiness about the whole affair, it was overwhelmed by the scent of enterprise. Website managers in sport coats passed out business cards with the eagerness of Times Square hawkers offering fliers. Thirtysomething men in Dockers spoke of "cross-media synergy" and the promise of "dashboard technology" (wherein a fantasy owner's Web portal features warning lights that turn red if, say, Jim Edmonds's average dips below .250). In all, 150 people paid $300 apiece to attend the conference, and representatives from major spenders of advertising dollars, such as Comcast, were among them.

The crowd could be delineated neatly into a) the many who were desperately trying to crack the fantasy market, a segment that included (somewhat surprisingly) *USA Today* and SI.com (which recently upgraded its fantasy engine but still trails the leaders); and b) the few from well-established sites, namely the big three of SportsLine.com, ESPN.com and Yahoo. Of that trio, SportsLine provides the most telling case study.

In 1996 SportsLine employed three people to run its fantasy operation; today 50 contribute to the site's fantasy portion, including an editorial staff of six (meaning six people are paid to ruminate upon whom you should pick up off the waiver wire). Of the company's $57.6 million in revenue in 2003, $15.9 million, or 28%, came from fantasy sports, a 34% increase over '02. Sports Line's NFL-partnered fantasy football attracted 1.3 million paid users last fall, according to a study done by Nielsen/NetRatings; that was more than the next four sites combined. As for what's driving the sports site's traffic, consider: Of the 2 million people who visited during the month of October, 1.32 million were fantasy players (who then stayed an average of one hour and 42 minutes, or long enough to see an awful lot of banner ads). Says Scott Engel, SportsLine's senior producer of fantasy sports, "I've seen our game go from having a minor cult following to being a major part of our success."

For its part Yahoo has built a reputation on its free games—more than a million people are playing free fantasy baseball this year—and recently upgraded its editorial staff by hiring Brandon Funston away from ESPN.com. Not that such a move will really hurt ESPN. The company doesn't disclose its revenue numbers, but ESPN.com senior vice president of business operations and programming John Kosner estimates that fantasy accounts for 15% to 20% of the site's traffic, and he speaks in glowing terms of its future, touting the potential of "easy fantasy," week-to-week games that appeal to casual fans. ESPN's big advantage, of course, is synergy. Eric Karabell, a former *Washington Post* writer who is now the network's fantasy expert, appears regularly on *ESPN News,* has a column in *ESPN the Magazine* and a weekly hourlong radio show online. His televised commentary drives people to the games on the website, and those games drive people to ESPN to watch "their" players perform. It is a neat little cycle of consumption.

The scary part is, this is just the beginning. Fantasy cricket is huge in India; fantasy football (that is, soccer) has caught on in England, and fantasy thoroughbred racing is the rage in Hong Kong. The fastest-growing fantasy sport is NASCAR. (In what business isn't NASCAR the fastest-growing segment?)

Already, major consumer companies are trying to capitalize on fantasy 25
sports. Best Buy, the home electronics chain, will unveil a fall marketing campaign centered on its own branded fantasy football game (to be powered by fanball.com and for which Best Buy will distribute more than $20,000 a week in prizes). The company's research found, not surprisingly, that men who bought high-definition TVs also played fantasy football. EA Sports, the video game maker that produces the *Madden NFL* series, is close to signing a deal with the NFL Players Association that includes a "fantasy license" under which future versions of *Madden* will potentially allow users to play with teams made up of their fantasy rosters. (The idea is as meta as they come: to play

a virtual game based on a virtual game based on an actual game.) Given the trend, it's not all that unrealistic to imagine that 10 years from now a league—say, something like Arena football or a circuit based on a previously obscure sport—will be founded by a partnership between a multinational company such as McDonald's and a fantasy provider. McFantasy Frisbee: I'm Lovin' It.

The original games have now been around long enough that today's pro athletes grew up playing them. While with the Phillies, Curt Schilling started a football league and rented out a hotel suite for a catered draft that was announced by Phillies play-by-play man Harry Kalas. Red Sox pitcher Derek Lowe, who plays in a NASCAR league (and used to be in a football league), says, "I can remember in 2001, when I was stinking as a reliever, people were yelling, 'You're killing me on my fantasy team!' I didn't understand it back then because I wasn't involved in this stuff yet, but now I do. I know I get pissed off when a guy on my football team is struggling or a NASCAR guy blows an engine." There's a French connection in a fantasy NBA league that includes Atlanta Hawks rookie reserve guard-forward Boris Diaw, San Antonio Spurs point guard Tony Parker and Gonzaga forward Ronny Turiaf (who played together on France's national team). Says Diaw, who averaged 4.5 points this season, "I chose to take myself—and I don't think it was a good choice."

No professional player has been accused of conflict of interest because of involvement in a fantasy league based on his own sport, and there are no rules about fantasy participation. The closest thing to a fantasy arrest came in 1991, when a firefighter in Florida was fired and charged with misdemeanor gambling for running a baseball league that had a $5,000 prize. (The charges were later dropped.) "The [main] legal issue is whether the games fall under lottery laws—games of chance—or whether they're games of skill, which are [not subject to regulation in most states]," says William Heberer, a lawyer with the New York City firm of Manatt, Phelps and Phillips who specializes in advising clients on sports gambling issues. "So far, they've always been considered games of skill, and there hasn't really been a challenge to that at all."

All this is fine—surely we will sleep better knowing that every Flyers fan with a cable modem can legally play in as many fantasy hockey leagues as he wants—but it doesn't address the larger question of whether fantasy sports are a good thing. It is a simple question with a complicated answer.

Fantasy sports might go against the nature of the true fan—that is, one who roots for a real-life team—but one could argue that they are merely a reflection of real sports in the age of free agency. When neither players nor owners feel any loyalty other than to their bank accounts, why should fans be any different? Maybe a fantasy team is the last vestige of control fans have, keeping them connected to a game in which a real team's players and uniforms change every season. Playing a fantasy game undeniably makes a fan more knowledgeable; pre-Rotisserie, there was little reason for anyone outside of Milwaukee or Atlanta to care who batted sixth for the Brewers or to track the assists of the Hawks' backup point guard (and, in the case of Atlanta, one could argue that even those in the city had no reason to care). Rotisserie players also gain an appreciation for the inner workings of the sport; after all, Okrent formulated his seminal eight categories by using the *Baseball Encyclopedia* and studying 10 years of NL East stats to see which indicators best correlated to winning percentage. (That's why stolen bases were included instead of on-base percentage.)

30 Then there is the camaraderie. Fantasy leagues are similar to pickup basketball games; they bring people together. In fact, one could even think of all those hours spent hunched over box scores as an investment in brotherhood. In one long-running New York City fantasy basketball league, there is a father-and-two-sons team that has used the game as a means to repair a relationship strained by the father's divorce. In the same league another player routinely flies in from Cleveland just for the draft, allowing him to see old friends.

In other respects, time "invested" in fantasy leagues is irretrievably wasted. Imagine what could be accomplished during the hours spent on fantasy—you could learn a new language, train for and run a marathon or, at the very least, significantly increase your bowling average. There are also the vacations that suddenly become dependent on Internet access (gotta change those starting pitchers!); the frantic long-distance phone calls asking for injury reports; the poor souls the fantasy player has afflicted with updates on his team (a habit that Okrent compares with the ritual display of baby pictures by new parents: "A fantasy team is something that's deeply your own," he says. "One sentence about it is too much"); and the friendships ruined over trade disputes that progress from the jocular *Hey, that deal smells fishy* to *Don't be surprised if someone firebombs your car.*

What does this say about the millions of men who play (and with 93% of participants being male, fantasy is an overwhelmingly masculine pursuit)? That's what Don Levy is trying to figure out. A doctoral student in sociology at Connecticut, Levy studies masculinity and male relationships; his previous work includes *The Friendships of White Middle-Class Men: A Dialectic of Gendering.* In fantasy sports he saw a microcosm of male relationships, and so last November he began a one-year study of men who play. He's interested in how they find meaning in fantasy, what it says about camaraderie and what can be deduced from the communities that spring up. "The friends that these men meet in these leagues might be some of their best friends, even though they only meet once a year," says Levy. "They've gone through divorces, had kids—some of them have been doing this for 12, 15 years. And they end up turning to each other for support, which is interesting." Levy has also seen the other side of the phenomenon. "Some of these guys have been in leagues for six years with each other and have no idea if another player is married or not," he says.

For Steve Wulf, fantasy has come too close to supplanting reality. Recently he decided to go Roto cold turkey. For him, the game used to be about fun, but then, he says, "the drafts got more serious, to the point where it was like a bunch of accountants, and if you cracked a joke, you were upsetting the karma." Okrent has also dialed it back. In 1995 he quit Rotisserie ball for five years and followed the continued rise of fantasy sports from afar. (He takes particular pride that Rotisserie has its own definition in the newest edition of the *Merriam-Webster's Collegiate Dictionary.*) Two years ago, however, he rejoined what he calls a "slo-pitch" or "AARP" league, where trades are allowed during only one week of the season.

Asked how his team fared, Okrent grimaces. "I was wire to wire in first place every day from Opening Day to Sept. 7 and then collapsed and finished fourth," he says. "I was"—he catches himself and emits a quick laugh—"I could tell you why, but then I'd be talking about my Rotisserie team, and it's not interesting." The father of fantasy sports shakes his head and smiles. "Really, it's not interesting."

DAVID SEDARIS

Giant Dreams, Midget Abilities

My father loves jazz and has an extensive collection of records and reel-to-reel tapes he used to enjoy after returning home from work. He might have entered the house in a foul mood, but once he had his Dexter Gordon and a vodka martini, the stress melted away and everything was "beautiful, baby, just beautiful." The instant the needle hit that record, he'd loosen his tie and become something other than the conservative engineer with a pocketful of IBM pencils embossed with the command THINK.

"Man, oh man, will you get a load of the chops on this guy? I saw him once at the Blue Note, and I mean to tell you that he blew me right out of my chair! A talent like that comes around only once in a lifetime. The guy was an absolute comet, and there I was in the front row. Can you imagine that?"

"Gee," I'd say, "I bet that was really something."

Empathy was the wrong tack, as it only seemed to irritate him.

5 "You don't know the half of it," he'd say. "'Really something,' my butt. You haven't got a clue. You could have taken a hatchet and cut the man's lips right off his face, chopped them off at the quick, and he still would have played better than anyone else out there. That's how good he was."

I'd nod my head, envisioning a pair of glistening lips lying forsaken on the floor of some nightclub dressing room. The trick was to back slowly toward the hallway, escaping into the kitchen before my father could yell, "Oh no you don't. Get back in here. I want you to sit down for a minute and listen. I mean *really* listen, to this next number."

Because it was the music we'd grown up with, I liked to think that my sisters and I had a genuine appreciation of jazz. We preferred it over the music our friends were listening to, yet nothing we did or said could convince my father of our devotion. Aside from replaying the tune on your own instrument, how could you prove you were really listening? It was as if he expected us to change color at the end of each selection.

Due to his ear and his almost maniacal sense of discipline, I always thought my father would have made an excellent musician. He might have studied the saxophone had he not been born to immigrant parents who considered even pot holders an extravagance. They themselves listened only to Greek music, an oxymoron as far as the rest of the world is concerned. Slam its tail in the door of the milk truck, and a stray cat could easily yowl out a single certain to top the charts back in Sparta or Thessaloníki. Jazz was my father's only form of rebellion. It was forbidden in his home, and he appreciated it as though it were his own private discovery. As a young man he hid his 78s under the sofa bed and regularly snuck off to New York City, where he'd haunt the clubs and consort with Negroes. It was a good life while it lasted. He was in his early forties when the company transferred our family to North Carolina.

"You expect me to live *where?*" he'd asked.

The Raleigh winters agreed with him, but he would have gladly traded 10
the temperate climate for a decent radio station. Since he was limited to his record and tape collection, it became his dream that his family might fill the musical void by someday forming a jazz combo.

His plan took shape the evening he escorted my sisters Lisa and Gretchen and me to the local state university to see Dave Brubeck, who was then touring with his sons. The audience roared when the quartet took the stage, and I leaned back and shut my eyes, pretending the applause was for me. In order to get that kind of attention, you needed a routine that would knock people's socks off. I'd been working on something in private and now began to imagine bringing it to a live audience. The act consisted of me, dressed in a nice shirt and tie and singing a medley of commercial jingles in the voice of Billie Holiday, who was one of my father's favorite singers. For my Raleigh concert I'd probably open with the number used to promote the town's oldest shopping center. A quick nod to my accompanist, and I'd launch into "The Excitement of Cameron Village Will Carry You Away." The beauty of my rendition was that it captured both the joy and the sorrow of a visit to Ellisburg's or J. C. Penney. This would be followed by such crowd pleasers as "Winston Tastes Good Like a Cigarette Should" and the catchy new Coke commercial, "I'd Like to Teach the World to Sing."

I was lost in my fantasy, ignoring Dave Brubeck and coming up for air only when my father elbowed my ribs to ask, "Are you *listening* to this? These cats are burning the paint right off the walls!" The other audience members sat calmly, as if in church, while my father snapped his fingers and bobbed his head low against his chest. People pointed, and when we begged him to sit up and act normal, he cupped his hands to his mouth and shouted out a request for "'Blue Rondo à la Turk'!"

Driving home from the concert that night, he drummed his palms against the steering wheel, saying, "Did you *hear* that? The guy just gets better every day! He's up there onstage with his kids by his side, the whole lot of them jamming up a storm. Christ almighty, what I wouldn't give for a family like that. You guys should think of putting an act together."

My sister Lisa coughed up a mouthful of grapefruit soda.

"No, I mean it," my father said. "All you need are some lessons and in- 15
struments, and I swear to God, you'd go right through the roof." We hoped this was just another of his five-minute ideas, but by the time we reached the

house, his eyes were still glowing. "That's exactly what you need to do," he said. "I don't know why I didn't think of it sooner."

The following afternoon he bought a baby grand piano. It was a used model that managed to look imposing even when positioned on a linoleum-tiled floor. We took turns stabbing at the keys, but as soon as the novelty wore off, we bolstered it with sofa cushions and turned it into a fort. The piano sat neglected in the traditional sense until my father signed Gretchen up for a series of lessons. She'd never expressed any great interest in the thing but was chosen because, at the age of ten, she possessed what our dad decided were the most artistic fingers. Lisa was assigned the flute, and I returned home from a Scout meeting one evening to find my instrument leaning against the aquarium in my bedroom.

"Hold on to your hat," my father said, "because here's that guitar you've always wanted."

Surely he had me confused with someone else. Although I had regularly petitioned for a brand-name vacuum cleaner, I'd never said anything about wanting a guitar. Nothing about it appealed to me, not even on an aesthetic level. I had my room arranged just so, and the instrument did not fit in with my nautical theme. An anchor, yes. A guitar, no. He wanted me to jam, so I jammed it into my closet, where it remained until he signed me up for some private lessons offered at a music shop located on the ground floor of the recently opened North Hills Mall. I fought it as best I could and feigned illness even as he dropped me off for my first appointment.

"But I'm sick!" I yelled, watching him pull out of the parking lot. "I have a virus, and besides that, I don't want to play a musical instrument. Don't you know *anything?*"

20 When it finally sank in that he wasn't coming back, I lugged my guitar into the music store, where the manager led me to my teacher, a perfectly formed midget named Mister Mancini. I was twelve years old at the time, small for my age, and it was startling to find myself locked in a windowless room with a man who barely reached my chest. It seemed wrong that I would be taller than my teacher, but I kept this to myself, saying only, "My father told me to come here. It was all his idea."

A fastidious dresser stuck in a small, unfashionable town, Mister Mancini wore clothing I recognized from the Young Squires department of Hudson Belk. Some nights he favored button-down shirts with clip-on ties, while other evenings I arrived to find him dressed in flared slacks and snug turtleneck sweaters, a swag of love beads hanging from his neck. His arms were manly and covered in coarse dark hair, but his voice was high and strange, as if it had been recorded and was now being played back at a faster speed.

Not a dwarf, but an honest-to-God midget. My fascination was both evident and unwelcome, and was nothing he hadn't been subjected to a million times before. He didn't shake my hand, just lit a cigarette and reached for the conch shell he used as an ashtray. Like my father, Mister Mancini assumed that anyone could learn to play the guitar. He had picked it up during a single summer spent in what he called "Hotlanta G.A." This, I knew, was the racy name given to Atlanta, Georgia. "Now *that,*" he said, "is one classy place if you know where to go." He grabbed my guitar and began tuning it, holding his head close to the strings. "Yes, siree, kid, the girls down on Peachtree are running wild twenty-four hours a day."

He mentioned a woman named Beth, saying, "They threw away the mold and shut down the factory after making that one, you know what I mean?"

I nodded my head, having no idea what he was talking about.

"She wasn't much of a cook, but hey, I guess that's why God invented TV dinners." He laughed at his little joke and repeated the line about the frozen dinners, as if he would use it later in a comedy routine. "God made TV dinners, yeah, that's good." He told me he'd named his guitar after Beth. "Now I can't keep my hands off of her!" he said. "Seriously, though, it helps if you give your instrument a name. What do you think you'll call yours?" 25

"Maybe I'll call it Oliver," I said. That was the name of my hamster, and I was used to saying it.

Then again, maybe not.

"Oliver?" Mister Mancini set my guitar on the floor. "*Oliver?* What the hell kind of name is that? If you're going to devote yourself to the guitar, you need to name it after a girl, not a guy."

"Oh, right," I said. "Joan. I'll call it . . . Joan."

"So tell me about this Joan," he said. "Is she something pretty special?" 30

Joan was the name of one of my cousins, but it seemed unwise to share this information. "Oh yeah," I said, "Joan's really . . . great. She's tall and . . . " I felt self-conscious using the word *tall* and struggled to take it back. "She's small and has brown hair and everything."

"Is she stacked?"

I'd never noticed my cousin's breasts and had lately realized that I'd never noticed anyone's breasts, not unless, like our housekeeper's, they were large enough to appear freakish. "Stacked? Well, sure," I said. "She's pretty stacked." I was afraid he'd ask me for a more detailed description and was relieved when he crossed the room and removed Beth from her case. He told me that a guitar student needed plenty of discipline. Talent was great, but time had taught him that talent was also extremely rare. "I've got it," he said. "But then again, I was born with it. It's a gift from God, and those of us who have it are very special people."

He seemed to know that I was nothing special, just a type, yet another boy whose father had his head in the clouds.

"Do you have a *feel* for the guitar? Do you have any idea what this little baby is capable of?" Without waiting for an answer, he climbed up into his chair and began playing "Light My Fire," adding, "This one is for Joan. 35

"You know that I would be untrue," he sang. "You know that I would be a liar." The current hit version of the song was performed by José Feliciano, a blind man whose plaintive voice served the lyrics much better than did Jim Morrison, who sang it in what I considered a bossy and conceited tone of voice. There was José Feliciano, there was Jim Morrison, and then there was Mister Mancini, who played beautifully but sang "Light My Fire" as if he were a Webelo Scout demanding a match. He finished his opening number, nodded his head in acknowledgment of my applause, and moved on, offering up his own unique and unsettling versions of "The Girl from Ipanema" and "Little Green Apples" while I sat trapped in my seat, my false smile stretched so tight that I lost all feeling in the lower half of my face.

My fingernails had grown a good three inches by the time he struck his final note and called me close to point out a few simple chords. Before I left, he handed me half a dozen purple mimeographed handouts, which we both knew were useless.

Back at the house my mother had my dinner warming in the oven. From the living room came the aimless whisper of Lisa's flute. It sounded not unlike the wind whipping through an empty Pepsi can. Down in the basement either Gretchen was practicing her piano or the cat was chasing a moth across the keys. My mother responded by turning up the volume on the kitchen TV while my father pushed back my plate, set Joan in my lap, and instructed me to play.

"Listen to this," he crowed. "A house full of music! Man, this is beautiful."

You certainly couldn't accuse him of being unsupportive. His enthusiasm bordered on mania, yet still it failed to inspire us. During practice sessions my sisters and I would eat potato chips, scowling at our hated instruments and speculating on the lives of our music teachers. They were all peculiar in one way or another, but with a midget, I'd definitely won the my-teacher-is-stranger-than-yours competition. I wondered where Mister Mancini lived and who he might call in case of an emergency. Did he stand on a chair in order to shave, or was his home customized to meet his needs? I'd look at the laundry hamper or beer cooler, thinking that if it came down to it, Mister Mancini could hide just about anywhere.

Though I thought of him constantly, I grabbed any excuse to avoid my guitar.

"I've been doing just what you told me to do," I'd say at the beginning of each lesson, "but I just can't get the hang of it. Maybe my fingers are too shor— . . . I mean litt— . . . I mean, maybe I'm just not coordinated enough." He'd arrange Joan in my lap, pick up Beth, and tell me to follow along. "You need to believe you're playing an actual woman," he'd say. "Just grab her by the neck and make her holler."

Mr. Mancini had a singular talent for making me uncomfortable. He forced me to consider things I'd rather not think about—the sex of my guitar, for instance. If I honestly wanted to put my hands on a woman, would that automatically mean I could play? Gretchen's teacher never told her to think of her piano as a boy. Neither did Lisa's flute teacher, though in that case the analogy was fairly obvious. On the off chance that sexual desire was all it took, I steered clear of Lisa's instrument, fearing I might be labeled a prodigy. The best solution was to become a singer and leave the instruments to other people. A song stylist—that was what I wanted to be.

I was at the mall with my mother one afternoon when I spotted Mister Mancini ordering a hamburger at Scotty's Chuck Wagon, a fast-food restaurant located a few doors down from the music shop. He sometimes mentioned having lunch with a salesgirl from Jolly's Jewelers, "a real looker," but on this day he was alone. Mister Mancini had to stand on his tiptoes to ask for his hamburger, and even then his head failed to reach the counter. The passing adults politely looked away, but their children were decidedly more vocal. A toddler ambled up on his chubby bowed legs, attempting to embrace my teacher with ketchup-smeared fingers, while a party of elementary-school students openly stared in wonder. Even worse was the group of adolescents, boys my own age, who sat gathered around a large table. "Go back to Oz, munchkin," one of them said, and his friends shook with laughter. Tray in hand, Mister Mancini took a seat and pretended not to notice. The boys weren't yelling, but anyone could tell that they were making fun of him. "Honestly, Mother," I said, "do they have to be such monsters?" Beneath my moral outrage was a strong sense of possessiveness, a fury that other people were sinking their hooks into my own personal midget. What did they know about this man? I was the one who lit his cigarettes and listened as he denounced the careers of so-called pretty boys such as Glen Campbell and Bobby Goldsboro. It was I who had suffered through six weeks' worth of lessons and was still struggling to master "Yellow Bird." If anyone was going to give him a hard time, I figured that I should be first in line.

I'd always thought of Mister Mancini as a blowhard, a pocket playboy, 45
but watching him dip his hamburger into a sad puddle of mayonnaise, I broadened my view and came to see him as a wee outsider, a misfit whose take-it-or-leave-it attitude had left him all alone. This was a persona I'd been tinkering with myself: the outcast, the rebel. It occurred to me that, with the exception of the guitar, he and I actually had quite a bit in common. We were each a man trapped inside a boy's body. Each of us was talented in his own way, and we both hated twelve-year-old males, a demographic group second to none in terms of cruelty. All things considered, there was no reason I shouldn't address him not as a teacher but as an artistic brother. Maybe then we could drop the pretense of Joan and get down to work. If things worked out the way I hoped, I'd someday mention in interviews that my accompanist was both my best friend *and* a midget.

I wore a tie to my next lesson and this time when asked if I'd practiced, I told the truth, saying in a matter-of-fact tone of voice that no, I hadn't laid a finger on my guitar since our last get-together. I told him that Joan was my cousin's name and that I had no idea how stacked she was.

"That's okay," Mister Mancini said. "You can call your guitar whatever you want, just as long as you practice."

My voice shaking, I told him that I had absolutely no interest in mastering the guitar. What I really wanted was to sing in the voice of Billie Holiday. "Mainly commercials, but not for any banks or car dealerships, because those are usually choral arrangements."

The color ebbed from my teacher's face.

I told him I'd been working up an act and could use a little accompani- 50
ment. Did he know the jingle for the new Sara Lee campaign?

"You want me to do what?" He wasn't angry, just confused.

I felt certain he was lying when he denied knowing the tune. Doublemint gum, Ritz crackers, the theme songs for Alka-Seltzer and Kenmore appliances: he claimed ignorance on all counts. I knew that it was queer to sing in front of someone, but greater than my discomfort was the hope that he might recognize what I thought of as my great talent, the one musical trick I was able to pull off. I started in on an a cappella version of the latest Oscar Mayer commercial, hoping he might join in once the spirit moved him. It looked bad, I knew, but in order to sustain the proper mood, I needed to disregard his company and sing the way I did at home alone in my bedroom, my eyes shut tight and my hands dangling like pointless, empty gloves.

I sang that my bologna had a first name.

I added that my bologna had a second name.

55 And concluded: *Oh, I love to eat it every day*

And if you ask me why, I'll say

Thaaaat Os-carrr May-errr has a way, with B-Oooo-L-Oooo-G-N-A.

I reached the end of my tune thinking he might take this as an opportunity to applaud or maybe even apologize for underestimating me. Mild amusement would have been an acceptable response. But instead, he held up his hands, as if to stop an advancing car. "Hey, guy," he said. "You can hold it right there. I'm not into that scene."

A scene? What scene? I thought I was being original.

60 "There were plenty of screwballs like you back in Atlanta, but me, I don't swing that way—you got it? This might be your 'thing' or whatever, but you can definitely count me out." He reached for his conch shell and stubbed out his cigarette. "I mean, come on now. For God's sake, kid, pull yourself together."

I knew then why I'd never before sung in front of anyone, and why I shouldn't have done it in front of Mister Mancini. He'd used the word *screwball,* but I knew what he really meant. He meant I should have named my guitar Doug or Brian, or better yet, taken up the flute. He meant that if we're defined by our desires, I was in for a lifetime of trouble.

The remainder of the hour was spent awkwardly watching the clock as we silently pretended to tune our guitars.

My father was disappointed when I told him I wouldn't be returning for any more lessons. "He told me not to come back," I said. "He told me I have the wrong kind of fingers."

Seeing that it had worked for me, my sisters invented similar stories, and together we announced that the Sedaris Trio had officially disbanded. Our father offered to find us better teachers, adding that if we were unhappy with our instruments, we could trade them in for something more suitable. "The trumpet or the saxophone, or hey, how about the vibes?" He reached for a Lionel Hampton album, saying, "I want you to sit down and give this a good listen. Just get a load of this cat and tell me he's not an inspiration."

65 There was a time when I could listen to such a record and imagine myself as the headline act at some magnificent New York nightclub, but that's what fantasies are for: they allow you to skip the degradation and head straight to the top. I'd done my solo and would now move on to pursue other equally unsuccessful ways of getting attention. I'd try every art form there was, and with each disappointment I'd picture Mister Mancini holding his conch shell and saying, "For God's sake, kid, pull yourself together."

We told our father, no, don't bother playing us any more of your records, but still he persisted. "I'm telling you that this album is going to change your lives, and if it doesn't, I'll give each one of you a five-dollar bill. What do you think of that?"

It was a tough call—five dollars for listening to a Lionel Hampton record. The offer was tempting, but even on the off chance he'd actually come through with the money, there would certainly be strings attached. We looked at one another, my sisters and I, and then we left the room, ignoring his cry of "Hey, where do you think you're going? Get back in here and listen."

We joined our mother at the TV and never looked back. A life in music was his great passion, not ours, and our lessons had taught us that without the passion, the best one could hope for was an occasional engagement at some hippie wedding where, if we were lucky, the guests would be too stoned to realize just how bad we really were. That night, as was his habit, our father fell asleep in front of the stereo, the record making its pointless, silent rounds as he lay back against the sofa cushions, dreaming.

DEBBIE L. SKLAR

Indiana's Potato Chip Lady

Myrtle Young of Seyfert Foods, Inc.

Mention potato chips, and Indiana native Myrtle Young will tell you her prized possessions have seen more than the insides of foil bags.

Young is a former potato chip inspector for Seyfert Foods Inc. in Fort Wayne. She says hers is the only potato chip collection in the world. Her chips feature likenesses of animals, cartoon characters and even profiles of famous celebrities.

"My most famous chip," Young says with excitement, "is my Bob Hope chip. He sits on cotton in a special velvet jewelry box with a lid that protects him. It's my favorite chip and it could never be replaced."

Other chips in Young's collection include the countenances of comedian Rodney Dangerfield, Yogi Bear, Mr. Magoo, Mickey Mouse, Tweety Bird, Ziggy and Moby Dick, to name only a few. "I used to have a chip that looked just like Alfred Hitchcock," says Young, "but it had an accident. It broke into a hundred pieces."

Young began taking the chips home to show her granddaughter, who 5
suggested starting a collection. "I really began to get serious about it in 1987," Young says. "That's when I started traveling with my chips and showing them on various television shows around the world."

Have chips, will travel? Says Young: "My chips have been all over the world; from the West to the East to Europe and Great Britain. Even Lady Di, Prince Charles and their sons have seen my chips." Young has been on *Late Night with David Letterman, The Tonight Show, CBS This Morning, To Tell the Truth* and many other programs.

When she was on Johnny Carson's *Tonight Show* in 1987, Carson grabbed a chip from a bowl under his desk when Young wasn't looking and chomped on it—she thought it was one of hers. "I thought I was going to have a heart attack," she laughs. When she was in New York for *The David Letterman Show*, the hotel changed the locks on her doors to ensure the safety of her chips. On a more recent trip to Oklahoma City, the producers of the television show on which she appeared insured her chip collection for $1 million, Young says.

Ripley's *Believe It or Not* currently has its eyes on Young's unique collection. "These institutions told me, once I notice any deterioration in my chips, I should let them know, and they will preserve them for me and put them in display units," she says. "This is a rare collection and there will never be another one like it in the world because chip inspectors are being replaced by electric eyes to weed out bad chips."

No longer a Seyfert chip inspector, Indiana's potato chip queen now gives tours at the 58-year-old company's Fort Wayne plant, which turns a million pounds of potatoes into chips each week. "I don't collect chips anymore," she says. "But every once in a while, I'll comb through the trash bins to see if any good ones have been thrown away. And every once in a while I get lucky!"

CHAPTER 13

THE SUPERNATURAL

Overview

Many people have experienced phenomena that the status quo does not accept as existing within the realm of possibility. This realm consists of the natural and rational world, and it is supported by science, precedence, and logic. Anything that defies the known laws or facts within this realm is deemed "supernatural" or "paranormal," meaning that the event, sighting, or occurrence cannot be explained fully within our understanding of the world. The questions that persist concern just how all-encompassing this known world is. In other words, do we have full knowledge of every crevice on this planet? Do we completely comprehend mental processes and powers? Do we understand the worlds outside our physical limitations?

Many people react to a person's claim of seeing a ghost or encountering a UFO with skepticism, if not outright ridicule. Authority figures try to explain away these and other supernatural incidents by claiming that witnesses have overactive imaginations or did not really see or hear what they reported. Sometimes, of course, skeptics prove to be correct. A family of mice probably did cause the strange noise you heard in the old house you just moved into. A sheet fluttering in the wind only looked like an apparition to you when viewed from afar. The spiritualists at the party most likely did not read your mind but rather made educated guesses based on your body language and basic profile.

Yet, we have all either experienced something strange that has not been explained as an effect of natural causes or have heard a story from a

This icon will direct you to web links and additional resources on the website college.hmco.com/pic/thelin1e

person convinced that supernatural forces came into play in his or her life. The power of rational thinking and natural explanations wanes when it does not quite relieve the terror or satisfy the curiosity aroused by supernatural experiences.

As a young adult, I spent a night in a house that had been plagued by strange occurrences. Our coworkers Dominique and Patty had noticed strange events in their house. Doors slammed when they tried to put up a crucifix on the living room wall. They had an eerie feeling of being watched, as if a presence followed them. They were uncomfortable about staying alone. Several of us thought they were crazy and spent the night to prove that the house was harmless. Long after the last of us had gone to sleep, I awoke, sensing someone staring at me, and saw a large silhouette standing at the foot of my sleeping bag. Startled, I rubbed my eyes and shook my head, thinking it nothing more than a bad dream. But when I looked again, it was still there. I yelled and scrambled toward the person closest to me, but when she awoke and looked around, nothing was there.

The next morning I described the silhouette as we drank coffee. Patty's face turned white as I relayed my impressions. She wanted to know the color of his hair. "He was like a shadow," I said. "I have no idea what color his hair was. What does it matter?" Patty remained silent. "Because you described him," she finally said. She explained that before Dominique had moved in, she had shared the house with a male friend who, she said, had been using some sort of magic to try to seduce her. He had told her that he could project his presence from far away.

Had I seen this presence? Had this person somehow haunted or possessed the house? I don't know. Our other friends talked about weird feelings and bad dreams they had that evening, but no one claimed to have seen what I saw. Logical explanations can account for my sighting. I could have imagined it. Night vision combined with imagination fueled by the adventure of sleeping in a supposedly haunted house could have twisted my interpretation of a mere shadow. Having been made to look skittish, Patty could have invented the story about the male friend projecting his image. He might have looked nothing like the silhouette I saw. I also could have mistaken a real person for a silhouette. One of the other people spending the night could have been looking for a glass of water or sleepwalking. Less likely, an intruder could have entered the house and have been frightened off when I awoke.

None of these explanations has ever satisfied me. I know my sight had adjusted to the dark, and I saw the silhouette clearly. No one could remember getting up in the night, and we saw no signs of an intruder. Unless some sort of hoax was being perpetrated, the rational, natural explanations involved too much coincidence for me to believe them.

Other people with better proof of supernatural episodes also have to strive to be believed. Marc Dewerth, the leader of the Multi-State Bigfoot Research Roundtable, filmed what he believed to be Bigfoot in Coshocton County in eastern Ohio. While the creature on the videotape initially looks like shadows in dense brush, subsequent movement shows a clear image of more than one primate. Dewerth took this tape to primate experts at the Cleveland Zoo, telling them that he had been on a trip, had caught the animal on film, and was wondering what it was. The experts assumed that Dewerth had been in Africa and had caught a glimpse of some relative of the mountain gorilla. When he told them the tape came from Ohio, they showed Dewerth other places in the video where the primates became visible. The experts could not identify the species.

Possible explanations? When a species that is not supposed to be in a part of the country appears suddenly, officials claim that the animal must have been somebody's pet that was released into the wild. Officials do not entertain the possibility that animals of the species escaped detection in that area all those years. So despite dung and fur samples, not to mention sightings from reliable witnesses, grizzly bears have been considered extinct in Colorado's San Juan Mountains for forty years. While alligators have been spotted in the Miami River through Ohio and Kentucky, a native population does not exist. In both cases, the escaped pet explanation follows the denials. Using this logic with Dewerth's experience, I suppose we should believe that the primates he caught on film were a family of mountain gorillas who used to be somebody's pets. That sounds too far-fetched for me, though. To read more about Dewerth and a different recounting of his sighting of Bigfoot, see "Four Stops on a Bigfoot Hunt" by Jeff Parker (page 379).

When people hear stories about the supernatural, they often deny that something exists outside our natural, logical world. No matter how convoluted a "rational" explanation becomes, no matter how many coincidences it relies on, people gravitate to it rather than embracing the possibility of supernatural forces. People who do accept the possibility of a supernatural explanation risk ridicule.

Yet, while we as a culture go to great lengths to deny the existence of the supernatural in cases like the ones above, we willingly give the supernatural credence in other places in our life. Popular talk shows feature mediums who claim to speak with, and for, the dead. The Catholic Church requires that miracles be attributed to individuals in order for them to be declared saints. Websites are devoted to people recounting their experiences with angels. While we do not want to confuse evidence of the existence of Bigfoot with our religious convictions, these beliefs nonetheless show a clear embrace of the supernatural, as do many aspects of our various faiths.

As a culture, we dare to explore by launching spacecraft, conducting experiments, and searching for the past. However, evidence of the natural extensions of these explorations seemingly panics us. We study psychology to gain understanding of the human condition but scoff at demonstrations of extrasensory perception (ESP). We land probes on Mars to look for signs of civilization but actively denounce accounts that suggest that our planet in turn has been visited by alien cultures. Fossils tell us that bipedal primates other than humans existed millions of years ago, but we greet signs of their present existence with skepticism. So while the supernatural fascinates many of us, it repels others and is dismissed as superstition and fancy.

But what happens when the logical explanation seems less reasonable than the illogical one?

Openings for Writers

1. **Rational explanations** At what point do logical, natural explanations for a supernatural event falter? What type of evidence would persuade you that a supernatural event occurred? What evidence would you need to convince somebody else? Look for consistent features that arise when you reflect on these questions.
2. **Hoaxes** Hoaxes include Internet rumors that are spread through email and jokes friends play to fool or scare somebody. Why are they committed? What is the pleasure in deceiving others? Decide on the connection between harmless fun, fraud, and hoaxes.
3. **Wanting to believe** Sometimes we say that a person wants to believe in the supernatural as a way of explaining an apparition or a UFO they saw. Why would people desire to believe they had supernatural encounters? If they were ridiculed when they recounted something supernatural, what would cause them to wish or want it to be supernatural?
4. **Faith and the supernatural** What other beliefs does our culture accept that, like faith, fall under the category of the supernatural? Think about how these beliefs pervade our culture and what effect they have. Do they provide comfort? Do they release people from responsibility? Do they raise possibilities?

Language

1. **Imagination** People are offended when told they have let their imaginations run away with them. Why? Hasn't imagination allowed us to envision ideas that have let us progress? Think of the different meanings of *imagination* and the connotations that go with them.
2. **Coincidence** What is coincidence? How does it differ from the supernatural? Think of ways that the definition of *coincidence* might extend or limit the definition of supernatural.
3. **Bigfoot** Does the naming of a supernatural creature or event cause you to become skeptical before you have heard the evidence? *Bigfoot* can connote many images, as do *Loch Ness Monster, Martians,* and *phantoms.* Are the connotations of these words positive or negative? Why do you react to them the way you do?
4. **ESP and UFO** People use these acronyms more than they do the words they stand for. Do you know what the words are? Do you get a different sense from the acronym than from the words the letters represent? Describe what the acronyms and the words connote and whether the connotations predispose you toward the subject matter of the supernatural.
5. **Miracle** How do you use the word *miracle*? Does it always represent something supernatural? Think of miracles you have heard about. Do you have the same reactions to those stories as you do to stories about ghosts, alien abductions, telepathy, and other supernatural events? Why?

ROBERT ELLIS CAHILL

Whitman's Haunted Bed

The ghost story here is archetypal of those recounted in many books about local legends. This tale, taken from New England's Ghostly Haunts, *involves contemporary, innocent citizens experiencing strange happenings in their home attributed to an ancient curse or death. Typical of these stories, the people isolate a particular cause and take steps to rid themselves of the paranormal link. In this case, the cure seems to have worked. In other cases, the hauntings continue. While reading, think about what you would need to hear, see, or feel to grant this account credibility.*

David and Barbara English, with their year old son, moved to Whitman, Massachusetts, from Delaware, in the autumn of 1972. They moved into a quaint, 18th century Cape Cod cottage, on Temple Street, where they expected to live happily ever after. A few months after they had moved in, their good friends—a couple from Delaware—came to visit them. David and Barbara had little furniture and only one bed, but David remembered seeing an old bed folded into a corner crawl space in the attic of the old house. It was truly an antique with a carved headboard and intricately designed footboard. David pulled it out of the crawl space and set it up in a spare room. On the evening their guests arrived, the Englishes allowed them to use their room, and the hosts slept in the ancient bed in the guest room. David had a fitfull night and kept waking up with the feeling that someone was choking him. Barbara, on the other hand, slept soundly.

Next morning things began happening to Barbara. Her china teapot in the kitchen cabinet would not remain standing upright. As many times as she would stand it up in the cabinet, she would find it a moment later lying on its side. Then she stood there and watched after setting it on its base for the thirtieth time—she saw it rattle and tip over again. Also, all the coffee cups slid off their hooks in the cabinet. "I tried continuously slamming the doors of the cabinet for a long time one day," said Barbara, "just to see if the pot would fall over or the cups would fall off, but they didn't, because they couldn't." This convinced Barbara that there was either a ghost in the house, or some large truck kept traveling by the house and causing the pot and cups to tremble and fall.

David concluded, one evening, that Barbara's first guess was right, even though he didn't believe in ghosts. He found that the door to the attic crawl space, located near their bedroom, was always open—no matter how hard he tried to keep it closed. Barbara swore she hadn't been near the crawl space. Neither Barbara nor David could explain who or what could continuously pull back the latch and open the door to the crawl space; it certainly couldn't have opened by itself, and it was too high for their, now two year old, son to reach.

One evening, while Barbara was out bowling and David was puttering in the cellar, he heard footsteps upstairs. Thinking Barbara was home early, he went upstairs to greet her, but there was nobody there. This happened every Monday night in the English household, while Barbara was out bowling—footsteps, but no one there when David investigated.

The incident that stimulated David into action, and thoroughly frightened him and Barbara, was when they invited a neighboring couple over one night to play cards. They played at the kitchen table, where David sat with his back to the upstairs stairway, while the other three could see it clearly. David's slippers were tucked between two posts of the stairway, where he could easily pick them up when he went to bed. Suddenly, the visiting couple and Barbara looked up in astonishment—the pair of slippers were floating in midair, and then they landed with a slap beside David's feet. One of their friends told them about a medium who lived in Brockton, who might help them rid the house of its ghost. David was somewhat embarrassed about asking a ghost chaser to come to their house, but when the Brockton spiritualist refused to come, David was angry.

His anger and fear increased a few days later, when he came home and found pieces of sandwich meat scattered over the kitchen floor. He shouted for Barbara, who was upstairs, and scolded her for messing up the kitchen. Barbara had left the slices of meat on the table only minutes before and it was too high for the baby to reach. David returned to Brockton and pleaded with the medium to come. The medium came, and, after sitting at the kitchen table for a few minutes, he asked Barbara and David to take him upstairs. He walked into the room where the old wooden bed which had been found in the attic stood, and he slapped the footboard with an open hand. Then he began mumbling. Soon, he was shouting, "You must go!" David then noted that the medium turned pale and looked as though he was going to faint. David and Barbara accompanied him back down to the kitchen where he told them what he heard and saw; although the Englishes had been standing beside him in the guest room they had neither seen nor heard anything unusual.

"The spirit is an old woman," said the medium, "who lived in this house over 100 years ago. She died in that old bed. Another old woman lived with her at the time," said the medium, "but did not aid your visitor while she was sick, and treated her quite brutally. She is very angry about this mistreatment, and, by the way," the medium added, "she does not like David."

The medium had insisted to the ghost that she leave the house and she, so he said, agreed. David and Barbara went to bed feeling a bit easier, but David did not sleep easy. Again, he felt that someone was choking him. Coughing and sweating profusely, he woke Barbara and they went downstairs. They sat at the kitchen table all night, and in the morning called the medium in Brockton. The medium was there at seven A.M., and, after going to the bedroom again, he told Barbara and David that the old woman's ghost had left, but returned during the night to choke David. The ghost intended to show David how she felt when she died in the bed by strangling on her own fluid, which filled her lungs. The medium suggested that the Englishes get rid of the bed, then the old woman was sure to leave.

That day, David sold the bed to a local antique shop, who, in turn, sold it to a ghost lover for over $100. David English, however, is happy to have the bed out of the house, and, although he now believes in ghosts, he sleeps soundly.

SUSAN MCCLELLAND AND JOHN BETTS

UFOs, Skepticism, and Belief

Many people who claim to have seen flying saucers or alien beings face ridicule and even sanctions when they persist in believing the paranormal or supernatural explanation. While authors Susan McClelland and John Betts sound almost whimsical in reviewing the controversies in the field of UFOlogy, the issues they touch on contain serious elements. A Harvard researcher has to defend his methodology in interviewing victims of alien abduction and still is scorned for granting credence to abductees' stories. An abductee frequently awakens with unexplained piercings and nosebleeds after being paralyzed for a night. A government investigating an unusual outer space phenomenon in 1967 has to classify its findings as a UFO incident. This article also alludes to profiteering, wherein a Canadian town cashes in on the history of UFO sightings. The conflict about whether to believe in supernatural events crystallizes in our views of possible extraterrestrial life, touching the boundaries that science keeps pushing.

To the first-time tourist, St. Paul, Alberta, could easily pass for a set from *The X-Files.* The billboard at the edge of the small farming community about 200 km northeast of Edmonton welcomes visitors to the world's first UFO landing pad—a circular cement deck attached to the Chamber of Commerce. The chamber itself looks like a spaceship. Businesses with names like Mama's Flying Saucer Pizza & Breakfast and the Galaxy Motel line the main street. Even the town's mascot, Zoot, is an extraterrestrial that looks like a large-eyed blue bug. The biggest surprise, though, may be just how long it's been since the townsfolk put out the alien welcome mat. "The landing pad was built during Canada's Centennial," explains Mayor John Trefanenko. "People wanted to create something that would be recognized around the world. Over the years, we kept building on that theme."

And build they have. UFO fervour has spawned an industry in the town of 5,000 that brings in some 30,000 visitors a year. Along the way, some townsfolk have developed otherworldly areas of interest. Fernand Belzil, for instance, a semi-retired cattle rancher, is one of Canada's few experts on a grisly type of animal mutilation in which all the blood has been drained and certain organs surgically removed. The lack of footprints surrounding the carcasses has led some to rule out natural predators and practitioners of satanic rituals. So that leaves, perhaps, creatures from outer space? "It's as if the body is dropped from the sky," says Belzil, who has investigated more than 60 mutilations, predominantly of cattle, in western Canada. "Six years ago, when the chamber got a call asking if they knew someone who could check out an animal, I went thinking no way. It wasn't killed by aliens. Now, well, I'm not going to come right out and say there are UFOs. But like a lot of people in town, I am a little more accepting of strange phenomena."

No joke, folks: turns out the residents of St. Paul aren't alone in believing the truth is out there. A 1996 Angus Reid poll found 70 percent of Canadians believe intelligent life exists elsewhere in the universe, and just over half of those sampled said they thought the planet had already been visited by extraterrestrials. Throughout the country, numerous UFO groups monitor alien encounters. They estimate as many as 10 percent of Canadians have seen unidentified flying objects—and reports of sightings are as numerous as ever. Last year, more than 500 people saw 263 UFOs—up 10 percent from 1989. "Am I surprised with the numbers of people who have these experiences?" says Errol Bruce-Knapp, host of *Strange Days . . . Indeed,* a radio program about UFOs on CFRB in Toronto. "No. From the moment our show begins, the phone lines are busy."

"They're letting us know we're not evolving," says [Dorothy Wilkinson] Izatt, who believes she's met many aliens, and whose movies have captured strange phenomena.

5 OK, but it's one thing to fess up to a little-green-men fixation when you're talking to an anonymous pollster or on the disembodied world of radio. What do you say to non-believers, who state categorically that flying saucers and creatures that drive them—and then abduct earthlings—do not, cannot, exist? These people cite reams of scientific data to prove their argument—and question the soundness of mind of the E.T. crowd. Groups like Heaven's Gate in San Diego and Quebec's Solar Temple, whose devotees committed suicide in the hopes their spirits would be taken by aliens, bolster the skeptics' contentions that only those on the lunatic fringe believe in UFOs.

Some reasonable souls, however, are troubled by the rigid orthodoxy of the two opposing camps. "The problem has been that you have the hard-nosed skeptics, who believe nothing, and the full believers, who see a light in the sky and are convinced it's a flying saucer," says Palmiro Campagna, an electromagnetics engineer and administrator with the Department of National Defence in Ottawa and author of 1997's *The UFO Files: The Canadian Connection Exposed.* "What is needed are investigators who take neither view, but just look at the facts." As it happens, an emerging breed of serious scholars is daring to do just that. And if, in the process, they answer the age-old question of whether humans are alone in the universe, so much the better.

One world-renowned figure who surprised his scientific colleagues by trying to take an open-minded look at the world of UFOs is Dr. John Mack, a professor of psychiatry at Harvard Medical School. Mack, an author of more than 150 scholarly articles, worked over the past decade with more than 100 people who claimed to have been abducted by aliens. He acknowledges he, too, was skeptical at first. "The psychiatrist in me is trained to distinguish mental states like when someone is hallucinating, having some kind of psychotic episode or confusion around a dream," he told *Maclean's.* "But the clinician in me said these people were talking about these encounters the way people talk about what is really happening to them."

In 1994, Mack, who won a Pulitzer Prize for his 1976 biography of T. E. Lawrence, published *Abduction: Human Encounters with Aliens.* The book, which relates the experiences of 13 self-described abductees, went on to become a best-seller—and to irritate Harvard officials. They questioned his research methods, forcing Mack to vigorously defend his work before a university review board. The board accepted his methodology, but not before his reputation was sullied in a number of major U.S. newspapers.

People in high places, though, have long been curious about extraterrestrials. In the 1950s, alongside civilian groups, the Department of National Defence and the RCMP investigated reported sightings of UFOs. Ottawa also funded the work of Department of Transport Engineer Wilbert Smith, who was trying to figure out how they made it to Earth. "Smith was studying anti-gravity propulsion—if something was travelling through the stars, how would it be able to manipulate gravity," explains Campagna.

The research grant was small, and Smith was soon forced to wrap it up. 10
Then in 1953, the federal government supported another one of his initiatives, providing Smith with a building at Shirleys Bay near Ottawa where he was developing an electronic device that could identify flying objects. Several months later, Smith reported his first detection of an "anomalous disturbance" to the media. But the resulting publicity spooked the federal agencies supporting Smith's work—they cut off his funding, and the engineer was forced to close shop.

Still, Defence continued to collect UFO reports until 1968, when it handed the task over to the National Research Council: after multiple changes at the NRC, it, too, got out of the UFO business. Since 1996, the task of investigating sightings has been left to nonprofit groups. Between 1989 and 2000, they checked into nearly 3,000 UFO reports. Most could be explained as aircraft or natural phenomena, including stars or meteors. But according to Chris Rutkowski, an astronomer who heads up one of the volunteer organizations, Ufology Research of Manitoba, about 5 percent can't be accounted for. This includes one outside Whitehorse, where in 1997 an object shaped like a satellite dish flew at tree-top level as it followed a mother and her three kids down the Klondike highway. "I know how unlikely it is for aliens to reach Earth," says Rutkowski. "But there is a certain percentage of cases that just can't be explained."

One of Canada's most famous—and still unexplained—incidents took place in Nova Scotia, on October 4, 1967. Hundreds witnessed an unidentified object fly erratically 300 km southwest along the coast from Dartmouth until it eventually crashed into Shag Harbour. "I saw this strange orange light tracing the shoreline," recalls Chris Styles, who was 12 at the time. "My first reaction was fear. I had never seen anything like this before."

And seeing, as they say, is believing. Styles and writer Don Ledger co-authored the 2001 book *Dark Object: The World's Only Government-Documented UFO Crash.*

In it, they interviewed RCMP and military officers who were involved in the official search for the UFO. Some recalled bringing odd-looking debris, including a yellow foam-like substance thought to be from the wreck, to the surface of the ocean. The authors discovered that RCMP records classified the incident as a UFO. "I know many people involved want an investigation," says Styles. "UFOs are a worldwide phenomenon and these few cases that are well corroborated should be looked into."

Others say they've had encounters of a much closer kind. Larry, a successful 50-year-old Ontario businessman, appears to lead a normal life in every respect except one: from the age of 6, he's been visited by aliens. "I realized my experiences were abductions when I was in my late 30s after I watched a TV show about abductees," he says. "Until then, I didn't have a clue what it was. I just kept it all to myself. As it turned out, what I was experiencing was textbook abduction."

And, yes, there is such a textbook—or at least a fairly standard—abduction scenario. One was spelled out in the 1987 book *Communion,* in which American writer Whitley Strieber earnestly recounted his own abduction ordeals. The abductee is taken every few months, usually at night, feels paralyzed, has visions of bright lights, and afterward has a sense of lost time. Some recount having had sexual encounters with their abductors, while other abductees feel they've been prodded and poked with strange objects. In Larry's case, he frequently awakens the next day with unexplained nosebleeds and piercings on his body. He admits he has no idea why this happens to him.

Harvard's Mack has his own theories about what's going on. He maintains, for instance, that much of the UFO experience occurs during an altered state of consciousness. "Through near-death experiences or deep meditation, the psyche can be separated from the body and can connect to deeper forces of the universe," he says. Although some may liken this to a spiritual experience, abductions, notes Mack, are unique because they appear to cross from one dimension to another. "What is distinct about UFOs and aliens is that they appear to go beyond a spirit that has no substance and show up as a physical body in the material world," he explains. "This is a problem for our Western mind-set because we are so based on material evidence. If it comes from somewhere else, it is hard for us to accept."

Canadian author John Robert Colombo, who has written three books on UFOs, doesn't doubt that the experiences are genuine—that is, in the person's mind. He points to the work of Laurentian University psychologist Michael Persinger, who has refitted a motorcycle helmet to expose the wearers' brains to a rhythmic bombardment of low-intensity electromagnetic waves. Although the gadget was developed to help people suffering from ailments such as depression and chronic pain, Persinger discovered that the wearers also have unusual visual sensations, like seeing angels. He suggests these experiences may be nothing more than a neurological accident. Epileptics, for instance, tend to have mystical experiences during seizures. What people make of the presence before them, Persinger says, depends on their own beliefs. "Some people may have visions of Mary," adds Colombo. "Others might say it is an alien."

Don't try to tell that to Dorothy Izatt. The 78-year-old great-grandmother from Richmond, B.C., claims to have seen just about everything there is out there. Izatt has met numerous aliens—some are little grey creatures, others are fair-skinned blonds—since she first saw a spaceship in 1974. She's also made more than 500 home movies capturing strange phenomena, and photography experts who have viewed the films say they haven't been doctored. "She happens to have a highly sensitive antenna," explains Lee Pulos, a Vancouver-based clinical psychologist who knows Izatt. "She is still rooted in this reality, but somehow she is able to tune into these extraordinary frequencies that most of us don't even know exist."

Like many others keeping the UFO faith, Izatt thinks extraterrestrials 20
are trying to tell us something: they're deeply concerned about mankind's future. "They're letting us know that we're not evolving," she says. "We have wars and then we forget so we have another war. We were put here to be guardians and keepers of the Earth, to look after it so that it will not die. So far we have failed." No argument there. But to true believers in visitors from the beyond, there's at least comfort in knowing they'll try, try again.

E.T., Check the History Books

Nearly every civilization since the beginning of time has told tales of visitors from space. The ruins of Tiwanacu in Bolivia, for instance, reveal a city fortified by walls made of blocks weighing up to 100 tonnes each. According to some writers, pre-Incan folklore maintained bearded white giants from the stars we now call the Pleiades built the walls in just one night. In the Canaima region of Venezuela, some local indigenous people point to the tabletop mountains, known as tepuis, they believe once ascended to heaven; the mountains were cut off, trapping some aliens on Earth, and their descendants still walk among us.

Then there's an Egyptian creation myth about the age of Tep-Zepi. Long before the pyramids were built (some today believe that they, too, were built with help from the great beyond), sky gods in flying boats came to Earth and raised the land up from under mud and water. And sand paintings by the Dogon of Mali in West Africa reflect the tribe's beliefs that they were once visited by extraterrestrials from the star sign tolo, known today as Sirius. The evidence: although the Dogon had no telescopes or other astronomical equipment, they possessed arcane knowledge about some aspects of the stars and planets.

In Canada, the first documented sighting of what is commonly considered a UFO was in the winter of 1792. David Thompson, a Hudson's Bay Company explorer, and a companion were camped out in an isolated area of what is now Thicket Portage, Manitoba, when they saw a large "mass of jelly" fly through the air and crash to Earth. As Thompson noted in his journal, they failed to find it. But several days later, he reported a second, similar sighting. Judging by the thousands of reported sightings since, the skies over Canada are a busy place.

Assignment Ideas

Reflecting on the ideas from Chapter 3 about audience will be important in responding to the following prompts. While the lure of writing about the supernatural stems from fun or childlike fancy, the topic lends itself to many serious discussions. Thus, you should realize that skepticism prevails in any investigation of the supernatural or paranormal. Do not assume that your audience will believe anything you say. Pay attention to detail, and be willing to scrutinize your own perceptions and desires.

1. Robert Ellis Cahill strongly suggests that the incident the Englishes experienced has supernatural origins. Compare the narrative of this story to something supernatural you might have experienced or a supernatural story a friend told you. Consider your prewriting about rational explanations. What makes more sense in the possible explanations of the Englishes's incident and the one you know about? Be specific about the criteria you used to reach your determination, and develop a thesis about the limits of belief. You might want to refer to the two brief articles about the courthouse ghost on pages 392–394 to see how rationality is used in cases like this.
2. St. Paul, Alberta, Canada, welcomes visitors and cheerfully makes connections to its history of UFO visitations. Many towns might not celebrate their connections to paranormal history. For instance, Danvers, Massachusetts, the town in which the Salem witch trials took place, has only scattered landmarks associated with the many historical and supernatural occurrences that took place in the seventeenth century. The town to its east, Salem, encourages tourism and a belief in its supernatural legacy. Using St. Paul, Salem, or any town that broadcasts connections to religious or other supernatural occurrences that you know of or can find in an Internet search, discuss the possible connection between marketing, profits, and belief. How do they feed into one another? At what point, if ever, is dignity compromised?
3. Do you distinguish between legends and folklore on one hand and the supernatural on the other hand? Why? Choose a legend, and compare it to a specific supernatural event. What characteristics do they have in common, and where do they differ? Theorize about a purpose for the propagation of this legend and the supernatural event. Why does belief persist in one or both, or in one but not the other? Does this shed any light on our culture's conformity to so-called established fact or anything that you pondered concerning the word *imagination*?
4. Do you hold religious beliefs? If so, how are they connected to aspects of the supernatural? Reflect on your freewriting about religion and the supernatural, and expand on your thoughts. Do you consider your religion more valid than a belief in supernatural phenomena? Why? Draw parallels between beliefs in the supernatural and your religion. How does such a comparison make you feel? Generate a thesis that explains or questions why we validate religious belief but remain skeptical about other supernatural phenomena. You might find it useful to consult one of the readings that follows, "Is God in Our Genes?" which investigates religious belief as a possible survival mechanism.

Group Work

Books, magazines, and Internet sources have multiple witness statements about differing types of supernatural occurrences ranging from the Loch Ness Monster to poltergeists. Focus on one supernatural phenomenon, and examine various narrative accounts of its appearance or activity. Establish reliable criteria for evaluating the observations in these published accounts, and scrutinize the claims made by the witness statements. "Talking to Heaven Through Television" (pages 394–404) might give you some clues about how to scrutinize such claims. Speculate about possible alternative explanations for the supernatural phenomenon, remembering to apply critical analysis. Are you comfortable with the conclusion your group reaches? Make sure to include your feelings—your wish to believe or lack thereof—in assessing the materials you find.

Additional Readings

This section follows up on many of the issues discussed in this chapter. Look at the tone and language the writers use. How do the tone and language shape your attitude as a reader? Which writer seems to present his or her critique with the most balance? Why do you think this is the case?

JEFF PARKER

Four Stops on a Bigfoot Hunt

1

We are not two minutes into our hike, the monthly sojourn of the Tri-State Bigfoot Study Group, when travel coordinator Marc Dewerth stops and shushes us. "Listen," he whispers. And because the six mostly average-looking middle-aged white men I'm with take his command so seriously, I do too.

The sound is the wind blowing through the trees, quiet basically. Then an odd groan from somewhere in the hills. Everyone looks at each other. Their eyes grow and grow. They extricate cameras—each researcher carries at least two—from holsters and shirt pockets and point them up and around. Dewerth shushes us again, the noise of cameras distracting him. He doesn't move. You can tell by his squint he's a little annoyed the others don't hike, like him, with cameras at ready.

Nowadays Dewerth keeps his video camera in hand at all times so he doesn't miss the beast ever *again*. If you're near him when he stops like this, and if you're on a Bigfoot hunt, you stop too and try to see what he sees, hear what he hears.

The sound registers once more, clearer this time: a guttural roar. Dew- 5
erth's eyes tighten at the corners.

Admittedly I am a little freaked out by this, having not seriously expected to run across anything. I have done time in woods, and this I've not heard. So I rationalize: this must be a trick. The sound is that weird.

On the way out here, as our minivan trailed a caravan of two other vehicles—one bearing the license plate *Yeti 2*—into the boondocks, past a big red barn with *Sasquatch Valley* painted on the side, I asked Bruce where exactly we were heading.

Bruce is 55. He drives the six hours from Michigan to tromp around the woods outside of Newcomerstown, Ohio, researching Bigfoot. He is an avid reader of *Fate* magazine (a publication that chronicles UFOs and Yetis and Devil Monkeys, among other unexplained phenomena) and proudly boasts that he was born in the very year the magazine was first published. He is a model Bigfoot researcher. In the car he listens to CDs of "vocalization recordings." The creature sounds sometimes like a screaming banshee, sometimes like Yogi Bear. For no apparent reason Bruce is given to proselytize on Bigfoot-related topics, such as the possibility the creature moves through creekbeds: "They say gorillas and chimps are afraid of the water. I believe the Sasquatch is a better swimmer than the average man."

"I don't know where we're hiking today," Bruce replied. The locations of the hikes are always kept secret from him and the other hunters, "in case there's someone who'd try and throw down some bogus tracks or something." So—this is before I understand the true nature of their ritual—maybe they're hoaxing me. You don't bring up hoaxing, I figure, standing there amid this strange bleating, unless you hoax.

10 I'd met Marc Dewerth several months back at the annual Newcomerstown Bigfoot Conference. It's what makes Newcomerstown the Vatican City of Bigfoot research east of the Mississippi. This year it attracted 350 people from all over the world, the biggest gathering of Bigfoot aficionados anywhere. He invited me to come sometime on their monthly hikes, and maybe, just maybe, we'd run across something, he said. I couldn't help but thinking that these hikes were like their Sabbaths, and he was trying to convert me.

This realization excited me because I'd been doubting the concepts of belief and faith in general. I hadn't grown up in a religious household and found myself starting to feel something was missing from my life. I wanted to be converted. I wanted to believe. Not that there aren't certain things I do believe in. Love, for one, I suppose. But then again, love is a far more tactile thing than a Bigfoot. At least you know when love is there in the woods with you. As far as religious faith goes, that's more intimidating, something people work at all their lives. It made sense in a way, to start with something small. Or in this case big.

"What is it?" Bruce asks Dewerth, who is looked up to by researchers much older than him, being the only one in the present company who's actually seen it. In every Bigfoot outfit around the world there's a guy or two who's run into the thing. The Bigfoot researcher equivalent of a hajj pilgrimage to Mecca, but less spiritual; the slots player equivalent of hitting the jackpot, but more spiritual. In any case, he's seen it, so he's the deacon.

"To me that sounds like a coyote," Dewerth suggests. "It doesn't sound like a Bigfoot. It doesn't sound like a primate call."

The group pauses for a moment to consider this.

"Could be an engine," Bruce offers. "It's too regular." 15

"Well, let's see," Dewerth says, and just like that, with doubt cast, he pushes on. Everyone gallops after him.

"Before you step in any soft mud, take a look," Bruce reminds us.

I witness a groundhog barreling through the brush away from us and point it out to Dewerth. "Look," I say. "Groundhog." They don't have groundhogs where I'm from, and they're something to see. Dewerth could not be less impressed. He is more interested in the ubiquitous volume of fresh deer and turkey tracks in the mud, and the fact that we have not and will not see a single deer or turkey today. He points out the density of the woods, how difficult it is to see anything in there. He emphasizes size. The toes on the turkey tracks, some of them—just the toes now—approaching three inches. Even the anthills are big as boulders. "There's all kinds of wildlife out here," he says. "Badgers, bald eagles, turkey vultures. And they grow huge. Some of the biggest deer taken from Ohio come from Coshocton and Muskingum Counties, monsters." Every now and then he mutters to himself about what in the hell that noise was.

2

"Stop!" Dewerth says, crouching slightly. "I just heard something running along that ridge away from us."

We stop and peer ahead. 20

There's an anxious silence. The leaves rustle again. "It's a blue jay," Bruce says.

A Bigfoot hunt is made up of moments like these. False stops. Just enough to get your heart racing, to make it exciting.

Dewerth divvies the group up, which increases the likelihood of a sighting. And when he splits off, I follow him. It's like Bigfootin' with a Steve Irwin, a Crocodile Hunter for Sasquatch. He talks the whole way. You imagine he'd even be talking (to it, to you, to the camera, to himself—just talking) if he ran across it again. *Now this here is a midwestern spotted Bigfoot. Look at him would you. Gorgeous, ain't he!*

He knows his field, though, and narrates with great flair while we search for this elusive of elusives. He explains why the wilds of Ohio are such a hot spot for the creatures, as opposed to the great Northwest and Canada, where they're normally assigned: those monster deer.

"One thing I used to wonder," he says, "is why Bigfoots . . . Bigfeet would live in Ohio. But after thinking about it, it's obvious. The deer aren't controlled naturally, and anything that needs to eat meat is going to come to where the pickings are thick." 25

There is disagreement among Bigfoot researchers on many aspects of their discipline. No one seems 100 percent confident as to how exactly to pluralize the name of their prey, and they switch often between *Bigfoots* and *Bigfeet.* Also, the fact that our journey today isn't a hunt in the true sense highlights a more telling schism. Dewerth and his minions only want to catch the creature on film, in hopes it will convince the mainstream scientific community to pursue it; many others believe the only way to accomplish this is to catch or kill one. In fact, most Bigfooters across the country have converted to the latter goal, partly because the biologists of the world, while they've come a long way the past 30 years in allowing for the possibility the beast exists, refuse to dedicate their research to it until the amateurs come up with a body. Even with a new documentary, *Sasquatch,* aired on Discovery this January detailing all the circumstantial evidence you could hope for (plaster casts of the animal's ass, footprints with nonhuman and nonprimate dermal ridges, blurry videos, petrified Bigfoot dung, indeterminate sound analysis on the spooky vocalizations), without a body or live capture there may never be bona fide scientific research into the Bigfoot phenomenon. Many Bigfooters nowadays carry guns instead of cameras in their holsters. The fact that Dewerth and his crew don't intend to haul the animal before the public puts them on the fringe of the fringe. Despite their claims, they know full well the evidence they're after is the same kind that's been refuted by scientists for years. What's one more footprint with impeccably sampled dermal ridges? What's one more low-resolution video with what could easily be a guy in a gorilla suit? It's as if they're after just enough to justify the continuation of their pilgrimage, just enough to keep alive the possibility. No more.

Dewerth has his Bigfoot Eats Deer Theory refined. The deer hunters have limits. They can only kill so many. The deer thus have no other natural predators, because coyote hunters *can* shoot all the coyotes they want, decimating that population. Also, this area is old mine country. Natural gas and sulfur. When the mining companies cleared out the land, they created meadows where the deer like to bed down. The old mine structures make for ready-made covert Bigfoot shelter.

We meet up with the rest of the group when two trails converge at a crossroads where hulking antique hinged structures grow from the hill, old mining equipment, a natural gas pump like a mini Texas oil well, and some other pumping apparatus with rusted steel doors aswing.

"You guys didn't hear any sounds?" Dewerth asks. "I wonder what the hell that sound was."

The woods out here smell of oil, and the bright orange sulfur water runs in small streams down to the river.

The crew shares granola bars and they talk about things like other people in other groups, clubs you might say, talk about things pertaining to their club when they get together: Dewerth asks Bruce about recent sightings and investigations in Michigan. IRS busts out his Peterson's track guide and scrutinizes a small track in the mud. ("I never seen one with three pads before," he says.) They reminisce about the three-hundred-pound guy they took on a nine-mile Bigfoot hunt at the recent conference. ("He was sweating white foam," Bruce says, "like a horse.")

Rusty, a red-haired disciple of Dewerth's, inspects the steel doors around the pump, which howl as they blow in the wind. He wonders out loud if this could be the culprit, the odd noise we heard earlier.

"It's possible," Dewerth says, his statement setting them all to serious, deliberative nodding.

So we walk away again without any conclusion.

"Wouldn't it be great to employ one of those buzzards as your camera in 35
the sky?" Dewerth says.

"Hey, anybody into falconing?" Bruce asks.

3

"Shshshshshhhhh," Dewerth says, stopping with his arms out at his sides, frozen in skanking position. He cocks his head. There's the sound again. And it's coming from behind us. "I think it's that pump."

There is a pause while his comment is again given its due consideration.

"It's something rhythmically turning, or blowing, like a windmill," Bruce adds.

Says Rusty, "It's those doors we saw—" 40

"Yep!" Dewerth cuts in. This is his careful Bigfoot researcher bit. "That's why I tell people, if you see or hear something unusual, it's just something unusual. We solved it. It's a pump. You'd get some people who'd say it had to be Bigfoot, had to be. And it's a pump."

He leads us on. No one acknowledges that six grown men—myself included— had mistook the sound of a rusty door blowing in the wind for that of a seven-foot man-ape until long after it should have been obvious. No one acknowledges that. We accept the setback and plow on.

"If we brought out a few bottles of Bigfoot testosterone we'd get him out here," IRS says.

IRS introduced himself to me just before the hike. He didn't say "Hello." Instead he stuck out his hand and said, "I'm an IRS agent." By this, he explained, after realizing I hadn't made the connection on my own, he meant that he's naturally suited to anything involving "research and discovery."

At first he seems like the wild-eyed crazy man you'd expect to see on an 45
expedition like this. One minute he's tapping me on the shoulder to say: "I was just kidding about the testosterone by the way. You've seen those 'Animal Encounters' videos where the guy puts the female deer scent on him and the buck about tore his leg off. In 'Nam you couldn't wear any perfume, had to go *au natural*." Then I look at him to see if he's laughing (he's not), and he seems to recognize that I'm looking at him to see if he's laughing. So he qualifies. "I'm a CPA," he says. "I got my feet on the ground. I'm not out chasing ghosts. Got a buddy from high school into multidimensional beings. I don't go for that."

He even reveals that he's not out here today because he expects to see it; he suggests that none of them are. "The number of sightings go far apart, people and the animal just happen to cross paths, just for that fleeting moment. I'm out here because I enjoy being with people who believe in the animal, catching up on new discoveries or rehashing old ones. I have no hope at all of seeing it today . . . But it would be interesting, wouldn't it?"

Dewerth confirms this when he and I split off from the group again. It's more of a gathering prior to the Tri-State Bigfoot Study Group meeting later this evening. (He warns me that that's where I'll meet the real freaks: "They'll tell you the reason we're not finding carcasses is alien ships are beaming them up. *Nooooo.* The reason we don't find them is because nature takes care of its own. Why don't we find them dead? Well . . . cannibalism is common among animals. Food is scarce. If you're hungry you've got to eat what's available, even if it's your own mother. Maybe they bury their dead. Who knows?")

"This is a leisure day," he says.

"Not even a print?" I ask. Dewerth tells me especially not a print. The animal is clever and cunning. It's not going to step into any wet mud and just leave incontrovertible evidence for us. We're more likely to get a sighting than to find a usable print.

50 "It's just so smart," he says. "It may never get caught unless it wants to be."

Dewerth goes on Bigfoot hunts four times a month; once with the group, by himself the other three. He came across the creature on one of these solo hikes in 1997. Most people, when they see it, happen to be alone. It was right in this area, Muskingum County. He was making his way up an incline and looked over at some *thing* with brown fur about thirty-five feet away.

At first he thought it was a bear, then it made its way up the steep hill in four humongous steps. He noticed the foliage shaking around it, as if it was keeping itself between him and something else—its family, he figures. He fumbled to get his camcorder out of his backpack and powered up just as it disappeared into the brush. He pursued it briefly, "until I came to my senses," he says.

The footage doesn't show much more than some shaking bushes. But this sighting is his street cred and also the saving grace of his Bigfoot researcher career. He was becoming disillusioned with the pursuit back then. All the reports coming in to the Eastern Ohio Bigfoot Investigation Center (EOBIC) were turning out to be hoaxes, or people calling—sometimes posing as Bigfoot—to make fun of him. The EOBIC follows up on sightings in eastern Ohio, checks them out, and if they're legitimate, posts them to its website. He criticizes other organizations for posting any reports that come in, no matter how unsubstantiated. He emphasizes that if a sighting is posted on the EOBIC site, someone of his ilk has been to the scene and done some poking around, has sought out the rational explanation, the swinging steel doors on the old pump say, if a rational explanation was to be found.

The sighting was his wake-up call, a renewal of his faith.

55 "Are you a religious man, Marc?" I ask him.

He has always been, he tells me, all his life. But recently his baby daughter died of sudden infant death syndrome, a tragedy that he's not yet come to terms with.

"So I'm at something of a standoff with God right now," he says.

After that we walk in silence awhile. The earlier excitability drains away.

Dewerth breaks the quiet with this word: "Coelacanth." Then he spells it—correctly my dictionary later attests—explaining that it's a fish thought to have been extinct for millions of years until a paleontologist glanced at a picture of two Chinese fisherman holding one. "Of course there's stuff out here we don't know about. Just cause you can't see it don't mean it's not there," he says.

4

There is this one point when Dewerth and I are way up ahead of the others. 60
He walks faster than the rest of them. He says he's happy I'm there to keep up with him. He fancies himself extremely fit, a woodsman of sorts in his matching khaki shorts and tan 2001 Annual Bigfoot Conference tee. But I think it's just that, at thirty-three, he's about a decade younger than most of the other Bigfoot hunters behind us a ways.

Suddenly he stops and points his camcorder into the brush.

"Look at this, Jeff," he says. "Look at this shit. Look at it, would you."

I look briefly to the ground. Just moments ago we'd scrutinized a couple pieces of trail scat. We'd knelt to the ground, the two of us hunched over them. Knowing nothing of trail scat myself I looked to him for illumination. He moved them around with a stick and declared them definitely non-Bigfoot herbivore output. (He hadn't seemed to even notice a bright orange butterfly, the same fantastic orange as the sulfur streams, the orangest butterfly I ever saw, fanning its wings atop the output, fluttering away as he disturbed it.)

He's not being literal this time, though. We are looking at dense deciduous forest in the unglaciated foothills of eastern Ohio. He is turning in circles, his video camera in one of his outstretched palms. Dewerth's point being, best I can tell: we cannot see shit.

"For all we know a Bigfoot could have just squatted down somewhere out there and is right now wondering what these humans are up to," he says, his zoom lens whirring, the foliage obscuring the wild turkey and deer and whatever other creatures might be lurking in there at this very moment, aware of us while we're oblivious to them.

Then he goes and pees off a ravine. He does not even look down but 65
keeps his eyes on the woods.

JEFF CHU, BROWARD LISTON, MAGGIE SIEGER, AND DANIEL WILLIAMS

Is God in Our Genes?

It's not hard to see the divinity behind the water temples that dot the rice terraces of Bali. It's there in the white-clad high priest presiding in the temple at the summit of a dormant volcano. It's there in the 23 priests serving along with him, selected for their jobs when they were still children by a bevy of virgin priestesses. It's there in the rituals the priests perform to protect the island's water, which in turn is needed to nurture the island's rice.

If the divine is easy to spot, what's harder to make out is the banal. But it's there too—in the meetings the priests convene to schedule their planting dates and combat the problem of crop pests; in the plans they draw up to maintain aqueducts and police conduits; in the irrigation proposals they consider and approve, the dam proposals they reject or amend. "The religion has a temple at every node in the irrigation system," says David Sloan Wilson, professor of biology and anthropology at Binghamton University in Binghamton, N.Y. "The priests make decisions and enforce the code of both religion and irrigation."

Ask true believers of any faith to describe the most important thing that drives their devotion, and they'll tell you it's not a thing at all but a sense—a feeling of a higher power far beyond us. Western religions can get a bit more doctrinaire: God has handed us laws and lore, and it's for us to learn and practice what they teach. For a hell-raising species like ours, however—with too much intelligence for our own good and too little discipline to know what to do with it—there have always been other, more utilitarian reasons to get religion. Chief among them is survival. Across the eons, the structure that religion provides our lives helps preserve both mind and body. But that, in turn, has raised a provocative question, one that's increasingly debated in the worlds of science and religion: Which came first, God or the need for God? In other words, did humans create religion from cues sent from above, or did evolution instill in us a sense of the divine so that we would gather into the communities essential to keeping the species going?

Just as a hurricane spins off tornadoes, this debate creates its own whirlwind of questions: If some people are more spiritual than others, is it nature or nurture that has made them so? If science has nothing to do with spirituality and it all flows from God, why do some people hear the divine word easily while others remain spiritually tone-deaf? Do such ivied-hall debates about environment, heredity and anthropology have any place at all in more exalted conversations about the nature of God?

5 Even among people who regard spiritual life as wishful hocus-pocus, there is a growing sense that humans may not be able to survive without it. It's hard enough getting by in a fang-and-claw world in which killing, thieving and cheating pay such rich dividends. It's harder still when there's no moral cop walking the beat to blow the whistle when things get out of control. Best to have a deity on hand to rein in our worst impulses, bring out our best and, not incidentally, give us a sense that there's someone awake in the cosmic house when the lights go out at night and we find ourselves wondering just why we're here in the first place. If a God or even several gods can do all that, fine. And if we sometimes misuse the idea of our gods—and millenniums of holy wars prove that we do—the benefits of being a spiritual species will surely outweigh the bloodshed.

Far from being an evolutionary luxury then, the need for God may be a crucial trait stamped deeper and deeper into our genome with every passing generation. Humans who developed a spiritual sense thrived and bequeathed that trait to their offspring. Those who didn't risked dying out in chaos and killing. The evolutionary equation is a simple but powerful one.

Nowhere has that idea received a more intriguing going-over than in the recently published book *The God Gene: How Faith Is Hardwired into Our Genes* (Doubleday; 256 pages), by molecular biologist Dean Hamer. Chief of gene structure at the National Cancer Institute, Hamer not only claims that human spirituality is an adaptive trait, but he also says he has located one of the genes responsible, a gene that just happens to also code for production of the neurotransmitters that regulate our moods. Our most profound feelings of spirituality, according to a literal reading of Hamer's work, may be due to little more than an occasional shot of intoxicating brain chemicals governed by our DNA. "I'm a believer that every thought we think and every feeling we feel is the result of activity in the brain," Hamer says. "I think we follow the basic law of nature, which is that we're a bunch of chemical reactions running around in a bag."

Even for the casually religious, such seeming reductionism can rankle. The very meaning of faith, after all, is to hold fast to something without all the tidy cause and effect that science finds so necessary. Try parsing things the way geneticists do, and you risk parsing them into dust. "God is not something that can be demonstrated logically or rigorously," says Neil Gillman, a professor of Jewish philosophy at the Jewish Theological Seminary in New York City. "[The idea of a God gene] goes against all my personal theological convictions." John Polkinghorne, a physicist who is also Canon Theologian at England's Liverpool Cathedral, agrees: "You can't cut [faith] down to the lowest common denominator of genetic survival. It shows the poverty of reductionist thinking."

Is Hamer really guilty of such simplification? Could claims for a so-called God gene be merely the thin end of a secular wedge, one that risks prying spirituality away from God altogether? Or, assuming the gene exists at all, could it somehow be embraced by both science and religion, in the same way some evolutionists and creationists—at least the less radicalized ones—accept the idea of a divinely created universe in which evolving life is simply part of the larger plan? Hamer, for one, hopes so. "My findings are agnostic on the existence of God," he says. "If there's a God, there's a God. Just knowing what brain chemicals are involved in acknowledging that is not going to change the fact."

Whatever the merits of Hamer's work, he is clearly the heir of a millen- 10
niums-long search for the wellsprings of spirituality. People have been wrestling with the roots of faith since faith itself was first codified into Scripture. "[God has] set eternity in the hearts of men," says the *Book of Ecclesiastes,* "yet they cannot fathom what God has done from beginning to end."

To theologians in the 3rd century B.C., when *Ecclesiastes* is thought to have been written, that passage spoke to the idea that while all of us are divinely inspired to look for God, none of us are remotely capable of fully comprehending what we are seeking. Scientists in the 21st century may not disagree, provided that "hearts of men" is replaced with "genes of men." The key for those researchers is finding those genes.

Hamer began looking in 1998, when he was conducting a survey on smoking and addiction for the National Cancer Institute. As part of his study, he recruited more than 1,000 men and women, who agreed to take a standardized, 240-question personality test called the Temperament and Character Inventory (TCI). Among the traits the TCI measures is one known as self-transcendence, which consists of three other traits: self-forgetfulness, or the ability to get entirely lost in an experience; transpersonal identification, or a feeling of connectedness to a larger universe; and mysticism, or an openness to things not literally provable. Put them all together, and you come as close as science can to measuring what it feels like to be spiritual. "This allows us to have the kind of experience described as religious ecstasy," says Robert Cloninger, a psychiatrist at Washington University in St. Louis, Mo., and the designer of the self-transcendence portion of the TCI.

Hamer decided to use the data he gathered in the smoking survey to conduct a little spirituality study on the side. First he ranked the participants along Cloninger's self-transcendence scale, placing them on a continuum from least to most spiritually inclined. Then he went poking around in their genes to see if he could find the DNA responsible for the differences. Spelunking in the human genome is not easy, what with 35,000 genes consisting of 3.2 billion chemical bases. To narrow the field, Hamer confined his work to nine specific genes known to play major roles in the production of monoamines—brain chemicals, including serotonin, norepinephrine and dopamine, that regulate such fundamental functions as mood and motor control. It's monoamines that are carefully manipulated by Prozac and other antidepressants. It's also monoamines that are not so carefully scrambled by ecstasy, LSD, peyote and other mind-altering drugs—some of which have long been used in religious rituals.

Studying the nine candidate genes in DNA samples provided by his subjects, Hamer quickly hit the genetic jackpot. A variation in a gene known as VMAT2—for vesicular monoamine transporter—seemed to be directly related to how the volunteers scored on the self-transcendence test. Those with the nucleic acid cytosine in one particular spot on the gene ranked high. Those with the nucleic acid adenine in the same spot ranked lower. "A single change in a single base in the middle of the gene seemed directly related to the ability to feel self-transcendence," Hamer says. Merely having that feeling did not mean those people would take the next step and translate their transcendence into a belief in—or even a quest for—God. But they seemed likelier to do so than those who never got the feeling at all.

15 Hamer is careful to point out that the gene he found is by no means the only one that affects spirituality. Even minor human traits can be governed by the interplay of many genes; something as complex as belief in God could involve hundreds or even thousands. "If someone comes to you and says, 'We've found *the* gene for X,'" says John Burn, medical director of the Institute of Human Genetics at the University of Newcastle in England, "you can stop them before they get to the end of the sentence."

Hamer also stresses that while he may have located a genetic root for spirituality, that is not the same as a genetic root for religion. Spirituality is a feeling or a state of mind; religion is the way that state gets codified into law.

Our genes don't get directly involved in writing legislation. As Hamer puts it, perhaps understating a bit the emotional connection many have to their religions, "Spirituality is intensely personal; religion is institutional."

At least one faith, according to one of its best-known scholars, formalizes the idea of gene-based spirituality and even puts a pretty spin on it. Buddhists, says Robert Thurman, professor of Buddhist studies at Columbia University, have long entertained the idea that we inherit a spirituality gene from the person we were in a previous life. Smaller than an ordinary gene, it combines with two larger physical genes we inherit from our parents, and together they shape our physical and spiritual profile. Says Thurman: "The spiritual gene helps establish a general trust in the universe, a sense of openness and generosity." Buddhists, he adds, would find Hamer's possible discovery "amusing and fun."

The Buddhist theory has never been put to the scientific test, but other investigations into the biological roots of belief in God were being conducted long before Hamer's efforts—often with intriguing results. In 1979, investigators at the University of Minnesota began their now famous twins study, tracking down 53 pairs of identical twins and 31 pairs of fraternal twins that had been separated at birth and raised apart. The scientists were looking for traits the members of each pair had in common, guessing that the characteristics shared more frequently by identical twins than by fraternal twins would be genetically based, since identical twins carry matching DNA, and those traits for which there was no disparity between the identicals and fraternals would be more environmentally influenced.

As it turned out, the identical twins had plenty of remarkable things in common. In some cases, both suffered from migraine headaches, both had a fear of heights, both were nail biters. Some shared little eccentricities, like flushing the toilet both before and after using it. When quizzed on their religious values and spiritual feelings, the identical twins showed a similar overlap. In general, they were about twice as likely as fraternal twins to believe as much—or as little—about spirituality as their sibling did. Significantly, these numbers did not hold up when the twins were questioned about how faithfully they practiced any organized religion. Clearly, it seemed, the degree to which we observe rituals such as attending services is mostly the stuff of environment and culture. Whether we're drawn to God in the first place is hardwired into our genes. "It completely contradicted my expectations," says University of Minnesota psychologist Thomas Bouchard, one of the researchers involved in the work. Similar results were later found in larger twin studies in Virginia and Australia.

20 Other researchers have taken the science in a different direction, looking not for the genes that code for spirituality but for how that spirituality plays out in the brain. Neuroscientist Andrew Newberg of the University of Pennsylvania School of Medicine has used several types of imaging systems to watch the brains of subjects as they meditate or pray. By measuring blood flow, he determines which regions are responsible for the feelings the volunteers experience. The deeper that people descend into meditation or prayer, Newberg found, the more active the frontal lobe and the limbic system become. The frontal lobe is the seat of concentration and attention; the limbic

system is where powerful feelings, including rapture, are processed. More revealing is the fact that at the same time these regions flash to life, another important region—the parietal lobe at the back of the brain—goes dim. It's this lobe that orients the individual in time and space. Take it off-line, and the boundaries of the self fall away, creating the feeling of being at one with the universe. Combine that with what's going on in the other two lobes, and you can put together a profound religious experience.

Even to some within the religious community, this does not come as news. "In India in Buddha's time, there were philosophers who said there was no soul; the mind was just chemistry," says Thurman. "The Buddha disagreed with their extreme materialism but also rejected the 'absolute soul' theologians." Michael Persinger, professor of behavioral neuroscience at Laurentian University in Sudbury, Ont., puts the chemistry argument more bluntly. "God," he says, "is an artifact of the brain."

Even if such spiritual deconstructionism is true, some scientists—to say nothing of most theologians—think it takes you only so far, particularly when it comes to trying to determine the very existence of God. Simply understanding the optics and wiring of the eyes, after all, doesn't mean there's no inherent magnificence in the Rembrandts they allow us to see. If human beings were indeed divinely assembled, why wouldn't our list of parts include a genetic chip that would enable us to contemplate our maker?

"Of course, concepts of God reside in the brain. They certainly don't reside in the toe," says Lindon Eaves, director of the Virginia Institute for Psychiatric and Behavioral Genetics at Virginia Commonwealth University in Richmond. "The question is, To what is this wiring responsive? Why is it there?"

Says Paul Davies, professor of natural philosophy at Macquarie University in Sydney, Australia: "I think a lot of people make the mistake of thinking that if you explain something, you explain it away. I don't see that at all with religious experience."

25 Those religious believers who are comfortable with the idea that God genes are the work of God should have little trouble making the next leap: that not only are the genes there but they are central to our survival, one of the hinges upon which the very evolution of the human species turned. It's an argument that's not terribly hard to make.

For one thing, God is a concept that appears in human cultures all over the globe, regardless of how geographically isolated they are. When tribes living in remote areas come up with a concept of God as readily as nations living shoulder to shoulder, it's a fairly strong indication that the idea is preloaded in the genome rather than picked up on the fly. If that's the case, it's an equally strong indication that there are very good reasons it's there.

One of those reasons might be that, as the sole species—as far as we know—capable of contemplating its own death, we needed something larger than ourselves to make that knowledge tolerable. "Anticipation of our own demise is the price we pay for a highly developed frontal lobe," says Persinger. "In many ways, [a God experience is] a brilliant adaptation. It's a built-in pacifier."

But the most important survival role religion may serve is as the mortar that holds a group together. Worshipping God doesn't have to be a collective thing; it can be done in isolation, disconnected from any organized religion. The overwhelming majority of people, however, congregate to pray, observing the same rituals and heeding the same creeds. Once that congregation is in place, it's only a small step to using the common system of beliefs and practices as the basis for all the secular laws that keep the group functioning.

One of the best examples of religion as social organizer, according to Binghamton University's Wilson, is early Calvinism. John Calvin rose to prominence in 1536 when, as a theologian and religious reformer, he was recruited to help bring order to the fractious city of Geneva. Calvin, perhaps one of the greatest theological minds ever produced by European Christianity, was a lawyer by trade. Wilson speculates that it was Calvin's pragmatic genius to understand that while civil laws alone might not be enough to bring the city's deadbeats and other malefactors into line, divine law might be.

Calvin's catechism included the familiar Ten Commandments—which, 30
with their injunctions against theft, murder, adultery and lying, are themselves effective social organizers. Added to that were admonitions to pay taxes, perform civic duties, behave in a civil manner and submit to the authority of magistrates. "You must understand religions very thoroughly in relation to their environments," says Wilson. "And one problem for Calvin was to make his city function."

The heirs to Calvinism today—Presbyterians, many Baptists and believers in the Reformed tradition in general—see the roots of their faith as something far more divine than merely good civic management. But even some theologians seem to think that a deep belief in the laws of God can coexist with the survival demands of an evolving society. "Calvin had a reverence for the Scriptures, which then became institutionalized," says James Kay, professor of practical theology at the Princeton Theological Seminary. "The Bible is concerned about justice for the poor, equity and fairness, and all of those things were seen to in Calvin's Geneva."

Other struggling cultures have similarly translated godly law into earthly order and in doing so helped ensure their survival. The earliest Christians established a rough institutional structure that allowed them to transmit their ideas within a generation of Christ's death, and as a result succeeded in living through the Roman persecution; the Jews of the Diaspora moved as a cultural whole through the nations of Europe, finding niches wherever they could but maintaining their identity and kinship by observing the same rites. "All religions become a bit secular," says Wilson. "In order to survive, you have to organize yourselves into a culture."

The downside to all this is that often religious groups gather not into congregations but into camps—and sometimes they're armed camps. In a culture of Crusades, Holocausts and jihads, where in the world is the survival advantage of religious wars or terrorism? One facile explanation has always been herd culling—an adaptive way of keeping populations down so that resources aren't depleted. But there's little evolutionary upside to wiping out an entire population of breeding-age males, as countries trying to recover from wars repeatedly learn. Why then do we so often let the sweetness of religion curdle into combat?

The simple answer might be that just because we're given a gift, we don't necessarily always use it wisely. Fire can either light your village or burn down the one next door, depending on your inclination. "Religions represent an attempt to harness innate spirituality for organizational purposes—not always good," says Macquarie University's Davies. And while spiritual contemplation is intuitive, says Washington University's Cloninger, religion is dogmatic; dogma in the wrong hands has always been a risky thing.

Still, for every place in the world that's suffering from religious strife, there are many more where spirituality is doing its uplifting and civilizing work. A God who would equip us with the genes and the smarts to cooperate in such a clever way is a God who ought to be appealing even to religious purists. Nonetheless, sticking points do remain that prevent genetic theory from going down smoothly. One that's particularly troublesome is the question of why Hamer's God gene—or any of the others that may eventually be discovered—is distributed so unevenly among us. Why are some of us spiritual virtuosos, while others can't play a note? Isn't it one of the central tenets of religion that grace is available to everybody? At least a few scientists shrug at the question. "Some get religion, and some don't," says Virginia Commonwealth University's Eaves.

But this seeming inequity may be an important part of the spiritual journey. It would be easy for God simply to program us for reverence; it's more meaningful when the door is opened but you've got to walk through on your own—however hard those steps may be for some. "I have never had a Big Bang conversion experience," says the Jewish Theological Seminary's Gillman. "My sense is that slowly and gradually, out of a rich experience of the world, one builds a faith."

Such experiences may ultimately be at least as important a part of our spiritual tool kit as the genes we're born with. A poor genetic legacy but lucky spiritual circumstances might mean more than good genes and bad experiences. "Fortune includes the possibility of divine grace as well as environmental influences," says Cloninger.

No matter how the two factors balance out, scientists may eventually find that trying to identify the definitive cluster of genes that serves as our spiritual circuit board is simply impossible—like trying to draw a genetic schematic of love. Still, they're likely to keep trying. "I am personally convinced that there is a scheme of things," says Davies of Macquarie University, "that the universe is not just any ragbag of laws." In the end, genes may prove to be a part of that scheme—but clearly one of very many.

ASSOCIATED PRESS

Courthouse Camera Captures a Ghost

Chestertown, Md. (AP)—The word "ghost" is hot on the lips of Kent County Courthouse employees.

A new $75,000 security system installed July 1 hasn't caught any criminals, but it did capture some haunting images of what appears to be a strange light "walking" in one stairwell.

"It didn't show up to the eye, but it showed up on tape," said security officer Phillip Price.

Security personnel first saw the light while looking at a surveillance tape recorded July 29, and it appeared live for more than an hour the next day.

After noticing the light, Mr. Price walked up the stairs and didn't see a thing. But downstairs, where by then a crowd of employees had gathered to watch, the video monitor revealed the strange light moving ahead of Mr. Price, stopping when he stopped and starting when he started.

At one point, those watching the video feed saw Mr. Price walk through the anomaly, they said. That was about the time that Mr. Price said he felt something.

"I felt a real chill, I will tell you that," Mr. Price said.

This time of year, the courthouse stairway is warm and muggy, and Mr. Price said he doesn't have much time for ghosts.

Officials in this Eastern Shore town are still trying to find a scientific explanation for the anomaly, such as dust spots on the camera lens or a malfunctioning battery. A digital copy of the data has been sent to Atlantic Security, the firm that installed the cameras.

Kent County Sheriff John F. Price said he doesn't believe in ghosts.

"There has to be a logical explanation," he said, adding, "I'm keeping an open mind."

Employees said they have seen odd shadows and heard unexplained noises, including the sound of closing doors when no one else was around.

For those who believe in the paranormal, the image on the courthouse security camera is described by the Maryland Ghost and Spirit Association as an "orb," which some believe represents the soul of a person who has died.

If that's true, there could be dozens of explanations, as the courthouse has been the site of executions dating back to 1746. A 1969 expansion was built over a forgotten 19th-century cemetery.

"If it is a ghost, it's a friendly ghost," said Mark Mumford, clerk of the circuit court. "If it's a friendly ghost, it's not hurting me."

ASSOCIATED PRESS

Courthouse Ghost Identified as Insect

Chestertown, Md. (AP)—It turned out to be just a bug on the lens of a security camera. The would-be ghost haunting Kent County Court House is an anomaly that's happened before, a security company said.

On July 29, for a little more than an hour, a courthouse security camera showed a round, translucent, white object that seemed to "walk" up and down a set of stairs inside the newer wing of the courthouse. A security officer first saw the strange light on a delayed video and then live on the video system.

"I've seen it so many times, it's not funny," said Brooke Eyler, general manager of Atlantic Security, which installed the courthouse cameras. "It's definitely a bug."

But a self-proclaimed "ghost investigator" wants to have another look.

5 Beverly Lipsinger, president of the Maryland Ghost and Spirit Association, said the descriptions she's heard don't sound like a bug. But she hasn't seen the video yet for herself.

"It's a ghost," said Lipsinger, a Randallstown resident. "They don't want to believe, so they're coming up with something."

She said she wants to view the video and bring in her "ghost detection equipment," including night vision, temperature gauges and an electromagnetic field detector.

Eyler said he has seen how bugs can be distorted on a lens. He said an insect would appear as a white spot due to the curvature of the lens that is focused on a distant spot.

Part of the courthouse dates to 1860, and the newer half was constructed in 1969 on top of a former cemetery. Some courthouse employees said the anomaly on the video confirmed what they believed—that the courthouse is haunted. They said they have heard strange noises such as doors opening and closing when they were alone in the building.

10 Kent County Sheriff John Price IV said he is satisfied with the technical explanation, which should put the matter to rest.

MATT NISBET

Talking to Heaven Through Television

How the mass media package and sell medium John Edward

When psychic medium John Edward appeared March 6 on CNN's *Larry King Live,* viewers deserved a balanced treatment of his claims, especially considering that the *Larry King Live* guest panel included two skeptics and a rabbi critic. Instead, quantitative and qualitative analysis of the program's transcript indicates that King and his producers offered viewers a carefully controlled and framed promotion of psychic ability.

CNN's *Larry King Live* is just the most recent example of the mass media's package and sale of John Edward and other psychics. Spirit mediums have emerged as top-grossing media personalities, the result of a synergy between recent trends in the media industry, and a likely increased public appetite for "crossing over."

"Gifted" Psychic Showman John Edward

John Edward speaks to dead people, or so he claims. According to the official bio on Edward's website, "John exhibited psychic abilities from an extremely early age, and was deemed 'special' by many in his family." Born and raised in Long Island, apparently no one in Edward's family made a "fuss" over his abilities, as Edward took up the habit of divining family history or events that took place before his birth. After college, Edward worked in the health care industry, and as a dance instructor, but according to his bio "due to the large demand for his time and ability, John now devotes his time to pursuing his psychic work full time."

For Edward, "full-time psychic work" translates into lectures and seminars across the country, and appearances on various afternoon television talk shows where he promotes his books including *One Last Time*, a "non-fiction" treatise on his abilities, and his new novel *What If God Were the Sun?*, an "account of a family that weathers tragedy, bonds together, and passes on healing messages of love from generation to generation."

In July 2000, the Sci Fi Channel premiered *Crossing Over with John* 5
Edward. The typical format for the half-hour program features fast-talking Edward in a darkened amphitheater, surrounded by risers packed with audience members. As various investigators have observed, Edward walks around the enclosure, pointing his attention to different sections of 20 or so audience members at a time, throwing out fast successions of general and random statements like "I'm getting something about a George over here. I don't know what this means. George could be someone who passed over, he could be someone here, he could be someone that you know," and then turning to focus on individuals that respond to Edward's guesswork by nodding their heads, breaking out in tears, or raising their hands in excitement (Shermer 2001).

Edward's psychic shtick is nothing new. He is the latest in a century-and-a-half lineage of full-time flamboyants that have laid claim to spirit communication, ranging from the nineteenth-century rappings of the Fox sisters to present-day media celebrities Rosemary Altea, Sylvia Browne, and James Van Praagh. But what is unique about Edward is that he has emerged as the right kind of psychic, in the right place, at the right time.

Part of Edward's current success may be attributable to an apparent increase in public fascination with spirit communication over the past several years. A Gallup survey conducted in 1996 indicated that 20% of Americans believe that it is possible to communicate with the dead, while another 23% are unsure about the possibility. There is a significant gender difference on the topic, with 24% of women indicating belief in comparison to 16% of men. There are also differences across religious affiliations, as 27% of Catholics believe in spirit communication in comparison to 16% of Protestants and 9% of Jews (Gallup 1996).

"Without a doubt, visiting spirit mediums is becoming amazingly popular," author Cathy Cash Spellman told the *New York Times* last October (La Ferla 2000). Spellman's novel *Bless the Child,* about a girl with psychic abilities, was released as a film with the same title by Paramount this past fall. Panned by critics, the film grossed a disappointing $30 million. *Bless the Child,* however, was the second major film featuring psychic mediums over the past two years. Walt Disney's *Sixth Sense,* starring Bruce Willis as a child psychologist who administers to a boy traumatized by visions of dead people, grossed an extraordinary $300 million in 1999.

Spellman attributes spirit medium popularity to a growing public embrace of the New Age. "We live in a world where many people have an acupuncturist, understand that there is energy, and practice the martial arts. People are so much more open minded about the unseen" (La Ferla 2000).

While a trend among the general American public is difficult to assess because of an absence of relevant polling data gathered since 1996, some observe that spirit mediumship has captured the fascination of the trendy urban elite. "Quite a lot of people in the fashion world are paying visits to people they have lost," Nadine Johnson, a New York publicist, told the *New York Times.* "I wouldn't call it booming, but it's harder to get appointments with mediums these days, so you know the business has increased tremendously. To hear it from the people I know, mediums are a hotter commodity than the Prada bowling bag" (La Ferla 2000).

So what is it about Edward that allows him to capitalize on a possible growing public appetite for his claimed abilities over other more established psychic mediums? For one, Edward as television show host holds certain personality and stylistic traits that lend advantages over contemporaries Van Praagh and Browne. Edward exhibits greater personal and physical charisma than the rotund and twitchy Van Praagh. He also doesn't attempt the arcane mysticism that typifies Browne. Instead, Edward offers audiences a brand of psychic "street smarts." To get a sense of his appeal, imagine a Brooklyn taxi cab driver who can channel your dead relatives. Or as one journalist observed of Edward's *Crossing Over* routine, "He's like a psychic short-order cook, barking out personal messages then moving on to the next person" (Brown 2001).

In terms of technique differences between Edward and Van Praagh, one critic estimates Van Praagh's hit rate at between 20 to 30 percent, while Edward only scores 10 to 20 percent of the time. What Edward lacks in accuracy, however, he makes up for in sheer volume of guesses. After a recent analysis conducted in conjunction with *ABC News,* the consulting skeptic wrote in an email commentary that "the advantage Edward has over Van Praagh is his verbal alacrity. Van Praagh is Ferrari fast, but Edward is driving an Indy-500 racer. In the opening minute of the first reading captured on film by the ABC camera, I counted over one statement per second (ABC was allowed to film in the control room under the guise of filming the hardworking staff, and instead filmed Edward on the monitor in the raw). Think about that—in one minute Edward riffles through 60 names, dates, colors, diseases, conditions, situations, relatives, and the like" (Shermer 2001).

Appearing five days a week, the Sci Fi Channel's *Crossing Over* follows on the success of the television talk-show format that includes programs like *Oprah, Leeza, Sally,* and *Montel,* all of which have packaged and sold New Age self-help. *Crossing Over* also mimics the more recent success of unscripted television programs like MTV's *The Real World* and CBS's *Survivor.*

For the producers of *Crossing Over,* the situation is ideal. Edward is the only actor on the payroll, the producers don't have to worry about employing writers, and they don't have to hassle with booking guests.

Since its premiere, *Crossing Over* has increased Sci Fi Channel ratings 33% over the same time period for the previous year, to a daily average of 533,000 households. The program is also attracting more female viewers to the network's traditionally male-dominated audience. While women generally make up 45% of the network's audience, *Crossing Over's* audience is comprised of 60% women (Brown 2001).

The popularity of *Crossing Over,* combined with Edward's well-oiled publicity machine, and the corresponding media attention across entertainment and news media outlets have made Edward's *One Last Time* a national best-seller. In order to measure a possible correlation between media coverage of Edward and sales of his book, I ran the keywords "John Edward" and "psychic or medium" through the Lexis-Nexis Universe database. My search identified for the past year the population of articles featuring Edward that appeared in major U.S. newspapers, and the population of relevant transcripts from major national television news programs, talk shows, or large media market local newscasts. The results provide an indicator of the amount of

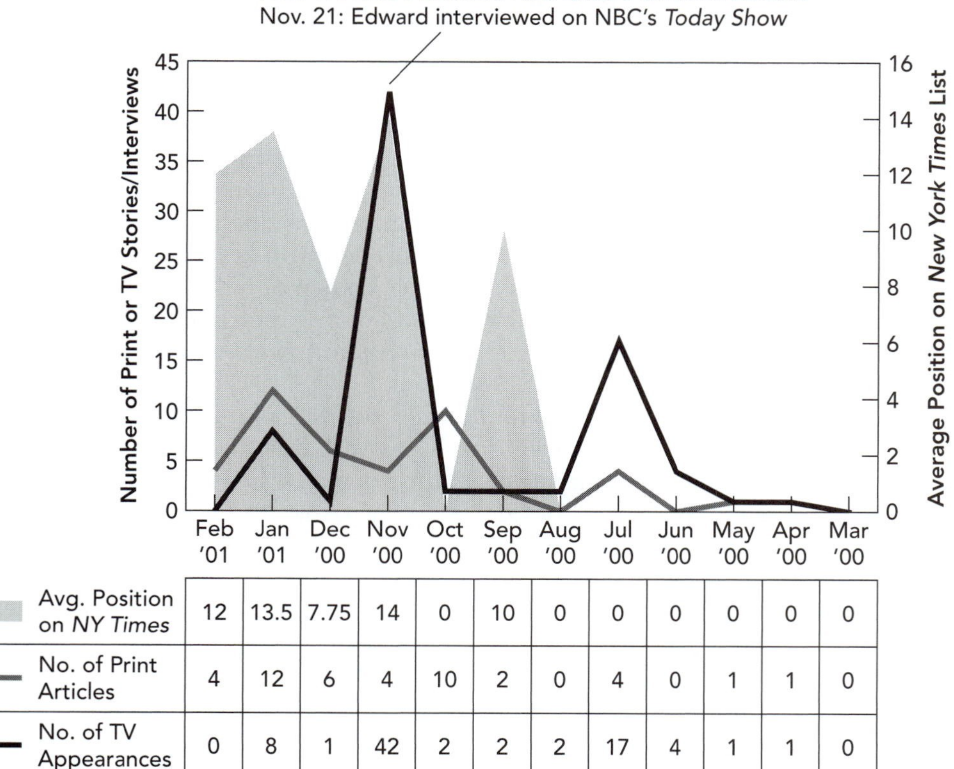

Avg. Position on *NY Times*	12	13.5	7.75	14	0	10	0	0	0	0	0	0
No. of Print Articles	4	12	6	4	10	2	0	4	0	1	1	0
No. of TV Appearances	0	8	1	42	2	2	2	17	4	1	1	0

Figure 1. Relationship Between Media Coverage of John Edward and Sales of *Crossing Over*

media attention to Edward across time. I also tallied the average position for each month that Edward's *One Last Time* appeared on the *New York Times'* weekly paperback non-fiction bestseller list, providing a less precise, indirect measure of book sales.

Figure 1 indicates that a spike in Edward's media profile over the past year precedes each of *One Last Time's* sales jumps. For example, after an increase in both print and television attention in July 2000, *One Last Time* appeared on the *New York Times* bestseller list for the first time. Later, after a major media blitz during the month of November, including appearances by Edward on NBC's *Today Show,* CBS's *Early Show,* and NBC's *Dateline, One Last Time* jumped for the month of December to its highest best-seller position to date. The pattern of increased media attention preceding a jump on the best-seller list occurred again for the months January to February 2001.

Journalist-Skeptic Leon Jaroff

John Edward's emergence on the public and media agenda has not gone without strong criticism from skeptics. Over the past two years, both Paul Kurtz (2000) and Joe Nickell (1998a; 1998b) of the Committee for the Scientific Investigation of Claims of the Paranormal (CSICOP) have critiqued Edward and other psychic mediums in articles published in *Skeptical Inquirer* magazine, and in press releases or public statements. In covering Edward, however, many mass media reporters have either favored the norm of "journalistic balance" in their coverage, or have honored the American media tradition of uncritical coverage of topics related to religion. The result has been a serious failure on the part of journalists to question Edward's claims.

Enter veteran science writer Leon Jaroff. "Clairvoyants who claim to communicate with the dead—and warnings not to listen to them—go back at least as far as the Old Testament, yet psychics continue to flourish in back parlors and storefronts across America," wrote Jaroff in his lead to a March 6 *Time* magazine feature. "None today is better known or more listened to than John Edward, a fast-talking former ballroom-dancing instructor who is cleaning up on his proclaimed ability 'to connect with energies of people who have crossed over.' Died, that is" (Jaroff 2001).

Jaroff is one of America's senior science journalists. Named *Time* magazine's chief science reporter in 1969, Jaroff has won numerous awards for coverage ranging from space exploration to anthropology. In 1980, Jaroff became the founding managing editor of *Discover* magazine, and like many science writers of his generation, he exhibits in his reporting a strong enthusiasm and appreciation for the scientific paradigm. A long-time fellow of CSICOP and friend of magician James Randi, Jaroff has reported on several controversies related to the paranormal and the pseudoscientific, including Randi's efforts to expose psychic Uri Geller.

20 Therefore, for Jaroff, Edward's performances were less than remarkable, and merited critical coverage. In the *Time* magazine article, Jaroff explained Edward's "psychic" success as a likely result of two very earthly techniques. First, there was the old fortuneteller's technique of "cold reading," a succes-

sion of quick generalizations about individual audience members made by Edward that were meant to elicit a response, followed by a series of educated guesses based on demographics. Second, there was what Jaroff referred to as a "hot reading," a variation on the cold reading in which the medium takes advantage of information surreptitiously gathered in advance. (For a full discussion of cold reading techniques, see Hyman 1977.)

In support of his assertions of Edward's possible hot readings, Jaroff detailed the experience of Michael O'Neill, a past audience member on *Crossing Over* who had been the subject of a reading by Edward. According to O'Neill's account, producers of the show had spliced into the final program clips of O'Neill nodding yes into the videotape after statements by Edward with which he remembers disagreeing. In addition, according to O'Neill, most of Edward's "misses," both in relation to him and other audience members, had been edited out of the final tape.

O'Neill also claimed that before the show, assistants to the producers had gathered information about audience members, including their names and family histories. O'Neill also told Jaroff that most of the conversations among the audience while they were seated in the stands waiting for the start of the show were about dead loved ones, information that could have been picked up by microphones strategically placed about the amphitheater.

As he notes in his article, Jaroff did not include in his article reaction from Edward, since upon contacting Edward's publicity people, Jaroff was informed that the medium does not respond to criticism.

The Psychics, the Philosopher, the Rabbi, the FBI Agent, and the Maverick Scientist

With Jaroff's article appearing in *Time* magazine, the stage was set for the March 6 edition of CNN's *Larry King Live*. Host Larry King has long been a promoter of psychic mediums, in recent years providing hour-long platforms for both James Van Praagh and Sylvia Browne.

King's failure in previous programs to include guests who could provide a scientific rebuttal to the psychic's claims has enraged many skeptics. Last year, CSICOP's Kurtz and Nickell sent a protest letter to King, provoking an angry response by telephone from the show's producers. Besides Larry King's preference for all things psychic, other factors likely contributed to the decision to air a special program on Edward. Jaroff's article provided an opportune moment for parent company AOL/Time Warner to promote both the company's flagship magazine and the longest running talk show on its leading television network. The line-up of guests and the ultimate format for the March *Larry King Live* program was subtly stacked against criticism of Edward. In his Los Angeles studio, King sat at his desk with Van Praagh and Browne, while Edward was interviewed via satellite hook-up from the CNN studio in New York City. Jaroff appeared via satellite from Boca Raton, while CSICOP chair and philosopher Paul Kurtz was interviewed via feed originating from Buffalo, New York. On satellite from London, England, the panel also included Rabbi Shmuley Boteach, author of various self-help books including

Table 1. Shared Publishers Among Edward, Van Praagh, Browne, and Boteach*

Author	Books Published by Penguin Putnam	Books Published by Signet	Books Published by Hay House
John Edward	*One Last Time* (2000)		*What If God Were the Sun?* (2001)
James Van Praagh	*Talking to Heaven* (1998)	*Reaching to Heaven* (2000)	
Sylvia Browne		*The Other Side and Back* (2000)	*Adventures of a Psychic* (1998) *God, Creation, and Tools for Life* (2000)
Shmuley Boteach w/ Deepak Chopra			*Integrating the Masculine and Feminine in the Spiritual Traditions of Judaism and Vedanta* (2001)

*Source: Amazon Books

Kosher Sex: A Recipe for Passion and Intimacy, and the forthcoming *The Psychic and the Rabbi: A Remarkable Correspondence,* co-authored with psychic Uri Geller and spiritual guru Deepak Chopra.

25 Boteach appeared on the program supposedly to present criticism from the perspective of a traditional religious leader, while Van Praagh and Browne were framed by King as an unbiased jury of Edward's "psychic" peers, able to objectively attest to the legitimacy of Edward's abilities. In reality, however, all three individuals have economic ties to Edward's success, as they all share a book publisher with Edward. Table 1 outlines the publishing links between Edward, Van Praagh, Browne, and Boteach.

Making a cameo appearance on the program was physicist Dale Graff, author of two books recounting his version of the CIA's attempt to use psychic "remote viewing" for spy purposes. Also appearing in a cameo role was Clint Van Zandt, a former FBI profiler able to offer first-hand familiarity with Bureau and police agency use of psychics to assist in crime solving.

Throughout the hour-long program, the in-studio, "stage center" presence of Browne and Van Praagh allowed the duo to dominate the program's dialogue. Both psychics took turns interrupting other guest's comments or reframing responses. Van Praagh appeared well-coached and practiced in his comments, while Browne, with a seat next to King, was able to maintain a visible screen presence throughout the program, often lowering her head as if in meditation, or frequently closing her eyes, cultivating a persona of mysticism for the studio cameras.

Larry King played the role of stage master, carefully controlling and managing commentary from Kurtz, Jaroff, and Boteach. If Van Praagh and Browne were stage center on *Larry King Live,* the other guests, including Edward, were side stage shows only to be revealed when King directed questions their way.

In order to measure the "talk time" allocated each guest, I analyzed the full text of the transcript of the television program using CATPAC, a software package developed by communication researchers at the State University of New York at Buffalo for use in quantitative content analysis. As an indicator of a guest's "talk time," I tallied the number of words spoken by each guest during the program. The total number of words for each guest can be considered a function of the individual's verbal speed, the number of opportunities to offer commentary afforded by King's questions, and the time allocated by King for a response.

Not surprisingly, Table 2 indicates that at 2,244 words spoken, Larry 30
King dominated the program, accounting for 26.3% of the total talk time. The three psychics combined for 36.6% of the total talk time on the program, in comparison to just 13.8% of the talk time afforded the two skeptics. The disparity was a likely result of the nearly twice as many questions asked by King of the psychics (34) than of the skeptics (18). The disparity may have also been caused by Van Praagh's and Edward's talent for quick speech, and Larry King's tendency to cut in on answers by either Jaroff or Kurtz. King's management of responses by guests and the impact of the fast-talking mediums are reflected by the measure of average number of words spoken per question asked, with "Ferrari-fast" Edward (153.3) and almost-as-quick Van Praagh (80.4), able to get more out of their allocated time on camera than either Kurtz (68.4) or Jaroff (62.4).

In addition to comparing the time allocated to each guest's perspective and input on the topic of psychic ability, I also used CATPAC to provide an indicator of the major themes that each guest emphasized. Table 3 indicates the most frequently used unique words for each of the seven guests and Larry King. The prominence of each individual's themes was measured by assigning a coefficient equal to the individual's percentage of talk time contributed to the program.

As host, King emphasized themes of "belief," the impact and import of the *Time* magazine "article," what "people" "think," "psychics," and aspects of "know"-ledge or certainty about the veracity of the psychic's claims. At a prominence coefficient of .26, King's themes carried greater weight than any other individual guest.

The psychics emphasized "people," but concentrated mostly on transcendental themes of emotions, "spirituality," "God," and "energy." The three psychics also highlighted the type of service that they promote, namely general "information" about "somebody" or "something." Combined, the prominence coefficient of the psychic's themes was a dominant .37.

Skeptics Kurtz and Jaroff emphasized themes of "reason," "science," "evidence," "testing," or "challenge" of claims, and what "people" might believe or "think." At a combined prominence coefficient of .14, the skeptics' themes

Table 2. Distribution of "Talk Time" Across Guests, Number of Questions Asked, and Average Length of Answer per Question*

Individual	"Talk Time" as Number of Words Spoken	Percentage of Total "Talk Time"	Number of Questions Asked by King	Average Words Spoken per Question
Larry King	2,244	26.3%	NA	NA
Psychic Mediums				
James Van Praagh	1,045	12.3%	13	80.4
John Edward	1,533	17.9%	10	153.3
Sylvia Browne	574	6.7%	11	52.2
Psychics (Total)	3,152	36.6%	34	92.7
Skeptics				
Leon Jaroff	616	7.2%	9	68.4
Paul Kurtz	562	6.6%	9	62.4
Skeptics (Total)	1,178	13.8%	18	65.4
Others				
Shmuley Boteach	1,037	12.2%	8	129.6
Clint Van Zandt	546	6.4%	1	546.0
Dale Graff	368	4.4%	2	184.0
Total	8,525	100%	63	99.7

*Note: Estimate of the average words spoken per question is approximate since part of the "total words spoken" for several guests is also accounted for by remarks that may not have been in direct response to a question by King. The "total" program estimate of average words spoken per question was calculated by dividing the total words spoken by guests only (6,281) by the total number of questions asked by King (63).

comprised a minority perspective on the show, and were almost three times less prominent than the psychic perspective.

While the skeptics offered criticism from a scientific viewpoint, Rabbi Boteach framed his criticism in the light of Judaism. He emphasized "religion" and "God" while highlighting the religious "elitism" of mediums promoting themselves as self-proclaimed chosen ones able to "communicate" with God. Boteach also emphasized "ethics" and a naturalistic spiritualism based on "earth," not in an "afterlife" or heaven. At a prominence coefficient of .12, Boteach's themes were only slightly less than the combined prominence of the two skeptics. FBI agent Van Sant emphasized that he was "open" to the possibility of psychic ability. He also highlighted his "experience" in police

Table 3. Individual Thematic Messages as Measured by Frequently Used Unique Words/ Prominence of Themes Based on Percentage of Talk Time*

Individual	Themes	Prominence of Themes
Larry King	believe; article; people; dead; psychic(s); know	.26
Psychic Mediums		
James Van Praagh	people; something; know; information; love; better; destroy; feel; God; spirit; hearing; understand; Earth	.12
John Edward	know; show; people; think; something; somebody; belief; energy; sense; dead	.18
Sylvia Browne	know; want; God; bible/biblical	.07
Psychics (Total)	NA	.37
Skeptics		
Leon Jaroff	think; people; believes; fact; reason; challenge; show;	.07
Paul Kurtz	claim(s); evidence; people; think; facts; extraordinary; science/scientific	.07
Skeptics (Total)	NA	.14
Others		
Shmuley Boteach	think; earth; God; religion; psychics; believe; communicate/ing; elitist; afterlife; goodness; people; ethical	.12
Clint Van Zandt	psychic; enforcement; law; experience; information; FBI; help; open; kidnapped; victim	.06
Dale Graff	phenomena; program; real; work; data; remote viewing; research; community	.04

*Note: The prominence of themes was assessed by assigning each individual's emphasized themes a coefficient equal to their proportion of talk time.

work, and his acceptance of psychic involvement in crime cases if it could "help" law enforcement efforts. Physicist Graff emphasized his "experience" working on the CIA "remote viewing" project, the general reaction of the scientific "community," and his belief that the "data" supported the claim that psychic ability was "real." As cameo guests on the program, the prominence coefficients of the themes emphasized by Van Sant and Graff were negligible at .06 and .04, respectively.

Eternal Life Through Syndication and Spin-off

Despite the appearance of balance in the guest line-up for *Larry King Live,* the analysis of the program's transcript presented here indicates that King and his psychic guests heavily dominated the hour-long debate, both in total "talk time," and in regard to the emphasis on themes highlighting the transcendental over the scientific or critical.

For television producers, spirit mediums are a new form of staged drama, able to capture audiences at a relatively low cost. *Crossing Over with John Edward* is already headed for syndication (Brown 2001), and based on the program's ratings, it doesn't take a psychic to predict that other television studios will attempt to mimic its success.

Sources

Brown, Ivy. 2001. "Hearing from dearly departed proves a hit on SciFi Channel." *Los Angeles Times,* March 5.

Gallup Organization. 1996. Phone survey taken September 3–6. Data archived at the Roper Center for Public Opinion Research, University of Connecticut–Storrs.

Hyman, Ray. 1977. "Cold reading: How to convince strangers that you know all about them." *Skeptical Inquirer* 1: 2 (Spring/Summer), 18–37.

Jaroff, Leon. 2001. "Talking to the dead." *Time,* March 6.

Kurtz, Paul. 2000. "The new paranatural paradigm: Claims of communicating with the dead." *Skeptical Inquirer* 24:6 (November/December) 27–31.

La Ferla, Ruth. 2000. "A voice from the other side." *New York Times,* Oct. 29.

Nickell, Joe. 1998a. "Review: Talking to heaven—Who's answering?" *Skeptical Inquirer* 22: 4 (July/August), 51.

Nickell, Joe. 1998b. "Investigating spirit communications." *Skeptical Briefs* 8: 3 (September).

Shermer, E. 2001. "Deconstructing the dead: Cross over one last time to expose medium John Edward." E-Skeptic. Archived at http://www.skeptic.com/.

CHAPTER 14

HUMOR

Overview

Is laughter the best medicine? Certainly, we all love to laugh. Whether or not scientific evidence supports the healing effects of laughter, we seem to be cheerier and livelier after seeing a comedy act, recounting old stories with friends, or watching televised satires of the day's news. What produces laughter, though? What constitutes humor? We differentiate between funny and not-so-funny, between tired gags and fresh material, but have we ever stopped to think about how we make these distinctions?

As an undergraduate, I took several literature courses from a professor who used humor effectively. Dr. Lane combined sarcasm with clever observations about humanity, making his humor relevant to our reading. Yet, he was also sensitive to the plight of others and could make stinging critiques about sexism and war. I was never confused about when he meant to be funny and when he meant to be serious.

In the last course I took from Dr. Lane, a student in the back row tried to match wits with him. During every class, or so it seemed, this student cracked jokes or punned based on remarks Dr. Lane made. The student was not disruptive or disrespectful, but his attempts at humor never received more than some smiles or light chuckles. His jokes stunk. I consistently felt embarrassed for him and wanted to laugh just to relieve the tension. His sense of humor just did not match my own or, apparently, anyone else's. Dr. Lane started making jokes in response, trying to rescue some sort of humor in the student's failed witticisms, but other students started groaning at the

This icon will direct you to web links and additional resources on the website college.hmco.com/pic/thelin1e

exchanges. Dr. Lane eventually steered the class back to the original conversation and tried to avoid embarrassing the student. It seemed, though, that Dr. Lane called on the student less and less.

Toward the end of the semester, it occurred to me that the student's failed humor came not from a lack of cleverness but rather from a limited sense of his audience. In other words, the rest of us in the class did not share his viewpoints. In another context, he might have been very funny.

In one of Dr. Lane's classes, we discussed Carolyn Forché's prose poem, "The Colonel." Forché recounts the terror she felt at a Latin American colonel who showed her the severed ears of his human victims, shook one of the ears in Forché's face, and placed the ear in a glass of water—all while Forché sat at his table immediately after having dined with him. Hearing this, we were horrified and could feel her fear for her own safety. The student who thought he was funny quipped, as I remember the remark, "Bet she didn't have dinner there again." His words might have been greeted with laughter in a different context, but he had seriously misjudged his immediate audience's sympathy for Forché's situation. Forché was not a character or caricature we needed to laugh at to distance ourselves from the unpleasantness of the situation. The student, therefore, came across as being insensitive or worse.

An attempt at humor that extended the cruelty of the colonel to ridiculous extremes, or that understated his crudeness to the point of absurdity, or that cut him down in some way might have worked. In such a joke, we would have seen sensitivity toward a basic code of right and wrong, and it would have lightened a grim moment. We can see an attempt in the student's joke to intentionally misunderstand the situation to reveal how ludicrous the dinner table scene actually must have been. But Forché's persona in the poem did not lend itself to ridicule of her actions unless we had a viewpoint, as perhaps the student did, that she was naïve or foolish for having dinner with the colonel.

Humor does not have to have underlying sensitivity to succeed, but the audience must perceive the target of the joke as deserving of scorn or ridicule. Successful comedians understand dominant ideology. By this I mean that they understand assumptions that are shared by the majority of the audience members. When people accuse a comedian of telling "tasteless" jokes, that comedian has, essentially, misunderstood the audience's assumptions, as discussed in Chapter 3. Of course, some comedians thrive on offensive humor—but so do their particular audiences.

The dearth of comedy routines about the terrorist attacks in New York and Washington, D.C., on September 11, 2001, is an example of understanding assumptions. No comedians tried to lighten the mood with jokes about the victims, the firefighters and police officers who rescued victims or became victims themselves, or affected family members. Few audiences would have seen these people as deserving of scorn and ridicule. Instead, jokes revolved around what was going to happen to the perpetrators, around the ethnicity of the hijackers, and, eventually, around criticism of the government's handling of the situation. The ideology behind patriotism imposed limits on humor.

If humor is linked to ideology, does humor reflect what society deems acceptable? How might humor reveal the dominant tensions in our culture?

Many of us might not want to expose these hidden implications of humor. Yet, the connection exists. While juvenile bathroom humor reflects the tensions of adolescence, we can also see how natural functions of the body, such as flatulence and sexual stimulation, have been stigmatized in our culture so that they seem unnatural. In this type of humor, we can see the tension between appropriate societal behavior—not mentioning bodily functions—and what is apparent to every human being—how our bodies work. The tension produces the laughter.

Comedians often make use of political tensions. Audiences seem to gain power from satire over dominant political discourse. Political comedians express publicly repressed angers and show the absurdity of decision making at the highest levels of government.

The Daily Show, for example, a parody of daily news shows, magnifies the inconsistencies in government leaders' speeches to poke fun at political figures as well as to make a point. In December 2006 there was much division in the government about withdrawing troops from Iraq. On December 4, Jon Stewart, the host of *The Daily Show,* engaged in a dialogue with the show's "senior foreign policy analyst," John Oliver, to supposedly interpret the president's strategy for the direction of the war. Oliver exaggerated the implications in President Bush's speeches by saying that Bush believed in fighting until the last possible second, "giving armed conflict every chance to succeed until all violent means have been utterly exhausted." Only then, according to Oliver, would Bush give "the grim task of talking" a chance. The segment was funny to those frustrated with the direction of the war and needing an outlet.

Many jokes that circulate on the Internet use gender and race. While the gender jokes sometimes center on crude sexual innuendo, many of them seek humor by exploiting gender stereotypes. Women forward lists of behaviors supposedly common to married men, such as leaving underwear everywhere but in the hamper. Men forward lists of the ten things married women do not need but stereotypically crave, such as twenty pairs of shoes. We seem to be able to laugh at ourselves in these caricatures. Do they suggest a truth or a conflict that we wrestle with? Race-based jokes, which often mock stereotypical attributes, evoke a different level of discomfort. An audience's involuntary laughter at such jokes shows an understanding of the stereotypes, but how much deeper does the understanding go? Does the audience unconsciously accept that a certain ethnic group is deserving of scorn or ridicule?

To analyze humor means to take a hard look at our beliefs and conduct. Why do some people find redneck jokes funny? Do the jokes not hinge on the poverty and struggles for dignity many working-class people endure? Jokes about blonde women should make us question why people need to see others as stupid. Gags about nerds should likewise make us wonder about our values and our need to conform to the standards of certain cliques. Humor based on obesity or other perceived physical defects could be a sign of how deeply media-generated images of beauty have corrupted our sensitivity to differing understandings of attractiveness. Perhaps we deflect some of our inner fears by targeting others.

No matter what conclusions we arrive at, humor cannot be considered innocent. While we need to laugh, our view of the world directs what we laugh at.

Openings for Writers

1. **Comedians** Identify comedians you find especially funny. Write about a routine by one of these comedians that exemplifies his or her humor. What was the subject matter in the routine? Can you identify a targeted group of people? If you saw the performance live or on film, how did the audience react?
2. **Puns** What is a pun? Do you ever find puns funny? Describe what a pun is, give examples of a few puns, and consider what makes them funny or unfunny. How does your reaction to puns reflect your sense of humor and even your worldview?
3. **Teaching and humor** Reflect on some of the best classroom experiences you can remember that involved humor. Do you distinguish between teachers who share humor with a class and teachers who use humor at the expense of students? Support your answer with specific examples. It might help to look at David Sedaris's "Me Talk Pretty One Day" (page 422) to see an example of a teacher who belittles her adult students with sarcasm.
4. **Humor and tragedy** Some people believe that the passing of time allows us to start laughing at incidents that were not funny when they occurred. At what point can you start making jokes about a painful or traumatic event? Have you had uncomfortable moments when you wanted to laugh at another person's misfortune? What happened, and how did both of you feel? Would your reactions have been more appropriate if they had come later?

Language

1. **Ridicule** What criteria do you associate with the term *ridicule?* Can you differentiate ridicule from humor? Are they related?
2. **Crudeness** What values do we as a community hold that allow us to designate some humor as crude and other humor as "clean"? In the overview's use of this term, do you sense any lines that a writer won't cross? If so, what are those lines, and how do they affect the writer's main ideas? If not, how does the designation of some humor as crude function in the other observations in the overview?
3. **Satire** Do you associate satire with political bias? Does it always function to critique or to undermine power? How does it differ from ridicule?
4. **Stereotypes** The word *stereotype* has negative connotations for most people. Describe these connotations. Can the word ever be viewed in a positive light? We all have seen connections between stereotypes and humor. What makes comedians' use of stereotypes acceptable and, at times, successful?

JOYCE CAROL OATES

Is Laughter Contagious?

This short story asks us to question the appropriateness and inappropriateness of certain types of social behavior, including laughter. Mrs. Delahunt tries to suppress giggling and chortles during a series of situations in which laughter might be seen as cruelty. Her lack of tact at the end and the readers' reaction raises issues about humor and its human targets.

Is laughter contagious? Driving on North Pearl Street, Franklin Village, Mrs. D. began suddenly to hear laughter on all sides, a wash of laughter gold-spangled like coins, just perceptibly louder issuing from the rear of her car, and she found herself smiling, her brooding thoughtful expression erased as if by force, on the verge of spontaneous laughter herself, for isn't there a natural buoyancy to the heart when we hear laughter? even, or particularly, the laughter of strangers? even an unexpected, inexplicable, mysterious laughter?—though Mrs. D. understood that the laughter surrounding her was in no way mysterious, at least its source was in no way mysterious, for, evidently, she had forgotten to switch off the car radio the last time she had driven the car, and the laughter was issuing from the radio's speakers, the most powerful of which was in the rear of the Mercedes.

What were they laughing about, these phantom radio-people?

Men's laughter?—and, here and there, the isolated sound of a woman's higher-pitched laughter?—delicious, cascading, like a sound of icicles touching?

Though laughing by this time herself, Mrs. D., who was a serious person, with a good deal on her mind—and most of it private, secret, not to be shared even with Mr. D.—switched the radio off, preferring silence.

There. 5

Christine Delahunt. Thirty-nine years old. Wife, mother. Recently returned to work—a "career." A woman of moral scruples, but not prim, puritanical, dogmatic. Isn't that how Mrs. D. has defined herself to herself? Isn't Mrs. D., in so defining herself, one of us?—determined, for no reason we can understand, to define ourselves to—ourselves?

As if we doubt that anyone else is concerned?

Mrs. D. was to tell us, certain of her friendly acquaintances. Last Thursday it seemed to begin. Did others in Franklin Village notice—that afternoon, sometime before six o'clock? The time of suburban car-errands, family-tasks, last-minute shopping, and pickups at the dry cleaners and drugstore, the pace of the waning day quickening, yes and Thursday is the day-preceding-Friday, when the week itself notoriously quickens, a panic-sensation to it, as a river seemingly placid and navigable begins to accelerate, visibly, as it approaches a cataract—though there is, yet, no clear sign of danger? no reason for alarm?

10 Outbursts of laughter. Gay infectious laughter. In the Franklin Food Mart, our "quality" grocery store, at one of the checkout counters when the deaf-and-dumb packer wearing the badge FRITZ (pasty-skinned, in his fifties; the Franklin Food Mart is one of several area businesses that have "made it a policy" to employ the handicapped) spilled a bag of fresh produce onto the floor, and Washington State winesaps, bright-dyed Florida navel oranges, hairy-pungent little kiwi-fruit, several pygmy-heads of Boston lettuce, a dozen Idaho red potatoes, a single California melon—all went tumbling, rolling, startling yet comical as the deaf-and-dumb packer gaped and blinked, standing frozen in a kind of terror that for all its public expression seemed to us, witnessing, to be private, thus somehow funnier, and the very customer who had paid extravagant prices for these items laughed, if a bit angrily; and other customers, seeing, burst into laughter, too; and the checkout cashier, and other cashiers, and employees of the store, peering over, craning their necks to see what the commotion is, their laughter tentative at first since the look in poor Fritz's eyes *was* terror wasn't it?—then exploding forth, an honest, candid, gut-laughter, not malicious surely, but, yes, *loud?*

Mrs. D. was at an adjacent checkout counter, methodically making out a check to the Franklin Food Mart, a weekly custom this is, perhaps it might better be called a blood-sacrifice, this week's check for—how can it be? $328.98 for an unexceptional week's shopping? for a family of four? no supplies for a dinner party? no beer, wine, liquor? not even any seafood? making out the check with resigned fingers when she heard the strange laughter rising around her, rising, erupting, childlike raucous laughter, and turning, smiling, wanting to join in, Mrs. D. saw the cause—a bag of groceries had overturned, things were rolling on the floor, and that look on that poor man's face, it *was* amusing, but Mrs. D. suppressed laughter for, oh dear, really it *wasn't* amusing, not at all, that poor man backing off and staring at the produce on the floor, paralyzed as everyone laughed so cruelly, what are people thinking of? how can it be? in the Franklin Food Mart of all places?

Are the Delahunts neighbors of ours? Not exactly.

We don't have "neighbors," in the old sense of that word, in Franklin Village. Our houses are constructed on three- and four-acre lots, which means considerable distance between houses, and with our elaborate landscaping (trees of all varieties, shrubs, twelve-foot redwood fences, electrically charged wire-mesh "deer-deterrent" fences) it's possible for the residents of one house to be unable to glimpse even the facade of the house next door, certainly it's possible to go for years without glimpsing the faces of the people who live next door, unless, of course, and this is frequently the case, we encounter one another socially—on neutral territory, you might say. Nor have we sidewalks in residential Franklin Village. Nor have we streets, in the old sense of that word—we have "lanes," we have "drives," we have "passes," "circles," "courts," even "ways," but we do not have "streets."

Are Mr. and Mrs. Delahunt friends of ours? Not exactly.

15 We don't have "friends," in the old sense of that word, in Franklin Village. Most of us are relatively new here, and a number of us are scheduled to

move soon. Spring is the busiest time for moving! (Of course there are residents in this area who are known as "old-time." Who can recall, for instance, when the Franklin Hills Shopping Mall was nothing but an immense tract of open, wild, useless land, and when Main Street in the Village was residential from Pearl Street onward, and when Route 26 was a mere country highway!) Thus the majority of us make no claims to have (or to be) "friends"—but we *are* "friendly acquaintances" of one another and we *are* social. Very!

The Delahunts, Mr. and Mrs., became friendly acquaintances of ours within days of their arrival. They are highly respected, warmly regarded, attractive, energetic, invited almost immediately to join the Franklin Hills Golf Club and the yet more prestigious Franklin Hills Tennis Club. Mr. D. moved his family here three years ago from Greenwich, Connecticut—or was it Grosse Pointe, Michigan?—when he became sales director at W.W.C. & M., and Mrs. D. has recently begun public relations work part-time, for our Republican Congressman Gordon Frayne—Gordon's the man whom the papers so frequently chide, urging him to "upscale" his image. The Delahunts live in a six-bedroom French Normandy house on Fairway Circle, their fourteen-year-old daughter, Tracey, and their eleven-year-old son, Jamey, both attend Franklin Hills Day School. Mrs. D., like many of us, tries to participate in parent-teacher activities at the school, but—when on earth is there *time?*

"Upscaling" Gordon Frayne's image is a challenge, Mrs. D. laughingly, if somewhat worriedly, confesses. But Gordy Frayne—some folks even call him Gordo—wins elections. He's a big-hearted ruddy-faced shooting-from-the-hip character, often in the headlines and on television, one or another controversy, last year he was interviewed on network television and made a statement warning that "ethnic minorities" had better man their own oars "or the venerable Ship of State's gonna capsize and sink"—which naturally led to protests from certain quarters but a good deal of support from other quarters. Mrs. D., like other associates and friendly acquaintances of Gordon Frayne's, has learned to frown as she smiles at his witticisms, just slightly reprovingly, as Franklin Village women often do, she has unconsciously mastered this response, this facial expression, as adroitly as any professional actress—"Oh Gordy! Oh *really!*" It was at a party on Saturday night (the Saturday following the Thursday) that Gordy launched into one of his comical diatribes, the guy could have been a stand-up comedian for sure, cruel but ingenious mimicry of Jesse Jackson (an old routine, but a favorite), and the latest of his AIDS jokes . . . and most, though not all, of the company laughed, Mrs. D. among them, shocked, yes, but not wanting to be a prude, or to seem a prude; but smiling, shaking her head, avoiding the others' eyes as in a communal complicity, but thinking why, why, why, and what will come of this?

Five girls from the Franklin Hills Day School jogging on Park Ridge Road, Monday after school, pumping legs and arms, high-held heads, shorts and loose-fitting school T-shirts and identical expensive jogging shoes, and according to the girls' testimonies after the "vehicular assault" they were running single file, they were keeping to the left side of the road, facing oncoming traffic, careful to keep off the road itself and to run on the asphalt-paved shoulder. As usual one of the girls was falling behind, there were three girls running close together, then, a few yards behind them, the fourth, and approximately twenty feet behind her the fifth, poor Bonnie, Bonnie S., fourteen years old, second year in the "upper form" at the Day School. Bonnie S. is a few pounds overweight, not fat, the most accurate word would be plump but who wants to be plump? who can bear to be plump? fourteen years old and plump in Franklin Village, New York?—poor Bonnie S., whom the other girls like well enough, feel sort of sorry for, she's sweet she tries so hard she's so generous but it's pathetic, Bonnie trying to keep up with the tall thin girls, the girls she envies, letting it be known at school that her problem isn't overeating it's glandular it's "genetic—like fate," and maybe that's true since none of Bonnie's classmates ever sees her eating anything other than apples, carrot sticks, narrow slices of honeydew melon, she'll devour fleshy-fruit and rind both—poor Bonnie S.! (But *is* her weight problem "glandular"? Maybe she binges?—in secret?—tries to stick her finger down her throat and vomit it up?—but can't quite *succeed?*—enough to make a difference?) In any case, there was Bonnie S. running fifth in the line of girls, breathless, clumsy, a sweaty sheen to her round flushed face, a glazed took to her damp brown eyes, and the carload of boys swerved around the curve, that curve just beyond Grouse Hill Lane, six older students from the Day School jammed together in a newly purchased white Acura. The girls could hear the radio blasting heavy-metal rock even before the car came into sight, they could hear the boys yelling and laughing as the car bore down upon them, they saw the faces of the boys in the front seat clearly, wide grins, gleeful, malicious eyes, a raised beer can or two, then the girls were screaming, scattering. It was Bonnie S. who was the target, poor Bonnie arousing male derision pumping away there twenty feet behind the others, poor plump sweaty Bonnie S. with her expression of incredulous shock and terror as the white car aimed for her, boyish-prankish braying laughter, she threw herself desperately to the left, the car skidded by, missing the screaming girl by perhaps a single inch, then righted itself, regained the road, on shrieking tires it sped away and there was Bonnie S., lying insensible in the shallow concrete drainage ditch like something tossed down, bleeding so profusely from a gash in her forehead that the first of her friends to reach her nearly fainted.

Tracey Delahunt tells her mother afterward, she'll confess to her mother solely, knowing her mother will understand, or, failing to understand—for who after all *can* understand?—will sympathize with the hungry wish to understand. "It happened so fast—oh God!—we looked back and there was Bonnie sort of *flying* off the road like something in a kid's cartoon—and it was horrible—it was just, just horrible, but—" lowering her teary eyes, thick-lashed tawny-green eyes Mrs. D. thinks are far more beautiful than her own, though closely resembling her own, "—sort of, in a way—oh God!—*comical* too."

20 Pressing her fingertips hard against her lips but unable to keep from bursting into a peal of hysterical laughter.

Three days later, the most upsetting incident of all.

Not that Mrs. D. allowed herself to think of it very much afterward.

Certainly not obsessively. She isn't that type of mother—the obsessive, neurotic mother. Fantasizing about her children, worrying, suspicious.

She'd entered the house from the rear, as usual. About to step into the kitchen when she'd overheard, coming up from the basement, the "family room" in the basement, the sound of juvenile laughter, boys' laughter, and ordinarily she would not have paused for a moment since Jamey and his friends often took over that room after school to watch videos, yes some of the videos the boys watched were questionable, yes Mrs. D. knew and, yes, she'd tried to exercise some restraint while at the same time she'd tried not to be, nor even to appear to be, censorious and interfering, but that day there was something chilling about the tone of the boys' laughter, and wasn't there, beneath it, another sound?—as of a creature *bleating?*—a queer high-pitched sound that worried Mrs. D. so she went to the door of the family room (which was shut) and pressed her ear against it, hearing the laughter, the giggling, more distinctly, and the other sound too, and carefully, almost timidly—she, Christine Delahunt, nearly forty years old, wife, mother, self-respecting surely?—self-determined surely?—opening a door timidly in her own house?—and saw there a sight that froze her in her tracks even as, in that instant, she was already shoving it from her, banishing it from her consciousness, denying its power to qualify her love for her son: for there were Jamey and several of his boy friends, eighth-graders at the Day School whose faces Mrs. D. knew well, Evan, Allen, Terry, red-haired impish Terry, and who was there with them? a girl? a stranger? and *strange?*—slightly older than the boys, with dull coarse features, eyes puckered at the corners, wet-dribbly mouth, no one Mrs. D. knew or had ever glimpsed before, and this girl was sprawled on her back on the braided "colonial"-style carpet in front of the fireplace, in the Delahunts' family room, her plump knees raised, and spread, naked from the waist down, and what was red-haired Terry doing?—poking something (too large to be a pencil, an object plastic and chunky, was it a child's play baseball bat?), or trying to poke something, into the girl's vagina?—while the other boys, as if transfixed, crouched in a circle, staring, blinking, grinning, giggling.

Mrs. D. cried, without thinking, "Oh what are you doing! Boys! Jamey! And you—you filthy, disgusting *girl!*"

Her voice was unlike any voice she'd ever heard springing from her. 25
Breathless, disbelieving, angry, wounded.

She slammed the door upon the children's startled-guilty-grinning faces and fled. Upstairs.

That evening, at dinner, not a word! not a word! not a word! to Jamey, who, frightened, subdued, ate his food almost shyly, and cast looks of appeal to Mrs. D., who behaved as—as usual?—knowing that the child *knew.*

"I'm so afraid."

Mrs. D. was sitting, yes in the family room, which Mr. D. preferred to call the "recreation" room, with a drink in her hand. Her voice was quiet, apologetic.

30 Mr. D. sipped his drink. Peered at the newspaper. Said, vague, but polite, "Yes?"

"Harry I'm so afraid."

"Well, all right."

Mr. D. was scanning the paper with increasing impatience.

"Christ, it's always the same! AIDS, crack, crime! 'Ghetto!'" He squinted at a photograph of several black youths being herded into a police van, he laughed harshly. "*I'm* a subscriber, for Christ's sake, d'you think these punks subscribe? Why the hell am I always reading about *them*?"

35 Upstairs a telephone rang. Tracey's private number.

Mrs. D. raised her glass to her lips but did not sip from it. She feared the taste of it—that first slip-sliding taste. She pressed her fingertips to her eyes and sat very still.

After a few minutes Mr. D. inquired, glancing in her direction even as his attention remained on the newspaper, "Chris—are you all right?"

"I'm so afraid."

"Cramps, eh? Migraine?"

40 "I'm *afraid.*"

Mr. D. was scanning the editorial page. A sudden smile illuminated his face. He nodded, then, suddenly bored, let the newspaper fall. "Everyone has an *opinion.* 'Put your money where your mouth is' my father used to say."

Mr. D. rose—majestically. A solid figure, ham-thighed, with a faintly flushed face, quick eyes. At its edges Mr. D.'s face appeared to have eroded but his mouth was still that "sculpted" mouth which Mrs. D., a very long time ago, so long ago now as to seem laughable, like a scene in a low-budget science-fiction film, had once avidly, ravenously, *insatiably* kissed.

Mr. D. said, walking away, "Two Bufferin. That'll do it."

After dinner, rinsing dishes and setting them carefully into the dishwasher, Mrs. D. smiled tentatively at her reflection in the window above the sink. Why was she afraid? Wasn't she being a bit silly? Where, so often recently, she was thinking of what she was *not* thinking of, now, abruptly, she was *not* thinking of what she was *not* thinking of.

45 Elsewhere in the house, issuing from the family room, and from Tracey's room upstairs, laughter rippled, peaked—television laughter by the sound of it.

Simple boredom with the subject, maybe.

Which subject?

Mr. H., father of one of the girls who had been jogging on Park Ridge Road on the day of the infamous "vehicular assault," telephoned Mr. D. another time, and, another time, Mr. D. took the call in private, the door to his study firmly shut; and, as they were undressing for bed that night, when Mrs. D. asked cautiously what had been decided, Mr. D. replied affably, "We don't get involved."

Mrs. D. had understood from the very first, even as Tracey was sobbing in her arms, that, given the litigious character of Franklin Hills, this would be the wisest, as it was the most practical, course of action; she gathered too, as things developed, despite Tracey's protestations and bouts of tears, temper, and hysteria, that Tracey concurred, as her girl friends, apart from Bonnie, concurred, perhaps even before their worried parents advised them, yet she heard herself saying weakly, "Oh Harry—if Tracey *saw* those boys' faces, Tracey wants to *say,*" and Mr. D., yawning, stretching, on his way into his bathroom, nodded vaguely in her direction and said, "Set the alarm for 6:15, hon, will you?—the limo's picking me up at 6:45."

50 Tracey no longer discusses the incident with Mr. and Mrs. D. *Ugly!—horrible!—nightmare!—never never forget!*—she restricts all discussions of it to her girl friends, as they restrict their discussions of it too.

That is, the girls who were witnesses to the incident, not Bonnie S., to whom it happened. Not pathetic Bonnie S., to whom they no longer speak, much, at all.

For weeks, red-haired Terry was banished from the Delahunts' house. Not that Mrs. D. spoke of such a banishment, or even suggested it to Jamey, who watched her cautiously, one might say shrewdly, his gaze shifting from her if she chanced to look at him.

No need to chastise and embarrass the poor child, Mrs. D. has begun to think. He's a good decent sensitive civilized child, he *knows* how much he has upset me.

Poor Mrs. K.!—poor "Vivvie"!

55 Since the start of her problem eighteen months ago, the first mastectomy, and the second mastectomy, and then the chemotherapy treatments, her circle of friendly acquaintances has shrunken; and those who visit her, primarily women, have had difficulties.

Yes it's so sad it's *so* sad.

Vivvie Kern of all women.

A few of us visited her at the hospital, some of us waited to visit her at home, it's awkward not knowing what to do or to say, it sometimes seems there isn't anything *to* do or to say, and there's the extra burden of having to exchange greetings with Mr. K., who appears almost resentful, reproachful, that's how men are sometimes in such cases, husbands of ex-prom-queen-type women, and Mrs. K. was, a bit boastfully, one of these. Of course it's wisest to avoid *the subject,* but how can you avoid *the subject* with that poor man staring at you unsmiling?—just *staring?*

But it's lovely in their new solarium, at least. So much to look at, outside and in, and you aren't forced to look at *her,* I mean exclusively at *her,* poor thing! chattering away so bravely!—and that gorgeous red-blond hair she'd been so vain about mostly fallen out now, the wig just sort of *perches* there on her head, and her eyebrows are drawn on so crudely, and with her eyelashes gone it's *naked eyes* you have to look at if you can't avoid it, but in such close quarters and with the woman leaning toward you sometimes even gripping your arm as if for dear life how can you avoid it?—except by not visiting poor Mrs. K. at all?

60 (Of course, some in our circle have stopped seeing her, and it's embarrassing, how painful, Mrs. K. joking to disguise her bitterness. Saying, "My God, it isn't as if I have AIDS after all, this isn't *contagious,* you know!")

Visiting Mrs. K. in late June, having procrastinated for weeks, Mrs. D. was nervously admiring the numerous hanging plants in the solarium, listening to Mrs. K. speaking animatedly of mutual acquaintances, complaining good-naturedly of the Hispanic cleaning woman she and Mrs. D. shared, perhaps half-listening was more accurate, not thinking of what she was not thinking but she *was* thinking of the ceremonies of grief, death, mourning, how brave of human beings yet how futile, how futile yet how brave, for here was a terminally ill woman now speaking aggressively of regaining her lost weight—"muscle tone" she called it—and returning to the Tennis Club, and Mrs. D. smiled at the woman's wide smiling mouth, a thin mouth now and the lips garishly crimson, yes but you must keep up the pretense, yes but you must be brave, and smile, and nod, and agree, for isn't it too terrible otherwise?

Sharp-eyed, Mrs. K. has noticed that Mrs. D. has another time glanced surreptitiously at her wristwatch, as a starving animal can sense the presence of food, however inaccessible, or even abstract, so does Mrs. K, sense her visitor's yearning to escape, thus she leans abruptly forward across the glass-topped table, nearly upsetting both their glasses of white wine, she seems about to bare her heart, *oh why does Vivvie do such things! with each of us, as if for the first and only time!* seizing Mrs. D.'s hand in her skeletal but strong fingers and speaking rapidly, intensely, naked bright-druggy eyes fixed upon Mrs. D.'s, thus holding her captive.

". . . *can't* bear to think of leaving them . . . abandoning them . . . poor Gene! poor Robbie! . . . devastated . . . unmoored . . . already Robbie's been having . . . only thirteen . . . the counselor he's been seeing . . . specializes in adolescent boys . . . says it's a particularly sensitive age . . . traumatic . . . for a boy to lose . . . a mother."

Mrs. D., though giving the impression of having been listening closely, and being deeply moved, has, in fact, not been listening to Mrs. K.'s passionate outburst very closely. She has been thinking of, no she has *not* been thinking of. What?

With a startled, gentle little laugh, Mrs. D. says, "Oh—do you really think so? *Really?*"

Frightened, Mrs. K. says, "Do I really think—what?"

Calmly and unflinching, Mrs. D. looks the doomed woman in the face for the first time.

"That your husband and son will be 'devastated' when you die? That they will even miss you, much? I mean, after the initial shock— the upset to their routines?"

A long moment.

A *very* long moment.

Mrs. K. is staring incredulously at Mrs. D. Slowly, her fingers relax their death-grip on Mrs. D.'s fingers. Her bright lips move, tremble—but no sound emerges.

It's as if, in this instant, the oxygen in the solarium is being sucked out. There's a sense of something, an invisible flame, a radiance, about to go *out*.

"Oh, my goodness!" Mrs. D. exclaims, rising. "I must leave, I still have shopping to do, it's after *six*."

She would tell us, confide in us, yes we'd had similar experiences lately, unsettling experiences, sudden laughter like sneezes, giggles like carbonated bubbles breaking the surface of something you'd believed was firm, solid, permanent, unbreakable, the way in her car that day, fleeing Mrs. K., Mrs. D. found herself driving like a drunken woman, dizzy-drunk, scary-drunk, but also *happy*-drunk as she never is in real life, she was hearing laughter in the Mercedes, washing tickling over her, so funny! so wild! you should have seen that woman's face! that bully! that bore! how dare she! intimidating us! touching us! like that! how dare! as if I wasn't, for once, telling the truth!

Hardly a five-minute drive from the Kerns' house on Juniper Way to the Delahunts' house on Fairway Circle, but Mrs. D. switched on the radio to keep her company.

There.

The Darwin Awards

The Darwin Awards website attracts many visitors. The website recounts how people end up accidentally killing themselves through actions that can only be labeled as stupid. Each story has been nominated for the annual Darwin Awards, which "commemorates those who improve our gene pool by removing themselves from it." The website investigates and verifies the stories before giving the posthumous award to the victims. The website's audience finds great humor in the stories even though each ends in the death of the key figure. The following is a sampling of recent nominations.

Shooting Blanks[1]

2003 Darwin Award Nominee Confirmed True by Darwin

(11 March 2003, Spain) Early one morning, police received a call warning that three robbers had invaded the bar of a Madrid brothel. The police dispatched several units, and confirmed that the call was true. Officers surrounded the building, and used a bullhorn to coax the offenders from the premises.

The robbers, understandably frightened, found themselves in an untenable situation inside a building surrounded by dozens of policemen. Their subsequent actions may have been influenced by the ready availability of alcohol. Instead of surrendering, they decided to go out in a blaze of glory, and tried to escape while shooting at everything in sight.

[1] Submitted by: Javier "RAM" Bringas, Mike Puchol. Reference: www.terra.es Terra Networks, South America

The policemen ducked, covered, and proceeded to shoot back at the running robbers. Two were fatally injured, and the third was wounded in his right leg.

Why was the gunfight over so quickly? The three robbers were carrying REAL guns loaded with FAKE ammunition. They were firing blanks, making enough sound and light to fool the police into shooting back, but not enough to actually help them escape.

What's That Sound?[2]

2002 Darwin Award Nominee Confirmed by Darwin

5 (2 August 2002, Kansas) Police said an Olathe man was struck and killed by a train after his vehicle broke down on Interstate 35. His attempts at repairing his car had failed, and he had stepped away from the busy freeway to call for help, when the train engineer spotted him standing on the tracks. The engineer said the man was holding a cell phone to one ear, and cupping his hand to the other ear to block the noise of the train.

> *Authorities are at a loss as to how to prevent train deaths. Long Island, New York, locomotive engineers recently formed a support group, as every year-plus veteran without exception has involuntarily killed someone in a grade crossing collision. The baffled engineers wonder how anyone could be so unaware of the laws of physics, which dictate that a train weighing hundreds of tons has too much inertia to stop on a dime—or even a football field.*

Depth of a Fisherman[3]

2002 Darwin Award Nominee Confirmed True by Darwin

(9 January 2002, New Zealand) A fisherman was swept away from the wild West Coast beaches of Auckland, pushed to sea by 12-foot swells encountered after ignoring warnings of the impending danger.

Onlookers could only look on in conditions too poor to allow for a rescue attempt. A Surf Lifesaver reported seeing the man standing and fishing as swells broke over his head in the wake of the oncoming gale.

His body was recovered not far from the rocks.

He is not the first fisherman to drown recently off the West Coast beach. Another man tied himself to the rocks to prevent being swept away, and was drowned by the incoming tide.

10 A story of yet another fisherman's odd capsize.

Mechanic Mayhem

2002 Darwin Award Nominee Confirmed True by Darwin

(15 January 2002, Washington) A 49-year-old Boeing worker was performing maintenance on a giant, computer-controlled machine that makes parts out

[2] Submitted by: Sharol. Reference: Kansas City Star & TV news
[3] Submitted by: Mike Peters. Reference: New Zealand Herald

of metal blocks using hydraulics to control its movement. The hydraulic lines are pressurized to 20,000 PSI even when the machine is shut off. Working on equipment such as this requires attention to detail, and a careless employee is liable to suffer dire consequences.

The potential for trouble should have been obvious to this sixteen-year member of the Machinists Union, and yet, despite redundant safety procedures, tags, warning signs, and a fearful co-worker, our Darwin Award hopeful began to remove a hydraulic line without relieving the pressure.

The bolts holding the line in place were so tight that he had to locate a 4-foot section of pipe to attach to his ratchet to give him enough leverage to loosen the bolt. For some, that would have been warning enough that the line was pressurized.

Four high-strength bolts attached the line to the machine. The soon-to-be-ex-employee had removed three, and loosened the fourth, when the over-stressed bolt snapped. A foot-long, 3″ diameter brass sleeve was inside the line to prevent the hose from kinking. It shot out and hit the mechanic in the forehead with such force that it knocked him back eight feet, ricocheted off his head, and hit a crane fifty feet overhead.

The maintenance worker never knew what hit him. 15

The details of this event come from eyewitness reports and a news release from Boeing. The precise details are disputed, but the story is written to take as many observations into account as possible. Eyewitnesses and knowledgeable parties are encouraged to step forward to confirm or dispute this account.

Think Before You Leap[4]

2001 Darwin Award Winner Confirmed True by Darwin

(21 July 2001, Idaho) When his brakes failed while driving down a steep mountain road, Marco bailed out on his eight passengers and leapt from his Dodge van. Too bad Marco didn't alert the others to the problem before he took flight so precipitously. Another passenger was able to bring the vehicle to a stop a short distance away. Marco struck his head on the pavement and died at the scene. No one else was injured.

Coke Is It![5]

2001 Darwin Award Nominee Confirmed True by Darwin

(12 December 1998, Canada) A man crushed beneath a vending machine while trying to shake loose a free soda? If you thought it happened only in Urban Legends, you're wrong!

Kevin, a 19-year-old Quebec student, killed himself at Bishop's University while shaking a 420-kilogram Coke machine. He had been celebrating the end of final exams with friends. He died beneath the soda machine, asphyxiated, with a blood alcohol level slightly over the legal driving limit.

---

[4] Submitted by: Sean Capps. Reference: South Idaho Press

[5] Submitted by: The Bitshipper, Dave Mann. Reference: The Canadian Press and Graeme Hamilton of the National Post

Kevin's last act was committed in vain. "Even as it fell over, the vending machine did not let out a single can," the coroner reported. Soda-holics take note! The report also states that toppled vending machines have caused at least 35 deaths and 140 injuries in the last twenty years.

For those with enquiring minds, I refer you to a website dedicated to the quest to clear Kevin's name. His family questions the official version on their website, aptly named cokemachineaccidents.com. They recently sued Coca-Cola, two related companies, and Bishop's University for "gross carelessness." Their website exposé proffers several explanations for why Kevin's death was not his own fault: shaking coke machines "was common practice at the University," and anyway, unknown persons might have crushed Kevin with the vending machine in a bizarre murder, as it "would be difficult for one person to move" the machine.

In response, a spokesperson for Coke said that Canadian machines are now labelled with a warning that "tipping or rocking may cause injury or death." They have also installed anti-theft devices in newer models to keep people from obtaining free drinks.

Blown Away[6]

2001 Darwin Award Winner Confirmed True by Darwin

(16 July, 2001, United States) An assistant plant manager for Blacklidge Emulsions died when he used an acetylene torch to cut a hole in a 10,000 gallon tank of asphalt emulsion. He was attempting to visually survey the amount of emulsion that remained in the tank, but "no safety precautions were taken before the cutting operation began," stated an OSHA representative. "[His] attention was twice called to a warning sign on the side of the structure which stated the contents were combustible. In complete disregard of safety procedures," the erstwhile manager "lit an acetylene torch and began cutting, causing an explosion that blew him 93 feet away."

Assignment Ideas

Writing about humorous events can be difficult for the very reason mentioned in the overview: your audience must share your viewpoint to be able to enjoy the humor. While you cannot control readers' sensibilities, you can be aware of their perspective and help them, through your language choices, clearly understand the situation you are discussing (review Chapter 3 about audience). Make sure to provide sufficient context for what you want your audience to find funny. The goal in these assignments is to analyze humor rather than to just get a laugh, but it will not hurt if you can make your readers smile!

[6] Submitted by: Jon Kade, Matt Newell, Gary Arbuckle, Chris Stockard, Dave. Reference: CCH Employment Safety & Health Guide Issue 1573, OSHA Regional News Release, Mississippi Sun Herald

1. Analyze differing forms of political humor. Describe some of the humor you read, heard, or saw, and explain why you found it funny or unfunny. Investigate whether your political sympathies make you enjoy the targeting of some political figures more than others. What does the nature of this targeting and your enjoyment say about you as a member of our society? Can humorist Dave Barry's observations in "All I Think Is That It's Stupid" (page 436) make you reflect more deeply on this?
2. The Darwin Awards show a common tendency to laugh at stupidity, something that "How Laughter Works" (page 428) refers to as the "superiority theory." Find additional examples of this type of humor. Analyze the examples to uncover why some people find them humorous. Describe the consistent patterns that pervade humor focusing on stupidity. Could this humor be an extension of the "observational" style of humor that Warren St. John discusses in "Seriously, the Joke Is Dead" (page 425)? Contrast laughing at stupidity with another type of humor, perhaps pulling some ideas from your brainstorming or freewriting about comedians, puns, or tragedy. Try to isolate the key elements in both types of humor, and compare their functions in society other than simply making people laugh.
3. Does humor maintain dominant ideology, or does it undermine the privileged and the powerful? Take examples from several different sources. Look for the tension in the jokes, and spot patterns that align with race, gender, or sexuality. Some critics suggest that even the positioning of a person in a film, such as the sidekick or comic relief, aligns with racist thought. Don't forget to investigate the historical uses of humor by black, female, and Jewish comedians to support or complicate your argument.
4. Referring to your brainstorming or freewriting about humor and tragedy, analyze "Is Laughter Contagious?" (page 409) in light of an experience in which you had to hold in laughter, regretted having laughed, or burst into laughter in response to insensitivity. Does this type of laughter serve a purpose in times of tragedy or pain? Can such laughter be good medicine? Or is such laughter a reflection of inability to care about others? You might want to consult "How Laughter Works" (page 428), but make sure to answer these questions with support from Joyce Carol Oates's story and your own experiences.

Group Work

Obscenity and humor often go hand in hand, starting with the juvenile bathroom humor heard in junior high school and culminating with famous entertainers who earn remarkable livings using profanity and crudity in their routines. Explore the different uses of obscenity by celebrities such as Whoopi Goldberg, George Carlin, Dave Chappelle, Chris Rock, Roseanne Barr, and Howard Stern. Provide background details on their careers, and describe their humor through the use of explicit details. Theorize about why they turned to the use of obscenity in their comedy, and generalize about the place of such humor in our society. Does obscenity serve a purpose other than shock value? Does it deliver a serious message better than other types of humor? Be sure to discuss with your teacher and your peer review group the level of obscenity they will find acceptable in your paper, especially if you plan to quote directly from a comedian's more provocative material.

Additional Readings

The chapter from David Sedaris's book "Me Talk Pretty One Day" demonstrates the observational humor that Warren St. John, in "Seriously, the Joke Is Dead," contends is replacing the joke. Does Sedaris's wit work for you? Looking at "How Laughter Works" might provide insights about the biological processes that produce laughter, but does the incongruity theory explain the wry laughter "All I Think Is That It's Stupid" alludes to—the humor produced not from obvious, silly situations but from the ridiculousness of a political or social situation?

DAVID SEDARIS

Me Talk Pretty One Day

At the age of forty-one, I am returning to school and have to think of myself as what my French textbook calls "a true debutant." After paying my tuition, I was issued a student ID, which allows me a discounted entry fee at movie theaters, puppet shows, and Festyland, a far-flung amusement park that advertises with billboards picturing a cartoon stegosaurus sitting in a canoe and eating what appears to be a ham sandwich.

I've moved to Paris with hopes of learning the language. My school is an easy ten-minute walk from my apartment, and on the first day of class I arrived early, watching as the returning students greeted one another in the school lobby. Vacations were recounted, and questions were raised concerning mutual friends with names like Kang and Vlatnya. Regardless of their nationalities, everyone spoke in what sounded to me like excellent French. Some accents were better than others, but the students exhibited an ease and confidence I found intimidating. As an added discomfort, they were all young, attractive, and well dressed, causing me to feel not unlike Pa Kettle trapped backstage after a fashion show.

The first day of class was nerve-racking because I knew I'd be expected to perform. That's the way they do it here—it's everybody into the language pool, sink or swim. The teacher marched in, deeply tanned from a recent vacation, and proceeded to rattle off a series of administrative announcements. I've spent quite a few summers in Normandy, and I took a monthlong French class before leaving New York. I'm not completely in the dark, yet I understood only half of what this woman was saying.

"If you have not *meimslsxp* or *lgpdmurct* by this time, then you should not be in this room. Has everyone *apzkiubjxow?* Everyone? Good, we shall begin." She spread out her lesson plan and sighed, saying, "All right, then, who knows the alphabet?"

It was startling because (a) I hadn't been asked that question in a while and (b) I realized, while laughing, that I myself did *not* know the alphabet. They're the same letters, but in France they're pronounced differently. I know the shape of the alphabet but had no idea what it actually sounded like. 5

"Ahh." The teacher went to the board and sketched the letter a. "Do we have anyone in the room whose first name commences with an *ahh?*"

Two Polish Annas raised their hands, and the teacher instructed them to present themselves by stating their names, nationalities, occupations, and a brief list of things they liked and disliked in this world. The first Anna hailed from an industrial town outside of Warsaw and had front teeth the size of tombstones. She worked as a seamstress, enjoyed quiet times with friends, and hated the mosquito.

"Oh, really," the teacher said. "How very interesting. I thought that everyone loved the mosquito, but here, in front of all the world, you claim to detest him. How is it that we've been blessed with someone as unique and original as you? Tell us, please."

The seamstress did not understand what was being said but knew that this was an occasion for shame. Her rabbity mouth huffed for breath, and she stared down at her lap as though the appropriate comeback were stitched somewhere alongside the zipper of her slacks.

The second Anna learned from the first and claimed to love sunshine and detest lies. It sounded like a translation of one of those Playmate of the Month data sheets, the answers always written in the same loopy handwriting: "Turn-ons: Mom's famous five-alarm chili! Turnoffs: insecurity and guys who come on too strong!!!!" 10

The two Polish Annas surely had clear notions of what they loved and hated, but like the rest of us, they were limited in terms of vocabulary, and this made them appear less than sophisticated. The teacher forged on, and we learned that Carlos, the Argentine bandonion player, loved wine, music, and, in his words, "making sex with the womens of the world." Next came a beautiful young Yugoslav who identified herself as an optimist, saying that she loved everything that life had to offer.

The teacher licked her lips, revealing a hint of the saucebox we would later come to know. She crouched low for her attack, placed her hands on the young woman's desk, and leaned close, saying, "Oh yeah? And do you love your little war?"

While the optimist struggled to defend herself, I scrambled to think of an answer to what had obviously become a trick question. How often is one asked what he loves in this world? More to the point, how often is one asked and then publicly ridiculed for his answer? I recalled my mother, flushed with wine, pounding the tabletop late one night, saying, "Love? I love a good steak cooked rare. I love my cat, and I love . . ." My sisters and I leaned forward, waiting to hear our names. "Tums," our mother said. "I love Tums."

The teacher killed some time accusing the Yugoslavian girl of masterminding a program of genocide, and I jotted frantic notes in the margins of my pad. While I can honestly say that I love leafing through medical textbooks devoted to severe dermatological conditions, the hobby is beyond the reach of my French vocabulary, and acting it out would only have invited controversy.

15 When called upon, I delivered an effortless list of things that I detest: blood sausage, intestinal pâtés, brain pudding. I'd learned these words the hard way. Having given it some thought, I then declared my love for IBM typewriters, the French word for *bruise,* and my electric floor waxer. It was a short list, but still I managed to mispronounce *IBM* and assign the wrong gender to both the floor waxer and the typewriter. The teacher's reaction led me to believe that these mistakes were capital crimes in the country of France.

"Were you always this *palicmkrexis?*" she asked. "Even a *fiuscrzsa ticiwelmun* knows that a typewriter is feminine."

I absorbed as much of her abuse as I could understand, thinking—but not saying—that I find it ridiculous to assign a gender to an inanimate object incapable of disrobing and making an occasional fool of itself. Why refer to crack pipe or Good Sir Dishrag when these things could never live up to all that their sex implied?

The teacher proceeded to belittle everyone from German Eva, who hated laziness, to Japanese Yukari, who loved paintbrushes and soap. Italian, Thai, Dutch, Korean, and Chinese—we all left class foolishly believing that the worst was over. She'd shaken us up a little, but surely that was just an act designed to weed out the deadweight. We didn't know it then, but the coming months would teach us what it was like to spend time in the presence of a wild animal, something completely unpredictable. Her temperament was not based on a series of good and bad days but, rather, good and bad moments. We soon learned to dodge chalk and protect our heads and stomachs whenever she approached us with a question. She hadn't yet punched anyone, but it seemed wise to protect ourselves against the inevitable.

Though we were forbidden to speak anything but French, the teacher would occasionally use us to practice any of her five fluent languages.

20 "I hate you," she said to me one afternoon. Her English was flawless. "I really, really hate you." Call me sensitive, but I couldn't help but take it personally.

After being singled out as a lazy *kfdtinvfm,* I took to spending four hours a night on my homework, putting in even more time whenever we were assigned an essay. I suppose I could have gotten by with less, but I was determined to create some sort of identity for myself: David the hard worker, David the cut-up. We'd have one of those "complete this sentence" exercises, and I'd fool with the thing for hours, invariably settling on something like "A quick run around the lake? I'd love to! Just give me a moment while I strap on my wooden leg." The teacher, through word and action, conveyed the message that if this was my idea of an identity, she wanted nothing to do with it.

My fear and discomfort crept beyond the borders of the classroom and accompanied me out onto the wide boulevards. Stopping for a coffee, asking directions, depositing money in my bank account: these things were out of the question, as they involved having to speak. Before beginning school, there'd been no shutting me up, but now I was convinced that everything I said was wrong. When the phone rang, I ignored it. If someone asked me a question, I pretended to be deaf. I knew my fear was getting the best of me when I started wondering why they don't sell cuts of meat in vending machines.

My only comfort was the knowledge that I was not alone. Huddled in the hallways and making the most of our pathetic French, my fellow students and I engaged in the sort of conversation commonly overheard in refugee camps.

"Sometime me cry alone at night."

"That be common for I, also, but be more strong, you. Much work and 25
someday you talk pretty. People start love you soon. Maybe tomorrow, okay."

Unlike the French class I had taken in New York, here there was no sense of competition. When the teacher poked a shy Korean in the eyelid with a freshly sharpened pencil, we took no comfort in the fact that, unlike Hyeyoon Cho, we all knew the irregular past tense of the verb *to defeat*. In all fairness, the teacher hadn't meant to stab the girl, but neither did she spend much time apologizing, saying only, "Well, you should have been *vkkdyo* more *kdeynfulh*."

Over time it became impossible to believe that any of us would ever improve. Fall arrived and it rained every day, meaning we would now be scolded for the water dripping from our coats and umbrellas. It was mid-October when the teacher singled me out, saying, "Every day spent with you is like having a cesarean section." And it struck me that, for the first time since arriving in France, I could understand every word that someone was saying.

Understanding doesn't mean that you can suddenly speak the language. Far from it. It's a small step, nothing more, yet its rewards are intoxicating and deceptive. The teacher continued her diatribe and I settled back, bathing in the subtle beauty of each new curse and insult.

"You exhaust me with your foolishness and reward my efforts with nothing but pain, do you understand me?"

The world opened up, and it was with great joy that I responded, "I know 30
the thing that you speak exact now. Talk me more, you, plus, please, plus."

WARREN ST. JOHN

Seriously, the Joke Is Dead

In case you missed its obituary, the joke died recently after a long illness, of, oh, 30 years. Its passing was barely noticed, drowned out, perhaps, by the din of ironic one-liners, snark and detached bons mots that pass for humor these days.

The joke died a lonely death. There was no next of kin to notify, the comedy skit, the hand-buzzer and Bob Newhart's imaginary telephone monologues having passed on long before. But when people reminisce about it, they always say the same thing: the joke knew how to make an entrance. "Two guys walked into a bar"; "So this lady goes to the doctor"; "Did you hear the one about the talking parrot?" The new humor sneaks by on little cat feet, all punch line and no setup, and if it bombs, you barely notice. The joke insisted on everyone's attention, and when it bombed—wow.

"A joke is a way to say, 'I'm going to do something funny now,'" said Penn Jillette, the talking half of the comedy and magic duo Penn & Teller and a producer of "The Aristocrats," a new documentary about an old dirty joke of the same name. "If I don't get a laugh at the end, I'm a failure."

It's a matter of faith among professional comics that jokes—the kind that involve a narrative setup, some ridiculous details and a punch line—have been displaced by observational humor and one-liners. Lisa Lampanelli, who describes herself as the world's only female insult comic, said that in the business, straight jokes were considered "the kiss of death."

5 "You don't tell joke jokes onstage ever," she said. "Because then you're a big hack."

But out in the real world, the joke hung on for a while, lurking in backwaters of male camaraderie like bachelor parties and trading floors and in monthly installments of Playboy's "Party Jokes" page. Then jokes practically vanished. To tell a joke at the office or a party these days is to pronounce oneself a cornball, an attention hog, and of course to risk offending someone, a high social crime. "I can't remember the last time I was sitting around and heard someone tell a good joke," Ms. Lampanelli said.

While many in the world of humor and comedy agree that the joke is dead, there is little consensus on who or what killed it or exactly when it croaked. Theories abound: the atomic bomb, A.D.D., the Internet, even the feminization of American culture, have all been cited as possible causes. In the academic world scholars have been engaged in a lengthy postmortem of the joke for some time, but still no grand unifying theory has emerged.

"There isn't a lot of agreement," said Don L. F. Nilsen, the executive secretary of the International Society for Humor Studies and a professor of linguistics at Arizona State University.

Among comics, the most cited culprit in the death of the joke is so-called "political correctness" or, at least, a heightened sensitivity to offending people. Mr. Jillette said he believed most of the best jokes have a mean-spirited component, and that mean-spiritedness is out.

10 "You used to feel safer telling jokes," he said. "Since all your best material is mean-spirited, you feel less safe. You're worried some might think that you really have this point of view."

Older comics tend to put the blame on the failings of younger generations. Robert Orben, 78, a former speechwriter for President Gerald R. Ford and the author of several manuals for comedians, said he believed a combination of shortened attention spans and lack of backbone among today's youth made them ill-suited for joke telling.

"A young person today has a nanosecond attention span, so whatever you do in a humor has to be short," he said. "Younger people do not wait for anything that takes time to develop. We're going totally to one-liners."

"Telling a joke is risk taking," Mr. Orben added. "Younger people are more insecure and not willing to put themselves on the line, so a quick one-liner is much safer."

(Asked if he had a favorite joke, Mr. Orben said, "The Washington Redskins," suggesting that even veteran joke tellers might have abandoned the form.)

15 Scholars say that while humor has always been around—in ancient Athens, for example, a comedians' club called the Group of 60 met regularly in the temple of Herakles—the joke has gone in and out of fashion. In modern times its heyday was probably the 1950s, but the joke's demise began soon after, a result of several seismic cultural shifts. The first of those, Mr. Nilsen said, was the threat of nuclear annihilation.

"Before the atomic bomb everyone had a sense that there was a future," Mr. Nilsen said. "Now we're at the hands of fate. We could go up at any moment. In order to deal with something as horrendous as that, we've become a little cynical."

Gallows humor and irony, Mr. Nilsen said, were more suited to this dire condition than absurd stories about talking kangaroos, tumescent parrots and bears that sodomize hunters. (Don't know that one? Ask your granddad.)

Around the same time, said John Morreall, a religion professor and humor scholar at the College of William and Mary, the roles of men and women began to change, which had implications for the joke.

Telling old-style jokes, he said, was a masculine pursuit because it allowed men to communicate with one another without actually revealing anything about themselves. Historically women's humor was based on personal experience, and conveyed a sense of the teller's likes and dislikes, foibles and capacity for self-deprecation.

20 The golden age of joke telling corresponded with a time when men were especially loathe to reveal anything about their inner lives, Mr. Morreall said. But over time men let down their guard, and comics, like Lenny Bruce, George Carlin and later Jerry Seinfeld, embraced the personal, observational style.

"A very common quip was, 'Women can't tell jokes,'" Mr. Morreall said. "I found that women can't remember jokes. That's because they don't give a damn. Their humor is observational humor about the people around that they care about. Women virtually never do that old-style stuff."

"Women's-style humor was ahead of the curve," he said. "In the last 30 years all humor has caught up with women's humor."

The mingling of the sexes in the workplace and in social situations wasn't particularly good for the joke either, as jokes that played well in the locker room didn't translate to the conference room or the co-ed dinner party. And in any event, scholars say, in a social situation wit plays better than old-style joke telling. Witty remarks push the conversation along and enliven it, encouraging others to contribute.

Jokes, on the other hand, cause conversation to screech to a halt and require everyone to focus on the joke teller, which can be awkward.

25 Whatever tenuous hold the joke had left by the 1990s may have been broken by the Internet, Mr. Nilsen said. The torrent of email jokes in the late 1990s and joke websites made every joke available at once, essentially diluting the effect of what had been an spoken form. While getting up and telling

a joke requires courage, forwarding a joke by email takes hardly any effort at all. So everyone did it, until it wasn't funny anymore.

"The Aristocrats," the documentary produced by Mr. Jillette and the comic Paul Provenza, says a lot about what the straight-up joke once was, and what it isn't any longer. The film, which was shown at Sundance in January and will be released in theaters this summer, features dozens of comics talking about and performing an over-the-top vaudeville standard about a family that shows up at a talent agency, looking for representation.

The talent agent agrees to watch them perform, at which point the family goes into a crazed fit of orgiastic and scatological mayhem, the exact details of which vary from comic to comic. The punch line comes when the agent asks the family what they call their bizarre act. The answer: "The Aristocrats!"

Much of the humor in the documentary comes not from the joke, which nearly everyone in the film concedes is lousy, but from watching modern-day observational comics like Mr. Carlin, Paul Reiser, and Gilbert Gottfried perform in the anachronistic mode of Buddy Hackett, Milton Berle, and Red Skelton. Imagine watching a documentary of contemporary rock guitarists doing their teenage versions of the solo in *Free Bird* and you'll get the idea; with each rendition it becomes more and more clear why people don't do it anymore.

"Part of the joke is that it's even more inappropriate because we don't do that anymore," Mr. Nilsen said.

30 One paradox about the death of the joke: It may result in more laughs. Joke tellers, after all, are limited by the number of jokes they can memorize, while observational wits never run out of material. And Mr. Morreall said that because wits make no promise to be funny, the threshold for getting a laugh is lower for them than for joke tellers, who always battle high expectations.

"Jon Stewart just has to twist his eyebrows a little bit, and people laugh," he said. "It's a much easier medium."

Some comics who grew up in the age of the joke say they are often amazed at how easy crowds are in the era of observational humor. Shelley Berman, 79, a comic whose career took off on *The Ed Sullivan Show* and who now plays Larry David's father on the HBO show *Curb Your Enthusiasm,* said these days even the most banal remark seemed to get a response.

"I don't tell jokes in my act," he said. "But if I tell an audience I don't tell jokes, I'll get people laughing at that line."

MARSHALL BRAIN

How Laughter Works

http://www.howstuffworks.com/laughter.htm

Bill Gates and the president of General Motors have met for lunch, and Bill is going on and on about computer technology. "If automotive technology had kept pace with computer technology over the

> past few decades, you would now be driving a V-32 instead of a V-8, and it would have a top speed of 10,000 miles per hour," says Gates. "Or, you could have an economy car that weighs 30 pounds and gets a thousand miles to a gallon of gas. In either case, the sticker price of a new car would be less than $50. Why haven't you guys kept up?"
>
> The president of GM smiles and says, "Because the federal government won't let us build cars that crash four times a day."

Why is that funny? Have you ever wondered about that? Human beings love to laugh, and the average adult laughs 17 times a day. Humans love to laugh so much that there are actually industries built around laughter. Jokes, sitcoms and comedians are all designed to get us laughing, because laughing feels good. For us it seems so natural, but the funny thing is that humans are one of the only species that laughs. Laughter is actually a complex response that involves many of the same skills used in solving problems.

What Is Laughter?

First of all, laughter is not the same as humor. Laughter is the physiological response to humor. Laughter consists of two parts—a set of gestures and the production of a sound. When we laugh, the brain pressures us to conduct both those activities simultaneously. When we laugh heartily, changes occur in many parts of the body, even the arm, leg and trunk muscles.

If you want to get specific about it, it works like this: Under certain conditions, our bodies perform what the *Encyclopedia Britannica* describes as "rhythmic, vocalized, expiratory and involuntary actions"—better known as laughter. Fifteen facial muscles contract and stimulation of the zygomatic major muscle (the main lifting mechanism of your upper lip) occurs. Meanwhile, the respiratory system is upset by the epiglottis half-closing the larynx, so that air intake occurs irregularly, making you gasp. In extreme circumstances, the tear ducts are activated, so that while the mouth is opening and closing and the struggle for oxygen intake continues, the face becomes moist and often red (or purple). The noises that usually accompany this bizarre behavior range from sedate giggles to boisterous guffaws.

Behavioral neurobiologist and pioneering laughter researcher Robert Provine jokes that he has encountered one major problem in his study of laughter. The problem is that laughter disappears just when he is ready to observe it—especially in the laboratory. One of his studies looked at the sonic structure of laughter. He discovered that all human laughter consists of variations on a basic form that consists of short, vowel-like notes repeated every 210 milliseconds. Laughter can be of the "ha-ha-ha" variety or the "ho-ho-ho" type but not a mixture of both, he says. Provine also suggests that humans have a "detector" that responds to laughter by triggering other neural circuits in the brain, which, in turn, generates more laughter. This explains why laughter is contagious.

Humor researcher Peter Derks describes laughter response as "a really 5
quick, automatic type of behavior." "In fact, how quickly our brain recognizes

the incongruity that lies at the heart of most humor and attaches an abstract meaning to it determines whether we laugh," he says.

One of the key features of natural laughter is its placement in speech, linguists say. Laughter almost always occurs during pauses at the end of phrases. Experts say this suggests that an orderly process (probably neurologically based) governs the placement of laughter in speech and gives speech priority access to the single vocalization channel. This strong relationship between laughter and speech is much like punctuation in written communication—that's why it's called the punctuation effect.

What Is the Purpose of Laughter?

Philosopher John Morreall believes that the first human laughter may have begun as a gesture of shared relief at the passing of danger. And since the relaxation that results from a bout of laughter inhibits the biological fight-or-flight response, laughter may indicate trust in one's companions.

Many researchers believe that the purpose of laughter is related to making and strengthening human connections. "Laughter occurs when people are comfortable with one another, when they feel open and free. And the more laughter [there is], the more bonding [occurs] within the group," says cultural anthropologist Mahadev Apte. This feedback "loop" of bonding-laughter-more bonding, combined with the common desire not to be singled out from the group, may be another reason why laughter is often contagious.

Studies have also found that dominant individuals—the boss or the tribal chief or the family patriarch—use humor more than their subordinates. If you've often thought that everyone in the office laughs when the boss laughs, you're very perceptive. In such cases, Morreall says, controlling the laughter of a group becomes a way of exercising power by controlling the emotional climate of the group. So laughter, like much human behavior, must have evolved to change the behavior of others, Provine says. For example, in an embarrassing or threatening situation, laughter may serve as a conciliatory gesture or as a way to deflect anger. If the threatening person joins the laughter, the risk of confrontation may lessen.

10 Provine is among only a few people who are studying laughter much as an animal behaviorist might study a dog's bark or a bird's song. He believes that laughter, like the bird's song, functions as a kind of social signal. Other studies have confirmed that theory by proving that people are 30 times more likely to laugh in social settings than when they are alone (and without pseudo-social stimuli like television). Even nitrous oxide, or laughing gas, loses much of its oomph when taken in solitude, according to German psychologist Willibald Ruch.

Laughter on the Brain

The physiological study of laughter has its own name—gelotology. And we know that certain parts of the brain are responsible for certain human functions. For example, emotional responses are the function of the brain's largest region, the frontal lobe. But researchers have learned that the production of laughter is involved with various regions of the brain. While the relationship between laughter and the brain is not fully understood, researchers are making some progress.

For example, Derks traced the pattern of brainwave activity in subjects responding to humorous material. Subjects were hooked up to an electroencephalograph (EEG) and their brain activity was measured when they laughed. In each case, the brain produced a regular electrical pattern. Within four-tenths of a second of exposure to something potentially funny, an electrical wave moved through the cerebral cortex, the largest part of the brain. If the wave took a negative charge, laughter resulted. If it maintained a positive charge, no response was given, researchers said.

During the experiment, researchers observed the following specific activities:

- The left side of the cortex (the layer of cells that covers the entire surface of the forebrain) analyzed the words and structure of the joke.
- The brain's large frontal lobe, which is involved in social emotional responses, became very active.
- The right hemisphere of the cortex carried out the intellectual analysis required to "get" the joke.
- Brainwave activity then spread to the sensory processing area of the occipital lobe (the area on the back of the head that contains the cells that process visual signals).
- Stimulation of the motor sections evoked physical responses to the joke.

This is different from what happens with emotional responses. Emotional responses appear to be confined to specific areas of the brain, while laughter seems to be produced via a circuit that runs through many regions of the brain. (This means that damage to any of these regions can impair one's sense of humor and response to humor, experts say.)

The Limbic System

When we look more closely at the areas of the brain involved with laughter, 15
the limbic system seems to be central. The limbic system is a network of structures located beneath the cerebral cortex. This system is important because it controls some behaviors that are essential to the life of all mammals (finding food, self-preservation).

Interestingly, the same structures found in the human limbic system can also be found in the brains of evolutionary ancient animals such as the alligator. In the alligator, the limbic system is heavily involved in smell and plays an important role in defending territory, hunting and eating prey. In humans, the limbic system is more involved in motivation and emotional behaviors.

While the structures in this highly developed part of the brain interconnect, research has shown that the amygdala, a small almond-shaped structure

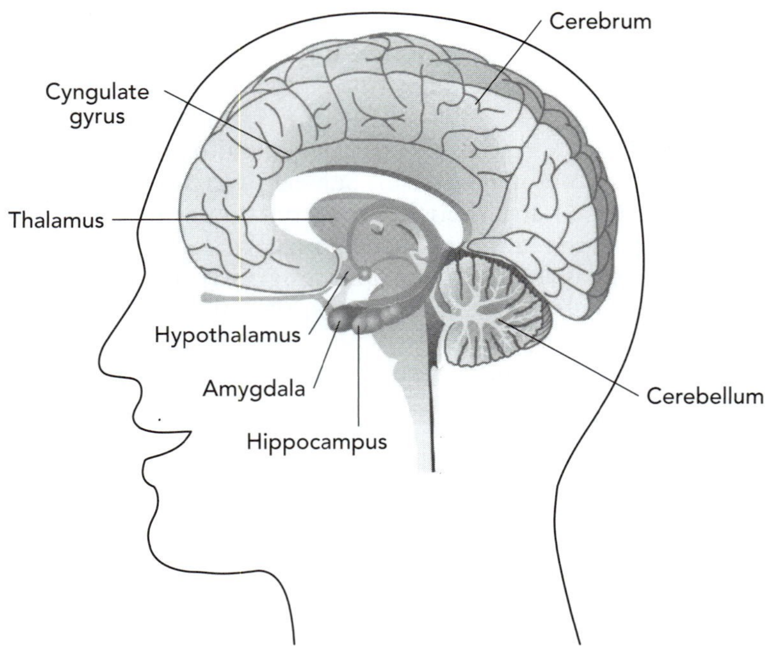

Structures in the brain's limbic system, which controls many essential human behaviors, also contribute to the production of laughter.

deep inside the brain, and the hippocampus, a tiny, seahorse-shaped structure, seem to be the main areas involved with emotions. The amygdala connects with the hippocampus as well as the medial dorsal nucleus of the thalamus. These connections enable it to play an important role in the mediation and control of major activities like friendship, love and affection and on the expression of mood. The hypothalamus, particularly its median part, has been identified as a major contributor to the production of loud, uncontrollable laughter.

What Makes Us Laugh?

Laughter is triggered when we find something humorous. There are three traditional theories about what we find humorous:

- The incongruity theory suggests that humor arises when logic and familiarity are replaced by things that don't normally go together. Researcher Thomas Veatch says a joke becomes funny when we expect one outcome and another happens. When a joke begins, our minds and bodies are already anticipating what's going to happen and how it's going to end. That anticipation takes the form of logical thought intertwined with emotion and is influenced by our past experiences and our thought processes. When the joke goes in an unexpected direction, our thoughts and emotions suddenly have to switch gears. We now have new emotions, backing up a different line of thought. In other words, we experience two sets of incompatible thoughts and emotions simultaneously.

We experience this incongruity between the different parts of the joke as humorous.

- The superiority theory comes into play when we laugh at jokes that focus on someone else's mistakes, stupidity or misfortune. We feel superior to this person, experience a certain detachment from the situation and so are able to laugh at it.
- The relief theory is the basis for a device movie-makers have used effectively for a long time. In action films or thrillers where tension is high, the director uses comic relief at just the right times. He builds up the tension or suspense as much as possible and then breaks it down slightly with a side comment, enabling the viewer to relieve himself of pent-up emotion, just so the movie can build it up again! Similarly, an actual story or situation creates tension within us. As we try to cope with two sets of emotions and thoughts, we need a release and laughter is the way of cleansing our system of the built-up tension and incongruity. (According to Dr. Lisa Rosenberg, humor, especially dark humor, can help workers cope with stressful situations. "The act of producing humor, of making a joke, gives us a mental break and increases our objectivity in the face of overwhelming stress," she said.)

Why Can't I Tickle Myself?

This is a little off the beaten laughter path, but believe it or not, some research is being conducted in this area. In fact, researchers at the University of California in San Diego have even constructed a "tickle machine."

Some scientists believe that laughing caused by tickling is a built-in reflex. If this is true, then, theoretically, you should be able to tickle yourself. 20
But you can't—not even in the same area and the same way someone else tickles you into hysteria! The information sent to your spinal cord and brain should be exactly the same. But apparently, for tickling to work, the brain needs tension and surprise—something that's obviously missing when you tickle yourself. How the brain uses this information about tension and surprise is still a mystery.

Why Don't We All Laugh at the Same Things?

Experts say that several obvious differences in people affect what they find humorous. The most significant seems to be age.

Infants and children are constantly discovering the world around them. A lot of what goes on seems ridiculous and surprising, which strikes them as funny. What's funny to a toddler consists of short and simple concepts, like an elephant joke. Along with the ridiculous and the surprising, children—much to their parents' dismay—also appreciate jokes where cruelty is present (it boosts their self-assertiveness) and what we refer to as "toilet humor." To children, a preoccupation with bodily functions is simply another way of exploring their fascinating new environment.

The pre-teen and teenage years are, almost universally, awkward and tense. Lots of adolescents and teens laugh at jokes that focus on sex, food, authority figures and—in typical rebellious style—any subject that adults consider off-limits. It is an insecure time of life and young people often use humor as a tool to protect themselves or to feel superior.

As we mature, both our physical bodies and mental outlooks grow and change. Since there is a certain amount of intelligence involved in "getting" a joke, our sense of humor becomes more developed as we learn more. By the time we're grown, we have experienced much of life, including tragedy and success. In keeping with these experiences, our senses of humor are more mature. We laugh at other people and ourselves in shared common predicaments and embarrassments. The adult sense of humor is usually characterized as more subtle, more tolerant and less judgmental about the differences in people. The things we find funny as a result of our age or developmental stage seem to be related to the stressors we experience during this time. Basically, we laugh at the issues that stress us out.

Another factor that affects what we find funny is the culture or community from which we come. Have you ever laughed at a joke and realized that if you were from anywhere else in the world, it just wouldn't be funny? It's a fact of life that culture and community provide lots of fodder for jokes. There are economic, political and social issues that are easy to laugh about, but only the people living in that culture may understand it. For example, a joke from a small country might not have universal appeal because it would be so little understood. The big, influential, much-observed United States might be the exception to this rule. Thanks to media and movies, most people around the world know what is going on here. So jokes about a situation in the United States can be enjoyed pretty much across the globe.

When people say "That's not funny," theorist Veatch says they mean either "It is offensive" or "So, what's the point?" For someone to find a joke or situation offensive, he must have some attachment to the principle or person being demeaned or put down in the joke. So racist and sexist jokes are offensive to many people who feel strongly about fighting bigotry and prejudice in the world. According to Veatch, when someone says, "So, what's the point?," it indicates the absence of any moral or emotional attachment or commitment to the joke's "victim."

Laughter and Health

We've long known that the ability to laugh is helpful to those coping with major illness and the stress of life's problems. But researchers are now saying laughter can do a lot more—it can basically bring balance to all the components of the immune system, which helps us fight off diseases.

As we mentioned earlier, laughter reduces levels of certain stress hormones. In doing this, laughter provides a safety valve that shuts off the flow of stress hormones and the fight-or-flight compounds that swing into action in our bodies when we experience stress, anger or hostility. These stress hormones suppress the immune system, increase the number of blood platelets (which can cause obstructions in arteries) and raise blood pressure. When we're laughing, natural killer cells that destroy tumors and viruses increase, as do Gamma-interferon (a disease-fighting protein), T-cells, which are a major part of the immune response, and B-cells, which make disease-destroying antibodies.

Laughter may lead to hiccuping and coughing, which clears the respiratory tract by dislodging mucous plugs. Laughter also increases the concentration of salivary immunoglobulin A, which defends against infectious organisms entering through the respiratory tract.

What may surprise you even more is the fact that researchers estimate that laughing 100 times is equal to 10 minutes on the rowing machine or 15 minutes on an exercise bike. Laughing can be a total body workout! Blood pressure is lowered, and there is an increase in vascular blood flow and in oxygenation of the blood, which further assists healing. Laughter also gives your diaphragm and abdominal, respiratory, facial, leg and back muscles a workout. That's why you often feel exhausted after a long bout of laughter—you've just had an aerobic workout!

The psychological benefits of humor are quite amazing, according to doctors and nurses who are members of the American Association for Therapeutic Humor. People often store negative emotions, such as anger, sadness and fear, rather than expressing them. Laughter provides a way for these emotions to be harmlessly released. Laughter is cathartic. That's why some people who are upset or stressed out go to a funny movie or a comedy club, so they can laugh the negative emotions away (these negative emotions, when held inside, can cause biochemical changes that can affect our bodies).

Increasingly, mental health professionals are suggesting "laughter therapy," which teaches people how to laugh—openly—at things that aren't usually funny and to cope in difficult situations by using humor. Following the lead of real-life funny-doc Patch Adams (portrayed by Robin Williams in a movie by the same name), doctors and psychiatrists are becoming more aware of the therapeutic benefits of laughter and humor. This is due, in part, to the growing body of humor and laughter scholarship (500 academicians from different disciplines belong to the International Society for Humor Studies).

Here are some tips to help you put more laughter in your life:

- Figure out what makes you laugh and do it (or read it or watch it) more often.
- Surround yourself with funny people—be with them every chance you get.
- Develop your own sense of humor. Maybe even take a class to learn how to be a better comic—or at least a better joke-teller at that next party. Be funny every chance you get—as long as it's not at someone else's expense!

GLENN GARVIN

All I Think Is That It's Stupid

Dave Barry on laughing at Very Big Government

A *New York Times* profile once said that *Miami Herald* humor columnist Dave Barry "makes his living by taking prosaic ideas to incongruous extremes." He is the only Pulitzer Prize winner to have a sitcom—CBS's *Dave's World*—based, very loosely, on his life. (They turned his one son and two dogs into just the opposite, but he enjoys cashing the checks.)

The Pulitzer Prize judges gave Barry the award for commentary in 1988 "for his consistently effective use of humor as a device for presenting fresh insights into serious concerns." His concerns include beer, Barbie, a "worldwide epidemic of snakes in toilets," exploding Pop-Tarts, and, perhaps most famously, "the worst songs ever recorded."

To be fair to the Pulitzer committee, the real Dave does devote more column inches than the average pundit to making Very Big Government look silly and obnoxious. This is a fresh insight in New York and Washington, and wildly popular with readers, who have bought more than a million copies of his books.

Taking prosaic ideas to incongruous extremes, he writes things like: "With the federal deficit running at several hundred billion dollars per year, Congress passed a transportation bill that, according to news reports, includes $30 million for a 'high-tech' moving sidewalk in Altoona, which happens to be in the district of Rep. 'Bud' Shuster, the ranking Republican on the surface transportation subcommittee.

5 "I don't know about you, but as a taxpayer, I am outraged to discover that, in this day and age, Altoona residents are still being forced to walk around on regular low-tech stationary sidewalks. I'm thinking of maybe organizing a group of us to go there and carry Altoonans on our backs until they get their new sidewalk. I'm also thinking that maybe we should donate an additional $10 million or so to build them a high-tech computerized Spit Launcher that will fire laser-guided gobs onto the moving sidewalk, so the Altoonans won't have to do this manually. 'What have I done today to help keep "Bud" Shuster in Congress?' is a question we all need to ask ourselves more often."

Contributing Editor Glenn Garvin interviewed Barry at his Miami Herald *office.*

Reason: You were in Washington recently to do a story. What was it like there?

Barry: It's like going to Mars. When you come back out no one is talking about any of the things the people in Washington are talking about.

If we're spending $853 trillion on some program now, and next year we spend any less, that's "budget-cutting" to them. For them, the question is always, "What kind of government intervention should we impose on the world?" They never think that maybe we shouldn't.

It gives me a real advantage as a humorist because I get credit for having insight and understanding—and I don't. I don't have any insight or understanding on anything about the government. All I think is that it's stupid—which is the one perspective that's almost completely lacking in Washington.

Reason: Did people there find your perspective peculiar?

Barry: They know this is what I do. Reporters aren't stupid. We were standing around talking about which of the 900 health-care proposals that nobody's going to accept is that day's hot news. They know how silly that is. But that's what they do. And if they don't do it, they'll get fired and someone else will do it. There's tremendous pressure, if you're in that system, to be involved and be interested and to care about it. There's no room to say, "This is stupid."

(One of the two tape recorders goes down. The reporter fiddles with it.)

Reason: I see why they wanted me to bring two. I'm totally humiliated. Virginia will be able to say, "Good thing I told you to bring two."

Barry: You know, if we had strict government standards about tape recorders, this kind of thing wouldn't happen. The consumer would be protected.

Reason: Was there anything surprising or unexpected about Washington?

Barry: I've been to Washington many times over the years for stories, and it always seems remarkably the same. More the same than the rest of the country. It's almost like they dress the same as they did 20 years ago. The same old guys are sitting outside the same dirty, dingy secret offices in the Capitol that you're not allowed to go in. But there's always this endless crowd of young, enthusiastic people who are in their Junior Achievement club or whatever, and someday they're going to be assistant to an aide to somebody. But they're making important contacts now that will serve them well the rest of their lives.

Reason: You're not sounding like a guy who has the fire in his belly for the '96 presidential race.

Barry: Oh, I never stop running. I'm not one of the weenies who drop out just because the electoral college votes. I'm still in the race. I'm an extremely corrupt candidate and I stress that in case anybody in our reading audience is interested in sending me money. You can have a naval base, is what I'm saying.

Reason: I would think that Washington would strain one's sense of humor. Sitting there listening to some imbecile like Paul Simon—the imbecile senator, not the folk singer—did you want to leap over his desk and cut his throat?

Barry: I'm a humorist. A guy like Paul Simon just makes my life so much simpler. When I was there, he had a hearing against hate. Steven Spielberg came and testified against hate. Paul Simon said hate was bad. Orrin Hatch was there, and he was against hate too. Everyone was opposed to hate. Is this really a wonderful way to spend our tax dollars, to have these men drone away about how against hate they are?

Reason: Did they make a token attempt to represent the pro-hate position?

Barry: No. But if the pro-hate lobby were to set up a PAC, I'm sure they'd be heard. It's not like they're not fair up there.

Reason: You've written in your columns about the strategic helium reserve the government keeps in case we have a sudden need for a fleet of dirigibles.

Barry: What bugs me when I write that is that I suspect 90 percent of my readers think I made it up.

Reason: What's something about the government that really pisses you off?

Barry: Well, that helium thing does. That's real money. All the tax money that I've ever, ever paid—and I've paid a lot of taxes—will not even begin to pay for one year of the strategic helium reserve. So when I sit and write a check out to the government, I can take it quite personally.

Reason: You don't sound like one of the people who fills out the IRS forms and then sends in voluntary contributions to alleviate the national debt.

Barry: No. Every year I write a tax advice column and I used to always make fun of that. One year, one of my favorite IRS commissioners, I think his name was Roscoe somebody, wrote that one of the most often-asked questions by taxpayers was, "How can I contribute more?" Well, I tell ya, ol' Roscoe's really been doing situps under parked cars again. I've heard a lot of people ask a lot of questions about taxes, but I never heard anybody say, "How can I, the ordinary person, send more money for no reason?"

Reason: Whatever happened to your $8.95 tax plan?

Barry: Oh, the $8.95 tax plan. Well, it was really popular with the average reader. It definitely reduced his taxes significantly. This was years ago, I think during the early Reagan years. I came up with a plan that everybody just pay $8.95 in taxes. Cheating would be allowed. But the incentive to cheat wouldn't be nearly as great if you only had to pay the $8.95. There were a few people who would have to pay hundreds of millions of dollars under this plan. I think it was Mark Goodson and Bill Todman, the guys who do the quiz shows. But almost everybody else would be off really cheap.

Reason: Do you ever get complaints that you're making people cynical?

Barry: Every now and then, when I write my annual tax column, some ex-IRS agent will complain, "There you go IRS bashing again." They're always saying that they're just doing their job. Someone I know once said, "You could get another job."

Reason: In your column I detect a certain skepticism at the notion that congressional spending creates jobs.

Barry: Of all the wonderful things government says, that's always been just about my favorite. As opposed to if you get to keep the money. Because what you'll do is go out and bury it in your yard, anything to prevent that money from creating jobs. They never stop saying it. They say it with a straight face and we in the press will write that down. We will say, "This is expected to create *x* number of jobs." On the other hand, we never say that the money we removed from another part of the economy will kill some jobs.

Reason: Have you ever had a government job?

Barry: No. I'm trying to think of what government job I would want. Maybe a disgruntled postal worker.

Reason: What's the most ridiculous government program you've ever written about or heard of?

Barry: I would really have a hard time just picking one. Anything at all in West Virginia is a good place to start. My favorite ones are when our own Defense Department says, "No, we really don't want you to build these weapons systems." Where do we stand now with the BI Bomber? We're going to build them but not put wings on them? We call it defense spending, but I wonder why we don't just hand the money to Lockheed and let them go out and spend it and not build a plane that might crash and kill somebody.

I don't think the press has done a very good job dealing with government spending. The Defense Department with the $9,500 toilet seat, that's not the problem anymore. Medicare and Medicaid and Social Security are the problem. That's us. That's our generation. There the press never says a word.

We certainly never require politicians to ever address those issues except really briefly sometimes during the New Hampshire primary, and then everybody falls asleep.

Reason: Have you noticed that baby boomers are showing alarming tendencies toward becoming safety Nazis?

Barry: I hate to speak for the whole society, but I will. I'm a journalist, it's my job. The real repressive, smug part of it seems to have passed. There's been something of a reaction against political correctness. Needless to say, the government hasn't caught up yet.

But when the boomers started to have kids reach adolescence, there was suddenly this feeling that they needed to protect their kids from all the same things they did when they were kids. Which I guess is a natural tendency, but it makes for a less fun society.

Reason: It strikes me as bizarre that a prospective Supreme Court justice has to get up there, in his 40s, and say, "No, I never smoked pot."

Barry: The whole thing about whether you smoke marijuana or not is so ridiculous. That and whether you protested the Vietnam War. Give me a break. Especially the marijuana thing. I'm inclined to think that anybody who never tried it should not be allowed in public office. But to make them get up there and lie, or at least be incredibly disingenuous, is just embarrassing.

After a while, the way this country deals with drugs is just not funny. What a waste of everyone's time and effort. What a waste of a lot of people's lives. The way we deal with drugs and sex. I saw one of these real-life cop drama shows, and they mounted a camera in this undercover agent's pickup truck, right under the gear shift, and they sent him out to pick up prostitutes.

So the whole show consisted of this guy, who's quite a good actor, driving to this one street, and young prostitutes come up to him and solicit him. He says OK. They get in. They're trying real hard to be nice. He's going to pay $23, that's all he's got and they said that's OK. Meanwhile, behind him the other cops, these fat men with walkie-talkies, are laughing and chuckling because here they are about to enforce the law and protect society. They take her to some street and then of course they come up and arrest her. This poor woman—I don't know whether she's feeding her drug habit or feeding her kids or whatever. And the cops are so proud of themselves, these big strapping guys.

It just made me sick to see this. To treat these people who are trying to make a living, one way or another, this way, and to be proud of it. It's on television and we're all supposed to watch this and feel good about it. It's just disgusting.

It's like when cops sell drugs to people and then arrest them. And then we reach the point where I think it was Sheriff Nick Navarro in Broward County [Florida] had his lab making crack so they could sell it. They couldn't get enough in south Florida, so they had to actually produce it themselves.

What politician would say, "This is really a waste of money to be doing what we're doing? It's ridiculous sending cops out to arrest prostitutes when we're supposed to be concerned about crime in this country." What politician would ever say that? What newspaper person would ever say that without getting stomped all over by all the other hypocrites?

Reason: *(Reporter fiddles with broken tape recorder, trying to fix it. It still doesn't work.)* I feel guilty sitting here knowing I don't have two tape recorders running like Virginia wanted. No one has ever crossed Virginia Postrel and lived to tell about it.

Barry: I can't help but notice that the Japanese product is the one working.

Reason: Didn't you once get a letter from someone on the Supreme Court?

Barry: I got a letter from [Justice] John Paul Stevens. I won't call it a serious letter. It was on his official John Paul Stevens stationery, though. He brought to my attention a product that I already knew about called Beano, which is an anti-flatulence product. I was very pleased to get a Supreme Court justice suggesting a column, so I went and did a column about Beano. I went with my wife and another guy to a Mexican restaurant which we thought would be the ultimate test for an anti-flatulence product. There's a reason most of Mexico is located out of doors. And it worked. Several newspapers refused to run that column. But they did run advertisements for Beano.

Reason: You write about Miami as a place filled with people from many different lands, cultures, backgrounds, walks of life all of whom want to kill each other. When they were going bring a pro basketball team, you suggested we call it the "Giant Blood-Sucking Insects." So why do you live here?

Barry: Well, for one thing the *Herald* is here. If the *Herald* was in Minneapolis, I'd probably be in Minneapolis.

That isn't the main reason. I actually like south Florida. I never lived in a more interesting place than this. I've never met such a wide range of people. I guess when I came here I thought there were Cubans and then there were people from New York and that was Miami. Now I know that it's Cubans, people from New York and some people from New Jersey.

Actually, there are people from all over—not just Latin America, certainly not just Cuba, but all over Europe, all over the United States. A lot of them just got here and have interesting stories to tell about where they are from. I like that. I like knowing a lot of different types of people. And I can afford to live in a relatively safe part of Miami.

Reason: Do you go along with the conventional Miami opinion that we should invade Haiti since they've sent all these dangerous rafts to our shores?

Barry: I guess like every other American I feel very threatened by the situation in Haiti. I know our own lifestyle here is hanging by a thread because of what's going on down there.

Reason: What about Cuba? What's the solution to this Cuban business?

Barry: Let them in! Look what they did for Miami. This was a pathetic little town and now it's a big city. It's just so silly. Let people come in and work, but come in and work. If we let them come in for the purpose of signing them up for government programs, I'm not too enthused about that.

Reason: One of the planks in your presidential campaign is the Department of Two Guys Named Victor.

Barry: This is one of those times I wasn't kidding. At the time, we were mad at Moammar Gadhafi, which resulted in us bombing all over Libya and killing a bunch of people, but not him. Then Ronald Reagan gets up and says we're not trying to kill him, we're just dropping bombs. You can kill all the Libyans you want, but legally you can't try to kill the leader.

The other one was Manuel Noriega. Here we have a problem with just one person, and we send all these troops down to deal with it. All these people get killed and hurt, but not Noriega.

So instead of messing around with armies, get a couple of guys named Victor. The president meets with them and has breakfast, or he goes to dinner with them at the restaurant of their choice, and suggests that he's having a problem. Then the next thing you know, you read in the paper that Saddam Hussein has suffered an unfortunate shaving accident resulting in the loss of his head. We don't involve a lot of 22-year-old kids in this dispute between George Bush and Saddam Hussein.

Reason: Let's talk about Vietnam. Did you think the war was evil, that we were fighting the wrong guys, or was it like, to paraphrase Muhammad Ali, "You didn't have any quarrel with no Vietcong"?

Barry: First of all I thought that was the best argument anybody ever gave against going to Vietnam. The most articulate, clear-cut, understandable, accurate, rational argument ever. To me, it showed a lot more wisdom than a lot of stuff I heard from anti-war people. There was a lot of talk about why we should be opposed to the war that was pro-totalitarian.

I felt ashamed at the time to say I didn't want to go. I didn't have any stake in that war. I didn't want to get killed; I didn't know anybody over there that I wanted to go over and kill on behalf of. I think the real gut-level reason was what Ali said. But at the time I felt that you had to have a moral justification. It didn't occur to me then that the moral justification is that other people can't tell you who to kill.

If they come for my kid, I'd say, "Go, if you want to go fight a war. If you don't, you don't. Nobody's got the right to tell you." I see that more clearly now than I did then. But in the climate of the times I believed the government did have the right to tell us all what to do, but that in this case they were just making a terrible mistake. I admire more the people who just said, "I'm not going because I don't want to."

But I had conscientious objector status. I got it because my dad was a C.O. in World War II. My dad was a Presbyterian minister. And I went to a Quaker college. Neither of those things had anything to do with me. But to my draft board—a bunch of plumbers in Peekskill, New York, making decisions about who should go and who shouldn't—that looked good.

I was really against that war, but to be a C.O., you had to believe that there was no circumstance under which you would ever kill anybody. And I can't say I honestly felt that. I would definitely kill people. I would have liked to have killed my draft board at the time.

This was in 1969 and it was getting harder to find jobs that were acceptable because they were all getting filled up with C.O.s. I ended up working for the Episcopal Church national headquarters in New York City as a bookkeeper. That's what I did for two years. But I was happy, because I knew guys who were getting shot. Sometimes I can't believe this actually happened in this country.

Reason: Let's play a little game.

Barry: You're not gonna ask me what kind of tree I would be?

Reason: That's the last question. Let's do a little word association. I'll give you the name of a political figure and you say the first thing that comes to mind.

Barry: Oh, I hate this.

Reason: Oliver Stone.

Barry: Am I only allowed to say one word? Shithead. Oliver Stone—did you mean Oliver North or Oliver Stone?

Reason: Oliver Stone.

Barry: Oh, Oliver Stone. Shithead.

Reason: Janet Reno.

Barry: Out of her depth. I actually kind of like Janet Reno. She seems like a nice enough lady. But when you're basically going through the entire phone book trying to find women lawyers who don't have maids to pick the attorney general of the United States, how well can you do?

Reno taking responsibility for the Waco thing made me crazy. It enraged. Seemingly nobody wants to know what actually happened. There were some gun violations and we end up in a situation where we are surrounding them. I kept saying, "Why don't they just walk away? Just walk away. Nobody has to die. Walk away. Later on, arrest them when they come out. But walk away."

But no, we can't do it. So we order these tanks to attack this building full of crazy people with kids, and lo and behold, bad things happen. Ha! Knock me down with a feather. It got me when Janet said, "I'll take responsibility." No. You can't say that. And if you mean it, then you have to resign your job right away.

Maybe what she meant was "I'll take political responsibility for it," which turns out to be a big plus. But if you're going to take real moral responsibility for those deaths, then take it. But don't take it and say you're still going to be the chief law enforcement officer of the United States.

That's not what you wanted. You wanted a one-word answer.

Reason: That's OK. Bill Clinton.

Barry: He's such a putz. He's basically my age; I knew a lot of people like him in college. It starts to really come home to you how inadequately prepared anybody is to be in charge of your life from a distance and to be given a lot of power when that person is basically your age and background. He strikes me as a pathetic figure. Because you can be the smartest person in the world—which he is, and if he's not, his wife is—and care more than anybody else in the world—which he does, I don't doubt that for a minute. And you can care so much that you're willing to be dishonest—you can tell people one thing but do another because you really know it's for their own good. And you'll still screw it all up. Because the whole premise of what you're doing's wrong!

Reason: I was talking to one of your editors as I did my lengthy—lengthy, Virginia!—preparation for this interview.

Barry: And it cost a lot, too!

Reason: One of your editors said, "Well, Dave's a libertarian, that's true. But he's not an irresponsible libertarian." Doesn't that kind of take the fun out of it?

Barry: I'm not sure what they mean by that. If you tell most people what libertarians think, they immediately assume that you cannot mean it all the way, that you're really just taking a position for argument's sake. When you say you don't think we should have public schools, they can't believe you mean that. You must mean that they should be smaller. But you can't really mean no public schools. Therefore, if I don't argue too much, they probably think I'm responsible. I don't think I'm particularly responsible. I resent that!

Reason: Last fall you wrote a piece in the *Tropic* and explicitly acknowledged being a libertarian . . .

Barry: John Dorschner, one of our staff writers here at *Tropic* magazine at the *Miami Herald,* who is a good friend of mine and an excellent journalist, but a raving liberal, wrote a story about a group that periodically pops up saying that they're going to start their own country or start their own planet or go back to their original planet, or whatever. They were going to "create a libertarian society" on a floating platform in the Caribbean somewhere. You know and I know there's never going to be a country on a floating anything, but if they want to talk about it, that's great.

John wrote about it and he got into the usual thing where he immediately got to the question of whether or not you can have sex with dogs. The argument was that if it wasn't illegal to have sex with dogs, naturally people would have sex with dogs. That argument always sets my teeth right on edge.

And I always want to retort with, "You want a horrible system, because you think the people should be able to vote for laws they want, and if more than half of them voted for some law, everyone would have to do what they said. Then they could pass a law so that you had to have sex with dogs."

I was ranting and raving about this here in the office. So my editor, Tom Shroder, said "Why don't you write a counterpoint to it?"

So I wrote about why I didn't think libertarians are really doing this kind of thing so that they can have sex with dogs. I discussed some of the reasons that a person might want to live out of the control of our federal, state, local, and every other form of government. Actually, I don't think I even called myself a libertarian in the article. I think Tom Shroder identified me as one.

Reason: Did that give you pause, coming out of the closet on this?

Barry: I guess libertarianism is always considered so weird and fringe that people assume that you're in the closet if you don't go around talking about it. Usually in interviews we're talking about humor writing and they don't bring it up. Because I don't write an overly political column, people just assume I'm not. I guess nobody assumes anybody is a libertarian. It's a more complex political discussion than most people are used to, to explain why you think the way you do about public education or drug laws, and why it's not as simple as being for or against something.

Reason: Did you get any mail about being a libertarian after that article?

Barry: I got a few letters, mostly pretty nice. One or two letters saying, "Here's why it wouldn't work to be a libertarian, because people will have sex with dogs." Arguments like, "Nobody would educate the kids." People say, "Of course you have to have public education because otherwise nobody would send their kids to school." And you'd have to say, "Would you not send your kids to school? Would you not educate them?" "Well, no. I would. But all those other people would be having sex with dogs."

Reason: How did you become a libertarian?

Barry: I can tell you the person responsible. His name is Sheldon Richman and he is still something of a wheel in libertarian circles. He's at the Cato Institute now. Sheldon and I were working for competing newspapers when we met in suburban Philadelphia in the early '70s. We were at municipal meetings, which were hell for Sheldon. He was a libertarian way, way back. I don't know what I was. I came out of college with lots of trappings of '60s radicalism which had been tempered somewhat by the fact that almost all the real radicals I knew were assholes. You know, the guys who were "for the people," but really just seemed to hate people. And guys who wanted to be in Weatherman mainly so they could get into fights.

Sheldon and I would argue. I mean, really argue. Well, what if a baby is born with no arms and no legs and his parents both die? Huh? Doesn't society have a obligation? Sheldon was wonderfully patient and had a excellent sense of humor and never lost his temper, which is not true of me. I'd yell at Sheldon and get furious at Sheldon, but we were still friends.

I left journalism for a while and I was working for a consulting company where I taught effective writing seminars and by my recommendation we hired Sheldon. We argued more. I was a middle-of-the-road Democrat more than anything else. I know I voted for Carter. Watergate taught me how bad the Republicans were. Then in the late '70s, I begin to see. I think the gas crisis had something to do with it. I began to realize, this is all happening because of the government. And I began to think about all the government people I knew, all the times I'd sat in meetings with Sheldon, watching people who were theoretically for the common good. Then I realized not one of them was and none of them ever have been. All these things Sheldon had said to me: There is no such thing as the common good, there is no such thing as society. He was right.

So I wrote him a letter. "Sheldon, I just wanted to let you know that in all the arguments you were right."

Reason: Here you are a libertarian and you work for the *Miami Herald,* conceivably the most anti-libertarian newspaper in North America.

Barry: You mean our editorial board. The eight or 10 people who nobody knows here who speak for this paper.

I don't like anything unsigned in a newspaper that purports to be the opinion of some group if we don't know who the group is. It's laughable to say that the *Miami Herald's* editorials or any newspaper's editorials represent any views other than those of the people writing them, so why don't we tell everybody who they are?

It bothers me greatly that we have this system of opinion pages that dates back to when you knew who the owner of the paper was and his editorial told you what he thought. We should call editorials what they are: columns written by committees. If you want to agree with the committee, that's great. But they don't speak for me and they don't speak for a lot of people who work at the paper. I want to gag sometimes when I see who "we" are recommending that people vote for, and not just as a libertarian.

Reason: Is this a reference to the First Lady's brother?

Barry: Yeah. We are recommending that people vote for Hugh Rodham for the Senate of the United States!

Reason: You write a lot about rock 'n' roll. From a philosophical standpoint, what's the worst rock 'n' roll song of all time?

Barry: My nomination right off the top my head is a song that was a hit in the '70s—"Signs, signs, everywhere signs, blocking up the scenery, breaking my mind, do this, don't do that, can't you read the signs?" Basically a diatribe against property rights.

Reason: That was by The Five Man Electrical Band.

Barry: It's a real smug self-righteous punk kid saying nobody has the right to tell him what to do and how dare you put a sign up saying that I can't go on your property? Hey, kid! Stick this sign up your ass.

Reason: You wrote a serious column about your son's bicycle accident, in which you concluded that he should wear a helmet even though he looks like a dork. Now a lot of states are considering mandatory bicycle helmet laws. What do you think about that?

Barry: I got a lot of mail about that column, which is the only serious column I've ever written that went out as a regular column. It was the only time I ever had anything to say, which is, "Make a kid wear a helmet."

I got a lot of mail from organizations concerned with bike safety. Then I got a couple from people who wanted my support for mandatory helmet laws. I can't support that. If you pass a law like that you'll do more harm than good, because you'll make people think they've done something about the problem when they haven't.

There's only one way kids will wear helmets, and that's if their parents are nagging them to. They will never wear helmets because some state passes a law requiring it.

I genuinely think in this case—just 'cause I know my son and I know his friends—that kind of legislation would focus responsibility in the wrong place. It's not up to the cops, for God's sake. So I know that all over America there's probably politicians sending out pictures of themselves signing that mandatory helmet bill, but it's bullshit. I say that as a parent.

Reason: As your son grew up and began getting into activities where he had the potential to break things and kill himself, did that cause you to rethink your views?

Barry: No. He does hurl that back in my face sometimes. I said, "Rob, as soon as you are paying your own way in life, I'll stop telling you what to do. But you're not. You're taking money from me, living in my house." I try really hard to make him a responsible person.

Reason: What if the 7-Eleven down the street put in a vending machine where you could get heroin for a quarter?

Barry: And then have sex with a dog? Meaning what? My son wouldn't go get heroin. If he did or didn't, it wouldn't have anything to do with whether it was legal or illegal. I did all this stuff that was illegal when I was a kid. I drank beer when I was 15. I smoked cigarettes when I was 13. I drove to New York City when I was 14—don't tell my son. Those things were against the law, but I did them anyway. I didn't become a heroin addict, although I probably could have gotten heroin somehow. I don't think my son would buy heroin at any price. He knows what it is, and he knows how stupid it is. Any parent that relies on any law to help him parent is an idiot.

Reason: Why did you leave Coral Gables, the Miami suburb that's the libertarian paradise?

Barry: God, you talk about a libertarian nightmare! We got a ticket for painting our own living room white. And they came to the door, a guy in a uniform.

Reason: This is inside the house?

Barry: The interior living room. It turned out you had to have a permit if the job cost more than $50. I don't know what you can possibly do for less than $50 to have somebody come in your house. I had to pay the painter to go down to the city hall. This is after I called up city hall and ended up actually screaming. The painter spent a day getting a permit to do a job that took about half a day to actually do.

Then I wrote a column about that and discovered that there were people in Coral Gables who would wait until 2 o'clock in the morning to replace a sink because to do it during the daytime you'd see the trucks outside. Two trucks. That's a carpenter and a plumber. So that's two different permits. People were not fixing their houses because they didn't know how to get the permits. It was crazy.

Reason: If you have a cat out of the house, it's supposed to be on a leash there.

Barry: Yeah, and you're not allowed to park a truck in your driveway. You're not allowed to work on your house on Sunday. The people who enforce these laws are nuts. After I wrote a column on this, I got I don't know how many letters from Coral Gables homeowners, story after story after story, wonderfully horrible stories. And the venom they felt for their own government! You cannot paint the exterior of your house. You have to take the paint chip down to show the paint chip Nazis. It goes on all the time and it's hilarious. People are afraid to own their own homes. People are afraid their own government will catch them fixing their houses.

Reason: Thank you.

CHAPTER 15

HONESTY AND DECEPTION

Overview

In many cultures honesty is one of the most appreciated qualities. People do not like to be deceived. Even so-called white lies taint our impressions of others. We ask ourselves, "Why couldn't she have told me the truth?" having discovered after treating a friend to an expensive lobster dinner, for instance, that she does not share our fondness for seafood. Or we might confront a friend who told us that we looked fine before we attended a party wearing an outfit that proved inappropriate by stating, "You could have saved me a lot of embarrassment if you had just spoken the truth." These small lies can lead us to mistrust others and make us doubt their judgment in the future.

Ethics implore us to be honest. Philosopher Martin Buber (1878–1965) suggested that ethical treatment involves maintaining relationships that do not objectify another person's humanity. Lying treats other people as objects. We do not bestow on those people the dignity of being told the truth. We act as if we know what they can handle or understand better than they do.

Since violating ethical standards by deceiving others and the consequences of deception often outweigh the minor hurt feelings that might occur if we are honest, it seems advantageous to always tell the truth. So why do we lie? Nobody I know can claim to have never deceived somebody, but most would claim to be honest overall.

If we distance ourselves from pathological embezzlers or frauds who make a living deceiving others—who lie to conceal wrongdoing from

This icon will direct you to web links and additional resources on the website college.hmco.com/pic/thelin1e

authorities—we might be able to see lying in a different light. Deception may serve a purpose that is not as nefarious as we have been taught to believe.

For one, people have a right to their privacy. Sometimes, we simply do not wish to reveal details about our lives when people ask us questions. We have comfort zones regarding our personal lives, so we set up invisible barriers between public and private knowledge that are impermeable to strangers and acquaintances. Most of us, for instance, do not open our dalliances to public inspection. We also prefer to keep information about some illnesses between our doctors and ourselves. Many people believe that household finances—especially if the family is struggling financially—are no one else's business.

The difficulty arises from people's curiosity. Often, maybe inadvertently, we ask about things that others consider to be private. For example, you might ask a classmate, "How did you do on that exam?" Whether the person received a passing or failing grade, the classmate might feel that grades do not constitute an open competition and that the information should remain strictly between herself or himself and the professor. The person should be able to say, "I'm sorry, I like to keep those things to myself." But this answer strikes most listeners as evasive, if not overly protective, and we start assuming that the person failed the exam.

Perhaps media, with their intrusive questions about public figures' lives, have led us to believe that if there is no shame to hide, people should give answers. This forces people to lie to protect the boundaries of the personal and private. The more personal the information others seek from us, the more likely we are to defuse the situation with a lie. The most innocent person will look guilty if he answers "Are you having an extramarital affair?" with "That's none of your business." The latter answer functions as an admission of guilt. Therefore, the answer always must be, "No, of course not."

Whether we want to cloak incidents that deviate from standard morality, conceal unruly desires that might reveal character weaknesses, keep unpopular opinions to ourselves, or simply keep a secret, we deceive others for privacy's sake. Our belief in the privacy of our lives outweighs our belief in honesty. For an honest society to exist, people would have to quash their curiosity and not ask questions that might intrude on other's privacy. Since the boundaries are so different among individuals and between subcultures, lying becomes the best available option.

The irrationality of others also forces us into protective lying. A rational person, by most people's definition, does not prod someone unduly or enter into confrontations when his or her agenda meets resistance. Unreasonable people intrude on private matters, and they also act aggressively in public or in the course of their jobs, perhaps trying to coerce us to do something we do not want to do. Not being able to articulate our doubts or not caring to fully share our reasoning, we invent lies that will satisfy these people and avoid further confrontation.

Experiences with some salespeople epitomize the need for this type of lying. We often have to choose between being rude or lying to free ourselves from sales pitches we have no interest in hearing. I cannot count the number of times I have said, "No, I am not interested in a free vacation" and "No, I have no interest in being a millionaire." Such lies end the conversation; the salesperson has nothing left with which to lure me. Similarly, I lie to people wanting me to donate to charities or to support their religious affiliations. Of course, I want to feed starving children, comfort leukemia sufferers, and aid earthquake victims, but I do not want to have to explain my priorities and reasoning to people who try to make me feel guilty through insistence. Thus, I fabricate stories about balloon payments on my house or flooding in my basement. Though I am actually fascinated by any type of religious discussion, when people preach their convictions at me, I feel forced to tell them lies to preclude possible confrontations.

Rational people can become irrational in certain sensitive areas—such as about sports teams, politics, and work-related matters—and cannot accept disagreement. To keep confrontations from escalating into physical violence, other reasonable people lie. We step out of such a situation, in other words, by feigning agreement or pretending that the person's points have made us think differently. In our relationships, we also find ourselves telling these types of lies to avoid heated exchanges or other forms of stress.

Another type of deception comes from wanting to draw attention to ourselves. Few of us want to be taken for granted or ignored. We want to believe that events in our lives have significance and that we influence these events to some degree. Few of us actually live action-packed lives full of excitement and relevance. We are far more likely to feel like cogs in machines. Thus, when someone tells an exciting story, we might be jealous or want to chip in, perhaps to take the spotlight away, perhaps to create an affinity with other listeners. Therefore, we exaggerate our involvement in a similar story or fabricate details of a conflict to make ourselves look heroic or victorious.

Exaggerated stories can be the source of amusement at a party or get-together. Many cultures have long traditions of telling tall tales to bring a sense of magic or mystery or to relieve boredom. We can teach children cautious behavior by pulling their legs with stories meant to illustrate the dangerous outcomes of activities they might otherwise pursue. Generally, though, such lies function as entertainment and give the teller an identity that denies the tedium or dreariness in his or her life and establishes some importance that, however illusory, grants privilege or status in a group setting. If people did not try to call attention to themselves, we might not enjoy get-togethers as much as we do. So lies can function in a positive way for both teller and listener.

A much more complicated form of deception comes from a conflict between larger truth and mere honesty. While the actual evidence and details of a situation might point to our blame, we might not feel that we did anything wrong. We might embrace such values as personal responsibility, sincerity, and fairness that conflict with how we felt we were treated. An honest retelling of the events might obscure the larger truth we find in these values.

One day, when I was a teenager, I waved and yelled hello to my friend George, who was driving by. George turned toward me and started shouting a question about whether I needed a ride. As he was doing this, another car pulled out of a parking space, and the front end of George's car crashed into the driver's side of the other car. Its driver, an older man, got out and started blaming George for the accident, saying that he wasn't looking where he was going. George had not been looking at the road; however, he had the right of way and could not have avoided the accident even if he had been looking. I was the only witness. If I had said that George had turned to look at me a second before the accident, the credibility of the experienced driver, as compared to the lack of credibility of seventeen-year-old George, would have persuaded insurance companies and even courts to believe his account of the story, which was that his car had been stationary, waiting for George to pass, when George swerved into him. So I lied, saying that I saw George traveling down the road, looking straight ahead, when the other car pulled out in front of him.

Some might see such a lie as merely protecting a friend, but to me it served the purpose of justice. It might have been best if we all admitted our roles in the accident. I had distracted George; he hadn't brought his car to a complete stop to ask me about a ride; and the older man had pulled out into traffic instead of first letting George pass. But if the other driver had used my honesty to escape responsibility, a larger deception would have emerged. Most of us, I think, do not want to allow such injustices, so we lie to try to bring about fairer conclusions to incidents like this one.

Ultimately, we feel compelled toward honesty, and we never want to present ourselves as liars to people we want to favorably impress. We anguish over our own transgressions of ethics. But situations demand that we lie. We cannot get around it. The question, then, is our personal code: How many of our lies spring from selfishness? How many will hurt others? How much worse will a situation be if we lie? The only way to judge the value of honesty and deception, it seems, is to understand them in the context of our other values.

Openings for Writers

1. **Privacy** How much privacy should a person have? What social or political circumstances might make people lie to maintain their privacy? Is there always something to hide? Why might a person lie about something about which she or he feels no particular shame but just thinks is none of anybody else's business?
2. **Embezzlers and frauds** What does a person have to do to be called an embezzler and/or fraud? What distinguishes embezzlement and fraud from other types of lies? Are there ways in which our culture—through movies, public endorsements, or political chicanery—validates embezzlers and frauds? If so, why would we do that? If not, what values separate their activities and those of other people who deceive?
3. **Prioritizing values** Make a list of the values you hold, starting from the most important and ending with the least important. Where does honesty rank? Why did you put other values above or below it?
4. **Tall tales** Think of stories told in your family that you believe stretched the truth (at least at some level). Were there purposes to the stories? Write about the way you feel when you hear the stories and whether different

feelings crop up now. If you can't think of any, analyze "The Lightning Struck Lost Mine" (page 469), which serves as a typical tale of a lost treasure that might be seen as fanciful when scrutinized.

Language

1. **Stretching the truth** Is the expression "stretching the truth" a euphemism (discussed in Chapter 5)? Compare it with other terms used for deception, and decide how the words you choose to describe lies shape the perception of a person or incident.
2. **Justice** Is justice predicated on honesty? Compare it to other concepts such as revenge, vengeance, and retribution. Do the differences shed light on the point the overview makes about larger truth?
3. **Honesty** How is honesty related to truth? What definition you can come up with, and what understandings of key terms must a person have for your definition to be acceptable?

STEPHEN L. CARTER

The Insufficiency of Honesty

In this 1996 article published in the Atlantic Monthly, *Stephen Carter argues that honesty does not require the ethical consideration that integrity does. He feels that people can use honesty as an excuse for performing the bare minimum under an agreement or for being forthright about beliefs without exercising proper judgment. His views about honesty complicate the understandings put forward in the overview.*

> *Honesty is not synonymous with integrity—and integrity is what we need*

A couple of years ago I began a university commencement address by telling the audience that I was going to talk about integrity. The crowd broke into applause. Applause! Just because they had heard the word "integrity": that's how starved for it they were. They had no idea how I was using the word, or what I was going to say about integrity, or, indeed, whether I was for it or against it. But they knew they liked the idea of talking about it.

Very well, let us consider this word "integrity." Integrity is like the weather: everybody talks about it but nobody knows what to do about it. Integrity is that stuff that we always want more of. Some say that we need to return to the good old days when we had a lot more of it. Others say that we as a nation have never really had enough of it. Hardly anybody stops to explain exactly what we mean by it, or how we know it is a good thing, or why everybody needs to have the same amount of it. Indeed, the only trouble with integrity is that everybody who uses the word seems to mean something slightly different.

For instance, when I refer to integrity, do I mean simply "honesty"? The answer is no; although honesty is a virtue of importance, it is a different virtue from integrity. Let us, for simplicity, think of honesty as not lying; and let us further accept Sissela Bok's definition of a lie: "any intentionally deceptive message which is *stated.*" Plainly, one cannot have integrity without being honest (although, as we shall see, the matter gets complicated), but one can certainly be honest and yet have little integrity.

When I refer to integrity, I have something very specific in mind. Integrity, as I will use the term, requires three steps: discerning what is right and what is wrong; acting on what you have discerned, even at personal cost; and saying openly that you are acting on your understanding of right and wrong. The first criterion captures the idea that integrity requires a degree of moral reflectiveness. The second brings in the ideal of a person of integrity as steadfast, a quality that includes keeping one's commitments. The third reminds us that a person of integrity can be trusted.

5 The first point to understand about the difference between honesty and integrity is that a person may be entirely honest without ever engaging in the hard work of discernment that integrity requires: she may tell us quite truthfully what she believes without ever taking the time to figure out whether what she believes is good and right and true. The problem may be as simple as someone's foolishly saying something that hurts a friend's feelings; a few moments of thought would have revealed the likelihood of the hurt and the lack of necessity for the comment. Or the problem may be more complex, as when a man who was raised from birth in a society that preaches racism states his belief in one race's inferiority as a fact, without ever really considering that perhaps this deeply held view is wrong. Certainly the racist is being honest—he is telling us what he actually thinks—but his honesty does not add up to integrity.

Telling Everything You Know

A wonderful epigram sometimes attributed to the filmmaker Sam Goldwyn goes like this: "The most important thing in acting is honesty; once you learn to fake that, you're in." The point is that honesty can be something one *seems* to have. Without integrity, what passes for honesty often is nothing of the kind; it is fake honesty—or it is honest but irrelevant and perhaps even immoral.

Consider an example. A man who has been married for fifty years confesses to his wife on his deathbed that he was unfaithful thirty-five years earlier. The dishonesty was killing his spirit, he says. Now he has cleared his conscience and is able to die in peace.

The husband has been honest—sort of. He has certainly unburdened himself. And he has probably made his wife (soon to be his widow) quite miserable in the process, because even if she forgives him, she will not be able to remember him with quite the vivid image of love and loyalty that she had hoped for. Arranging his own emotional affairs to ease his transition to death, he has shifted to his wife the burden of confusion and pain, perhaps for the rest of her life. Moreover, he has attempted his honesty at the one time in his life when it carries no risk; acting in accordance with what you think is right and risking no loss in the process is a rather thin and unadmirable form of honesty.

Besides, even though the husband has been honest in a sense, he has now twice been unfaithful to his wife: once thirty-five years ago, when he had his affair, and again when, nearing death, he decided that his own peace of mind was more important than hers. In trying to be honest he has violated his marriage vow by acting toward his wife not with love but with naked and perhaps even cruel self-interest.

As my mother used to say, you don't have to tell people everything you 10
know. Lying and nondisclosure, as the law often recognizes, are not the same thing. Sometimes it is actually illegal to tell what you know, as, for example, in the disclosure of certain financial information by market insiders. Or it may be unethical, as when a lawyer reveals a confidence entrusted to her by a client. It may be simple bad manners, as in the case of a gratuitous comment to a colleague on his or her attire. And it may be subject to religious punishment, as when a Roman Catholic priest breaks the seal of the confessional—an offense that carries automatic excommunication.

In all the cases just mentioned, the problem with telling everything you know is that somebody else is harmed. Harm may not be the intention, but it is certainly the effect. Honesty is most laudable when we risk harm to ourselves; it becomes a good deal less so if we instead risk harm to others when there is no gain to anyone other than ourselves. Integrity may counsel keeping our secrets in order to spare the feelings of others. Sometimes, as in the example of the wayward husband, the reason we want to tell what we know is precisely to shift our pain onto somebody else—a course of action dictated less by integrity than by self-interest. Fortunately, integrity and self-interest often coincide, as when a politician of integrity is rewarded with our votes. But often they do not, and it is at those moments that our integrity is truly tested.

Error

Another reason that honesty alone is no substitute for integrity is that if forthrightness is not preceded by discernment, it may result in the expression of an incorrect moral judgment. In other words, I may be honest about what I believe, but if I have never tested my beliefs, I may be wrong. And here I mean "wrong" in a particular sense: the proposition in question is wrong if I would change my mind about it after hard moral reflection.

Consider this example. Having been taught all his life that women are not as smart as men, a manager gives the women on his staff less-challenging assignments than he gives the men. He does this, he believes, for their own benefit: he does not want them to fail, and he believes that they will if he gives them tougher assignments. Moreover, when one of the women on his staff does poor work, he does not berate her as harshly as he would a man, because he expects nothing more. And he claims to be acting with integrity because he is acting according to his own deepest beliefs.

The manager fails the most basic test of integrity. The question is not whether his actions are consistent with what he most deeply believes but whether he has done the hard work of discerning whether what he most deeply believes is right. The manager has not taken this harder step.

Moreover, even within the universe that the manager has constructed for himself, he is not acting with integrity. Although he is obviously wrong to think that the women on his staff are not as good as the men, even were he right, that would not justify applying different standards to their work. By so doing he betrays both his obligation to the institution that employs him and his duty as a manager to evaluate his employees.

The problem that the manager faces is an enormous one in our practical politics, where having the dialogue that makes democracy work can seem impossible because of our tendency to cling to our views even when we have not examined them. As Jean Bethke Elshtain has said, borrowing from John Courtney Murray, our politics are so fractured and contentious that we often cannot even reach *disagreement.* Our refusal to look closely at our own most cherished principles is surely a large part of the reason. Socrates thought the unexamined life not worth living. But the unhappy truth is that few of us actually have the time for constant reflection on our views—on public or private morality. Examine them we must, however, or we will never know whether we might be wrong.

None of this should be taken to mean that integrity as I have described it presupposes a single correct truth. If, for example, your integrity-guided search tells you that affirmative action is wrong, and my integrity-guided search tells me that affirmative action is right, we need not conclude that one of us lacks integrity. As it happens, I believe—both as a Christian and as a secular citizen who struggles toward moral understanding—that we *can* find true and sound answers to our moral questions. But I do not pretend to have found very many of them, nor is an exposition of them my purpose here.

It is the case not that there aren't any right answers but that, given human fallibility, we need to be careful in assuming that we have found them. However, today's political talk about how it is wrong for the government to impose one person's morality on somebody else is just mindless chatter. *Every* law imposes one person's morality on somebody else, because law has only two functions: to tell people to do what they would rather not or to forbid them to do what they would.

And if the surveys can be believed, there is far more moral agreement in America than we sometimes allow ourselves to think. One of the reasons that character education for young people makes so much sense to so many people is precisely that there seems to be a core set of moral understandings—we might call them the American Core—that most of us accept. Some of the virtues in this American Core are, one hopes, relatively noncontroversial. About

500 American communities have signed on to Michael Josephson's program to emphasize the "six pillars" of good character: trustworthiness, respect, responsibility, caring, fairness, and citizenship. These virtues might lead to a similarly noncontroversial set of political values: having an honest regard for ourselves and others, protecting freedom of thought and religious belief, and refusing to steal or murder.

Honesty and Competing Responsibilities

A further problem with too great an exaltation of honesty is that it may al- 20
low us to escape responsibilities that morality bids us bear. If honesty is substituted for integrity, one might think that if I say I am not planning to fulfill a duty, I need not fulfill it. But it would be a peculiar morality indeed that granted us the right to avoid our moral responsibilities simply by stating our intention to ignore them. Integrity does not permit such an easy escape.

Consider an example. Before engaging in sex with a woman, her lover tells her that if she gets pregnant, it is her problem, not his. She says that she understands. In due course she does wind up pregnant. If we believe, as I hope we do, that the man would ordinarily have a moral responsibility toward both the child he will have helped to bring into the world and the child's mother, then his honest statement of what he intends does not spare him that responsibility.

This vision of responsibility assumes that not all moral obligations stem from consent or from a stated intention. The linking of obligations to promises is a rather modern and perhaps uniquely Western way of looking at life, and perhaps a luxury that only the well-to-do can afford. As Fred and Shulamit Korn (a philosopher and an anthropologist) have pointed out, "If one looks at ethnographic accounts of other societies, one finds that, while obligations everywhere play a crucial role in social life, promising is not preeminent among the sources of obligation and is not even mentioned by most anthropologists." The Korns have made a study of Tonga, where promises are virtually unknown but the social order is remarkably stable. If life without any promises seems extreme, we Americans sometimes go too far the other way, parsing not only our contracts but even our marriage vows in order to discover the absolute minimum obligation that we have to others as a result of our promises.

That some societies in the world have worked out evidently functional structures of obligation without the need for promise or consent does not tell us what *we* should do. But it serves as a reminder of the basic proposition that our existence in civil society creates a set of mutual responsibilities that philosophers used to capture in the fiction of the social contract. Nowadays, here in America, people seem to spend their time thinking of even cleverer ways to avoid their obligations, instead of doing what integrity commands and fulfilling them. And all too often honesty is their excuse.

AL FRANKEN

I'm a Bad Liar

In this chapter from Lies and the Lying Liars Who Tell Them, Saturday Night Live *alumnus Al Franken recounts duping people at Bob Jones University into believing that a young man accompanying him on a visit was interested in attending the conservative Christian college. Franken's ruse exposes some of the extremes of the mission of Bob Jones University, but it also raises questions about the ethics behind deception and gags. What was Franken hoping to accomplish with this gag, and at whose expense?*

I never lie. That is, unless it's absolutely necessary. So the story I'm about to tell you is a little embarrassing.

It starts two and a half years ago. My son, Joe, a junior in a very high-powered, expensive New York City private high school, was beginning his college search. We started to put together a list of schools to visit during spring break. The boy wants to be an engineer, so M.I.T., Michigan, Washington University, and Princeton were early contenders.

My wife, who, I have to tell you, is not usually funny, had a hilarious idea. Why don't I take Joe down to Bob Jones University as a prospective student (which, technically, he was) and have fun at their expense?

Great idea, honey! Hilarious! We could ask them all kinds of snarky questions in the information session. Like about their interracial dating policy. Because of bad publicity, Bob Jones had changed the policy since Bush's visit. Now, according to news reports, they were allowing kids to date interracially *with their parents' permission.* "Yeah, um, I understand the students need their parents' permission to date other races. I was wondering. My wife is fine with Joe dating a black girl. But I'm against it. How would that work out?"

5 Or "Yeah, um, on your interracial dating policy, I have a theoretical question. Tiger Woods? Could he date *anyone?* Or *no one?* Could he even go out by himself?" Oddly enough, the answer to that last question, I would learn, was no, unless Tiger was leaving campus either to go home or on a mission.

Excited about all the comic possibilities, I immediately asked my assistant Liz to call BJU, which is what they call themselves. Find out when they have information sessions and tours. Liz called, and found the people in the BJU admissions office to be incredibly friendly. I mention this because it will become a leitmotif for the rest of this chapter.

Of course, there were plenty of information sessions and tours! Come down anytime! We'd love to get to know Joe! What's he interested in? Liz did her best—the boy's into history. Great!

That afternoon, when Joe got back from his fancy, two-thirds-Jewish high school, I told him the good news. We were going to go on a little comedy adventure. Joe—and in retrospect, this is to the boy's credit—was *absolutely appalled.* "No!"

"What?" I said incredulously. This was my son, who grew up in a comedy household. Didn't he recognize a great idea?

"Leave these people alone!" he said angrily. "What did they do to you?"

"Well, they're racist and nuts, and—"

"Dad, they just have a different belief system. Leave them alone."

And that, I thought, was that. What I didn't understand was that when you contact an evangelical organization, they will not stop mailing you shit. Did you know that BJU has quite a history department? Did you know that the BJU cheerleaders wear skirts down to their ankles? It's in their brochure.

And then there were the calls.

"Hi! Is Joe there?"

"Um, who may I say is calling?"

"Josie Martin from Bob Jones University."

"Oh. Joe's not here now."

"When will he be back?"

"Um, hmmm, I . . . don't know."

This happened a lot. A lot. And because I'm a busy man and my wife wasn't vigilant enough, Joe actually answered a few times, getting angrier and angrier at me because he was now being forced to lie. Something we Frankens don't do. Unless it's absolutely necessary.

The last straw was the call from a junior at BJU who was from Manhattan. "Where," he asked Joe, "do you go to church?"

"I don't go to church," Joe answered reflexively. On the other end of the phone, he heard a shocked GASP.

". . . in Manhattan," he quickly recovered. "I go to church on Long Island."

"Oh," said the very nice young man whom my son was lying to.

Joe charged out of his room and confronted me. "This has got to stop! I don't like lying to people!" He told me to call Bob Jones and tell them he had decided to go to a secular college. Which was, of course, entirely true.

So the next day, I had Liz call and tell BJU the bad news. They were disappointed, but understood. And were extremely nice about it.

Cut to: TeamFranken. Present day. A good idea never dies. I needed a kid without Joe's integrity. Fortunately, I was at Harvard. Among the fourteen members of TeamFranken, I had fourteen volunteers, including Owen Kane, a thirty-eight-year-old mid-career Kennedy School grad student.

But to maximize the chances of our little scheme working, it was important that my "son" or "daughter" be able to pass for a high school junior. Owen was out.

Andrew Barr was in. A sophomore at the college, Andrew was perfect. Fresh-faced, eager, he could easily pass for seventeen. Valedictorian at Boston Latin, the top public school in Boston, Andrew was razor sharp and quick on his feet. Only one problem. The Jewish thing. Neither Andrew nor I knew jack about Christianity, particularly the weird, freakish kind practiced by these incredibly nice people at Bob Jones University.

We decided to do our homework. Learning about Christianity would be too difficult and time-consuming. Also, boring. Instead, we checked out BJU's website, hoping not just to learn enough to pull off our scam, but also to find stuff to make fun of.

Unfortunately, we discovered that the interracial dating policy had been discarded altogether. Shit. There went the Tiger Woods joke.

But not to worry. There was plenty of other fodder. First of all, the "university" is not accredited. That's right. They have the same degree-granting power as Schlotsky's Deli. *They* claim it's because they don't *want* to be accredited. We think it's because they don't believe in *science.* You see, they stand without apology for the absolute authority of the Bible. God created the Earth in six days. And He didn't put gays in it, either.

Then, there's the BJU policy on student use of the Internet, which is "a source of much content antagonistic to Godliness." No argument there. Chat rooms, instant messaging, and web-based email accounts are banned. Students are not allowed to access websites with "Biblically offensive material." In addition to the usual pornography and violence, this includes "crude, vulgar language or gestures, tasteless humor (excretory functions, etc.), and graphic medical photos." Fortunately, BJU has an automatic filter, updated *daily,* to block these websites. And since nobody's perfect (i.e., we're all sinners), if the filter picks up a student attempting to access one of these websites, the "incident" is logged for an Internet administrator. In fact, all Internet use is constantly monitored by the "university," giving parents real peace of mind. Like the incredible friendliness, "constant monitoring" would also become a theme of life at BJU.

And speaking of parents, Andrew and I found the linchpin for what would become "our elaborate ruse." On the BJU website is a letter telling parents that it is their "God-given responsibility" not to allow their children to choose their own college. The consequences of that are made clear in the vivid and terrifying stories of the "Three College Shipwrecks," written by Bob Jones, Sr., the founder of the "university."

The first two "shipwrecks," known as "His Only Daughter" and "The Pride of His Mother," come to alarmingly similar ends. In each, a promising, God-fearing student is allowed to go off to a secular university. After returning from their freshman years, both have lost their way, their faith shattered. The Only Daughter "rushed upstairs, stood in front of a mirror, took a gun, and blew out her brains." Whereas the Pride of His Mother, having contracted "an unspeakable disease," announces his intention to "buy a gun and blow out my brains."

The third shipwreck, "The Son of an Aged Minister," is less violent, though certainly just as tragic. He had been "a great boy, bright, clean, obedient, Christian." Unfortunately, although the boy makes the life-saving decision to attend a Christian school, it isn't BJU. "A skeptic had got in the Science Department" of the less-Christian Christian school, and when the boy returns home, he has lost his faith and becomes "a drunken, atheistic bum."

So. Parents could save their kids from suicide, alcoholism, and the clap by forcing them to go to BJU. Excellent. This was our key. Since neither

Andrew nor I could pull off being devout evangelical Christians, it would be Andrew's *mother* who desperately wanted him to go to Bob Jones. Instead of being Andrew's father, I would be a friend of the family—in fact, the best friend of Andrew's father, who had died tragically of brain cancer—no wait, boating accident—three years ago. Andrew's mom had sunk into a deep depression, then miraculously found Christ.

It was perfect. Neither Andrew nor I would have to know anything. But why wasn't Mom there? Sick? No. Threw out her back carrying boxes of blood at a blood drive. At church. As you can see, we started putting *way* too much thought into the back story, and way too little into the fact that I have been on television for nearly thirty years.

Seeing as how we did spend the time on the back story, you really should 40
hear it. Because it's pretty good. Andrew's father, Hank, my college roommate and financial advisor, ran an incredibly successful hedge fund. Andrew's mother, Ellen, therefore, was not just a stunningly beautiful widow—she looks like Naomi Judd—but also fabulously wealthy. Now for the delicious spin. I was more than just a family friend. I had my eye on the Widow Barr, and seeing to it that young Andrew would agree to attend Bob Jones would be a feather in my cap.

Andrew's part was equally delicious. Eager to please his mother, he had happily agreed to visit what he thought was just a typical, fun-in-the-sun Christian school. Our plan, as you can clearly see, was brilliant. Neither of us would have to know anything about either Christianity or Bob Jones University. We had thought of everything.

And, yes, I considered the possibility that I would be recognized. A disguise? Nah. I'd just cut my hair extra short. Yeah, that would do it.

"Hi, Mr. Franken! Big fan!" "Good to see you, Mr. Franken!" "Loved you on SNL!" These were the security guards at La Guardia. Nothing to worry about. We were still in New York. Didn't mean the haircut wasn't working.

We arrived in Greenville. The Hertz rent-a-car gal, also a big fan. That's good, I explained to Andrew. It's good to have a fan base. But this Hertz woman, she wasn't a nutcase evangelical. She watched secular TV. Don't worry.

So we got there around 11 A.M. Drove through the gates. Didn't set off 45
the Jew alarm. We're in.

Took a look around. Not an unattractive campus. Buildings, grass—nice day. But the place was eerily devoid of human activity. We'd soon learn that everyone was at chapel, this being a weekday. Out of the car and into the Administration Building. At the desk, an extremely friendly, well-scrubbed, wide-eyed young man greeted us and sent us along into the admissions office, where we were met by an extremely friendly, well-scrubbed, wide-eyed female staffer. Like every woman at BJU, she wore a skirt that covered not just her upper thigh, but her lower thigh, and her knee, and her calf, and her either well-turned or not well-turned ankle. No real way of knowing. But she was *really* nice and showed us the official admissions video, which featured two miniature pirates who introduced themselves as "your guardians." At BJU, they told us, you're never alone. Remember I said "constant monitoring" would be a theme? The creepy mini-pirates weren't kidding.

We scheduled a 1 P.M. interview with "Gerald"[1] and decided to grab some lunch, joining the mass of students pouring out of chapel and into the dining commons. There were thousands of them, young men in shirts and ties and khakis, young women in their ankle-length skirts. You could say we stood out. We were about to face our first test.

His name was Doug, an intense, though extremely nice, finance major. In an effort to appear as if I had nothing to hide, I said hi. Doug squinted, looked me over skeptically, and decided to keep an eye on us. Very nicely, he offered to help us get lunch and sit with us, and then asked us lots and lots of questions about who we were and why we were there.

I took this as an opportunity to take our elaborate ruse out for a little test drive. Andrew's dad, dead. Mom, depressed. Mom finds Jesus. Wants Andrew at BJU. Throws out back carrying boxes of blood. Doug asked if Andrew wanted to go there. Andrew didn't know, but I pointed out that his mother really, *really* wanted him to. Doug said that Andrew shouldn't go unless he really wanted to. Hadn't Doug read "The Three Shipwrecks"?

50 Then things started getting sticky. Doug was asking *me* questions. Like, what did I do for a living? And why did I look familiar? I told him I was a writer, which is true, by the way. Remember, I lie only when it's absolutely necessary.

To get us off a potentially incognito-blowing line of questioning, I cleverly changed the subject to creationism. You really believe it? Doug said he did, and so did all his friends sitting around us. According to Doug, evolution made no sense at all. No mutation, he insisted, had ever been beneficial. I looked at my thumb, but said nothing, as I used it to hold my fork and shove the worst lunch I've ever had into my mouth. It was some kind of creamed broccoli on a bun. But then again, you don't go to Bob Jones for the food!

Doug told us that the chances of protoplasm evolving into a human being were infinitesimally small: one over ten to the 256th, or something like that. Duane, an intense, but extremely nice, business administration major, came up with a vivid analogy. "The chances," Duane said, "of protoplasm turning into a fully formed human being are worse than the chances of an explosion in a junkyard yielding an intact Boeing 747."

Doug could tell that I wasn't buying. "So, Alan," he said. Oh, I forgot. I had changed my name to "Alan" as part of our undercover operation. My name really is Alan—remember, only when absolutely necessary. "So, Alan," he said, "why do you believe in evolution?"

"Well, Doug, I'm not a scientist. But it seems that every scientist in this field at an accredited university [heh, heh] believes in evolution. You know, at M.I.T., Stanford, Wisconsin, Arizona State, Wake Forest, you know, everywhere."

55 Doug had a good answer. "So, just because everyone believes something, you think it's true. Well, remember, the Catholic Church taught for hundreds of years that the sun revolved around the Earth. Then they persecuted Galileo for saying the opposite."

---

[1] All names have been changed to protect me.

"I think you're making my point, Doug. The Church based their conclusions on faith, just as you are. Galileo was an empiricist, like all those scientists at the accredited universities."

Andrew was growing more and more uncomfortable. Though he was thirty-two years my junior, he felt that I was exhibiting poor judgment by questioning the fundamental belief of the entire institution while attempting to remain inconspicuous. After a lot of eye contact between the two of us, we decided it was time to bail.

We told Doug and his friends that we had an appointment with an admissions officer, which again was true. Doug offered to walk us to the admissions office, but we told him that first we had to pick up something at a pharmacy, which while not true, was a necessary lie. We had to ditch Doug. Otherwise, our cover would be blown.

On the way to the "pharmacy," I was recognized by several students, some of whom yelled out, "Al Franken!" I waved. And gave out some autographs. The kids were very nice.

There was still thirty minutes until our appointment, so we did the only 60
thing that made sense. We hid.

At 1 P.M. sharp, we slipped into the Administration Building for our appointment with Gerald Fortenberry. We were praying that Gerald hadn't been alerted to the presence of a liberal satirist on campus. It was our only hope.

We were unbelievably lucky. Gerald had no idea who I was. Clearly a recent graduate of the university, he was a sweet, almost innocent young man. A perfect patsy. He bought our elaborate ruse hook, line, and sinker.

Moved by the story of young Andrew's father's death (boating accident), he understood totally Mom's depression and subsequent salvation. "It sounds like your mother's life has been transformed."

"Yes," Andrew said. "And now she wants me to come here."

"Well, you're the one who really should want this." 65

Hadn't *anyone* read "The Three Shipwrecks"?! Even in the *Admissions* Department?

"Well," Andrew replied, "I'm not into the whole religion thing as much as my mother."

"That would be impossible," I offered. "She's very beautiful. She looks like Naomi Judd."

Gerald nodded.

"But I'm okay with it," Andrew continued. "I haven't really developed 70
my own personal relationship with Christ, but I think it would be good to work on that. Plus, I'm really pumped about going off to college. I have a friend at Syracuse, and he's having a blast."

Gerald moved past the blast at Syracuse and came back to Mom. "She sounds like she's happier than she's ever been."

"Yeah," Andrew nodded. "Well, at least since Dad died."

I had a couple questions. Andrew was interested in premed. "I know you teach creationism as opposed to evolution. How does that work out with medical schools?"

"Oh, it's no problem," Gerald reassured. "In fact, we have a higher percentage of students accepted to medical school than the national average."

"Really? And what would that percentage be?" I wanted to know.

"I don't have that offhand," Gerald replied. "Perhaps I can get it for you."

Then Andrew pounced. At the airport in New York, we had picked up a *U.S. News & World Report Guide to the 1400 Top Colleges and Universities.* "Maybe it's in here," Andrew suggested innocently, pulling it out of his backpack.

Gerald blanched, knowing, as we did, that Bob Jones was not listed among the one thousand, four hundred top colleges and universities in the United States. Andrew flipped to South Carolina. "Hmmm . . . maybe it's under J."

"Give me that." I took the book and examined it thoroughly, as Gerald looked on uncomfortably. "It's . . . it's not here."

"No," said Gerald. "A lot of colleges pay to get in that thing."

"Really?" I asked.

"Yes." He nodded authoritatively.

Andrew understood. "So it's like an advertisement?"

"Yeah."

That was quite a relief for me. Until that moment, I had been feeling more and more guilty. But now that Gerald was lying about the college guide, I felt a lot better. Putting the book aside, I smiled at Gerald. "Well, at least we know Bob Jones is an accredited university."

"Uh . . . no."

"No?"

"No. Actually, we *choose* not to be accredited. I can give you a pamphlet on that."

Assured that the pamphlet would explain everything, we moved on. Andrew expressed an interest in theater. Gerald got very excited. Every year Bob Jones's theater department presents what Gerald called a "Shakespeare-play." Gerald told us that before he came to BJU, "I wasn't much for operas and Shakespeare-plays."

One concern. Mom, the one that looks like Naomi Judd, was worried about a certain element that Andrew might be exposed to in the Drama Department. Did Gerald understand what I was getting at? To make it even clearer, I used the magic phrase, "alternative lifestyle." Any of that here at BJU?

"Oh, no, no, no, no." Gerald shook his head. "No, no, no, no. No." None of that here. We could be absolutely certain of that.

Good, good. Because Andrew was looking forward in particular to the heterosexual experience of college life.

"Yeah, my mom doesn't like me dating, because of, you know . . . but college is the time that, you know . . ."

"Oh, yes. We want you to meet girls here," Gerald smiled. "We encourage that."

"So, the dating scene," I asked on behalf of the boy, "what's that like?"

Before Gerald could respond, Andrew expressed some mild concern. "Yeah, I was talking to some guys outside and they said there were some . . . rules."

"Yes," Gerald nodded. "You cannot leave campus with someone of the opposite sex, unless you are accompanied by a chaperone."

Andrew raised his eyebrows. Then, looking for a ray of hope, "But on campus, you know . . ."

"We have a snack shop. You can sit and have a snack together."

Andrew and I looked at each other. How to put this? 100

I took it upon myself. "In terms of, um, you know, um—how far can he go?"

Gerald understood. "Well, obviously, there's absolutely no physical contact."

A numbed silence from the two of us.

"None?" finally came out of Andrew's gaping mouth.

"That's right. No holding hands, hugging, kissing, anything like that." 105

"Backrubs?" Andrew asked for clarification.

"No."

"Oh, you mean in public? Well, that's understandable," Andrew conceded.

"No. No physical contact anywhere. At all."

Andrew slumped. 110

Maybe Gerald had seen this reaction before. He knew just what to say. "Because, Andrew, you know what hand-holding leads to."

Andrew took a wild stab. "Sin?"

"That's right. You see, our rules are like guardrails that keep you on the path of Christ."

So far, our plan was working beautifully. Young Andrew, who at first seemed amenable to, even excited about, pleasing his mother, was now reeling. It was time to set up the kill.

"You know, Gerald, Andrew's mother really wants him to come here. I 115
read that you have to be in the dorms by ten-twenty for the ten-thirty prayer group, and then lights out at eleven. But how about weekends?"

Andrew perked up. "Yeah, how far is it to Atlanta? Because my mom might let me bring my car, and a lot of the bands I like don't play here in Greenville."

"Well, you can have a car on campus, but you can only use it on weekends to go home or if you're going on a mission," Gerald explained helpfully.

"Oh, I see." Andrew nodded. "I guess it wouldn't be so bad to take the bus. Because Weezer didn't play in Greenville last time out."

"No, no. We don't want you going to rock concerts. There's no rock and roll."

"No rock 'n' roll?" I asked. 120

"No, we don't endorse that, obviously."

"What if I don't play it too loud?" Andrew said, becoming upset.

"No. We don't allow it in the dorms at all."

"I could use headphones," Andrew suggested.

"No." 125

Things were getting a little tense. "How about country music? That's good clean fun," I winked.

"No."

"*Christian* rock?" I tried. Certainly they must allow *Christian* rock.

Gerald shook his head. "We don't endorse that."

By now, Andrew was visibly shaken. No hand-holding. No road trips. No tunes. Lots and lots of prayer.

130 That's when I spoke up. "Gerald, could I have a word with you alone?"

"Sure, Alan."

I nodded to Andrew, who excused himself and stepped into the nearby men's room. I waited for the door to close, then turned to Gerald, suddenly in his face.

"Listen. This kid's mother is *extremely* wealthy. She has *tons* of money. She wants him to come here. If he comes here, I'm talking another *building.* Okay?! And you're blowing it!"

Gerald recoiled. His eyes opened wide. It was as if he had seen Satan himself.

135 I was pleading. "Don't tell him everything. You said before 'nobody's perfect.' Certainly there are kids who do stuff here."

"Well, I said that because we're all sinners. And the rules are guardrails to keep you on the path of Christ. I can't withhold anything from Andrew. That would defeat the whole purpose. Which is to live a life in Christ."

Aw, hell. Gerald was absolutely, totally, without question incorruptible. Screw it.

We had our story. The place was weird, but the people extremely nice. A good honest day's work done, lying to God-fearing people. We'd sleep well tonight. But we decided to poke around a little more since we had some time to kill. Off to the museum, where BJU houses the largest collection of sacred art in the Western Hemisphere.

And let me tell you, it's a lot of sacred art: Botticelli, Granacci, Tintoretto, Dolci, Rembrandt, Ribera, Rubens, Van Dyck. Twenty-seven rooms full. A priceless collection. Donated by wealthy alums? Not quite. Most of it was purchased by Bob Jones, Jr., himself, the second of the three Bob Joneses.

140 You see, Dr. Bob II had spent some summers in the 1930s as a tour guide in Rome, Paris, and Vienna, and had acquired a taste for fine art. Luckily, when he returned to Europe in the late forties, he was able acquire quite a bit of it at very reasonable prices. Hmmm, I thought. What do you suppose would be the chances of a white supremacist who came to Europe in the thirties knowing someone who knew someone who had recently come across some "misplaced" art in the late 1940s? In fact, I thought I recognized a couple pieces that used to belong to my grandfather, who was a big collector of sacred Christian art before he was hauled off to Buchenwald. Nah. Maybe I was jumping to conclusions.

Still with some time to kill, we decided to hop on the three o'clock tour with a delightful Christian family of four. We had a lovely time, even had some laughs, until we got to the theater, where our bluff was finally called. On the stage were several gigantic crosses, scenery for what they call "The Living Gallery." This involves recreating great works of sacred art using real people in tableaux. I was very excited about getting Andrew to take a picture of me hanging from one of the crosses. Then we met R.J. From the public liaison's office.

"I'll take them from here," R.J. told our tour guide. We didn't like the way he said that. Nor the way he said, "Let me tell you a little about the theater. The floor is from Rockefeller Center. But it's no *Saturday Night Live.*"

The jig was up.

"Can I just ask what you're down here looking for?" he inquired pointedly.

"Well, it's a long story," I said, willing, but not really eager, to go into the whole boating-accident-depression-salvation-boxes-of-blood thing again.

"Uh-huh. Look. We've had enough of being made fun of," R.J. said with more than a touch of bitterness. Then turning to Andrew, he added, "I hope this isn't awkward for you."

"Oh no," said Andrew cheerfully. "We've been getting this all day." Actually, we hadn't. But I thought it was a nice touch.

R.J. continued. "If you're legit, I'd be happy to show you anything you want to see. But we're not going to put our heads on the chopping block again." I had to admire his directness and his willingness to call us on what should have been obvious to everyone all day. And yet he had the manners to leave open the remote possibility that we were, as he put it, "legit." And even while being hostile, he was extremely nice about it.

Accompanied by R.J., we made a show of being interested in the alumni building, the least interesting building on campus, and then were walked to our car.

And as we bid farewell to old BJU, we realized that we had learned something, not just about Bob Jones University, but about ourselves. We'd come to Bob Jones expecting to encounter racist, intolerant homophobes. Instead, we found people who were welcoming, friendly, and extremely nice. A little weird, yes. And no doubt homophobic. But well-meaning. Kind of.

More important, we learned that while we were happy that we had successfully executed our ruse and relieved it had worked on Gerald, it was not something we were particularly proud of. Yes, we got a good story out of it. But while there's a certain subversive thrill in deceiving people, it also left us with an unsettled feeling in our stomachs that a trip to the Waffle House only exacerbated. It made us wonder what kind of person can lie like that every day of his life. How do the lying liars do it?

In a way, I was glad that R.J. had cut short our tour before I got up on one of those giant crosses. (Although if he hadn't, you'd be looking at a pretty cool picture right now.) I don't begrudge them their religion. Hell, I admire it. No, I don't. But it's their right to have it. Just as it's my inherent right to invade their privacy under false pretenses. No, it isn't.

Doug, Duane, R.J., and especially Gerald, when you finally read this—we're very sorry. Also, we stole some stuff from the gift shop. No, we didn't.

Yes, we did.

No, we didn't. We're not crooks.

Assignment Ideas

Moving away from clichés toward more profound insights about honesty and deception is the key to successfully responding to the assignment options below. While you might ultimately settle on a fairly standard view of the topic you choose, the method in which you explain your thinking must demonstrate sufficient complication. Reviewing methods of critical analysis in Chapter 2 will help you explore the topic and relate your decisions to your audience.

1. Summarize Stephen L. Carter's ideas from "The Insufficiency of Honesty" so that you convey a firm grasp of his concerns. Extend, limit, confirm, or negate his views by giving other examples, whether personal or public, that show the tension between honesty and integrity. Try to find a word or virtue of your own—perhaps from the list of values you brainstormed—to replace Carter's reliance on *integrity*. Look at the way Eric Dezenhall uses the term *hypocrisy* in "We Like Our Bad Guys to Be Honest About It" (page 481).
2. Compare two incidents in which you told lies, exploring the reasons that made you choose to deceive. Were the lies completely self-serving and no better than those told by embezzlers and frauds? Or can you categorize them into one of the four groups discussed in the overview? Explore the effects of your lies. For example, the lies Jim Ladd talks about in "The Big Lie" (page 472) spelled the end of a profitable radio station. See if your reasons for telling lies were better than reasons you can think of for telling the truth, and reach a conclusion based on your analysis of whether some situations are better handled by lying.
3. Franken had difficulty sustaining his charade; after being exposed he asks how people can lie like that every day. He is alluding to politicians, but the question has application to people who continually lie in their social circles. In an essay, describe a person you know who tells a lot of stories or makes a number of claims that you don't believe or have found to be untrue. Recount some of the lies, and theorize about why the person continually deceives others, using your analysis as a generalization about lying and honesty in our culture.
4. Research con games, keeping in mind your brainstorming or freewriting about embezzlers and frauds. Describe some of the deception that goes into typical con games, such as pyramid schemes, bait and switch, and desert land schemes. Draw a parallel to Franken's prank. Since Franken profits from his deception by generating material for his comedy routine, how are his motives different from those of people who face imprisonment should they be caught? Is misrepresentation harmless? Think about ways you can supplement this parallel with examples from your own involvement in a practical joke or scheme. Do the justifications outweigh the harm of the deception?

Group Work

Deception and basic dishonesty have cost taxpayers billions of dollars, have bilked innocent people out of retirement funds, and have even caused the deaths of thousands. Each group member should investigate an example of large-scale deception. One deception should have been perpetuated by politicians, another by corporate executives, and a third by an ordinary individual. Look into the motives of the people involved. What did they stand to gain? Why did the possible gain matter more than the consequences of the deception? Place each incident in a context that shows the American reaction to it, including the punishment of the people involved, and use this to build a thesis about our cultural response to deception. Do we tolerate it? Do we make excuses for it? Does who is involved matter more than what he or she did? Do we hold individuals accountable to the extent that we should?

Additional Readings

The selections that follow extend our understanding of deception and, more implicitly then explicitly, make us yearn for honesty. "The Lightning Struck Lost Mine" reminds us of tall tales that somebody believes and acts on, looking for hidden riches and losing more money, even his or her life, in the pursuit of the treasure. In "The Big Lie," Jim Ladd, a legendary FM radio disk jockey in Los Angeles, recounts the playing out of a simple untruth that the KAOS programmer would retain control over format after a consultant had been hired to improve ratings. The initial deception led to the dismantling of the most progressive radio station in the Los Angeles area and the loss of musical integrity to corporate greed. "Censor or Victim of Censorship?" also involves radio broadcasting, but attends to the lies that prevented the Fairness Doctrine from being reinstated, showing how a talk show host "spun" the issue to make it appear like a politically motivated and biased personal attack when he was actually preventing free speech and balanced programming. The last article, "We Like Our Bad Guys to Be Honest About It," compares the dishonesty of mobsters to the dishonesty of the Enron executives who swindled millions from investors and employees. All the readings have common elements of greed, ego, and ambition that might make you wonder about other virtues and their relationship to honesty.

ROGER HENN

The Lightning Struck Lost Mine

Great ranches now spread across the valley of Cow Creek: Sleeping Ute, Chimney Rock, and others. Some have their own private jet landing strips. Their ranch houses are pretentious, spreading to tens of thousands of square feet. Cow Creek and its valley is greatly different from what it was like in the nineteenth century.

One early map calls Cow Creek, Bache Creek, which was the Spanish word for buffalo. It is also a term for cow. Could it have been possible that early Spanish explorers found the valley filled with grazing buffalo? There is one old, old building in Cow Creek that has a buffalo skull mounted over the door. Could it be that the skull might have been found nearby? The Spanish name suggests that Cow Creek was known to their trappers, miners, or explorers far earlier than we have acknowledged. We do know that the Escalante explorers reached the Uncompahgre at about the present-day location of Colona in 1776.

When the Ute reservation was moved to Colona, Cow Creek became the grazing grounds for the Ute cattle herds. Chief Ouray and his key sub chiefs were working to change the Utes from hunters to cattle raisers—a change Ouray recognized would be necessary if the Utes were to survive in the white man's world. If the Utes had another ten years in the Uncompahgre Valley before their expulsion, they might well have become successful agrarians.

My story of the lost mine of this Cow Creek country must begin with the first white man we have record of exploring it. Charlie Hall came to the San Juans with the ill-fated Baker parties. Having no success in finding placer gold in Baker's Park near present-day Silverton, Hall and two companions left to look at the Uncompahgre Valley in 1861. In the bowl that is today Ouray they found no gold in their panning so they proceeded down the stream, panning as they went. Like others of the Baker parties they watched where their feet walked looking for evidence of free gold; if they had raised their eyes, they would have seen gold and silver veins all around them. Free gold, which can be collected by panning, is almost non-existent in the San Juans. Going downstream they encountered the recently abandoned camp of the Doc Arnold party that had spent the winter of 1860–61 a mile south of present-day Ridgway. The Arnold party was headed for Baker's Park and the hubbub there but got lost and ended up in the Uncompahgre Valley trapped for the winter by heavy snow. Although they did find some gold, when spring came they left to travel on to the exciting Baker camp which had always been their goal.

5 Charlie and his two friends continued down the river to the junction with Cow Creek. Running out of food they headed up Cow Creek hoping to find a shortcut back to Baker's Park. Thus they became the first white men of record to have entered Cow Creek. Starving, they were so anxious to get back that they did no prospecting. In the years that followed Cow Creek remained unprospected.

And so we turn to our tale of the lost mine. First, however, much confusion exists in histories of Ouray as to two men named Long. As one of these is the center of our story we need to clarify this confusion. Robert F. Long was one of the group of thirteen men to first winter in Ouray. Long is first recorded as coming into the San Juans in early spring of 1875. With his small party he brought a number of wagons from Del Norte and started up Stony Pass, but the remaining heavy snow made it impossible to bring wagons over the pass. The wagons and supplies were left at Lost Trail Camp with a packer named Frank Blackledge who used Lost Trail as his headquarters. Long and his associates struggled up through the snow and then down to Cunningham Gulch and Howardsville. When the snow melted Long returned to Lost Trail, but to his dismay found the wagons burned and the valuable supplies missing. Blackledge had a number of conflicting stories, but Long never recovered the missing supplies.

Long worked his way up to Mineral Point (which with grandiose ideas was calling itself Mineral City) and joined a party of men setting out to explore the Uncompahgre. . . . Long helped stake out the town site of Uncompahgre and with the Cutler brothers built the third of three cabins that were to constitute the entire community that first winter. Long's cabin was selected by the La Plata County Commissioners to be the polling place for all of the sparsely settled Uncompahgre country. The La Plata Commissioners recognized the new community as Uncompahgre, but the post office designated it as Ouray. It was at Long's cabin that he cooked the famous Christmas dinner for the thirteen men wintering in Ouray. In celebrating the men drank from a gallon jug of vinegar. The hill where the cabin was located is still called Vinegar Hill. Long was petitioner for the 1875 application for the Town of Uncompahgre, was elected Trustee at the first town meeting of Ouray in 1876, and County Judge when Ouray County was formed.

Treatment of ore to free gold and silver was a real problem in the San Juans. The first ore from the Wheel of Fortune had to be packed on burros over the ridge of Imogene Basin, down to Silverton then over Cinnamon Pass to Lake City. To pay for that very long trip took very high ore values so ore was carefully sorted and the less valuable left on the dump. In 1877 it cost twenty-five dollars a ton to pack ore from Ouray to Silverton for treatment and then the result had to be carried by wagon to Pueblo for smelting. One mine was reported using 270 burros for that haul.

Long went back to Silverton, bought the equipment and works of the Brown, Epley & Company smelting plant, and hauled it to Ouray. He bought other equipment from outside the San Juans and placed in operation the mill and smelter named San Juan & St. Louis Smelting Company, a name suggesting his ties to St. Louis. The plant was located just short of four miles north of Ouray.

Unfortunately for Ouray, enterprising Robert F. Long died in 1882 at age 10
forty-one. He was a veteran of the Civil War, his wife a New Orleans belle. Their eleven-year-old son died in St. Louis a month later. So it was not Robert Long who found the mine in Cow Creek which has been lost for so many years. It was Alfred E. Long who made the discovery. A. E. Long must have come into the San Juans before 1876 because he was well known enough to run for county clerk of the new San Juan County in that year. He lost in a three man race for the position. He was still involved in Silverton in 1879 when he was one of three men who incorporated a Silverton, Ophir, and Rico Toll Road Company which never turned a spade of rock.

By this time A. E. Long's interest had been transferred to Ouray and he ran again for county clerk, but this time for newly formed Ouray County, and he was elected. He held public office on and off for many years. In 1891 he founded the *San Juan Silverite,* a newspaper largely dedicated to his political aspirations. The short-lived paper was described as "a political paper with no party and a religious paper with no church."

Almost twenty years after his experiment of prospecting in the Animas country, Long decided to go gold hunting again. Most all the mountains deemed worthy of prospecting had been thoroughly covered and staked with mining cliams. But Long knew of one area that had been largely overlooked. He enlisted an acquaintance to go with him.

The two set out to prospect in Cow Creek country. Finding some promising float (rock that had rolled from higher up) led them to climb a high stony ridge leaving their horses below. There on the top of this bare ridge they found a six inch vein of quartz carrying good gold values. A heavy thunderstorm came up, and as there was no place on that barren ridge to seek shelter, the two men just continued to work at extracting gold-bearing quartz. A lightning bolt struck knocking Long's companion unconscious. When he recovered he found the bolt had killed Long. He packed Long's body across the back of a horse and led the animal with its burden back to Ouray.

Severely shocked, he told his story, climbed aboard the first train leaving Ouray, and was never heard from again. He left behind the story of a rich gold mine and some ore to prove it, but no direction as to how to find it. The Cow Creek drainage is immense, but somewhere in that vastness, on a rocky ridge, is a rich lost gold mine.

JIM LADD

The Big Lie

Nineteen eighty-four—the perfect moment in history for the Orwellian nightmare that was about to engulf RADIO KAOS. The computer, the consultant, and the consequences of the two, were all about to come crashing into KAOS.

It was late afternoon as I sat in Terri Belle's office. The book had come out and the station had gone back up a little, but there was no celebration. The powers that be had decided to bring in the consultant anyway. Terri was extremely upset, and so was I. Although Ira swore that Terri would retain final say over programming, we both knew this consultant's reputation for slick repetitive formats, not to mention what it really meant whenever Ira used the words "Trust me."

"We can't let this happen Terri," I said, as she stared blankly out her office window. "This guy hasn't got a clue as to what RADIO KAOS stands for, not to mention how it works."

"Ira swore that if we went back up in this book we wouldn't have to do this," she said, still gazing out toward Hollywood. "It's the first time in eight years that we haven't been number one, and they won't even give us a chance to fix it."

5 "Terri you know me, if this guy tries to bring in a format I won't do it. I can't do it."

"I know, Jim," said Terri, now turning to look at me, her eyes devoid of the happy glint of rebellion they usually contained. "I'll do everything I can to keep him away from your show. Fortunately the nighttime numbers are still strong, so he can't say that you need to change what you're doing."

"We can't let this happen," I repeated, not knowing what else to say. "We can't let this guy turn almost twenty years of progressive radio into a jukebox."

For nearly two decades, from 1968 to 1984, RADIO KAOS had been the outlaw, a thorn in the side of the establishment, and now they wanted us to put on a suit and tie like everybody else. We were the last bastion of real rock radio in L.A., a station that had built its reputation on pushing the boundaries of ideas and culture. If RADIO KAOS went, there would be no freedom left on the dial—no place for experimentation, no one to champion social causes or push the boundaries of bad taste. There would be nothing left but the automatic drone of safe prepackaged entertainment.

I decided to call a friend of mine who was working at our sister station in New York. Dean Brady did afternoon drive at the biggest FM rocker in the Big Apple. They too had been sentenced to work with the same radio consultant who was about to be forced on us.

"Dean, it's Jim, how ya doing?" 10

"Fine I guess, what's happening on the Coast?"

"They did it, Dean, they hired that same radio genius you guys got."

"So Ira finally gave in to the front office, huh? I'll bet that took all of thirty seconds."

"Dean, give me the lowdown on this guy, what does he want you to do?"

"You ain't gonna like it. It's the same old thing—tight playlists, strict 15
format rules, and lots of slick promotions."

"You're kidding. Terri was told that he was just going to provide her with music research, and that we wouldn't have to do his format."

"Oh yeah, we got that same rap at the beginning, but two weeks after he started we lost all freedom of choice over the music. Now we just sit here and do our shows off of a computerized list."

"You're kidding, you guys?" I asked in disbelief. "He makes you follow a *list?*"

I could hear Dean tense up at the other end of the phone. "Song by song, cut by cut, in order, twenty-four hours a day."

"Man, it's like a disease eating up FM from the inside out. I'll bet that 20
RADIO KAOS and WBCN are the only two major market stations left in the country that aren't robot controlled. And from what you're saying, that may not last long."

"Haven't you heard? Reagan has declared that it's okay to do anything for money. In fact, it's downright unpatriotic *not* to sell out."

After the deregulation of the broadcast industry, radio stations could be bought and sold like junk bonds, by people whose idea of a hero for the eighties was Ivan Boesky. Prior to deregulation, anyone purchasing a station was required to hold on to it for at least three years. This ensured that those who would be broadcasting over the public airwaves must take a long-term, responsible approach to the community they served. But once deregulation opened the floodgates to speculators, owning a station no longer carried the responsibility of "servicing the community." The get-rich-quick guys who came into the field were not interested in buying a broadcast facility; to them, it was merely investment property. If you had the bucks, you could treat a radio station like any other hotel on the Monopoly board.

Freed from the constraints of "broadcasting in the public interest," the Reagan administration had unleashed a buying frenzy that drove the price for an FM station through the roof. These new owners were not interested in broadcasting, merely the buying and selling of "broadcast properties," and the *quicker* you got numbers, the faster you could resell the station for a profit. This resulted in the use of every get-rated-quick scheme in the world, by hungry investors whose only concern was to drive up the market value of their facility.

By this time the other stations in town were literally trying to requisition an audience. KASH, who now had a consultant of their own, had totally debased itself with a big hoopla Porsche giveaway, in an attempt to bribe its audience into listening. They must have given away over $750,000 worth of German sports cars to get people to tune in to KASH—this at a time when American autoworkers were being laid off in droves. There was a new Top 40 dance station at the far end of the dial, and their idea was even more to the point; if you want listeners, go out and buy them. They gave away ten thousand dollars a week in cash as ransom for the ratings.

There were no ethics in FM anymore. The frequency modulation band was no longer an alternative to the AM Top 40 approach; the only difference now was that they did it in stereo. But the worst part, the most disheartening part, was that the audience of the eighties fell for it.

In this best of all yuppie worlds, money and Porsches were what it was all about. Fuck Bob Dylan and all that social consciousness bullshit. Yuppies wanted the cash and the cars. Music to them was just something else to consume, like tofu and fashion. This, above all, was the hardest part for me to accept. Hypnotized by the Great Communicator, and worn out by almost two decades of social upheaval, the audience had become bored with issues like ecology and civil rights. Social activism was now "totally out of fashion."

It was the era of the credit card and corporate takeovers and the photo opportunity. The audience bought into Reagan's greed creed like a junkie who'd just won an all-expense-paid trip to the poppy fields of Turkey. And FM radio was tripping over itself to get in on the new smoke and mirrors prosperity, which trickled down from the top, and polluted everything.

The first thing the consultant did when he arrived in town was rape the KAOS music library. The Southland's most extensive biblioteca of rock music was reduced overnight to a couple of hundred hits. From Chuck Berry to Bruce Springsteen, the Jefferson Airplane to U2, anything that wasn't a national Top 40 hit was eliminated, taking away not only the variety but the very character of KAOS.

Two weeks after that, he had convinced the gentlemen in New York to force Terri Belle into implementing his Super-schlock format—a tight computerized list of songs calculated to repeat like dull clockwork, with no regard for how or why one cut followed another. It would be one thing to take over some middle-of-the-road station that had been dying in the market, but this guy was dicking with RADIO KAOS. To him, of course, we were just another customer on his national client list of jukebox outlets.

30 Terri did her best to juggle this guy's plastic approach, the front office's demands for numbers, and Ira's career paranoia, while still trying to keep some semblance of KAOS alive. But it was useless. The consultant kept *saying* how much he respected RADIO KAOS's reputation, and that he wouldn't do anything to lose that "image of integrity." Only a consultant could look at a station like RADIO KAOS and come up with a phrase like "image of integrity." Meanwhile, of course, he was systematically dismantling the very essence of what had earned RADIO KAOS that "image."

Needless to say, the magic was gone. Life at RADIO KAOS was now a humiliating daily struggle of justifying techniques we had crafted over the years to a bureaucrat whose only concept of magic was card tricks. Never once did this guy even try to figure out what had made RADIO KAOS so important to its listeners. All he was interested in was a quick hit in the ratings, so he could add KAOS to his list of "winners."

As the other members of the air staff struggled with the shackles of a sterilized playlist, I continued to do my four hours as best I could with the skeleton record library left to me. It was like working with both hands tied behind my back. Every set was a compromise, every song a substitute for something that would have worked better. For the first time since my days at KASH, I was actually embarrassed to go on the air. I felt like I was lying to my audience every time I opened the mike. The only thing that kept me going was that I didn't have to follow his inane format. Even though we had only a tenth of the songs to choose from, at least I was still picking my own music. I kept telling myself that if I could maintain the ratings at night, and the rest of the station went down, they would have to give us KAOS back.

This went on for the next two ratings books—six months of Ira Steinberg kowtowing to his bosses instead of standing up for his troops, while Terri Belle placated the bean counter who called in his ill-calculated musical statistics from a hotel room on the road. And what were the results from the absentee consultant's brave new plan? After all his charts and graphs and spreadsheets, after plundering the most carefully compiled record library in Southern California, the ratings went down.

Somehow I was able to maintain my audience at the pre-consultant level, and after the second disastrous book came out, I thought surely that the guys at corporate headquarters would see the light, and discontinue this misdirected experiment in simulated chaos. It was obvious now that if I was able to maintain my audience while the format's numbers went down, that it was the format that didn't work, not KAOS.

35 Reversing their decision, however, would mean that somebody at the corporate level would have to admit they had made a mistake. And no matter how much history was on the line, or how many social causes we had fought for, or how many careers were affected, or even how badly the ratings fell, no one at corporate headquarters was going to admit even a slight error in judgment.

So instead of returning power to the people who had built the station, they fired Terri Belle. After all, it couldn't be the fault of this genius they were renting, and it certainly wasn't the fault of the person three thousand miles away who'd hired him. Something must be wrong with the people who had been there, made RADIO KAOS the number one FM station in L.A., and were struggling against bad leadership and increased competition to keep it afloat.

Like Raechel Donahue, and B. Mitchel Reed, and hundreds of others across the country, Terri Belle had been used up and spit out. All she had to show for her eight years was the obligatory bullshit memo about "moving on to other opportunities." It's hard enough to lose your job, but when you've put your heart on the line for something like RADIO KAOS, leaving is like losing a loved one.

Terri had made her share of mistakes, to be sure. Like most of us, success had bred a level of complacency and an interest in extracurricular activities, which clouded her judgment and dulled her concentration. But for eight years she had helped to make RADIO KAOS a broadcast legend, and with a little support, she might have done it again. In the end, however, Terri Belle was thanked for building the most successful FM station in the Micromedia chain, with a pink slip.

Even though the ratings were going down, the consultant had won. The charts and graphs had triumphed. All that remained was to insert the first in a long string of programming puppets, who would simply take orders from the consultant and pass them along to the staff.

Ira's first choice for the job turned out to be a walking Napoleon complex, called Lucifer Le Rock. At first I was relieved when Ira told me that he was promoting someone from inside the station. Lucifer had been doing an early morning talk show on the weekends for the past few years, and although we weren't close friends, I'd always gotten along well with him. He seemed like one of us, someone who was knowledgeable about music and cared about the station. But something happened to Lucifer when he got into a position of power.

Lucifer was a guy who knew in his heart of hearts that he was a genius, and now, as the leader of RADIO KAOS, he would have the opportunity to get back at all those who'd not yet acknowledged his obvious mental gifts. Now he was the program director of a 58,000-watt radio station in Los Angeles, and he would show them all.

Lucifer had been a weekend jock all his life, a fringe player, envious of anyone who had achieved the recognition he had been denied. He was a guy who actually thought "Lucifer Le Rock" was a cool radio name. Lucifer's very first act as program director was not to rally the air staff, or replenish the record library; no, Lucifer's first priority was to get his voice on the air as much as possible. To him, this is what the L.A. audience had been praying for: the wit and wisdom of Lucifer Le Rock. Every promotional announcement, every station identification, and every local commercial now began, "This is Lucifer Le Rock speaking," twenty-four hours a day, seven days a week. Never mind that he had the best-known staff of voices in L.A. He wanted to hear himself on the radio, and this seemed to take precedence over everything.

Lucifer saw himself as the commanding general of an undisciplined military unit, which he and the power of his voice were going to whip into shape. RADIO KAOS would no longer be a collective effort of pooled knowledge and team play. It was now a group of employees who were to fall into lockstep behind his vast leadership capabilities. And like the consultant whose ass he was kissing while pretending to be in charge, Lucifer wanted the station to be "regulated, repetitious, and redundant."

Lucifer and I mixed like oil and water. He hated the fact that I refused to give up creative control of my show; I hated him for trying to transform what was left of this special family into his personal company of robots. The station began to change immediately under Lucifer's megalomania, and almost overnight, RADIO KAOS was catalyzed into a gimmick-riddled, boot-licking joke.

Under Lucifer's leadership genius, RADIO KAOS plummeted to its lowest level in seven years, and mercifully, Lucifer Le Rock was sent back to his own private hell of obscurity.

The next guy they tried was a twenty-five-year-old suit from Chicago who had never heard RADIO KAOS in his life. Bill Kelly was from the "games, glitz, and giveaways" school of radio, and to him, the consultant (still providing his invaluable absentee research) was the kind of guy who knew the score. Kelly's goal, as he was so often found of saying, was to "make KAOS the McDonald's of radio": uniform, convenient, predictable.

We fought it out tooth and nail, five days a week. I'd taken my stand against selling out RADIO KAOS a long time ago, and I wasn't about to lay all that aside now to become a Big Mac. Besides, I had Ira's word that no one would ever be allowed to interfere with how I did my show, as long as I maintained the ratings. As with all systems freaks, this lack of direct control over one of his jocks drove Kelly nuts. What made me crazy was having to discuss FM radio with someone who had never even heard of Tom Donahue. One night on the air, the hotline rang inside the studio, and I found myself engaged in one of our typical debates.

"Hello?"

"Jim, this is Bill Kelly, what the hell are you playing?"

"You mean the song on right now?"

"Yes, who is that?"

"This is some kind of joke, right? You're recording this conversation aren't you?"

"I'm dead serious. We had this discussion twice this week. If you're going to pick your own music, you at least have to confine yourself to the most recognizable artists. This is the very reason you should be following the format like everybody else!"

"Bill, this is Jimi Hendrix."

"Well I've never heard it before, what is it?"

"It's 'Voodoo Chile' from *Electric Ladyland.* You must have heard this song before."

"It's much too obscure for our station. We should be banging out the hits. I want this place to be the McDonald's of radio. This song isn't even on the format."

"Look, for the last time, I don't do the fucking format! And as for this song, it may not have been a hit single in Chicago, but it was one of the biggest FM hits ever in L.A. It's *Hendrix* for Christ sakes!"

"I still say it's too obscure for our audience. The days of people listening closely to the radio are over. Nowadays people just want to feel good, and it makes them uncomfortable when you play something they aren't familiar with."

60 "Bill—it was a listener's *request*."

So there we were: me trying to explain why after fifteen years on the air in L.A., I wanted to do the show my way, and he, two weeks off the plane, just as convinced that what Southern California really needed was McRadio.

Over the next two years, Ira Steinberg hired three more of these guys, each with a worse new idea than the last, each a carbon copy of somebody else's image of what a "winner" should be, each in turn driving the station further and further into the toilet. They kept hiring variations of the same guy, a systems man who played the consultant's game and followed the blind path of statistical research without ever bothering to see where it was leading.

The irony is that the problem did not lie in the data, or even the methodology. There is nothing inherently wrong with using call-out research, or focus groups, or statistical trends, or any of the rest of it. Both Terri Belle and Jack Snyder had relied on a highly sophisticated formula of local sales, national record charts, and the like to determine what songs were appropriate for RADIO KAOS, and which tracks should get the most airplay. The key is what you *do* with that information.

Consultants, believing that an audience can be herded like sheep, seek to create a rigid structure that never varies. They would take the results of their lab tests, print them out on a computer spreadsheet, and demand that the jocks on the air play the data in the prescribed manner.

65 What we had done at KAOS was to take that same data and go one step further. We provided a staff of highly creative professionals with the information, and it was their job to *interpret* the data and transform it into a living, breathing radio show.

In the broadest of terms, RADIO KAOS and KASH were both playing the same music, so why had RADIO KAOS been so dominant for so long? KASH had an air staff of great jocks, talented people who, left to their own devices, could have done wonderfully inventive shows. The difference was that the jocks at RADIO KAOS were encouraged to explore new frontiers with the music, while the people at KASH were forced into the role of assembly line workers. The curious thing was that the more Ira Steinberg and Micromedia tried to make RADIO KAOS fit the bureaucratic mold, the more the ratings went down.

By 1987 morale was at an all-time low, and I was getting fed up with the daily battles over creative control of my show. I was torn between losing my job and the loss of artistic freedom, and each day became a struggle within the very studio which had once set me free. How could I go on the air and *not* speak my mind? They wanted us to smile while we lied to our listeners, and that was something I just could not do.

By the time Ira and the corporate brain trust in New York had gone through their *fifth* program director following Terri Belle, the station had lost all semblance of KAOS. No longer a beacon of the L.A. airwaves, RADIO KAOS was now merely a whisper amongst the cacophony of hucksters and pitchmen that crowded the FM dial.

STEVEN RENDELL, JIM NAURECHAS, AND JEFF COHEN

Censor or Victim of Censorship?

Few Americans can be said to enjoy freedom of speech more than Rush Limbaugh, with his 17 1/2 hours of national broadcast time each week. Yet he constantly complains that he is a victim of persecution and "censorship"—at the hands of the Pentagon, Congress, gays, etc. On his TV show, the muzzled one even gave an award for "the best attempted censorship of me during 1993" to the Pentagon—*after* he'd become the most forceful partisan voice on Armed Forces Radio.

Limbaugh can be a stirring defender of free speech—when it's his own or that of someone he agrees with. Limbaugh calls his daily savaging of President Clinton the essence of patriotism, but that's hardly his position on criticism of former presidents Reagan or Nixon.

When a Limbaugh fan in Orange County, California, was dismissed from a Catholic high school after, among other things, accusing women teachers of "feminazi tactics" (in a school, ironically, where teachers would be fired for advocating abortion rights), Limbaugh used his broadcasts to defend the student as a martyred fighter for the First Amendment. That's also how Limbaugh hailed another high school student in Northern California who faced obstacles in setting up a Rush Limbaugh Club on campus: "My friends, we have here another classic example of discrimination and hypocrisy. . . . He's fighting for his First Amendment rights."

Classic hypocrisy, indeed. Calling himself Rush "Warmonger" Limbaugh, he had used his national radio show to applaud schools in Pasadena, Texas, that prohibited students from wearing peace symbols because school officials believed they were the mark of devil worshipers (*Washington Post,* 6/27/89). That same week, he denounced the Supreme Court ruling that flag burning is free expression protected by the First Amendment. And, during a public lecture, when his condemnations of artists Robert Mapplethorpe and Andres Serrano provoked a heckler's cry of "censorship," Limbaugh defended censorship: "It has been used throughout this nation's history as a means of maintaining standards." (*New York Times,* 12/16/90)

The "Hush Rush" Hoax

"I, Rush Limbaugh, the poster boy of free speech, am being gang muzzled." 5

The broadcaster was crying censorship over congressional efforts in 1993 to reinstate the Fairness Doctrine, which he labeled "The Hush Rush

Bill," "The Get Limbaugh Act," and "The Rush Elimination Act of 1993." Limbaugh's daily on-air crusade generated thousands of calls to Washington and helped derail congressional action. As usual, Limbaugh's followers were mobilized through misinformation and deception.

The Fairness Doctrine—in operation from 1949 until it was abolished in 1987 by Ronald Reagan's deregulation-oriented Federal Communications Commission—called on broadcasters, as a condition of their licenses from the FCC, to cover some controversial issues in their community, and to do so by offering some balancing views.

Reinstating the Fairness Doctrine can hardly be a "Hush Rush" bill aimed at silencing him, since it was broadly and actively supported on Capitol Hill *well before anyone in Washington had ever heard of Limbaugh.* In 1987 (when Limbaugh was still in Sacramento), a bill to inscribe the Fairness Doctrine in federal law passed the House by 3 to 1, and the Senate by nearly 2 to 1. Such "commie-libs" as Representative Newt Gingrich (R-GA) and Senator Jesse Helms (R-NC) voted for the bill, but it was vetoed by President Reagan.

In 1989 (when Limbaugh was just emerging as a national host), the Fairness Doctrine easily passed the House again, but didn't proceed further, as President Bush threatened to veto it. In 1991, hearings were again held on the doctrine, but interest waned due to Bush's ongoing veto threat. Yet when the same Fairness Doctrine emerged in 1993, with a new president who might sign it, Limbaugh egotistically portrayed it as nothing but a "Hush Rush Law." And his followers believed him.

10 And they believed him when he claimed the Fairness Doctrine was aimed at censoring conservative talkshow hosts: "It's the latest attempt by the United States Congress to legislate against me, and talk radio hosts." Remarked Limbaugh: "Why is 'fairness' so needed now? Because there's too much conservatism out there." In reality, not one doctrine decision issued by the FCC had ever concerned itself with talkshows. Indeed, the talkshow format was born, and flourished, while the doctrine was in operation. Right-wing hosts often dominated the talkshows, but none was ever muzzled.

The Fairness Doctrine did not require that each program be internally balanced or mandate "equal time." Nor did it require that balance in the overall program lineup be close to 50/50. It merely prohibited a station from blasting away day after day from one perspective, without opposing views. It would not "hush Rush," but it might get stations that offer only a constant diet of Limbaugh and fellow right-wingers to diversify their lineup a bit. Limbaugh was uttering nonsense when he said that to balance his show under the Fairness Doctrine, station owners "will have to go out and get two liberal shows. Or maybe three. Even three might not be enough." (Perhaps what Limbaugh meant to say was how difficult it is to find a host far enough to the left to balance his far-right views—especially since Mao is dead.)

A wide variety of citizen groups have used the Fairness Doctrine as a tool to expand speech and debate—not to restrict it. For example, it prevented stations from allowing only one side to be heard on ballot measures. (The abolition of the doctrine, a study found, had a disastrous impact on democratic debate around 1992 ballot measures.) Over the years, the doctrine has been supported by hundreds of grass-roots groups across the political spectrum, including the ACLU, National Rifle Association, and the right-wing Accuracy In Media.

"The Fairness Doctrine isn't going to take Rush Limbaugh off the air," remarked Larry King. "Be fair: What's wrong with that? If I were Rush, I would want a liberal host following my show."

Limbaugh argues that there should be no government "fairness" stan- 10
dards on broadcasters, since there are none on the print press: "You can buy a newspaper, and start it all you want, and they wouldn't dare try to do this [establish a Fairness Doctrine]" (TV, 9/17/93). He misses the key difference: If we want to compete with Limbaugh's publication in the marketplace of ideas, we can start our own publication right next to his. But if we set up our own competing broadcast program right next to a Limbaugh station on the radio dial—without acquiring a government license—we will be prosecuted. Broadcast frequencies are limited, and government licensed; printing presses are not. That's the legal underpinning of the Fairness Doctrine.

ERIC DEZENHALL

We Like Our Bad Guys to Be Honest About It

When I watched Enron's former chief executive, Jeffrey K. Skilling, testify recently before Congress, it sparked a decades-old memory of—don't laugh—the televised testimony of a very different kind of honcho, my hometown mob boss, Philadelphia's Nicodemo "Little Nicky" Scarfo.

As a kid, I used to see Nicky and his boys talking on the beach in Margate, N.J., and thought I was pretty cool when I got an acknowledgment, a "Yo, kid," from Nicky or one of his killers. Years later, in the mid-1980s, I was a former White House aide still gaga over the political process, and I couldn't wait to see how Nicky defended his corner in a congressional hearing about racketeering. The highlight of Nicky's testimony was when he was asked if he swore to tell the truth. Nicky — visibly ticked, his South Philly pompadour bouncing — glanced at his lawyer for a little help. The lawyer urgently nodded a yes. In Nicky's business, lying was currency, and he appeared, well, betrayed, by the very pretense that the proceedings would be on the level. In contrast, Enron's Skilling, when questioned, conveyed an earnest, helpful demeanor and stayed "on message" in the spirit of a true wise guy: Wasn't me.

Lots of people have said they don't believe Skilling, and one of my friends even huffed that the ex-CEO was "worse than a gangster." I don't agree; I have always been amazed by how our culture grades corruption on a curve of moral relativism. Most scandals are called "Watergates," military conflicts become "Vietnams" and human rights horrors "Holocausts" when they're not.

Nor do I believe, in any legal or moral sense, that an accused corporate huckster is comparable to a convicted psychopath like Nicky Scarfo. Nevertheless, the Scarfo and Skilling testimonies point to an interesting cultural distinction. Everybody I've talked to seems to want the Enron guys to do hard time. I can't remember the last time I heard the same dark wishes expressed about the Mafia.

5 On the contrary, American culture often romanticizes the wiseguys of organized crime. *The Sopranos* became a TV show beloved both by cable viewers and the Emmy judges. Mobsters preen in beer commercials, asking "How ya doin'?" Successful films such as *Analyze This* and *O Brother, Where Art Thou?* portray professional killers as comic, even heroic characters.

The simultaneous vilification of Enron and glorification of organized crime makes me wonder what kind of bad guys America wants? Answer: honest ones. A thief pointing a gun at your head makes no pretense about his intentions, but a thief armed with a laptop and a smile is out to fool you, and Americans absolutely hate to be fooled.

The real sin of the Enron executives is their hypocrisy. They portrayed themselves as model corporate citizens, society's pillars, deeply concerned about their community. Meanwhile, it has been alleged, they were helping themselves to millions of dollars at the expense of their employees and shareholders. Murderous Little Nicky and his Mafia cronies have never tried to pretend to be anything other than what they are: wiseguys.

I suspect there's another reason we go easy on street-corner buccaneers, one tied more deeply to the roots of American culture. We like the Mafia because it is cheating the system from the outside. It's no coincidence that Butch and Sundance are lionized just as Don Corleone's Godfather is—though all are violent criminals.

Often the glorification is tinged with nostalgia. Last month, the front page of the *New York Daily News* revealed that prosecutors say mob boss Vincent "the Chin" Gigante—who for years roamed Greenwich Village in his bathrobe, feigning insanity to dodge the clink—is still running the Genovese Crime Family from prison. And when aging mobster Raymond "Long John" Martorano was mortally shot while driving on a busy street in Philadelphia, the newspaper articles reported the grisly details—but also reminisced that he was one of the last of the old-timers, whose killers didn't appreciate the power he once held. Ah, the old days, when grown men dispatched one another more discreetly. In the past year, barely a week has gone by when the networks haven't reported a "death watch" at the bedside of cancer-stricken mob boss, John Gotti, as if we were all waiting for puffs of white smoke to waft from the Vatican.

10 Chronicling the toughs is less a cry for justice than a spectator sport. Friends who know I write about the mob, including a priest and several rabbis, no less, contact me from time to time, thirsty for old yarns and gossip about South Philly rogues such as "Al Pajamas" (in prison), "Chicken Man" (blown up on his front porch with a nail bomb), Harry "the Hunchback" (recently died in prison), and "Nicky Crow" (in the witness protection program).

Despite the steady cavalcade of Mafia coverage, there are no letters to the editor asking that prosecutors take action. No demands to "Lynch the Chin." There's no public outcry, because most readers would just as soon write to the producers of *General Hospital* to complain about loose morals. Sensational behavior is the whole point of the show. But where Enron is concerned, the outraged public, understandably, wants blood. As for mobsters, dare I suggest that many of us do want their crimes to pay?

Maybe that's because of some warped spinoff of the American Dream, the idea that one can accomplish anything on rogue instinct and back-alley cunning. After all, isn't that our perception of the Founding Fathers themselves: hell-raising outsiders who took what was theirs? We somehow see thieves who operate outside the system as being more, well, honest than thieves who operate from within. Many of us love the mob because it beats the system; we hate Enron because it bought the system.

Americans have a long track record of celebrating wily subversives. What was vaudeville, after all, but shtick after shtick of immigrants slamming bluebloods in the face with a pie? What of National Lampoon's *Animal House,* where the piggish Deltas cheat the system by trawling through Faber College's trash for the exam answers (and flunk out anyway), while the priggish Omegas become "outstanding campus leaders" by doing Dean Wormer's dirty work? Is it lost on anyone that in the epilogue, the film's writers reward the Deltas' John Belushi, who resembles a Mafia thug, with a U.S. Senate seat, and punish the preppy Omega house honcho by revealing that he becomes a Nixon White House aide who is later "raped in prison"?

In the end, even if the Enron honchos are proven to have swindled anything resembling the mob's booty, there was something chillingly respectable about how they did it, which is the part, I think, that provokes our most furious wrath. I think I've got a good business sense, but like most investors I was reluctant to question the imperious, blue-chip facade of "limited partnerships" and "audited balance sheets." As a kid who grew up around green felt and velour beach wear, who was I to ask?

15 We'll see what happens to the Boys of Enron, who made fortunes, perhaps legally, without spilling a drop of blood. As for Little Nicky, he's doing life in Marion for directing a reign of terror that left dozens dead, including "Frankie Flowers," who was a friend of my family. Nicky swears he's innocent. His associates—the guys I saw hugging him on the beach—ratted him out and are living under assumed names, trying to blend into the yellow prairies and small towns of rural America. The lawyer who advised a reluctant Nicky to tell the truth at the congressional hearing did some time himself for racketeering. John Gotti, who was caught on tape, apoplectic, saying that the FBI was persecuting him, will soon be gone. On one hand, I'm thinking, good riddance. On the other, I am very much a part of the phenomenon that I'm judging, not because I admire the bad guys, but because I miss the days on the boardwalk when we all knew who the bad guys were.

You got a problem with that?

CHAPTER 16

PETS, PESTS, AND BEASTS

Overview

The animal kingdom often fills us with wonder. Few people do not admire the beauty, grace, or physical abilities of at least some type of animal. Some individuals feel affinity with a certain animal group; the worship of animals, especially predators, can be traced to virtually all early human cultures.

Human cultures distinguish among animals, having domesticated certain breeds, controlled or destroyed others as pests, and forced still others to keep their distance from us. Based on these groupings, we have endowed animals with certain rights and have determined a moral code by which to judge their behavior. In this code, we can see some self-defeating beliefs that might make us look more closely at our own actions.

The animals known as pets or companion animals reflect a relationship to the animal kingdom that sees humans as the supreme beings on Earth. No other animal owns another species, nor does any other animal try to change the eating habits of another species. It is true that animals try to deter other species from eating them, but they do not exert a concerted effort to prevent scavengers from scavenging, hunters from hunting, and grazers from grazing. No animal other than the human tries to control the breeding habits of other species, nor does any other animal cage, chain, or fence in other species. Only humans try to train other species to respond to commands and groom them to please human perceptions of beauty.

While we clearly love our pets, we cannot deny that our actions represent a belief in our innate superiority and the right to dominance. While some

This icon will direct you to web links and additional resources on the website college.hmco.com/pic/thelin1e

pet owners might refer to themselves as "mommy" or "daddy" when interacting with pets, especially kittens or puppies, the term often heard is "master," as in a dog should obey its master. Where there is a master, there must be a slave.

The most obedient members of the animal kingdom garner the greatest rewards in this system of domestication. The less wild an animal is, the more likely it is to receive bountiful meals, medical attention, and regular exercise. The more the animal performs services—as a watchdog, for instance, or a racehorse—the more acclaim it receives. On the opposite end of the spectrum, domesticated animals unable to learn tricks or lackadaisical in their duties earn scorn. They are derided as stupid, do not receive treats, and sometimes are even abandoned or given away. The many incidents of neglect and ill-treatment of pets have led to the establishment of animal welfare laws, demonstrating that when some pet owners transgress the boundaries of humane treatment, other people respond protectively.

While many different types of animals can be owned as pets, we tend to grant fewer rights to smaller animals. The less they resemble us and the less we can project personalities onto them, the more we feel free to respond whimsically to our dominance. So while some people keep rabbits, snakes, and frogs as pets, other people treat these animals as unworthy of concern. Teenagers use rabbits for target practice with BB guns and .22s. Children capture frogs in jars, suffocating or dehydrating them, sometime unintentionally, sometimes not. Because of superstitions and phobias about snakes, some people automatically kill them, even if the snakes are nonpoisonous and present no danger.

Many cultures believe that animals exist for the benefit of humans. The use of lab animals in the developed world evinces this point. Scientists experiment on animals to find cures for human diseases more than to find cures for animal diseases. Animal rights activists receive support when they protest against pain inflicted in testing perfume or cosmetics on animals, but the public is much more tolerant of cruelty to animals when the testing is for diseases. That is, when the results might alleviate human suffering from cancer or bacteria, the animals' suffering is seen as necessary.

Animals that get in the way of progress, pose imagined or real threats, or interfere with our comfort are considered pests. Their very right to life is secondary. Some legitimate reasons for killing pests exist. Mosquitoes can carry disease. The bite of a brown recluse or a black widow spider contains enough poison to cause considerable swelling and discomfort in a fully grown human. A fly invades our personal space. Mice and rats invade food supplies, and the feces and other possible contaminating agents they leave are unsanitary. Bats or other creatures that fly can disrupt and foul a household, and they are difficult to remove without force. These smaller creatures, then, constitute a nuisance that we take proactive measures to stop. We feel little moral remorse in eradicating them.

On the opposite end of the spectrum are the animals that leave us alone, basically, but that we nonetheless consider threats. While they have mammalian characteristics, their size, strength, and ferocity frighten us, and we want to remove them if they get too close. While humans are not the natural prey of any animal, certain animals will stalk and kill humans given the opportunity. One in every hundred tigers is a man-eater. Polar bears, due to the sparse availability of food in their domain, hunt human travelers within the region. Great white sharks do not distinguish between human and other types of prey, even though their reputation far exceeds the number of human kills attributed to them. These predators, like most animals, also protect their young and attack when they perceive danger. Outside of, perhaps, the unpredictable behavior of the North American grizzly bear, though, the reaction of most larger animals to human presence is flight. They do not seek confrontations with us.

Despite the overwhelming documentation of this fact, human predation has caused the number of very large animals to dwindle, and many species will not survive to the twenty-second century. Big-game hunting accounts for part of this, as does poaching for treasures like ivory, but these activities alone would not doom a species. Rather, ever-increasing human encroachment on the terrain of wild animals poses the worst threat. We place our comfort above the existence of other species, refusing to curtail our expansion of settlements, to place limits on growth, or to modify our use of the land. And when human development of a wilderness area brings humans and animals in closer proximity, the animal that accidentally or deliberately kills a human will be hunted down and killed, as will many others of its kind in preemptive strikes against perceived dangers (see Scott McMillon's "Treat It Right" on page 499 for an example).

Humans, indeed, might have been ordained the caretakers of the world long ago by a higher being. Our actions could be the subconscious recognition of our destiny. But if so, our treatment of animals shows abuse, not stewardship. We need animals, from the smallest to the biggest and surliest of beasts, to survive. Their complex world must be understood beyond the immediate comforts and needs of humans. How do we reverse trends and scale back our expansion to allow ecosystems full of large and small animals to flourish? Must we suffer the inconveniences of pests when we head outdoors to ensure that an ecosystem persists? Should we allow predators such as cougars and alligators to enter our domain? Do we need to question elements of our relationships with domesticated animals? The questions outweigh the practical solutions, but perhaps the first step is to look at the moral code we enact on the animal world and spot the inconsistencies that, if not rectified, will lead to our doom as well.

Openings for Writers

1. **Relationships with pets** How would you describe your interactions with your pets? Have you ever given priority to the pet's needs? Judge your own actions regarding pets in light of the overview's claims of a relationship based on dominance.
2. **Animal rights** While the animal rights movement mostly seeks to protect animals from the fur trade and laboratory experimentation, its boundaries can be expanded to the right to live. Do species have an innate right to exist freely in the world as dictated by their instincts? What other rights

should they have? What should be done to strengthen the chances of survival of threatened species?

3. **Human destiny** Are humans superior to other life forms? Is it possible that animals know about life in ways that elude us? Think about the basis on which we grant ourselves an elevated position in the animal kingdom, and consider the possibility that we might be wrong. What changes would we have to make if we considered ourselves equal to members of the animal kingdom? You might want to consult Edward Abbey's "The Snake" (page 495) for a different perspective.
4. **Dealing with pests** How do you try to deter insects and rodents from creating a nuisance in and around your house or apartment? Have you ever felt guilty about killing pests? Why?

Language

1. **Master and owner** Do you use the term *master* when talking about a pet, or are you more comfortable with *owner*? What words do you associate with these terms? Are there any opposites other than *slave* and *laborer?* Develop complex definitions of *master* and *owner* that investigate positive and negative connotations of the words, and see whether a deeper understanding of the terms reveals anything about the topic of pets, pests, and beasts.
2. **Obedience and disobedience** Do the terms *obedience* and *disobedience* have meaning outside of a hierarchical relationship? What do they connote to you? Does *obedience* always have positive associations and *disobedience* negative ones?

DAVID QUAMMEN

Face of a Spider

This article extends the question of dealing with pests by putting actions into a philosophical context. Quammen tries to develop a guideline on when to act violently against another species. Although Quammen claims to have squandered his opportunity for moral growth, his reflections demonstrate a keen mind that does not accept easy answers.

One evening a few years ago I walked back into my office after dinner and found roughly a hundred black widow spiders frolicking on my desk. I am not speaking metaphorically and I am not making this up: a hundred black widows. It was a vision of ghastly, breathtaking beauty, and it brought on me a wave of nausea. It also brought on a small moral crisis—one that I dealt with briskly, maybe rashly, in the dizziness of the moment, and that I've been turning back over in my mind ever since. I won't say I'm *haunted* by those hundred black widows, but I do remember them vividly. To me, they stand for something. They stand, in their small synecdochical way, for a large and important question.

The question is, How should a human behave toward the members of other living species?

A hundred black widows probably sounds like a lot. It is—even for Tucson, Arizona, where I was living then, a habitat in which black widows breed like rabbits and prosper like cockroaches, the females of the species growing plump as huckleberries and stringing their ragged webs in every free corner of every old shed and basement window. In Tucson, during the height of the season, a person can always on short notice round up eight or ten big, robust black widows, if that's what a person wants to do. But a hundred in one room? So all right, yes, there was a catch: These in my office were newborn babies.

A hundred scuttering bambinos, each one no bigger than a poppyseed. Too small still for red hourglasses, too small even for red egg timers. They had the aesthetic virtue of being so tiny that even a person of good eyesight and patient disposition could not make out their hideous little faces.

5 Their mother had sneaked in when the rains began and set up a web in the corner beside my desk. I knew she was there—I got a reminder every time I dropped a pencil and went groping for it, jerking my hand back at the first touch of that distinctive, dry, high-strength web. But I hadn't made the necessary decision about dealing with her. I knew she would have to be either murdered or else captured adroitly in a pickle jar for relocation to the wild, and I didn't especially want to do either. (I had already squashed scores of black widows during those Tucson years but by this time, I guess, I was going soft.) In the meantime, she had gotten pregnant. She had laid her eggs into a silken egg sac the size of a Milk Dud and then protected that sac vigilantly, keeping it warm, fending off any threats, as black widow mothers do. While she was waiting for the eggs to come to term, she would have been particularly edgy, particularly unforgiving, and my hand would have been in particular danger each time I reached for a fallen pencil. Then the great day arrived. The spiderlings hatched from their individual eggs, chewed their way out of the sac, and started crawling, brothers and sisters together, up toward the orange tensor lamp that was giving off heat and light on the desk of the nitwit who was their landlord.

By the time I stumbled in, fifty or sixty of them had reached the lampshade and rappelled back down on dainty silk lines, leaving a net of gossamer rigging between the lamp and the Darwin book (it happened to be an old edition of *Insectivorous Plants,* with marbled endpapers) that sat on the desk. Some dozen others had already managed dispersal flights, letting out strands of buoyant silk and ballooning away on rising air, as spiderlings do—in this case dispersing as far as the bookshelves. It was too late for one man to face one spider with just a pickle jar and an index card and his two shaky hands. By now I was proprietor of a highly successful black widow hatchery.

And the question was, How should a human behave toward the members of other living species?

The Jain religion of India has a strong teaching on that question. The Sanskrit word is *ahimsa,* generally rendered in English as "noninjury" or the imperative "do no harm." *Ahimsa* is the ethical centerpiece of Jainism, an absolute stricture against the killing of living beings—*any* living beings—and it led the traditional Jains to some extreme forms of observance. A rigorously devout Jain would burn no candles or lights, for instance, if there was danger a moth might fly into them. The Jain would light no fire for heating or cooking, again because it might cause the death of insects. He would cover his mouth and nose with a cloth mask, so as not to inhale any gnats. He would refrain from cutting his hair, on grounds that the lice hiding in there might be gruesomely injured by the scissors. He could not plow a field, for fear of mutilating worms. He could not work as a carpenter or a mason, with all that dangerous sawing and crunching, nor could he engage in most types of industrial production. Consequently the traditional Jains formed a distinct socioeconomic class, composed almost entirely of monks and merchants. Their ethical canon was not without what you and I might take to be glaring contradictions (vegetarianism was sanctioned, plants as usual getting dismissive treatment in the matter of rights to life), but at least they took it seriously. They lived by it. They tried their best to do no harm.

And this in a country, remember, where 10,000 humans died every year from snakebite, almost a million more from malaria carried in the bites of mosquitoes. The black widow spider, compared to those fellow creatures, seems a harmless and innocent beast.

But personally I hold no brief for *ahimsa,* because I don't delude myself 10
that it's even theoretically (let alone practically) possible. The basic processes of animal life, human or otherwise, do necessarily entail a fair bit of ruthless squashing and gobbling. Plants can sustain themselves on no more than sunlight and beauty and a hydroponic diet—but not we animals. I've only mentioned this Jainist ideal to suggest the range of possible viewpoints.

Modern philosophers of the "animal liberation" movement, most notably Peter Singer and Tom Regan, have proposed some other interesting answers to the same question. So have writers like Barry Lopez and Eugene Linden, and (by their example, as well as by their work) scientists like Jane Goodall and John Lilly and Dian Fossey. Most of the attention of each of these thinkers, though, has been devoted to what is popularly (but not necessarily by the thinkers themselves) considered the "upper" end of the "ladder" of life. To my mind, the question of appropriate relations is more tricky and intriguing—also more crucial in the long run, since this group accounts for most of the planet's species—as applied to the "lower" end, down there among the mosquitoes and worms and black widow spiders.

These are the extreme test cases. These are the alien species who experience human malice, or indifference, or tolerance, at its most automatic and elemental. To squash or not to squash? Mohandas Gandhi, whose own ethic of nonviolence owed much to *ahimsa,* was once asked about the propriety of an antimalaria campaign that involved killing mosquitoes with DDT, and he was careful to give no simple, presumptuous answer. These are the creatures whose treatment, by each of us, illuminates not just the strength of emotional affinity but the strength, if any, of principle.

But what is the principle? Pure *ahimsa,* as even Gandhi admitted, is unworkable. Vegetarianism is invidious. Anthropocentrism, conscious or otherwise, is smug and ruinously myopic. What else? Well, I have my own little notion of one measure that might usefully be applied in our relations with other species, and I offer it here seriously despite the fact that it will probably sound godawful stupid.

Eye contact.

15 Make eye contact with the beast, the Other, before you decide upon action. No kidding, now, I mean get down on your hands and knees right there in the vegetable garden, and look that snail in the face. Lock eyes with that bull snake. Trade stares with the carp. Gaze for a moment into the many-faceted eyes—the windows to its soul—of the house fly, as it licks its way innocently across your kitchen counter. Look for signs of embarrassment or rancor or guilt. Repeat the following formula silently, like a mantra: "This is some mother's darling, this is some mother's child." *Then* kill if you will, or if it seems you must.

I've been experimenting with the eye-contact approach for some time myself. I don't claim that it has made me gentle or holy or put me in tune with the cosmic hum, but definitely it has been interesting. The hardest cases—and therefore I think the most telling—are the spiders.

The face of a spider is unlike anything else a human will ever see. The word "ugly" doesn't even begin to serve. "Grotesque" and "menacing" are too mild. The only adequate way of communicating the effect of a spiderly countenance is to warn that it is "very different," and then offer a photograph. This trick should not be pulled on loved ones just before bedtime or when trying to persuade them to accompany you to the Amazon.

The special repugnant power of the spider physiognomy derives, I think, from fangs and eyes. The former are too big and the latter are too many. But the fangs (actually the fangs are only terminal barbs on the *chelicerae,* as the real jaw limbs are called) need to be large, because all spiders are predators yet they have no pincers like a lobster or a scorpion, no talons like an eagle, no social behavior like a pack of wolves. Large clasping fangs armed with poison glands are just their required equipment for earning a living. And what about those eight eyes—big ones and little ones, arranged in two rows, all bugged-out and pointing everywhichway? (My wife the biologist offers a theory here: "They have an eye for each leg, like us—so they don't *step* in anything.") Well, a predator does need good eyesight, binocular focus, peripheral vision. Sensory perception is crucial to any animal that lives by the hunt and, unlike insects, arachnids possess no antennae. Beyond that, I don't know. I don't *know* why a spider has eight eyes.

I only know that, when I make eye contact with one, I feel a deep physical shudder of revulsion, and of fear, and of fascination; and I am reminded that the human style of face is only one accidental pattern among many, some of the others being quite drastically different. I remember that we aren't alone. I remember that we are the norm of goodness and comeliness only to ourselves. I wonder about how ugly I look to the spider.

20 The hundred baby black widows on my desk were too tiny for eye contact. They were too numerous, it seemed, to be gathered one by one into a

pickle jar and carried to freedom in the backyard. I killed them all with a can of Raid. I confess to that slaughter with more resignation than shame, the jostling struggle for life and space being what it is. I can't swear I would do differently today. But there is this lingering suspicion that I squandered an opportunity for some sort of moral growth.

I still keep their dead and dried mother, and their vacated egg sac, in a plastic vial on an office shelf. It is supposed to remind me of something or other.

And the question continues to puzzle me: How should a human behave toward the members of other living species?

Last week I tried to make eye contact with a tarantula. This was a huge specimen, all hairy and handsomely colored, with a body as big as a hamster and legs the size of Bic pens. I ogled it through a sheet of plate glass. I smiled and winked. But the animal hid its face in distrust.

JANE GANAHL

Women Like Men Who Like Cats

Western culture tends to associate men with dogs and women with cats. A common stereotype suggests that men who own cats tend toward effeminacy. In a light-hearted article from the San Francisco Chronicle, *Jane Ganahl challenges this stereotype and proposes that men who own cats appeal to women because they demonstrate a certain sensitivity. Does the ability of our culture to shift away from the gender stereotypes associated with cats and dogs offer some hope for changing other ideas about animals in our lives?*

It seems as if single men are discovering what single women have known since ancient Egyptian times: Cats are worthy of worship.

At least unmarried British men say so, in a recent survey conducted by Cats Protection, a leading animal welfare society in the United Kingdom. And judging by the delirious worship that single men I know lavish on their kitties, I'd like to think American men—those brave enough to stand up and be counted— feel the same way.

The survey showed that 85 percent of men, and 94 percent of women, don't think it's wimpy or needy for a man to love his cat. In addition, just as many single men as single women said they enjoy "lavishing care" on their cat.

And yet there are still gender differences in how we view the often puzzling feline species. Given their choice of characterizing their cat as a good friend, a child, a baby or a partner, men chose good friend (aww), while women said they considered their cats either a child or a baby. And men chose a cat's "independent spirit" as the animal's most desirable trait, while women thought that trait was a cat's least desirable trait.

More than anything, the survey showed that unmarried laddies go as 5
delightfully off the deep end over their pets as women have been teased for

doing for centuries. Single male cat owners are more likely than their female counterparts to have made, or consider making, a sacrifice for their cat, including giving up a vacation and going into debt. Three-quarters of male respondents say their cats fulfill their cuddle requirements, and single men are also almost as likely as single women to consider choosing their cat over their partner.

It's long been said by women that cats are excellent guy-o-meters—capable of spotting a bad one with a sniff. I always found the converse to be true: Men who were good to my cats—and not in a manipulative, let's-impress-her-with-my-sensitivity kind of way—were going to be good to me.

Noodge has always been easy to like. A bulldozer of a Maine coon cat, he is like a dog in cat's clothing. He's fearless, assertive, funny and loud. He possesses, as his vet said recently, more attitude than any other 16-year-old cat she'd seen. I've never looked to him to be an impartial judge on the men in my life; he liked anyone who would feed him and stay out of his chair.

But Bunny was harder to warm up to. She came to us in 1991, on the day of the Oakland hills fire—a tiny, ragged survivor of a brood most likely born in the field nearby. Terrified but plucky, she hung out behind the water heater in the garage for two days before she finally allowed my daughter to hold her. I came home from work and Erin was doing her homework on the concrete garage floor, beaming and ecstatic at the gray fur ball curled up in her lap.

Although we were able to tame her feral nature, Bunny (named for the rabbitlike way she would nestle under your chin, purring loudly) bonded only with the two of us, and was terrified of everyone and everything else—from the UPS man to the vacuum cleaner. Only a few boyfriends in the past 13 years have been patient and loving enough to coax her out of her hiding places with sweet words and smiles. Those were good men indeed.

10 Bunny loved her food—OK, OK, she was a bit of a porker. Erin would admonish me when she came home from college for letting her get fat, while I would argue back that Bunny was merely big-boned. She loved Erin fiercely and even if they didn't see each other for months, the cat would recognize her instantly and burrow under her chin, relieved and happy.

After watching Bunny slow down in recent months, I should not have been surprised that she timed her collapse for the night Erin came home for Christmas. She knew the wagons were circled; she knew we'd be able to go through this together. At the vet hospital the next day, Dr. Heidi McClain noted that with a kitty this fat ("She's just big-boned!" I mouthed to Erin to keep her from crying), it was hard to get a sense of what had gone wrong inside. But it soon became apparent: kidney failure.

After five days of Christmas-week back-and-forth visits to the hospital, which saw her improve to the point of almost coming home, Bunny's heart unexpectedly gave out. I held her still body and called Erin. Through the tears we knew Bunny was better off without the tubes and the monitors, and all the scary things that had daunted her.

It's been two weeks and Noodge is confused and alarmed that his mate is gone. I watch him closely to see if his tough attitude softens and he starts to die, too. At that point, I will find him a new friend.

In the meantime, if a new man comes into my life, I guess I'll have to suss him out the old-fashioned way. And hope that any new kitty I get will be as difficult to love as Bunny was.

There is a moral to this story. Men, if you want many good things in life, 15
get a cat. Why? So many reasons. There is the unconditional-love thing, the way science has proved that stress levels come down drastically when one is stroking a pet, etc. But here's additional incentive: They are babe magnets.

Yes, according to this same British survey, women love men with cats. Ninety percent of single women surveyed thought men who like cats are "nicer"—i.e., more caring and sensitive—than those who don't. A quick poll of my cat-loving single girlfriends bears this out.

Additional points were awarded to those who adopted mature felines from shelters, rather than adorable kittens that have a much easier time finding homes. I suspect I shall find myself doing that very thing quite soon.

More than anything, I'm pleased to find that single men might just be warming to the notion of single-with-cat as a worthy lifestyle. It might help deflect the endless guff single women with cats have taken over the centuries. And it will certainly be good for cats.

And rightly so. They rock. Even when they break your heart.

Assignment Ideas

Writing a critical analysis of issues related to animals will push you toward examining some of your most basic beliefs about hierarchy and moral behavior. You might assume that an animal's rights are secondary to human rights based on unquestioned views of human intelligence, progress, and religious beliefs. As a writer, be careful not to dismiss any position too quickly, and try some of the suggestions for analysis from Chapter 2. Also practice your critical reading skills when you peruse the selections in this chapter to help you avoid clichés and produce a relevant thesis.

1. Have you ever been in a situation, like David Quammen's, where the threat from an animal or insect was not imminent, but you considered preemptive action to prevent future problems? Describe the situation. Through a comparison with Quammen's experience, develop a thesis about animal (or insect) rights that outlines specific ethical measures humans can use in behaving toward members of other species.
2. Write about an animal on the endangered species list, which can be found on the Internet at http://endangered.fws.gov/wildlife.html. Describe the animal, providing background information about its physiology, habits, and distinctive features. Have humans associated any qualities with this animal that strike you as either accurate or inaccurate? Do legends surround the animal? How and why were its numbers reduced? Talk about specific ways that the species could recover that take some people's belief in human destiny into account.

3. Are you a "dog person" or a "cat person"? The study cited by Jane Ganahl suggests that men and women find different characteristics of cats appealing, making gender an important criterion for understanding how we grow an affinity for certain animals. Using your personal experiences or observations, develop this and other generalizations about the differences between dog and cat people and discuss the human traits that attract or draw certain types of people to particular pets. "The Indian Dog" on page 495 depicts a young boy's transference of traditional male traits onto an animal. Do we really know something about a person by the type of pets he or she has? Do we know anything more about the pet?
4. Ecosystems can be delicate, and slight disruptions produce chain reactions that cause the depletion of species. We also have an emotional reaction when an old-growth forest is cut down or a river is dammed. Talk about an experience you had when nature and human needs collided, causing the destruction of part of an ecosystem. Did this destruction produce a chain reaction? Did you notice fewer animals than before? Look at Thomas McNamee's "Drainage Ditch" (page 512) to see how he describes the before and after as well as his reaction to the changes.

Group Work

Cartoon depictions of different animal species can tell us much about the qualities we associate with animals. They also can reveal our fears and, often, our sense of superiority. Study different television cartoons or animated movies that have talking animal characters. Describe the traits attributed to these animals. Can you find patterns that reveal conflicts in our culture's relationship with animals? For instance, do we admire a particular animal for strength and guile but still hunt it beyond what the species can sustain? Do we associate innocence with certain herbivores and castigate carnivores? Develop a thesis that takes a position on human relationships with the rest of the animal kingdom.

Additional Readings

This cluster demonstrates our broad view of different animals. The first two selections offer perspectives on domestication. While "The Indian Dog" deals specifically with a pet, "The Snake" suggests our anthropomorphism when we see animals enter our lives. The third selection takes a decidedly different view of animals in its recounting of a grizzly bear attack and the subsequent reaction of Glacier National Park officials. In "Drainage Ditch," Thomas McNamee reminisces about the old creek he used to play in and what happened to the ecosystem as a result of progress. Think about the ways these perspectives, from a boy's acceptance of a pet wanting to be free to the destruction of wildlife for resources, reflect our relationship with animals.

N. SCOTT MOMADAY

The Indian Dog

When I was growing up I lived in a pueblo in New Mexico. There one day I bought a dog. I was twelve years old, the bright autumn air was cold and delicious, and the dog was an unconscionable bargain at five dollars.

It was an Indian dog; that is, it belonged to a Navajo man who had come to celebrate the Feast of San Diego. It was one of two or three rangy animals following in the tracks of the man's covered wagon as he took leave of our village on his way home. Indian dogs are marvelously independent and resourceful, and they have an idea of themselves, I believe, as knights and philosophers.

The dog was not large, but neither was it small. It was one of those unremarkable creatures that one sees in every corner of the world, the common denominator of all its kind. But on that day—and to me—it was noble and brave and handsome.

It was full of resistance, and yet it was ready to return my deep, abiding love; I could see that. It needed only to make a certain adjustment in its lifestyle, to shift the focus of its vitality from one frame of reference to another. But I had to drag my dog from its previous owner by means of a rope. It was nearly strangled in the process, its bushy tail wagging happily all the while.

5 That night I secured my dog in the garage, where there was a warm clean pallet, wholesome food, and fresh water, and I bolted the door. And the next morning the dog was gone, as in my heart I knew it would be; I had read such a future in its eyes. It had squeezed through a vent, an opening much too small for it, or so I had thought. But as they say, where there is a will there is a way—and the Indian dog was possessed of one indomitable will.

I was crushed at the time, but strangely reconciled, too, as if I had perceived intuitively some absolute truth beyond all the billboards of illusion.

The Indian dog had done what it had to do, had behaved exactly as it must, had been true to itself and to the sun and moon. It knew its place in the scheme of things, and its place was precisely there, with its right destiny, in the tracks of the wagon. In my mind's eye I could see it at that very moment, miles away, plodding in the familiar shadows, panting easily with relief, after a bad night, contemplating the wonderful ways of man.

Caveat emptor. But from that experience I learned something about the heart's longing. It was a lesson worth many times five dollars.

EDWARD ABBEY

The Snake

As mentioned before, I share the housetrailer with a number of mice. I don't know how many but apparently only a few, perhaps a single family. They don't disturb me and are welcome to my crumbs and leavings. Where they came from, how they got into the trailer, how they survived before my arrival (for the trailer had been locked up for six months), these are puzzling matters I am not prepared to resolve. My only reservation concerning the mice is that they do attract rattlesnakes.

I'm sitting on my doorstep early one morning, facing the sun as usual, drinking coffee, when I happen to look down and see almost between my bare feet, only a couple of inches to the rear of my heels, the very thing I had in mind. No mistaking that wedgelike head, that tip of horny segmented tail peeping out of the coils. He's under the doorstep and in the shade where the ground and air remain very cold. In his sluggish condition he's not likely to strike unless I rouse him by some careless move of my own.

There's a revolver inside the trailer, a huge British Webley .45, loaded, but it's out of reach. Even if I had it in my hands I'd hesitate to blast a fellow creature at such close range, shooting between my own legs at a living target flat on solid rock thirty inches away. It would be like murder; and where would I set my coffee? My cherrywood walking stick leans against the trailerhouse wall only a few feet away but I'm afraid that in leaning over for it I might stir up the rattler or spill some hot coffee on his scales.

Other considerations come to mind. Arches National Monument is meant to be among other things a sanctuary for wildlife—for all forms of wildlife. It is my duty as a park ranger to protect, preserve and defend all living things within the park boundaries, making no exceptions. Even if this were not the case I have personal convictions to uphold. Ideals, you might say. I prefer not to kill animals. I'm a humanist; I'd rather kill a *man* than a snake.

5 What to do. I drink some more coffee and study the dormant reptile at my heels. It is not after all the mighty diamondback, *Crotalus atrox*, I'm confronted with but a smaller species known locally as the horny rattler or more precisely as the Faded Midget. An insulting name for a rattlesnake, which may explain the Faded Midget's alleged bad temper. But the name is apt: he is small and dusty-looking, with a little knob above each eye—the horns. His bite though temporarily disabling would not likely kill a full-grown man in normal health. Even so I don't really want him around. Am I to be compelled to put on boots or shoes every time I wish to step outside? The scorpions, tarantulas, centipedes, and black widows are nuisance enough.

I finish my coffee, lean back and swing my feet up and inside the doorway of the trailer. At once there is a buzzing sound from below and the rattler lifts his head from his coils, eyes brightening, and extends his narrow black tongue to test the air.

After thawing out my boots over the gas flame I pull them on and come back to the doorway. My visitor is still waiting beneath the doorstep, basking in the sun, fully alert. The trailerhouse has two doors. I leave by the other and get a long-handled spade out of the bed of the government pickup. With this tool I scoop the snake into the open. He strikes; I can hear the click of the fangs against steel, see the strain of venom. He wants to stand and fight, but I am patient; I insist on herding him well away from the trailer. On guard, head aloft—that evil slit-eyed weaving head shaped like the ace of spades—tail whirring, the rattler slithers sideways, retreating slowly before me until he reaches the shelter of a sandstone slab. He backs under it.

You better stay there, cousin, I warn him; if I catch you around the trailer again I'll chop your head off.

A week later he comes back. If not him, his twin brother. I spot him one morning under the trailer near the kitchen drain, waiting for a mouse. I have to keep my promise.

This won't do. If there are midget rattlers in the area there may be dia- 10
mondbacks too—five, six or seven feet long, thick as a man's wrist, dangerous. I don't want *them* camping under my home. It looks as though I'll have to trap the mice.

However, before being forced to take that step I am lucky enough to capture a gopher snake. Burning garbage one morning at the park dump, I see a long slender yellow-brown snake emerge from a mound of old tin cans and plastic picnic plates and take off down the sandy bed of a gulch. There is a burlap sack in the cab of the truck which I carry when plucking Kleenex flowers from the brush and cactus along the road; I grab that and my stick, run after the snake and corner it beneath the exposed roots of a bush. Making sure it's a gopher snake and not something less useful, I open the neck of the sack and with a great deal of coaxing and prodding get the snake into it. The gopher snake, *Drymarchon corais couperi,* or bull snake, has a reputation as the enemy of rattlesnakes, destroying or driving them away whenever encountered.

Hoping to domesticate this sleek, handsome and docile reptile, I release him inside the trailerhouse and keep him there for several days. Should I attempt to feed him? I decide against it—let him eat mice. What little water he may need can also be extracted from the flesh of his prey.

The gopher snake and I get along nicely. During the day he curls up like a cat in the warm corner behind the heater and at night he goes about his business. The mice, singularly quiet for a change, make themselves scarce. The snake is passive, apparently contented, and makes no resistance when I pick him up with my hands and drape him over an arm or around my neck. When I take him outside into the wind and sunshine his favorite place seems to be inside my shirt, where he wraps himself around my waist and rests on my belt. In this position he sometimes sticks his head out between shirt buttons for a survey of the weather, astonishing and delighting any tourists who may happen to be with me at the time. The scales of a snake are dry and smooth, quite pleasant to the touch. Being a cold-blooded creature, of course, he takes his temperature from that of the immediate environment —in this case my body.

We are compatible. From my point of view, friends. After a week of close association I turn him loose on the warm sandstone at my doorstep and leave for patrol of the park. At noon when I return he is gone. I search everywhere beneath, nearby and inside the trailerhouse, but my companion has disappeared. Has he left the area entirely or is he hiding somewhere close by? At any rate I am troubled no more by rattlesnakes under the door.

The snake story is not yet ended. 15

In the middle of May, about a month after the gopher snake's disappearance, in the evening of a very hot day, with all the rosy desert cooling like a griddle with the fire turned off, he reappears. This time with a mate.

I'm in the stifling heat of the trailer opening a can of beer, barefooted, about to go outside and relax after a hard day watching cloud formations. I happen to glance out the little window near the refrigerator and see two gopher snakes on my verandah engaged in what seems to be a kind of ritual dance. Like a living caduceus they wind and unwind about each other in undulant, graceful, perpetual motion, moving slowly across a dome of sandstone. Invisible but tangible as music is the passion which joins them—sexual? combative? both? A shameless *voyeur,* I stare at the lovers, and then to get a closer view run outside and around the trailer to the back. There I get down on hands and knees and creep toward the dancing snakes, not wanting to frighten or disturb them. I crawl to within six feet of them and stop, flat on my belly, watching from the snake's-eye level. Obsessed with their ballet, the serpents seem unaware of my presence.

The two gopher snakes are nearly identical in length and coloring; I cannot be certain that either is actually my former household pet. I cannot even be sure that they are male and female, though their performance resembles so strongly a *pas de deux* by formal lovers. They intertwine and separate, glide side by side in perfect congruence, turn like mirror images of each other and glide back again, wind and unwind again. This is the basic pattern but there is a variation: at regular intervals the snakes elevate their heads, facing one another, as high as they can go, as if each is trying to outreach or overawe the other. Their heads and bodies rise, higher and higher, then topple together and the rite goes on.

I crawl after them, determined to see the whole thing. Suddenly and simultaneously they discover me, prone on my belly a few feet away. The dance stops. After a moment's pause the two snakes come straight toward me, still in flawless unison, straight toward my face, the forked tongues flickering, their intense wild yellow eyes staring directly into my eyes. For an instant I am paralyzed by wonder; then, stung by a fear too ancient and powerful to overcome I scramble back, rising to my knees. The snakes veer and turn and race away from me in parallel motion, their lean elegant bodies making a soft hissing noise as they slide over the sand and stone. I follow them for a short distance, still plagued by curiosity, before remembering my place and the requirements of common courtesy. For godsake let them go in peace, I tell myself. Wish them luck and (if lovers) innumerable offspring, a life of happily ever after. Not for their sake alone but for your own.

20 In the long hot days and cool evenings to come I will not see the gopher snakes again. Nevertheless I will feel their presence watching over me like totemic deities, keeping the rattlesnakes far back in the brush where I like them best, cropping off the surplus mouse population, maintaining useful connections with the primeval. Sympathy, mutual aid, symbiosis, continuity.

How can I descend to such anthropomorphism? Easily—but is it, in this case entirely false? Perhaps not. I am not attributing human motives to my snake and bird acquaintances. I recognize that when and where they serve purposes of mine they do so for beautifully selfish reasons of their own. Which is exactly the way it should be. I suggest, however, that it's a foolish, simple-minded rationalism which denies any form of emotion to all animals but man and his dog. This is no more justified than the Moslems are in denying souls to women. It seems to me possible, even probable, that many of the nonhuman undomesticated animals experience emotions unknown to us. What do the coyotes mean when they yodel at the moon? What are the dolphins trying so patiently to tell us? Precisely what did those two enraptured gopher snakes have in mind when they came gliding toward my eyes over the naked sandstone? If I had been as capable of trust as I am susceptible to fear I might have learned something new or some truth so very old we have all forgotten it.

> They do not sweat and whine about their condition,
> They do not lie awake in the dark and weep for their sins. . . .

All men are brothers, we like to say, half-wishing sometimes in secret it were not true. But perhaps it is true. And is the evolutionary line from protozoan to Spinoza any less certain? That also may be true. We are obliged, therefore, to spread the news, painful and bitter though it may be for some to hear, that all living things on earth are kindred.

SCOTT McMILLION

Treat It Right

Put yourself in Buck Wilde's shoes. You're hiking alone in Glacier National Park in Montana when you find a blue hat lying in a trail. Then you spot a camera on a tripod, laid carefully down, the tripod legs neatly folded, the lens cap on. There's a small red backpack there, too, and this makes you suspicious and curious and you start to pay some serious attention. You move thirty feet or so back the way you came and there about three feet into the brush you spot the bad news: a pool of blood, a foot or more wide and still fresh.

Then you notice more blood, spots of it leading down the trail, and you see some grizzly bear tracks, claw marks scratched into the hard-packed ground. You follow them, making plenty of noise and moving downhill very slowly for about five hundred feet, until you find a bunch of scuff marks on the trail, a place where something heavy has been swept back and forth a few times. You keep going and you find more blood, then little pieces of what must be human flesh. You find some coins, you find a bootlace, you find more blood. Puddles of it, and a blood trail leading into the woods. You have spent a lot of time around bears and you know how dangerous they can be, but you also know they rarely kill people. Somebody is hurt very badly and the blood trail is there and you have only a can of pepper spray with you and you know somebody will surely die if you don't help so you go into the brush where you find more coins and a wristwatch and a boot and then you find a man lying on his left side.

The man is bitten and clawed from head to toe and the bear has eaten the meat from one arm and one buttock but his body is warm and he might still be alive even though you can't find a pulse and still there is nobody here but you and this dead or dying man. Surely you can do something so you hustle back to the red backpack only a few hundred feet and get a coat to cover him and keep him warm and when you get back to him after maybe five minutes the man is gone.

Not just dead. Gone.

5 Smears of blood tell you the bear has come back, probably after watching you follow its tracks, and has taken the man away, so you follow this grisly trail for a few steps and you see that it leads into a patch of timber really thick where you can't see anything at all.

Put yourself in Buck Wilde's shoes.

What are you going to do?

"That's when I knew I had really been more foolish than I thought I was being," Wilde recalls of that day, the third of October, 1992, a sunny Saturday in the high country. "I had the pepper spray in my hand the whole time, with the safety off. I was scared shitless. That was the point when I made the decision that I was in over my head and I had to get out. It was time to think about myself and other people, who I knew were alive."

Wilde was just off the Loop Trail, a vigorous four-mile hike that leads from the Going-to-the-Sun Road to the Granite Park Chalet, a popular backcountry destination. But it was late in the season—the first days of October can be the early part of winter in some years—and as far as Wilde knew, there wasn't another person around for miles. Still, it was a pleasant Saturday, only about noon, and there was a good chance that other hikers would arrive soon and walk into an ugly situation. So Wilde backtracked to the trail, walked downhill a quarter-mile, and pinned a note to the middle of the trail with a small rock.

10 "A man has been attacked by a bear," the note said. "Turn around and go back to the highway. Shout and make noise every hundred feet or so. Don't run, but move fast. Send help."

Wilde left his bear spray with the note and gave instructions on how to use it. Then he moved back up trail to the chalet, closed at the time, and met some other hikers who had just arrived. He sent them back to Logan Pass, a relatively flat eight-mile hike away, but a place with lots of traffic and a visitor center, the quickest source of help. He gave them a note for park rangers.

"Help," it said. "Discovered signs of bear mauling about a quarter to a half a mile downhill from chalet backcountry campsite. Followed another quarter-mile and found body. He was in bad shape but alive. Went back to get coat to cover him and body was gone.

"Met these people at chalet. I plan to stay here for two reasons.

1. To turn people back toward Logan Pass visitor center.

2. To take National Park Service personnel to site I last saw victim." 15

He signed the note "seriously, Buck Wilde" and asked the hikers to turn back anybody they met coming toward the chalet.

After the messengers left, Wilde left another note at a second trail intersection, then climbed to the chalet's second-story deck to settle in and wait, scanning the area with his binoculars, looking for bears and watching for any hikers who might be coming in. At one point, he heard a scream somewhere down on the Loop Trail. He didn't investigate. He had already spent an hour or more too close to a grizzly bear's fresh kill. He'd already pushed his luck. Enough was enough.

Wilde is an unusual man. Forty-three years old at the time, he had given himself his name when, at the age of forty, he gave up a lucrative career as an electrical engineer and launched a new one in wildlife photography. He spends several months a year in the wild, moving between places like Yellowstone National Park and Alaska, Florida and Southeast Asia, with periodic stays in his hometown of Julian, Pennsylvania. It's a tough way to make a living but he's been successful, publishing ten photo books. He lives a lifestyle he readily describes as "eccentric," one that often brings him into close contact with grizzly bears. He's been charged a few times but never attacked.

Wilde had walked into the Granite Park area the previous afternoon and spent the night in the backcountry campground. There were no other campers. He hoisted his food high into the air on the food pole there, then went to bed early and slept late. He walked around the area for an hour or so after he got up in the morning, then went back to the campground to fix breakfast in the designated cooking area, which is separate from the sleeping area to keep from attracting bears to the tents.

Sometime during the meal of hot cereal and tea, he caught a quick 20
glimpse of a small grizzly bear. He heard a woof, probably from the cub's mother, and the little bear took off running toward the Loop Trail. Wilde hastily cleaned up his breakfast and raised his gear back up on the food pole. He found fresh grizzly tracks, small ones, covering the footprints he had left less than an hour earlier, grabbed his camera, and took off in the direction he had seen the bear going. It was about half past eleven in the morning.

By then, the bears probably had already attacked John Petranyi, a forty-year-old jazz buff from Madison, Wisconsin, who had hiked up the Loop Trail that morning.

"It was no more than five minutes to put the food up the pole, plus another ten to fifteen minutes to get to the point of the attack," Wilde says. "That's how quickly things unfolded there.

"In my mind, what happened was, the bears came in and saw me and smelled my food. They were looking at it, but did the good bear thing and split when mama saw one of the cubs getting too close to me and took off running down towards that trail."

Wilde knows a lot about bears, knows that grizzlies will almost always avoid an encounter with people if they have a chance. He had spent the previous summer guiding photographers to places in Alaska where they could watch, up close, as grizzlies fished for salmon. Less than a year earlier, a sow had bluff-charged him on Kodiak Island after he inadvertently came between her and one of her three cubs. She came close enough, charging from a hundred feet away, that he could feel her hot breath, and she got there fast enough that he never even had time to reach for the shotgun on the ground at his feet. That's when he decided guns weren't much good in a bear encounter, and he hasn't carried one since. He studies bear behavior, is a fanatic about keeping a clean camp, and is a self-professed "pain-in-the-ass person to go into bear country with."

25 "You've got to read the bear safety books. You've got to convince me you've read the books. You've got to obey the rules. And pay attention. Any time you're not, I'm giving you shit about it."

He was paying close attention as he walked toward the Loop Trail that morning, mostly because he was hoping for a good photograph. But he wasn't paying much attention to the trail itself. Rather, he was watching and listening for bears.

That's when he stumbled across Petranyi's cap, then the blood and the other grim evidence of bad trouble. That point in the trail is a narrow corridor between thickish stands of pine trees, a place where visibility reduces to twenty feet in some places. It's also where Wilde started paying even more attention.

He had walked right past the big pool of blood just off the trail, the largest amount of blood he would find, even when he finally located Petranyi. "It was pretty much his life in that pool of blood."

After that, he noticed the small spots of blood leading down the trail. Then he got to the bootlace, the coins, the place where it looked like the bear had taken the two-hundred-pound man in its mouth and shaken him, leaving the scuff marks in the trail.

30 Following the evidence was not something he had to force himself to do, he later said. But it wasn't easy either, and it got even harder when the blood and other sign pulled him off the trail and into the woods.

"I was spooked out of my mind, but I had every reason to believe I was alone in that situation and that this guy's life was on the line. It was a weird thing, but all my senses were heightened to the nth degree. I was hearing four times better than I normally do. And I was seeing and smelling four times better than I normally do. So I just set on the logical track and tried to do things as logically as I could. I mean I took my time.

"It wasn't like I had to force myself, it was like what had to be done. But I didn't just go whistling in there either. I mean I was scared. I looked. I observed everything. I heard everything. I continuously rotated in 360 degrees to make sure I wasn't missing something, and I made noise all the time. I expected the guy was, if not dead, then on his way to dying from the evidence I was seeing. But you don't know. I still don't know if he was actually dead when I found him."

Wilde could find no pulse, no breath. The blood around the man's wounds was turning dark when he left to get the coat.

Moving the 750 feet—rangers would later measure the distance—between the backpack and where the bear first left Petranyi's body took about fifteen minutes the first time, Wilde said, because he was moving so carefully. But he made the round-trip from Petranyi to the pack and back in about five minutes, goaded by the faint hope of trying to keep somebody alive. Moving fifteen hundred feet in five minutes is no sprint, but it's no dawdle either, especially when there's a grizzly in the area.

When he returned to the spot where the body had disappeared, there was no doubt in Wilde's mind that he was in the right place. The blood, his own tracks, and other evidence were too clear to be mistaken. Petranyi had been lying under a small tree, the only one in the area, and now he was gone.

That meant the chances of him still clutching to life were even smaller, and Wilde knew what he had to do then: Back off, warn other people, and wait for help.

The help arrived at 5:02 P.M. in the form of a helicopter bearing two rangers armed with 12-gauge shotguns, loaded with heavy slugs. A pair of hikers had found Wilde's note on the Loop Trail (they were probably the source of the scream he had heard earlier) and hustled back to the trailhead to call rangers. The lead man in the helicopter was Charlie Logan, a Glacier veteran with long experience in managing grizzly bears.

But the rangers weren't the first ones on the scene. As Wilde waited at the chalet, scanning the hillsides and trying to control his tension, a group of four hikers arrived. They had walked in on the Highline Trail, ignoring the warnings from the people Wilde had sent that way with another note.

"They came in, like, 'Hey, let's go see that bear that killed that guy.'

"When they got in there I was irate," Wilde recalls. "I lectured them like I probably shouldn't have. I was all over them and they came right back at me. They said they were from Montana and live with this kind of thing all the time and wanted to see it."

The rangers were almost as disgusted with the people as Wilde was. The hikers no longer were having much fun either. They got to thinking about the bear they had seen on the hike to the chalet, and one of them asked for a ride out on the helicopter. They were in the air within moments.

It took about thirty minutes for Logan to interview Wilde and organize gear. Then the two of them, along with ranger Curt Frain, hit the trail, hoping to find Petranyi's body before the approaching darkness fell. Stopping to inspect and photograph evidence along the way, it took them twenty-four minutes to reach the body. Wilde had found Petranyi's body 175 feet from the trail. The bear had moved it another 500 feet by the time the three men found it the second time. If Wilde hadn't been there, it would have taken the rangers a lot longer to find it.

"After seeing what he had seen, it was remarkable that he offered to go back," Logan says. "It took a lot of courage."

Logan's reports described the brief trip as "challenging tracking while watching our flanks." The bear carrying Petranyi's body changed course a couple of times. Along its trail they found Petranyi's sock and bits of his shirt, but Logan, a trained medic, found no evidence of life in Petranyi. The body was cold, the eyes glazed, the injuries massive.

45 Considering all of this and "that a real danger to us (including civilian Buck Wilde) still existed at this late hour, I decided that we quickly document and mark the scene and exit the area," Logan wrote in his reports of the incident.

Frain flagged the area and took notes while Logan stood guard, shotgun at the ready. Very fresh sign indicated the bear or bears were probably still close at hand. At this point, nobody knew for sure how many or what kind of bears were involved, but dirt had been shoved on the body, indicating the bear had claimed it as its own and was protecting it from scavengers.

The men then backtracked, continuing to photograph and document evidence, moving back to Petranyi's backpack, which they checked for food. They looked for identification, and they wanted to know if Petranyi's lunch had lured the bear. But there was no food in the pack.

That's when the bears charged.

Frain was searching the backpack "when I heard heavy, rapid pounding of feet on the trail section below us, followed by repeated woofing sounds," Logan wrote in his report. "I could not see what was running up the trail at us but guessed it was a bear so began yelling 'back bear.' Within a moment a grizzly appeared at the bend in the trail below us and stopped. I caught a glimpse of a smaller bear just behind but did not take my eyes off the larger bear, now squarely in the sights of my shotgun."

50 The adult bear bounced back and forth on its front paws several times, a sign of stress and agitation, looked back at its offspring, and "woofed" a few times. It was fifty feet away, later measurements would show, and Logan said later that if the bear had taken one more step he would have pulled the trigger. He did not believe the bear had run upon the men by surprise, he says. It was charging.

The charge "looked like a pretty deliberate deal on the bear's part," Logan says. "But there were three of us there and we were yelling at her. I think she sized us up and decided we were too much."

Then the bears took off, but the men could still hear them, woofing and crashing in the nearby brush, tearing through the area where they had first attacked Petranyi, moving around the men in a quarter-circle. By then, it was getting dark fast.

Logan later would call the incident one of the biggest scares of his life, but his report is written in the deadpan style of official documents. Wilde remembers the charge a little more vividly. He says he doesn't believe that guns do much good in bear encounters, that attacks almost always happen too fast for most people to draw a weapon. But in this case, Logan and Frain were ready and probably could have killed at least the sow, had they chosen to.

"We heard the bears before we saw them," Wilde says. "It was like a freight train coming up that Loop Trail, coming on full speed.

"Charlie is on the left and [Frain] is on the right. I'm in the middle and we're standing right on the trail. And Charlie says, safety off, one up in the chamber. Bead down. Start yelling."

So the men started yelling. "Stop bear, stop bear." And the bears turned away.

"I don't know Charlie much outside this situation," says Wilde. "But the judgment he used right there, to not shoot those bears, I thought was very commendable. Most people would have been throwing lead. Trust me, I mean those bears were close and coming fast. But he gave them more than a fair chance and they did enough to avoid getting shot."

Logan says he didn't shoot for a couple of reasons. First, the bear stopped when he started yelling at it. Second, he had no idea if these bears were the ones that killed Petranyi.

"I certainly didn't want to kill the wrong bear, especially one with cubs."

The men then decided, as Wilde had earlier in the day, that enough was enough. They left the pack and tripod where they lay and "cautiously retreated" to the chalet area, where Wilde broke down his camp in the increasing darkness as the rangers stood guard, shotguns at the ready.

They took Wilde to a nearby backcountry ranger station with them—he had been ready to catch what sleep he could on the second-story deck of the chalet—and spent a long, long night filling out reports, reliving the day, and trying to figure out what had happened to Petranyi. About four in the morning, they caught a couple hours of sleep.

John Petranyi had lived a quiet life in Madison, Wisconsin, where he was a supervisor of custodians for the city government and shared a home with his father, a Hungarian immigrant. He loved jazz music, fine beers, good books, and riding his bicycle, commuting on it the six miles to his job in all kinds of weather.

But his greatest passion was getting out into wild country, according to his brother, Mark. Every year, he spent his three-week vacation in the wild country of the West: climbing volcanic peaks in Oregon, exploring Alaska, mountain biking in the canyons of Utah. In 1992, he took an auto tour of the Canadian Rockies, visiting Banff, Jasper, and other national parks, camping and hiking. Glacier was the last stop on his itinerary. Had he survived the day hike to Granite Park, he would have turned toward home the next day.

"That's what he worked all year for," Mark Petranyi says. "His three-week journey into the woods."

Stocky and strong, his five-foot-eleven-inch frame carried almost two hundred pounds. Bicycling, jogging, and cross-country skiing kept him in good shape. He was the oldest of three sons and his death was not the first sadness in the family: A brother had died in an accident in 1974 and his mother passed away in 1990. He was a bachelor, childless.

The evening after the day he died, a Sunday, a police chaplain came to the home of his father, also named John, and delivered the heartbreaking news. The next day, as Mark and John senior were preparing to fly to Montana to retrieve the body, a postcard arrived at Mark's house. It was postmarked from Kalispell, just outside Glacier.

"He said he hadn't seen any bears yet but had heard they were around," Mark says. "My wife almost didn't give me the card. It was a hard one to read."

John Petranyi liked to take pictures, but he wasn't an avid wildlife photographer. Almost all of his photographs were of landscapes, Mark says, a statement backed up by the film in John's camera, developed later by rangers. The pictures were all of the jagged peaks and cliffs that make Glacier so famous. No bears were on the film.

Mark says neither he nor his father blame the bears for John's death.

"He was just in the wrong place at the wrong time," Mark says. "It's unfortunate but he was in their home. You really can't blame the bears."

He and his father flew to Montana, where John's remains were cremated, and drove the dead man's car back to Wisconsin.

It was, as Mark recalls, a long drive.

Back in Glacier, Charlie Logan was getting ready to pull some long shifts himself.

As the bad news circulated around the park that Sunday morning, Logan, Frain, and Wilde rose in the ranger cabin to find the weather had gone to hell. Plans had called for a helicopter to arrive at first light and carry the body to park headquarters, but fog had cut the visibility to about one hundred feet when the sun rose at a little after seven. By half past eight, the temperature had fallen ten degrees, the wind had picked up, and snow was coming down in big round flakes. It wasn't until half past eleven that the weather cleared enough to bring a helicopter into the alpine bowl. On the way in, rangers spotted the bears on Petranyi's body. The sow had a distinctive marking—a light-colored collar around her neck and descending onto her chest.

More armed rangers came in on that flight, and Buck Wilde rode the helicopter back to park headquarters. His role was over, but the rangers' work had hardly started.

It took a couple of hours to get the six rangers and helicopter pilot Jim Kruger organized and a strategy worked out. Five rangers would walk to Petranyi's body. One would fly in the helicopter with Kruger, to observe the operation from the air. The ground crew arrived at the site at 2:15 and found Petranyi's body had been moved another seventy-five feet, where the bears had eaten more of it.

Pilot Kruger found the bear family—a sow and two cubs—still near the body. The bears didn't want to leave and kept trying to get closer, so he started hazing them with the helicopter, trying to keep them away from the body and the ground crew. "He'd get her going one way and then she would come back another way," Logan says. All this information was traveling to the ground crew via radio, but it was still hard to pinpoint the bear's exact location. It took only twenty minutes to load the body in the airship—four men carrying and one standing guard, keeping a close eye on the bushes—but it was a long twenty minutes. Then the ground crew continued documenting all the evidence they could find, working under a constant guard. With the helicopter gone, nobody knew where the bears were. As they back-tracked to the site of the backpack and camera and fanned out to search some more, the crew found Petranyi's wallet in the woods, a dozen steps from his backpack.

The wallet allowed the rangers to positively identify him and also provided a crucial piece of evidence. It had been torn by bear teeth, gouged deep enough to puncture the plastic credit cards inside it. There were a few traces of blood on the wallet and a little more blood on a nearby tree. That was enough to indicate that Petranyi had initially been attacked there and had then moved closer to the trail, where Wilde had found the pool of blood. Probably he had rested there, bleeding, and then moved down the trail the way he had come, hoping to find help.

Buck Wilde believes Petranyi met the bears in a surprise encounter, that the bears were running from the cooking area of the campground (tracks showed one bear had come within fifteen yards of him while he ate breakfast) and that, when they ran into Petranyi, the mother attacked to defend her cubs.

Rangers, who had more time to investigate, came up with a handful of possible scenarios.

Since the pack and camera appeared to have been laid carefully down, and because Petranyi's pants and underwear were around his ankles when he was found, they said it was possible that he had placed his things beside the trail and moved into the woods for a bowel movement or to urinate. That's where the bear hit him first. Then, either she let him go or he escaped and moved back to the trail, where he stopped long enough to leave the pool of blood before moving downhill, back toward his car and the only source of help he knew about.

It's also possible that he saw the bears on the trail and set his gear down before running into the woods, where the bears caught up with him. Under this scenario, they may have charged before or after he started running.

Maybe he saw the bears and put his things down, preparing to photograph them, and they attacked.

Or he could have heard a noise and moved into the woods, leaving his gear behind, to investigate.

The bowel movement theory seems likely, but is not conclusive. The only evidence backing it up is that his pants were down around his ankles. But being dragged by a bear shredded his shirt and pulled a boot off his foot. It could easily have pulled his pants down, too. Plus, if he had stepped into the woods to relieve himself, why would he leave his hat in the trail? Unless, of course, he dropped the hat after being attacked, as he stumbled back to the trail. Rangers found his glasses and some other items in the woods, indicating considerable movement in a small area.

It's clear that the initial assault didn't kill him.

The blood spots that Wilde followed down the Loop Trail were round, indicating Petranyi probably walked down the trail under his own power. If the bear had dragged him down the trail, the blood would have been smeared. Also, the bear left claw marks on the trail but no pad marks, indicating the bear was up on its toes, running.

Less than six hundred feet from the pack and camera, the bear caught Petranyi again, causing the "thrashing" marks in the trail. That's probably where he died. Then it dragged him down the trail a few steps and into the woods, where Wilde would find him.

It's possible that the bear chased Petranyi down the trail, but "he probably bumped into the bear again there," Logan says.

90 It is those last six hundred feet of his brother's travels that bother Mark Petranyi the most.

"Apparently he attempted to get away," Mark says. "Maybe that was the wrong thing to do. We'll never know. But that time from the first attack until she finally got him . . . it must have been sheer terror. Why didn't the bear go away? I've asked myself that question a thousand times."

Rangers asked themselves the same question. A grizzly bear had killed and eaten a man. It was an incredibly rare situation. In the ninety-year history of Glacier Park, where thousands upon thousands of people walk through grizzly country every year, Petranyi was only the ninth person to be killed by a grizzly bear. And in most of those cases, the bear left the body alone after the attack. During the same period, forty-eight people drowned in the park, twenty-three fell to their deaths from cliffs, and twenty-six died in car wrecks. Clearly, grizzly bears are only one of many perils in the park.

"In all my other cases, the bear attacks, neutralizes the threat, and leaves," Logan says.

The National Park Service met Monday morning to discuss the situation. Logan and the other rangers flew to park headquarters to participate. Chief Ranger Steve Frye called some outside bear experts for advice. After a few hours, the group of rangers and administrators decided the bears must die.

95 A combination of circumstances led to that decision. The initial attack on Petranyi may have been a defensive reaction by a surprised bear, and that is not normally a death sentence for a bear in Glacier National Park. But it quickly turned into a "predatory" situation when she started eating him. Add the bear's aggression on the trail, the way she had tried to buck the helicopter to get back to the corpse, and the way she had partially buried the body. Then add public and political perceptions.

"By removing that bear we perhaps saved many bears," Logan says.

That sounds like stilted logic at first, but it makes sense in the highly charged political debates over grizzly bears and their place in the modern world. If the bear had been allowed to live, "then," says Logan, "every attack after that would have been the man-killing grizzly" in the public mind.

"We're trying to have an atmosphere where people and bears can coexist," he says. But having a bear around that has earned a food reward by killing a person "is not consistent with what we want to achieve here. It was terrible to have to remove that grizzly bear, but I never had any second thoughts about it."

Logan and several other rangers packed up their weapons and flew back to the chalet at Granite Park.

The rangers searched from the air for as long as the weather held out 100
that day but couldn't find the bears they were looking for. A family group was spotted a few miles away, but they were the wrong bears.

That night, snow fell, and by the next morning—day four of the incident—a couple of inches of fresh dust coated the high country.

Kruger flew in part of a rancid deer carcass to use as bait, carrying it in a sling beneath his helicopter. Rangers on the ground had to adjust the bait, manipulating the smelly carcass and knowing there were hungry grizzlies in the area. Later that afternoon, a large, chocolate-colored grizzly came in, sniffed the bait, and disappeared with the whole bundle in less than five seconds as rangers watched through binoculars. Bait would be staked to the ground in the future.

The hunt was marked with frustration. Several snares were set and baited with more deer carcasses but they didn't do the job. The rangers caught a grizzly one day, but he was the wrong animal, a subadult male, so they let him go. Bear biologists with the Montana Department of Fish, Wildlife and Parks flew in to help. Bear sign was everywhere. Rangers on foot patrol found tracks of the bear family in one of the places where Petranyi's body had lain, along the trail where he had been dragged, and in nearby meadows. They found places where bears had "rototilled" their previous day's footsteps as they dug up roots. Rangers spotted the bears a couple of times over the next several days, but nobody could get a shot at them.

It wasn't until October 11, day nine of the incident, that they were finally killed. Kruger had spotted them while shuttling rangers in and out of the chalet area. But there was a problem. Another family of bears was in the same area. The rangers had to make sure they were shooting the right bears, so Logan and ranger Regi Altop climbed in the helicopter and buzzed over the bears several times until Logan saw what he was looking for: that light-colored collar around the sow's neck.

Kruger dropped the two rangers off about two hundred yards from the 105
bears, and they crept closer while the helicopter hovered overhead. The bears paid little attention to the noisy chopper and focused on digging up roots, a testament to the single-minded quest for food that grizzlies display in the fall.

When the rangers approached within one hundred yards, they took careful aim at the feeding sow with their. 300 H&H Magnum rifles. Logan started counting. When he hit three, both men fired. The sow took a couple of steps and fell dead. Then they opened fire on the cubs. One dropped and the other took off into the woods, wounded but still scampering.

More rangers arrived to help Logan and Altop search for the wounded animal, and after about an hour Kruger spotted it from the helicopter. The four rangers spread out and went after it, walking uphill.

That's when the second bear family showed up.

Kruger had to take his eyes off the cub and haze the second family away with his helicopter, trying to keep them away from the rangers, trying to keep a bad situation from getting worse fast. It worked, but the men lost the cub.

110 Kruger, always sharp-eyed, spotted the cub later in the day with a spotting scope that was set up at the chalet. It had come back to the area where its mother had died, wounded and alone. Kruger flew Steve Frye and another ranger to the area. It was almost dark by then, but they walked into a thick stand of trees and finished the animal off with a final shot.

At 6:43 P.M, on the eleventh day of October, 1992, after nine bloody and grueling days, Kruger loaded the cub in his helicopter and lifted off for the last time. The whole unpleasant business was finally over.

The three bear carcasses were shipped to the Montana Department of Fish, Wildlife and Parks diagnostic laboratory in Bozeman, Montana, where veteran biologist Keith Aune performed a necropsy, an autopsy for animals.

The National Park Service wanted to know if there was any evidence of Petranyi inside the bears, any hair or flesh or fiber. Bear scat collected near Petranyi's body contained human remains and two different types of cloth. But when Aune examined the bears, he found nothing unusual. Not that he had expected much. The bears had been passing huge amounts of food through their bodies in the days since Petranyi died. Each of them had a belly full of roots when it died.

Rangers singled these bears out for death working on the best possible evidence. They had seen these bears near the body and trying to get closer. There was no other family group in the area with cubs that size. But had they killed Petranyi? The rangers were sure, but they wanted scientific evidence, something to remove absolutely all doubt about whether they had killed the right bears. Aune couldn't give it to them.

115 "There was no evidence in the stomach or gastrointestinal tract which can confirm the presence" of the bears at the scene of Petranyi's death.

A niggling doubt would remain forever, and that's the kind of thing that can bother a park ranger. People don't sign up to be rangers because they enjoy killing grizzly bears.

"It's beyond a reasonable doubt," says Glacier spokeswoman Amy Vanderbilt, whose husband, Gary Moses, helped investigate the incident. "But we'll never be able to absolutely verify it."

Aune did, however, provide some information about the bears. The sow was at least fifteen years old, in good general health, and weighed 251 pounds. She harbored a normal load of parasites, was seventy-four inches long, and carried a layer of fat an inch thick along her back, indicating she was only in moderate shape. Bears often have two to four inches of fat along their backs at that time of year. Her two cubs, both females, weighed thirty-nine pounds and fifty pounds.

The sow's left front foot had been injured recently, which could have caused an attitude problem, but the most interesting thing Aune found was in her mouth: deep cavities in her molars.

"They had to be very painful," Aune says. Plus, one of her front teeth 120
had rotted away almost entirely.

Did a constant and severe toothache make the bear more cantankerous? Aune, who has studied grizzlies for decades, thinks it probably did.

But why did she run away from Buck Wilde as he ate breakfast, then attack Petranyi twice and feed on him? Seeing Wilde was probably no surprise to her. She knew the area, knew that people were often seen in the campground and cooking area. Whether she first saw Petranyi on the trail or in the woods, it likely was a surprise encounter, which triggered an instinct to protect her cubs. The toothache probably reduced her tolerance level at least a little. That, combined with her intense focus on calories prior to denning for the winter, could have triggered some kind of switch that made her see Petranyi as food rather than as a nuisance or a threat, made her attack a second time and begin to eat him.

Buck Wilde says it took him five years before he could talk about the incident with any comfort.

When the helicopter took him to park headquarters, rangers interviewed him again and then repeated Logan's earlier advice to get some psychological counseling, "to make sure from a shrink point of view that everything was sort of okay," is the way Wilde puts it.

He declined. Rather, he shouldered his backpack and slipped out the 125
back door of the headquarters building, dodging the reporters waiting for him at the front door. Then he walked to the highway, stuck out his thumb, and caught a ride with a couple he had met two days earlier while hiking in to Granite Park. He told them the story, and the man bought him a bottle of Wild Turkey whiskey ("It's one of my poisons, especially in high-stress situations") before dropping him at a trailhead on the east side of the park.

Wilde was seeking his own mental therapy.

"I decided I was going back into bear country."

It was an area new to him, the Triple Divide Pass, where waters run to the Atlantic, the Pacific, and Hudson Bay.

"I wasn't just scared, I was scared to death. I had been shaken, fundamentally, to the core. I wanted to handle my shakiness in a way that would be constructive, and I thought the most constructive thing to do, for my psyche, was to get back in bear country. Fear management, I guess you'd call it."

He's had other big scares since then. A couple more charges by grizzlies 130
and a canoe wreck that left him stranded on an island in the raging North Fork of the Flathead River for six days.

He doesn't like to talk about that one much either, for the same reason he's avoided talking much about the Petranyi incident.

"It's taken me five years to get to the point where I'm ready to do that. You get kind of weird when you spend as much time in the woods as I do. I understand firsthand what is meant by the word 'taboo'. Taboos are things that the Native Americans dealt with in special terms, by whispering or whatever."

He's still a little uncomfortable talking about it. It brings things back, he says, and he wants to treat the situation with respect for the bears and for Petranyi's family. And there is another matter. Call it practical spirituality. Long-term physical survival in the wilderness depends on having the right attitude, Wilde believes.

"I felt that if I didn't give this situation enough respect, spiritually, and with all the time I spend in bear country, that the bears would get me. That sounds pretty weird, but it's really the way I look at it. One thing you should get is that I was scared shitless. It scared me enough to make it very special."

135 He says he doesn't expect people to understand him, but he believes what he believes. It's important to him.

The trip into Triple Divide Pass lasted five days. He saw lots of bear sign, tracks, and evidence of fresh digging. But he didn't see a bear during the whole trip, and today he's comfortable in the woods.

Put yourself in Buck Wilde's shoes.

What would you have done?

THOMAS McNAMEE

Drainage Ditch

When my family moved to Whitehaven, Tennessee, in 1954, it was an unincorporated hamlet of a few thousand people, and just beginning to serve as a suburb of Memphis, several miles to the north. We were surrounded by country.

To the south lay the Mississippi Delta, destination of the early-morning busloads of black children turned out of their schools each spring to chop cotton and each fall to pick it while we white children stayed at our desks. The Delta was my daddy's ancestral home, and his kin all still lived there. When we drove down to see them, Highway 61 would plunge from the wide bright cottonfields into dark bayou bottoms, and the windshield would be so spattered with bugs that we had to stop to scrape them off. Dead deer and snakes and owls and opossums lay sprawled on the bridge sides. Ospreys nested in the cypress tops, and there were alligators in the mud.

To the east of my home rose the scrub-and-clay uplands of Fayette County, Tennessee's poorest county, pig country, Klan country, buzzard country. West was the river, too huge and too strong to be quite real to a boy of seven.

What was real was closer to home. A big Hereford bull lived across the road, a chaser of children. Down our side of Oakwood Drive there was a row of seven new houses, and beyond its dead end a deep forest began, with swamps and lakes and mysteries in it. Spring nights, the frog chorus there sang loud. In an abandoned barn pulled half down by honeysuckle vines, mud daubers built their terrible castles, tube on tube of wasp-brick. Because I was allergic, my mama said, one sting could kill me. I grew to dread all insects—June bugs, yellowjackets, bumblebees, dragonflies—alike.

5 The hedge, the lawn, the big hollow sweetgum in the front yard, the maples and dogwoods and pines, even the scruffy bushes that screened our garbage cans were wildlife habitat. Hundreds of songbirds squabbled at my mother's feeders. A family of rabbits every spring, shuffling quails and burbling doves, and countless reptiles and amphibians all thrived around our house. At lightning-bug time, my friends and I had toadfrog-catching contests. You could catch three dozen of those warty, poison-peeing monsters in an hour, some of them fat as a softball. Terrariums, their glass walls slimed with the leavings of mudpuppies, skinks, snails, and prize toads, were my pride. I also tried to keep box tortoises and various snakes, but they always escaped, often inside the house.

Behind our house was a sharecropper's shack, with a friendly old retired workhorse. Later, when the shack had given way to the grounds of a grandiose white-columned pseudo-mansion, there came a fancier horse, who would eat my father's Chesterfield cigarettes from my hand. At the bottom of the pasture, a little creek had its source.

I cannot remember when I first began to follow that creek downstream. It flowed slowly and opaquely along the bottom of a deep winding gouge cut through layers of the wind-deposited silt called loess. Loess is a very fine and viscid stuff, and it makes one hell of a mud. Where the water backed up, the muck could be waist-deep on a boy.

Miraculously, there were at least a dozen boys within a year of my age all living on one sparsely settled square-quarter-mile quadrangle of roads (and only one girl). I was small, and bad at sports—nearly always last to be chosen for a team—but in the swamp I often led our expeditions, and was usually first to test the footing. My mother always said I was the muddiest boy of all when we came trudging home at suppertime.

Above a pool perhaps a mile downstream, we would swing on grapevines and do cannonballs into water the color of coffee with cream, where the bottom was a bottomless ooze. Snakes swam there, including the dread cottonmouth. Kingfishers laughed in the willows and tall tulip trees. Catfish took hooked bits of hot dog we dangled from cane poles on lines bobbered with porcupine quills. Once, a gang of us blundered on a hobo camp so freshly abandoned that a half can of beans was still warm on the coals.

10 As we grew older, I often went into the swamp by myself. I was a melancholy boy, sometimes lonely even among my friends. My solitary wanderings began, I think, as flights, from games in which I could not excel, from an uncomprehended restlessness, from the sweat and tumble and perplexity of social boyhood; but before long my long after-school afternoons alone in the woods had grown into pilgrimages, my weekends and summers rhapsodic quests: I felt that I was seeking something, and sometimes, I know, I found it, though I still could not tell you what it was.

Beyond the tangled muscadine and honeysuckle jungles, beyond the canebrakes in which whole chattering flocks of birds could hide, beyond the old overgrown fields snarled with blackberries and cocklebur, there came an even, easy, open floor of dead leaves and low, soft plants, pillared with trees of awesome girth and height. The canopy was far above, punctured only intermittently by the sun. I believe that this forest had never been logged, although, like some of these others, that memory may be colored by desire. I remember the air as very humid, very hot, very still. I remember the buzzing of wasps in that air, and, in response, the beating of my fretful heart.

My little creek (did it have a name? I never wondered) fed a larger one that fed Nonconnah Creek, which in turn fed the Mississippi River. Nonconnah was occasionally so audacious as to flood its own flood plain, and the Army Corps of Engineers dealt severely with such impertinence. Their chosen instrument of correction was the dragline, a great toothed scoop on a crane. It could rip out a ton of root-riddled earth in one bite. The messy, inefficient eccentricities of Nonconnah Creek—the oxbows, the riffles and pools, the braided channels, the islanded swamps, the tupelo bottoms—were chastened into an orderly, straight-running ditch. The rate of flow was thus increased, and flooding prevented, and development of previously unusable land made possible. That thousands of such acts of discipline would bring on anarchy downstream was not particularly a worry, for quelling the Mississippi's rebellion farther south would mean more contracts for the contractors, one of whom was the father of one of my neighborhood pals. Racing ever faster, full of the sediment that the old flood bottoms and swamps used to retain, the Mississippi today wants to crash through its banks down near Natchez and pour into the Atchafalaya basin—and leave New Orleans sitting on a mudflat. To prevent this will require one of the most expensive public-works projects in the history of the United States.

The dragline first came when the old one-lane wooden bridge at Mill Branch Road was to be replaced. Growling and grunting, it chewed out the bridge pool and left on the bank two alps of mud. They were the only steep hills we ever had, and they made a splendid place for dirt-clod fights—just the kind of thing my friends loved and I hated. In that deeper water the fishing improved, but where once a boy could sit all day undisturbed but by an occasional truckload of cotton banging over the planks toward the gin, now there was constant traffic: workers and materials for the tract-house subdivisions springing up to the south. I took my cane pole farther now, to the lakes.

My prey was mostly smaller here than the catfish of the creek, but better eating—bream, and crappies, and once in a while a largemouth bass. No matter how early I might come or how late stay, the best fishing spots always seemed to be occupied by an elderly black man or woman with little to say to a white child. I wonder now, did they fear that I might be the landowner's son? And who did own that land? The thought never crossed my mind. They would nod, and keep on fishing, catching ten fish to my one. For them, of course, it was not sport.

15 There was a place on the creek we called the rapids—it was just a gravelly riffle, really—and there, one day, my best friend, Bobby Towery, and I came upon the most stupendous animal we had ever met outside the zoo. I knew at once, from my avid reading in field guides, that this was the mighty *alligator snapping turtle*—you could tell by the three mountainous keels on

his carapace—the largest species of freshwater turtle in the world, sometimes surpassing two hundred pounds. He was very far from his home, which was supposed to be the Mississippi River.

Snappers are swimmers, not walkers, and this one seemed to have run aground. A gingerly probe with a stick elicited only a slight drawing-in of his huge plated head. We agreed that there was only one thing to be done: we had to capture the turtle. With my trusty Boy Scout hatchet we cut down a small tree and laid the trunk, about two inches thick, across the gravel shallows to block him from escaping into the opaque pool below. While Towery stood guard, I ran home for my green coaster wagon. When I got back, the turtle had not moved a muscle.

We had the idea that if we could get him to bite the pole he would not let go, and then we might haul him to land. How to get him into the wagon we would worry about later. But even with some pretty rowdy poking at his great hooked beak, the snapper could not be tempted to do more than flinch.

We sat on the bank and considered waiting him out. How hideous, how beautiful, how fierce, how still he was! How primitive, how ancient. What was time to a creature like this? Two boys could never outwait such a turtle.

We decided we would try to flip him onto his back. And then what? We'd see. At least he would be immobilized. Prying and pushing and sweating and slipping—and terrified that one slip would tumble us in on top of him—we got our pole beneath him, and the alligator snapping turtle came to life. He whirled—I know, turtles aren't supposed to whirl, but this one did—and bit our two-inch pole in half, and clawed his way into deep water and was gone.

Corpses of frogs, fish, snakes, and crawdads were ranged along my bed- 20
room bookshelves in jars of denatured alcohol. Then my wild bachelor uncle from the Delta, to my mother's horror, gave me a BB gun. No songbird was safe. The first shot usually only knocked it senseless from its perch, and I would seek it out in the brush to administer the coup de grâce to the brain. I made no pretense of collecting them; I left my victims where they lay. My favorite target was the mockingbird, the Tennessee state bird, illegal to kill. What could have possessed me? Remembering this makes my throat clench with shame.

The pursuit of Eagle Scouthood led me to gentler concerns. To take casts of animal tracks for my nature merit badge, I traveled deeper into the old forest than I had ever gone. There were mysteries at every step. Why did the mother raccoon and her family stop here? What made the heron take flight? Fox prints at the edge of the water: did the fox swim, or leap? Hence, slowly, my rage to possess wild creatures was displaced by empathy.

In a little pasture far back in the woods I found a dead calf. The head was twisted half around, the eyes staring into the sky. The skin was peeled back from the rib cage, which was crawling with flies. One leg had been eaten down to the bone. The day was hot, but the flesh had not yet begun to stink, so the kill must have been very recent, and the predator nearby. Crows called. A sharp hind edge of cloud-shade swept across the grass, and in the sudden brightness there was a clarity that I had never seen before, as if a veil had been lifted from the face of the world.

I looked for tracks, found one, and took its cast. It was big, three inches across. My field guide said, unbelievably, cougar! Mountain lion! *Panther.*

Not until years later, when the cast was long lost, did I realize what a find that may have been. *Felis concolor* is extinct now in the Mississippi valley. Indeed the cougar may be gone everywhere east of the Rockies, except for the minuscule and dwindling population of the Florida panther subspecies. Could this have been one of the last eastern cougars? Or was it, as a wildlife biologist suggested to me recently, the hybrid of a calf-killing dog and a boy's eager imagination?

The old-growth forest was cut down, and not even for lumber: the great trees were bulldozed into piles and burned. Most of the topsoil washed away, and the red clay beneath it required laborious cultivation to sustain the newly unrolled swaths of zoysia and Bermuda grass sod. Saplings were planted, and wired upright. The lakes were drained, and the black people moved out. The last hobo known to have visited Whitehaven was found dead beneath a hedge. We got a shopping center, and an interstate highway. Fluoridation of our drinking water was fought, thought to be a Communist plot to curb the birth rate. I had my first summer job as a carpenter's helper, putting up drywall in new houses.

Improved pesticides came onto the market, and it was possible now to drive through the Delta bottoms with no more than an occasional sweep of the windshield wipers. My wild uncle, who kept bongos and a conga drum in his den closet, got married. The ospreys disappeared from the cypresstop nests, the alligators from the bayous. The only lake left was appropriated by tough teenagers as a beer-drinking hideout; they raped a girl there. Quails no longer shuffled in the leaves on the lawn.

What had been done to Nonconnah Creek was done now to its tributaries. New sewers leaked into the stagnant trench that was all that remained of my creek's headwaters. Our grapevine-draped swimming hole and the alligator snapping turtle's riffle lasted longer, but we could get there on bicycles now, on smooth blacktop. Often I didn't make it that far, having stopped off to chew gum and laugh in Mary Scott Moyers's or Joellen Krayer's yard and lost track of time. When the last of my creek was ditched out, I believe I did not notice.

Twenty years later, home one Christmas from New York, I saw a dragline working in the parking lot of the cabana apartments that stand where my old creek went under the old wooden bridge. I was astonished to see that there was still some life in what the people there now called the drainage ditch: each time the great machine took a bite, the muddy water boiled with creatures forced downstream before it. The V-shaped ditch was being made into a box-shaped one. A chain-link fence was being built along both sides, to keep children safely out. The walls and floor of the drainage ditch were being lined with concrete.

· CREDITS ·

Chapter 1. 6: Learning to Read, from THE AUTOBIOGRAPHY OF MALCOM X by Malcolm X and Alex Haley, copyright © 1964 by Alex Haley and Malcolm X. Copyright © 1965 by Alex Haley and Betty Shabazz. Used by permission of Random House, Inc.; **15:** Reprinted by permission.

Chapter 2. 29: "Introduction" from LOOKING GOOD: MALE BODY IMAGE IN MODERN AMERICA by Lynne Luciano. copyright © 2002 by Lynne Luciano. Reprinted by permission of Farrar, Straus and Giroux, LLC; **35:** Reprinted with the permission of The Free Press, a division of Simon & Schuster, Inc. from THE SILENT TAKEOVER by Noreena Hertz. Copyright © 2001 Noreena Hertz; **41:** © 2004 Time, Inc. Reprinted by permission; **43:** Copyright © 2004 John Wiley & Sons, Inc.; Reprinted with permission of John Wiley & Sons, Inc.; **47:** Reprinted by permission.

Chapter 3. 60: Reprinted from Columbia Journalism Review, September/October 2004 © 2004 by Columbia Journalism Review; **65:** Copyright © 1986 by The New York Times Co. Reprinted with permission; **67:** "From Outside, In" originally appeared in The Georgia Review, Volume XLI, No. 2 (Summer 1987), © 1987 by The University of Georgia/© 1987 by Barbara Mellix. Reprinted by permission of Barbara Mellix and The Georgia Review.

Chapter 4. 91: Reprinted by permission; **95:** Reprinted by permission of Basic Books, a member of Perseus Books Group; **101:** Copyright © 1993 Time, Inc. All rights reserved. Reprinted by permission; **109:** Reprinted by permission of The Philadelphia Inquirer; **113:** "The Lottery" from THE LOTTERY AND OTHER STORIES by Shirley Jackson. Copyright © 1948, 1949 by Shirley Jackson. Copyright renewed 1976, 1977 by Laurence Hyman, Barry Hyman, Mrs. Sarah Webster and Mrs. Joanne Schnurer. Reprinted by permission of Farrar, Straus and Giroux, LLC; **121:** Slate.com and Washington Post Newsweek Interactive Co. All rights reserved; **123:** Reprinted by permission of Sll/Sterling Lord Literistic, Inc. Copyright 1986 by Gloria Naylor.

Chapter 5. 131: © 2003 Cable News Network LP, LLLP. A Time Warner Company. All Rights Reserved; **132:** Reprinted by arrangement with the Estate of Martin Luther King, Jr., c/o Writers House. Copyright 1963 Martin Luther King, Jr., copyright renewed 1991 Coretta Scott King; **138:** "Introduction: Mind and Work," from THE MIND AT WORK by Mike Rose, copyright © 2004 by Mike Rose. Used by permission of Viking Penguin, a division of Penguin Group (USA) Inc.; **141:** Excerpt from THE LOST GRIZZLIES: A Search for Survivors in the Wilderness of Colorado by Rick Bass. Copyright © 1995 by Rick Bass. Reprinted by permission of Houghton Mifflin Company. All rights reserved; **144:** "When the Old Man Is Dead and Buried" from PERFECTLY LEGAL by David Cay Johnston, copyright © 2003 by David Cay Johnston. Used by permission of Portfolio, an imprint of Penguin Group (USA) Inc.; **148:** Reprinted by permission of the Jean V. Naggar Literary Agency on behalf of William Lutz.

Chapter 6. 165: Reprinted by permission.

Chapter 7. 178: Copyright © 1999 by Marcus Laffey (Ed Conlon). Reprinted by permission of William Morris Agency, LLC on behalf of the author; **194:** © 2004 Time, Inc. Reprinted by permission; **195:** © 2004 Time, Inc. Reprinted by permission.

Chapter 8. 207: Reprinted by permission. Dr. Jack Rasmus, PhD, Political Economy, is author of THE WAR AT HOME and FROM US TO THEM: THE TRILLION DOLLAR INCOME SHIFT, and may be contacted at www.kyklosproductions.com; **215:** Reprinted by permission; **220:** From THE VANISHING HITCHIKER: AMERICAN URBAN LEGENDS AND THEIR MEANINGS by Jan Harold Brunvand. Copyright © 1981 by Jan Harold Brunvand. Used by permission of W.W. Norton & Company, Inc.

Chapter 9. 247: Reprinted by permission of the author; **254:** Reproduced with permission from BLACKBEARD AND OTHER PIRATES OF THE ATLANTIC COAST by Nancy Roberts, published by John F. Blair, Publisher; **257:** Reprinted by permission of The University of Georgia Press.

Chapter 10. 266: Reprinted by permission of Project Censored; **278:** Reprinted courtesy of The Green Party of the United States; **281:** Reprinted courtesy of SPORTS ILLUSTRATED, "Questioned Marks," by Rick Reilly, October 4, 2004, Copyright © 2004 Time, Inc. All rights reserved.

Chapter 11. 298: "The Symbols of Halloween," from THE PAGAN BOOK OF HALLOWEEN by Gerina Dunwich, copyright © 2000 by Gerina Dunwich. Used by permission of Penguin, a division of Penguin Group (USA) Inc.; **303:** Reprinted by permission; **307:** Reprinted by permission of the publisher from "Festivals, Rites, and Presents" in CELEBRATING THE FAMILY: ETHNICITY, CONSUMER CULTURE, AND FAMILY RITUALS by Elizabeth Pleck, pp. 2–9, Cambridge, MA: Harvard University Press, Copyright © 2000 by the President and Fellows of Harvard College; **314:** Reprinted with the permission of Simon & Schuster Adult Publishing Group, from AT LARGE by Ellen Goodman. Copyright © 1981 by The Washington Post Company. All rights reserved; **315:** Reprinted by permission of the author; **323:** From EARTH FOR SALE: Reclaiming Ecology in the Age of Corporate Greenwash by Brian Tokar. Reprinted by permission of South End Press.

Chapter 12. 330: Reprinted with permission from PSYCHOLOGY TODAY. Copyright © 1994 Sussex Publishers, Inc.; **337:** Reprinted with the permission of Simon & Schuster Adult Publishing Group from "Leonard Lauder: The Beauty of Small Things" from THE BANANA SCULPTOR, THE PURPLE LADY, AND THE ALL-NIGHT SWIMMER: Hobbies, Collecting, and Other Passionate Pursuits by Susan Sheehan and Howard Means. Copyright © 2002 by Susan Sheehan; **343:** Reprinted courtesy of SPORTS ILLUSTRATED, "Con Games" by Michael Bamberger, May 31, 2004, Copyright © 2004 Time, Inc. All rights reserved; **350:** Reprinted courtesy of SPORTS ILLUSTRATED, "Fantasy World" by Chris Ballard, June 21, 2004, Copyright © 2004 Time, Inc. All rights reserved; **358:** From ME TALK PRETTY ONE DAY by David Sedaris. Copyright © 2000 by David Sedaris. By permission of Little, Brown and Co.; **365:** Reprinted by permission of Indiana Business Magazine.

Chapter 13. 371: Reprinted by permission; **373:** Reprinted by permission; **379:** Reprinted by permission; **385:** © 2004 Time, Inc. Reprinted by permission; **392:** Reprinted by permission; **393:** Reprinted by permission; **394:** Used by permission of the Skeptical Inquirer.

Chapter 14. 409: Copyright © 1991 Ontario Review. Reprinted by permission of John Hawkins & Associates, Inc.; **417:** Copyright © 2007, www.DarwinAwards.com. Reprinted with permission; **422:** From ME TALK PRETTY ONE DAY by David Sedaris. Copyright © 2000 by David Sedaris. By permission of Little, Brown and Co.; **425:** Copyright © 2005 by The New York Times Agency; **428:** Reprinted courtesy of HowStuffWorks.com; **436:** Reprinted by permission.

Chapter 15. 453: Stephen L. Carter, "The Insufficiency of Honesty," The Atlantic Monthly, February 1996, pp. 74-76; **458:** Al Franken, "I'm a Bad Liar," from LIES AND THE LYING LIARS WHO TELL THEM (Dutton Adult, 2003), pp. 261-276; **469:** Roger Henn, LIES, LEGENDS, AND LORE OF THE SAN JUANS, 1999 Western Reflections, Inc., Lake City, CO; **472:** From RADIO WAVES by Jim Ladd, Copyright © 1991 by the author and reprinted by permission of St. Martin's Press, LLC; **479:** © 1995 by FAIR. This piece originally appeared in THE WAY THINGS AREN'T: RUSH LIMBAUGH'S REIGN OF ERROR by FAIR. Reprinted with the permission of The New Press. www.thenewpress.com; **481:** © 2006, The Washington Post. Reprinted by permission.

Chapter 16. 487: Copyright 1987 by David Quammen. All rights reserved; **491:** Copyright 2005 by SAN FRANCISCO CHRONICLE. Reproduced with permission of SAN FRANCISCO CHRONICLE in the format Trade Book via Copyright Clearance Center; **495:** From THE MAN MADE OF WORDS by N. Scott Momaday. Copyright © 1997 by the author and reprinted by permission of St. Martin's Press, LLC; **495:** Reprinted by permission of Don Congdon Associates, Inc. Copyright © 1968 by Edward Abbey, renewed 1996 by Clarke Abbey; **499:** Scott McMillion, MARK OF THE GRIZZLY: True Stories of Recent Bear Attacks and the Hard Lessons Learned. Copyright © 1998 by Scott McMillion. Used by permission of The Globe Pequot Press; **512:** Drainage Ditch from the RETURN OF THE WOLF TO YELLOWSTONE by Thomas McNamee. Copyright © 1997 by Thomas McNamee. Reprinted by permission of Henry Holt and Company, LLC.

· INDEX ·

"2006 Green Party Candidate Spotlight" (Green Party website), 278–279

Abbey, Edward, "Snake, The," 495–499
Academic achievement, 224–225
  learning for future application, 225
Action, calls for, 120–121
Ad hominem attacks, 50–51
Agendas
  behind websites, 277–278
  unearthing, 40–41
"All I Think Is That It's Stupid" (Garvin), 436–448
Allusions, 75–76
Alternative magazines, 265–266
Analysis, 171–173
"Analysis of the Dietary Habits of a Known Bookworm, An" (Badar), 226–228
APA (American Psychological Association) style, 288
Argument, 77
  bandwagon fallacy, 251, 260, 280
  criteria and, 249
  straw man fallacy, 253
Associated Press
  "Courthouse Camera Captures a Ghost," 245, 392–393
  "Courthouse Ghost Identified as Insect," 393–394
Assumptions
  investigating, 39–42
  questioning, 53
Attacks against others, 50–51, 53
Audience, 54–86, 166
  anticipating reader needs, 63–76
  forging relationship with, 99
  peer feedback and, 83
  responding to possible objections by, 76–82
  revision and, 84–85
  targeting potential readers, 58–63
  using real readers in peer groups, 82–84
  writing and, 3–4
Authors, website, evaluation of, 276–277

Badar, Mandy, "Analysis of the Dietary Habits of a Known Bookworm, An," 226–228
Ballard, Chris, "Fantasy World," 350–358
Bamberger, Michael, "Con Games," 343–350
Bandwagon fallacy, 260, 280
Bandwagon mentality, avoiding, 250–251
Banks, Anna, "Sexuality Orientation," 55–56
Bannatyne, Leslie Pratt, "Reformation and Guy Fawkes Day, The," 303–305
Bass, Rick, *Lost Grizzlies, The* (excerpt), 141–143
Beliefs, verifying information about, 252–253
Betts, John, "UFOs, Skepticism, and Belief," 373–377
Bias, 264
Bibliographies, 291
"Big Lie, The" (Ladd), 472–479
Blackbeard and Other Pirates of the Atlantic Coast excerpt (Roberts), 254–256
  student essay on (extract), 256–257
Blackboard (online), 186
Blake, Mariah, "Voices: The Damage Done," 60–63
Blogs, 13, 264
"Bloody Footprints" excerpt (Dunbar), 59
Books, evaluating for research, 265
Boreta, Trish, "Top Censored News Stories of 2005–2006, The," 266–275
Brain, Marshall, "How Laughter Works," 428–435
Brainstorming, 130, 161
Brunvand, Jan Harold, *Vanishing Hitchhiker, The* (excerpt), 220–224
Bulletin boards (online), 186

Cahill, Robert Ellis, "Whitman's Haunted Bed," 371–373
"Car Accident, The" (Robinson), 23–24, 25–27
Career options, writing and, 19
Carter, Stephen L., "Insufficiency of Honesty, The," 29, 453–457
"Censor or Victim of Censorship?" (Rendell, Naurechas, and Cohen), 479–481
Charged language, 139–140

Chat rooms, 186
Chicago Manual of Style, 288
Chu, Jeff, "Is God in Our Genes?," 385–392
Citations
  documentation systems and, 288, 291
  in-text, 289–290, 291
  of online sources, 277
  of sources, 156, 260
Citizenship
  letters to the editor and, 14–15
  political action and, 15–17
  reading, critical awareness and, 214
Civic engagement, reading and, 214–215, 216–217
Claims
  ensuring relationship of evidence to, 250
  establishing criteria for, 249–251
  supplying evidence for, 241
Class, assumptions about, 39–40
Clichés, 25, 29, 164
  avoiding, 53
  twisting, 28–29
Cohen, Jeff, "Censor or Victim of Censorship?," 479–481
Collaboration, 86, 155
  uses of, 176–204
College, developing reading strategies for, 225–226, 228–229
College writing, 18–19
  emphasis on grammar, 19
  five-paragraph theme, 18
  formal thesis statements, 19
  modes of discourse, 18
Common ground, in introductions, 99
Complaints, letters of, 12
"'Computer Ate My Vote' Scores Coast to Coast Wins" (TrueMajority), 15–17
Conceding, to objections, 81–82
Conclusions, 113, 120–121, 126
  call to action, 120–121
  of essays, 4, 172
  last part of narratives and, 123
  purpose of, 113
  selecting powerful images in, 123
  tying points together in, 120
Condescending tone, avoiding, 59
Conflicting evidence, in sources, 280, 282–283, 286–287
"Con Games" (Bamberger), 343–350
Connotations, 137–138
Consensus building, 112, 130–131, 135
Consumer awareness, reading and, 212–214
Cooperative strategies, for peer review, 192–193
Corliss, Richard, "How to Live to Be 100," 195–201
Corrie, Rachel, 131
Course management systems, 186
"Courthouse Camera Captures a Ghost" (Associated Press), 245, 392–393
"Courthouse Ghost Identified as Insect" (Associated Press), 393–394
Credibility, 139, 153
  of online sources, 214, 291
  of websites, 278
Credits, in acknowledgement pages, 288, 289
Criteria, 260
  for claims, 249–251
  substantive, 250
Critical analysis, 50, 53, 54, 172, 251
  asking who profits, 47
  breaking through writer's block and, 164
  developing meaningful thesis and, 3
  development of, 282
  effective arguments and, 77
  interrogating the obvious, 28–39, 53
  revision and, 166
  thesis and, 108
  value systems and, 64
  for writing, 23–53
Critical knowledge, locating, 263–266
Critical thinking, 5
Cultural considerations, 59–60
Cultural literacy, 5
"Curriculum Is a Political Statement" (Meyer), 47–50
"Curse of the Ouija Board," 78–81

"Darwin Awards, The," 417–420
"Death Penalty's False Promise" (Quindlen), 65–67, 81, 82
Deception
  avoiding, in workplace writing, 21–22
  honesty and, 449–483
Decision making, peer groups and, 85
Definitions, verifying information about, 252–253
Describing and shaping, 136–138, 139–141
  charged language, 139–140
  connotations, 137–138
  slang and obscenity, 140–141
  vague words, 136–137
Dezenhall, Eric, "We Like Our Bad Guys to Be Honest About It," 76, 481–483
Documentation systems, 288, 291

Drafts, 19, 57, 83, 157, 159, 160, 171, 175
  creating options, 169–170
  initial, 191–192
  strategies for, 165–166, 169–170
  writing out of order, 170
"Drainage Ditch" (McNamee), 512–516
Dunbar, Roxanne A., "Bloody Footprints" (excerpt), 59
Dunwich, Gerina, "Symbols of Halloween, The," 298–303

Editing, 157, 159, 160, 165, 166, 171–174, 175
  group projects and, 195, 204
Egan, Molly, focused freewrite, 232–233
Email, 20
Essays, 171
  arrangement of, 4
  shaping, 91
  synchronous discussions of, 186
  thesis placement in, 108–109, 112
Ethos, 54, 57, 58, 99, 150
  establishing, 63, 86
Euphemisms, 135, 144, 146, 153
  bureaucratese, 147
  filler words, 146
  sanitizing, 147–148
Evaluations, individual, in group projects, 202–203
Evidence
  accounting for, 287
  avoiding bandwagon mentality, 250–251
  for claims, 249–251
  ensuring relationship of, to claims, 250
  examining, 243–247
  facts and, 245
  popularity as, 251
  proof *vs.*, 243
  writing with, 156, 237–260
"Executive Pay in the U.S." (Rasmus), 207–210
Exemplification, 105, 106

"Face of a Spider" (Quammen), 247, 487–491
Face-to-face groups, 185–186
Facts, 245, 260
  as examples, 47
Fallacies
  bandwagon, 260, 280
  straw man, 253
"False Controversy of Stem Cells, The" (Kinsley), 41–42
Fanatical approaches, in websites, 279–280
"Fantasy World" (Ballard), 350–358
Fairness and Accuracy in Reporting, "Smearing Anti-War Activists?," 215–216
"Festivals, Rites, and Presents" (Pleck), 307–313
Field-specific journals, analyzing, 264–265
Finding your voice, 150–152
  active sentence constructions, 152
  choosing your words, 151–152
  types of words, 152
Five-paragraph theme, 18
"Four Stops on a Bigfoot Hunt" (Parker), 379–385
Franken, Al, "I'm a Bad Liar," 458–467
Freewriting, 130, 161, 162, 172
  comprehension and, 232, 233
  focused, 163–164, 232
Freire, Paulo, 132
"From Outside, In" (Mellix), 67–75

Ganahl, Jane, "Women Like Men Who Like Cats," 491–493
Garvin, Glenn, "All I Think Is That It's Stupid," 436–448
Gender, assumptions about, 39–40
"Giant Dreams, Midget Abilities" (Sedaris), 358–365
Goodman, Ellen, "Thanksgiving," 314–315
Green Party website, "2006 Green Party Candidate Spotlight," 278–279
Group projects, 155, 176–177
  assigning tasks in, 187–191
  individual evaluations in, 202–203
  instructor intervention in, 190–191
  progress logs for, 188–190
  selecting secretary for, 187
  strengths and weaknesses of, 187–188
  taking responsibility in, 202–203
  teamwork and, 203
  types of, 191
Groups
  face-to-face, 185–186
  online, 186
Guang, Ding, "Negative Cliques in Schools," 128–129

Henn, Roger, "Lightning Struck Lost Mine, The," 469–472
Hertz, Noreena, *Silent Takeover, The* (excerpt), 35–38, 40
"History of Anglo-Saxon Wedding Customs, A" (Ranger), 315–323
"How Laughter Works" (Brain), 428–435

"How to Live to Be 100" (Corliss/Lemonick), 195–201
"Humor in Society" (Windhorst), 87–90

Ideas
  generating, 161
  new twists on, 108
  synthesizing, 191–194, 195
  transitioning from, 101, 105–107
"I Have a Dream" (King, Jr.), 132–135
"I'm a Bad Liar" (Franken), 458–467
"Indiana's Potato Chip Lady" (Sklar), 365–366
"Indian Dog, The" (Momaday), 495
"'Indians,' Textualism, Morality and the Problem of History" excerpt (Tompkins), 166–168
Information checking, 251–253
  beliefs, histories, and definitions, 252–253
  dictionaries, encyclopedias, and websites, 253
  straw man fallacy and, 253
Information retrieval, 219–220
  competition, 219
  hobbies, 219–220
  social discourse, 220
"Inside Dope" (Laffey), 178–184
"Instincts vs. Rules" (Turner), 240, 241–242
Instructions, 212–213
"Insufficiency of Honesty, The" (Carter), 29, 453–457
Integrating sources, 254, 256, 257, 259–260
  extricating information, 254, 256
  paraphrasing, 257, 259
  tag phrases, 259–260
Internet, evaluating sources on, 276–278, 279–280
Interrogating the obvious, 28–39, 53
  finding what's not there, 35
  focusing on interrelatedness of key elements, 29
  twisting the cliché, 28–29
In-text citations, 289–290, 291
Introductions, 126
  description of, 98
  in essays, 4, 171
  finding common ground in, 99
  general to specific, 99–100
  pivotal scenes and, 100
  writing last, 98–99, 170
Investigating assumptions, 39–42
  race, class, and gender, 39–40
  unearthing agendas, 40–41
"Is God in Our Genes?" (Chu, Liston, Sieger, and Williams), 385–392
"Is Laughter Contagious?" (Oates), 409–417

Jackson, Shirley, "Lottery, The," 113–120
Job-related writing, 20, 21–22
Johnston, David Cay, *Perfectly Legal* (excerpt), 144–146
Journals, 13
  field-specific, 264–265

Kaplan, Fred, "Worst-Laid Plans, The," 121–122
King, Martin Luther, Jr., "I Have a Dream," 132–135
Kinsley, Michael, "False Controversy of Stem Cells, The," 41–42

Ladd, Jim, "Big Lie, The," 472–479
Laffey, Marcus, "Inside Dope," 178–184
Language
  choices with, 127–153
  power of, 4
  precision in, 129
Lau, Charley, Jr., *Lau's Laws on Hitting* (excerpt), 162–163
Learning
  academic, 224–225
  for future application, 225
"Learning to Read" (Malcolm X), 6–9
Lemonick, Michael D., "How to Live to Be 100," 195–201
"Leonard Lauder" (Sheehan/Means), 337–342
Letters
  of complaint, 12–13
  to the editor, 14–15
"Life Under the Chief Doublespeak Officer" (Lutz), 148–150
"Lightning Struck Lost Mine, The" (Henn), 469–472
Limbo excerpt (Lubrano), 43–46
List of works cited. *See* Works Cited (MLA) list
Liston, Broward, "Is God in Our Genes?," 385–392
Logical fallacies, 50
Lost Grizzlies, The excerpt (Bass), 141–143
"Lottery, The" (Jackson), 113–120
Lubrano, Alfred, *Limbo* (excerpt), 43–46
Luciano, Lynne, "Male Body Image in America," 29–35
Lutz, William, "Life Under the Chief Doublespeak Officer," 148–150

Magazines, alternative, 265–266
Mainstream sources, analyzing, 264
Malcolm X, "Learning to Read," 6–9
"Male Body Image in America" (Luciano), 29–35
McCarthy, Terry, "Nowhere to Roam," 194–195
McClelland, Susan, "UFOs, Skepticism, and Belief," 373–377
McMillion, Scott, "Treat It Right," 100, 499–512
McNamee, Thomas, "Drainage Ditch," 512–516
"Me Talk Pretty One Day" (Sedaris), 107, 422–425
Means, Howard, "Leonard Lauder," 337–342
Mediating experiences, 130–132, 135
  consensus building, 130–131, 135
  figurative language, 132, 135
  naming the world, 132, 135
Mellix, Barbara, "From Outside, In," 67–75
Meyer, Richard, "Curriculum Is a Political Statement," 47–50
Mind at Work, The excerpt (Rose), 138–139
MLA (Modern Language Association) style, 288
Momaday, N. Scott, "Indian Dog, The," 495
"Mommy, What Does 'Nigger' Mean?" (Naylor), 99, 123–125

Narrative voice, 150
Narratives
  believable voice in, 140
  evidence and, 246
  last parts of, as conclusions, 123
Naurechas, Jim, "Censor or Victim of Censorship?," 479–481
Naylor, Gloria, 99
  "Mommy, What Does 'Nigger' Mean?," 123–125
"Negative Cliques in Schools" (Guang), 128–129
Nisbet, Matt, "Talking to Heaven Through Television," 394–404
"Norming Groups" (Thelin), 20–21
"Nowhere to Roam" (McCarthy), 194–195

Oates, Joyce Carol, "Is Laughter Contagious?," 409–417
Objections
  refuting and conceding to, 81–82
  responding to, 76–78, 81–82
  self-reflection and responding to, 77
  tone and responding to, 78
Observations
  evidence and, 246–247
  writing from, 11–12
Ohio Department of Public Safety, "Where to Ride on the Road," 217–218
Online research, 261–263
Online sources
  agenda of, 277–278
  author of, 276–277
  citation of, 277
  evaluating, 276–278, 279–280, 291
  fanatical approaches and, 279–280
  testing credibility of, 214
  updates of websites, 277
Organizing your ideas, strategies for, 87–126
O'Rourke, P. J., "To Hell with Lipitor," 247–249
Outlines, 161

Parker, Jeff, "Four Stops on a Bigfoot Hunt," 379–385
Patterns, 159–161
  comparisons and, 52
  facts and events as examples of, 46–47
  noting what you do not do, 160–161
  seeing, 42–43, 46–47
  tracking your steps, 160
Peer feedback, 82–83, 86
  receiving more than once, 85
Peer groups, 184, 185, 204
  decision making and, 85
  using real readers in, 82–84
Peer review reader's discussion guide, 84
Peer review writer's discussion guide, 83
Peers' work, critiquing, 192–193
Peltier, Leonard, "Statement to Judge Paul Benson," 283–286
Perfectly Legal excerpt (Johnston), 144–146
Personal inspiration
  complaints, 12–13
  gratitude and good cheer, 13–14
  observation, 11–12
  reflection, 13
  writing from, 11–12
Persuasion, 64
  tone and, 78
Phillips, Peter, "Top Censored News Stories of 2005–2006, The," 266–275
Place
  orienting audience to, 106–107
  reading and choice of, 229

Plagiarism, 257, 288
Pleck, Elizabeth, "Festivals, Rites, and Presents," 307–313
Prewriting, 19, 157, 159, 160, 161, 162
"Problem with Being a Thing, The" (Wise), 95–97
Progress logs, 188, 204
  example of, 188–190
Proof, evidence *vs.*, 243
Proofreading, 160, 165, 166, 171, 173, 175
  group projects and, 195, 204
Public interest, 216–217
Public presentations, 17

Quammen, David, "Face of a Spider," 247, 487–491
"Questioned Marks" (Reilly), 281–282
Questioning assumptions, 53
Quindlen, Anna, "Death Penalty's False Promise," 65–67, 81, 82

Race, assumptions about, 39–40
Ranger, Arden, "History of Anglo-Saxon Wedding Customs, A," 315–323
Rasmus, Jack, "Executive Pay in the U.S.," 207–210
Readers
  anticipating needs of, 63–64, 67
  common knowledge and, 58–59
  cultural considerations of, 59–60
  potential, targeting of, 58–60
  vocabulary and, 60
Reading, 155
  academic achievement and, 224–225
  information retrieval and, 219–220
  knowledge, safety, consumer awareness and, 212–214
  literacy and, 210–211
  prediction and, 211
  reasons for, 212
  in short spurts, 228–229
  social and civic engagement and, 214–215, 216–217
  strategies for college, 225–226, 228–229
  surroundings and, 229
Reading planner, 229–231
Reasonable (or rational) thinking, 50
Reasoning, poor
  attacks against others, 50–51, 53
  avoiding, 50–53
  diversions, 51–52, 53
  overgeneralizing, 52–53
References (APA) list, 289
Reflection, 13
  responding to objections and, 77
"Reformation and Guy Fawkes Day, The" (Bannatyne), 303–305
Refuting objections, 81–82
Reilly, Rick, "Questioned Marks," 281–282
Religion, 237–239, 251–252
Rendell, Steven, "Censor or Victim of Censorship?," 479–481
Reports, workplace, 20
Research, 156
  alternative magazines, 265–266
  books, 265
  field-specific journals, 264–265
  mainstream sources, 264
Revision, 57, 58, 84–85, 157, 159, 160, 171, 175
  collaborative, 193–194, 204
  creating options, 169–170
  critiquing peers' work and, 192
  focus on, 169
  making decisions about, 85
  receiving peer feedback more than once and, 85
  strategies for, 165–166, 169–170
  writing out of order and, 170
"Right Chemistry, The" (Toufexis), 101–105
"Risk" (Roberts), 330–337
Roberts, Nancy, *Blackbeard and Other Pirates of the Atlantic Coast* (excerpt), 254–256
  student essay on (extract), 256–257
Roberts, Paul, "Risk," 330–337
Robinson, Sam, "Car Accident, The," 23–24, 25–27
Rose, Mike, *Mind at Work, The* (excerpt), 138–139

"Same Difference, The" (Wang), 109–112
Sedaris, David
  "Giant Dreams, Midget Abilities," 358–365
  "Me Talk Pretty One Day," 107, 422–425
"Seriously, the Joke Is Dead" (St. John), 425–428
"Sex and Religion" (Springfield), 237–239
"Sexuality Orientation" (Banks), 55–56
Sheehan, Susan, "Leonard Lauder," 337–342
Shepard, Paul, *Tender Carnivore, The* (excerpt), 257–259
  student essay on (extract), 259
Sieger, Maggie, "Is God in Our Genes?," 385–392

Silent Takeover, The excerpt (Hertz), 35–38, 40
Singer, Peter, "Tools for Research," 91–94
Sklar, Debbie L., "Indiana's Potato Chip Lady," 365–366
"Smearing Anti-War Activists?" (Fairness and Accuracy in Reporting), 215–216
"Snake, The" (Abbey), 495–499
Sources, 260
  accounting for all evidence in, 287
  author, title, and publication information for, 289
  conflicting evidence and, 280, 282–283, 286–287
  finding and evaluating, 156
  integrating, 254, 256, 257, 259–260
  mainstream, 264
  primary, 288
  questioning credibility of, 51
  status quo and, 282–283
Springfield, Julie, "Sex and Religion," 237–239
St. John, Warren, "Seriously, the Joke Is Dead," 425–428
"Statement to Judge Paul Benson" (Peltier), 283–286
Status quo, evaluating sources and, 282–283
Stereotypes, 41, 59
Straw man fallacy, 253
Subjects
  finding what's not there, 35
  introducing, 98–100
"Symbols of Halloween, The" (Dunwich), 298–303
Synchronous discussions, 186
Synthesizing ideas, 191–194, 195
  critiquing peers' work, 192–193
  initial drafts, 191–192
  stabilizing the voice, 195
  weaving sections together, 193–194

"Talking to Heaven Through Television" (Nisbet), 394–404
Tender Carnivore, The excerpt (Shepard), 257–259
  student essay on (extract), 259
"Thanksgiving" (Goodman), 314–315
Thelin, Bill, "Norming Groups," 20–21
Thesis, 53, 98
  clichés in, 25
  critical analysis and development of, 3
  interrogating the obvious and, 28–39
Thesis placement, 108–109, 112
  building toward consensus, 112
  new twist on an old idea, 108
  Oreo cookie method, 108–109
Thesis statements, 98
  formal, 19
"To Hell with Lipitor" (O'Rourke), 247–249
Tokar, Brian, "Twentieth Anniversary of Earth Day, The," 323–326
Tompkins, Jane, "'Indians,' Textualism, Morality and the Problem of History" (excerpt), 166–168
Tone, 120
  responding to objections and, 78
"Tools for Research" (Singer), 91–94, 99, 120
"Top Censored News Stories of 2005–2006, The" (Phillips, Boreta, and Project Censored), 266–275
Toufexis, Anastasia, "Right Chemistry, The," 101–105
Transitions, 101, 105–107, 193
  contrast, addition, summary, and exemplification, 105
  increasing levels of specificity, 101, 105
  repeating keywords, 106
  subheadings, 107
  time and place, 106–107
"Treat It Right" (McMillion), 100, 499–512
TrueMajority, "'Computer Ate My Vote' Scores Coast to Coast Wins," 15–17
Turner, Brad, "Instincts vs. Rules," 240, 241–242
"Twentieth Anniversary of Earth Day, The" (Tokar), 323–326
Twisting the cliché, 28–29

"UFOs, Skepticism, and Belief" (McClelland/Betts), 373–377

Vanishing Hitchhiker, The excerpt (Brunvand), 220–224
  check marks in margins of, 233–236
  highlighting, 233
  student's freewrite on, 232–233
Vocabulary
  building, 132
  growth in, 129
  targeting audience and use of, 60
Voice
  finding, 150–152
  stabilizing in group projects, 195
"Voices: The Damage Done" (Blake), 60–63
Voting, reading and, 214

Wang, Amy, "Same Difference, The," 109–112
Web-based research, 193
Websites, 261–262
  citation of sources within, 277
  evaluating, 291
  verifying information in, 253
"We Like Our Bad Guys to Be Honest About It" (Dezenhall), 76, 481–483
"Where to Ride on the Road" (Ohio Department of Public Safety), 217–218
"Whitman's Haunted Bed" (Cahill), 371–373
Williams, Daniel, "Is God in Our Genes?," 385–392
Windhorst, Steve, "Humor in Society," 87–90
Wise, Peter, "Problem with Being a Thing, The," 95–97
Witnesses, 260
  evidence and, 245–246
"Women Like Men Who Like Cats" (Ganahl), 491–493
Word choice, editing, proofreading and, 172–173
Workplace writing, 20, 21–22
  avoiding deception in, 21–22
  cautious, not skimpy style of, 20
  finding importance in, 21
Works Cited (MLA) list, 289
Workshopping, peer, 82
"Worst-Laid Plans, The" (Kaplan), 121–122
Writer's block, 175
  breaking through, 161–162, 163–165
  discovering why you are blocked, 162
  drawing a tree, 164–165
  focused freewriting, 163–164
  starting with the critical analysis, 164
Writing
  as a citizen, 14–17
  in college, 18–19
  critical analysis for, 23–53
  with evidence, 156, 237–260
  language choices in, 127–153
  out of order, 170
  from personal inspiration, 11–12
  purposes of, 3, 6
  reasons for, 11–22
  in the workplace, 20, 21–22
Writing process, 155
  discovering, 157–175